KAHLIL GIBRAN

His Life and World

Self-portrait with likeness of Mary Haskell in the background, oil, 1911. (Authors)

KAHLIL GIBRAN

HIS LIFE AND WORLD

Jean Gibran and Kahlil Gibran

New York Graphic Society
Boston

The illustration on the dedication page was drawn by Kahlil
Gibran for an issue of *as-Sayeh*.

International Standard Book Number: 8212-0510-2
Library of Congress Catalog Card Number: 73-80368

First published 1974 by New York Graphic Society Ltd.
11 Beacon St., Boston, Mass. 02108
First printing 1974

Designed by Betsy Beach

Manufactured in the United States of America

Contents

For
Concord
Souls

Introduction

The need to explore the world of Kahlil Gibran began for me in 1932 when I was ten years old. His death the year before had profoundly affected my family; N'oula Gibran, my father and the poet's cousin, felt most bereft. They had grown up together in Lebanon, and when my father finally made the long voyage to America ten years after Kahlil and his sister Marianna, he also gravitated to Boston. There he met and married my mother Rose Gibran, another cousin. Kahlil not only was their best man, he also named their five children—Horace, Susan, Kahlil, Hafiz, and Selma.

We grew up huddled in the Lebanese–Syrian enclave of Boston's South End. Poor during the twenties, we hardly noticed the difference when the Depression became official. The only event that relieved the dreariness of those tenement days was a visit from Gibran, who was then living in New York. We would all descend upon "Aunt" Marianna's Tyler Street apartment, and for days there would be feasting, laughter, and talk.

I remember his room late at night, dense with smoke, redolent with the licorice smell of the *arak* liquor; I can hear the melodies of the native *oud* (lute) and *nay* (flute) played by neighbors in homage to the man who was celebrated as a writer and artist. Many mornings I would deliver bread to the Tyler Street studio, when it was deserted except for Kahlil and his sister. He talked with me and encouraged me. Once he gave me parts of a broken clock to reassemble. I can visualize the paintbox in which he taught me to mix colors, and even the slippers he wore as I sat and watched him at his easel or writing table. One especially vivid picture remains. We all attended the Quincy School, as he had. It had just let out and as I was rushing away I spotted him. He was standing across the street, in front of the Denison House, our local settlement center, dressed in a white suit and holding a cane. He looked far removed from my dingy world—but he saw me and shouted to me in Arabic, and I knew somehow that he was not apart.

When he died we lost someone who had brought a certain flair and style to our life. I treasured the little trinkets he had given me, but it was not the material gifts I really missed. After his death Marianna left for Lebanon. When she returned, the liveliness that I had known in her house was replaced by her memories and her tears. She was close to us and good to us; and in return we treated her, the closest one of all to the poet, like a matriarch.

She had moved out of the South End, and we made trolley-car pilgrimages to her house in Jamaica Plain. There, one weekend, I became an unwitting conspirator in the destruction of evidence about the man we had all revered. While Marianna was abroad we saved her mail, some of which was addressed to Gibran. Enough accumulated to fill a shopping bag. When she returned she at first ignored the letters, but one drowsy afternoon she asked me to go through them with her. She could not read, and I was her eyes. I would dip into the cavernous bag, retrieve an envelope, and read aloud the name of the sender and return address. If she did not recognize the source she laid aside the envelope, unopened. That night we burned the voluminous unread correspondence—probably two hundred unexplored letters, decorated with stamps from all over the world. All of these deliciously perfumed, sealed, and embossed covers encased documents that attested to Gibran's life beyond us. They were destroyed, and I stood and wondered what I had done.

Years passed. My childhood adulation of an exciting relative was superseded by my own concerns as an art student and then in my own work as an artist. Yet an urge to understand the man I had known, whose name I bore, was always present. Oddly, the growing body of publications about him made it harder for me to reach this understanding. The books and articles were either embarrassingly reverential or offensively lurid. My curiosity had to be content temporarily with the material remnants of his life given to me gradually by Marianna: his clothes, his watch and cigarette lighter, the pigment chest, the paintings stored in Boston, letters and manuscripts, even his death mask, all became mine. Neither owning these things nor listening to the endless reminiscences of my family was an answer to my questions. How did a penniless immigrant not only adapt to the Boston slums but within a few years have enough of a following to bridge the social chasm between the South End and the Back Bay? I knew that his literacy was no magical happening, as one biographer stated, nor was it due to an enlightened family environment.

As my personal career developed, my quest for Gibran's identity became more imperative. As his namesake and a creative artist in an allied field, I was constantly besieged by inquiries about the man. Inevitably confusion arose. I even considered changing my name. Somehow pride prevented me.

By 1966 the complexities of my own life had been resolved. I was recognized professionally, and independently of my relative. Entrusting me with articles, books, and letters, my father had added to Marianna's gifts. I had my own family, and the time to stop and assess what to do with the mass of Gibran material had arrived.

I turned to an outside depository. Years before, Marianna had showed me letters from Gibran's friend and mentor, Mary Haskell Minis, in which she stated her decision to give all her Gibran correspondence, as well as her journal, to the University of North Carolina. At last I could begin to put together the pieces. At this stage my wife Jean joined forces with me, and we began to explore the 615 letters and 47 diaries that spanned the years from

1904 to 1931. Reading the material through twice, we learned about Gibran's beginnings in Boston and achievements in New York from a fresh perspective. Although the long passages of the Haskell journal abounded in leads, the basic puzzle of Gibran's earliest introduction into the world of arts and letters remained unsolved.

Finally, in the early seventies, my wife and I decided to stop mid-career and devote ourselves full time to research, however long it might take. We were in possession of two primary clues, an extraordinary photograph and a packet of letters. The stunning large print of a young Kahlil dressed as a Bedouin had hung over Marianna's sofa as long as I could remember; when I asked her about the photographer, she responded with vague stories of an impressively elegant Mr. Day. Fred Holland Day's significance in the poet's life had always been limited by biographers to his role as the owner of a studio in which Gibran's drawings were shown in 1904. However, Gibran's youthful appearance in this portrait convinced us that Day was an important force at a much earlier period. The letters were mostly written during the most obscure time in Gibran's life—when his mother, his sister Sultana, and his half-brother had died—and were addressed to an unidentified "Brother." How Marianna had received them or why she had so carefully saved them had never been clear.

We made inquiries about Day, and Peter Bunnell, then working in the Alfred Stieglitz Archive at Yale University, suggested that we visit the Norwood Historical Society, formerly Day's home. In 1972, at the Day House, our serious research began. On our second trip there, we verified that the packet of letters, written in stilted English, were unquestionably addressed to Day. Moreover, although we could locate no further correspondence from Gibran (leading us to suspect that Day had returned such notes either to the poet himself or to Marianna after Gibran's death), other letters to Day demonstrated his early sponsorship of the precocious adolescent. One note linked the entire chain of people responsible for Gibran's success. In 1896 a sympathetic social worker had requested Day's collaboration in helping "a little Assyrian boy Kahlil G." No discovery in all our research moved us so much as this early letter.

Also at the Day House was correspondence from Josephine Preston Peabody to her publisher. As early as 1898 it began to mention Gibran's name. We then realized that at the turn of the century Day, photographer, publisher, and avid collector, did not deserve characterization as an "opaque" figure; on the contrary, when Gibran met him, he was a colorful tastemaker and entrepreneur whose function and significance had disappeared as the twentieth century became louder and bigger.

With the engaging personality of Josephine Peabody added to our list, we began to look for material relating this talented poet to Gibran. We were led eventually to Harvard University's Houghton Library, where her beautifully executed diaries revealed a completely new dimension of his experience.

Through her sympathetic eyes were recorded his most tragic years. The myth was becoming reality. The story of Gibran would necessarily be the story of Gibran and his contemporaries. To reflect accurately the period and set his life firmly in a meaningful world, we would have to describe and re-create the vivid characters of Day, Josephine Peabody, Mary Haskell, Charlotte Teller, Emilie Michel, Ameen Rihani, Rose O'Neill, and others, by now nearly all obscure.

Gibran, admittedly a secretive man, was ambivalent about his background, and his desire to refashion his own past long frustrated serious study about it. Small wonder that some of his biographers resorted to imagined conversations about the major events of his life. With the discovery of the Peabody diaries and the wealth of material in the Haskell journal, fiction became unnecessary —all conversations and descriptions appearing in our text originate from either eyewitness accounts or contemporary letters. Previous allusions to relationships and incidents that have not been corroborated by primary source material have remained unmentioned. For the most part we have footnoted only direct quotations. Aware of previous tendencies to edit Gibran's English letters, which abounded in grammatical errors and misspellings, we decided to publish them as they were originally written. We have not noted his obvious mistakes unless they interfere with textual meaning.

Both Josephine Peabody and Mary Haskell kept two sets of diaries, the second set being more private "page-a-day" or "line-a-day" books. We have depended heavily on these intimate accounts. In them, unlike the more self-consciously literary journals, one may trace visits, mail, and the pertinent details of daily life. When Mary relied upon the phonetic spelling of names we have supplied the correct version.

A major difficulty that we encountered with Gibran's Arabic-speaking world was how to deal with proper names. Admittedly, modern methods of transliteration have made early twentieth-century attempts at Americanizing Arabic surnames obsolete. However, we have consistently presented names as they were written at the time. We hope our decision to rely on newspaper usage and established precedent will satisfy scholars who have so often questioned these Americanized versions.

Probably the greatest problem in dealing with Gibran's life was his duality. Constantly the theme of divided loyalties to two languages, two careers, two often conflicting sets of associates, dominated his development, with the result that biographers and historians have been biased, aware of one perspective and neglectful of the other. The hundreds of articles appearing posthumously in Middle-Eastern publications have analyzed his contribution to modern Arabic literature, while American accounts, flawed with careless scholarship and little documentation, have concentrated on the implications of his popularity. We have attempted in our work to show Gibran's several worlds, and the way he lived in them all.

Many individuals have shared their memories, stories, and material. First, of course, were Gibran's relatives in Boston. His sister Marianna, N'oula Gibran, Rose Gibran, Assaf George, Maroon George, Zakia Rahme (my mother's sister, often referred to as Rose Diab), and Joseph Rahme all have made invaluable contributions to this study. Also important as an eyewitness of Gibran's last years in Boston is Mary Kawaji (known as Mary Kellan), whose anecdotes and recollections have been most helpful.

For making available their extensive holdings of the Minis Family Papers, Haskell–Gibran series, we are most grateful to the entire staff of the Southern Historical Collection, The University of North Carolina Library at Chapel Hill. Our rewarding correspondence with J. Isaac Copeland, director of this collection, and its curator of manuscripts, Carolyn A. Wallace, has been marked by their limitless patience and understanding.

We also wish to thank Richard Teller Hirsch for his cooperative attitude toward our project and his permission to publish previously unpublished writings by Mary Haskell and Charlotte Teller Hirsch, now deposited at the Southern Historical Society.

Our appreciation is similarly due to the librarians, especially Carolyn E. Jakeman, assistant librarian for reference, at Houghton Library, whose holdings of the Josephine Preston Peabody Papers and Gibran letters to Witter Bynner and Corinne Roosevelt Robinson added immeasurably to this work.

In researching contemporaneous newspaper and magazine accounts, we have spent two years at the Boston Public Library, where numerous staff members have been helpful and enthusiastic. We also wish to acknowledge the staff of the Boston Athenaeum, particularly Donald C. Kelley, assistant in the art department, for their consideration shown our project.

Personnel at the New York Public Library, especially John L. Mish, chief of the Oriental division, and his assistant, Francis W. Paar, deserve our thanks. We also want to acknowledge John D. Stinson, research librarian at that library's manuscripts and archives division, where Gibran's letters to James Oppenheim are held.

It would be impossible to list all the helpful librarians and manuscript curators with whom we have corresponded in our search for unpublished documents by or about Gibran. We especially wish to thank David A. Randall, librarian at the Lilly Library, Indiana University, for his steadfast encouragement and advice during the past several years.

We also acknowledge the following archivists for their special attention: David Farmer, assistant to the director, Humanities Research Center, The University of Texas; Donald Gallup, curator, The Beinecke Rare Book and Manuscript Library, Yale University; Reverend Eugene J. Harrington, S.J., curator of manuscripts at Dinand Library, College of the Holy Cross; Paula Lichtenberg, senior reference librarian, The Public Library of Newark; Eva Moseley, curator of manuscripts, The Arthur and Elizabeth Schlesinger Library on the History of Women in America, Radcliffe College; Mary Faith

Pusey, assistant in manuscripts, Alderman Library, University of Virginia; E. Rosenfeld, curator, Abernethy Library, Middlebury College; Joseph W. Slade, editor of *The Markham Review*, Horrmann Library of Wagner College, Staten Island; Wilma R. Slaight, archivist, Wellesley College Library; Ronald S. Wilkinson, manuscript historian, The Library of Congress (where Gibran's letters to Margaret Lee Crofts are on deposit); and Walter W. Wright, chief of special collections, Baker Memorial Library, Dartmouth College.

Because it has been our intention to present a richly illustrated account of Gibran's life, we wish to thank Alan McNabb, director of the Telfair Academy of Arts and Sciences, Savannah, and his assistant, Feay Shellman, for their cooperation in making available reproductions from their Haskell collection of Gibran's art. For granting us permission to reproduce photographs or art, we are also grateful to Gail Buckland of The Royal Photographic Society of Great Britain; Jerald C. Maddox, curator of photography, The Library of Congress; Grace B. Mayer, The Edward Steichen Archive, The Museum of Modern Art; also the Museum of Fine Arts, Boston; the Fogg Art Museum; Harvard College Library; Peter A. Juley & Son, New York; The Metropolitan Museum of Art; the Lebanon Tourist and Information Center, New York; and The New-York Historical Society.

We are also grateful to countless individuals in private life. Our search at the Day House was greatly facilitated by Margaret Alden, Miriam and Charles Lennon, George Mahoney, then president of the Norwood Historical Society, and Francis Morrison. For supplying further information on Day, we would like to thank James Baker, Lilla Cabot Leavitt, Nathaniel Hasenfus, Anna E. Tanneyhill, Clarence White, and Ruth Rüyl Woodbury.

Stephen Maxfield Parrish, whose unpublished dissertation, "Currents of the Nineties in Boston and London: Fred Holland Day, Louise Imogen Guiney, and Their Circle," has caught the fragrant essence of that elusive period, deserves our special acknowledgment.

Our work concerning Josephine Preston Peabody Marks has been one of the most rewarding experiences in this search. This is due to the generous sharing of the Peabody material owned by Alison P. Marks and Lionel P. Marks. To them we are profoundly grateful. We also want to acknowledge the efforts of Nancy Lee Lewis, president of Wellesley College's Tau Zeta Epsilon society in 1973, for locating material about Gibran's first public exhibition in 1903.

In our efforts to portray justly Mary Haskell as the great intellectual force in Gibran's life and Charlotte Teller as the catalytic personality of his early New York days, we have interviewed and corresponded with many people who knew either woman or who could comment on some biographical fact. We are especially indebted to the following individuals: Elizabeth Belcher, Mrs. William B. Clagett, Adelaide Collier, Jean E. Crossman of the Wellesley College Alumnae Association, Suzanne Davis Durham, Gertrude Elsner, Dr. David McLean Greeley, Hetty Shuman Kuhn, Agnes Mongan, Marion Raoul

Stewart, Gladys and William Teller, and Hilda Washburn, guidance counselor at the Cambridge School of Weston (formerly the Cambridge School).

Most of Gibran's associates have died. However, we were fortunate in having interviewed or corresponded with several of his friends who recalled him during his Greenwich Village days. For their recollections we are grateful to Margaret Lee Crofts, Alice Raphael Eckstein, Philip K. Hitti, Hope Garland Ingersoll, Mariita Lawson, Matta and Birger Lie, Dorothy Maadi, Madeline Mason, and Mikhail Naimy.

Also contributing to our understanding of Gibran's friends have been Henry Bragdon, Mrs. Malcolm S. MacKay, and Madeleine Vanderpool. We want especially to acknowledge Jean Cantwell, president of The International Rose O'Neill Club, for her efforts in finding references to Gibran from her vast material on Rose O'Neill. For her cooperation in making Barbara Young's background available, we wish to acknowledge gratefully Marcia Sullivan.

In many instances William Koshland, president of Alfred A. Knopf, Inc., has cooperated with the writing of this biography. To him and Alfred A. Knopf we are especially appreciative for their contributions of letters from Gibran to his American publisher.

Our goals to compile and synthesize all the disparate articles and material by or about Gibran would never have been possible without the assistance of Charles H. Flanigan, who also transcribed the Haskell and Peabody papers for us. Nabila Mango of the Oriental studies department, University of Pennsylvania, has retrieved and translated all the voluminous Arabic material consulted. Unless otherwise noted, all translations are hers. To these loyal workers we shall always be grateful. For her many hours spent locating articles at libraries in New York, we are indebted to Susan Holcombe. We should also like to acknowledge Elizabeth Lansing for her research at the rare book section of the University of North Carolina Library, Chapel Hill, and Martine Loufti for her work at the Bibliothèque Nationale.

Mention of our good friends must be made. Francesco Carbone, Liz Clauhsen, Stuart Denenberg, and Paul Ward English have always responded whenever an unexpected research problem has arisen. The photography by Morton Bartlett and Stephen F. Grohe has been invaluable.

To the entire staff at New York Graphic Society we express our gratitude. For three years we have been encouraged and sustained by the sincere interest of the editor-in-chief, Donald A. Ackland. We thank him, our perceptive editor, Robin Bledsoe, and the designer, Betsy Beach, for their patience and expertise. Our appreciation is due Irene Bracchi for her typing.

Our final acknowledgment is to the many friends and countless strangers who have articulated a desire to read our interpretation of Gibran. To all these and many more, we are deeply indebted.

Boston, July 1974   KAHLIL GIBRAN

Besharri and Mount Lebanon. (*Aramco World Magazine*, July-Aug. 1940)

I

Poor in Besharri

The date of my birth is unknown," Kahlil Gibran once said. In an isolated village like his birthplace of Besharri, Lebanon, births and deaths were as ordinary as the tasks of the seasons, events imprinted only in the memories of men and women who later told their stories without regard for written history. It is only by such tales that we may deduce, with a fair amount of accuracy, that the poet was born on January 6, 1883.[1]

Besharri then was still very much like what it had always been: almost a fortress-village, secure in itself in high, lonely, limestone hills. Five thousand feet above the Mediterranean, tucked in the northern corner of the 120-mile strip that is today the Republic of Lebanon, it is an ancient place whose origins lie far back in prehistory when men first settled there in caves that still exist today. As Phoenicia, this land introduced the phonetic alphabet. In the centuries since, Egyptians, Babylonians, Assyrians, Persians, Romans, Byzantines, crusading Europeans, Arabs, and Turks have known and used the fruits of Lebanon's earth and the crafts of her people. The village knew and endured them all, but always her people insulated themselves against the destructive winds of change, clung to their pastoral habits, and went on living, dying, and surviving in their own traditional way. Always there was a symbol in their world which was at once the source of their life and the means of their living, an unchanging presence with which their identity had always been and always would be linked: the looming white apparition of "the Mountain."

Literally known as "the White" from the Semitic word *Lubnan*, which evokes the whiteness of milk, Mount Lebanon dominates and describes the entire range that rises so abruptly from the sea. In a country that is only some 4,000 miles square—about half the size of the State of New Jersey—it can be seen from every house and village. Below it, a careless confusion of cultures, religions, and languages streamed by through the millennia, but the mountain dominated them all—remote and white with the snows that cover its summit six months of the year, white with the sedimentary rock that shimmers in a perpetually white horizon. It was in the shadow of the Mountain that Kahlil Gibran was born.

At the time when she was delivered of her second son, his mother, Kamila, was thirty years of age. Herself the offspring of a priestly, and important, family, Kamila had married into a small and undistinguished clan. Only seven or eight Gibran families lived in the town, and they were not known for either industry or leadership. The root of their name, *jebr*, had been linked to the word *al-gebra*, based on the introduction to a thesis on equations by the ninth-century Arab mathematician Al-Khwarizmi. A nineteenth-century missionary, discussing the origins of proper names, reinforced this linguistic deduction with the mention of a boy "called Jebr or Al-jebra." [2] Time has a way of lending substance to such theories: Kahlil Gibran himself traced his name to the same source.

The few scanty records mentioning the Gibrans indicate that they arrived at Besharri toward the end of the seventeenth century. Where they came from, no one knows for sure. A family myth links them to Chaldean sources, an ancient Semitic people who were the dominant element in Babylonia. A more plausible story relates that the men named Gibran came from Syria in the sixteenth century, settling on a farm near Baalbek and moving to Bash'elah in 1672. Somewhere in their history a brother was condemned to death for religious reasons and died in Tripoli, only twenty-five miles from Besharri. Yet another version places the Gibran family originally in Acre, Palestine, and then traces their migration in 1300 to Bash'elah. There, a document exists which quotes a Patriarch, Boulos Massaid: "Those people called Gibrans are from Bash'elah and at the end of the seventeenth century moved to Besharri." [3]

There is enough evidence, in any event, to allow the poet, when he became a man, to make up for his own comfort a story of distinguished origins. He had need of that, for in his own immediate past the Gibran story left much to be desired. His great-grandfather's name appears in a petition from the townspeople of Besharri asking for protection from the Turks during the bloody Druze and Christian massacres of 1860. Tannous, Said, and Issa Gibran all signed it. It was Said who fathered Michael, who in turn fathered the poet's own father Khalil.

This Khalil was a bully and a gambler, but he was not without a certain charm. A man of lordly pretensions whose status symbol was an amber cigarette holder, he owned a walnut grove on Gibran land in Mar Sheen, near Baalbek, some thirty-five miles from Besharri. He had a mercurial temper, extravagant habits, and a contempt for hard work, preferring the gambling game of *domma*, or checkers, to the demeaning labor of a peasant. As a small boy, of course, Kahlil Gibran saw his father differently. To him he was proud and imperious, a big man with a domineering manner who came from a background which Kahlil, as a young man, described as "lofty." But it was Kamila, the mother, who brought such qualities of character to the family—these, and an enduring strength of character of her own.

Besharri was a stronghold of Maronite Christianity, that ancient sect which traced its origins as far back as the fifth century A.D. when the early Christians of Syria pledged their allegiance to a legendary monk, St. Marun, whose memory is perpetuated in a monastery at the source of the Orontes River. Kamila Rahme came from a family of priests in that sect. Despite an alliance with the Church of Rome, the Maronites always preserved for their priests the right to marry. The Rahme clan was large and, as a result, a power in the town of 2,000 souls. Kamila, graceful, pretty, and strong willed, was the youngest and favorite daughter of Istifan Abd-al-Qadir Rahme.

The story that is told of Kamila's father's origins emphasizes the intermingling of religions that was so typical of Christians and Moslems in the nineteenth century before the disputes that led to the massacres beginning in 1860. Two Moslem horsemen were said to have entered Besharri one day and, liking what they found, they settled in the town. Their names were Abd-al-Qadir and Abd-al-Salaam. Both married into the Rahme clan and, turning Christian, abandoned their Moslem background and took the name of Rahme.

Istifan, the male child of Abd-al-Qadir, grew up to be a priest. When his daughter Kamila reached marriageable age, she was betrothed to her cousin Hanna, the son of her father's brother Abd-al-Salaam. Such inbred interfamily alliances were common in Besharri, where for generations bloodlines crossed and strengthened the insular clans. It was considered better to marry "one of us" than "one of them," even if "they" were neighbors from a nearby town.[4]

But Hanna Abd-al-Salaam Rahme proved to be an undependable spouse and a restless man. In his native village he had little to sustain him and his bride but empty dreams of glory. Kamila bore him one son, Peter, before he abandoned her to venture out into the world beyond the Mountain. Motivated by his lack of everything and the hope of something, he went to Brazil to seek his fortune. Like so many of the pioneer emigrants whose immunity to foreign disease was fragile, he died in the alien climate. Kamila and Peter were left in Besharri.

All this happened before Kamila reached the age of thirty, and she was a provocative and witty girl. One day, in the shop of Isaac Gibran where the villagers bought herbs and potions, she met Isaac's nephew, Khalil, when she came to buy some ointment for an infected finger. Isaac introduced them; with her flirtatious wit Kamila aroused the interest of the handsome man with the amber cigarette holder. Some time between 1879 and 1882—the date is lost to posterity—they were married, and in 1883 Kamila bore her second son. No records survive attesting to the hour, the day, or even the month of his birth; if a literate priest happened to note it, the pages he wrote on have not survived. In accordance with the tradition of naming a boy by prefacing his father's name with the surname of his father's father, the child was called Gibran Khalil Gibran.

The man Kamila met in the apothecary's shop, for all his wayward charm, proved no more reliable a spouse than her first husband. In the four years following Khalil's birth, she gave him two daughters, Marianna and Sultana, but his growing responsibilities did not spur their father to earn an honest wage. His lack of ambition and his propensity for seeking to solve his financial problems at the *domma* table rather than in the fields were by now common talk in the village. Even their simple stone house with its mud roof proved too burdensome for the elder Khalil to keep up, and when the neglected home began collapsing around them, he found one level of a four-story house on publicly owned land near the center of town for his family to live in. The overseer, a town official named Raji Beyk, gave the Gibrans free living quarters in exchange for Khalil's fealty in local politics.

It was here, in this precarious situation, that the family's shaky foundations began to come apart. To be poor in Besharri was normal, but to be destitute and without pride, deserting the last remaining shreds of respectability, was shameful. Through her attitude, Kamila conveyed a sense of inferiority to the children. The children also felt the incompatibility of the marriage. "There was a subtle, silent gap in understanding between the two," Kahlil remembered later when as a young man he reminisced about his childhood. "My father had a very imperious temper and was not a loving person." [5]

The elder Gibran was irresponsible and extravagant, and Kamila, while she lacked a formal education, was worldly enough to spurn her expected role as a traditionally subservient woman. She was aware of her qualities and refused to bear the browbeating of her captious husband. Thus his powerful ego had to suffer the indignity of a bold wife who never hesitated to look seductively at other men in the village, and who deliberately flaunted her lusty singing voice and attractive presence at local feasts and dances. And if her behavior soured him, he retaliated in kind. He was a believer in the easy life, and far from modifying his desires to suit the needs of a growing family, he increasingly squandered at the gambling table what little he gained from his walnut groves. He also gave himself over to drinking, cursing, and boasting, in which he was ably assisted by his alcoholic brother E'd. Both brothers were town legend, and twenty-five years after Khalil's death Besharri villagers, uncertainly recalling stories about two ne'er-do-wells, tended to combine the two personalities into one.

It was not a happy family, and it lacked two elements essential to the spiritual welfare of a growing boy: security and love. But Khalil had, all around him as well as within him, wellsprings of strength upon which he could draw. One of the most important of these sources of solace was the magnificence of the countryside. It was a place to inspire any small boy, particularly a boy given to romantic dreaming. The solid cliffs near which he lived were split by yawning gorges; there were the clear and gushing torrents of the town's four rivers, and the cascading waterfalls. All his life he would remember the dramatic beauty of those places he sought out. Even the names exalted their magic and mystery: Wadi Qadisha, the Blessed Valley; Nahr Qadisha, the Blessed River; Nahr Nabaat, the River of the Springs; Nahr Ruwayyis, the River of the Leader; Nahr Simon, the River of Simon. Even at an early age, the child reveled in the ancient lore of his birthplace and sensed the holiness which emanated from the crystal waters and the eternal greenness of the forests. As an adult, he looked back on its idyllic perfection.

At the heart and center of this world in which he dreamed were the neighboring giant Cedars of Lebanon. Like the Mountain itself, the Cedars

The Gibran family tree, drawn by Kahlil in pen and ink at around age eight. "The Gibran Tree is adorable—such care! and beauty, too," wrote Mary Haskell. "Only the males counted of course and 'you see when I came to myself I made a somewhat different kind of leaf.'" His name is in the serrated leaf near the top. (Authors)

were both symbol and source to those who lived near them. The simplest of peasants felt awe at beholding these ancient testimonials to long-dead civilizations, and drew spiritual strength from them. Since biblical times they had been casting their black shadows on the mountain snows, and though their numbers were diminishing, they seemed as eternal as the Mountain.

The Cedars also provided a link for isolated towns like Besharri with the wider world beyond the Mountain and the sea. For hundreds of years they had attracted travelers visiting the Holy Land, travelers who brought with them intimations of other civilizations and cultures. During the eighteenth and nineteenth centuries, Europeans made a ritual of pilgrimages to the giant groves. In 1836 one such pilgrim set down his impressions of them in words that reflect the romantic meaning which the Cedars had for Westerners:

> The trunks of the old trees are covered with the names of travellers and other persons who have visited them. . . . They are difficult to approach, and are surrounded with deep snow, which is not passable until the middle of summer when it begins to melt away; the ground on which they stand is uneven, being covered with rock and stone, with a partial but luxuriant vegetation springing up in the interstices; their position, on the brow of the mountain, surrounded on every side by deep and solemn valleys, rocky and almost perpendicular descents, waterfalls and dreary dells, has something sacred and awful in it; they seem as if placed in their splendid and perilous site, like sentinels between time and eternity—the sad and deathless memorials of the days of the first temple, when God dwelt among His people, in the visible glory between the cherubim, and in the blessings of earth and heaven, the proofs of his love.[6]

The boy Khalil was profoundly moved by such symbols of God's love and by the wonders of the natural world. Retreating from parental tirades at home, he found shelter there, and solace, and as he grew, he came to identify with the timeless spirit of the places in which he worshipped his own childish gods. Much later, he recalled his impressions:

> The first great moment that I remember was when I was three years old—a storm—I tore my clothes and ran out in it—and I've been doing that in storms ever since. . . . And there were other great moments of new perception in my child life. Do you remember when you first saw the sea? I was eight when I first saw it. . . . My mother was on a horse, and my father and I were on a very beautiful, large Cyprian donkey—white. We rode up the mountain pass, and as we came over the brow, the sea was before us. The day was one of those when the sea and the sky are of one color. There was no horizon visible—and the water was full of the large Eastern sailing vessels—four- and five-masters with sails all set. As we passed across the mountain, suddenly I saw what looked like an immeasurable heavens [sic] and the ships sailing in it. I cannot describe what I felt. . . . And I remember when I was taken to the ruins of

Baalbek—the most wonderful ruins in the world. I was about nine then. We stayed about four days at Baalbek and when we left I wept. I have a notebook of the sketches I made there.[7]

It is important to be able to identify the means by which Khalil first developed the discipline to express later his personal vision of the land as a sanctuary. Where did he learn the basic skills of reading and writing? In villages like Besharri, as the nineteenth century was drawing to its close, public schooling as Westerners know it was nonexistent. The level of literacy was low among men; most women never learned to read or write at all. The only education to be had came from the ubiquitous priests, who taught a chosen few how to read Arabic, form the Arabic script, and do elementary calculations. But this meager learning was offered only for a purpose: to train young boys so that they could become familiar with the Scriptures and the liturgy and assist the clergy during masses and religious services. Although many of his friends and relatives attended these classes, no one in the disorganized Gibran household was interested in providing young Khalil with a religious education, and so for his first twelve years formal schooling was denied to him.

In later years, when the subject of his early education came up, he would refer vaguely to "tutors." But the concept of a personal tutor for the boy in the straitened circumstances of the Gibrans' existence is clearly incongruous; it was certainly another product of the defiance with which he cloaked the drab facts of a disappointing childhood. The truth remains that his primary education never included the discipline of a teacher or a classroom, and all his life long the poet never really learned to spell.

Yet there was someone. If a tutor can be seen as an older, wiser, and significant person to whom a child turns for information and for guidance just as a friend, then Khalil Gibran did indeed have a tutor who was an important influence in his formative years. His name was Selim Dahir. Just who he was and how he came into the boy's life is a mystery, but it is enough to know that he was a man who clearly perceived the young boy's loneliness and felt his thirst for knowledge. Even as a somewhat remote child, Khalil must have accepted his friendship gratefully and with some awareness of what it meant, for in his later years he recalled Selim Dahir, in terms that glowed with love and admiration, as a truly creative individual:

But some people are so wonderful that I wonder whether their life isn't creation after all. You remember Selim Dahir? He was a poet, a doctor, a painter, a teacher, yet he never would write or paint as an artist. But he lives in other lives. Everybody was different for knowing him. All Becharry [sic] was different. I'm different. Everybody loved him so much. I loved him very much, and he made me feel very free to talk to him. Once I asked him, in great confidence, whether if a company of the learned physicians came together, they couldn't find means to graft the human head on the horse and make centaurs. I may have been about seven years old then.[8]

Khalil learned the rudiments of the alphabet and language from Selim Dahir. But the older man gave him more—he opened up a wide world and showed the boy how he could discover it through history books, atlases that described the shape of continents and the spread of seas, and scientific instruments that measured the universe. The debt that the poet owed his friend was remembered and acknowledged when, in 1913, he wrote an elegy to Selim Dahir:

> The son of the Cedars has died.
> Arise, o youth of the Cedars.
> · · · ·
> The son of the Mountain has died.
> Gird him with his father's sword.
> · · · ·
> Your sage, o youth, has died.
> Do not lament him.
> Do not flood his corpse with tears.
> Recall the words of his days and nights.
> Repeat the memory of his virtues.
> For every man there will be a day.
> In that day the design of his life
> Is reflected on the faces of his people.[9]

To any teacher with an understanding of the development of a young human being, Khalil must have seemed a complex and compelling child. He was lonely, he was thoughtful, he seldom smiled or laughed as children should. But his inner resources were many, and he knew how to draw upon them. He was not satisfied with mere dreams; he also wanted to make dreams come true. An aspect of this is seen in his almost compulsive drive to fill his days by thinking up and building the toys he never had—toys which utilized whatever came to his hand, but which sometimes went far beyond what one might consider for a small boy. He remembered them with nostalgic affection:

As a child I did not know I was sad. I just knew I was longing to be alone, making things. And they could never get me to play.

When I was a little boy, five or six or seven, I had a room all my own, filled with things I collected. . . . It was a perfect junk shop . . . old frames and bits of clear stone and rings, and plants—and pencils—I had hundreds of pencils—and little ones that I wouldn't throw away. Later it became colored pencils. I drew swiftly and covered dozens of sheets of paper. And when there were no more sheets I drew on the walls of the room. . . . And I wrote compositions. I remember one on an old man, a poor, old man, old and miserable—and I said over and over again how old and cold and miserable he was—and then how another man came and helped him and did him good—a real Good Samaritan story.

Casting was my greatest delight when I was about eight years old, in the simplest and easiest of metals—lead. I would use sardine cans and sand. . . . I wasn't always successful. . . . But I made gods and goddesses in this way, and I loved it.

I was the busiest boy that ever was—Yes, indeed, all the town knew it. When I had finished a thing, I'd bring it down to be shown. But I liked them to look at it while I was not there. The pleasure was while I was doing the thing. The result was never what I wanted. . . . It was always that way from the time I was nine or ten—and so I was never happy. Once I planned a great work, a garden, 14 or 15 yards square—and all laid out and planted, and I was going to carve all the gods and goddesses—in wood—for it—and each was going to make an appropriate gesture. Then when all was ready, I was going to pull the string, and every god at the same time would make his or her gesture. . . . I was deeply interested in flying. And [I] bought yards and yards of stout cloth and rope and made a big thing to fly off the roof with. They let me finish it and then they wouldn't let me try it. . . . But wheels were my chief joy. I made them myself—and waterwheels were the greatest. I made a big wheel that ran many little wheels by belts. But I was always unhappy because my vision was so far beyond anything I could do.[10]

The manipulated gods and goddesses, the mechanical devices, the kite-flying vehicles of escape were all manifestations of young Khalil's desire to design a universe which he could control. But they also show another aspect of his character as a boy: he was no idle dreamer, but a child of active work, and he equated work with love. And, finally, he was always conscious that the objects and stories of his own devising invariably gained him praise and attention. This desire to win respect for things accomplished remained with him and was probably instrumental in driving him, once in America, toward that sector of society which recognized genius and talent in even its most exotic forms.

Meanwhile, other events befell him that made indelible impressions on his life. One of the most significant was an accident that occurred shortly before the family sailed for America. He later told the story:

When I was ten or eleven years old, I was in a monastery one day with another boy, a cousin, a little older. We were walking along a very high place that fell off more than a thousand feet. . . . The path had a hand rail, but it had weakened—and path and rail and all fell with us—and we rolled probably one hundred and fifty yards in the landslide. My cousin fractured his leg, and I got several wounds and cuts in the head down to the skull, and injured my shoulder. The shoulder healed—but healed crooked—too high and too far forward. So after it was well and sound, they pulled it apart again and strapped me to a real cross with thirty yards of strap and I stayed wrapped to that cross forty days. I slept and all sitting up. I was not strong enough to take ether when they broke the shoulder again. If it had hurt less, I should probably have cried out. But it hurt too much for me to cry. My father and mother were with me talking to me and that helped.[11]

This candid story of a youthful mishap is true, and the cousin, N'oula Gibran, remembers all the details of the prolonged mending of Khalil's shoulder. In the poet's mind, however, the event acquired mystical overtones. An ordinary splint became a cross, and the painful period of convalescence stretched out to forty days—the period Christ spent in the wilderness. The transposition eloquently illustrates the degree to which biblical legend imbued the thinking of the Maronite Christians.

Religious awareness permeated the life of the people of the Mountain. Since they first banded together in the fifth century A.D., the Christians of Syria, joined in allegiance to the monk St. Marun, had learned to live introspectively and defensively within the concepts of their own sectarian thought. In 685 they were already known as Rebels, and they defied the Third Council of the Byzantine Church in Constantinople and set themselves up as a separate body headed by their first Patriarch, John Maron. The step was a decisive one; the schism has lasted to this day.

While the schism was tearing apart the Catholics of the Byzantine Empire, another religious eruption in the East was beginning to threaten the Church's domination of the Mediterranean world from Mecca to Palestine. The forces of Islam were pouring down the Holy Lands, and where they conquered they held sway for centuries afterward. But while large numbers of Christians readily accepted the Moslem faith, a majority chose to resist, pay tribute, and retreat to the safety offered by the Mountain. There they held fast. Throughout the period of Moslem ascendancy the physical remoteness, the indomitably fanatic spirit of the Maronites, and their warlike reputation protected these pockets of Christianity and allowed them to cherish their separate creed.

Although the native Aramaic and Syriac languages were being replaced by Arabic, the language of the Maronites, even among those who would never be able to read the Scriptures, remained laden with the sayings and symbols of Christ. Legends, tales, and songs perpetuated the ancient stories of saints and holy men from generation to generation. To a child in nineteenth-century Lebanon, the asceticism of St. Marun, the visits of St. Anthony to the land of the Mountain, and the feats of St. George were like contemporary events. And strengthening this emphasis on spiritual folklore was the mysticism of local landmarks—strangely inscribed stones, the caves which were everywhere, the mysterious grottos.

Thus when the poet Gibran recalled his siege of early pain, the most direct device with which he could describe his suffering was the Cross, the most eloquent way of explaining his time of convalescence the forty days which, like Jesus, he spent in the wilderness of pain. Throughout his life, when searching for a suitable simile or a pertinent image, he would revert to the biblical traditions of his background. His early experiences, steeped as they were in the metaphor of the Gospels, served as the link in his poetry between East and West, the source from which he drew the inspiration and the language for his experience with the soul.

Politically, Lebanon in the years of Khalil Gibran's childhood was the most modern of the Turkish provinces under the Ottoman Empire. This was an ancient dominion, going back to 1516 when the Turks first extended their empire beyond the borders of Anatolia, and it contributed scarcely less than the Moslem invasion to a sense of isolation among the Maronite Lebanese. For since their first contact with the Papal See in Rome in 1201, the Maronites had been open to the influence of the West. When this rapprochement with the Roman Church culminated in official union at the Synod of 1736, which recognized Maronite allegiance to Rome but acknowledged their right to the Syriac liturgy and the tradition of their noncelibate priesthood, the trend toward westernization was strengthened even more, and Franciscan, Carmelite, and Lazarist monasteries were established in the most remote areas of the country. Although the complex loyalties of the native population were eventually divided and factionalized by this intrusion of Western thought, the Maronites continued to flourish in their cherished independence, and under the reigns of two powerful Lebanese leaders who attempted to unite the country against any kind of foreign domination, they attained a fair measure of political power.

The first of these leaders was Fakhr al-Din II, a feudal lord of the Druze sect who in 1590 was the first emir of Lebanon to command a united front of Christian and Druze leaders. The Druze, a sect combining elements of Christian, Moslem, and Jewish religious thought, were open to Western persuasions, particularly since their leader, Fakhr al-Din, had spent five years of exile at the Tuscany court of Cosimo II, where he observed firsthand the arts of Western diplomacy, economics, and administration. Upon his return, he entrusted state offices, land grants, and military commands to enterprising Maronites, and he opened Lebanon to the westernizing agents of missionaries, traders, and teachers.

A century and a half later, a second period of westernization was launched by the emir Bashir II, who ruled Lebanon from 1788 to 1842 and brought the country to the threshold of modern times. Breaking up the pattern of feudalism and undermining Ottoman authority wherever possible, Bashir introduced machinery and other engineering achievements of a modern

Western society and strengthened his authority by the swift dispensation of impartial justice.

Bashir's rule was in many ways like a long-delayed flowering of Lebanese culture, but in 1830 the old threat of foreign interference once again brought strife and dissension to the land of the Mountain. Imbued with a new sense of nationalism and outraged by Bashir's increasing misrule, Druze, Christians, and Moslems united against him and deposed him.

For all the fact that he proved to be a tyrant in the end, however, Bashir II was a genuine national hero in the minds of many Lebanese. The young Khalil was profoundly influenced by the tales he heard of him, and as his feelings for his native country grew, he came in young adulthood to transfer qualities of the heroic emir to his own father. Such feelings were all the stronger because of the events which overtook the unfortunate Lebanese in the years following Bashir's downfall.

In Europe, the tide of colonialism was now in full surge and with the deposition and exile of Bashir II, the way was open for the direct intrusion of the European powers into the affairs of Lebanon. Under these outside pressures, the brief alliance between Lebanese factions soon began to crumble. Where Druze and Christian had shared the Mountain under a carefully observed, symbiotic understanding, they now once again began to look upon each other with mutual suspicion and distrust. By 1845 this unrest had increased to the point of open hostility, and a series of atrocities finally shattered their hard-won cooperation completely. In Constantinople the Turkish authorities did nothing, secretly encouraging the slaughter which could only be of benefit to the Ottoman rule. Offstage in Europe, the English were unacknowledged allies of the Druze, while the French, also seeking to capitalize on the religious schism, were outspoken protectors of the Maronites.

For the next twenty years ambush, slaughter, and pillaging weakened the Lebanese peasantry and countryside. Scores of Christian villages were laid waste while the Christian world watched in horror and blamed the Moslem population as a whole for the acts of vengeance perpetrated by a fanatic few. In 1860 France at last openly intervened, supported weakly by the other European powers. French troops occupied Beirut for ten months, and in that time helped to shape a constitution for Lebanon, but the peace it was supposed to produce never materialized, the Turkish rule remained as inept and exploitative under a Christian governor as it had been before under a Turk.

Meanwhile, Besharri, Khalil's native village, in these times of Byzantine intrigue, plotting, and destruction, reverted once again to its instinct for survival. The town drew in upon itself, shunned outsiders, and sought only to protect itself in ancient isolation in the steep hills shadowed by the Mountain.

In so doing, the Besharrians also raised a wall against a new invader from the Western world: the American Protestant missionary.

The heyday of these proselytizers, who sought to "revive pure Christianity among the Eastern Christians and to make 'spiritual conquests' among the Muslims," was now beginning.[12] Based in Boston and espousing a policy of "disinterested benevolence," the zealous band, products of the New England divinity schools, fanned out all over the world, and the closed boundaries of the Levant only provided a further incentive to their work. Their early attempts to settle in Palestine, the Holy Land, were frustrated by disease, death, and native hostility. They finally chose Beirut as the center of their missionary efforts, and here they managed to lure a few Eastern Catholics to their first primitive schools. For years their spiritual goals were limited to the establishment of schools, the offering of much-needed medical aid, and the publication and distribution of Bibles and tracts in Arabic. Soon aware that their efforts were punishable by death to both Moslem converted and Christian converter, and thwarted in the dissemination of the New Testament by Jewish resistance, the evangelists were forced to content themselves with "nominal" Christians.

But in towns like Besharri, the Protestants from faraway America never gained even the semblance of a foothold. Mindful of an 1826 Maronite encyclical which forbade any transactions with the atheist "Biblishiyyun," and remembering the fate of Asaad Shidiaq—the earliest of Syrian Protestants who was imprisoned in a monastery near Besharri, tortured, defiled, and finally put to death for his heretical beliefs—Besharri aggressively resisted any Protestant intrusion. For their part, the missionaries, frustrated in repeated attempts to bring enlightenment to the hinterland, contemptuously rested their case on native stupidity: "Besharri, near the Cedars of Lebanon," the dean of the mission wrote home in 1874, "is one of the places where the people are so ignorant that the other villages laugh at them." [13]

For the young Khalil Gibran, religious persecution, atrocities, and such instances of biased snobbery were only a generation removed, and as such very much alive to him. He could still see all about him the evidence of religious hatred, and even though the Maronite Christians no longer were forced to wear black, or were denied the privilege of Moslem testimony in court, or were forbidden to own horses, the memory of these harassments and the terrors of bygone massacres haunted them. In his later search for some meaning to the deep antagonisms which divided his country's various sects, Khalil was finally to depart from all forms of orthodoxy, which he considered to be destructive to man's freedom and growth.

To the poverty of knowledge, which Khalil sought so desperately from a man like Selim Dahir, was added in his childhood a second poverty—that of material things, beginning with food, which could no longer be produced in sufficient quantity by the meager soil of his homeland. When he was born, it was no longer possible to depend on the rocky earth of the Lebanese hillsides to produce what the growing population needed to sustain itself. The infant economy fostered by Bashir II had slipped into a severe depression: shipping was diverted from Lebanese ports by the new Suez Canal, the silk industry was hurt by competition from Japan, the export of wine all but destroyed by a disastrous fungus disease. Under these conditions, many Lebanese for the first time considered emigration as a way out of their difficulties. Kamila's first husband, the father of Peter, had been among the earliest of these to seek prosperity abroad through peddling and storekeeping. Others from Besharri followed him, and by 1890 a small Gibran caravan headed by Khalil's cousin, Melham Gibran, his wife M'ssahia, and their daughters Rose and Zakia, ventured to Boston, where they settled down to live.

At this same time the family of young Khalil received the final blow that led to its total collapse. Exactly what happened will never be clear because no one wanted the details to be known outside the Gibran clan, but the broad outlines of a scandal are nonetheless incontrovertible. The elder Gibran, the gambler and wastrel, probably to at least a degree by his own foolish act, somehow became involved in a small-town political racket.

It came about because the powerful head of the town, Raji Beyk, of the Hanna Dahir clan, had introduced a policy of petty graft and extortion in Besharri. It finally grew to be intolerable for the citizenry, and a committee of outraged villagers turned to the Patriarch and demanded Beyk's removal from office. The Patriarch, beset in other areas by challenges to his authority, reviewed the case and ousted Beyk.

Khalil Gibran was inevitably caught up in the consequences of this scandalous affair. He had long since undertaken certain duties for the political boss, and he was not liked in the town. Possibly he had misused taxes which, on behalf of Raji Beyk, he had collected. Whatever the case, he was accused of embezzlement, arrested, and arraigned for trial.

For Kamila, proud daughter of a family of standing, this was more than she could bear. Long afterwards, her son Khalil remembered "the morning when the summons was served on his father—how the crowd rode into the courtyard of the big old house and how his mother stood bravely smiling. At the end of three years Gibran was found guilty and all his property was confiscated except the clothes on their backs . . . so that they became guests of the government in their own house." [14]

At the time of the arrest, Khalil was eight years old. His youth and innate sense of pride probably combined to prevent his ever learning all the details of his father's downfall—even whether he was jailed or not is unknown today. In any case, it was the boy's strong-willed mother who now became the center of his life. Her family suggested America as the best avenue of escape from the ignominy of a disgraced husband; the younger Khalil later protested that before she accepted this way out, she tried "to move heaven and earth to absolve her innocent husband from the crime of which he was accused." [15] As for the elder Gibran, he viewed the whole affair, including his family's departure, with equanimity. He even offered to give some money of his own to make the trip possible. Kamila allegedly refused. "I have money to equal your own weight," she said, and this retort reflects the breach that split the family.[16]

Shortly before the family left, a photograph was taken which showed them together for the last time. In the center is Khalil Gibran, whose uncowering expression dramatically displays the boisterous defiance with which he met any and all attempts to restrict his indomitable spirit. At his left is Kamila, attractive still and silently sullen. In front of them is the older of the two daughters, Marianna, clutching a bouquet of flowers. Beside her is an unfortunate gap that probably showed the younger Sultana. Behind the mother towers Peter, alert and alive to the potential of a beckoning New World. Khalil, defying his frailty and aloofness in a particularly stalwart stance, clutches in his left hand a pencil, in his right a scroll.

It is a touching photograph, one that mirrors somehow the mingled pain and hope which mother and children must have felt in that difficult hour. But their hope, however fragile, had much to sustain it in the background of their lives and the long history of the homeland they were now forsaking. In the ancient tradition which fortified their spirit, the Arabic word *al-mahjar* described a city to which pilgrims had traveled in those times when the Mediterranean's first cities were symbols for the Phoenicians who colonized settlements in search of prosperity. In 1895 *al-mahjar* was "al-New York" for the widening flow of Lebanese emigrants departing on a similar search, of whom Kamila and her family formed a part.

On June 25, 1895, Kamila Gibran and her children disembarked in America after a voyage of some 5,000 miles.[17] What would happen to this family in their American experience would deeply impress each one of these expectant lives, either through the fragility of a new existence or the splendor of success.

The Gibran family in Lebanon shortly before their departure to America. (Authors)

2

A City Wilderness

When Kamila and her children finally landed, their first American experience was the long wait at Ellis Island, where every immigrant was processed by the Immigration and Naturalization officials. Here they spent their first night, Marianna recalled some ten years afterward; and she remembered, too, the last lap of their hegira, the journey northward to Boston the next day.

Boston was a logical place for the Gibrans to settle. Next to New York it was the second largest Syrian community in the United States, and it was also the home of Melham Gibran and his family, as well as many other cousins and friends who had emigrated from Besharri. Oliver Place is a part of Chinatown today, but at the turn of the century it was a small, thriving, Levantine enclave hidden at the edge of Boston's populous, impoverished South End. Protected on four sides by tenements from the surrounding streets, it was reached by a narrow brick entrance that tunneled between two tall buildings which faced out onto Beach Street. Whether immigrants chose the security of this Casbah-like retreat, forced again to protect themselves as they had in towns and villages like Besharri, or whether they were simply shunted there by officials is debatable. But here Kamila would find a familiar tongue, accustomed ways, and the understanding of voyagers like herself.

To Bostonians of the day, the teeming South End was at once too close to the center of the city to ignore, and too complicated in its cultural diversity to understand. The chosen home of immigrants of many countries and religions, it lacked the solidity and identity of one national population like the Italian North End, or the aspiring middle-class values of residents in the outlying Charlestown and Dorchester sections. By 1892 its inherent social problems were being compared unfavorably to the notorious slums of East London: "But the picturesque features which light up the gloom of East London are wanting in the South End where life is characterized by a pathetic monotony." [1]

In the 1890s, pioneering and well-meaning social scientists were beginning to examine, as objectively as their puritan consciences allowed, the indignities of the South End that awaited thousands like the Gibrans—crowded housing, disease, and poverty. One of them, Robert Woods, in his book *The City Wilderness*, has left us a description that is as revealing of the attitude of the early social workers as it is of the area and its 40,000 inhabitants:

> The nearness of the district to the city's throng, together with remoteness from its best life, allows the irresponsible class of people to come and go, who throw aside the ordinary restraints and give reins to their worst impulse. . . . This South End which once rose out of the water, as it were, to become a refuge for the older American families, has now become a common resort for all nationalities. . . . In this wide variety, however, a comparatively small number of nationalities make up the greater part of the population. The Irish, Jews, British Americans, Americans, and Negroes are its chief constituents; but the English, Germans, Greeks, Armenians, Austrians, and a few other nationalities are represented, though in considerably smaller numbers. And if we add to these Chinatown and the Syrian settlement in Oliver Place, both on the outskirts of the district, we supply an appropriate finishing touch to the group, a population as complicated as it is inharmonious. [2]

Obviously the Syrian community, mentioned by Woods almost as an afterthought, was an incomprehensible presence to the social surveyors. They could more easily describe Irish and Middle European ways than account for the behavior of swarthy Levantines who called themselves Christians, fingered strange-looking prayer beads, and showed a suspicious resistance to becoming Americans. Oliver Place was an equally alien territory to the overseers of the Associated Charities of Boston, who wrote:

> The Syrians are nearly all peddlers if they are anything. Some are persistent candidates for charity. There are very few of them in the South End outside of Oliver Place. Next to the Chinese, who can never be in any real sense American, they are the most foreign of all our foreigners. Whether on the streets in their oriental costumes, or in their rooms gathered about the Turkish pipe, they are apart from us. They are hospitable in their homes, but they are also deceitful, and out of all the nationalities would be distinguished for nothing whatsoever excepting as curiosities. [3]

Kamila began to earn a living in the expected way. Laden with a fifty-pound pack of laces and linens, she began the daily trudge back and forth to the grand houses of the Back Bay, and even worked her way to the suburbs of

Brookline and Cambridge. By the time of the Gibrans' arrival, peddling was a way of life for Syrian immigrants. Except for some sporadic, missionary-sponsored visits in the 1850s and 1860s, Syrian immigration to America was negligible until relatively late, 1878, with the well-documented arrival of a Protestant family to New York. In the next decade there arrived a widening trickle of Syrian petty merchants, who hawked olivewood trinkets popular for their associations with the Holy Land, and colorfully embroidered native handiwork. These wayfaring bands, finding a market for their exotic wares at country fairs and expositions, slowly worked their way westward until, perhaps, they took up homesteading along the frontier or settled down in a midwestern farming town. In time, they were assimilated into the American background.

Not so with those who followed. In the 1890s small colonies of Syrians began to form in the cities, from which they fanned out into surrounding areas and huckstered their growing selection of dry goods, laces, hardware, or whatever would satisfy the antimacassar vogue of the American public. More than their dress, speech, or religion, it was this lack of interest in the kind of hard work which, according to the New England ethic, was the principal path to salvation, that set the Syrians apart and made them incomprehensible to even the charitably inclined social workers.

> They come . . . thinking to sweep up money in the street. . . . They have little idea how to work, for they have never had to stick to anything at home. They have worked when it pleased or when the crops demanded it. Work in our sense of the word they have never done. Regular hours throughout the year is a thing unknown to them. Even those who start in at factory work often prefer peddling. . . . They peddle in nearly all the suburbs of Boston. . . . Who has not seen these dark-complexioned women with black kerchiefs over their heads and baskets under their arms, getting in or out of electric cars? How many families of Boston have not had them at their doors, peddling so-called Syrian silk and Oriental goods (which are usually made in Paris or Constantinople), or with their baskets filled with needles, pins and other small wares? . . . They seem to need money, are thinly clad, and footsore.[4]

Perhaps most outrageous and repellent to the Puritan New Englanders was the practice of the mothers going out to work and leaving their children at home "to be looked after by their idle husbands." A woman who was little more than a drummer or packhorse—although, like Kamila, she was likely to be the financial support of her family—could not have been more foreign to the Yankee understanding of an industrious woman. This reversal of roles was considered the first step of a descent into moral iniquity: "The idle husbands . . . can be seen at almost any hour of the day by going into Oliver Place and

Tyler Street, Boston. From the right are the two wings of the Quincy School, the Our Lady of the Cedars Maronite church, and number 76 where the Gibrans lived. (Schlesinger Library, Radcliffe College)

looking around. It is not the custom in this country to let the women work and have the men remain idle at home. When girls and young men go out on the streets to peddle, they fall into bad company, and, as one who understands his people well, says: 'They often end by going to houses of ill repute.' And all this is encouraged by buying of and aiding these people." [5]

Thus Boston's five hundred Syrians were especially visible in their unconventionality and, perhaps more than other immigrants of the day, unfairly stereotyped. "Every time a kind-hearted individual buys of a Syrian something he does not want—or gives food, clothing, or money for doctors' bills without investigating the case—he encourages begging, lying, idleness, neglect, exposure, and a future increase of 'Syrians to sweep up money from our streets,'" said an Associated Charities report.[6] Even the wretched living conditions of Oliver Place were blamed on the Syrians' innate turpitude: "The desire to appear poor encourages a mode of living which is alike unhealthful physically and morally. . . . They overcrowd tenements to avoid high rents, and dirt and squalor are their companions. Things are permitted in Oliver Place, which if it were a public way, could not exist." [7]

In this setting the twelve-year-old Khalil, who was always to display a thin-skinned reaction to the slightest slur upon him or his family, soon became aware of the scorn that often accompanied the distribution of food, clothing, and medicine. What he thought of this charity in terms of specific instances we will never know, because he rarely spoke of it in later years. Instead, he denied the hardships and hurts of Oliver Place in so thorough a way that a clear understanding of the social forces and the early influences that molded him becomes nearly impossible. In the squalid surroundings of his first years in America, there began an ambivalence about his private life and thoughts which was to continue all his life long. Possibly because the truth of the indignities which were the daily fare of his family was too much for his fragile ego to bear, he overlaid the filth and stench of Oliver Place with a veneer of imaginary stories of a privileged childhood suitable to the son of noble parents. Even then he had a way of removing himself in his own thoughts, which came to light once in a conversation with a friend, who noted, "All Kahlil's life he has been remote." [8]

One of the avenues that would lead Khalil, and many other immigrant children, out of their "offensive conditions" and into a life of useful employment and productivity was the public school system. For every enclave of foreigners there existed a nearby school ready to immerse the children into the indoctrinating waters of the American dream. Close to Oliver Place on Tyler Street was the Quincy School, a boys' school whose ethnic make-up was becoming as diversified as that of the South End. One-third of its pupils were Irish, one-third American, and the remaining third consisted of Jews and "other foreigners." Among the latter was a mixture of Central and Eastern Europeans along with a scattering of Chinese children. It was in this polyglot environment, brief records tell us, that Gibran Khalil Gibran first went to school.[9]

In one respect, at least, the experience marked him for life. Due either to the impersonal registration procedures or to clerical impatience with a too-foreign name, his name was misspelled and shortened to Kahlil Gibran. And so, except for a few attempts to continue calling himself Gibran Khalil Gibran, the Americanization of the little boy began with his ultimate acceptance of the abbreviated name which was obviously more compatible to the American bureaucratic ear and eye. After his death, efforts to realign his name to a transliteration acceptable to Arabic scholars failed, frustrated by the simple reality of turn-of-the-century decisions that anglicized not only names but attitudes and manners. These surgically swift gestures penetrated more deeply than the unwary victims realized.

When he entered school on September 30, 1895, Kahlil had been in America just a little more than two months. He was placed in the ungraded class reserved for immigrant children who had to learn English from the beginning. In this no-man's-land environment where the pupils might chatter in half a dozen or more different languages, a child could progress as fast as his "admirable traits" would allow, that is, if he were "ambitious, quick witted, and imitative." [10] Kahlil, apparently, both reached the expected levels of achievement and further impressed his teachers by the bravura with which he sketched and drew. Marianna, in fact, always remembered her brother's performance as outstanding. Whether the family story of his interrupting a chalkboard lesson and showing the teacher how a figure should be drawn is true or not, the Yankee and Irish women who remained to teach another generation of Gibrans recalled Kahlil vividly in later years.

Kahlil's own thoughts about Quincy School and the teachers who helped him to adjust during his first months in America were later expressed when once he was asked what was the most difficult period in his lifetime. He replied, "The two years when I was first in Boston. They were my most miserable. I had only the teachers in the school. And they were so loving to me, so kind. When I was in college, I had letters from all of them. You see, I had gone through so many of the grades while I was there. And they really loved me. And I felt it. But we had nothing in common." [11]

School was an opportunity open to Kahlil alone; Marianna and Sultana were not allowed to participate in a school program. The cloistered traditions of Middle Eastern women as well as economic need prevented their going, and neither ever learned to read or write. Instead, they became part of a new family enterprise: they joined their older half-brother Peter in the operation of a store.

This exciting expansion of the family's commercial activities was entirely the result of Kamila's hard work, perseverance, and thrift. Within a year she had been able to save up enough money to enable Peter to open a small dry goods store at 61 Beach Street. Marianna and Sultana helped out as sales girls, and Marianna later remembered it as fun—particularly when Peter was occupied and she would reach into the cash box and filch a penny for her and her sister to squander on a Syrian sweet or sherbet. But despite a flurry of effort and activity, Peter's business never thrived.

Yet if ever one of the Gibran children was to succeed in the American world, Peter seemed destined to be the one. Of all the children, he was the most personable, the most socially talented, and considered the most handsome. He played the lute with feeling and had a large repertoire of native songs. People liked him for his charming manners and easy approach to life. Marianna and Sultana adored him; it was no secret that they, and others, preferred Peter's life style to Kahlil's introspection. Years later Marianna fondly recalled Peter's verve and spirit, and loved to tell how proud she had been to walk through the South End streets with her dashing older brother.

Kahlil, especially, recognized and respected Peter's popularity within the family. "Father loved Peter, his stepson, very much, much more than me," he once said. "He had a good head, though there was nothing that was great in him. And everybody loved him. He was so courteous, and sweet and upright and gentle." [12]

Peter's worldly ease was somewhat shared by the youngest daughter, Sultana, whose own beauty and personality were emerging. Marianna's reminiscence of the childhood alliances within the family is worth noting: "Marianna and Kahlil used to be together against Sultana because everything was Sultana, Sultana. 'She was so lovely, and she and my mother had such lovely voices.'" [13]

It was a good and close family, despite the poverty and the occasional despair about ever being able to surmount the problems of getting along in America. Kamila's energy was unflagging, and her courage seldom faltered. She had an intuitive respect for her children's spiritual development, and for Kahlil's in particular. His fragmented impressions and memories of this period point to his deepening sense of withdrawal from the social life around him and to his effort to discover some interior route of escape that would compensate for the abrupt change from a rural to a city wilderness. Kamila must have protected her introverted son, and later he often recalled her sympathetic understanding of his need to be alone. "My mother understood [my remoteness]. When I was a boy, say from nine to thirteen, sometimes she would smile at someone who came in and look at me and lay her finger on her lip and say, 'Hush. He's not here.'" [14]

At the same time, Kamila conveyed to Kahlil a spirit of independence and fostered in him a will to develop outside the family's narrow mercantile existence. Her attitude, which was remarkable for its open-mindedness, allowed him to meet other people and form acquaintanceships beyond the tightly knit confines of Oliver Place. The sequence of events that would lead to Kahlil's early familiarity with the Boston world of art and letters was only possible for an independent boy who felt free to explore the adjacent neighborhood. Later he remembered his mother's wisdom with gratitude and love: "My mother was a most remarkable being . . . she was always doing little things that put me on the way to love others besides myself—always, as it were, pushing me away or out a little. She freed me from herself. And she said things to me when I was twelve years old that I'm just realizing now—prophetic things. She knew things very wonderfully." [15]

The colorful South End streets must have fascinated Kahlil, as they would most adolescent boys. This emerging street culture was a phenomenon that also intrigued the benevolent social scientists. To them, the omnipresence of unsupervised children, gutter-fast and alley-wise, was a sign of family breakdowns. In their preoccupation with youthful gangs, they observed: "The term 'street children' is used advisedly, for as a matter of fact, most of the children of this locality live on the street when they are not asleep. The streets educate with fatal precision. Sometimes in a little side street, you will see a hundred children at play. In this promiscuous street life, there is often every sort of license that can evade police authority. Juvenile rowdyism thrives." [16]

While overestimating the percentage of "incorrigible truants" with "criminal tendencies," the social scientists finally conceded that "a small minority of these children manage to keep an obedient, law-abiding spirit, in spite of 'street education,' although one does not know how." [17] The Gibran children, if noticed, would probably have been classified within this latter group. One story survives to attest to the man Gibran's memory of the boy Kahlil's city escapades. Years after he had left Boston and was studying in Paris, a flock of birds reminded Gibran of the streets where he had played, and he told a story of trying to fly a kite in a crowded South End street. He was stopped by a policeman. Certainly this fleeting encounter with the law cannot be interpreted as participation in "promiscuous street life."

But Kahlil, if he did not participate often in the life of the street, nonetheless developed street wisdom of his own. Like thousands of other South End immigrant children, the shy, introverted country boy from the land of the Mountain adapted to his new surroundings, finding the instinct and will not only to survive but to succeed in the context of city life.

Around him, all the time, the city was expanding even as he grew up. Attractions of all kinds were burgeoning in the South End. Kahlil's youthful freedom and curiosity no doubt took him to the surrounding entertainment rows. There was Washington Street where the Grand Dime featured lurid melodramas, while its rival, the Grand Opera House, advertised its vaudeville shows as "entertainment expressly suited for women and children . . . every day a bargain day." The Columbia catered to an audience that demanded Irish comedy. Along with the varied and cheap theater, close to Oliver Place there were the bawdier attractions of numerous public dance halls and "a variety of minor attractions . . . of a catch-penny character"—shooting galleries, a poorly stocked aquarium, a flourishing series of merry-go-rounds on a vacant lot, waxwork shows, and the sidewalk fantasy of "Barnum's What Is It?" As a contemporary account described it, "the noise of discordant music, the glare of electric lights, and the gaudy decorations of tents and booths" contrasted with "the dimly lit, squalid neighborhood." [18] Kahlil's first encounter with American culture was in this colorful sidewalk world, just a few blocks away from the self-consciously uplifting culture of Brahmin Boston, where eventually he would walk as an equal.

But in the meantime the invisible barriers that prevented social congress between the South End and the neighboring Back Bay were more impenetrable than the railroad that physically divided them. The chief contact between the two areas came from the South End servants who worked in the mansions of Beacon Street and Commonwealth Avenue. Robert Woods well described the breach between these geographically close yet culturally distant worlds: "Though the lack of friendly association between the Back Bay and the South End is so complete that there is no direct street car communication, yet it must not be said that the two sections have no dealings with each other. The Back Bay which sometimes 'investigates' the South End would probably be surprised to know how constantly it is being in turn investigated by means of back-door and below-stairs points of approach." [19]

Still, the Back Bay residents did not completely ignore their less fortunate neighbors. The record of Boston's charity-minded citizens was already a long and generous one. The influential Associated Charities of Boston, founded in 1879, had been strongly supported by the "fiery inspiration" of Phillips Brooks, the distinguished Episcopalian minister. In the 1890s the illuminating stewardship of the great reformer Robert Treate Paine was guiding the association's efforts toward a "new charity." Socially conscious leaders like Paine were finally recognizing themselves in Emerson's words about the "foolish philanthropist" and were beginning to understand that in "miscellaneous popular charities . . . men do what is called a good action, as some piece of courage or charity, much as they would pay a fine in expiation of daily non-appearance on parade. . . . Their virtues are penances." [20] By the 1890s men of conscience were demanding more than money to relieve human distress.

Parts of the South End by this time could already be justly described by Edward Everett Hale as "the most charitied region in Christendom." The "new charity," by contrast, was based on "reconstructive" principles which aimed "to build up a better life for the district out of its own material and by means of its own reserve of vitality." [21] This call to neighborhood pride was designed to erase the earlier images of outdoor work relief and the degrading poorhouses. It demanded individual involvement on the part of the charity-minded, who were to "endeavor by personal friendship and counsel and co-operation to help them upward and onward." [22] In short, Back Bay Boston was about to enter the South End slums and work side by side with the immigrant population to improve their lot. The consequences for Kahlil Gibran were to be far-reaching indeed.

The principal means for carrying out this new form of charity were the "settlement houses." Established within needy neighborhoods, these clusters were to serve to "lighten the burdens of discouraged fathers and mothers, so that it shall be possible for them to have homes as bright and happy as our own." [23] In 1891 a group of dedicated men began an experiment in social living at 20 Union Park and founded the South End House. One year later another settlement house followed when a four-story brick house on Tyler

Street across from the Quincy School was converted for service. Sponsored by the College Settlement Association, it was managed by a group of college-educated women who in years to come were to set a distinguished example of dedicated, practical, and positive charity.

Denison House soon became a South End landmark. Children were encouraged to visit and play in its backyard; mothers were invited to tea; even the parish priest, anxious lest these Protestant women evangelize his parishioners, became involved in the dialogue. In the next two years the Denison House "family," under the guidance of headworker Helena Stuart Dudley, made significant inroads into the social life of the community, and their South End neighbors began to trust the motivations and ministrations of these well-bred, educated social workers and even to seek their aid.

Kahlil Gibran discovered Denison House sometime in the winter of 1895. At that time, its social workers were endeavoring to entice neighborhood children with a variety of diversions based on their own genteel notions about culture. Poetry readings, dramatic recitals, and instrumental performances were used to lure the children in from the streets. Arts and crafts classes, social studies groups, and Shakespeare clubs were also introduced. Wellesley College students who contributed to the settlement's financial resources also volun-

Municipal playground on Tyler Street, one block from the Denison House, as it was in 1917. (Schlesinger Library, Radcliffe College)

34

teered their services, soon establishing a pattern of shared musicals and plays with their newly found audience in the slums. Before long, young boys and girls who were barely familiar with English were performing in *As You Like It*, *Twelfth Night*, and *Julius Caesar*.

Kahlil must have been one of the first Syrian visitors. The chief concern of the Denison House women at the time were the Irish Catholics of the South End, and judging from the carefully kept notes in the house's daybook, the presence of a Syrian child must have been unusual. Not until the turn of the century does the daybook show evidence of a growing Syrian attendance. He was unique also for his innate talent in drawing, which the women at Denison House recognized. As he sketched in classes there and at Quincy School, his skill grew, and he began to seek out other places where he could enrich his knowledge. In doing so he was unexpectedly brought to the center of a controversy that was famous in Boston in the closing years of the century.

Boston's latest contribution to the cultural enrichment of its citizens was its imposing public library, designed by the New York firm of McKim, Mead and White, and completed in 1892. Not only did the exterior of this imposing edifice rival that of any other existing library in the country, but its interior, decorated with works by Puvis de Chavannes, Edwin Austin Abbey, and John

Singer Sargent, proclaimed as well the city's determination to be a leader in "the great movement toward popularizing art culture." [24] To the impressive frescoes decorating the halls the architect Stanford White contributed in 1895 what he thought would further enhance the library's aesthetic position: a life-sized statue of a bacchante by Frederick MacMonnies, which was placed in the courtyard as a fountain ornament.

The Bacchante proved to be a controversial beauty. Clasping a lively babe in one arm and holding aloft a bunch of grapes with the other, the dancing nymph was an immediate and sensational attraction. Her heel-kicking posture and general air of abandonment became a cause célèbre for the censors of Boston's morals—the whole city took sides, one way or another, on the question of whether her provocative nudity was a fit subject for public exhibition. The publicity brought thousands to the library's courtyard. "The Bacchante continues to draw great throngs," reported one contemporary wit. "Suburbans are now coming in battalions, and Bacchante special trains are shunting the regular theater trains onto the sidings." [25]

The youthful Kahlil, now going on thirteen years of age, was as enthralled as anyone else by the sculptured maiden's obvious joie de vivre, and in the winter of 1896 he drew an admirable likeness of her, which is now lost. It was fortunate that he was attracted to her early on, because late in the same year a phalanx of outraged citizens petitioned for her removal, and she was exiled to the more libertine corridors of the Metropolitan Museum in New York.

With this perspective on the history of the spirited figure who in Victorian eyes was "the incarnation of drunkenness and lewdness, a goddess of shame," [26] Kahlil's interest in the statue seems all the more significant. He must have been aware of the controversy which swirled around the subject of his drawing; thus, one of his earliest encounters with formal art was made possible by the rise of American public institutions and colored by the tinge of Victorian prudery that still inhibited these cultural efforts.

Since 1887 another effort to edify Boston's immigrant children had been carried out—the distribution of books throughout the city. Jessie Fremont Beale, a social worker at the Children's Aid Society, had devised and continued to guide the project known as the "home libraries." Its aim was to develop local stations in the homes of the poor, each one consisting of a "neat little bookcase filled with fifteen carefully selected juvenile books and five bound collections of suitable magazines." [27] Along with instilling a love for the care and reading of books, it was hoped that the home libraries would give poor children a chance to act as their own librarians with the help of an interested outsider or "friendly visitor" who would meet the children weekly, lead them in group discussions, initiate games, and occasionally sponsor outings. By 1896 some sixty-seven home libraries were scattered throughout

Boston, and their success in keeping children off the streets was being publicized.

In her efforts to reach out and discover new ways to bring refinement and literature to the children of the shadows, Miss Beale organized a formidable group of volunteers who spread all over Boston. She also used her position as librarian of the Children's Aid Society to enlist the help of the Boston establishment. The wealthy, the artistic, the literary, and the academic were included in her blueprint to bring enlightenment to the poor. In this context, she would in time introduce Kahlil Gibran to a man whose literary tastes and aesthetic leanings would stamp the little Syrian boy for the rest of his life. The link to this introduction was Kahlil's art teacher at Denison House.

We know her name, but little more. Florence Peirce, a resident at Denison House from 1894 to the spring of 1896, has remained an almost featureless shade. Brief entries in the house's daybook record only her entrance and departure. Her unassuming role included attendance at meetings, visits with families in the Tyler Street area, and helping the ailing get to hospitals. Whether she was a college student interested in social science or an artistically inclined girl who volunteered her services is not clear. What is certain is that Florence Peirce belonged to that growing clan of self-effacing women who were sincerely "distressed" and "made restless" by a "sense of privilege unshared." [28] Her early presence in Kahlil's life and the important role she played in it foreshadowed the female prototype with whom he would always be associated in later life. Liberated and liberating, interested and interesting, the emerging type of emancipated women whom Florence Peirce represented would profoundly guide Kahlil Gibran throughout his career.

Recognizing some spark emanating from the thirteen-year-old boy, Florence Peirce brought him to the attention of the older and more influential Jessie Fremont Beale. Thereupon Miss Beale wrote to the one person whom she knew she could most depend on to guide a child with artistic promise.

November 25, 1896

My dear Mr. Day:

. . . I am wondering if you may happen to have an artist friend who would care to become interested in a little Assyrian boy Kahlil G——. He is not connected with any society, so any one befriending the little chap would be entirely free to do with him what would seem in their judgment wise. He strolled into a drawing class at the College Settlement on Tyler Street last winter and showed a sufficient ability to make Miss Peirce feel that he was capable of some day earning his living in a better way, than by selling matches or newspapers on the street, if some one would only help him to get an artistic education.

His future will certainly be that of a street fakir if something is not done for him at once. The family are horribly poor, living on Oliver Place, and will insist upon having some financial assistance from this little boy just as soon as the law will allow unless he is on the road to something better. Next year he will be fourteen, beyond the school age, so we are specially interested to start the little fellow this year in his drawing, if such a thing is at all possible.

A drawing which he made in the cloisters, at the library, of the Bacchante made quite a sensation.

I fear you will feel this request in regard to Kahlil almost an intrusion, but I am so interested in the little fellow myself, and yet so utterly helpless, that I feel as if I must try to find some one else who can be of real use to him.

Very cordially yours,

Wednesday   Jessie Fremont Beale[29]

The close of Jessie Beale's letter to Day. (Norwood)

3

The Sick Little End
of the Century

Fred Holland Day, the man to whom Jessie Fremont Beale had addressed her letter, was one of Boston's end-of-the-century curiosities. He was properly not a Bostonian, and certainly not a proper Bostonian. He was a financially independent man-about-letters, a sometime setter of artistic tastes, a supporter of the avant-garde, and at this time engaged in one of the few truly successful ventures of his career as partner in the prestigious publishing firm of Copeland and Day. In this capacity he had not only supplied Jessie Beale's home libraries with many donations of sumptuously illustrated books, but also played the role of weekly "friendly visitor," reading aloud to the slum children, helping to introduce them to the classics, and generally acting as a literary mentor.[1] His interest spurred the involvement of other influential people.

To understand what was now about to happen to Kahlil Gibran, it is necessary to understand Fred Holland Day, the man who was to have so profound an influence on the life of the small Syrian boy. But to understand Fred Holland Day, it is necessary to know what was happening in the artistic world of Boston at the "sick little end of the century," to borrow a phrase frequently used by Day and his followers.[2]

Day was the only son of a prosperous tannery owner and a mother who loved him too much, and his many-sided talents were cultivated in a hot-house setting in suburban Norwood, thirty miles south of Boston. Born in 1864, in the 1880s he managed to loosen the laces of his restricted Victorian upbringing sufficiently to head for Boston, where he aspired to a literary career. His education at Chauncy Hall, the city's fashionable preparatory school, had given him a passionate love of literature and some insight into the nature of the flame of creativity. Upon these cornerstones he hoped to build a literary life in a style he fancied as uniquely his own.

Unfortunately, Day as an adult proved to be a mixture of talent and mediocrity. His infallible instinct for the magic of words surpassed his intellectual ability to cope with them, and expressing himself verbally was a lifelong struggle for him. His endless difficulties with pernicious details of grammar and spelling prevented him from ever authoring the brilliant letters he should have written, the critical articles he imagined, the witty epigrams he so admired.

Though hobbled by this poverty in literary talent, he had a keen sense of beauty and aesthetic judgment which enabled him to realize some notable achievements in related fields. His vocation began as a mania for collecting exquisite volumes and the memorabilia of writers whom he revered. He not only coveted rare first editions of writers such as Shakespeare, Keats, and Balzac, but he also possessed an instinct for the new and controversial. Only eighteen when Oscar Wilde toured America in 1882, he did not hesitate to approach the high priest of aestheticism and managed to extract a cherished autograph. This brief encounter with the "apostle of the lily" made a lifelong impression on him. He adopted some of Wilde's outrageous finery, and within ten years he was importing to unsuspecting Bostonians Wilde's writings and the ambience of English decadence. When he was ready to publish, he chose Wilde's everpresent lily as part of his printer's logo, and he distributed the scandal-tinged *Yellow Book* throughout the land.

The corner of bohemian Boston in which Day thrived became mostly forgotten before the new century was very old. But for a brief decade this small and curious figure in Vandyke beard and contrived costumes provided the city with genuine entertainment and enlightenment. He fancied himself as "the Day that God hath made,"[3] and his jousts with the staid and conventional pierced the prudish and incited the complacent. In 1896, when Miss Beale wrote to him about Kahlil Gibran, he was thirty-two and at the zenith of his poetaster's pursuits. He had already a mildly colorful reputation as a bibliophile, publisher, amateur photographer, and general entrepreneur. His financial means allowed him to tour extensively England and the Continent, where "he devoted all his spare time to gathering literary and illustrative material regarding his favorite heroes in literature and art."[4] He captured in photographs the homes and countryside haunts of his literary idols as eagerly as a young girl pressing flowers from her favorite suitors. He used these prints in his search for literary souvenirs, distributing them as bait, and before long, editors and academics, impressed by his evocative documents, began to consider him a semi-serious scholar. In short, he had established himself as an artistic bridge between American and English letters, and he was about to play an important and influential role in shaping a renaissance in poetry—a role that he managed to undercut with his languid flair for procrastination and an infirmity of too many goals.

40

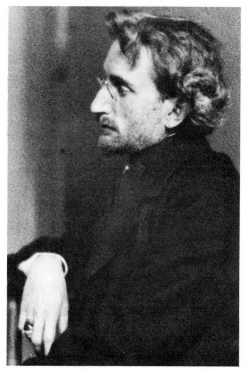

Above left: Day in a turn-of-the-century
photograph by Reginald Craigie. (Norwood)

Above right: Day as photographed by
Frederick H. Evans in England. (Norwood)

Day's involvement with the children of the streets did not stem from the usual feelings of guilt shared by other do-gooders; he was honestly attracted to the exotic and unusual drama to be found on the bazaar-like streets of the South End. He enjoyed the dizzying varieties of local color, and the multiracial features of the street children inspired him in his experiments with the new art of pictorial photography. Italian, Chinese, Negro, and Mediterranean types alike fascinated him, and he seriously searched for new and interesting models. Precisely at this time came Jessie Beale's catalytic letter, which was to plunge Kahlil Gibran into the Boston art world and was to provide Day with the boy who, of all his models, became the most famous.

Supporting Day in all his literary ventures was another minor star in Boston's dimming galaxy: Louise Imogen Guiney, who was a distant relative. An Irish Catholic piper among Yankee drums, she was the daughter of an extraordinary immigrant named Patrick Guiney who in the Civil War rose from the ranks of private to become one of Lincoln's generals. She was three years older than Day, and during their association her strengths compensated

41

for many of his weaknesses. Her natural eloquence and easy use of well-turned phrases balanced his awkwardness; her single-minded devotion to literature offset his occasionally haphazard passions; and her pragmatism, based on a threadbare poverty, contrasted with his casual freedom with the purse.

When they were very young, Louise Guiney and Fred Holland Day almost fell in love as they followed a wayfaring life and tramped the English countryside. But the need to make difficult adjustments in religion and temperament cooled their vague notions about marriage, and by the time they reached their thirties their ardor had cooled. He became more and more attracted to the thoughts and trappings of aestheticism; she spent much of her life in Oxford, withdrawing to the cloistered solitude and security of books, from which she occasionally issued unrequited poetry and elegantly obscure essays. She lived to perpetuate the memory of unfashionable men of letters, especially the recusant poets of the seventeenth century. They were her idols, discovering their weed-grown graves her pleasure, restoring their fame her passion. But before the couple's affection became merely a mutually convenient relationship between publisher and author, they launched together a memorable literary venture which elevated hearts as well as eyebrows on both sides of the Atlantic Ocean, and strengthened Day's image in the Anglo-American world of letters.

Both Day and Louise Guiney shared an unbridled enthusiasm for John Keats, whose memory they considered painfully neglected in England. In 1891 they proposed an American memorial to him, a marble bust by the Boston sculptor Anna Payne Whitney, which would be installed in the parish church in Hampstead, England. The two embarked upon a three-year search for funds to finance the Keats Memorial. In persuasively worded announcements they begged subscriptions from literary America, waging their campaign as a "sort of pleasant revenge" to remind the English of how they were disregarding their beloved "brother Johnny." [5]

Both recognized the need for a "big gun" to lend prestige and dignity to their plan, and Louise urged Day to approach Charles Eliot Norton, the distinguished professor of fine arts at Harvard. "Write to him yourself in your best wheedling fashion," she advised, "and you'll bag that lovely man. Be sure to write plain, O son! and to spell conventionally."[6] Day instead concocted a wordy, bumbling epistle in which nothing better shows up his own shortcomings as a writer than the hopelessly involved first sentence: "I hope the subject upon which I address you now will serve as pardon for a lack of conventionality that will, perhaps, win for the cause a frank and full expression of your feeling, which had I approached you through the office of mutual friends, would perhaps have been due to kindlyness." [7] It is to Professor Norton's credit that he managed to divine Day's meaning and agreed to lend his name to the proposed memorial.

The list of sponsors finally assembled was impressive enough, and by spring 1894, though still occasionally hindered by Day's disorderly methods, the project had progressed to the point where plans could be made for the dedication. Day went to England to arrange for this, but without Louise's watchful presence to prod him, he proceeded on his task with alarming casualness. Just as the final details of the unveiling were being worked out, he sauntered off to Venice for a month's vacation. Edmund Gosse, the critic and journalist who was the arbiter of literary achievement in England at that time, had agreed to deliver an acceptance speech on behalf of the English. He suddenly found himself also having to coordinate the ceremony with the unsuspecting vicar of the Hampstead church, arrange for the wording and design of the invitations by William Morris and their printing by the Kelmscott Press, and engage the presence of English notables. "Things don't work out without a good deal of trouble being taken," he wrote in mild reproof to Day in Venice. Two weeks before the event he wrote more bluntly to Day, who by this time had wandered up to Berlin: "You have really been very negligent of what is necessary. Your punishment must be an implicit acceptance of whatever we arrange." [8]

When the day came, a rainy July 16, somehow the dedication went off smoothly before an audience of more than a thousand people who crowded into the church. Gosse's presence attracted a stellar group of English speakers; Day's reputation brought out poets and artists of a younger and more colorful plumage, such as Aubrey Beardsley, William Butler Yeats, Arthur Symons, and Coventry Patmore. The ecclesiastical procession to the memory of the free-spirited Keats included one vicar, one primate, two bishops, and fourteen choirboys. For lack of a participating American celebrity, Day was forced to deliver the presentation speech, which was brief and astonishingly simple. Gosse gave an academic and lofty address, a letter from Swinburne was read, and other tributes were given. The gathering was a dramatic triumph, and Day's role as its promoter was acknowledged and reported throughout the English-speaking world.

Along with rousing Americans to help establish the Keats Memorial, Day had also been busily preparing to enter the world of publishing. His interest in bookmaking stemmed from the 1880s, when he had worked for a time in the Boston office of the New York publishing firm, A. S. Barnes. Now he had become a moving spirit in the crusade by Boston's intellectual elite to stamp out mediocrity, mammonism, and hypocrisy. Three preeminent poets had only recently died—James Russell Lowell in 1891, John Greenleaf Whittier in 1892, and Oliver Wendell Holmes in 1894—and younger writers and intellectuals from the academic worlds of Boston and Cambridge were seeking to take their places. They were aware that the commemorative tide which was flooding their city might well drown out the new voices, and they rallied to

Left: Louise Guiney and Day, probably at Five Islands, Maine. (Norwood)

Right: "Solitude," a study of Fred Holland Day by Eduard Steichen, Paris, 1901. (Museum of Modern Art)

meet it by recapturing the mystical spirit of Concord, without its Calvinistic overtones.

Searching for causes which might relieve the intellectual torpor, the dull grayness, of the ebbing century, these latter-day transcendentalists dabbled with the arcane, flirted with the medieval, and even expressed sympathy for a restoration of the Stuarts to the British throne. They toasted the memory of Charles I, wore the white rose in their buttonholes, and formed "social controversial-inspirational groups." [9] Bright young men met in Elizabethan conviviality at favorite restaurants like Marliaves and the Pi Alley taverns; they called themselves "The Pewter Mugs," the "Visionists," or "The Procrastinarium." As much as any English dandy or French avant-gardist, they favored the intellectuals' symbols of the day: "the implements of Decadence," as one essayist called them, "—cushions, cigarettes, incense, wine, turkey carpets, jade bowls, Burne-Jones' pictures, French novels, Oscar Wilde's complete works." [10] All these became their emblems.

Out of these strange societies, these midnight meetings, these flirtings with outrageous causes, came something real and valuable. For it was this freewheeling resurgence of intellectual creativity that fathered the "little

magazines" and the good literature that was to come in the United States. Herbert Stone and Ingalls Kimball of *Chapbook* fame; Herbert Small of Small, Maynard & Co.; Herbert Copeland; and, of course, Fred Holland Day were all part of the inner circle.

The revolt against genteelness and sentimentality was embodied in the birth of two new magazines which presaged the late-nineteenth-century fad for "ephemeral bibelots": *The Mahogany Tree* and *The Knight Errant*. Day was an important force in each of them.

The Mahogany Tree first appeared in January 1892. Its editorial goals promised everything a young literary revolutionist might dream of: a "paper that shall be unlike all other papers in existence—one devoted solely to the 'fine arts' from which all Philistinism shall be banished, even the Philistinism of advertisements and the hope of making money." [11] The editorial staff was made up of Harvard graduates of the classes of '91 and '92, including the youthful Herbert Copeland. Day contributed articles under the pseudonym of "Bibliophile." The prevailing philosophy was allied "with the deeper side of American life," which meant "away from the narrowing rush of business; away from all shallow trivialities." [12] The editors demanded a spiritual realignment against the ever-encroaching industrial world. Their fears about the nightmare of the machine which stalked their idealistic dreams of America were summarized in the final issue:

> The world is going at too rapid a pace for its own good as a world, and far too rapidly for the individuals who make up this, our boasted nineteenth century civilization. . . . We have tried of course to reform the world, to induce mankind to turn now and then from the mad chase after the Almighty Dollar, and smoke cigarettes and read Oscar Wilde. We have taken sides against electric cars, bicycles, and Mr. Howells. We have played at theosophy because we found it amusing, and we have exalted Mr. George Meredith because we have an honest admiration for him. We have sung the praises of cigarettes and coffee, not for themselves alone, but because they stand for a mood opposed to that prevailing one of our times which turns life into an express train and makes old men at forty.[13]

From January 1892 to July 1892 *The Mahogany Tree* appeared in twenty-six weekly issues. Shortly before its demise, Day was already collaborating on a more elaborate venture, the magazine called *The Knight Errant.* Created by the combined talents of Bertram Grosvenor Goodhue, architect and designer; Ralph Adams Cram, architect and critic; Francis Watts Lee of the Elzevir Press; Herbert Copeland; and Day, who provided bookmaking taste and financial aid, *The Knight Errant* aimed its lance at lofty goals. Cram outlined its direction many years afterward in his memoirs: "What we aimed to do was to take the English *Hobby Horse* and, in a manner of speaking, go it one better. It was to be not only an expression of the most advanced thought of the time (the word meant then something radically different from what it means today) but as well a model of perfect typography and printer's art. We had special handmade paper prepared for us, and a new and beautiful fount of type."[14]

Writers for the elegant editions included Charles Eliot Norton, the English artist Walter Crane, and the poets Bliss Carman and Richard Hovey. Essays on Oriental and Renaissance art were submitted by Ernest Fenollosa and Bernard Berenson, Boston's expatriate aesthetes in Japan and Italy respectively. Still, Boston did little more than smile at these "men against an epoch." Even Louise Guiney described the handsome result with what seems faint praise: "[*The Knight Errant*] is as medieval as possible, by way of representing the rebound from progress and science and agnosticism and general modernity."[15] One newspaper snickered at the editors' indiscriminate idol-smashing and commented on the magazine's effeteness:

> The mission of the new quarterly is to promote a love for art and to contend for spiritual rather than material good. With this it combines a

wish to reinstate U in such words as 'honor', to substitute Roman numerals for Arabic, and to spell certain words with capital letters. These are harmless oddities. But if an old journalist may advise younger ones, I should say, Concentrate your attack—do not shoot at too many enemies at once and with the same gun. So far as I can discover the writers in this first number think ill of (1) the art of printing, (2) the Renaissance, so called, (3) the Protestant Reformation, (4) the American Constitution, (5) Puritanism, (6) Realism, Impressionism, Eclecticism (so-classed), (7) Agnosticism and Rationalism, (8) Democracy and Mammonism, (9) Individualism, which seems to be the root of all evil.[16]

The Knight Errant was a quarterly, and its quest was brief. From April 1892 to July 1893 it appeared in only four issues. Its short life paralleled too closely the exhortation in Miss Guiney's dedicatory poem: "A short life in the saddle, Lord! / Not long life by the fire!" [17]

Such failures left Fred Holland Day undaunted. The practical experience of putting out the magazine, in fact, only served to increase the interest in publishing he had already gained from his social involvement with English publishers and booksellers during his frequent visits to London. An especially important contact for Day was Frederick H. Evans, who ran a bookstore devoted to the avant-garde and was a prominent architectural photographer. Credited with introducing Aubrey Beardsley to John Lane, he probably also introduced Day to that innovative publisher of the Bodley Head.

Day also began to take stock of the friendships he had formed with poets he met at the Rhymers Club in London. Recognizing that there was an American audience for the new breed of English talent, and that the 1891 Copyright Act signed by the United States and Britain permitted joint publishing in the two countries, he became the American publisher of the John Lane books. He was ready now to undertake his most meaningful and lasting endeavor.

Day chose as his partner Herbert Copeland, then on the staff of the magazine *Youth's Companion*, and the publishing firm of Copeland and Day was born. It was run from an "aesthetic little office" [18] at 69 Cornhill, a location famous for its bookstallish associations. From the outset, there was nothing of the playful dilettante about this venture. Copeland and Day became a serious and successful publishing house, quickly respected for introducing "a higher standard of integrity in craftmanship and in commercial standing as well as in the character of the literature issued." [19] Embellished with the symbolic imprint of lilies and roses, which recalled the marks of the sixteenth-century printers Richard Day and Robert Copeland, the ninety-eight books that the firm issued in its five and a half years of existence pioneered the way for modern typography and bookmaking in America. A colleague later recalled Day's contributions by including him "in the brief list of those artist-publishers and artist-printers who by their work and influence have

Drawings by Kahlil in a dummy copy of *The Arabella and Araminta Stories* which contained Ethel Reed's illustrations. (Authors)

restored printing to its rightful place among the Fine Arts." [20]

The initial offerings of Copeland and Day appeared in December 1893, and they included several co-editions originating from the London firm of Elkin Mathews and John Lane. Most notable was Oscar Wilde's *Salome* (gracefully and decoratively illustrated by Aubrey Beardsley), Francis Thompson's *Poems*, and Dante Gabriel Rosetti's *The House of Life*. The first unmistakably American contribution was *The Decadent*, by Ralph Adams Cram. This fascinating manifesto of the leading fin-de-siècle movement portrayed New England lotus-eaters, languidly gathered around opium-gurgling *nargilehs* and saturated with burgundy wine, while they railed against the urban incubus, "this gigantic abortion," and yearned for the new life promised by the twentieth century.

As Copeland and Day's list grew so did the tastes and attitudes of the firm's proprietors. Their first books directly reflected the English literary scene, and they introduced to the American public the poetry of Richard Le Gallienne, Lionel Johnson, Alice Meynell, William Butler Yeats, and others. But their most celebrated achievement was the joint publication with Mathews and Lane of ten volumes of *The Yellow Book*. These books, compiled by Henry Harland as literary editor ("the Yellow Dwarf") and Aubrey Beardsley as art editor, were studded with essays and stories by such leading talents as Max Beerbohm, Anatole France, Edmund Gosse, Henry James, George Moore, Kenneth Grahame, and Arthur Symons. The *Yellow Books*, which featured

48

Beardsley at his naughtiest, were the quintessence of the nineties, their jaundiced tone the symbol of an emancipation from all that was dreary and dull. Copeland and Day distributed the daffodil-covered editions for three years until John Lane opened a New York office in 1896.

As time went on, the Cornhill house became increasingly involved in sponsoring poets of the New World. While Herbert Copeland was leading American literary tastes toward American and Canadian poets, Fred Holland Day was replacing the ornamental but archaistic designs of Bertram Grosvenor Goodhue with more contemporary and direct images. The evolving tastes of both of the firm's partners were exemplified in *Songs from Vagabondia* by Bliss Carman and Richard Hovey. This slim, small volume, on whose cover portraits of the authors and the illustrator Thomas B. Meteyard were encircled in a striking medallion, featured endpapers boldly lettered and decorated in a manner that echoed the free style of the verse. Its immediate success gratified Day, whose long-held conviction that attractive trade editions could be made and sold to an American audience was now justified.

By 1895 the firm was well established, and with the Keats Memorial dedication a year behind him, Day could devote his full energies to publishing genuinely new and interesting works. Copeland induced many of his Harvard friends, and colleagues from *Youth's Companion* days, to submit their manuscripts. Louise Guiney, one of the firm's literary advisers, unabashedly championed her own and her good friend Alice Brown's poetry and stories. A lively juvenile series called The Yellow Hair Library was successfully launched. Gertrude Smith's Arabella and Araminta stories were deliciously embellished by Ethel Reed's saucy and surprising illustrations.

Mid-career, Herbert Copeland and Fred Holland Day, "the high priests of the new creative movement and the new revival of the old," were being regarded with esteem. Their success was summarized in a Boston journal: "Their three lilies are stamped upon many quaint, musical, fantastic works, some ultra-modern, some medieval, but all strongly picturesque and original. . . . Poetry is their specialty, and names which are becoming almost classical already are numbered in their short but shining list. Some of their typography has equalled the best Kelmscott."[21]

One barely known writer who did indeed gain classic stature after he was introduced to the public by Copeland and Day was Stephen Crane. Although his starkly agnostic verses jangled Louise Guiney's ecclesiastical nerves, Day saw merit in his protests and published *The Black Riders and Other Lines* in 1895. These poems significantly affected the shape and style of the vers libre of a generation yet to come. They also profoundly aroused the young Kahlil Gibran.

The world into which the barely literate young Syrian boy was about to be introduced was the antithesis of anything he had ever known. Compared to his early life in the countryside of the Mountain and his present life on South End streets, it was the perfumed essence of culture and breeding.

Doubtless, Fred Holland Day had felt some sense of obligation when he was moved to enlighten the children of the slums. But beneath these charitable feelings there also lay a deeper challenge. The men of the late nineteenth century were waiting for something—something that would lead them into the approaching century with a glimmer of hope. Like all the bright young men around him, Day was searching for relevant movements and causes at the "sick little end of the century," and he was now about to find them. After exploring Jacobism, spiritualism, and decadence, and after dressing young poets' words in fine new packages, he would explore one more art form—pictorial photography. It was here that the "potential street fakir" referred to him by Jessie Beale would perhaps inspire him. He, in turn, with his carefully acquired predilections in poetry and art would challenge and direct the boy in ways that Jessie Beale could not possibly have imagined.

The final decade into which Day had squeezed so much of his rarefied talent was too high strung with delicate, quivering nerve fibers, too inbred, to produce a lasting popular poet. Perhaps he recognized this, and recognized, too, that it was a time for sowing rather than for gathering the harvest. But the seeds of his carefully cultivated lilies and roses did not fall on sterile ground. The young Kahlil was to graft these initial and most important artistic influences onto his own simple cedar stalk. Long after Alice Brown's *Meadow Grass*, Father Tabb's *Poems*, and Louise Guiney's *Patrins* were generally forgotten, their essences would be remembered and emulated by the young artist. As a result of what Fred Holland Day bequeathed to him, Kahlil Gibran would become one of the most complex and consequential of the immigrant hybrids.

Copeland and Day colophon, designed by
Bertram Grosvenor Goodhue.

4

The Young Sheik

It was November 25, 1896, when Jessie Beale first wrote to Fred Holland Day requesting his help with the education of Kahlil Gibran; it was two weeks later before a meeting could be arranged between the two. Florence Peirce worked hard to pin down the supreme procrastinator on the one hand, and on the other to find the elusive boy. Finally she was able to write to Day, "Through the ministrations of Denison House, Kahlil has been seen and promises to come to us Thursday evening. I trust we may not be disappointed." [1]

Kahlil did come, and he brought along a selection of his drawings. He had been working hard and had begun to see the advantages of the opportunity being offered to him. As he waited, Miss Peirce leafed through the drawings; a few days later she penned another note to Day: "Kahlil has brought his sketches which I send you. Unfortunately he has given many of them away. The boy is here now and if you can see him, I hope you will do so." [2]

That Day saw and liked the drawings is evident from the context of Miss Peirce's next note to him and from the uncharacteristic alacrity with which he expressed a willingness to meet Kahlil. The two were introduced on December 9, 1896, and the meeting was undeniably stimulating to both of them. Day's sense of the picturesque and sensitive was satisfied by the quiet, olive-skinned, brown-eyed youth. Kahlil, for his part, must have reacted to the elegantly clad dandy with wide-eyed wonder.

The publisher waited for the holiday season to pass before he followed up on the initial meeting, requesting Kahlil's address from Miss Peirce. "Kahlil Gibran's address is 9 Oliver Place," she replied. "Have you heard anything concerning his future? I am anxious to know if a decision has been reached. It will be most interesting to hear the boy's comments. May I be there too?" [3] And within a few weeks the boy was sitting for the camera of his new-found friend.

An early photograph of Kahlil by Day. (Library of Congress)

Day's interest in photography was by this time his primary concern, taking precedence even over his publishing activities at Copeland and Day. His aims, as always, were high: he saw the camera not just as an instrument that recorded faithfully the subjects on which its lens was trained, but as the vehicle for a new art form. Where he had begun by using photography to record literary scenes, he now sought a painterly style, inspired by his knowledge of "composition, of light and shade, of proportion, of outline, of the intermediate links," [4] which he found in the paintings of Velazquez, Whistler, Sargent, and Rembrandt. The result—called "coal mine" effects by some[5]— was a sharp image surrounded by misty tones. To this end he commissioned from a Boston firm a special lens which was "deliberately uncorrected, rendering photos similar to that of a wet lens. The image was quite sharp but all the light tones had a halo around them." [6] His artistic results did indeed amount to a new kind of picture, and his models and their poses complemented the effect. Deriding the shallowness of contemporary "Art Photographic" and the current vogue of "hideous caricatures of the human figure . . . disarrayed in all states of nakedness, postured in impossible attitudes against commercial back-grounds and surrounded by papier-mache columns, fruit, or trees," Day sought "the most striking, unusual, and weirdly picturesque set of models, black, white and yellow, that ever posed before a camera" and rushed to join the emerging school of "the painterly photograph." [7]

Just how Kahlil reacted to Day's world is uncertain, but, in a strange reversal, he might not have been as shocked by the man's strange mannerisms and costumes as were the gaping Bostonians. The publisher Elbert Hubbard once described a visit to Day, who "wore a fez and turned-up Turkish slippers, worshipped a squat number ten joss and wrote only by the light of thirteen candles." [8] The critic Sadakichi Hartmann told an anecdote about the time when Day was waiting at his parents' home for a visitor whom he had never met. When the stranger knocked, "he heard a most cheerful 'come in,' but entering found to his great astonishment nobody present. He looked around everywhere, but could find no trace of Mr. Day, then suddenly he heard a clucking sound, he looked up and saw Mr. Day sitting on a shelf right under the ceiling, wrapped in an oriental costume, smoking a water pipe!" [9]

Such accessories—waterpipes, fezzes, pointed slippers, embroidered robes, and incense, that dispeller of evil spirits which was continually burned in the most ordinary of Syrian homes—were to Kahlil common objects of everyday life. The boy was delighted that a well-educated American enthusiastically responded to his country's symbols. In turn, he was able in many ways to help his patron's Oriental fancies become more authentic and elaborate. While Bostonians may have believed that these fantastic props were all imported at great cost from faraway lands, they more likely were found locally at places like Peter Rahme's "Fancy Goods" store on Beach Street in the heart of Boston.

Kahlil was entering his adolescence now, and his recollections of the many and long sessions he began to spend before Day's camera allude vaguely to a prevailing mood of sadness. "Mr. Day made a great many photographs of me," he once said. "He was fond of me." But he also recalled that once "Mrs. Day said to her son, 'I like that young man very much, but I don't want to be with him because he never smiles.' I never smiled." [10]

Day's countless photographs show this very clearly: the pictures are of a serious, unsmiling, proudly dignified, and almost arrogant boy. He taught Kahlil, along with the Negro, Armenian, and Chinese children who posed for him, to suit their poses to his mood, and the portraits that resulted, with their mysterious tones, were beginning to stamp Day as a "veritable Rembrandt of the camera." Already British and American photographic journals were linking him with another innovator, Alfred Stieglitz. The two were characterized as "artistic photographers [who] like the true artist . . . only depict what pleases." [11]

None of the critics who wrote with such feeling about Day's photographs speculated on where he got his models. Had they done so, they would have found an interesting story. Day, concerned for the fate of underprivileged children, had by now become a Pied Piper of the South End. Dressed in a dashing cape and a broad-brimmed hat, he took children by the streetcar-load on country outings or to cultural entertainments, selecting from their ranks the precise type he sought for a particular picture.[12] He indulged in no discrimination; he saw only what he wanted for his camera. "You're no reflector of color," a cousin once said to him. "Remember the night at Symphony Hall we heard 'em say, 'Let's see who he's got *this* week; last week he had a Chinaman!' " [13]

Day's methods were as patient as they were occasionally bizarre. A year after he met Kahlil, he wrote, "I once knew an enthusiast who, after discovering in the scantily-clad figure of a street urchin what he supposed to be almost the unattainable perfection for the subject he was at work upon, waited six weeks while the little fellow was letting his hair grow into the required condition, being all the time paid by my friend for the concession he was required to make, that he might become more nearly the classic ideal. In this case all proved well and the results more than justified the means." [14] Day's syntax had obviously not improved with the years, and adding to the obscurity of his prose was the fact that in writing he often referred to himself in the third person. But there is little doubt that he could easily have been the "friend" who paid a daily sum and waited for his subject's hair to grow.

Kahlil could well have been the boy; surviving photographs show that he let his hair grow. Day posed him in mysterious Arab burnooses, just as he dressed

Armenians in turbans, blacks in Ethiopian regalia, Chinese with flutes, Japanese in kimonos. The children must have viewed such artifices as make-believe games, but they were much more than that. A magical transformation took place, and through Day's lens ghetto waifs became "Armenian Princes," "Ethiopian Chiefs," and "Young Sheiks." Day's titles infused the children with an unexpected sense of privilege and dignity. Kahlil in particular fortified his self-image and sought to overcome the reality of a poverty-stricken childhood with a vision of nobility and lineage. With Day's lofty labeling, he was no longer a slum child who lived in a dark alley; the silvery image of himself which he saw on Day's platinum-coated plates showed far more. Within a year, he was striving to live up to the grand illusions which Day had caught.

Spring came, and Florence Peirce was satisfied that Day was providing young Kahlil with some security. She wrote that she was going on a trip to Europe and thanked him for a gift he had proffered her: "Kahlil's photograph was most acceptable." [15]

Now that Kahlil's assimilation was underway, the social planners who had helped him turned their attention to his sisters. On June 10, 1897, Jessie Beale announced a plan to take the three children to the country. Her letter shows the delicacy and care which sensitive social workers of that time had found were necessary to allay the fear and distrust which many foreign families felt toward outside meddlers in their affairs. "My dear Mr. Day," she wrote, "Miss Johnson, the lady who has charge of the country week outings, tells me that Kahlil and his two sisters are to go for their visit about July first. Shall she not send the invitation to you? It seems that it will seem a little more personal coming that way. The Christian Union is specially anxious to have them seem to the children like any other invitation. It was kind of her to arrange for them all to go together. This is unusual but being foreigners she feared they might be homesick if separated." [16]

The gentle conspiracy of having Day extend the invitation did not work. In spite of his personal sponsorship of the offer, Kahlil, Marianna, and Sultana did not go to camp that year. Kamila knew that the damp, dreary confinement of Oliver Place held no joy for children, but she considered the separation of the three children from herself to be unnatural. It was as Jessie Beale had thought: these "foreigners" were wary of interference with the family unit, especially separation planned by Protestant outsiders. But she tried again. On July 9 she wrote to Day, "I have just heard indirectly that Kahlil and his little sisters did not get off on the sixth. Is this true I wonder? And if so can we do anything about getting Miss Johnson to arrange a second outing." [17]

The Gibrans had disappeared, and Day must have combed the Syrian quarter for word or sight of Kahlil or his family. Vanishing suddenly, then surfacing again just as unexpectedly, they were typical of the mobile poor who

BOSTON CHILDREN'S AID SOCIETY.

PRESIDENT, GEORGE S. HALE, 10 Tremont Street.
TREASURER, I. TUCKER BURR, Jr., Exchange Bldg. 53 State St.

GENERAL SECRETARY, CHARLES W. BIRTWELL.   TELEPHONE, HAYMARKET 1241.
ASSISTANT SECRETARY, WILLIAM H. PEAR.   OFFICE OPEN 9 A. M. TO 5 P. M.

43 Charity Building, cor, Chardon and Hawkins Sts.

Boston, Mass., *July 9th, 1897*

Miss Beale's letter to Day.
(Norwood)

dropped in and out of the precarious life in the tenements, following instincts few Americans could understand. But by mid-September the family had been located again. "My dear Mr. Day," Jessie Beale wrote on September 22, "I am so much obliged to you for your trouble and interest in Kahlil's behalf, but I am exceedingly sorry that I caused you the bother when investigation proves there was no need of such anxiety. . . . These people are so apt to suddenly disappear from our sight, that I feared Mrs. Gibran might be one of those quiet mortals, who tell their plans to no one, but silently move off and are lost sight of." [18]

Obviously Day did finally find the boy and managed to win his confidence and his family's, for the next few months were a whirlpool of activity at the studio, with Kahlil observing it all. He eagerly absorbed the exhibitions, book productions, literary discoveries, and general antics. Alert, becoming more open, and greedy to learn, he was an apt pupil for the indoctrination which Day gave him in his own tastes and affinities. The fact that he was then barely literate in English or Arabic made little difference; he learned fast.

In the fall of 1897 a new interest came into the fourteen-year-old boy's life. Under the guidance of Day, who often read to him, he began to make his first discoveries in the world of literature. *The Treasure of the Humble*, a new work by Maurice Maeterlinck, one of Day's favorite authors, had just been

56

translated. This series of brooding Neoplatonic essays appeared at a good time to feed spiritually hungry Americans with the hope that "we are on the verge of a wonderful spiritual awakening which will come near to laying bare the soul of one man to another." [19] A poet friend related in her journal Day's account of how he introduced the young Kahlil to the thoughts of the Belgian symbolist: "Mr. Day read to him out of the newly translated *Trésor des Humbles* of Maeterlinck one day, and the boy would not let him go till he had read the whole volume at a sitting. Then he borrowed it. Then he had to own it himself. . . . One day Kahlil Gibran came back with a copy of Lemprière which Mr. Day had lent him and said: 'I am no longer a Catholic: I am a pagan.' " [20]

The book that inspired the half-grown Maronite Christian to thus renounce his religion was the *Classical Dictionary* by the English scholar John Lemprière. Published in 1788 and widely used as a reference work in the nineteenth century, it outlined classical mythology and history. Perhaps Kahlil's infatuation with Olympian gods and goddesses was predictable, but his simultaneous response to Maeterlinck was surely unusual. As the poet-diarist wrote of him: "His aptitude for literature is like his drawing: his mind is in every way marvelous." [21]

In this last decade of the nineteenth century, Maeterlinck's intuitive meditations were so popular that he was often called "the Belgian Shake-speare." Because he believed in the "oneness of the individual with the absolute" his idealistic concerns were often compared with the earlier message delivered by Boston's own Ralph Waldo Emerson: "We live in the lap of an immense intelligence, which makes us organs of its activity and receivers of its truth." [22] Soul-searching Bostonians in particular, always conscious of the transcendental legacy bequeathed to them by Emerson, recognized and took to heart the parallel beliefs of Maeterlinck.

Kahlil by this time had some of Boston in him and was in any event very much a child of his time. Twelve years after Day had read him the essays in *The Treasure of the Humble*, he recalled the intensity of that experience: "Maeterlinck is of the first rank. . . . In the early nineties big men were finding unlimited form. Maeterlinck perceived the current. . . . From fourteen to eighteen he was my idol . . . *The Treasure of the Humble* is his masterpiece." [23]

Maeterlinck's preoccupation with "death that is the guide of our life," his conviction that "a spiritual epoch is perhaps upon us," his mysterious allusions to a predestined love "in the impenetrable regions of almost astral humanity" profoundly affected the young Syrian boy in the early stages of his introspective journey of the soul. Throughout his career, Gibran never completely abandoned the Belgian writer's attempts to penetrate into the "souls of all our brethren . . . ever hovering about us, craving for a caress, and only waiting for the signal." [24]

But along with his introduction to the classics and Maeterlinck's veiled mysteries, Kahlil was also exposed to the contemporary literary scene through the activities of Copeland and Day. In 1896, capitalizing on the popularity of Carman and Hovey's *Songs from Vagabondia*, the firm published a sequel. The first two poems in *More Songs from Vagabondia* alluded to remote regions which Kahlil must have delightedly recognized as belonging to his own country. In "Jongleurs" the images evoked immigrants who "Wandered at noon / In the valleys of Van, / Tented in Lebanon, tarried in Ophir." Kahlil must have hungrily absorbed such romantic pictures which cloaked his homeland with magical meaning. If American poets sang about the land where he was born and grew up, did not his closeness to and reverence for that place confer on him some heretofore unimagined stature?

Again, in a stanza of "Earth's Lyric," he could identify with the symbols, recalling their majestic impression from times when he was very small: "A golden flute in the cedars, / A silver pipe in the swales, / And the slow large life in the forest / Wells back and prevails." Did not his experience in this land of prophets endow him with a special knowledge? Instead of abandoning his origins completely, as so many first-generation immigrant children did, he began to understand that his exotic background could help him in his artistic development.

Another influence in Kahlil's life which would profoundly affect his development as a poet was his growing familiarity with the ideology expressed in an article by Richard Hovey. Entitled "Decadence—or Renascence," it was a significant statement on the "decadence" with which the contemporary poets were being charged, lucidly spelling out the "gospel-crusade" that characterized the "children of one mother—Today." [25]

"The younger poets," Hovey wrote, "are not, strictly speaking, a school at all. . . . They cannot be catalogued under one formula. . . . Their greatest unity lies in the stress of individuality." Analyzing the beliefs held by his contemporaries, Hovey stated, "The right to live involves the right to love, and the freedom of man must include the freedom of woman." Referring to the strong influence of Emerson on the new poets, he noted, "Materialism seems almost without a representative, the tendency being to the other extreme of mysticism as in the native symbolism of Carman or Maeterlinck's strange new development of Neo-Platonic thought." He went on to explain the new religion: "From the brave agnostic faith of Watson's 'The Unknown God' to the passionate Catholic rhapsodies of Francis Thompson. . . . Through almost every shade of creed or creedlessness, these poets are filled with the sense of God and the spirit of worship." Predicting a commitment of future poets to

"It is Finished," Day's portrait of Maeterlinck with a crystal ball, 1901. (Royal Photographic Society)

blank verse, he saw their form of expression as "leading to a greater freedom of technique—impelling the poets . . . toward the flexibility, complexity, and naturalness of vers libre."

In Hovey's challenges to the orthodox, he defended the liberalizing tendencies which would characterize twentieth-century creativity: "Now there are some who will have it that because we are democrats we are dynamiters; who, because we find nothing shameworthy in the love of man and woman, but look with reverent eyes upon its holy mysteries, accuse us of eroticism; who call our worship of joy paganism, our love of the virile coarseness, our mysticism obscurity, our religion superstition, and our technique a violation of all the rules of Art."

Day no doubt supported this closely reasoned and farsighted analysis; he especially favored Walt Whitman and his English counterpart Edward Carpenter, both of whom were included in Hovey's discussion of vers libre poets. The impression made on the young Kahlil is unmistakable: in years to come he would include all of the prototypes discussed by Hovey in his own pantheon of people whom he had admired and trusted in his youth. Moreover, the attitudes and convictions proclaimed by Hovey also became part of the young writer's future principles. It is apparent that Gibran's sources and early influences lay not with the early-nineteenth-century romantics of France and England to whom they have so often been attributed, but with the philosophy prevalent in Boston in the 1890s. The boy of the Cedars recognized a common chord on which to build, and from his new country he himself adopted anything and everything with which he could identify.

Nevertheless, reading the literature of the day was less important to Kahlil at this time than making pictures. The sketches saved from this period show his ravenous appetite for copying anything he saw before him. On the blank backs of the public library call cards, he drew countless heads and figures which he derived from Blake, Beardsley, and Burne-Jones.[26] He also laboriously printed the new Roman alphabet he was learning, trying to perfect the letters by copying the most ordinary forms and titles. "I promise to return this book to the Public Library," he spelled out again and again, interspersing the words with Beardsley-like heads of gnomes and Blake-like dancing figures. In the student's notebook which he began to keep are carefully wrought letters copying the titles of Copeland and Day books. Once, looking over these early attempts in later years when he was a mature artist, Gibran remarked on his stylistic indebtedness: "Wasn't I having a good time with Blake then?"[27]

The Copley Square library served the boy as a grand studio, for the modern art that decorated its halls was still the talk of artistic Boston. In 1897–98 he also took advantage of the weekly exhibits organized by the library's active

60

fine arts department. Fred Holland Day frequently lent new issues from Copeland and Day and his own Kelmscott Press editions. In the spring of 1897 the library sponsored an extensive showing of William Morris's medievalizing works, comprised mostly of items from Day's collection. A year later a large exhibition of American and European book and magazine covers included contemporary work by Maxfield Parrish, Edward Penfield, and Will Bradley. The growing availability of photographic reproductions allowed the library to acquire "the fine Hollyer platinotypes of the . . . English Pre-Raphaelite school," [28] as well as prints of Assyrian, Egyptian, Greek, and Roman sculpture in the British Museum.

Stimulated by this wealth of visual images, Kahlil was by now beginning to develop his own technique and vision in design. Not only did his patron Day encourage this, but he eventually permitted Kahlil to work on covers for some of the publications scheduled by his firm—unlikely as this might seem for a publisher who was commissioning illustrations from artists like Will Bradley, Ethel Reed, and John Sloan. That Kahlil was actually involved in Copeland and Day's publishing program by 1898 is proven by a pen-and-ink illustration which he drew for a book of poems published that December. It was one of the boy's first attempts to make an original illustration, and although it was never used, it serves to show the progress he had made in the three years since he had been introduced to Day.

Earlier that year he had made a pictorial representation of Duncan Campbell Scott's "Labor and the Angel," the long title poem of Scott's latest book. Kahlil picked out every detail of the pastoral scene described by the

Kahlil's pencil drawings on the backs of library call cards. (Authors)

61

Canadian poet—"The angel that watches o'er work," while "Down in the sodden field / A blind man is gathering his roots / Guided and led by a girl." The girl who "touches his arm with her hand" is there, radiant and golden, and so are the "dark colored beets in the barrow," and the angel, a full-winged Pre-Raphaelite female embracing the peasant couple. Tight in execution and detail, this uncharacteristic drawing shows some knowledge of composition and perspective, and much familiarity with the Pre-Raphaelites. It bears printer's marks, which indicate that it was prepared for reproduction.

Day did not hide his protégé; convinced of the boy's talent, he shared his find with other artists who needed a model and could, in return, offer Kahlil guidance. Through the interchange, Kahlil was able to enter precociously the front doors of Back Bay houses, which were ordinarily accessible only through an elaborate system of protocol and introductions. It was, perhaps, too easy and premature for the boy to enter so casually into this lofty world.

One of the generous and benevolent individuals he met in this fashion was Lilla Cabot Perry, a versatile painter who had studied with Pissarro and Monet and a poet whose book *Impressions* would soon be published by Copeland and Day. Her husband, Thomas Sergeant Perry, was descended on his father's side from the two commodores Oliver Perry and Matthew Perry, and he was related on his mother's side to Benjamin Franklin. Everything surrounding the Perrys—his former careers as instructor of literature at Harvard and editor of the *North American Review*, her translation of Turgenev's poetry, the family's extended tours throughout Europe—was rich with the heaviest of Bostonian and Cantabrigian cream.

But Kahlil entered their house at 312 Marlborough Street with ease. Lilla Perry's affection for her young model, and her interest in his career, began with his first day's posing. She later gave him gifts, including what was probably his first set of paints, writing to Day: "I only gave Kahlil a part of the paints I had for him the other day, and I send the remainder in this little box with your things. I also send him the robe he posed in, as I thought he would like to own it and that you might like to photograph him in it." [29] Kahlil immediately experienced a feeling of being wanted and liked; his softly sad eyes and his half-learned English, colorfully laden with romantic images, obviously intrigued and pleased the right people. And he soon learned the manners and deportment expected of any Back Bay visitor.

Within a year the Perrys had departed for Japan, where Thomas Perry was to lecture on English literature at Keiogijiku University. But Kahlil was able to maintain his acquaintanceship with Back Bay society by a sort of public debut, which he remembered vividly for years. In the winter of 1898, Day's photographic work had been featured in an exhibition at the New York Camera Club; now it opened on March 8, 1898, at the Boston Camera Club on Bromfield Street. It was an astoundingly successful showing—the three hundred prints on display were acclaimed not only for their unusual presentation but also for their subject matter. "Mr. Day has displayed exquisite taste in the selection of his mats and his backgrounds," wrote the critic Charles Peabody. More noteworthy was the fact that the photographer courageously showed nude studies of males and females along with his array of exotic models. "The photographs pass over the merely pictorial and become almost as sculpture. Myron would have delighted in them, and Michael Angelo would have made many compliments." [30] The critic of the popular *Transcript* described the models in a way that presaged the poignant photograph that Day would make a few years later of Kamila, Sultana, and Marianna: "Give Mr. Day a girl or two with long chins and almond eyes and an expression of anxious long-suffering and hunger, and he can make a better pastiche of an Italian primitive altar-piece than most of the English pre-raphaelites." [31]

Kahlil was featured in a number of Day's most successful pictures, and he and his family attended the opening. No effort was spared to show him off to his best advantage. He later recalled,

> I was invited to his exhibition of course. There I met a great many fine people. It was an event and mother dressed me with especial care. She had wonderful taste and she always chose the richest and best of everything. I was all velvet—knickerbockers—with silk stockings; my hair was longish. Mr. Day introduced me to Mrs. [Joshua] Montgomery Sears, who took photographs herself, and she carried me home after the exhibit. I met Miss Peabody, too, and she said to me, "I see you everywhere," for to my surprise, I had found seven or eight studies of myself, mounted and framed on the walls. "But you look so sad—why are you sad?" she said.[32]

Fine clothes had probably meant sacrifices for the whole family, but Kamila and her daughters viewed the exhibit as Kahlil's own private triumph. And it was, for through it he met more "fine people." Sarah Choate Sears, the talented widow of Joshua Montgomery Sears, one of the city's wealthiest real estate men, liked the portraits of Kahlil well enough to buy one, and she was to invest in his own art as he grew older. Josephine Preston Peabody, the other "fine person" he referred to, was to become a friend whose loyalty and advice would affect his life for the next several years.

"Why are you sad? Why are you sad?" The question rang through the mind of the fifteen-year-old boy from the day of the exhibit. It was with him through that spring, it chased him when he left for his homeland in late summer, and it entered his thoughts as he studied in Lebanon for the next four years. Kahlil worked and waited to become a man—an educated man—so that he could match the brilliance he saw in his questioner and in time answer her not as a solemn, charity-bound waif but as an artist and an equal.

One cause of his sadness may have been that success came early to him, while he was still an immature artist. In retracing his Boston years during a

"Labor and the Angel," pen and ink, 1898. (Authors)

period later in his life when he was deliberately obliterating the memory of the social workers and his earliest patrons, Gibran wrote: "Most men would gladly repeat at least their boyhood and youth from six–eighteen; they had such a good time playing and running and enjoying themselves. I think I was first made to realize this by other people. When I was thirteen or fourteen, there were articles in papers and pamphlets about my work, my drawings and designs." [33] Elsewhere he again referred to the public recognition of his earliest designs. "Do you know that you've a book in a binding which I designed when I was fourteen years old? The Maeterlinck books all have that binding—I did several of them—but I've never been able to trace any of the others. Probably they were used on books that passed and were forgotten." [34]

Although these statements seem to be mere dreams piped out of the intricate fantasy life of a man unwilling to admit the facts of a deprived childhood, they begin to be corroborated by a journal entry written by Josephine Peabody, four months after he had left for Beirut: "Mr. Day told me of a lovely thing that happened. In New York, just before he sailed, the boy tried to sell some of his designs for book covers. He sold many, not knowing what [books] they were to be used for. Only a fortnight ago, there came to Mr. Day from Macmillan, I think, the new volume of essays—*Wisdom and Destiny*

64

by Maeterlinck—with one of the boy's designs for a cover. 'That,' said Mr. Day—and I would have hugged him for it—'is one of the pleasantest things that ever happened to me.' " [35]

Evidence that Kahlil had sold his designs to a New York publishing house is also confirmed by a letter from Lilla Cabot Perry, then living in Japan. On March 2, 1899, she wrote Day to acknowledge a package which contained

> your wonderfully beautiful photograph of "It is finished," the Maeterlinck with its delightful inscription, and the first copies I have seen of my book [*Impressions*]. . . . Mr. Perry who is as you know a great book lover is delighted with the form which you have given to my fugitive fancies and agrees with me in liking also Kahlil's cover very much as also the other cover of his. Please tell him this with my affectionate remembrances. . . . I wish I knew what Kahlil is doing and that I could be where I could take a look at his work from time to time, especially if he has begun to work at oil painting when my advice might be of some use to him. [36]

But the most graphic allusion to Kahlil's book designs appeared in the April 2, 1898, issue of *The Critic*, a New York weekly review of literature and art:

> Some days ago a Syrian youth not more than sixteen years of age walked into the office of Mr. S. W. Marvin of Messrs. Scribner's. He carried a letter of introduction in his hand and a portfolio of drawings under his arm. In very good English, he asked Mr. Marvin to read the one and glance over the contents of the other. Mr. Marvin did as requested. The appearance of the boy interested him. His large dark eyes and olive skin made him remarkable amid his American surroundings. The boy sat modestly by while his portfolio was being examined. It was found to contain a collection of the most striking Oriental designs for book covers. When Mr. Marvin had run his critical eye over them, the boy asked him if there were any that he might find worth using. "Have you any more?" inquired Mr. Marvin, to which the boy replied that all he had were there.
> "I will take them all," said Mr. Marvin, "and when you have any more, bring them along and I will take them also."
> I happened in some time after, and was shown the designs. They are certainly striking, and remind one, not unnaturally, of the designs of oriental stuffs. Only one was Americanized, and that was the least successful. Now I wonder why more Syrians, Turks, and other Orientals with whom New York abounds have not tried their hands at this sort of work before. This particular Syrian said that he had never studied the art of design but had simply picked it up. [37]

The journal excerpt, Lilla Perry's letter, and the anecdote in *The Critic* all point to Kahlil's precocious entrance into the world of art. That spring of 1898 foreshadowed the man Gibran's lifelong ability to enter successfully American intellectual and artistic circles, and reveals also the indefinable charisma that was beginning to surround him. He had talent, good looks, verbal glibness, modest manners, and an indomitable will to succeed.

In March 1898 Aubrey Beardsley died of consumption. Louise Guiney and Fred Holland Day mourned this self-taught prodigy and felt that some commemorative effort should be made by a few "select Bostonians" who had admired his feverishly brilliant fancies. Just before he died, Beardsley had converted to the Catholic faith, and so they arranged for a requiem low mass to be celebrated on April 23, at the Roman Catholic convent at 620 Massachusetts Avenue, for the departed artist's soul. Unlike their earlier memorial effort for Keats, this event embarrassed Irish Catholics and papal-wary Yankees alike: to them, Beardsley was indelibly associated with decadence and Oscar Wilde, and a posthumous mantle of Christianity seemed to fit him ill.

Whether Kahlil was present at this occasion is unknown, but it must have been of some importance to him. The fact that Louise Guiney and Day had arranged for it was testimony to the responsibility they, and other Boston bohemians, felt toward the task of ridding America of the trappings of respectability which for so long had mummified liberal forces and thoughts. Being close to Day and his works, Kahlil could not escape some involvement in the struggle with popular censorship and prudishness in America. "Today there are self-appointed rulers the world over who attempt the handcuffing of Art," Day wrote in 1898. "Here in America the censors of art and letters are flourishing as the proverbial green bay tree." [38] The role of the artist as iconoclast was being made clear to the boy, and he learned not to be afraid of controversy.

But with his small successes came problems for Kahlil. Kamila and Peter were unhappy about how quickly he was gravitating toward the outside world, far beyond their control, and the old specter of worldly influences that might be tainted with heresy, with Protestantism, was rising. Kahlil himself missed the town of Besharri and even the authoritarian presence of his father. The family decided that he would return to Lebanon and there finish his education.[39]

Before he started on the long journey home, Kahlil benefited again from the attention of Day and his friends. To supplement a meager income, Louise Guiney had been acting as postmistress for the town of Auburndale. In 1897, seeking escape from the job's bureaucratic rigors, she had bought a spit of bayberry-covered land far up on the Maine coast, Five Islands near Bath. In July 1898 she invited Kahlil and some other young city boys to visit her in her isolated seaside wilderness, an opportunity which was rare indeed for any child of the Boston slums.

The arrangements were made through Day. To ensure that the unsupervised boys would not wander off or miss train connections, the trip was made by sea, in an old sailing vessel called *The Headchance*. The fresh air and healthy living that Kahlil had been denied the previous summer were his now, in a concentrated dose, on that vacation just before he left America. In a letter to Day, Louise Guiney assured him that "everything was OK" with the boys. Then she mentioned that Kahlil had told her of his coming departure. "Is he really going for *good?* I hope not," she wrote.[40]

Miss Guiney was not the only one who was perturbed about the family's unexpected decision. Clearly, Day had also notified Florence Peirce, and from her comment, it seems that Day was also collecting money to help pay for the boy's trip. "Will you let me contribute the enclosed cheque toward Kahlil's expenses?" she wrote. "Can you not dine with us tomorrow at six o'clock? I have asked Kahlil to come at that hour, and you can then have an opportunity to get the desired information from Miss Beale." [41]

Thus it was that Kahlil enjoyed a farewell supper given by his earliest and most perceptive sponsors. We know that he sailed from New York to Lebanon sometime before September 4, for on that day Louise Guiney conveyed a message to him in gratitude for a farewell drawing: "When you write Kahlil," she asked Day, "pray thank him for me. Tell him I'll cherish the ethereal baby! It is modelled, I see, on Van Dyck's little Duke of York, James II. Is the boy not coming back at all?" [42]

Writing later in September from the Adirondacks, where she was staying for a "troublesome cough," Miss Peirce expressed a similar concern about Kahlil's departure from the United States. "Kahlil, I suppose, is on his way to Syria. I fear his going is a mistake but possibly now since he has recognized his artistic tendencies, he may renew the local coloring and return to us benefited by a visit to his nation." [43]

A few days later, a poet who was waiting eagerly for her first book to appear under the Copeland and Day imprint of lilies and roses recorded in her journal the day's mail:

> Cheered by the mail which brings me the third proof of *The Wayfarers* and a note from F. H. Day with a delicate little drawing which he says was left for me by a little Syrian boy (a protege of his whom I saw for a few moments last winter at the photograph view)—Kahlil Gibran. Says FHD, "He is now on his way to —— where he will study Arabic literature and philosophy. He always kept a bright memory of you and wished that you would not forget him." What a sweet little happening is such a thing as this. I had not forgotten the boy; but there were crowds of people there and I only had a word or two with him because I saw that he was shy, and we smiled at each other once or twice across the rooms.[44]

That same day she wrote her publisher about the proofs. But anxious as she was to establish a firm date for the long overdue publication of her book, she first acknowledged the slip of a drawing with its "au revoir" message:

My dear Mr. Day:
This delicate little drawing is a pretty happening. Indeed I had not forgotten Kahlil Gibran; but I am much astonished that he should have remembered me. Are you quite sure that it was I? I will not dispute anything so pleasant, though. . . .

Very sincerely yours,
Josephine Peabody[45]

26 King Street
Dorchester

"Kahlile" by Day, ca. 1898. A similar photograph hung for years above Marianna's sofa. (Royal Photographic Society)

5

Miss Beabody

Josephine Preston Peabody, who was so surprised and gratified at receiving Kahlil's likeness of her, would in any time and place be considered an unusual young woman; in Boston at the turn of the century she was little short of extraordinary. In thanking Day for sending her the drawing before she turned to the matter of business which was her most pressing concern, she was being true to the primary force that had sustained her for ten years: her love of beauty. She had been beauty's disciple even before the age of fourteen, when her first poem was published, and it was beauty that fortified her, as an adult, against the trying circumstances of a life for which her childhood had in no way prepared her.

Life for this girl, "Posy," had been a paradox of surplus and denial. Her earliest memories were of a perfect and privileged childhood in New York, dappled—like the watercolors her talented mother taught her how to use—with sun-shot idylls in Central Park, loving nannies, and genteel private schooling. Her Boston-bred parents, Charles Kilham Peabody and Susan Morrill Peabody, shared all of their devotion to good literature and the theater with their three daughters. It was a singing household that showered applause on budding infant talent and encouraged the girls to express themselves through pageantry, tableaux, and poetry writing. Tales from Grimm, Hawthorne, and Dickens were daily fare, and Shakespeare was the vehicle of their earliest home drama. The whole family recited his words, just for the pure delight of hearing them over and over again.

The idyll was broken in 1882 when the youngest of the three little girls died. Two years later, when Josephine was ten, the fairy tale ended forever with the sudden death of her father. Her mother, bewildered, was left without the means to sustain the life they had known, and the Peabodys began a gradual descent into genteel poverty. Adapting their graceful style of living to the reality of meager finances, they moved to Massachusetts, where they settled in with Mrs. Peabody's mother. Cramped though Mrs. Peabody's circumstances suddenly were, they allowed her to build a modest house in the respectably dull Dorchester section of Boston. Here the family lived "in Darkest Suburbs," as Josephine was later to remember it, deprived of all the music, the plays, the paintings that had nourished their spirits in New York.[1]

Coping with the unaccustomed pressures of impersonal public schools and adjusting to a fatherless household, Josephine withdrew into a private world of words, which she caught and spun into countless stories, plays, and poems. "Lately words have taken the most appalling significance for me," she wrote in her diary.[2] She used and understood them with a special talent: by age fourteen, she was sending her sonnets to editors in New York and Boston. Several of the poems had been published by the time she was near to completing the rigorous classical curriculum of the Boston Girls' Latin School. However, a chronically weak constitution and nerves which were always stretched taut forced her to leave school in her junior year.

She abandoned neither Greek nor literature. She read voraciously, six hundred books in all between 1888 and 1893. She strengthened her admittedly "patch work education" by "going to the [Boston] Athenaeum several mornings a week and making use of the Greek there." [3] Writing once to a friend about what she would like to do in the staid reading rooms of the Athenaeum, she betrayed the whimsical side of her scholarly preoccupations: "We will walk up the precious corkscrew staircase that winds past the French highlands and the Biography perch and the Mathematics catacomb, to Religion, Witchcraft, and Demonology. . . . We will creak about in the gallery and drop books on the librarian's head; we will come down and pass 'Wharton on Homicide,' and traverse the dark staircase in search of a sensation." [4]

She was a girl of an irrepressibly exuberant spirit, and during her maturation as a poet, she revealed this most alluringly and compellingly in her journals. Here her external stresses and her internal longings came alive with style and with the intensity of a lonely, bittersweet girlhood:

> *May 1894.* I want some fun, some fun, and there is none to be had; good times I have, reading. But oh! I want young people and gaiety and something droll. . . . I go in town full of the May feeling, wanting to laugh and talk, and there is nobody at all to laugh and talk with; and I just have to sit and read all by myself, and I can't always do that in comfort; and then I come home again and feel like crying out of sheer caged-up youth. . . . The sky is so blue and the trees are budding—and I want somebody to PLAY WITH![5]

Josephine Preston Peabody at eighteen. (Alison P. Marks)

Unhampered by rhyme or cadence, Josephine's candid introspective writings transcend dutiful diary entries. Evoking her muse—her "Guardian Angel"—she wrote: "I seem to live in a state of continual *ecstasy*. I feel as if there were an angel at my side, always whispering to me." She confided secrets: "Even if you loved anyone enough, it would be imprisonment in a garden! How can you *belong* to anybody, *anybody!*" Sometimes she laughed at her own vain expectations: "One does not expect things in this world; one hopes and pays car-fares." [6] Her journal was, quite literally, her best friend. Here she made up for all the giggling, gossiping, and confiding she yearned for.

Her interior conversations revealed her as alternately retiring and aggressive. In August 1893 she wrote: "I cannot become accustomed to wearing a human shape and having the birds afraid of me, when I come near. They hurt my feelings." In November, still nineteen, she proclaimed: "I should like to be a Positive for a while. Oh, that is just it, you Egoist! Of course you would. You would like to harness up the Crab, the Serpent, the Bear, and the Scorpion to the wain of Boötes: you would like to don Orion's belt and take a long-tailed comet for a lash and go racing meteors in August—wouldn't you? (Yes I would.)." [7]

When she was nearly twenty, Josephine's verses came to the attention of Horace E. Scudder, editor of the *Atlantic Monthly*. Scudder not only agreed to publish one of her Arcadian fancies, "The Shepherd Girl," but was so impressed by her brilliant effervescence that he arranged for her to study at Radcliffe College as a special student.

Cambridge welcomed her and gave her far more than she had ever dreamed. She was able to indulge her "unendurable thirst for music" at weekly "stand-ups" at the Boston Symphony where "people of my age will walk in, Friday afternoons, and buy apotheosis for twenty-five cents." Her visionary imagination transformed human events into miracles. Of a concert by Paderewski she wrote, "He played so that the whole city rose new and perfect in a larger symmetry. This I know because the streets were crooked when I went into Music Hall; but the way was straight before me when I came out: and there were vanishing points and divine perspective everywhere." Her yearning to meet and talk with people who were directly engaged with creative minds was satisfied. Her professors of English literature—William Vaughn Moody, Lewis Gates, Francis Child—found her insouciance refreshing, and she was able to experience "a strange new-made Spring of occasional comradeship, of several genuine 'Good Times' (things that I haven't known too much of in the world's way), of new sights and insights, new helps and new inspirations: I have met with almost unvarying kindliness and affection . . . and I have been patted on the head to excess." [8]

Although she read Homer in the original and soaked up the deliciousness of modern writers in their own tongues—Whitman, Rossetti, Leopardi, de

Musset, Verlaine—Josephine was the antithesis of the blue-stockinged, short-haired, spectacled female scholar. She recoiled from the current stereotype of "maiden huntresses" who charged at their professors' desks with "O Mr. Gates! or O Mr. Baker! at the close of the lecture." She charmed scholars with guileless, unspoken gestures: "*April 1896.* Yesterday Professor Child read at the open meeting of the English Club. We talked to him in the parlor for a few moments before the reading and I put some of my trailing arbutus in his buttonhole." [9]

These impulses, coupled with her sincere frenzy in seeking the "winged thing" that prompted poetry, art, and music, identified Josephine Peabody even then as potentially a great woman. But it was only natural that her high spirits were countered from time to time by wretched sloughs of depression. The comradeship and stimulation that she found at Radcliffe buoyed her for two years, but then, as if stricken with a sudden awareness of the pedantic uselessness of it all, she left the academic halls. "The things we have been reading have become almost a bore, under the present *régime,*" she wrote. "The class is stupid, and the instructor—I can picture him carving a phoenix, with conscientious precision, and remarking, 'Wings are unimportant, but here is a drumstick, my dears.' " [10]

Even the famed lectures of Charles Eliot Norton began to pall:

> *October 1895.* I wonder if these dear and reverend people realize what an impression they give the younger ones when they beg them to believe that there is nothing high and lovely in this country or this age. I put down most of his lectures in quotation marks; some of it I tried to listen to respectfully and with patience. But my hope scorched me. I could not resist scribbling . . . while he talked: "The great inscrutable Day winds its arms around the world and smiles down upon that particular ant-hill wherein Professor Norton expounds the pitiful degeneracy of things and the hopeless unloveliness of our country." [11]

In June 1896 Josephine left Radcliffe. "I desire above all things to deal with things that concern all people. I don't want to be a 'literary' poet. Heaven forbid!" [12] Although no one really understood what prompted her to go, her rejection of the training that would groom her talent was a carefully considered decision. She saw herself as a "maker of (bad) paragraphs and much verse" and wanted to "see a little more life to make them out of! For God knows I hate life-at-hearsay and call the life of letters merely a despicable thing." She left knowing that an illustrious career, "a situation where one must have one's degree and one's experience and one's letters of introduction," would perhaps be denied her.[13] This knowledge at once terrified and exhilarated her: "Of late it has amused me (and made me shiver a little too) to hear Cambridge people express their horror at my departure. Not coming another year—Have I lost my wits? This one opportunity—I may have this and that—but surely I must see that I need the Training—hopeless outlook if I don't return, etc. It is so much like what the Latin School teachers said when I had to leave. Was that to be the end of my education? They had hoped that I would amount to something." [14]

Returning to Dorchester, she reentered the daily routine of a female household where her ailing grandmother, her endlessly grieving mother, and her two-year-older sister Marion, by now an art student, were enduring the embarrassing privations of rapidly dwindling capital. Her circumstances depressed her; a feeling of guilt at being a financial burden dogged her. She suffered violent headaches and devastating recurrences of "azure blues." Nevertheless, she was able to produce a continuing stream of stories, poems, and a retelling of the classical myths, *Old Greek Folk Stories*. Best of all, the Cambridge intellectuals did not forget her. Her physical radiation and the sparkle of her wit lured Harvard graduates out to her suburban refuge, and suddenly 26 King Street became a sort of salon, accessible by trolley car, for bright and talented young men.

Josephine was fast becoming an adored darling, but she held out for more than that. She genuinely wanted a different and more satisfactory relationship between the sexes than existed in turn-of-the-century America. Wanting to establish and maintain warm friendships with men, she mourned the artificial barriers that prevented true communication between men and women:

> We cannot seem to befriend each other. I never felt the piteous helplessness of it more than I did the other evening—nor the possibility of a true affection for a man-friend as for a woman-friend, the will to be sympathetic and comradely in vital, unworldly childish ways if you like; and anxiously tender of temperamental trials and sadness. Yet people insist that all this is impossible for men and women. . . . I *do not see*, and I *will not believe* that there is nothing for men and women between Love and the purely intellectual impersonalities that we are forced to call friendship.[15]

Defiantly emotional and unforgivably pretty, she made herself known. Within a year, she was being introduced to the older women poets who flourished in Boston's several authors' clubs and poetry societies. Louise Guiney, her friend Alice Brown, Louise Chandler Moulton, and even the august personalities of Julia Ward Howe and Annie S. Fields welcomed her. When finally she summoned up enough courage to submit *The Wayfarers*, a collection of her favorite poetry, to Copeland and Day, Herbert Copeland assured her that as editor of *Youth's Companion* he had admired her juvenile work for years. In fact, he and Day had been about to invite her to publish these early poems.

Left: Pencil drawing Kahlil left with Day to present to "the dear and esteemed Lady Josephine Peabody," August 23, 1898. (Lionel P. Marks)

Below: Opening and close of Josephine's letter to Day. (Norwood)

15 September 1898.

My dear Mr. Day:
 This delicate little drawing is a pretty happening. Indeed I had not forgotten Kahlil Eiban: but I am much astonished that he should have

could come so far: and I shall be at home every evening, and as usual, Sunday afternoon.
 Yours sincerely,
 Josephine Peabody
26 King Street
Dorchester

When Kahlil Gibran first saw Josephine at Fred Holland Day's opening, she was admittedly full of "gush and bubble" and neither looked nor felt her years: "Twenty-three: and not grown-up yet. Why should I be?" she wrote then.[16]

Kahlil, attracted by her radiance and her diminutiveness, remembered her and tried to capture in a drawing the ruffles of dark hair piled above the heart-shaped face, the bright brown eyes, and the bewitching mouth. He showed this attempt to Day who, provocateur that he was, probably urged the boy to inscribe it to her and leave it as a memento of himself. Gibran wrote his dedication in Arabic—a mischievous gesture that he may have known would evoke more mystery than his painfully written English. It read, as a Harvard scholar later translated it for her, "August 23, 1898, to the dear and esteemed Lady Josephine Peabody." [17] Day gave her the drawing two weeks after Kahlil had left.

When he reached Beirut, Kahlil spoke Arabic fluently and understood it perfectly; he could read it fairly well, but he could barely write it. On his voyage he studied a copy of Bulfinch's *Age of Fable* which Day had given him. Inside it he wrote in colloquial Arabic: "This book I studied between Nairik [New York] and Beirut and all the studying I did was with great zeal." On the last page he practiced his Arabic script again: "I arrived on [*sic*] Beirut in good health. Nothing is missing." [18]

Kahlil chose Madrasat-al-Hikmah as the college where he would complete his education. Established in 1875 by Yousef Dibs, a Maronite priest, the school offered a strongly nationalistic curriculum biased heavily in favor of church writings, history, and liturgy. Kahlil tried to persuade those in charge that he was ready to study at the college level. Even though his Arabic was so poor that he could not arrange his courses without help, he complained to Father Joseph Haddad, a resident teacher, about having been put into the most elementary class of the school because of his weakness in Arabic grammar. Father Haddad explained patiently that learning was like climbing a ladder; one must climb each rung, one at a time. The dark-complexioned youth stared back at him unblinkingly with his sleepy brown eyes. Birds, said Kahlil, did not need ladders to fly. Exaggerating his background, he claimed that he had just completed his English lessons in America and adamantly stated that since he, and not his parents, was responsible for his tuition, he was also responsible for his own studies. If he could not choose his own curriculum, he would go to the American University in Beirut.[19]

This arrogance implied heresy. The Maronite Madrasat was vigorously competing for Lebanese students with the Protestant-run American University, and Kahlil's American upbringing lent weight to his threat. Father Haddad made a special effort on his behalf and secured the headmaster's agreement that Kahlil's curriculum be tailored to his special needs. Impressed by the youth's seriousness of purpose and his unusual self-confidence, he also agreed that Kahlil could audit lectures and read the assigned literature for three months before being called upon to answer questions. The result was a seminary-like course of study created in no small measure by Kahlil's own powers of persuasion. Within it, his Arabic consciousness developed rapidly. Father Haddad encouraged his creative efforts at writing and assigned him Arabic literature that would fill the appalling gaps in his background. Prominent were selections from the Arabic-language Bible, especially the Gospels, in whose style and cadence Kahlil immersed himself.

Again he made a vivid impression at school. Long after he had departed, he was remembered by the teachers as a strange boy marked by extravagances in style and attitude. He still wore his hair long, and his tastes were distinctly out of the ordinary. He told strange stories, lacing his conversations with references to American and English writers, and plays that he had seen. If he was candid enough to describe his Boston experiences, his unconventional patron, the American poets he had personally known, and the designs that he had made and sold for book bindings, it would be scarcely surprising that such stories were only half believed.

Meanwhile, as Kahlil tried to accommodate his American experiences to a classical Arabic training, the poems of his "dear and esteemed lady" were published in the first week of December 1898. Josephine Peabody had agonized for a year waiting for this event—a year in which she fretted at the languid pace of Copeland and Day and was nonplussed by the premature publicity in October: front-page headlines proclaiming, "Boston has a new poetess." [20] When she finally held in her hands the first thin green volume, embossed with golden wings designed by her sister Marion, she was disappointed. "It looked dead and full of hurts," was her first impression. But two weeks later she forgot the error in the quotation from Dante on the frontispiece, forgot the painfully long delay: *December 1. Here come six copies and a note saying that it is to be published on Saturday. Te Deum laudamus."* [21]

On December 3 Josephine visited 69 Cornhill to discuss with Day her apprehension about her publishers' casual attitude toward the distribution of her book. Day entertained her and slyly distracted her from her pressing concerns. For half an hour he showed her "a whole sheaf of drawings of the Syrian boy, Kahlil Gibran: I can hardly tell of them." [22] Seeing how visibly moved she was, he then told her all about Kahlil—about his response to Maeterlinck, and Lemprière, about the designs he had created and sold, about his return to the land of the Bible. When Josephine left Day's office, her anxiety had vanished.

Her book was in her hands now; she could do with it what she wanted. Her first act was to mail a copy to Maurice Maeterlinck, who was recalled to mind by her conversation with Day. She not only admired his *Treasure of the Humble*, but an entry in her diary reveals how an unusual incident strengthened her feelings for him still more. She had been sitting in an open trolley car reading, in the original French, the essay on silence. Just as she came to the sentence about "Silence, ange de rivite supremes . . . where he says that our souls seem to beg to put it off—and to implore yet a few hours of harmless lies . . . I felt a flutter in the folds of my gown. I looked and saw a young sparrow in my lap. I could hardly believe my eyes, took him in my hand; he did not try to escape, but rested passim and looked at me with bright uncurious eye." [23]

For Josephine this visitation had been full of symbolic meaning. She sought always for signs from the winged muse—what could be more appropriate than this? Her visit with Day had reminded her of it, and so in a spirit of teasing, almost of flirting, she sent Maeterlinck some sign of herself. Simultaneously, convinced that the young Syrian artist was weaving similar spells with his drawings, she determined to signal him. It was another game, and she was still looking for someone to play with.

She recounted her conversation with Day: "*December 12, 1898*. Today I mean to write a letter to Kahlil Gibran! The very idea of him is like a well-spring and locusts and wild honey. . . . His father is a sheik, a tax collector, says Mr. Day. . . . He is only fifteen years old." Learning of Kahlil's assertion that after reading Lemprière he was now a pagan, she had interrupted Day: " 'Ah,' said I, 'how many changes of heart he will go through.' 'He will indeed,' said Mr. Day." [24]

She asked Day if he knew whether Kahlil had ever kept sheep, and

> he touched me by looking unsurprised and not inclined to laugh. It opened my eyes to him: and I saw that he believes what I believe—that the boy was made to be one of the prophets. This is true. His drawings say it clearlier [sic] than anything else could. There is no avoiding that young personality. You are filled with recognition and radiant delight. Great spiritual possessions. These you can see in every sketch and a perception, a native-born wisdom that is second sight. I bless the day I saw these things, for there is nothing that so warms one's heart and cheers the thoughts that are growing down in the dark as to meet one of these creatures who are dear to God.[25]

Two months later in Beirut, Kahlil received a decorative letter from Josephine:

12 December 1898

My Dear little Friend:
    A lovely surprise came to me, some time ago in the shape of the drawing that you left for me, before you sailed away. At first I found it hard to

78

believe that it really was for me, or that you could have kept me in mind so long. But since the picture is in my hands, be very sure that I mean to keep it.

It lies before me as I write; and, if I can, I am going to find somebody wise enough to tell me what the inscription means. I have not hurried to find that out, because the face itself says so much to me: my ears can hear a lovely voice from it, whenever I stop and listen.

Very lately I saw and talked with your friend Mr. Day. We spoke of you; and he let me see many more of the drawings that you had left with him. I wish to tell you that they made me feel quite happy for the rest of the day. Why? Because I seemed to understand you through them clearly: and I felt sure that you will always have within yourself, a rich happiness to share with other people. You have eyes to see and ears to hear. After you have pointed out the beautiful inwardness of things, other people less fortunate may be able to see too, and to be cheered with that vision. I think that your spirit lives in a beautiful place: and to believe that of anyone always makes me happy.—May it always live there.

To my mind, it is thus with people who can truly make lovely things, whether pictures or pottery or music or anything else: whoever they are, they are sure of a daily bread which is nothing less than the Bread of Life: and they have the perfect happiness of giving that Bread away to others, poorer than themselves, who might go hungry and unbefriended.

I wonder what your country is like, and whether you have some quiet place to grow in. I am sometimes so perplexed with the noises and crowded sights of the city, that I feel like a lost child hunting after my own true self. I remember how many prophets have grown up in solitude, even perhaps tending the sheep (like Apollo in the story, keeping the flocks of King Admetus!) and I wish that all people who *must* be in a lonely country-place for a time, could know how to find the blessing in solitude, like a spring hidden in the desert. (Have you ever seen the Desert? I have wished to know what it is like.)

You know what Maeterlinck says of silence in *The Treasure of the Humble*. Well I think you listen to silences: and I hope that you will come back someday and tell us what you have heard.

If you should ever tell me something of your life in a country far and strange to me, how gladly will I listen! And if you want news of anything that goes on here, ask me, and I will tell you all I know. This is but a little of my thanks for the drawing.

Your very sincere friend,
Josephine Peabody[26]

Now it was Kahlil's turn to be impressed. Small wonder he boasted about the American poets he had met! Josephine's message, full of references to her own works ("Daily Bread" became the title of a poem that would be published in 1900 in her *Fortune and Men's Eyes*), treated him as a fellow artist. Day had sent him a copy of *The Wayfarers*—but this letter, in her own hand, was like manna.

Anxious to live up to Josephine's expectations, while unaware of the predictions being made about him, the boy tried to command his impoverished written English for a heartfelt reply. His uncertain spelling and unconventional punctuation were just naive and fresh enough to delight her: he called her "Miss Beabody" because the letter P is nonexistent in Arabic. His confusion in simultaneously learning to write in two languages is evident; his need and determination to express himself figuratively simply transcended his ability.

When his answer reached her in March 1899, Josephine was delighted by its simple ardor. This woman who had memorized twenty-one Shakespeare sonnets, "sundry Italian things," plus a "number of English lyrics" so that she would never be alone, who read Dante for relaxation and took Herodotus to her bath, was overjoyed at the half-literate attempts of her youthful Lebanese admirer. Fortunately, she carefully copied this "marvel of a letter" in her journal, "to keep it safe." [27] The transcribed letter, with all of its errors preserved, reads thus:

> My dear Josephine,
>   It seems that if I have gained you for a friend after all, "Have I?" the hope of that was near the side of its graive.
>   Of course I was so pleased when I saw your picture and what they says about it but not so much if it was just little letter from you to me which will open the door of our friendship. And as I says that the hope of getting a letter from you was allmost dead, till your letter arrived which did tell me great more that was what was in it of words. O, how hapy I was? How glad? So hapy that the tongue of poor pen can not put my joy in words.
>   You can see that I allway feel disconted when I come to write English because I know not how to translate my thought as I want, but perhaps you won't mind that, and I think I know enough to tell you (that I will keep your friendship in middest of my heart, and over that many many milles of land and sea I will allways have a certane love for you and will keep the thought of you near my heart and will be no sepperation between you and my mind) O, if I know better English or if you know Arabic it will be great pleasure to us still I will prommis that I will write to you all what I know and do, hoping that you will write to me sometime telling me about you, andall what you write will give me pleasure.
>   Yes, I did kept you in mind so long, as you said in your letter "for I allways keep things of that sort" and for a certane thing I am just like a camera and my heart is the plate, why? I kept you because your face seems to tell me somethings when I ever thinks of it, not that I will forget when you spoke with me by your own self that night in Mr. Day's exhibition. At the same night I asked Mr. Day who is the lady in black he said "She is Miss Beabody a young poet and her sister is an artist" What a hapy family" said I, I love to know them." And after that time, days past so readily that I did not seen you to know you more, untell the love of wisdom caryed me

Kahlil at college in Beirut, ca. 1900. (Authors)

over that long distance and put me in Byrouth in a college studying Arabic and French and many things beside.

Syria is very nice country so old ruen [ruins] found in many places it so defrance to America it is very silence more in the country in the villages like mine where people are all of one kinde of heart they love eachother and they dont do very much work like the people in America for they only work in their ground, Rich and poor are seems to be very happy.

I wonder what make you know that I love silence and quite pleaces, why, yes I do and I realy could hear its beautiful music, I wonder do you ever set in a dark silence room lessening to the music of the rain so calm that is (won't you write me?? I will tell you many thing in my next litter) From your far far friend

Kahlil Gibran

So "hapy" was "Miss Beabody" with this adventure in writing by a spirit unfettered by grammar, spelling, or conventional style, that on March 25 she wrote to Day: "This last week brought me a letter from Kahlil Gibran: English as broken and sense as perfect as I have ever seen. It was a great pleasure. I wonder if you would mind showing his drawings to my friend Mrs. Prescott and me, if we should come to Cornhill some day after Easter." [28]

Thus while Kahlil was struggling with the intricacies of classical Arabic form, Josephine was already perpetuating her belief in his giftedness. Long before he was able to present lucidly his thoughts in any language, an audience was being prepared to listen to his message. Josephine had been studying clay modeling with Kate Prescott, as a "desperate effort at self-help," [29] and her early efforts to get her teacher interested in Kahlil's work were prophetic of things to come. When he returned to Boston three years later, her relentless quest for aesthetic satisfaction and expression would be essentially secured, and she would take it upon herself to ensure Kahlil some place in the creative sun. Meanwhile, in Beirut he was accelerating his studies, hurrying to fit into the singer-artist mantle that others—and he himself—wished him to wear.

Adjustment to the strict discipline of the school was difficult at first. As he later described it:

> The first two years in college were hard, because of difficulty with the authorities. The college was strict—they keep a far more rigid hand on the students than colleges do here—and I didn't believe in their requirements and I wouldn't obey them. I was less punished than any other student would have been, however, because I made it up in other ways—I studied so hard. And the last year was good—because of the magazine that Hawaiik and I were getting out, and the many occasions for poems—and they made me the college poet.[30]

Joseph Hawaiik represented to Kahlil the embodiment of prestige and culture. He was a nephew of the Maronite Patriarch, and he enjoyed all the privileges accorded to a relative of an influential churchman. Easygoing and sophisticated, he was open and responsive to the intense and anxious spirit of the youth from Besharri. Together the two started a magazine called *al-Manarah* or *The Beacon*.[31] This literary venture, in which Kahlil's experience at Copeland and Day allowed him to assume a certain leadership, enabled him to offset his inferior economic and social position with a talented performance, and it was a source of satisfaction to him. His later account of how Hawaiik supported and admired his skills is an example of how, early on, he insisted on visualizing himself always as the innovator: "In college [Hawaiik] was my sort of spiritual child. I first got him to draw. He thought I was wonderful because I could draw a cat & a tree—We published a paper together: he was manager and I was editor. At first we printed it on one of those metal and gelatin machines and in our senior year the president let us use the college presses." [32]

Hawaiik's later memories of Kahlil included a description of the magazine which they had conceived and for which Kahlil wrote and drew illustrations. He also recalled Kahlil as "lonely, obstinate and strange in appearance." [33] Resisting as he did the routines thrust upon the students by the priests, Kahlil's defiance took many forms. He skipped classes, he filled his school notebooks with drawings and satirical sketches of his teachers, he flouted religious duties, and when forced to receive communion, he would forgo the obligatory confession. It is a measure of the understanding of Father Haddad that he recognized the ambitious boy as more than a defiant student.

The recognition that Kahlil craved came in his final year when his poetry was selected for merit. Later he described how important this award was to him:

> The year before I finished college I was trying very hard in the poetry contest. That is a great thing in the college life, because the successful man is the college poet for his last year and a great many honors are shown him. I was very much excited and very eager to get the prize. About ten o'clock I was in my room and one of my teachers came by and knocked at the door.
> "Gibran Effendi," said he, "are you still awake?"
> "Yes," said I, "I don't want to sleep."
> "Now," said he, "you go to bed, and go to sleep, and dream good dreams."
> I knew they were even then holding a meeting in the prefect's room and probably deciding about the poems. "Probably," I said to myself, "probably he just came by to give me that knock and that word"—and it made my hopes firmer, and I went to bed, and to sleep.
> In my dream I was in a little garden. Near the wall—the wall is of marble and you know how strange beautiful colors come in marble with time—the soft red and the blue lines. Well, instead of looking outward towards the flowers as I usually did, I found myself looking towards the wall. Then Christ was there. There was no way for him to come—at the wall—but he was there. And he said the very words of my teacher, "Go to sleep and dream good dreams." I did not wake then—but in the morning I remembered I was successful in the poem—and very very happy. It was ecstasy. I suppose in all my life I shall never know such an uplift again.
> [The poem was] a description—of a place—we were all given the same subject. It was just school work—but it meant a great deal to a boy.[34]

The satisfactions Kahlil received at the Madrasat were in stark contrast to his reception at Besharri. He returned to his home town during summer vacations, only to encounter again the obduracy of his father, a man whom time had not mellowed in any way. Still arrogant despite his besmirched reputation, still indifferent to the intellectual pursuits of his son, Gibran's personal indulgences and disregard for the feelings of others were if anything worse than they had been. Kahlil found himself in a conflict of emotions with regard to his father: on the one hand, he could not help admiring the man's strength of will, on the other, he could not escape a deep resentment at the antagonism that his father displayed toward him.

> I admired him for his power, his outspokenness & refusal to yield—that got him into trouble eventually. But if hundreds were about him he could command them with a word. He could overpower any number by any expression of himself. . . .
>
> My father hurt me often. I remember once especially. I had just written a poem—I was in college—about sixteen or seventeen. And it had been published—and I was very proud and very conceited and thought everybody would be so interested and would speak to me about it when I went home. Well my father gave a dinner party—& one of the guests was Salima [Selim Dahir] a literary man I was very anxious to see. I longed to appear well in his eyes. During the dinner one of the ladies told me she had read my poem—and liked it so much—and then several spoke and praised it. The lady said, as a woman of 50 would to a boy, to encourage him, "And shall you write more, Kahlil?"
>
> "Yes. In fact, I wrote one last night"—glad to say it in the happiness of her commendation.
>
> "Oh! how interesting. I'd like very much to hear it. Won't you read it to us after dinner?" Then the others joined in & said, "yes, Kahlil—Read us your poem."
>
> I looked at my father, & he made a face—of contempt for it all.
>
> After dinner when we went out into the hall where coffee was served, presently one of the men asked me to read my poems—& the lady said, "Especially the one you wrote last night." My father said, "I don't believe, Kahlil, that our friends will find such things interesting"—
>
> Then they insisted—& I said to myself that I would *be* myself—& I got the poem & read it.
>
> They all listened—& I shall never forget it—They liked it—it touched them—they all looked kindly at me—It was my first reading ever to a selected audience—I cannot describe what it was to me. But they all were with me—they were loving me. And my father said—"I hope we shall never have any more of this stuff—this sick-mindedness."
>
> That hurt deep into my inner most being.[35]

The schism between father and son widened, and Kahlil at last left his father's house. When in Besharri, he shared a room with N'oula Gibran, the cousin who had been with him when he had his childhood accident, and was now an apprentice to the village carpenter. N'oula remembered those long summers when he and Kahlil, who was penniless but no doubt full of grand stories about life in Boston, lived a simple life in a shabby room in the house of Kahlil's earliest childhood days—the house that was still managed by Raji Beyk. The condition of that room, as far as Kahlil was concerned, was part of the dark side of his life which he never spoke of in his later descriptions of Besharri. Its shabby dilapidation symbolized the grim reality which he always submerged. But N'oula in later years had no hesitation about recalling the damp, vermin-infested quarters, and the horror which he and Kahlil always felt upon entering. When they opened the door, hordes of bedbugs clinging to a rope which hung from the ceiling would drop and scuttle to their beds. And Kahlil, fastidious about his personal cleanliness, would curse the poverty that forced them to endure such skin-crawling degradation.[36]

In contrast was the splendor of the out-of-doors. Just as when he was a child, Kahlil found solace along the cliffs, in the gorges, and in the dark shadows of the Cedars. His friendship with the poet-physician Selim Dahir also sustained him, more than ever. In his newly learned calligraphy he began to record the stories and poems that Dahir recited. The older man's deep knowledge about the traditions of local history and memorable personalities enriched the youth's understanding of his background and provided him with the colloquial vocabulary which he would use when he himself began to write.

In Besharri, Kahlil was dependent on the hospitality of friends and relatives for food, and he often visited the home of an influential family related to both Raji Beyk (who belonged to the Dahir clan) and Selim Dahir. Here, in the house of Tannous Asad Hanna Dahir, warmth and material comfort offered him a pleasant refuge, and in return, he began to help the Dahir daughters with their chores. The oldest sister, Hala Dahir, was particularly attractive to him. She responded to the aloof, poetic youth, walked with him, and listened to his reveries. The friendship blossomed and was noticed. Gossipers began to speculate on the possibilities of a betrothal—which, was, of course, impossible. Not only was Hala older than Kahlil, but her brother Alexander, legal scribe and town official, strongly discouraged the "son of the goat tax farmer." He made it clear that Hala could do much better.

Ten years after Kahlil's forest trysts with Hala Dahir, he published *The Broken Wings*, a story about a Lebanese student's unrequited love for an unhappily

Pencil drawing of sleeping angel made in Besharri around 1900. (Photo Juley)

married woman, which caused speculation among his readers about the real-life identity of his heroine, Selma Karema. There is little doubt that this interlude in Besharri affected him, and that in portraying Selma he tenderly recalled Hala Dahir. Remembering her, Gibran could describe his ideal of the Lebanese woman, her physical appearance and social concerns. But the impetus for the story was found not in the mountain town of Besharri; it came from the civilized drawing rooms of Cambridge and Boston. His subsequent friendship with Josephine Peabody would prove to be far more consequential.

Once while N'oula and Kahlil rested on the banks of the river Ruwayyis, Kahlil drew a picture of a sleeping angel lying in a meadow filled with flowers. "What are those flowers?" N'oula asked. "They are the flowers that put you to sleep," was the reply.

Kahlil no doubt based the winged figure lying in a poppy field upon images of Greek mythology. But an even more direct source was one of Day's own photographs. In July 1898, shortly before the boy departed for Beirut, an article in *Camera Notes* described the photo: "Possibly Mr. Day's most successful effort . . . is the study entitled 'Hypnos' in which sleep is represented by an Ephebe with closed eyes, breathing the soporific odor of a poppy. In this the idealism is wonderfully aided by the wing of a bird, a pigeon's possibly." [37] Far removed from Boston, Kahlil recalled this symbolism when he made his own version of an elongated child-nude surrounded by poppies. The naturalistic flowers differed considerably from the photograph's artificial prop of a copper flower, but the ideas coincided.

That same article on Day pointed out the influence on him of the English painter George Frederic Watts: "In fact, in loftiness of aim Mr. Day bears no slight resemblance to that great painter of mysteries." [38] Kahlil's youthful expression was thus a curiously hybrid rendering, conceived in northern Lebanon where he recalled the idealizations of a Boston pictorial photographer who in turn owed his aesthetic roots to an English painter.

Kahlil carefully saved all the drawings he made in Besharri and sent a package of them to Day. If N'oula had been incredulous about Kahlil's stories of this miracle of a friend who took hundreds of photographs of him, brought him to concerts, and gave him books, he and the whole village became believers when Day's answer finally arrived from Boston. Not only did it acknowledge receipt of all the drawings, but it contained a check for $50.

Fifty dollars was an unbelievable sum in Besharri, and nobody in the town could cash this sort of paper. So Kahlil set out for Tripoli, twenty-five miles away, to convert his patron's payment into cash. While he was there, he bought a tan suit with pearl buttons and a splendid pair of high leather boots. When he returned, the townspeople envied him for his opulence, his success, his mysterious rich friend. N'oula resolved that he, too, would go to

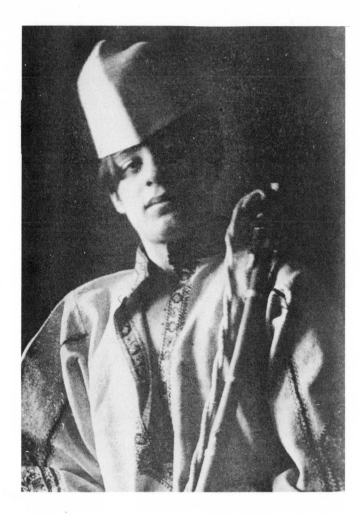

"The Young Sheik,"
ca. 1897. (Authors)

America—not with dreams about gold-paved streets but because he, too, might meet a big man who would pay cash dollars for some pencil pictures.

Fred Holland Day, meanwhile, was becoming more and more involved with his camera work. As early as 1898, he wrote to Louise Guiney that he was considering the dissolution of his publishing house. She replied, "Your prognostication about C & D didn't boggle me much as I knew well enough your heart hasn't been in it for a long while. When Evans 'broke jail' [Frederick H. Evans, the English architectural photographer, had closed his bookshop recently], I said: . . . This is exactly what Sonny would like to do, and will do 'ere long. I believe, moreover, that I remarked this summer that you would yet turn yourself loose in Palestine, with Kahlil for dragoman." [39]

Copeland and Day by now had an established reputation as a house of broad and imaginative tastes. But sustained success had always been uncomfortable to Day, and he decided to retire from the publishing world. By June 1899 Copeland and Day was nothing more than a list of remainders, acquired by the Boston firm of Small, Maynard & Co. Within a few years it would be merely a fleeting memory for a small group of cognoscenti.

Day now threw all his taste and energies into making photographs and writing about photography. His articles were in demand, and in 1899 the *American Annual of Photography* published his essay on "Portraiture and the Camera," illustrated by his portrait of "The Young Sheik." It shows a young Kahlil, probably in the first year that they met.[40]

Not long after this, Day became embroiled in a fierce controversy over a series of "sacred studies" he had made, including several sensational scenes of the Crucifixion and the Entombment. They intrigued and shocked the general public, and critical opinion was sharply divided on their merit. Rumors of just how Day had achieved the realistic pose of Christ nailed to the Cross were no doubt exaggerated, but beyond question the citizens of Norwood were aghast at his sacrilege. Stories flew of "the rehearsing of his company, and [how] the sacred tragedy was played more than a hundred times on the top of that hill, while curious farmers on their wagons with their families came from far and near to gaze at the strange spectacle." [41] Whether they were true or not, Day did in fact create a furore.

Part of the uproar was about whether Day himself had posed as the Savior. One critic suggested that "he seems in this case to have been his own model: his lithe and slender form, his intellectual and expressive face, adorned with flowing hair of the traditional color of a ripe filbert." Another writer found this hard to believe: "I can hardly associate the appearance of this man, carrying always a portfolio with prints under his arm, almost as large as himself, with the idea of his impersonating such an august personality, and yet his Christ in the sepulchre looks very much like him." [42] Norwood residents and Day himself remained forever silent on the identity of the cast.

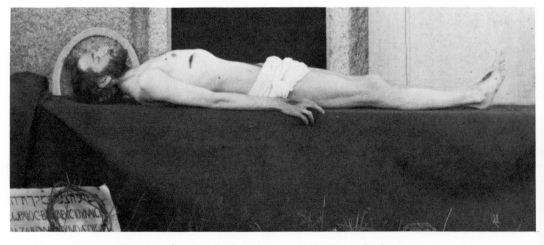

Day as Christ in the Entombment, ca. 1899. (Royal Photographic Society)

Day, of course, thrived on the publicity and shortly afterward invaded England with a collection of his own and other American photographers' art. His membership in The Linked Ring, a splinter group of the Royal Photographic Society devoted to the principles and advancement of photography as a fine art, gave him some influence in British photographic societies. By the fall of 1900, he had organized two shows in London. Under his influence, the first, the Eighth Photographic London Salon sponsored by The Linked Ring, devoted one-third of its exhibit to American photography.

The second show, held at the Royal Photographic Society's gallery on South Russell Square, was completely Day's endeavor. On the walls were the works of forty-one artists of "The New School of American Photography Supplemented by An Additional Collection of One Hundred Examples of the Work of F. Holland Day of Boston." [43] Although Day's work predominated, the notably successful exhibition included the work of photographers such as Alvin Langdon Coburn, Frank Eugene, Gertrude Käsebier, Eduard Steichen, and Clarence White.

Day's pictures included not only his scenes of Calvary but also portraits of his fellow artists and of his South End models. At least three photographs of Kahlil were shown: catalogue numbers 323, "Kahlile," 343, "Syrian Boy," and 363, "Portrait of Master G. K. G." [44] Also shown was "Portrait of Miss S. G.," one of Day's efforts to capture Sultana Gibran's solemn beauty.

The surviving Day portraits of Sultana, Marianna, and Kamila attest that the photographer did not forget the Gibran family while Kahlil was away. He used mother and daughters as models for the type of somber study that some hailed as "plastic psychological synthesis" and others called "plastic psychological fiddlesticks." He was accused of leading "this Cult of the spoilt print," but also credited with having "done more to the creating of the 'new school' than any other individual photographer." [45]

Immediately following his English success, Day moved to Paris, where he stayed at the Montparnasse studio of the young painter-photographer Eduard Steichen. Labeling Day as "un raffine," [46] Paris responded favorably to his and Steichen's mission to prove that a photograph was a work of art. At this point, however, Day's restlessness finally caused him to give in to his longtime yearning for travel in the Middle East. By April 23, 1901, he was writing to Louise Guiney from Algiers: "And here I am . . . veritably in the anti-room [sic] of the East, bewildered, enchanted, hypnotized by the strange beauty of architecture, the radiance of the atmosphere and the ever changing K (or C is it) aleidoscopic quality of costume which everywhere and at all times of day and night confronts one." [47]

One wonders if Day did indeed venture further East to visit Kahlil. There is an undatable letter from Kahlil to his father, which implies the possibility of his traveling with Day. "I am still in Beirut," he wrote, "although I might be

"Master G. K. G." (Royal
Photographic Society)

away from home for a whole month touring Syria and Palestine or Egypt and
Sudan with an American family for whom I have great respect. For this reason
I do not know how long my stay will last in Beirut. However, I am here for
personal benefit which makes it necessary for me to remain in this country for
a while, in order to please those who care for my future." [48] Although the
"American family" was quite possibly Day, no source exists which can place
Kahlil along with Day during the photographer's Oriental travels or even trace
the exact route of the youth's return to the United States in 1902. We do know
that he went by way of Paris, for it was there, quite unprepared, that he
learned of the death of his sister Sultana.

The elder Gibran had, in fact, earlier received a letter from Boston which
said that Sultana was ill. But Kahlil, in the same letter that mentioned "an
American family," had tried to tell him that this could not be true: "During
the last seven months I have received five letters from Mr. Ray [Day] who
assures me that both of my sisters Marianna and Sultana are in excellent
health. He extols their fine characters, marking Sultana's refined manners, and
speaks of the resemblance between her and me both in physique and
character." Yet Sultana was more gravely ill than anyone could possibly have
realized. Marianna's portrayal of the tragedy, as recorded by a friend twelve

Sultana by Day, sometime before April 1902. (Authors)

years later, tells the story in detail and is moving in its direct simplicity:

[When she died] Sultana was 14. When she was 12 glandular swellings came on both sides of her neck. The doctor gave her medicines. He said she would not live long anyhow, therefore he would not operate, since she might die under the operation. Peter had taken her to the hospital—for her mother spoke no English. He did not tell her or Mrs. G. what the doctor said—but simply followed instructions as to treatment. Consumption of the bowel set in—and after 7 months in bed Sultana died. Two months before her death, when Marianna came home one day S. showed her feet & legs, swollen to the knee—& said with bitter tears, "Now I can never get up at all." And she never did again. It was a terrible illness in every possible way—& felt in every possible way by the child & all who loved her & nursed her. . . .

The night before Sultana died had been very bad. They had been up all night—In the morning Peter went upstairs to rest. Marianna asked Miss Teahan when she got to work, not to keep her but to let her go back home and Miss Teahan did [Marianna was working as a seamstress for Miss Teahan's Dressmaking Shop]. When she came in again, S. said, "Why aren't you going to work?" "You know we were up all night," said Marianna, "so I thought I'd rather sleep this morning." "All right" said S. Then she said "Call Peter"—& Marianna did. The aunt was in the room. Peter tried to

Left to right, Kamila, Sultana, and Marianna as photographed by Day, ca. 1901. (Authors)

make Sultana take a little hot beef wine—& after a great deal of coaxing she did. Then she asked for her mother, & Marianna went to her. She was helping a woman who had come in to wash—& she told Marianna to hang out the basket of wet clothes while she went to Sultana. In little more than a minute Marianna heard her aunt scream. She ran back to the room. Sultana, who had been resting on her aunt's arm, was dead. Marianna started to scream like the aunt. She had never seen anyone dead before. "Hush!" said her mother. "That is not a right thing to do." [Marianna said:] "Then I cried quietly, like my mother. Peter had gone into the little room. For three days & nights he cried. He couldn't eat nor sleep." [49]

On the death certificate the name of Sultana Gibran, whose solemn face just two months before had been included in a display of Day's photos in his Boston studio, was changed to "Annie Gobran." The official cause of death was noted as "chronic diarrhea and interstitial nephritis." She died on April 4, 1902. Marianna's description of Kahlil's arrival to the bereaved family two weeks later showed him stunned and completely inarticulate:

Kahlil was away at college. He knew Sultana was ill—but not how ill. Shortly before her death he wrote to his mother that he had finished at college & wanted to come back. She answered, Come. He started at once—they had not expected that—& in Paris he read in a paper of S's death. The family meanwhile had written him the news but to Beirout. For sometime before her death S. had said she longed only to see Kahlil & her father, & then to go. When he came, she had been dead nearly two weeks. It was the 2nd Sunday afternoon after her death when a telegram came for Peter, about 4: he was out walking, till 6. Then he got it. "Mother!" he cried, "Kahlil's coming!" & for very joy wept as if his heart would break. "And my mother didn't speak for two hours—she was crying so for joy Kahlil was coming and for sorrow that Sultana's not here."

K. was coming by boat. [That morning] at 4 a.m., they were all up. Marianna wanted to stay at home from work, but her mother said, "You'll have plenty of time to see your brother at noon—and maybe Miss Teahan can let you stay at home for the afternoon." But Miss Teahan was too busy, & gave her only a whole hour at home at noon.

"Lots of company were there to see Kahlil just come from home," when Marianna got in. Mother was getting dinner—The aunt was with them. The company were invited to stay for dinner, but did not. Peter could not control himself, but all through dinner was running out to dry his tears. Kahlil talked of everything else—but did not mention Sultana—did not at any time of that home-coming. "Because he knew if he began to cry he couldn't stop," said Marianna.

Two or three weeks later, Marianna said to him, "as children will say, talking to one another—'Kahlil, I think it was awfully hard, you did not even ask about your sister that day.' 'Why should I?' said he, 'I knew she was dead; I knew my mother loved her, & my brother loved her, & you; and I knew all their hearts were aching. And they knew I loved her & my heart was aching. I didn't want to make it just harder for my mother.' " [50]

From Marianna's recollections one can see that Kahlil's immediate reaction to his family's grief differed from the sorrow in which Peter, Marianna, and their mother had lingered. Even to those closest to him, he was building an exterior shell. He also had the return to the Boston slum to contend with—certainly a rude awakening, although the family was now living at 7 Tyler Street instead of Oliver Place.

But Kahlil did observe the conventional signs of bereavement. Marianna remembered him with a moustache and she said: "He got a black suit & a black hat & black shoes for mourning . . . for all the clothes he brought back from college were light with a brown hat & tan shoes." [51] No one dared to suspect how necessary his mourning apparel would become, for they could not realize how the Angel of Death would continue to overshadow that household with its beating wings.

Self-portrait, pen and ink, ca. 1902. (Authors)

94

6

Pegasus Harnessed
to an Ash-Wagon

November 6, 1902. This morning I had a note from whom in the world but Kahlil Gibran, the Syrian boy, now grown up I suppose—and returned to America." [1]

If a surprised Josephine Peabody thought the boy grown up, so had she. Since she had copied his letter almost four years before, she had written and published two books: *The Singing Leaves*, a collection of poems, and *Fortune and Men's Eyes*, a one-act play centered around an Elizabethan tavern scene involving Shakespeare. In 1901 *Marlowe*, her first full-length play, appeared.

She had long felt a desire to contribute to American dramatic verse. "Oh, if I could only have a hand in the tug at the Drama in America," she wrote in 1901. "If I could only pull and haul and boost and kick and push—and hear one responsive onward squeak!" In actuality response to her poetry was louder than a squeak, but with the high praise came little material benefit. "I devoutly wish this work might in time bring in something beside honor," she wrote to Horace E. Scudder when Houghton Mifflin accepted *Marlowe* for publication, "for I shall have to make a laurel-salad to live on." [2]

In May 1899 the house on King Street was sold at public auction. Josephine hid behind the shutters and heard the proceedings from her room. As she listened to "Going, going—gone at fifty-five hundred, that's settled," she had second thoughts about moving. "I'm very sorry it went for so little; it never showed pleasanter, roomier, sunnier than today: as a House." But she and Marion wanted to be part of the Cambridge excitement. The family rented a house at 36 Linnaean Street, although this advantageous location did not lessen the pressures of their encroaching pennilessness. "Appearances—appearances—appearances! Our bogy till death. Little remnant of a family that we are, we cannot split up, and we cannot be stubborn and eccentric by ones in the same household. We must cling together, keep up traditional appearances, look thoroughly presentable, and answer all Philistine demands, while the moneys grow less." [3]

Knowing and genuinely caring about other poets was integral to Josephine's aims. She had met Edwin Arlington Robinson, then trying to fill a minor academic role at Harvard, in March 1899—the same month she had received Kahlil's letter. Even the taciturn Robinson, whom she understood to be "a thinker and a poet who escaped the infectious self-consciousness of Cambridge," responded to her artlessness. "I find it easy to get on with him," she wrote to a friend, "but he affects me with the sense of almost pathos that any creature does who seems fated to wait for an interpreter. . . . It is queer, isn't it, that anyone so distinctly gifted to create should seem to suffer a kind of helpless imprisonment within his own personality—like the poor prince in the iron stove. This mission of scraping people out of the stove is a thing that absolutely seems to pursue me; and as long as it does that, I shall scrape away." [4]

The kind of struggle that Robinson endured in his early career turned Josephine into a soul of empathy, and this sensitivity made her drawing room a shelter for poetic waifs. In September 1900 she gleefully counted up eight friends who were publishing books that winter. [5] Included in the list were William Vaughn Moody, Gelett Burgess (another Copeland and Day discovery who was famous for his comic verses and his dada-like publication *Lark*), the poet Lewis Gates, and Daniel Gregory Mason. Mason, who became a composer and professor of music at Columbia, remembered Josephine at this time: "Bard with a capital B was the nickname, alternating sometimes with 'the little singer,' that Robinson, Moody, and I applied to [her]. . . . Whenever Josephine could forget herself enough not to be a bird, or a flower, or a martyr, or anything else except a woman with a passionate, a truly consecrating love of beauty, she rose to heights of loyalty, both as friend and as artist, of which few are capable." [6]

Trying, and almost succeeding, to get Robinson's epic *Captain Craig* published at Small, Maynard & Co., Josephine proved that she was capable of being more than an ornamental fixture in men's lives. She even began to earn a regular salary, nine months after the twentieth century was born. (That occasion was observed by her and thousands of others in front of the golden-domed statehouse amid trumpet reveilles and solemn anthems. She held a red rose "for the sake of having a Rose see two centuries.") In September she began lecturing at Wellesley College, where she taught two courses on "Victorian and Georgian Poets" and "Modern Masterpieces." Except for "the thrilling experience;—to be a wage-earner *and* to get your wage," she regarded teaching as a back-breaking, nerve-straining chore. Her yearning for a reprieve at the end of the first dragging year was satisfied when Lillian Shuman Dreyfus, a poetically and generously inclined patron of hers, sent her to Europe. In London she visited such personalities as Wilfrid and Alice Meynell, Swinburne, and John Singer Sargent; in Oxford she saw Louise Guiney and reverently toured the university with her. Stratford was naturally the holiest of sanctuaries, and she sent her gratitude to Mrs. Dreyfus in the form of "three green things . . . a sprinkle of rose-leaves from Anne Hathaway's garden; . . . a holly leaf from Charlecote, where he surely poached . . . and a sprig of yew from the loveliest churchyard in the world." [7]

For all of her new maturity and acquired sophistication, she clung to her original awe of and perpetual search for self-knowledge. Writing to her close friend Mary Mason, later the wife of Daniel Gregory Mason, she touched on this unending quest: "I regard Kahlil Gibran's drawing, above this desk: and last night I transferred it to a little peg beside my bed, where I should see it as soon as I woke up: and perhaps it will help me to grasp on my Identity (which is to say—'what God meant when he made' Posy Peabody)." A few months later, just to remind herself that she was indulging in an excess of introspective posturings and verbal protestations of self-sacrifice, she again analyzed her charitable instincts:

> I have just found out what I am and why I am so funny. (And why did I never see it before?) And it is also why people who think I'm very-nice-indeed find me so inhumanly impossible to understand; and it is why I am so old and so very young. *I am a bankrupt Fairy Godmother.* I have nothing much to give; but I have the giving mania, and I go about trying to make people be Up and Doing on an illimitable capital of Faery Gold . . . I love them ineffectually—(Dare I say ineffectually though? That's my foible again)—I *shine* at them in my feelings, though they don't see it. Yes, and when they understand, I feel as if I appeared suddenly in all my glory; yes—I have a sense of sudden physical irradiation.[8]

Kahlil was sensitive to this shining aspect of his friend, and he wanted to be part of the creative group who gained strength and affirmation from her muse-like qualities. He waited until November, half a year after his return, to contact her. Perhaps he had been preoccupied with his family's bereavement, or he may have known that she had spent the summer in Europe, or he might simply have needed the intervening months in America to himself, in order to renew his courage and familiarity with his adopted culture.

Whatever the reason, he now wrote to her, and she answered his note the day after she received it. Two weeks later she summoned him to an evening of conversation and international camaraderie. If the nineteen-year-old Kahlil expected to have her sole attention, he was disappointed. If he was to charm her, he had to come prepared to contribute to the conversation within a socially aware and intellectually keen circle. She noted his first appearance at her Sunday salon:

Nothing more or less than some undertone talk with the Syrian Kahlil Gibran, who came to see me yesterday; along with a string of callers that we had. For our Sundays, now, are very different from our Sundays in the dark ages; and yesterday we sat about in a circle of Arts and Sciences, Mr. Gordon and Mr. Michaelis coming back in the evening to stay some more after staying the afternoon; and with Semitic-Swiss Fleischer dropping in between seven and eight—and Scotch Gordon and German Denghausen and Syrian Kahlil Gibran. We were all lively, interested and full of talk. . . . I have thought so many things about that boy's drawing and the beautiful letter, that it was wonderful to hear him, back from his own country, "touch a foreign country," saying these things to me. Spiritual substance again.[9]

That night she expertly drew out Kahlil, who impressed her with his answers and appearance, and she recorded their conversation.

"Do you remember me at all?" he asked her.

"Of course I do."

"For I only met you once, and that was five years ago at Mr. Day's."

"I have never felt quite sure that you meant the drawing for me," she said. "Because I had several friends with me. And I thought you might have confused my name with somebody else—I'm not sure even that I spoke to you; did I?"

He laughed at this. "Oh yes! you have spoken to me. And you thought I might have meant it for somebody else? Well you believe me now, don't you? And I have seen you three times in all: that time; and once on the street; and once, I think it was the Public Library; but you have not seen me then!"

He told her that he had received her two letters and that he had sent her three, of which two were lost in the mail ("Talk of lost treasures," she commented). He went on to say how glad he was of her letters and her remembrance, because although he had met her only that once, when he looked at her it had seemed then that they had known each other "long, long many years before."

At this declaration Josephine smiled. "He being then fifteen years old—this was rather comical; but I knew what he meant, and I was filled with comfort, because of the realness of these things to children of a certain consciousness, and I am blessed to be such a one, and knowing what the boy's consciousness was—I felt it as a shining honor all over me."

Kahlil apologized for his hesitant English. "I felt when I wrote you, trying to write in English, that I sent you my wrong self."

"Oh no. . . . Your English was as close as possible to me. I understand it perfectly."

"But it was in a bad language!" While in college, he said, he had written a very long letter to her, and when it was done he found it was in Arabic, not

98

English. "Your English was much clearer . . . than most spoken English," she reassured him. Because some of us people in the world who are conscious of certain things, . . . We have a *patois* of our own; and if you know but two words of my tongue, or I know two words of yours, we can understand."

"Yes, that's so!" he responded with relief and "a kind of joy."

"And," she continued, "when in speaking to a foreigner, we use our own common daily words more freshly, more reverently; and we go to the simplest truth of things."

After Josephine had bolstered the uncertain ego of Kahlil, whom she realized was still a boy, she playfully introduced her learned circle: "There's Scotch Mr. Gordon who digs up things in Mexico and Central America—mummies and palaces you know. And here's Mr. Denghausen who knows all about music and sings like an angel too. . . . And Mr. Michaelis who finds out everything anybody wants to know . . . and my sister who designs." She adroitly included the Syrian in the entourage: "—and you who are writing and drawing all the time."

He was not intimidated by the illustriousness of the group and cleverly turned the attention back to Josephine. "And you. What shall we say of you?" This retort, with its implied allusion to her own talent, "pleased me inexpressibly." The fact that he was able to contribute to the conversation also delighted her, and she noted that he "has read my books, even Marlowe, and was not at all upset by the old English things in the latter because he had read a great deal of Shakespeare. He knew something about everything that we mentioned from the script of the Book of Kells to Duse and to the Slugger [murder] case."

That first entrance by Kahlil into Posy Peabody's world was an exciting evening for him. No longer worshipping or struggling to communicate from a "far, far land," he was finally able to enjoy her at first hand in her own milieu. As for Josephine, her enthusiasm about him was startling. Her comments convey a sense of renewal of her own spirits and a resurgence of her youth:

> Maeterlinck he has lived on, and at present he is drawing and writing Arabic poems and essays. As for the drawings, we shall see them. If they have developed in any proportion at all to the early ones, he will shake up the world. I do not in the least believe that his writing can be anyway as remarkable. How can it? I told him, last night, something (but a very little) of the impression that his drawings had left me. And he was surprised with that much and deeply pleased. But his surprise was as nothing to mine when I found that he had delighted in my poetry. . . . The knowledge of his beautiful heart of a young prophet has been a comfort to me all these years; and how beautiful to know again that all the things I desire to be have taken shape and gone about with a foreign soul to comfort it likewise. I cannot doubt now from the boy's drawing, this letter and his story, that it

was given me to be remembered as something beautiful; and indeed it was a draught of wine to me, J.P.P. who has felt of late her identity fading from her in a kind of bewilderment of dying. He reminds me of that old fresh assurance I used to have, like a boy David, that I was somehow dear to God; and that He cared about my singing, if no one else did.

Elated over his reception, Kahlil returned a week later and brought a portfolio of his latest drawings. "Well of odd reappearances," she wrote, "here is the Syrian back again, whom I hardly expected to see in this life." [10] This time he did not have to compete with brilliant conversationalists, for they were mostly alone and "talked and looked at the drawings and talked again with much quietude." Marion was sick in bed, and Josephine sent the drawings upstairs to her artist sister for a comment. They excited the whole household. Mrs. Peabody reported Marion's approval: "Do you know you're entertaining an angel?"

Basking in the warmth of this attention, Kahlil grew bolder. When Josephine tried "a little to make Gibran say what things my face had seemed always to be telling," he proposed drawing her, explaining that "his English was not equal to some things." This time he promised to make it a portrait of her mind, although, he added, "The best portrait of you is your books." Before he left it was understood that they would see each other again.

That night Josephine realized what their mutual attraction was and what it would be. She defined the relationship that she, a twenty-six-year-old recognized poet, and he, a young immigrant of unfulfilled promise, would share for the next four years:

> There were other remarks of this young mystic that set me thinking much: What ever-lasting symbols women are! I know so well, now, when these beautiful moments happen, that it is none of it for me. I know so well that I am a symbol for somebody; I am a prism that catches the light a moment. It is the light that gladdens, not the prism. And yet for that moment, the prism, the symbol, the bringer of tidings, the accidental woman, becomes perforce an $\alpha\gamma\gamma\epsilon\lambda o_S$, a messenger of God, an angel truly, wonderfully, most humbly. And if she stops to know it, she knows how and why and for how long, and she must choose between the humbleness of real angelhood or the bitter pride of self-love that is bound to hurt sooner or later.[11]

Just as she considered herself a muse for Kahlil, so was he a source for her own inspiration. "Return," a poem she wrote between November 25 and 27, obviously resulted from their first two meetings:

> This word from long ago, can it be true?
> For you have told me that I gave you bread,
> Even as I would, in that young joy, have fed
> All souls and hungers with the joy I knew. . . .[12]

As if they had always known each other, they grew more and more close. Their notes increased; the time between his visits to her decreased. She had been out of touch with Fred Holland Day since he had dissolved his firm—now, suddenly, spurred by Kahlil's interest, she was back in the world of pictorial exhibits. On December 6 they met at a show in Day's Irvington Street studio and enjoyed "a good talk." [13] Two days later she finished the first draft of an eleven-stanza poem initially entitled "His Boyhood" and later changed to "The Prophet." It described Kahlil's life as she imagined it in Besharri. Written a month after he had first sought her friendship, it was eventually included in her collection *The Singing Man* (1911). The first version differed little from the final poem that begins:

> All day long he kept the sheep:—
> Far and early, from the crowd,
> On the hills from steep to steep,
> Where the silence cried aloud;
> And the shadow of the cloud
> Wrapt him in a noonday sleep.

Twenty years later, when Gibran was ready to publish his own most important work, which he had been calling "The Counsels," Josephine's earlier label of what she believed him to be, repeated often in her diaries, must have been inescapably before him. The seeds for his *The Prophet*, as he often asserted, were germinated just this side of the twentieth century as a result of the tenderness and respect shown to him by this remarkable woman.

What exactly was his kind of charisma that caused her to endow him with such giftedness? That December he plied her with presents of drawings and letters. "*December 11.* Mail: 2 drawings and 2 notes from K. G. and E. A. R. [Robinson]. *December 12.* Evening: Kahlil Gibran with drawings, a) Death b) Love and Hunger. *December 17.* 2 p.m. Go to F. H. Day's studio to have my portrait done. 4–5 p.m. Meet the Syrian." Kahlil, always more mature in appearance than in years, no longer appeared a boy to her. "This time he was yet another three years older than last week." Even his periods of silence, whether studied or simply the result of bashfulness, pleased her. "We two had some twenty minutes of tremendous quiet and cryptic conversation, before talk became general; and again I was not amazed and . . . not appalled at the boy's way of assuming that I know all things, and that it isn't necessary to tell me things in English or even to talk at all. If I see much of him I shall become a Buddha." [14]

Josephine was beginning to identify with her newest friend. Although he was only nineteen, he had seen the world from its other side, which she always knew existed but never could explore: he had faced poverty not with gentility but in the rawness of the slum, he had lived in the mysterious biblical lands, he had even known personal tragedy. She needed his exposure to life, and at this

101

"Inspiration," Josephine's portrait, pastel, 1902. On the
back Kahlil wrote in Arabic, "Give heed, oh Soul, for love
calls thee: so listen/Open the doors of thy heart and receive
Love and the King." (Harvard College Library)

stage he needed her wisdom and experience in her craft. More than anyone
else's example, her command of English strengthened his own expression.

Still pondering his sudden hold on her thoughts, she wrote, "But it was
strange enough, in one way to have the boy tell me quite simply his relation
with this world, as I have very often thought of mine (when we were alone). It
made me feel more than ever the inescapable identity of an $\alpha\gamma\gamma\epsilon\lambda os$ $K\nu\rho\iota o\nu$
[angel or messenger of God]. It does not look quite simple either. But I will do
my best." Nine days later she added, "What is my best going to be, I wonder?
This is the most unprecedented of all things, for three reasons. The boy is
Syrian; he is also a prophet which is to say an absolute genius. The third reason
I forget. But there are more than three." [15]

One day Kahlil met Josephine and her sister in Marion's Boylston Street studio. She read her poems aloud to him while he drew, and he told her "some of the thoughts that came to him from my face." She called his drawing "a transcendental portrait"—for he had promised that it would mirror her mind. "It was wonderful, the things we talked about," she wrote. "And to hear of the cedars of Lebanon that have been sweet in my mind ever since I was born. I was going to write of it. But I cannot. I must sleep and gather some wisdom out of the rest and learn how to disentangle twentieth-century responsibilities from deserts and date palms and natural things and the cedars of Lebanon." [16]

A year later her poem "The Cedars" appeared in her book *The Singing Leaves*. That she imagined the trees through Kahlil's eyes was certain. The fact that she wrote at all about them was a special tribute for which he felt blessed and grateful. He pledged "that all he had drawn or written, and all whatever he should yet draw or write was mine and of me and belonged to me." The things he had done before were "little things." "But," he said, "they were very little, and I did not know what they were or what I meant to myself." Her first letter had opened to him all the "bigness of things," and now with her support he was sure of himself. He knew "what he wanted to do and to be." [17]

On Christmas Eve he sent her a Syrian shepherd's flute. On Christmas night he visited her and they talked beside the fire. He drew her again at Marion's studio two days later. Then on the first day of the new year she recorded a special gift. "Evening brought in a magic cylinder from the Syrian ؏؏ —a drawing! Inspiration—all colors of pale flame and lines of music." Magic names and secret symbols had always embellished her diaries. Now she adopted Kahlil's own design of his initials G. K. G. in Arabic, the monogram with which he had signed the pastel drawing "Inspiration." Her first attempt at copying it was flawed, but soon the pages in her diary constantly show the correct version: "The Syrian keeps on being ؏؏." [18]

On January 5, the eve of his twentieth birthday,[19] Gibran spent the evening with her and she told him about a plan she had for him. One of her friends at Wellesley was Margarethe Müller, a well-liked German teacher and faculty adviser to a college society, Tau Zeta Epsilon. At Wellesley Greek-letter societies were more than social clubs, and Tau Zeta Epsilon, which was dedicated to "the study of the beautiful wherever found, whether in realms of painting, sculpture, architecture, music, or literature," naturally attracted Josephine's participation. Now she thought that she might get her friend "Tante" Müller to include some of his drawings in the society's annual spring exhibition and reception. He quickly agreed to submit his work. "Nothing would please me more than to give your friend some pleasure if I could." [20]

Day also noted Kahlil's birthday. His message was carefully formed, half in a primitively rendered Arabic and half in English. It read, "To thee little soul brother a present is given from the bottom of the heart—thy big brother—6th January—thy birthday." [21]

Doubtless this attention was distracting Kahlil from the pressures at home. Living conditions in the South End had not greatly improved since the Gibrans' arrival eight years before. In 1902 the Associated Charities reported, "Sickness was the 'chief cause' [of referral] in about forty-two per cent of our families and one-third of all the sick were consumptive." [22] The Gibrans were moving from tenement to tenement within the Syrian quarter, almost as though they were trying to elude the disease that was stalking them. Peter still tried to hold the dry goods business together. Kamila, so ambitious when she had first arrived, felt her strength giving out.

When Day made portraits of Sultana and Marianna early in 1902, he also photographed their mother. Suddenly now she appeared old. Framed in black, her face showed traces of tension and pain. Her heavily lidded eyes, which had radiated such willful determination, were now shaded with resignation. She no longer canvassed the streets with her pack. Even the period of mourning for her youngest child was to be cut short by the dreadful sickness that was invading Peter and herself. Marianna remembered the following details of the awful months that followed Kahlil's return.

> Peter had been consumptive for some months at the time of Sultana's death—but he had been taking care of himself & building up. . . .
> He was wonderfully careful about guarding the others from contagion. Now he got worse—& in the fall the doctor told him to go to Syria. Instead, he decided on Cuba, where he had friends in business—took some samples—& left on Dec. 13. "In two days he was ill—& he was never well again. He kept losing & losing & all the time he wrote to my mother that he was gaining, & to me that he was gaining—& to Kahlil that he was gaining. Only to the fellow that worked for us he wrote how sick he was."
> He left on Saturday—& on Monday Mrs. Gibran went to the Mass. Gen. Hosp. for a tumor. Smallpox developed in the hospital & no visitors were allowed for 6 weeks. When they were allowed at last to visit her, Marianna said to Kahlil, "I'll go the first day, because it is Sunday & I am free; then we will each go every other day"—for only 1 daily was allowed.
> "Oh Marianna!" said her mother when Marianna got there. "My tongue feels thick in my mouth—for someone to speak to"—for she could not speak English. And her first words were, "How's Peter?"
> "Peter's fine," said Marianna—for she thought he was.
> In 6 wks. Mrs. G. was operated on. Minnie [a family friend, Munni Sabagh] was staying with Marianna & K., & she went with Marianna that day to the operation—& the doctor told Minnie the mother would not live. He told her it was cancer, & told her much else. Marianna overheard "will not live" & got Minnie to tell her all. "I did not know what cancer was so when I got home I asked Kahlil to explain it to me in Arabic. And he did, & when we knew there was no hope we cried together & consoled each other all that night. And Minnie cried with us. And Kahlil said, 'Let us

Day's study of Kamila, 1902. (Authors)

bring our mother home as quickly as we can—so that she can be with us'—and we did. We brought her home in ten days." [23]

In these most anxious days Kahlil was becoming deeply involved with Josephine. The chasm between her cultivated drawing room and his own disease-filled home was almost unbridgeable. But the drawings which permitted him to cross into her world were the passport to his survival.

During all of January he did not reveal to her the pitiful conditions at his home. Such secrecy, so typical of his personal insecurity, could have been due simply to a dread that she might reject him if he admitted to a life surrounded by infection and death. It was enough merely to enjoy each other's company. Her diary revealed the extent to which their lives were becoming entwined: "*Jan. 15, 1903*. A. M. Late train to Wellesley, studying Arabic alphabet on the way. Class. P. M. To see M. Müller and show her drawings. *Jan. 19.* 10° below. ﻭﻭﻭ & Mr. Denghausen. Songs and drawings." [24]

The temperature that Josephine recorded on the nineteenth, a day when two of her admirers braved the cold to vie for her favor, described that winter of 1903. Along with the tuberculosis that was plaguing the crowded South End tenements, the exceptionally bitter cold and a crippling shortage of coal and other fuel caused unexpected hardships. Whether or not the Gibrans were relieved by the Denison House or any official agency, the outstanding purveyor of solace and warmth for Kahlil was obviously Josephine. Throughout that frigid winter she welcomed him, and he in turn welcomed his one chance to escape.

Although unaware of his troubles, she did notice his tendency to remoteness and abstraction. During January, when she of course did not know that Kamila was hospitalized, she wrote, "I noticed last evening that whenever I spoke to the boy, I seemed—in spite of my candor, to be wilfully assuming alien speech and hard to understand. And I am wondering if it is not true that when people understand each other intimately, they [cannot] speak at all without suffering some sort of disguise." [25]

Despite such misgivings, their understanding appeared to thrive. Her project of including Kahlil in the Wellesley exhibit was developing. On January 25 Miss Müller met him in Marion's studio, where "he pinned the drawings up one by one and two by two, on the big dark green screen." Miss Müller's comments supported his assertion that all of his faces were inspired by Josephine's own face. Both the artist and the poet greeted her opinion with a naive sort of glee. "Didn't you have her in mind when you drew 'Consolation'?" she asked guilelessly. "Why yes, of course," he remarked. And in her diary Josephine added, "But yet this thing he drew last summer before I had come home from Europe; and he had not seen me for four years!" [26]

Now that she was reassured in her judgment of him, Josephine began

106

Josephine, dressed for an artists' festival, January 1903. "I was *Legend*," she wrote, "in a most heavenly fair get-up, as nearly old Egyptian as the clad may be: strait, stiff yellow stuff stencilled up and down with silver and gold lotuses." (Alison P. Marks)

further to broadcast her faith in her latest discovery. "I have a marvelous and beautiful tale to relate of a genius of a creature I'm trying to god-mother now," she wrote Mary Mason. "He is a Syrian boy. He writes Arabic poetry all night; and he draws (much better than William Blake) all day. And if E. A. Robinson will come to Boston, he shall see that I speak truly." [27]

Kahlil and Josephine became publicly identified with each other during February. She took him out to suburban Milton where he met Mrs. Barnard, a former sponsor of hers. They also attended concerts together. And so, guiding her diminutive figure, he learned how to be a proper escort in Boston society. Not much taller than she, he still sported a foreign look. The appearance of this strangely matched couple must have drawn attention as they strolled through the Back Bay streets.

While Josephine's diaries reflect the exuberance of their midwinter friendship, Kahlil's surviving copybooks testify to his distraught mood at this time. Still using dummy copies of Copeland and Day books, he was writing at night, crowding the pages with random thoughts in English and Arabic. As he strained to find the proper vehicle for his expression, he described in Arabic the advantages of mountain life for those scourged with tuberculosis, as opposed to the city, and he attempted to describe his experiences in Maine (in all likelihood, Five Islands). Probably the most significant passage in these uneven ramblings was set down soon after Peter's return from Cuba. Written in Arabic, it reflects both his despair over his brother's health and a tentative belief in the significance of his own thoughts. "I write strange thoughts. Ideas pass like flocks of birds. This is my life. Who would buy it? . . . All these are great hopes, a lot of books and strange drawings. What is this learning that walks with me? And I do not know where I stand. What is this earth with gaping mouth and bared chest demanding more?" Two pages later he made a prophecy concerning Peter: "Wednesday night falling between the seventeenth and eighteenth of the month of February in the year A.D. 1903: I heard a bodyless voice which came, and I felt inspired, and the truth I felt is that the soul of my brother Peter would take to its God and Creator in eternity after five days. I write these words so perhaps the world would witness a truth I saw while in bed, and others will witness by putting their hands on this paper written with the ink with which I write these words." [28]

Kahlil's nighttime vision was not borne out. However, within the five days he did admit to Josephine the secret tension that he had been harboring. "These are bitter days for ٱلْعَبْد," she recorded. "I learn from him—only by asking—that his mother and his half-brother are dying, undoubtedly of two different illnesses beyond hope; and he 'has not drawn at all lately' and 'written very little,' because he has been nursing the two, writing business letters, and keeping watch over them at night. A terrible ordeal for my Genius, and one that makes my mind dizzy. He is watching these two die; and when that is over, he has one knows not what of hardship and struggle to face, all the time caring so little about this world but with the dreadful necessity—every year heavier upon us all—of finding wherewith to be fed and clothed and housed in order to give to this same world what must be given." [29]

A few days later she heard by mail from him. He had fled the city and his responsibilities and was staying with relatives at the seaside town of Gloucester, forty miles north of Boston. There "wretchedness and misery compelled him to be just then," she wrote.[30] But he soon returned to Boston and saw her on February 25.

To revive his spirits she granted him what she considered the greatest privilege: she let him into her innermost self by allowing him to read her old journals. This record of her entire creative life had previously been shared by no one. The boy was drowning, though, and needed a raft that would buoy him through the storm. Revealing to him the chronicle of her oldest joys and sorrows seemed to help. The next day they went to a concert, and the day after that they met at Day's studio.

By the first week in March, Kahlil had taken over Peter's business. Obviously the decision had not been easy and he had tried to escape it by going to Gloucester. Even the refuge he constantly sought in Josephine's company was a partial shirking of duty. She analyzed his venture in her journal:

> *March 7.* Ğ Ŏ ʒ was here yesterday and most unhappy. But he had done a very fine thing—entirely against his strongest inclinations—to save the business honor of his brother who is hopelessly ill. He thought it would be dishonorable—or at least "very easy" to fail (in the business his brother had started with several loans) so he made up his mind to work up the business if he could, till those men at least could get their money back; and he has persuaded the chief creditor to be his partner. Behold Ğ Ŏ ʒ a business man for the time—fast bound in misery and iron? I know with all my heart, the anguish it will be to him; and yet I'm filled with pride that my Genius was strong enough to grasp the situation that hurts him most and grasp it strongly. Win out of it—he must and then soon; and when 'tis over how sevenfold realer he will feel and be.

Feeling personally triumphant over a hundred-dollar check received that day from *Harper's* for six poems, she ended her entry, "So I am refreshed indeed. And may heaven bless the prophet also very soon." [31]

The money allowed her to stay at the Wellesley Inn for a few days instead of repeating the long trip by trolley car back and forth to Cambridge. Before she left she relayed the latest story of her "Genius" to her confidante Mary Mason:

> My poor Prophet (whom I am anxiously watching)—the Syrian Ğ Ŏ ʒ—is going through a soul-forcing process rare to witness (I'm glad to think), namely, watching his mother and elder brother die, slowly, of different incurable illnesses, himself forced to step into his brother's little business (of importations) because he does not think it would be honorable to go bankrupt—(although it would be very easy of course); Pegasus harnessed to an ash-wagon would suffer less. It's enough to make angels weep; but the timely grasp of the bitter old nettle by this visionary creature (a born Ravi Yogi) does my heart good to see. I wonder why we should all have to suffer so that most hideous anguish, a grinding service of work for the base privilege of food and raiment—when you don't care a D—— about living to eat or be clothed—if you can't be yourself and make your own work. But I am much wiser, I know—by all that wretchedness of last year (if it did knock the music out of me for a long time)—and I comfort the poor prophet with such living witness—song of the Bondages, so to say. He will win out splendidly, and that before long, in some manner, I feel sure. But just now he resides in Beach Street.[32]

Peter Rahme, probably by Day, sometime before 1903.
(Authors)

If Josephine so pronounced her faith in Kahlil to a friend, her words to him must have been at least as strong. Her entire romantic concept of the artist as truly unselfish "giver" and of the indomitable spirit of creativity became his credo, and it helped him endure and understand the next few months.

Peter's last days as related by Marianna were indeed as difficult for everyone close to him as Josephine had foreseen. He came home from Cuba around the first of February, one week after Kamila returned from the hospital.

It was six o'clock in the morning. "The cabman rang the bell, and my mother said to me, 'There is the bell. You'd better go to the door.' So I went down—and O how Peter had fallen away! I didn't know him. I said to the cabman, 'What do you want?' and he said, 'This man wants to get in.' And I said, 'We don't have any furnished rooms,' & I shut the door. Then the cabman rang the bell again—and when I opened the door Peter said, 'I'm your brother, dear. Don't you know me? Tell Kahlil to come help me upstairs'—for he was so weak he couldn't walk up by himself. So I ran up and got Kahlil out of bed & he came down in his night gown and slippers—and he & the cabman got Peter upstairs. And Peter went to mother's room, and he said, 'Mother will you get up & let me stay in your bed till sister can get mine ready?' Then I said, 'Mother can't get up, Peter dear.' And he said, 'Why? Is she ill?' 'Yes,' I said, 'she's ill.' And I explained to him. So he got in my bed till I fixed his.

"Peter was in the front room, and mother was in the back room—and I put my bed between the two, so that I could hear if either of them moved. Peter lived four weeks. And every morning & noon & evening when I'd take him his food he'd say, 'Marianna, have you had your breakfast?' & 'Marianna, have you had your dinner?' and 'Marianna, have you had your supper? You know you must take care of yourself now, Marianna, because you are all we have to take care of us. What would happen to us if you got ill?' "

All the night before Peter died, Marianna was anxious & fearful. Sultana had not changed in appearance before death—but Peter's look grew different. "His eyes were larger & his face had a dead look—& he looked at me differently. And I said, 'What's the matter?' And Peter said, 'Only a little pain, dear—& it will pass. Don't be afraid. Just go & try to get a little rest.' " The aunt was there, & she said to Marianna, about three a.m., "Get your brother's clothes out, & his black suit." Marianna questioned. She did not realize he was dying, & she thought it absurd to get out his clothes when he could not dress & get up. So her aunt took his closet key & got his suit herself. Several of Peter's friends were there, in friendly way & they & Kahlil were in the room when he died.

All through this double illness, Kahlil was in the store.[33]

Later that day, March 12, Kahlil wrote of his grief to at least two of his American friends. He sent a note to Josephine at Wellesley, and to Day he wrote, "The dear brother went home, at 3 o colock this morning, leaving us in the dept of sorrow, wounded hearted. I am to console the poor sick mother. Ah, she is as [Marianna] and I, looking on the darckness of the future." [34] The signing of the death certificate—official acknowledgment that "Peter Rahmeh" of 35 Edinboro Street, twenty-five years old, a salesman, had died of congested lungs and exhaustion—and the burial at Mt. Benedict cemetery were hurriedly observed.

Josephine expressed her sympathy and wrote of her inadequacy during this sorrowful time, "My genius has lost his brother, I suppose the poor mother can hardly live longer now. And what to do for him I am helpless to know—There is nothing in the world to do; I can only be." [35] Four days later Kahlil visited her in Cambridge, breaking with the Lebanese tradition of mourning at home for at least a week. Ferris Greenslet, her editor at Houghton Mifflin, and a Mr. Boynton were also there. She secluded him in another room while she entertained them: "ح‌ﺟ‌ﻞ rests in my study while I see them all evening." [36]

A week later he visited again, "looking somehow older and with sad cheerfulness in his eyes and his black tie and his more foreign look." This time they were able to talk undisturbed the whole evening. Listing their strengths, they convinced themselves of being "blessed and rich again." Josephine admitted that when she saw him thus she seemed to feel "all over my soul as soft as snow, as soft as a rain of cherry petals on the pass." Tenderly she held his hand "with both of mine . . . and when we sit down, all is changed. I do not understand it: nor does he. But it is true that I feel it in myself, even as he says it is about me; and I cannot doubt—it has been proved so often—that I am an almoner somehow; and glad and grateful and filled with wonder above all that life lets me know these things."

He again vowed that he would reward her for the compassion she was bestowing on him: "for that you are giving me, all the time, all the time." She shrugged this off. "I have all my reward and more, because you make me believe that everything I wish towards you is a gift, and spirit turns to substance for you. You make me great by help from my wishing. For I am great indeed if I can turn my thoughts into gifts whenever I choose." Her explanation "seemed to make him feel happy."

Supported by each other's sorrow, they were able to sustain themselves through an escape into romanticized emotions and ideas. Josephine surrendered her properly worded world of language for a fuller realization of her feelings. Every pain of which Kahlil spoke gave her a twinge, and her interpretations in turn dulled his ache. "I feel his bondage, I believe, more than anyone else can, for I have more knowledge of his genius than any save Mr. Day perhaps; and I, unlike Mr. Day, know what it is to be parted from one's own soul and sent to the galleys. My heart bleeds for him." [37]

Even if Day could not provide the instinctive warmth that she could, he did insure that Kahlil was sustained during his death watch. "Mother blesses you for the refreshing gift, dear Brother," Kahlil wrote on April 13. Whether the gift was fruit, which Day loved to send to people he liked, is not known, but the note is proof that the Gibrans were not completely isolated in their last days together. Small, sympathetic gestures extended to Kamila by persons who lived outside the community helped the family to understand they were not alone.

Day also made an effort to include Kahlil in musical and theatrical events. On April 10 the youth wrote, "Yes I can hear music on Saturday, send me the ticket if you will, and I shall come to the Symphony Hall, for I cannot leave the store before half past seven on Saturday." [38] Three days later they made arrangements to see *Hamlet*. In some ways Kahlil's insistence on continuing to socialize with his American friends during a time when he and Marianna were so sorely beset was selfish and thoughtless. Certainly Marianna had no comparable escape valve. But this strain of self-preservation and indulgence in his own pursuits, no matter how they conflicted with propriety or considerate behavior, was a particular mark of his personality. Even though Marianna was fearful and even though he was needed at home, he would not completely sacrifice his other life.

Day's interests in literature were still profoundly influencing him. In April Josephine was invited to Chicago to lecture and read at poetry groups and women's clubs. Although she noted, "Mamma was very loath to have me go; equally so was MMM," she left by train on April 18.[39] He gave her a book to read during the trip, *Towards Democracy* by Edward Carpenter. His recommendation of the writings of the thinker who led England's "back to nature" Sheffield socialists, was a direct result of Day's admiration of English social reform. Carpenter's prose poems, so close to Walt Whitman's in style and feeling, were more spiritual than political, and the cult surrounding his exhortations to abandon the strictures of Victorian morality was now at its height. His view of a world freed from the hypocrisy of man-made restrictions played an important part in the growth of Kahlil's personal philosophy.

When Josephine returned, exhausted from two weeks of lecturing, it was Kahlil's turn to comfort her. The minute she arrived she learned from her mother that the Peabody family would have to move again—they could no longer afford the monthly rent. She tried to react as she had seen Kahlil do: "I must learn of عبد to take misfortune on trust." [40] Actually she stayed in bed for a week, blaming the flu, and brooded. By May 8 she was able to sit up, and her first visitor was a "disproportionately anxious" Kahlil. This time it was he who encouraged Posy. "He was very old and wise; and I was very young and docile and pleased to be revived with news of how great and glorious I am. We were almost funnier than ever."

Her description of this wooing of a convalescent poet by her Syrian genius evokes an Edwardian scene furnished with floral tokens, albums, and fervent

Marianna by Day, ca. 1901. (Authors)

gestures. While she talked she twirled a large pink daisy. Then she "got tired" and "handed it to ꙮ." He took her coquetry seriously, remarking, "It came off your dress," and matching it with the tracery of pink on her "flowered white empire." "With a benign air" they held hands. He worried about how pale hers were. Then he drew a picture. "Now, shall we look at the Picture Book?" she suggested—which mannered activity they carried out "with nods of satisfaction over each." The evening ended with a gift for him: "And then after much more talk we look at the vase of white roses that had been sent to me—critically. And I give him one, and he goes home." [41]

With knowledge of this interlude, a page of English in one of Kahlil's notebooks becomes meaningful. Perhaps a first draft of a note to Josephine, it reads, "I have just said good morning to the rose which you gave last night and I kissed its lips, you kissed them too." [42] Whether this was written shortly after this meeting or not, her documentation of that summer-sweet evening permits the inference that it was.

With the academic year at Wellesley coming to an end, Tau Zeta Epsilon's exhibition and studio reception took place in mid-May. Josephine's scheme had worked, and Kahlil's drawings were included. It was his official debut as an artist. On May 21 they attended the reception. The brief critique of his art that appeared in *The Iris*, the society's annual publication, was gently encouraging: "Mr. Gibran's work shows a wonderful originality in conception and an exquisite delicacy and fineness in execution." [43]

Kahlil enjoyed still more kindness at Wellesley that spring. May 30, Whitsun Eve, was Josephine's birthday, and that evening she invited him, Marion, and her mother out to the college where a series of open-air plays was being performed. They sat with Margarethe Müller, and "with joss-stick fire-flies, and stars overhead, and no wind" watched the play *The Sad Shepherd*.[44]

But the happy circumstances of the exhibit and the distracting hours of theater marked an end to their halcyon hours. The events of June crushed Josephine and Kahlil simultaneously. Still involved with the business of selling dry goods and imported merchandise, he was preparing for his final death watch, and she was too depressed to rally to his cause. She had rashly decided to give up the security of teaching at Wellesley. The question of how her family would survive without her regular stipend terrified her, and she cursed their growing financial tangle that demanded a salaried position and choked a poet. "That devil's own lure of drudgery for someone's sake, to put off every risk and to be some incalculably silent, deaf and blind and safe part of the Machine; . . . O you Devil of the times I live in, you Devil in a monk's hood too—Poverty, Poverty, Poverty, how long, how long?" [45]

"Dark within and without," packing and preparing to leave the house, she even derided herself for her former innocence and eagerness: "that bundle of unconsidered energies, that feathered monkey." Her gloom was only temporarily relieved by a visit. "*June 24.* Yesterday evening  came out, after a long interval of these same miseries. We had a wood fire in the grate, for bitter chill it was." After some interruptions they were "able to talk as we used to do." She gave him "a little old keepsake" (which she called a charm in her diary) and "told him something of the things it made me think of and remember, when I looked at it." [46] Three days later they walked through her neighborhood for the last time. By now the household was broken up and its members ready to live their disparate lives, alone for the summer. Josephine and Marion planned to visit various friends, while their mother and grandmother boarded in a suburban home.

Kamila died the next day. Kahlil immediately notified Day: "Mother suffer no longer, but we poor children are suffering and longing for our loving Mother. Write to me and bless me dear Brother." After the funeral he left another note at his patron's door. This time the hand was much shakier than in any of his English writing at this time: "And I came to see you dear Brother, so unlucky I am not to find you here! The funerale took place yesterday at two, your note came much later. Tell me when shall I see you, for my poor soul is tired of other things around me." [47]

Marianna's report of Kamila's last suffering and Kahlil's collapse is once again the only eyewitness account of all that happened.

> Mother lingered till June 28. That day she was incessantly restless. "Marianna, lift my head; Marianna, turn me this way; Marianna, turn my foot; Marianna, fix my arm." She had not tasted food or water for a week. Now, she asked for something. "I always had chicken broth ready for her. And I brought some. But when I put a spoonful in her mouth, she said, 'Marianna, take it out.' She couldn't swallow it, & she couldn't get it out by herself. I was frightened & after I had helped her I ran for the doctor. Then I told him how restless she was—& I suppose he knew it was the end. He gave me some things to give her, & then she was quiet & went to sleep. Kahlil was going out to dinner, & he said to me, 'Marianna do you think I ought to go?' And I said, 'Yes, Kahlil. Nothing will happen to mother. You see she's sleeping now. Go but don't stay late. Come back at six.' Neither of us had any idea she would die soon now. So Kahlil went.
>
> "My aunt was there. I didn't want her—because the other time when I had wanted her to stay with me & help me she had refused. But they sent for her. So she was there. And late in the afternoon two friends came in to help with Mother—and they were so glad to see her asleep. And they said, 'How nice to see your mother better.' And I was glad, & I was telling them about her day & how the doctor had given me something to quiet her. And my aunt said, 'I shouldn't think you'd be talking now. Look at your mother.' And mother was so"—(Marianna breathed a moment like one who is dying very quietly)—"Then she was gone. And then I felt I didn't have anything in the world. And about five minutes after that Kahlil came in. And there he saw his mother dead. And he fainted away. And the blood came out at his nose & mouth." [48]

7

A Gallery of Gracious and Novel Heads

Kamila died on June 28, 1903, and Josephine's departure for New Hampshire two days later prevented Kahlil from bathing in his usual fount of sympathy. Neither he nor she would ever completely recover from the events of that last week in June. The words and smiles of the winter and spring no longer served as balm. Bitterness over her family's dispossession and anxiety about her own future did not completely exclude Kahlil from Josephine's thoughts, but the couple's former closeness was never again quite equaled.

That she still considered him a special being is revealed in a letter to Louise Guiney written soon after she heard of Kamila's death:

> And do you remember the Syrean boy Kahlil Gibran? Of course you do. He remembers you so well. And he is back again, as you may know, and drawing more than ever wonderfully or rather he *was* doing such things before this winter had set upon him with all manner of disasters. . . . Now the poor prophet is left all alone with one younger sister in dire poverty and tied to a trade which his soul endures for the time. But the drawings and poetry go under for lack of time and thoughts. I wish you could see some of the big things he drew last autumn. The childish ones of five years ago cannot be outdone for sheer inspiration and marvelousness. But it would please you, I know, to see for yourself that the "child" of the mind has developed only, not altered in any respect; and that his imagination is as shiningly unspotted from the world as ever it was then.[1]

Louise, who had "an affectionate memory of that nice boy," expressed sympathy for his losses through letters to Day. Her answer to Josephine was more specifically directed to his plight: "Poor little Kahlil that I remember! I am so grieved to hear how illy things go with him. Can it be possible, that that shining talent can go under for long, in a place like Boston, where there are many of the generous and appreciative who are able to help? If I thought so, even at this distance, I should start an agitation in the Transcript. F. Day, whom I have known since the borderlands of childhood, who used to keep me well-advised of the ups and downs of our friends, has fallen unaccountably silent of late; and your word of Kahlil was the first real detail I have had." [2]

All through July while Josephine stayed in New Hampshire, she and Kahlil corresponded regularly. Returning on August 5, she rented a room on Maple Street in Arlington, a town north of Cambridge, across the street from where her mother and grandmother were temporarily boarding. Although he was ill at the time, Kahlil traveled out to their quarters the next day—a ten-mile trolley-car journey over the Charles River. When she saw him she was concerned over his appearance: "K. G. has been ill (no wonder) for a time; in spite of which, he came out . . . looking pale and shining, in a furious storm of rain." From now on the slightest cough or fever would terrify both Kahlil and his sister, and Josephine gave him medicine. Their visit was uncomfortable: "We could not talk of the mysteries; for we had to sit in mamma's room. But I told him about the country and my brook and all those things I've had but lately." [3]

A day later he re-established the ritual of sending her a drawing, and he came out to Arlington again on August 10, when they sat in the summerhouse and talked. Shortly afterward he left for Five Islands, Maine, at Day's invitation. Day had fallen in love with Louise Guiney's seaside property there, which provided the perfect setting for his photographs, and he had bought it from her. Just as she had invited city boys there, so did he. He satisfied his dramatic flair by buying flags representing the different countries from which the boys came and flying Greek, Italian, or Chinese banners at the appropriate times.

Kahlil stayed at Five Islands for about nine days. His thank-you note documents his worry over his own health and his reliance on opportunities to get away from the South End, now in the perpetual shadow of the elevated railroad that was choking off air and sun. Although his English was still flawed occasionally, its construction and organization had greatly matured since the primitive message he had sent to Josephine six years before. Moreover, his handwriting was firmly formed in the style that he would use throughout his adult life. On August 20 he wrote Day:

> Home again, beloved brother, in darkness where no green pines nor the blue sea caressing the gray rocks. It seems all but a dream.
>
> It was a calm night while coming—still I did not slept at-all—for it was very beautiful to sit up watching the stars all night.
>
> You do not know how bad it seems to be under the elevated railroad while thinking of the calmness of Fife Islands.
>
> I think I have gained two pounds in spite of everything and I surely feel much stronger—than before we start. . . .

au revoir

One of Kahlil's "au revoir" drawings to Josephine. (Harvard College Library)

Beloved brother, think of me when the waves caresses the gray rocks, and when the pines streches their arms to the waves below.[4]

Kahlil's dependence on his American friends for companionship became compulsive. He made several determined trips out to Arlington, and Josephine was too kind to protest his too-frequent visits. Once when her friends Daniel and Mary Mason came to see her and discovered that she was not alone, she was embarrassed and apologetically wrote them, "It was a great pity that my Syrian charge chanced to journey out at the same time; and I would have sent him home or left him out, if he were less of an afflicted lamb at present—surely one of the Lord's sheep whom it is my good fortune to feed, in some sort, now and then." [5]

The dwindling summer evenings that they spent in the tree-shaded summerhouse were the last recorded episodes of their "beautiful and childish times." Withering and nearly dead was the romantic symbolism that had embellished her journals earlier that year. Never again would she write as ecstatically about her prophet: "And to this child of God chiefly my gratitude is due because to him my Soul is no poor foreigner, without the franchise. The gifts it holds out wistfully, expecting not to be heard, he takes with joy, and to him they are substance, richness, gifts indeed. Out of its wishing hands he takes thought, joy, and fullness; and it stands regarding him hearing his thanks—and for all set free—a glorious and liberated life. God bless him that he takes of me my gifts that I would give." [6]

By the end of August she had literally no more gifts—spiritual or material. She learned "with my ears that we have lost practically everything." No longer a specter, real poverty now sat boldly on the Peabody threshold. Kahlil's powerlessness to help her affected him strongly. Her story so "upset his trust in things—that he had felt positively ill." He went to Gloucester for a while "so I could think and think," he told her, "and be apart so I should not feel so little." [7]

This realization of his littleness—his diminutive size, position, and fortune —was paralyzing him. Despite the spiritual solace he could offer, he recognized that his was an ineffectual presence which professed devotion and gave nothing. When he returned they still tried to conjure up their old buoyancy: "*September 13, 1903.* Yesterday K. G. was out, and we sat discoursing in the summerhouse, while the last of the harvest-moon made the earth light and the crickets sang and sang of summer-going, and the clematis vines stirred and swayed. We both talked very much. . . . I discoursed to him of the advantages of the situation and of my own momentary readiness to hear and see and learn all that it might show me, till I felt quite happy; well knowing that I should yet suffer many things of dread—perhaps despair—but bound that I would not forget what I was telling myself and him." [8]

No matter how she reassured him, it was with sorrow and frustration that he watched her sell her gold jewelry for $7.50, and then her study table. She was even willing to part with her books. The family found a cheaper apartment in north Cambridge, on "the wrong side of the [Massachusetts] Avenue," and moved in on September 17. When Kahlil first came to 20 Forest Street, two days later, he found his muse staining floors, painting walls, and doing "all the repairs by personal labor that Landlord wouldn't do." [9]

Weary of advice from well-meaning friends, she did make one compromise for the freedom for which she was fighting. Her hasty resignation from Wellesley gave her the leisure she needed to write, but with a bank balance totaling $105, plus $10 in her pocketbook, she desperately needed some regular stipend. And so she agreed with her old friend Agnes Irwin, the dean of Radcliffe, to tutor privately a young girl with literary aspirations. She met her pupil, Frances Gibbs, and the girl's teacher, Mary Haskell, on September 27.

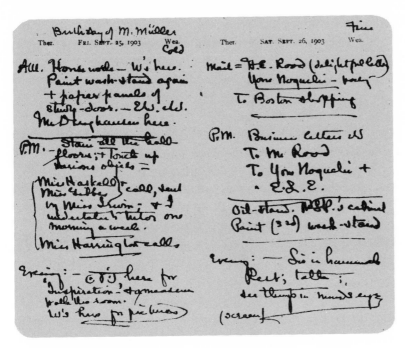

Pages from Josephine's diary, noting a visit from Kahlil.
(Alison P. Marks)

Seeing Mary Haskell recalled to Josephine her association with Mary's sister Louise during their Radcliffe days. The two Haskell sisters had traveled from Columbia, South Carolina, to receive the benefits of New England scholarship. Although their original purpose of coming North—Louise to Radcliffe and two years later Mary to Wellesley—was to return and educate Southerners, they stayed there, drawn by the powerful magnet of Boston–Cambridge intellectual life. After graduating Louise began Miss Haskell's School for Girls at 314 Marlborough Street, Boston, where Mary joined her in 1901. By 1903 Louise had met and married Reginald Daly, a brilliant young geologist, and Mary became headmistress. Josephine's renewed friendship with the Haskell sisters prefaced a series of circumstances and alliances that would in three years drastically realign her and Kahlil's careers. The inevitability of this diverging of their life's paths seems apparent in retrospect, but at the time the way was not clear.

For almost a year Kahlil's relationship with Josephine had radiated a gentle warmth. In October he began resorting to a more reckless stance. When he brought her a drawing and a pair of "Turkish slippers" with turned-up toes, he was certainly sweet enough, and the atmosphere was still placid the night he and Josephine sat in her "blue study," and he drew and she made him laugh ("for the first time in his life, too, he sketched a face with mirth in it").[10] But the mood had begun to change.

The rupture began on October 10 with a letter from him. She commented tersely about it: "Infuriating suggestion more or less." Two days later she described a visit from him with two disenchanted words, "Everyone depressed." The next day, October 13, her feeling of estrangement reached a climax: "Look over old letters and tear up." [11]

Obviously Kahlil had ruffled her, but the exact content of his suggestion disappeared when she destroyed evidence of their correspondence. Although she did not specifically mention his name in conjunction with her action, his frequent presence, his regular communications to her, and the timing of his last disquieting note indicate that he precipitated the destruction of the letters. What purpose or trait did he reveal that she had not perceived before? Until now their friendship had survived a series of devastating personal crises, and throughout the year he had assumed a passive, accepting role. We can only surmise that he now decided to become assertive, to insert himself even more obtrusively into her life.

Although it is natural to conjecture that he proposed a deepening of their relationship—possibly an affair or even marriage—it would be unjust to assume this on the evidence of her brief comments. The one apparent fact is that he was resoundingly rejected. Pride, prudery, or common sense may have motivated her unexpected coolness. She suddenly may have realized that what to her had been a pleasant dalliance with an exotic youth in need of help was becoming more than she could handle. As for Kahlil, rebuffed for his suggestions, whether inspired by passion or not, he was learning the strictures imposed upon forward young men in the genteel drawing rooms of Cambridge.

Even if he had angered Josephine, he was not completely banished from the Forest Street home, for a week later he spent an apparently normal evening sketching there. But the next day he wrote her and again upset her. Her laconic journal entry suggests her further disenchantment: "*October 23. [Wrote] letter to ⌢⌢—very curious coincidence—Emerson's Hermione and ⌢⌢ last note.*" [12]

Her cryptic inference was that Kahlil, trying to regain her favor, identified with the hero of Emerson's poem "Hermione," which opens, "On a mound an Arab lay, / And sung his sweet regrets." The hero speaks of redemption by a beautiful muse:

> . . . I am of a lineage
> That each for each doth fast engage;
> In old Bassora's schools, I seemed
> Hermit vowed to books and gloom,–
> Ill-bested for gay bridegroom.
> I was by thy touch redeemed;
> When thy meteor glances came,
> We talked at large of worldly fate,
> And drew truly every trait.

A pencil portrait of a winged angel, 1903. (Harvard College Library)

But if he foolishly usurped these lines to portray his own personal circumstances, Posy Peabody—his Hermione—was far too knowledgeable to let him borrow so flagrantly.

His answer to her note questioning the curious resemblance was called "astonishing" by her. Both letters are now lost. He hurried out to Cambridge the next night and for the first time in a year found her not at home. But he clung to the friendship stubbornly. A few days later he again ventured to Cambridge and that night sat and listened to her definition of their relationship. "Much making clear of many things," she noted.[13] As their involvement with each other developed precarious overtones, her deliberate condensation of the actual events reveals a stiffening of purpose on her part.

Her sudden implacability evoked in Kahlil a flurry of determined activity, but he suddenly found himself competing with men far beyond his own admittedly still small stature. Edwin Arlington Robinson visited her on November 3, and Kahlil rushed to her side the following evening. On November 6 he forwarded by evening express a peace offering of three pomegranates, and the gift of this mythical and sensuous fruit seemed to soothe her feelings. However, his position was no longer charmed. She continued to see him but ceased to sing about him. When they stopped play-acting in November, each retreated into his or her private creative world, and they never met again with the intimacy they had known before.

Kahlil's dummy copy of *Lyrics of Earth*. (Authors)

Still struggling to express himself, Gibran recorded in his notebooks his disentanglement from the nagging shreds of his shopkeeper's life. "The firm of P. Rahmeh & Co. is no more, I placed it in the hand of an assigner, so you can see that I am in trouble, which I hope will be the end of troubles." This passage, in English, ends with a hastily formed signature and appears to be a draft of a note, probably to Josephine. It closes, "I realy do'nt know how late it is; it must be after midnight. I am waiting for the morning sun. Bless me beloved I am very wretched." Next to a pencil drawing of a radiant face he again blurted out in English a fragment from the ruins of his heart: "I loved you with confidant—now I love you with fear—I love more than I ever did but I am afraid of you. Love life."

At this time he was concentrating on writing in both Arabic and English and on making accompanying drawings. In Arabic he addressed his soul as his last refuge: "There is nothing left except you, soul—so please judge me with justice—which is your glory—or call death upon me. You have burdened me with love I cannot handle. I am weak in regard to material things. She lying on the throne—on the mountain—showed me happiness. You and happiness are above the mountain. I and misery are in the depths of the valley. Will the high meet the low?"

And in English he called upon a lofty, unnamed person and then admitted how bewildered he was:

> And why did I not write sooner? Why did I not poured my self with ink as soon as I came to my room. Why? Ah such wounding questions. You see, my—my what? What shall I call you? Learn me your name for the gods sake and save me.

> You see: there was a cup of wine, a poem, and your sad eyes—one pain in three formless forms; one tale in three chapters—three sad flowers in a vase—So when I came to write that same evening, I found how little one can say. For who can speak of the soul—Who can reduce the infinite into five lines?

> Write me a word and wound if you will for I love a beautiful pain. Alas this letter is incomprehensible but you understand because your eyes are sad.[14]

Kahlil was straining to express himself meaningfully in an alien tongue. His "cup of wine, a poem, and your sad eyes" is suspiciously reminiscent of Edward FitzGerald's popular *Rubaiyat of Omar Khayyam*. But he was still constantly exposed to Josephine's highly romantic and sophisticated tastes as he continued to escort her to cultural events. They saw David Belasco's Japanese-inspired production, *The Darling of the Gods,* and at Wellesley they heard the high priest of the Celtic revival, William Butler Yeats, lecture on Irish poets.

Her book *The Singing Leaves* had just come out, and he showed her an Arabic review of it. Since her song to "The Cedars" was included in it, it is reasonable to believe that he had brought her poems to the attention of the emigrant Arabic press in America. But her comment is more significant as an early reference to his new preoccupation with the writings of the Arab emigrés. Until that November his growth in her eyes had been that of a talented foreigner—albeit an idealized Arab—on whom European and American influences were superimposed. But in the next year he would turn from trying to express his feelings in English, a language which he still could not handle, to writing almost solely in Arabic. By this deliberate means his thoughts could now be transmitted to an audience composed of 20,000 or more Arabic-speaking immigrants.

For the next ten years he would balance a two-sided career. To the nucleus of responsive American intellectuals who had discovered and nurtured his earliest artistic expression, he would remain a talented and precocious visionary who could draw like an angel. These earliest admirers saw him not as the son of an immigrant peddler but, as Josephine had written, a "born Ravi

Yogi." At a time when the spiritual sons and daughters of Emerson and Thoreau were fascinated with "psycho-physics" and "mental chemistry," when it was fashionable for Boston Brahmins to enter "the mystic atmosphere of the Oriental Circle" by flocking to private lectures given by Siddi Mohammed Tabier on "The Book of the Dead" or by Swami Vivakananda on "The Karma Yogi," the young Syrian fitted well into the transcendental atmosphere. The city which had recently spawned the spiritual movements of Christian Science, the Society of Psychical Research, and Theosophy smiled benevolently at young prophets. When Josephine proclaimed that she would become a Buddha if she spent much time with this silent boy who, perhaps enthralled with her loveliness, seemed to meditate in her presence, she was merely reflecting the temper of her times. "Going into the silence"—a popular occupation and a phrase very much in use—was considered to represent "a real and vital spiritual experience." [15]

Along with the general fad for things mystical and Oriental, Kahlil's patronage by Fred Holland Day was enormously important. For years Day had ritualized the cult of the "unspoilt genius." No doubt his passion for Keats, the tubercular genius who arose from an ordinary hostelry, and his admiration for the similarly untrained talent of the sickly Beardsley, triggered his instinctive faith in the young Kahlil. All his life he had waited to discover such a primitive in Boston, and at last he had found one of the right background and circumstances. The youth's perception, his life in Lebanon, and his family's tragic deaths by corrosive disease fitted all the circumstances he found necessary for the making of a poetic creature. One early indication that he was introducing Kahlil's work to the public comes from a letter written to him by Gertrude Smith, a Copeland and Day author. "I have some friends who want to see your Syrian genius pictures. Are they at your studio? One may be of real aid to him?" [16] Josephine's susceptibility to Kahlil's magic aura reinforced Day's belief in him.

Since 1896 Gibran had been under the watchful gaze of a small circle of giant-weary Americans who discovered him, it seems, so they could believe in him. For the next ten years he worked hard to fulfill his promise. He did this in an unexpected way. He digested all of his influences—the English romantic poets, the Boston decadents, Maeterlinck, Carpenter, Yeats—and then set about to write in his own colloquial Arabic. He first addressed his countrymen in America. Eventually his Boston-based philosophy penetrated the Middle East, and by the time he was ready to write in English it reappeared in America, this time heralded as the writings of an Arabic philosopher. By then he was in New York, and the critics never paused to remember that short period of the nineties in Boston which truly provided his literary roots.

As his involvement with Josephine slowly and painfully diminished, he returned to his ethnic background and explored there the possibilities of expressing himself. By Christmas of 1903 he was becoming ready to write. Just as she had invited him on Christmas the previous year, Josephine again asked him to spend some time with her. This time he refused and explained the sense of duty which prompted him to stay home in the South End with Marianna: "I am asked to dine with friends on Christmas Eve—'unlucky Kahlil'—and on Christmas day most of the Syrians will come and visit the man who lost his mother, brother, and sister in one year. It is the custom among us to go and comfort the friend. I will tell you all about it." [17] For the holiday he sent her a pot of white cyclamens, and Josephine, always pleased by gifts of flowers, happily recorded his gesture along with mention of another floral tribute even more romantic, "—and some edelweiss in a box from Mr. Marks who gathered it in Switzerland himself." [18]

Lionel Marks, English born and educated at the University of London and Cornell, was then a restlessly brilliant associate professor in mechanical engineering at Harvard. During the Christmas holidays he had traveled with Mary Haskell to Ottawa to visit his best friend and colleague Reginald Daly. Louise Haskell Daly was delighted that her husband's closest associate found Mary attractive. Frequently calling upon her at the Marlborough Street school that winter, he enjoyed her inquisitive mind and devotion to social causes. In Ottawa on New Year's Eve he presented her with a belt buckle—"my style," she approvingly noted in her diary.[19]

Back in Boston, that same night Kahlil gave a little silver ring to Josephine. She described it a week later:

> ᏩᎻᎫ gave it to me: a little old, old Eastern ring of silver with "a store of mysteries" in it. For almost two hundred years it was on the hand of a certain image of the Virgin in a little old church of hers in Bisherri of Mt. Lebanon. And it was there with scores of other rings and votive offerings. And when ᏩᎻᎫ was born and taken to be christened there, his great grandfather, then a pontiff, took this little gift from the Madonna, to bless the baby with, (choosing silver as luckier for a baby) and tied it on his finger for a few hours. It was laid way for him till he was seven: and he wore it then till he was fourteen. And now he gives it to me. The ring part of it is battered but not worn. The stone and the setting are worn down with the kisses of pilgrims. No wonder I think it is a blessed ring.[20]

Despite her delight over the ring and its elaborate story, her relationship with Kahlil, who was now twenty-one, remained stalemated. But he still came and entertained her as usual and tried valiantly to pull her out of her "dark of nothingness." "*January 27.* ᏩᎻᎫ was out here yesterday evening to see what my spiritless—not to say woeful—note of the day before could mean. I was sickish and dismal and unspeakably discouraged over the impossibility of writing anything in this upside-down high strung and nervous home: and the bitter necessity of writing, . . . for to earn support of it. And for once I almost dismayed him with my inability to sit up straight and laugh more than forlornly. In fact, I'm afraid I upset him; and that has vext me further." [21]

Although her outbursts obviously disturbed him, he was at least able to observe at firsthand the predicament of the American artist, unprotected and unsponsored in a world that heeded him but little. He himself was preparing to enter that unstable arena in the spring of 1904 under the sponsorship of Day, who offered him an introductory show in his own studio, along with paintings by Langrel Harris, an artist whom Day had known in Paris and who had died the year before.

Day's studio in the Harcourt Building on Irvington Street was now increasingly devoted to exhibits of American and English photographers. His suzerainty over the school of pictorial photography, however, was beginning to wane. In 1901, still full of plans for cooperative efforts among artistic photographers, he had approached his New York rival, Alfred Stieglitz, with a grand plan for a show at the Boston Museum of Fine Arts. To procure the museum facilities he used the considerable influence of Sarah Choate Sears, who collected and sponsored the work of young artists, had exhibited widely and with some success as a watercolorist herself, and was a student of Day's at the turn of the century. He helped her outfit an ideal photographic studio in her Back Bay mansion and included her work in his exhibitions in England.

Stieglitz, however, always suspicious of Day's enthusiastic excesses, rejected his plan for "An American Association of Artistic Photography." When a year later Stieglitz was ready to form a New York-based group, Day sulked and refused to ally himself with it. This decision not to join the Photo-Secessionists was the beginning of his international decline. All his friends and students— Gertrude Käsebier, Alvin Langdon Coburn, Clarence White, Eduard Steichen—and even his Boston disciples, including Mrs. Sears, jumped on the New York bandwagon. Day began to retreat into his peculiarly Boston shell. In 1904 he was still locally active, and in March he showed Gertrude Käsebier's work. Kahlil and Josephine "had a good time" at the opening.[22]

That winter Gibran was working furiously for his projected show. Several notes to his patron indicate that he made regular trips to Day's studio to check the reaction to the stream of drawings he was producing. "I am very sorry, dear brother, for being unable to come Saturday to hear music. I have an engagement and there is no possible way of breaking it. But I shall come Monday and perhaps with a drawing under my arm." In the same letter he also described the kind of grippe-like malaise he would experience annually throughout his life: "I have not been well for days—very little sleep and less food—but I am not in bed." Josephine corroborated his midwinter sickness on March 9.[23] Later that month he took her to the Tremont Theater where they saw Nance O'Neill in the "scriptual drama" *Judith*.

She was busy writing a one-act play based on Anglo-Saxon legend, and Day

Invitation to Day's exhibit. (Authors)

was getting together a list of interested patrons for the show. First he secured
the blessing of Mrs. Sears. Because she had purchased a Gibran drawing, "The
Past: The Present: The Future," her name was prominently included in the
catalogue. Day issued an elegantly simple invitation which is significant mainly
because it shows that he preferred to introduce his youthful artist by the
formal and romantic name of Gibran Kahlil Gibran.

In April Josephine, who lent five works to the exhibit, went twice to Day's
studio to help mount and hang pictures. She offered to send out the
announcements to her many friends. From her diary and surviving notes it
appears that her earlier illusions about her "genius" were now fading. To
Lillian Shuman Dreyfus she merely stated, "In case you care to see the
Syrian's larger drawings any time this week, here is an invitation to his
exhibition in Day's studio." [24] Still, she tried actively to attract as many
viewers as possible. On May 2 she begged Lionel Marks to insist to Mary
Haskell that she see the show. He relayed her message the following night.

That same evening a review of the drawings appeared in the *Evening
Transcript*. This first major critical attention was all that a twenty-one-year-old
artist could hope for.

Mr. Gibran is a young Syrian, who, in his drawings, manifests the poetical
and imaginative temperament of his race, and a remarkable vein of
individual invention. The ponderous beauty and nobility of certain of his
pictorial fancies are wonderful; and the tragic import of other conceptions
is dreadful. All told, his drawings make a profound impression, and,
considering his age, the qualities shown in them are extraordinary for
originality and depth of symbolic significance. The series of drawings

129

entitled "Towards God" (20), recently executed, is perhaps as remarkable as any of the works in the exhibition. In spite of some crudity in the draughtsmanship, the drawing called "Earth Takes Her Own" (20f), in this series, is fairly majestic in its meaning and expression. It reminds one of William Blake's mystical works. Similar qualities are to be remarked in "The Souls of Men" (11), "The Past: the Present: the Future" (25), loaned by Mrs. J. Montgomery Sears, "Memory" (16), loaned by Mr. Day, "The Lost Mind" (24), "The Dream of Life" (13), "The Descent of Wisdom to India" (1), "One of the Worlds" (18), loaned by Miss Josephine Preston Peabody, and "Light" and "Darkness" (22 and 23).

All these drawings are, as their titles imply, spiritual allegories of the most solemn character and import. The earnest desire to give expression to metaphysical ideas has triumphantly prevailed over technical limitations to the extent that the imagination is greatly stirred by the abstract or moral beauty of the thought. There are faces here which haunt the memory with something of the spell cast upon the fancy by the visions of dreamland; and, mingled with some almost grotesque and repulsive types, incomplete realizations of the artist's conceptions, wherein the hand has not been able to answer to the idea, there is a whole gallery of gracious and novel heads which express the purest aspirations and the most subtle shades of moral moods.[25]

Left: Probably "Good Friday: A Study," a pencil drawing
which Josephine lent to the show. (Harvard College Library)

Above: A pencil drawing, whose title is not known, exhibited by Day. (Photo Juley)

The allegorical titles were probably chosen under Day's and Josephine's aegis. A predictable flurry of interest followed this publicity. A neighbor of Day's on Pinckney Street, William Bustin, purchased a drawing, and Mrs. Sears bought another one. On May 8 Dr. Charles Peabody (not related to Josephine) saw and expressed enthusiasm over the work.

Charles Peabody was a versatile man of several accomplishments. Trained in classical philology and archaeology, he was also interested in the fine arts and had for a time served as a critic for the Boston weekly *Time and the Hour*. Both he and his wife Jeannette were amateur photographers; he had joined the Photo-Secessionists, and like Mrs. Sears was greatly influenced by Day's concept of the art. By 1904 he was an assistant professor in European archaeology at Harvard. On the day he came to the Harcourt Studios he bought a drawing later described as a "man and a woman with closed eyes hand in hand and a bambino 'in nimbus.' " [26]

The next day Lionel again pressured Mary. "Tomorrow is the last day of that exhibit. You must go." Josephine too was making last-minute efforts on Kahlil's behalf. On May 10 she brought another distinguished Harvard professor, Hugo Munsterberg of the German and psychology departments. Kahlil and Day were there, and she also saw Mary, who had finally found time to take from girls' basketball games, teacher recruitment, and the women's labor movement to heed Lionel's advice. Gibran's first meeting with her did not visibly impress Josephine, who observed the headmistress's presence with disinterest: "Tuesday I took Mr. Munsterberg to see drawings . . . also Miss Haskell and E. Puffer there." [27]

Mary likewise made the following matter-of-fact observation: "Carried school circular to Foster. Mr. Gibran's pictures and Mr. Harris's—young man died in Paris. Mr. Day had both exhibits at his studio." Six years later she recalled the day in more detail. "I went and was deeply interested. I looked slowly—and while I lingered before a red pencil drawing, a little dark young man came up and said in a very gentle voice, 'Are you interested in that picture?' When I said I was indeed, he offered to explain them all to me and did." [28]

Gibran's own version of this scene came much later and, with the benefit of hindsight, outlined objectively the way he saw himself when he was the darling of the Brahmins. He told Mary:

> I was drawn to you in a special way the very first time I saw you. It was at the exhibition of my drawings in Mr. Day's studio. You were wearing black—and it was very becoming to you—and a silver something around your waist—I loved talking to you that day. . . . I knew many people in Boston at that time—some of them among the very finest there were. . . . The others found me interesting. They liked to get me talking, because I was unusual for them. I said, they liked to watch the monkey. And they

Probably "The Vision of Adam and Eve," colored chalk, which Charles
Peabody purchased. Mary Haskell later wrote Kahlil, "I saw your
boyhood sketch . . . at the Peabodys the other day . . . and of course
knew whose it was. Blood seemed to burst from my heart—for the
others lost." (Telfair Academy)

would have people meet me, as someone who was interesting. But you
really wanted to hear what was in me—and you weren't even content to
hear what I had to say—you kept making me dig for more. That was very
delicious to me.[29]

Mary at this time was the particular friend of Lionel, the man who had sent
edelweiss to Josephine the past Christmas. Now the involvements of the two
women and the two men were to be reversed. Gibran—half tutored, long
coddled by a precious group, and nurtured by Josephine's special romanticism
—had perhaps tired of his monkey-on-a-string role. He was in need of the
analysis and direction of a pragmatic soul. Mary Elizabeth Haskell, unsenti-
mental, a woman of reason, was so endowed. As her interest in the "little dark
young man" grew, Lionel, her man of intellect, moved away from her just as
Josephine, the woman of emotion, was moving away from Kahlil. These
uncanny exchanges of sensibility for reason progressed during the next two
years, and with the eventual marriage of Josephine and Lionel, Kahlil and
Mary were thrust together closely for the rest of their lives.

Miss Haskell's School for Girls, 314 Marlborough Street,
Boston. (Authors)

8

Strange Music

Four days after he met her Kahlil was summoned to 314 Marlborough Street to see Mary Haskell. This excellent woman of action was constantly looking for anything that might enlighten her teenage students, and showing the works of a young artist coincided with her philosophy of bringing the outside world to her classrooms. Her art teacher Frances Keyes encouraged her to bring Gibran's exhibit to the school "because it would be good for the girls to see the work of a man of promise before he won recognition." [1]

His first impression that Mary was different from "the others" was essentially correct. For the first time he met an American who was not Yankee born and bred. Although outwardly at home in Boston, Mary was in some ways an alien. Her father, Alexander Cheves Haskell, known as "the Marshal Ney of the Confederate Army," had been an outstanding cavalry officer.[2] At twenty-eight he surrendered the Confederate Cavalry at Appomattox. After the war he enjoyed some political success in South Carolina before his career was curtailed by the carpetbagger take-over.

By the time he had met and married Alice Alexander, sister of General E. P. Alexander, Colonel Haskell was teaching law at the University of South Carolina. Mary, the third child of this marriage, was born on December 11, 1873, during the shameful period when the South, especially her father's beloved South Carolina, was suffering the humility and rigors of a conquered nation. Her early years were frugally spent on a large farm near Columbia. The family rapidly grew to four boys and six girls, while her father's role in assuring the economic and political rebirth of his state expanded.

Mary's adulation of him grew as he methodically and wisely worked to repair the ruptures of war and occupation. She saw the family's fortune evolve by the turn of the century from postwar poverty to a comfortable prosperity. When she met Kahlil her mother had been dead for two years, but her father, then vice-president of a Columbia bank, was still an esteemed figure of reason and progress in the South. Within this context of divided national and state allegiances, she emerged a strong and selfless personality. From her father she inherited a cerebral sense of reality and a passionate yearning for justice for the downtrodden, no matter what their origin.

Kahlil's first meetings with Mary contrasted sharply with his initial encounters with Josephine. Instead of the incandescent beauty of the poet, he was confronted by a capable, forthright woman who saw herself as part of the "new breed" of women. Although she had lived near Boston during its frivolous fin-de-siècle years, dalliance with the decadent and decorative did not amuse her. At thirty she was a strongly built woman of five feet six who subscribed to a regimen of fresh air, exercises, and cold brisk showers. Pulling back her light brown hair in the style most suitable for her profession, she did not pretend to feminine allure, preferring to use her steady blue eyes as discerners of honesty and purpose. Indeed she had always considered herself plain and awkward, as is candidly illustrated by her autobiographical poem:

> Louisa, the elder, was lovely,
> With golden hair hanging in ringlets,
> With blue eyes and fair white complexion,
> A beautiful child was Louisa,
> But Mary, the younger, was homely,
> A tall and cadaverous maiden,
> With head that was large and ungainly,
> With eyes far apart like the owlets',
> With mouth that stretched wide like young robins,
> A parchment complexion had Mary—
> In short she was naught of a beauty.[3]

Gibran, well aware of Josephine's adoration of nature, found a new and far more forthright kind of nature worshipper in Mary. In contrast to Josephine's reverent description of shining brooks in which she symbolically immersed strings of amber—"I never doubted the naiads" [4]—Mary viewed the out-of-doors as a challenge to her abilities. She had spent the previous summer camping with the Sierra Club in the White Mountains, where she assaulted Mount Washington and exulted in long, hard hikes. Within the standards imposed by long skirts and stays, her athletic stance might have been considered awkward. Gibran, growing up with the twentieth century, learned to admire her hurried stride and back-flung shoulders, but his first impressions at the school, when he saw her dynamically and competently directing the students, entertaining flocks of visiting relatives, and articulating the most liberal and advanced social or political causes, must have staggered him.

Even her intellectual development differed radically from Josephine's interests. Gibran, at home with Josephine's essentially literary preferences, was confronted with a woman who vocally expressed disdain for Latin and

Mary on the right, with a Sierra Club hiking companion. (University of North Carolina Library, Chapel Hill)

Greek in schools and who much preferred to discuss anatomy and current events with her students. As a student at Wellesley College, she had revealed her essentially self-effacing personality when she had stated that her desire to learn to write was motivated by a wish to "do something for the South, by collecting such materials of history, localities, ideas as might be available for others to use in a work that should tell and should be a help to our people." [5]

Probably the most significant role she played there was as associate editor of *The Wellesley Magazine* and conductor of "The Free Press" column in which students criticized school policy. Her published writings in the magazine show the development of a didactic conscience. Through a series of exhortations to "live a larger life"—whether at Wellesley, which as a freshman she contended was "peculiarly out of touch with the rest of the world," or within the nation itself when she described "the deplorable condition in our country" at a Republican rally in 1896—her evangelical tone always called for a spirit of reform. In contrast to Josephine, she joined the Agora society, which encouraged "intelligent interest in the political questions of the day" and held that "woman must be broad enough to have a place in her heart and in her life not only for her home but for her country and for the world." [6]

In addition to her expository writing she concentrated heavily on the sciences, taking chemistry, physiology, zoology, and botany. She welcomed the challenge of realism and while still a freshman wrote, "Now for a march upon the fort of philosophy. If only I knew that I should love the *reality* of hard scientific work as I love the *idea* of it. N'importe. I must stick to it." [7] German was her one constant elective. Her interest in it was largely based on her admiration for "Tante" Müller, whom she had met in her freshman year and who continued to influence her long after she graduated.

Ever inhibited when it came to her own feelings, Mary had started a diary in 1894, inspired by the example of Col. Thomas Wentworth Higginson. Unlike Josephine she precisely defined her humanistic purpose as a recorder: "the idea of writing something that might serve years hence to furnish me with a setting of the customs and circumstances and ideas of my youth, if such a setting should ever be sought by some writer or chronicler." After this uncanny prediction of what her diaries would eventually become, she firmly stated that her chronicle would never be merely a repository for pure emotion. "As for the record of my innermost self: If I write my deeds, it will be folded up within them, the spirit prompting and informing them. For I am not one thing, and my deeds something apart; but my life is the truest expression of myself." [8]

By 1904 her habits of daily record keeping had not changed. She dryly recited the racing pace of her days, and her first brief meetings with Kahlil were noted without emotion. When he came to the school on Saturday, May 14, she recorded his visit as a minor detail in preparation for a school occasion. "Aleck and Laura [her oldest brother and his wife] came. Mr. Gibran to see about pictures—Lucinda and Mr. Farwell [Arthur Farwell, composer and musicologist] with rest to anniversary. Alice [her sister, then staying at the school] gave Mr. F. four Negro songs. To Art Museum with Laura and Aleck." [9] During the week of the exhibition, which opened on May 17, she noted his several appearances between perfunctory comments on Lionel Marks's presence at dinner, school demonstrations of the latest fire extinguisher, and the theater.

Apparently Mary invited outsiders to the show. She noted the attendance of twenty-five to forty-five visitors a day, despite some days of "pouring rain." [10] On Wednesday she dined with Kahlil and a friend, Henry Schofield. On Thursday she again invited Kahlil to dinner along with her brother Adam and three other friends. Afterward he entertained the company: "Gibran drew 'Melancholy' and 'The Voice of Love.' " She was too busy examining and interviewing new girls on Friday to write about the show other than "Mr. Gibran's pictures thirty people." And in the following week, the hectic last few days of school, she was too preoccupied with buying summer silks, completing school reports, and attending festivities even to mention Kahlil, who obviously came and removed his pictures.

Although all her students and faculty and at least a hundred of her acquaintances saw the show, Kahlil did not sell anything from it. Margarethe

Müller, probably coaxed by Josephine and Mary, decided to support the young artist who had shown his works the previous year at Wellesley. She reserved a pastel titled "The Dream of Life," which was priced at $150. But her interest in just one of his works did not cheer him. On the following Monday Josephine went to Fred Holland Day's studio and found Kahlil "in a low state of mind." [11] He was experiencing the sinking letdown so common to young artists after the first brief interest in their work subsides. His discouragement must have been complete a few days later when Josephine—always sensitive to any financial setback to an artist—no doubt told him that Miss Müller had confessed to her that she could not afford "The Dream of Life."

Kahlil's first venture into Mary's crowded life, then, was lacking in the intimacy so characteristic of his friendship with Josephine. Except for her interest in showing his work, her extension of the exhibition was not immediately significant for his way of life. His involvement with Day's world and Josephine continued at a far deeper level than his acquaintance with the headmistress.

Later that month, after she had returned from a trip to New York to recruit teachers, Mary relaxed her rigid schedule. On June 17 Kahlil paid her a call. They took a walk down Marlborough Street toward the Public Garden and were able to talk uninterruptedly for the first time since they had met in early May. He told her about life in his native country. When she returned home that night, for the first time she was interested enough to refer to him by his first name and to mention their conversation: "Kahlil at 8. Sat by Swan Pond. Difference between Syria and America." [12]

Meanwhile Kahlil and Josephine were tearing at each other's frayed nerves: "*June 27.* ꙮ here. Untuneful time." Two days later he showed none of the irritability with which Josephine was contending, when he saw Mary for the last time that season. On that evening they stayed at the school, which was being redecorated. She had painted the kitchen and hall earlier that week, and he helped her make a "screen for kitchen out of clothes-horse and burlap." She made a note of his summer addresses: "Kahlil Gibran through July c/o Mr. Field [Day's caretaker], Five Islands, Maine. Then back to 35 Edinboro." [13] A day later, always the consummate sightseer, she was traveling west toward the latest in world expositions, the St. Louis World's Fair.

Kahlil, however, did not immediately go to Maine. On July 5 he saw Josephine at Forest Street, where they sat on the piazza and argued in the midsummer heat. A few nights before, she had listened to a similar tirade from "Il Signor Marks." Chastising her for her "foolish [ways] or New England ways or Cambridge ways," Lionel had lectured her about her negligence in building a sensible career. She "rallied through" that unpleasant scene in which he "wished her some kind of awakening." But when Kahlil similarly chastised her, she was completely abashed and confessed how deeply his words had cut her. "I hear some more harsh sayings and know not what to do. . . . And the third disquieting interview . . . reduced me to tears. But that was about other things; or rather the same thing from another point of view." [14]

Kahlil and Lionel were vying to pull Josephine out of the depression in which she wallowed. She admitted the extent of her gloom when she wrote, "Some person is undoubtedly roasting a waxen image of me." Lionel's maturity and sophistication obviously were more persuasive than Kahlil's emotional strainings. Just as she had given the young artist a crystal the previous year, Josephine bestowed a token upon Lionel before he left for the summer. "I gave him a moon-stone for a safeguard, with some exhortations for him." [15] But to Kahlil, who was also going away, she gave nothing.

During this period a description of Kahlil was given by a visitor to Day's studio. Working there, away from the protective skirts of his two women supporters, he appeared as a self-assured and outgoing artist. "I arrived at the studio of Mr. Day about 3:15 and expected to stay until four. While walking in the work room, I chanced to come across a piece of brown paper which I took and started to sketch a girl's head, but a young fellow of Sirian nationality who was looking over my shoulder beheld the sketch and said it wasn't just right. He took the paper and started to draw a sketch of my head in which he did first rate." [16]

Along with helping Day with his photographic tasks, Kahlil was simultaneously looking for another logical outlet for his art, something that would supplement the meager income that Marianna was earning at Miss Teahan's dressmaking shop. He was by then aggressively assertive when it came to his career, and so when the editor of a New York Arabic-emigré newspaper visited the Syrian community in Boston that spring, he quickly made himself known.

Ameen Goryeb had started his newspaper in 1903. Its title—*al-Mohajer*, or *The Emigrant*—was significant to every Arabic-speaking person in America. The word *mahjar* contains the root *hegira*, meaning journey, and it evoked all the emotional implications associated with the long journeys which Syrian traders had made since the days of the Phoenicians. *Mahjar* was also synonymous with New York City, the ultimate mecca in the New World. At the beginning of the twentieth century the competition among Arab publishers for readers was intense, especially in New York where at least three newspapers provided political and social forums for the 5,000 or more immigrants.[17]

When Goryeb first met Gibran he was impressed by the youth's literary background and unusually articulate presence. Kahlil showed him the reviews of his exhibitions, and the editor recalled later that he was especially intrigued to read that "the drawings were admired in the newspapers of Boston, the esteemed city of arts and sciences." [18] Kahlil even invited him to his Edinboro

Street tenement and showed him his notebooks. And although the editor admired the talent shown in the sketches, he was more interested in the possibility of publishing some of the prose poems.

The exact date is uncertain, but sometime between that summer of 1904 and the spring of 1905, Kahlil's first published work appeared in *al-Mohajer*. He called this attempt "Vision." Typical of the string of romantic essays that followed it, "Vision" was laden with the symbolism of disillusion. It described a caged bird "in the midst of a field on the banks of a limpid stream," which died for lack of food and water "like a rich man locked in his treasury who dies of hunger in the midst of his gold." As the poet's vision sharpened, he saw the cage become "the dry skeleton of a man, and the dead bird was turned into a human heart." Resembling "a deep wound," the heart spoke and proclaimed that its imprisonment and neglectful death were due to the captivity "in this cage of laws fashioned by men." "I am the human heart which is imprisoned in the darkness of the multitude's edicts and fettered by illusion until I am arrived at death's point" was the underlying theme that ran through Kahlil's essays for the next three years.[19]

Goryeb's encouragement of the twenty-one-year-old immigrant was in turn reinforced by the continued support of Josephine and Day. By mid-August Kahlil and Josephine had returned from their summer vacations, during which they had continued to write often to each other, and in the fall he still visited her frequently. Although her diary shows that the two continued to quarrel, she was apparently helping him with his writing. "*Oct. 11.* Arabic poem from ͡ɛ͡ծ͡ͻ. *Oct. 15.* Evening ͡ɛ͡ծ͡ͻ here with a poem in Arabic. LSM [Lionel] here also. Me stupid likewise dismal." [20]

If we assume that he translated his poems in order to get her opinion, it is important to understand her influence on his development as an Arabic writer. She was obviously able to help him with the content and his evolving thought, but she could offer no criticism of the language itself. He had to wrestle with his linguistic problems alone. Four years of college in Beirut had not fully equipped him to perfect his writing in Arabic, and there is no record of any friendship with an Arabic scholar in Boston to whom he might have turned—indeed, he had formed no strong attachments within the Syrian community. He was forced to resort to his essentially peasant's ear when putting down his thoughts. Ignoring much of the traditional vocabulary and form of classical Arabic, he began to develop a style which reflected the ordinary language he had heard as a child in Besharri and to which he was still exposed in the South End. This use of the colloquial was more a product of his isolation than of a specific intent, but it appealed to the thousands of Arab immigrants who responded to this unique and simplified treatment. Many in his audience, barely literate in their native tongue, felt comfortable with his unconscious modernization of their language.

Day in his studio in the Harcourt
Building, 1900. (Norwood)

While Kahlil sought out Josephine for affirmation, he still depended heavily on Day. The background for his first published pamphlet, *al-Musiqa*, or *Music*, can be traced directly to Day's invitations to the Boston Symphony. The following letter to Day shows how he was beginning to formulate some ideas about the concerts he was hearing. It was written on October 29, 1904; within six months he would publish his Arabic essay on the subject.

> The overture to Tannhäuser, dear brother, is indeed a sublime music. Its end has moved every bit of my better self. To analyze such work is simply to be as great as the tone-poet himself, nay, for Wagner himself knew not all the glory of his works; like all big men.
>
> The fourth symphony of Beethoven is very wonderful, and I even thought that I could understand the work of the "miracle of man" until last Saturday when every note of his sought its echo from the innersmost of me.
>
> Mr. and Mrs. Ruyl are going to leave that beautiful little corner on Salem Street and they asked me to come tomorrow, and take a farewell dinner with them. So, you see dear brother, you must forgive me for not being able to come.[21]

Kahlil had met Beatrice Baxter Rüyl and her husband Louis, both of them illustrators for the Boston *Herald*, through Day. When they were first married they combined their artistic vocations with social work and lived at the North End Union settlement house at 183 Salem Street. The Rüyls also visited Day at Five Islands, and Kahlil continued to admire them for the next several years.

He still did not number Mary among his circle of American friends. When she returned from her whirlwind tour of the Midwest and South, she again threw herself headlong into a full schedule. In October she entertained her father at the school, and she was actively involved in the Women's Trade Union League. Her diary continued to note visits from Lionel, frequent theater-going, reunions with members of the Sierra Club, and visits to the Agora at Wellesley. Kahlil was simply not a part of her life.

On November 7 Josephine was invited to Ottawa by Mary's sister Louise Daly. The invitation was prompted by the forthcoming production of her *Pan, A Choric Idyl*, which had been set to music and was to be produced on November 15 at a state farewell concert for Lord Minto, the retiring governor general of Canada. Josephine decided to attend the elegant function even though it would strain her budget, and on November 12 she departed. She probably left too early to read the morning papers that Saturday.

"Fire! Loss $200,000 in Harcourt Studios," was the substance of all the Boston headlines that day. The four-alarm fire started at seven o'clock on Friday evening, turned into a devastating series of explosions during the night, and smoldered on well into Saturday. Threatening the nearby St. Botolph studios and the armory, and hindering the progress of trains on the adjacent railroad track, the holocaust attracted hundreds of onlookers from the Back Bay and the South End. Surely Kahlil must have heard about the disaster sometime Friday night or Saturday morning and gone to see the building where all of his drawings were stored.

The destruction of the work of a young and relatively unknown immigrant was far less consequential to the Boston art world than the sensational loss of "one thousand paintings by famous artists." And although the morning papers recorded the forty artists who had studios in the gutted building, Kahlil's name was not mentioned. On Saturday morning all the tenants assembled to watch the fire, "which clung stubbornly in the basement of the ruined building." "All Bohemia was there," and Kahlil stood forlornly with "other artists who came around and gazed unhappily at the smoking ruin and wondered when they would get together again, where the inspiration for another picture would ever come." [22]

Day, who "had stored in his studio pictures and prints upon which he placed great value," was one of the occupants who agreed to talk with reporters. "It was practically the work of twenty-five years," he grieved. "And I have not the slightest conception of the value of the collection." He referred to other well-known exhibitors like William Paxton, Edmund Tarbell, and Joseph De Camp, "who were like myself, without insurance and . . . must have suffered a great loss." [23] Two days later, after the last embers had been extinguished, nothing was found that was salvageable, and Day was ordered to vacate the condemned building. For the publisher-turned-photographer, a complete recovery from this loss was never possible. He suffered far more deeply than his passing comments to the press revealed. But if his morose decline began with the debris of his ruined plates, Kahlil—whose bereavement of a sister, a brother, and a mother was less than two years old—stubbornly retained some sense of stability throughout this latest shock.

He wrote Josephine immediately. She received his version of the fire on the very day of her Ottawa production. Dazzled by the opulence and excitement of a vice-regal performance in which her own poetry was the central theme of a splendid spectacle, she waited four days before she answered him. She also wrote Margarethe Müller and begged her to "help out something that is being patiently borne" by sending him a "written word from you." But only when she returned from her triumphant stay did she finally and with reluctance face the latest tragedy. "*November 26.* I did not want to write it down; it is such a dreadful thing. . . . The Harcourt Studios here burned to the ground . . . including F. H. Day's works and, in some ways the most poignant loss of all, Kahlil's great portfolio with all his best drawings—yes, *Consolation*, that whole record of an inspired childhood, that picture of the divine heart of Youth. All gone; burned to ashes. I cannot tell what I felt and still feel about it. But he replied to my letter with such fortitude and sweetness, that I was amazed and reassured. And after all, the most glorious thing that one can have . . . is surely this knowledge that one Lives Again."

She relayed her sympathy to Day, her friend and first publisher of her poetry, the next day. "I know, too, that according to your beautiful hospitality of spirit, you will doubtless be grieving even more over the loss to your friends—of the work which has always had house-room with your own. But I hope you will comfort yourself with the knowledge that everyone appreciates poignantly the sharpness of that special circumstance, and must feel keenly that it is a burden brought upon you, strangely enough, by your most generous interest in others." Mary, who had dined with Lionel the night of the fire, in time sent Day a rather formal note of regret, adding, "I am almost a complete stranger to you—perhaps quite so by this time—but the memory is still bright and grateful with me of an afternoon in your studio last spring when the work of Mr. Gibran and of your young friend Harris was on exhibition—when you kindly took pains to illuminate to me out of your own friendship the sketches of the man who was gone."

She also wrote to Kahlil, whom she had not seen that fall. Fortunately she kept his answer, which is possibly the first letter he ever wrote her, and certainly the first one she bothered to save. "My dear Miss Haskell," he respectfully addressed her. "It is the sympathy of friends that makes grief a sweet sorrow. And after all, the perishing of my drawings—the years of Love's labor—the flower of my youth—must be for a beautiful reason unknown to us. Few days ago I thought of seeing you but I had not the strength, but I shall try to come sometime soon. I do not know what to do with my coloured pencils at present; perhaps they will be kept in the chest of forgetfulness. But I am writing. Your sweet letter is indeed a consolation. Your friend, Kahlil." [24] Although his promised visit to Mary did not take place that winter, he still loyally paid homage to Posy. On Christmas Eve he brought her some Syrian sweets and on January 6 celebrated his twenty-second birthday with her.

"After the Harcourt Studios fire . . . I set to work," Gibran told Mary in 1916. Josephine's comments on his visits during the winter of 1905 confirm his resolute immersion in work. When Edwin Arlington Robinson came to her house on February 19, she enthusiastically showed him Kahlil's latest drawings. Four days later " ـﺒﺟ here with poetry to read and pictures to show and I read aloud to him somewhat." On March 1 it was "English translation of a poem by ـﺒﺟ." [25]

The Arabic essays that Gibran was busily dispatching to Goryeb's newspaper were providing him with a weekly sum of two dollars. In a first draft of a letter to Goryeb, he wrote, "Until now I did not understand what you want. If it is a must, then I would write two articles or more a week for two dollars." [26]

Perhaps in recognition of his indebtedness to Day, he called one of these early pieces "Letters of Fire" and began his soliloquy with the immortal lines inscribed on Keats's grave in Rome: "Here lies one whose name was writ in water." He went on to question the fragility of man's worldly efforts: "Shall death destroy that which we build / And the winds scatter our words / And darkness hide our deeds?" Reversing Keats's premise of the impermanence of man's deeds, he optimistically ventured, "The air bears every smile and every sign arising from our hearts and stores away the voice of every kiss whose source and spring is love. . . . If that sweet singer Keats had known that his songs would never cease to plant the love of beauty in men's hearts, surely he had said: 'Write upon my gravestone: Here lies the remains of him who wrote his name on heaven's face in letters of fire.' " [27]

Undoubtedly Day was pleased with Kahlil's youthful interpretations of his beloved Johnny's words. In pursuit of the romantic image, the Syrian was, by Western standards, a latecomer to the nineteenth-century ideal that "Beauty is truth, truth beauty." But in light of the limited literary and intellectual background of the immigrants for whom he was writing, this romanticism should be interpreted not as a restatement but as an introduction. Unconsciously he was creating for his transplanted countrymen a bridge on which they could cross over to the vast field of English literature. In the spring of 1905 his articles, published by now in a column entitled "Reflections," conveyed the theme of love. Often genteely erotic, they proclaimed the joys of physical and mental union. On April 1, 1905, there appeared "The Life of Love," a poem that depicted the four seasons of love. Nothing in these stanzas betrayed disenchantment with his beloved. In fact the poet admitted a separation from her only by the "icy breath" of death and winter.[28]

Kahlil was still competing with Lionel for Josephine's attention. On March 18 when he brought her some new drawings, he was forced to share the entire evening with Lionel, who finally walked him to the 12:25 trolley car. The relationship was still not running smoothly even when he had her to himself: "*April 7.* The ⟨⟩ solus and some mistaken talk."[29]

Many of Kahlil's contributions to "Reflections" contained references to a muse who counseled and consoled him. At times she personified the rapture of dreams, as in "The Queen of Fantasy," where the "mistress of regions of fantasy" caused "the earth to open and the firmament to tremble." She also loomed importantly in "A Visit from Wisdom," when she gazed upon the poet "like a tender mother and wiped away his tears." She answered his confused despair by pointing "to the wild places" and beseeching him "to learn pity through sadness, and knowledge by way of darkness." Similarly, her omniscience emerged in "Before the Throne of Beauty," where she became a "nymph of paradise . . . on her lips was the smile of a flower and in her eyes the hidden things of life." She defined beauty as "that which draws your spirit . . . that which you see and makes you to give rather than to receive."[30]

Could this provocative yet maternal image be anyone but Posy? Certainly she was not Mary, whom Kahlil barely knew. Nor can her words of wisdom be attributed to the Lebanese mountain girl Hala Dahir. Only Josephine could have imbued him with her code of beauty and her credo of giving. His acknowledgment was to exalt her presence in his life. She became the mirage who entered his dreams and spoke through his consciousness.

The spring of 1905 had gone well for Josephine. She delivered six lectures on "Symbolism of the Present," which included readings from Ibsen, Maeterlinck, and Yeats, and her analyses of their writings. Her play *Marlowe* was produced at Radcliffe in honor of the opening of Agassiz House. Public acceptance stimulated her inner thoughts, and she was able to finish *Chameleon*, a play based on the follies of marriage.

Gibran contrived to create for her birthday on May 30 a beautiful tour de force—something that perhaps would halt her gradual drift away from him and recall to her the extravagant opinion which she had once held of him. First he wrote a story, a parable that transparently revealed his deep feelings for

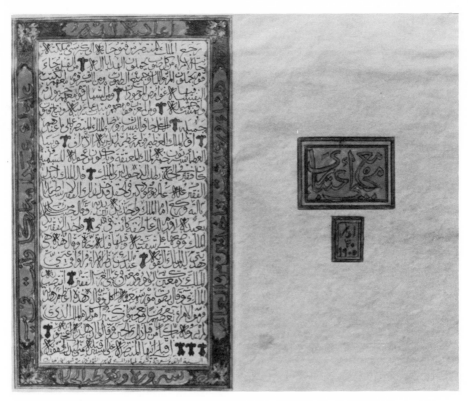

Kahlil's birthday greeting to Josephine, ink and watercolor,
May 30, 1905. (Lionel P. Marks)

her. The tale contrasted the lavish treasures presented to a victorious king and
the simple homage of a beggar—"I come from a distant land to offer you a
feeling from my heart." Thus honored, the king was moved to tears and
announced that the "poor one's" gift was his greatest tribute. In the final
sentence Gibran portrayed himself as the beggar and Josephine as the
monarch: "Accept, victorious one JPP in accordance with these customs a kiss
on your strong hand—the year 1905 A.D.—on the thirtieth of May." [31] Then he
dressed his story in the most beautiful garment he could render: he carefully
illuminated a double page of Arabic calligraphy and dedicated it to her. "May
the gods bring back this day many times with much happiness and joy so that
you may take from this beautiful world as much beauty as you give it. ﻙ ﻙ ﺩ."

Josephine loved the decorated message, but if he had expected to win her
forever with his preciously fashioned evocation of the Arabian Nights, he was
disillusioned. Whenever he voiced his fantasy of a serious alliance with his
muse, she was quick to point out his "mistaken talk." The disparity in their age
and background and the sad similarity of their poverty would have ruled out
any substantial plans for a future together.

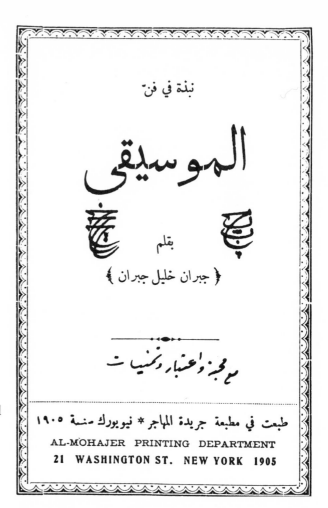

نبذة في فن

الموسيقى

بقلم

﴿ جبران خليل جبران ﴾

مع مجموعة واعتبار وتمنيات

طبعت في مطبعة جريدة المهاجر * نيويورك سنة ١٩٠٥
AL-MOHAJER PRINTING DEPARTMENT
21 WASHINGTON ST. NEW YORK 1905

The cover of *al-Musiqa.* Kahlil added the two intertwined monograms below the title and the inscription between the two horizontal lines. (Harvard College Library)

Shortly afterward *al-Musiqa* was published by Goryeb, and on July 1 he brought a copy to Josephine. To enhance the ordinary salmon wrappers he designed a parchment cover embellished with red letters spelling out MUSIQA. On the title page he wrote in Arabic his initials GKG and the equivalent of hers, GBB. He added in Arabic, "With love and respect and best wishes." [32]

She accepted this special copy—which she later described as "dedicated to me"—and listened as he read the opening lines. [33] The introduction was yet another attempt by the young poet to declare his open admiration for his anonymous beloved, safely disguised in a language that could be interpreted by few if any of the Boston–Cambridge circle. "I sat by the one I love listening to her conversation. I was speechless and felt her voice was a force that moved my heart. My soul was electrified and swam in a boundless atmosphere— seeing the world as a dream and the body as a prison. Strange music mixed with the voice of my beloved and so involved was I with her conversation that I was struck dumb. When my beloved sighs, o people, I hear music. I listened

148

when she spoke with halting speech and again with flowing sentences and again with her words half uttered between her lips."

But the embroidered preface soon turned into a didactic essay. He instructed his immigrant readers in the history of music and its role in ancient Chaldean, Egyptian, Persian, Greek, Hebrew, and Hindu cultures. "Music is like poetry and photography—representing the conditions of man," he continued, and then described the tone-poem qualities of four technical Persian modes.

But before he reached the end, where he naively called upon mortals to glorify Orpheus, David, Beethoven, Wagner, and Mozart, and especially urged his fellow Syrians to remember the equally great musical tradition embodied in the Arabic composers, he was interrupted twice. As Josephine wrote, "While he is translating it (kneeling on the floor beside my chair) enters Mr. G. J. Phelps and stays a while. Next Mr. Francis Dean of Baltimore. Later ٿٿٿ talks to me contentedly on the piazza." [34]

Except for occasional notes and visits throughout the next fall and winter, appearances of the symbol for Kahlil in Josephine's diary decreased. In their place materialized   the Hunter, the Grand Duke. She walked with this strong and romantic figure, and he took her for long rides in the country. Before long she was able to write about her emerging feelings for Lionel, by now her faithful protector and open suitor, "But everything has sailed into new regions of the air. The stars are different; and so is he; and so am I. Everything slow appears to be going fast and I am a me I never met before." [35]

If these developments left a void in Kahlil's life, so was Mary's life affected by Lionel's intense courtship of Josephine. That autumn the two renewed their acquaintance. He visited her during the first week of October and heard about her summer adventures in California, where she had explored Yosemite Park with the Sierra Club. She told him about being arrested in Illinois "for fast driving," and about an even more notorious escapade in the seaside village of nearby Cohasset, where in front of a good-sized crowd she had dared to ride a horse bareback and walk in tightrope fashion across some playground equipment. In years to come she would attribute to this lack of decorum part of the resistance of many Brookline mothers to sending their daughters to her school. Still she continued to defy the usual concept of the proper schoolmistress. That fall she "celebrated Russia's being given a constitution by hanging out the flag." Then she "gathered the girls into the library, told them about Russia, read the Czar's proclamation and sang America." [36]

A month later Kahlil, over dinner at Marlborough Street, told Mary his reading preferences. "Nineteen best books," she recorded, unfortunately specifying none of them. Josephine's and Mary's diaries reveal that in November he visited Josephine only once, just as Lionel saw Mary only once. In December Mary traveled to South Carolina for a family reunion. While she was there she refused a suitor, the second within a year. Attractive to men, she enjoyed their company until faced with their serious intent. She still described dancing until 2:30 A.M. as "blissful" and managed to exude an energetic sexuality that men admired.[37]

Instead of spending some time with Josephine during Christmas week, as he had done since his return from Lebanon, Kahlil sent her a note on Christmas Day. "My beloved Godmother: May all your days be birthdays of songs and all your years be new as the newly strung harp." If it was meant as a gesture toward reunion, it was in vain. By the advent of the new year, Josephine was able to write: "It has all come true. I feel still as if I were walking in my sleep." [38] At the Wayside Inn in Sudbury—the setting of Longfellow's tales—Josephine and Lionel, with Margarethe Müller as chaperone, openly toasted the year 1906 and secretly drank to their engagement.

Unaware of her decision, Kahlil visited Josephine shortly after his birthday, which was pointedly unobserved by her. The desultory talk was about "things occult," for in her darkest hours she had faithfully consulted fortune tellers and astrologers for some encouraging signs.[39]

Slowly Josephine's and Lionel's secret was dispersed among their friends. "Glorious," exclaimed Mary. She congratulated Josephine on her choice: "There is no other man I know so close to the deepest life of the human heart as Lionel." [40]

Kahlil did not officially hear about it until February 20, three days before the public announcement, when Josephine told him and other close friends. Five days later he sent his best wishes:

> May happiness enfold you with her gentle arms, godmother.
>
> May heaven fulfill your heart's desires, godmother.
>
> I rejoice with you and I bless you always, godmother, always.[41]

Always is a long time, particularly for a twenty-three-year-old man who already had known wells of suffering and had been promised heights of satisfaction. In spite of all his previous losses, 1906 was probably the saddest he had ever known.

Two days after Josephine received his note, she told Lionel how close she had been to the young artist. "I tell him about جبران" [42] By then he was so far removed from their social world that he was excluded from the several dinners and dances held in honor of the couple. Mary, on the other hand, played a major role throughout the four-month engagement. "*March 1.* Lionel & Jos to dine. . . . *March 6.* Dinner for Jos & Lionel at Shumans. . . . *March 13.* The crowd to dinner; L. & Jos. . . . *March 14.* Lunch at Colonial Club—Louise, Lio, Jos. . . . *March 18.* Louise to Ottawa; Lionel, Jos & I saw her off. . . . *March 28.* Jos to dinner"

Suddenly everything was blossoming for Posy. On April 17 her one-act play *Wings*—a subtle piece mourning the thralldom of womanhood and starkly set in Anglo-Saxon times on the mystical Welsh shore—was performed at the Boylston Street Colonial Theater. Boston loved the performance, and for the first time in her adult life, she knew a surfeit of material as well as emotional wealth.

Wedding gifts poured in, and she rhapsodized over every shimmer of silver, every sparkle of crystal. On May 2 Kahlil visited her one last time. Once again he showed her some "new pictures" and lingered for a while to listen to the voice which had inspired his youthful dreams. He followed this final "good talk" with a birthday note on May 30, and then, unable to play the well-bred game required of rejected admirers, retreated from her life, and from Mary's circle as well.[43]

On June 21 Josephine and Lionel were married at Harvard's Appleton Chapel. Marion Peabody and Mary Haskell were bridesmaids. The ceremony was simple, with "no obeys." Over three hundred of the Boston–Cambridge artistic and literary elite were invited to the reception at the Colonial Club. Among those who accepted were President and Mrs. Charles Eliot of Harvard, Mrs. Julia Ward Howe, Col. and Mrs. Thomas Wentworth Higginson, Professor and Mrs. William James, Professor and Mrs. G. L. Kittridge, and Professor Charles T. Copeland. Edwin Arlington Robinson and other poets collaborated in sending an inscribed silver loving cup. Louise Imogen Guiney came, back from London for a visit, and Fred Holland Day sent an artistic print of a boat. Notably absent and sending no gifts was "Mr. G. Kahlil Gibran of 55 Beach Street," who neither answered his invitation nor sent his felicitations.[44]

Mary sailed to Europe five days after the wedding, and on July 7 the newlyweds departed for Italy and Germany, where they would spend Lionel's sabbatical year. Kahlil Gibran, for the first time in his life, was singularly alone.

Mary, 1910. (Telfair Academy)

9

The Presence of
a She-Angel

The principals of his Boston days were retreating from Kahlil's life—Josephine forever, Mary for a while, and Day more and more as he suffered from a deteriorating personality. Left alone, Kahlil sought the companionship and support of his Syrian friends. He spent some time during the summer of 1906 at Five Islands, but then, determined to write about his growing alienation and inner conflict, returned to Boston.

Marianna and he had lived for the past three years in various apartments in the Syrian-occupied South End streets. By Syrian standards his sister, now a handsome woman of twenty-one, had developed admirable qualities. Associating the dread tuberculosis with dirt and squalor, she had become an immaculate housekeeper, and he was proud of her efforts to maintain an apartment in which he could entertain friends and relatives. From Kamila and later from older women in the community, she had learned secrets and short cuts in preparing the favorite national dishes, and she was gaining a reputation for her culinary excellence. Most important, she was the chief wage earner in that small household. Her deftness with a needle made her Miss Teahan's favorite employee. She made hats and sewed fine seams during the day, and at night she fashioned her own clothes and shirts for her brother. Thus he was completely free to stay at home and work.

Marianna was entirely dependent upon him for her own social life. Only he could tell the jokes and stories that made her forget the tragedy that was still fresh in her memory. Afraid of the world outside, she let him venture beyond and waited at home for him to return and tell her about the Americans he had met.

Despite all her accomplishments, Kahlil resented Marianna's one failing. She still could not read. She obstinately refused to attend the classes for immigrants at the Denison House. At first her illiteracy was only a small inconvenience, but it gradually assumed more important proportions as she tried to cope with subway and street signs, identify products in stores, or make out letters addressed to herself or her brother.

Kahlil alternately begged her to try and taunted her for her ignorance. He bribed her with a dollar to learn to write her name, which she did, but when he offered to pay fifty cents for every page she read to him, she balked. For the rest of his life, Gibran, who so admired the education and opportunities available to women in America, was ashamed of her obduracy. Her negligence of the written word became a symbol of contention between them. It rankled him that she could not read his words in any language. She, in turn, became silently protective of this shortcoming and tried to hide it.

He was equally concerned that N'oula, his cousin and playmate from Besharri, should succeed in learning the language that was so necessary for assimilation into American society. When N'oula was due to arrive in New York in 1905, Kahlil tried to arrange for him to be met at the boat, and in a letter told him how to succeed in the New World and offered to help him raise some cash:

> About work in Boston, like any other place in the U. S. A., there are lots of shoe factories, also lots of men who are unemployed. Be aware of this fact if you come, because that is a big complaint, and I do ask you not to give up, but be brave and work hard so that you can speak the language. After that you will find America is the best place on earth. You are young and should look to the future. If a year goes by with no results, have no regrets, because gains are available for those who use their brains and not for those who work day and night. . . . I am still heavy with the costs so I can continue to write, and I beg you to care for your health. I know by experience because my health is no good and hinders my studying. . . . Keep the antiques with you and maybe they will be of some value. When a friend comes back from Europe, I will show them.[1]

As his role changed from one who was helped to one who could help, Kahlil assumed a more respected position in the Syrian community. Undying feuds between Maronite and Orthodox Christians had followed members of the sects to New York. The split significantly affected the social and business lives of both Syrians and Lebanese, and extended even to the newspapers. But unlike some of their colleagues, the editors of *al-Mohajer* took a moderate stand in this bitter urban war. In a conciliatory effort the newspaper ran a front-page drawing by Gibran, which showed an angel extending both hands to the conflicting factions. Ameen Rihani, an influential immigrant writer, wrote an article decrying the strife and clerical dependence which cleft his community in two.

In the writings of Rihani, who was seven years older, Gibran found an ally. He responded with "The Poets of *al-Mohajer*," an essay on contemporary

154

Arabic writers, in which he mildly chastised his fellow immigrant writers for mimicking the traditional Arabic poets and for using poetry for mere financial gain instead of as a mirror of the soul. The article was interpreted by several older poets in both Syria and America as a personal attack, and its rather shaky literary analysis was criticized as linguistically weak and artificial. However, the ensuing notoriety lent prominence to the young Boston iconoclast. Soon his column, by now called "Tears and Laughter," was carefully read by all of the Arabic literati in America.[2]

He began to fashion in his writings a more complex Garden of Eden—one choked with painful thorns, in contrast to the earlier blooming roses. Irony tinged with bitterness came into his work; life and love became double edged. His stories were often built around a simple hierarchy of a society peopled with good and evil, in which the poets and simple folk were arrayed against the rich and powerful. Nature remained the constant truth, and death the final liberator. In one "Vision" the poet, mired in the "fields of perplexity," encountered Melpomene, the goddess of tragedy, who showed him "the world and its sorrows, for who has not seen sorrow cannot see joy." He saw "an earth strangled by priests, sly like foxes, and false messiahs . . . lawmakers trading their garbled speech in the market of shame and deceit," an earth where "the wretched poor sowed" and the "powerful rich" harvested.[3]

In other poems he abandoned himself to a surfeit of self-pity. This indulgence is especially apparent in "The Poet's Death is His Life," whose title character waited for his "hour of deliverance from the bonds of existence." Death became the ultimate love affair—a longed-for-release—and, in the end, a triumph for the neglected creator when the people erected "in the center of the town a great statue" to his memory.[4]

Along with these brief sorties into a utopia where men "knew the manner of the flower's breathing and the meaning of the songs of the thrush,"[5] Gibran was organizing his thoughts into a series of longer, more realistic stories. Three of these allegories took place in northern Lebanon. In "Martha" and "Yuhanna the Mad" the title characters were again victims of society's oppressors. The orphan Martha was seduced from the innocence of her isolated village to Beirut, city of dirty streets "wherein the air was leavened with the breath of death." She fell into a life of prostitution and squalor. As she finally lay dying, Gibran, as the first-person narrator, tried to ease her sense of shame: "It were better that a person should be the oppressed than that he should be the oppressor . . . fitter that he should be a victim to the frailty of human instincts than that he should be powerful and crush the flowers of life." Thus consoled, she found at last the ecstasy of death. Gibran helped her son and another boy, "whom the adversaries of existence had taught compassion," bury Martha "in a deserted field . . . for the priests would not pray over her remains, neither would they let her bones rest in the cemetery." [6]

If Gibran chose death as the escape for Martha, madness was the refuge for the hero of "Yuhanna the Mad." Tyrannical priests became tormentors of Yuhanna, a poor herder who had allowed his calves to stray into a monastery's pastures. Pleading for mercy from the monks, who demanded payment for trespassing on religious property, Yuhanna desperately resorted to his Bible "as the warrior draws out his sword. . . . 'Thus do you make a mockery of the teachings of this Book,'" he cried.

Yuhanna's secret reading of the Bible and his use of it as a weapon, his subsequent imprisonment, and the brutal beating by the sadistic monks paralleled the life of the Lebanese religious martyr Assad Shidiaq. In 1829 Shidiaq, an early convert to Protestantism and a believer in the Gospels, was captured and brutally murdered in a monastery not far from Besharri. Kahlil had grown up aware of the horror of his persecution. He knew also that the message of the Scriptures was still ignored by most of the local religious orders in the mountain towns of Lebanon. But Yuhanna the Madman suffered less spectacularly than his real-life model. The governor, condemning his Christ-like sermons as the words of one deranged, finally pardoned him, and he lived out his days as a madman beleaguered by the jeering hypocrites of his village.[7]

The last story in the trilogy, "Dust of the Ages and the Eternal Fire," dealt with reincarnation and pre-ordained love, themes that had obsessed Gibran ever since he had first made Josephine laugh by saying they had known each other "long, long many years before." The hero appeared not as the usual Maronite figure but first as Nathan, the son of a Phoenician priest in Baalbek, and then as Ali Al-Husaini, a Bedouin nomad. Nathan had been promised by his dying beloved that she would return to this world. The vow was fulfilled nineteen centuries later when, amidst the ruins of the ancient temple city, the shepherd Ali experienced haunting "distant remembrances" of life in Baalbek as it had been in Nathan's times before Christ. "He remembered those pillars standing upright in greatness and pride. . . . He felt the impressions of sleeping things stirring in the silences of depths." Consumed by this magical memory, Ali returned to his sheep and within a few minutes beheld a girl before him. She seemed to share his sense of *déjà vu*, and their reunion "was the act of one who finds an acquaintance who has been lost." Gibran's innocent and anticlimactic message was that love had conquered the onslaught of time and was finally and victoriously consummated.[8]

Ameen Goryeb wrote an afterword to these three stories and published them together in 1906. The original title was literally *Brides of the Prairie*, but it became *Nymphs of the Valley* when translated years later. The fresh approach of the tales—their ironic and anticlerical tone, their realism and use of lower-class heroes—was in sharp contrast to the formalistic, mannered Arab writing of the day. They immediately appealed to the emigré writers in New York. Gibran, although living in relative obscurity in Boston, was noted as a fascinating youth who through his drawings was already known to certain Americans.

But his countrymen knew little about his life. Already he was cloaking his origins and acquaintanceships with a compelling sense of mystery. The younger brother of Goryeb later recalled Kahlil's description of a day in the country when he had worn an Arab costume so that his rich American friends could see him in his native garb. It was undoubtedly one of Fred Holland Day's extravagant affairs, but it seems that Gibran's romantic flair, emphasizing his role of an Oriental poet, fascinated his fellow emigrés as much as it had his Bostonian audience.

Shortly after the publication of *Nymphs of the Valley*, Kahlil visited New York. While he was getting to know the Syrian community there, he was asked to be the godfather of an Orthodox child. Upon learning that the poet was a Maronite, the bishop raised objections as to his spiritual fitness. In the end, however, it was agreed that he could share the honorary parenthood with an Orthodox member, and both men participated in the christening.[9]

Certainly this conciliatory attempt made little impression on a people to whom religious dissension was a way of life, but to Gibran, by then determined to preach the doctrine of brotherhood, the incident confirmed his deepening dream of humanitarianism. Naive and sentimental though his messages seem, he sincerely believed that the readers of *al-Mohajer* needed a spokesman who could say with conviction, "For the earth in its all is my land. . . . And all mankind my countrymen." [10] He firmly believed he was destined to be that spokesman.

As he identified increasingly with his own ethnic roots, Kahlil, who four months before her marriage had promised Josephine he always would be indebted to her, now deliberately ignored her. She and Lionel had spent a blissful winter in Germany. There she was able to be the complete woman of letters for the first time in her life. She took advantage of her freedom to write a play about the Pied Piper of Hamelin, and she faithfully corresponded with everyone left behind in Boston and Cambridge.

Kahlil answered none of the letters she sent to him. Finally in May 1907 she wrote to Day, asking if he could arrange a letter of introduction to Maeterlinck. But something else was troubling her. "The other thing is: where is Kahlil Gibran? And is he well?—And working? I have written several times to him in the summer, and since, with no reply whatever, which is quite unlike the boy. It would be most kind of you to send me word." [11] Whether Day answered Josephine or not can only be conjectured. However, Kahlil's defiant silence can be interpreted as an act of building a protective shell to hide imagined grievances.

As for Mary, Kahlil did not see her during 1906. When she returned from her European tour that year she brought a partner, Sarah M. Dean, into her school, and for the next six years it was called the Haskell-Dean School. She was quietly pioneering several educational reforms. Concerned with the insular atmosphere of the classroom, she introduced field trips into her curriculum, such as visits to the nearby Massachusetts General Hospital to see X-rays being taken, or to the Boston Navy Yard to inspect its rope factory. She encouraged her girls to develop a kind of student government which they called "self-government meetings." In an even more progressive move she obtained permission from the mothers to teach the revolutionary concept of sex education.

Dr. Richard Cabot and his wife Ella Lyman Cabot were among those who advised Mary in her teaching experiments. Dr. Cabot, who had introduced a social service program to the Massachusetts General Hospital as early as 1905, advised her on her hygiene courses. Ella Cabot, a member of the state board of education, was a prominent ethicist and author of many books, including *Everyday Ethics* (1906). When Mary had first become principal of the school, she had frequently visited this remarkable couple at their Cohasset summer house. There she had studied anatomy with Richard every morning before breakfast and ethics with his wife later in the day.

As far back as her freshman days at Wellesley, Mary had admitted that she was no longer "an orthodox Evangelical Christian." [12] Organized church services still had little appeal for her. However, she remained deeply interested in the moral responsibility of the individual in modern society, and her deep, long-lived friendship with the Cabots greatly influenced her own life. She increasingly devoted more time to preparing "sermons" for her school assemblies. Covering a wide range of moral issues, these talks often specified the importance of honesty, charity, and tolerance in daily life.

Another friend who guided her was Sarah Armstrong, a school principal who had retired to New Hampshire. How dependent she had become on the older woman for support is illustrated in eight rambling letters that she wrote her from Scotland and England in the summer of 1906. This solitary, contemplative pilgrimage, along with Miss Armstrong's inspiration, profoundly changed Mary's attitude toward life and her role as an educator. After years of neglecting spiritual concerns, she was suddenly overwhelmed by the necessity of "religious devotion." She described to Miss Armstrong her spiritual reawakening: ". . . how after a lapse of several prayerless years, I first began once more to turn pretty often to God, and of how gradually . . . I came back to constant thought of Him, so that it was not until a year ago I began to speak of Him to my girls to any extent that could be called acknowledgment of Him." [13]

In October 1906 Sarah Armstrong died unexpectedly. The event shattered Mary's accustomed serenity. She who had so matter-of-factly recorded deaths within her family and at school now succumbed to a deep and prolonged

Charlotte Teller, around the time she met Kahlil. (University of North Carolina Library, Chapel Hill)

depression. She openly mourned this woman for the next two years and, strangest of all, she wrote a series of letters to the deceased in an apparent effort to contact her spirit.[14] Although this obsession did not immediately change her external life, she began gradually to withdraw from her many outside interests—the women's labor union movement, Wellesley activities, and waning family responsibilities. Most of her friends were by now married, and her independent personality rejected any intrusion into their domesticity.

At thirty-four she was at a crossroads of personal development. She was ready for new acquaintances and renewed interests. Her zest for life was restored by an unlikely triumvirate of characters whom she now gathered about her. They included a worldly divorcee trying to succeed as a playwright, a French teacher aspiring to be an actress, and Kahlil, an artist with a vision.

In 1904 Mary had become friendly with Charlotte Teller, then a freelance writer for Hearst publications such as the Chicago *Tribune* and the New York *Journal*. If Mary was intellectually involved with socialism and the women's rights movement, Charlotte—recently separated from her husband—was enjoying the emancipation of an active suffragette. The daughter of James B. Teller, who eventually became attorney general of Colorado, and niece of U.S. Senator Henry Teller, she had gone East in search of fame and fortune. At the University of Chicago she had been the favorite student of John Dewey, who once accused her of hypnotizing her pupils, not teaching them. By 1907 she was becoming known for her articles on contemporary issues and personalities. National magazines—*The Crisis, The Independent, The Arena, Everybody's Magazine*—liked her forthrightness in tackling progressive social movements, whether at Jane Addams's Hull House, in the Colorado labor wars, or in the Chicago sweatshops.

Charlotte's first novel was also published in 1907. *The Cage* was set in the Chicago lumberyards and documented the explosive labor situation in urban America. A reviewer who described its heroine could have applied his words to the author as well: "The right heroine of the new order . . . is slim, pretty, adorable. She has an epic sense of what is happening about her . . . is enchantingly feminine with a new kind of archery fitted better to that life which shall come after The Cage [i.e. "the tyranny of the law"] has been broke." [15]

Charlotte's witty ebullience contrasted with Mary's strange combination of spirituality and pragmatism, but somehow they became close confidantes. Soon she was regaling the high-minded schoolteacher with accounts of her adventures in New York, Washington, and Chicago. Full of breathless malapropisms, her letters about socialist meetings and union rallies veered between "The Perils of Pauline" and the antics of a wacky aunt. The wilder the letters the more Mary welcomed them and took vicarious pleasure from them. Slowly the women's friendship by correspondence strengthened into a much deeper relationship. Charlotte was convinced that the theater needed an emancipated woman playwright to interpret the new society. Mary's role became one of ensuring that she would have the money to support her aspirations, so with this security she tried to settle down and write the Great American Play.

Charlotte's letters did not completely satisfy Mary's yearning to know the world beyond Boston. And so when Emilie Michel, a young French teacher whom she had interviewed in June 1906, arrived at the school that fall, she found another companion.

As for Kahlil, he saw Mary twice in 1907. Their first meeting took place on his birthday, when he was invited to tea and stayed until ten. He brought her a copy of *Nymphs of the Valley*, which he had respectfully inscribed, "With the love of a strong child to Mary Elizabeth Haskell, from Kahlil, January 6, 1907." Although she saved the small volume, she did not bother to record it in her diary. That evening he drew two sketches for her; she called them "The Blessed Seed" and "Love, the Giant." He did not come to the school again until December 7, when she invited him to supper. Afterward he "drew his own picture from the looking glass" on her desk.[16]

Mary was cultivating the friendships of her three romantic figures individually. To each one her stability and receptivity to their ideas represented a refuge. Little is known about Mlle. Michel, but by the beginning of 1908 she was the highest paid and favorite teacher on the Haskell staff. Even so she was restlessly confiding to Mary that she wanted to be an actress. Charlotte, who was forever vowing that "opportunity must come to me and I will await it like a lover," was celebrating the freedom of her divorce, supported mostly by Mary's checks.[17] It was time, Mary realized, to introduce her three protégés to each other.

"They clicked," she later recalled about her first dinner for them. They all drank "porter to sustain us," and Kahlil's first effort to draw Charlotte was well received. "Very good," noted Mary. Girls delighted with picture." [18]

Mary was also engineering another reunion for that week. She had seen Josephine and Lionel Marks a few times since their return from Europe in the fall of 1907, and knowing of Kahlil's previous friendship with Josephine, she thought that his presence would be welcomed at a dinner for them. Kahlil responded cautiously to her invitation for dinner on January 30: "I shall be delighted to come Thursday and meet the Markses. I say 'meet' because I have not seen them as man and wife yet. . . . I too must fulfil an engagement after 7:30 on Thursday. A thousand goodnight from Kahlil." [19]

The evening was not a success. In her diary Mary did not mention his presence, merely noting, "Lionel and Josephine to dine and took me to 'The Great Divide.'" But Josephine, still radiant and now joyously anticipating the birth of her first child, was more candid: "We take a holiday now. . . . Then to dinner with Mary (who has ☾☉☽ there and a rather dissatisfying time with him)." [20]

Never again did Mary arrange an event which would include both Kahlil and Josephine. In fact, her growing involvement with him seemed to preclude further association with the Markses. They began to drift apart, and except for occasional visits from Marion Peabody, Mary completely dropped out of the "Cambridge crowd" to which Lionel and Josephine belonged.

In the space of a week she had observed both a charming and confident Kahlil—of whom Charlotte wrote glowingly, "Kahlil's letter was a poem; he is a boy in spirit, and delicate in all his contours of thought" [21]—and an arrogant young man ill at ease at an unhappy reunion. Four years later he would admit to her that until she had concerned herself with his future he had been too self-centered. "Why didn't I know you at fourteen—or someone like you?" he complained. "I ought to have been painting in oil all these years. I stayed naïf so long—so long after I was a man in writing." Mary replied that she understood that he had refused to study painting formally when he returned

from Lebanon "lest his individuality, his 'genius' be destroyed." Kahlil agreed. "Yes, so it was, but [it was] because that idea had been drilled into me. Mr. Day and the other friends who seemed wonderful people then told me not to study . . . that I would be spoiled."

When he claimed that "no one told him his drawing was bad," she suggested that he "might have been unready to hear" criticism. "Perhaps," he said, and went on to explain that the "whole stress of my environment was not for training but for self admiration. Mr. Day's exhibit of my work in 1904 was the worst thing that ever happened to me. . . . Some really big people actually bought things: Mr. Buxton [Bustin], Mr. Charles Peabody, Mrs. Montgomery Sears—And of course I thought I was big too, and all right." [22]

By 1908 the coddling of his boyish "genius" was beginning to pale. At twenty-five Kahlil was no longer the adolescent prodigy. His innate talent for illustration and decoration was not maturing. He was still timid about using oils and was beginning to realize the necessity of a better understanding of anatomy and a need to work with live models.

162

Left: Self-portrait, pencil, 1908.
(Telfair Academy)

Right: Emilie Michel, ca. 1908.
(Telfair Academy)

Mary—who had recently learned from her partner that Brookline mothers were dropping the school because the headmistress was "opinionated and imposed [her] views on them"—was well aware of her tendency to intrude.[23] Yet she could not resist a worthy cause. Both Kahlil and his career were wallowing, and she was confident that he needed her. On February 2 she wrote to him and suggested that he draw from life at the school at least once a week. She also began actively to solicit critical appraisals from those who saw his work there.

He appeared at a life class four days later. His first model was Emilie Michel, and although his first attempt was "not good of her . . . will try again," both artist and model enjoyed the experience. Mary described their encounter with the pleasure of a voyeur: "Wonderful to see these two; each just what other needs now." When he returned to draw the charming brunette on February 11, she again showed unusual interest in their interaction. "Kahlil and Mlle. again. Result much better. She read French poetry aloud. Exquisite." [24]

163

Sometime during those first two weeks in February Kahlil and Mary reached an understanding about his future. He agreed with her evaluation that his artistic development was stalemated. Furthermore, he gratefully accepted her offer to send him to Paris for at least a year. On February 12 he exultantly wrote Ameen Goryeb about this projected journey and even obliquely referred to the woman who was making it possible.

> Only my sister Marianna knows something about this bit of news which I am going to tell you . . . I am going to Paris, the capital of fine arts, in the late part of the coming spring, and I shall remain there one whole year. The twelve months which I am going to spend in Paris will play an important part in my everyday life, for the time which I will spend in the City of Light will be, with the help of God, the beginning of a new chapter in the story of my life. . . .
>
> I never dreamed of this voyage before, and the thought of it never did enter into my mind, for the expense of the trip would make it impossible for a man like me to undertake such a venture. But heaven, my dear Ameen, has arranged for this trip, without my being aware of it, and opened before me the way to Paris. I shall spend one whole cycle of my life there at the expense of heaven, the source of plenty.
>
> And now, since you have heard my story you will know that my stay in Boston is neither due to my love for this city, nor to my dislike for New York. My being here is due to the presence of a she-angel who is ushering me towards a splendid future and paving for me the path to intellectual and financial success. But it makes no difference whether I am in Boston or in Paris, Almuhager will remain the paradise in which my soul dwells and the stage upon which my heart dances. My trip to Paris will offer me an opportunity to write about things which I cannot find or imagine in this mechanical and commercial country whose skies are replete with clamor and noise. I shall be enlightened by the social studies which I will undertake in the capital of capitals of the world where Rousseau, Lamartine, and Hugo lived; and where the people love art as much as the Americans adore the Almighty Dollar.[25]

Kahlil's direct acknowledgment and thanks for the opportunity Mary was offering him seem to be embodied in a brief note he wrote her sometime during the same month. "And am I to have all of that happiness? A subject worth studying, and some coffee and cigarettes, and the faint song of burning wood? Am I to enjoy all these things while resting under your great wings? This is more than happiness. I am indeed a child of Light—Till Thursday, dear friend." [26]

Mary enjoyed supervising the evening art sessions with Kahlil and Emilie more and more. She offered $100 for two of his drawings, "Dance of Thoughts" and "Fountain of Pain," and one night she invited her sister Louise to watch. Kahlil was becoming the resident entertainer who told stories while he sketched. It was all very reminiscent of his earlier Cambridge perform-

Margarethe Müller, 1908.
(Authors)

ances. Meanwhile, in New York Charlotte learned that he thought her to be "indeed a strangely beautiful woman . . . one of the blessed few to whome is given the joy of looking into the eyes of things." Leaning herself to the occult, she was sympathetic to him and to his theories of reincarnation. "I wrote a little note to Kal'l too as I have meant to all along. I certainly do believe in the re-incarnation: He seems like an early-age brother of mine—as though if I were often with him I might recall actual scenes in those Egyptian times in which I *know* I lived—as I wrote him—I never think of Greeks or Romans with so real a sense of their existence—Nor do I have any Teuton or Anglo Saxon memory. I have: Hungarian (+ Celt)—and French. Some day we will understand these things: I expect to after death—don't you." [27]

Charlotte was somehow able to incorporate "battling wordily the Wall Street fortress" and the revolt of the middle class with "psychic" sessions "in the most scientific sense." Mary, her intellect notwithstanding, was intrigued by this "new Socialism—an actual Socialism of the spirit." [28] She made attempts at divination, which Charlotte always encouraged. Whenever they got together she would insist that Mary analyze handwriting and facial expression or read palms. Often she would forward to her a sample of a new acquaintance's writing to receive a kind of assurance and prediction of the subject's intent. In March Mary's diary began to show that while she was still responsible to her school it no longer challenged her as did the emerging relationships about her.

She began to introduce Kahlil to other friends in her circle. Coincidentally, the first person she brought to Marlborough Street was an old acquaintance of his, Margarethe Müller. He drew her while Mary corrected a manuscript for her. Two weeks later he returned and made a portrait of another of her friends. This time he brought Mary a "little bronze Osiris" sent to him by an acquaintance in Egypt.[29]

His gratitude for her growing attentions had also been shown on March 21. That night he brought her copies of his three published books, inscribing and signing them "Gibran Kahlil Gibran" all in Arabic. In *Music*, which he had not given her in 1905 when it was published, he wrote, "To Mary Elizabeth Haskell, who inspired the muses to fill my soul with songs—With my deep love." In a second copy of *Nymphs of the Valley*, this one covered with a hand-decorated jacket, he referred to her patronage: "To Mary Elizabeth Haskell, who wants to make me closer to the world now through her love and generosity and who wants me to see myself and bring it out to the people." Finally he presented his just-published *Spirits Rebellious*: "With my deep love to Mary Elizabeth Haskell, who has initiated and will initiate life in myself and who gave and will give strength to my wings and who granted and will grant beautiful deeds to my fingers." [30]

Frustrated by her inability to read the books or their dedications, she contented herself the next day by rereading his favorite book, *The Treasure of the Humble*. Four days later an ecstatic letter from him affected her immeasurably. He wrote,

> My soul is intoxicated today. For last night I dreamt of Him who gave the Kingdom of heaven to man. O if I could only describe Him to you: if I could only tell you of the sad joy in His eyes, the bitter sweetness of His lips, the beauty of His large hands, the rough woolen garment, and the bare feet—so delicately veiled with white dust. And it was all so natural and clear. The mist that makes other dreams so dim was not there. I sat near Him and talked to Him as if I had always lived with Him. I do not remember His words—and yet I feel them now as one feels in the morning the impression of the music he heard the night before. I cannot name the place. I do not remember having seen it. But it was somewhere in Syria.
>
> The hunger of my heart today is greater and deeper than all days. I am intoxicated with hunger. My soul is thirsty for that which is lofty and great and beautiful. And yet I cannot write nor draw nor read. I can only sit alone in silence and contemplate the Unseen.[31]

The sequence of events following his gifts, together with this letter, was to trigger an expression of emotion never before recorded by Mary, not even upon Miss Armstrong's death. For the past ten years she had carefully adhered to her philosophy of logic and objectivity in life. But the restraint of her diaries vanished during the last week in March.

On March 27 they visited Mlle. Michel's apartment. The ambience that evening moved Mary to rhapsodize over the French teacher's appearance— "she in tan wrapper, with red velvet stripes"—the "exquisite white wine," and the conversation. Kahlil walked her home from Copley Square to Marlborough Street under "angel tower, bare trees, flushed city sky" and talked about his "previous existences. . . . a life in Chaldea; one in India; a short one in Egypt, dying very young." [32]

Her romantic mood continued the following evening. After dining together they visited the Dalys, now back in Cambridge. Her efforts to capture the spirit that motivated him grew to a crescendo of feeling as she revealed herself and the artist:

> I never felt him so vividly before. But much more vividly on Sat. when he dined here. He spoke of his sense of being a divinity, his incarnation of a being and his work which he did not describe and of which he said he had not much spoken. He could hardly speak at all: it was his soul's secret—what keeps him from spoiling as a lion—I felt he was safe to be unspotted by slow stain while that vision is his and it is of his essence. . . .
>
> Kahlil is quietly and calmly usurping a place in my thoughts and consciousness and my dreams—at times more vividly than even Charlotte, who is constant background in all my life. It is only by *slow* degrees that I have come to feel a sense of companionship with him in little ordinary details, jokes, etc.—as in the big ones—and he has learned to talk of other than "winged things" though the latter remain his chief joy—consisting chiefly in his visions or one interchange of philosophy.[33]

Her allusion to "one interchange of philosophy" is clarified in a letter of Kahlil's dated April 2. First he wrote about his productive days, calling them dearer than the "pearls of the sea" and vowing that "I will not permit the tide to carry them back to the silent depth. Have you not heard of the tribe in Arabia that once worshipped a huge white pearl as a symbol of the soul?" He went on to reveal his awareness of Buddha's teaching: "I am waiting for that word even as Sakyia Muni waited for the descent of wisdom to India." [34]

Although Mary admittedly was more and more taken with Kahlil, she was encouraging him to meet regularly with Mlle. Michel. He had access to the Chestnut Street studio of the young artist Leslie Thompson, and Emilie may have sat for him there. The two were plainly falling in love. By now he had met all of Mary's relatives in the Boston area, as well as most of her local friends. But his portraits of them which she commissioned did not exhilarate her as much as seeing him and Emilie together. "*April 17.* To Micheline's. She

167

and Kahlil dined, he early to Royals [Rüyls], she till home in cab at 11:30. Exquisite." [35] Following this typical evening "Mademoiselle" became known as Micheline. Hereafter this musical name which so suited her loveliness would be used by the Marlborough Street habituées.

On Sunday, April 26, the day after he had finally drawn Mary at Thompson's studio "with half success," Kahlil introduced his sister to her. Marianna came with him to the school for supper. The headmistress, who anglicized her name to Mary, wrote, "She is dear." And in an effort to point to something they held in common, she added, "Knows Thayers, Fays etc. for whom has worked at Miss ——'s." [36]

In light of Kahlil's constant exposure to Mary's relatives, and now his final and unprecedented sharing of his own family with her, how did he view his relationship with this older woman? Several letters make it clear that he looked to her as a dependent son toward a giving mother. In one he asked, "Do you know what it is to feel like a found child? . . . Perhaps someday I will be able to bring to you the flowers and the fruit of your motherly love and tenderness. Today my hands are empty." And in another, "I work with desire much like that of a lost child for his mother. I believe now that the desire of revealing the *Self* is stronger than all hungers and deeper than any thirst." [37]

In turn Mary nurtured the interplay between him and Micheline. In May her comments reflected a candidness and openness on the part of all three who were involved in the infatuation. One night after dinner he confided some of his life's most vivid experiences: "K's becalming in boat on lake into the night . . . the woman who left him letters etc. while student." Mary and he also made a "compact about visiting from next life if possible," and he gave her some photos of those Boston days when Day had made him a sheik.[38]

Three days later Mary invited Micheline to dinner. Because they talked until one Micheline spent the night. On the following Sunday Mary summarized the conversation. For the first time she needed a larger notebook, and she continued to use this expanded format whenever a passage about Kahlil or his work demanded it.

> Micheline came to dinner. We spoke French, because the servants are always about and we always talk of Kahlil; and they will think us both mad on the subject if they hear us say "He" any more. For if it is not Kahlil it is still "He" with Micheline, who so inevitably holds the hearts of men—and the servants would fail to distinguish.
>
> She told me of his depression because his former friend and professor at Beyrout has called him a "false prophet". . . .
>
> Micheline: "Did he find fault with your style, Kahlil, with your words or music?" K: "No, No! they said that was beautiful." Micheline: "Then they found fault with your ideas?" K: "Yes." Micheline: "Oh! I'm so glad! I'm so

glad!" K: "Are you glad to have me called a false prophet?" Micheline: "O yes, Kahlil! If they had called your poetry bad I should have been sorry—but if your ideas were any good that's just what I should expect. You can't expect people to accept your ideas—That is asking more than people can give. . . .

"That boy is so easily hurt [continued Micheline] . . . and I want to prepare him if I can for some of what he must meet in the world. Here he is surrounded by love. He has near friends. But he will not always find people to love him this way—tenderly and truly and for himself. They will love him for what they can get out of him. He has many illusions—and they are very beautiful. But they cannot last. Life will crush them—and then I tremble for him. He will suffer so—and what may he not lose with his illusions?

"K. has many sides. He has a very strong side—and a side not so strong. He thinks he is invulnerable—and I would not try to undeceive him, because that belief lends him strength. But he is vulnerable. He is very much influenced by the atmosphere around him—and that student life in Paris is terrible. It breaks the health of some strong men—and what will it do with him? He is not strong, and that life can burn him up.

"We have talked frankly about the changes that may come. Two years—one year—from now, there may be only a memory between us. But I have said to him, 'Kahlil, there is one thing I want you to keep about Micheline. You may forget everything else, but remember, that I give you my affection because you merit it. Guard those qualities that were worthy of Micheline's heart, so that in the future you may merit the hearts of other women.'

"He is getting clever. At first when I used to tease he never knew quite how to take it, and I had to be so careful not to hurt him. But now that he knows he has nothing to fear, he mocks me and plays too and sometimes he's just as cute as I am. I say, 'O Kahlil, you're getting clever.' And he says, 'Am I not clever? Have I not always been clever?' 'O yes indeed!' I say. 'You've always been very clever.' And then we laugh." [39]

Two days later Mary had Marion Peabody to dinner. Perhaps the strained silence which Mary described was due to the fact that she was closely questioning Marion about Kahlil and Josephine. What Marion did reveal about him as a very young man, Mary noted in her supplementary book: "Marion Peabody told me on Thursday that before he went back to Syria he was the most beautiful boy she had ever seen. He was Mr. Day's model—and in one picture especially, in which he wore just a tiger skin, he was lovely beyond words. She and Josephine knew him then, tho' he did not then use to come to their house." [40]

She thrived on the excitement of that busy period. On Saturday she and Kahlil went to see *Countess Coquette* and then he stayed at Marlborough Street until one in the morning. They decided that she was to be his business

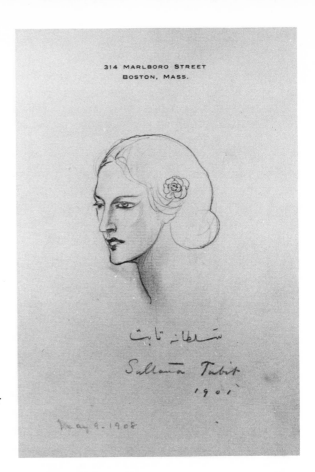

سلطانة تابت

Sultana Tabit

1901

May 9. 1908

Sultana Tabit, as Kahlil recalled her
in 1908. (Telfair Academy)

agent while he was in Paris. "He will send his pictures here and I am to sell
them or not, as I see fit and he suggests." Then she spoke of her inability to
recall the faces that she loved best. "He seemed moved and presently said: 'I
will tell you something in my life . . . that will remain with you.'" The
following story that he told "simply, gently, softly" was of his school days in
Lebanon and a woman he had known named Sultana Tabit. She was "a widow
of twenty-two . . . beautiful, accomplished, poetic, charming. She seemed
wonderful to him. He thought much about her. Four months they knew each
other. They exchanged books and notes with them. Her notes were brief, to
the point, cool, impersonal. Then she died. Her friend sent for Kahlil and gave
him, unopened, a silken scarf, some bits of jewelry, and a packet of seventeen
letters, sealed and addressed to him by the dead woman. Those were love
letters—tender, near-beautiful. 'And cannot you imagine what a sorrow that
was to me? What a pity? Why did she not send them before? It was many
many months before that ceased to fill my mind.'"

When Mary asked him to draw a picture from memory of Sultana, he did,
saying that her eyes were the longest he had ever seen and that he had "got
them well when it was done. . . . I'd like to put in a white rose just above the
ear—she used to wear one."

He mentioned how uncomfortable the American collar and tie made him

170

feel. "In America everyone has to wear certain things—but at home I never wear one." "Take them off," Mary suggested. "I'd like to see you without them." "Yes I'm glad to," he responded. His appearance moved her to write,

> I hope I shall always remember the simple and shadowy beauty which no picture will ever convey—The boy still tender in the man—with shirt turned in and coat still on. . . . There is a rapt, spiritual quality about him when he is released in mind. . . . These things are apparent whenever he is happily at work and conscious that love is about him—But the bared neck and throat brought out all the warmth and glow of them. His eyes have the longest silkiest lashes I have ever seen—and a sudden scoop in the lower lid when opened which he has not yet got into any of his pictures of himself. They are truly like stars reflected in deep water—so radiantly soft in quality. His face changes like the shadows of leaves—with every thought or feeling. I have seen it redden, contract, grow drawn, and unfold like a broad beam of light, all within a few moments. It is a study in living beauty.[41]

They talked about his settling in a studio in Paris, and the possibility of his going to Italy. Then she urged him to do a portrait from memory of Micheline. But he failed.

All during May Kahlil and Micheline were obviously experiencing the pain and pleasure of being in love, and Mary benevolently approved. "*May 19.* (M + K hard time, both sobbing broken heartedly). . . . *May 21.* All well for K + M. . . . *May 30.* Micheline till 4 gloriously happy. . . . *June 1.* K to dine and talk with two finished pictures. Talked of Micheline, of death, etc." [42]

That death still pursued him is evident from the Arabic poem, "Death Beautiful," he brought to Mary on May 14. Together they worked on an English version of it. Mary had helped other friends with translations and manuscripts, but this was the first time she had collaborated with Kahlil, and the shaky result was full of alternative phrases and ambivalences. It bore little resemblance to the English translation made some years later, in which he beheld "Death's bride standing as a pillar of light" between his "bed and the void." [43] However, it was the beginning of a new and enduring commitment, and he dedicated the version published that spring in *al-Mohajer* to "MEH."

In June Mary was busily arranging last-minute details for his trip to Paris, as well as her own, for she and her father also were looking forward to a European adventure that summer. Micheline, too, was booking passage to France to see her parents. When Kahlil came to the school for a final dinner on June 9, the farewells were not prolonged. He left his portfolio with Mary, and knowing they all would meet soon in Paris, they said good-bye.

The next day Mary left for the South and her sister Marion's wedding. Kahlil waited in Boston until June 25. While he prepared for his journey he remembered to write his old friend and mentor who was slowly disappearing from the Boston art world. Fred Holland Day was no longer an influence on him, but his letter to him was written out of respect for the life they had once known. "I leave Boston on the twenty fifth of this month, dear Brother. My steamer sails on the first of July from New York. I hope I will be able to see you before entering into the 'New Life.' I have so many things to say and so many questions to ask: and you, dear Brother, who first opened the eyes of my childhood to light, will give wings to my manhood. I hope we will meet before the sea calls me. But if it is not possible, just send your blessings to your little brother. Kahlil." [44]

The studio of Marcel-Béronneau, 1909. The bearded man standing at the left is probably the artist; Kahlil is in the front row, second from left. (Madeleine Vanderpool)

IO

Le Jeune Ecrivain Arabe

Kahlil sailed from New York on July 1, 1908. Although he claimed that he had "no zest for travelling alone," he also had boasted to Mary about his earlier voyages, particularly the one on which he had made "three hundred friends on the way to America. . . . People just come to me—I do nothing first." [1] Micheline's perception that he was susceptible to prestigious social surroundings was correct. He could not resist the good company which he now encountered on the *Rotterdam*. Whenever people responded to his pleasant looks and charm, he welcomed their attentions.

Still "between the infinite depth and the infinite hight, the sea and the sky," he sat down a few hours before the boat docked and described his trip to Mary.

"The ocean and the heaven were good friends, and I enjoyed them both. . . . I made many studies of fine faces during the journey. The most beautiful woman on the steamer is a Greek born in France. She knows Micheline very well. I made a drawing of her head. . . . She is sad and thoughtful; that, of course, adds something to her beauty." [2]

Mary and her father were by this time "doing" Ireland with great dispatch. On July 13 they sailed to England. The same day Kahlil, finally settled into "the heart of the world," wrote of how Micheline had helped him find a temporary fifth-floor room on the Avenue Carnot. He admitted to Mary his dependence upon his young French friend and how he would miss her when she left to visit her family in Nevers. "But if she is going to find herself on the stage, as I am finding myself in Paris, then it is all well and good—She must not stay and I must not ask her to stay." [3]

Micheline also assured Mary that all was well, in a letter that became a spirited joint effort. It began with her salutation, "Mary dear, Dear Mary, Kahlil is here with me looking very fine! He has just shaved!!!" This drolerie

173

"And is there any one who dose not want to know you?" asked Kahlil at the end of the joint letter, dated "samedi soir," July 1908. (University of North Carolina Library, Chapel Hill)

was interrupted by him: "And yet he is serious and his soul dwells in an unknown island." Another friend joined in in French, and then Micheline begged Mary to hurry to Paris and share their joie de vivre.

By the end of July this ebullience had not faded. Kahlil had moved to Montparnasse where he found a small studio at 14 Avenue du Maine, and he was even learning how to prepare his own meals there. More important, he enrolled in an art school, the famous Academy Julian, where he worked every afternoon. He wrote Mary, "I have already seen the two sides of Paris, the beautiful and the ugly. I am here to study both sides so that I may understand Life and Death. Yes, the spirit of decay is stealing it's way through this wonderful city: but we are apt to forget the existence of a hideous worm in the heart of a lovely apple. . . .

"My heart is full of wingged things: I shall keep them there untill you come." [4] In choosing the same winged symbol with which he had signed the communal letter, he began a custom he would follow intermittently for the next sixteen years. Mary had already noticed his passion for "winged things," although she failed to remark that other poets, including Josephine (who had often signed her letters "Wings" or with a winged sign), shared the same obsession.

When he saw Mary on July 31 and again four days later, he had little time to reveal his philosophical flights. Her anticipated arrival was somewhat of a letdown, for she became so involved with sightseeing and meeting old friends that she had no opportunity to stroll quietly through the streets with him as he had romantically envisioned. On August 4, the last morning of her stay, she and her father went to the Avenue du Maine and saw him at home, but she recorded the visit merely as one of the day's several activities.

Her rather obvious neglect of her protégé was understandable in the press of travel. Still, Kahlil, who always expressed a wistful awe of the entire Haskell clan, probably felt rejected. Whenever he saw her away from school, phalanxed by a distinguished father and other admirers, the growing rapport that he felt vanished. For Mary, too, the reunion was uncomfortable. The differences in their background and culture became irreconcilably magnified when observed by the people with whom she belonged.

Kahlil's creative life seemed to thrive on the very set of alienating circumstances that dogged his personal life. He had been in Paris only a brief time when his recently published *Spirits Rebellious* received much attention and solidified his position in American-Arab letters. The book was a collection of four narratives that had originally appeared in *al-Mohajer*.[5]

Like the tales in *Nymphs of the Valley*, they dealt with the oppressive social conditions in Lebanon. This time, however, Gibran fashioned different fates for his rebellious heroes and heroines. In "Wardé Al-Hani" a married woman abandoned her wealthy husband for "a youth who walked the highway of life alone and who dwelt alone among his books and papers." Unlike Martha, who paid with her life when she defied convention, Wardé openly expressed her emancipation from the "corrupt laws" of man. Not only did her act allow her happiness but she could proclaim, "Woe to them who would judge and weigh! I was a harlot and a faithless woman in the house of Rashid Nu'man because he made me the sharer of his bed by virtue of tradition and custom. . . . But now I am pure and clean, for the law of love has set me free."

Similarly, a triumphant fate was created for the hero of "Khalil the Heretic." Instead of suffering madness as did his prototype Yuhanna, Khalil when maltreated by monks retaliated with leadership and strength. The villagers heeded his exhortation and staged a bloodless revolution against the usurpers of clerical and political power. The utopian community that the evangelical hero created was the embodiment of Gibran's own desire for recognition. Somehow he saw himself as a reformer who through the authority of his words could show the path toward justice and liberty.

In the third story, "The Bridal Couch," a desperate bride slew her lover and herself on the night of her forced marriage to a man she never loved. But even these bloody consequences were not treated as a defeat. As the dying bride challenged a frantic wedding guest, the deaths became synonymous with release. "You shall not come near us, reproachful ones, neither shall you separate us lest the spirit hovering above your heads seize you by the throat and put an end to you. Let this hungry earth consume our bodies in one mouthful. Let it conceal and protect us within its heart."

Gibran recalled the brutal and ruthless injustice of nineteenth-century Lebanon in his fourth and most powerful allegory. The narrator in "The Cry of the Graves" observed a malevolent "ameer"—reminiscent of Emir Bashir II—sentence to death three prisoners. As the background of each criminal was revealed, the crimes were shown to be society's responsibility. The murderer condemned to be decapitated was a man who had protected a woman's honor by killing a lustful tax collector; the adultress destined to be stoned was revealed as a woman wrongfully accused; the thief sent to the gallows was a poor farmer who had snatched two sacks of flour from the monks' swollen granaries. The unfortunate trio was executed and left for carrion. Later they were surreptitiously buried and above their graves were placed a sheathed sword, flowers, and a cross—symbols of man's salvation by courage, love, and the "words of the Nazarene."

In evaluating the inequities of crime and punishment, Gibran, who had grown up believing that his father was unjustly accused by corrupt authorities, vehemently challenged the law. "What is the law? Who has seen it descend with the sunlight from the heavens? . . . In what age have angels walked among men, saying: 'Deny to the weak the light of existence and destroy the fallen with the edge of the sword and trample upon the sinner with feet of iron'?" But throughout these stories his hope of spiritual reform remained constant.

Years later he mused with Mary about the black period when *Spirits Rebellious* was written. "At that time life was full of terrible things for me. It seemed as if everything was piled up—illness and death and loss—and things that don't seem part of the inevitable lot of man—but just extra—I'm thankful for all of it. I'm on my knees a thousand times with gratitude. But that doesn't change the fact that it was hard." [6]

Early in 1908 Ameen Goryeb wrote a long and almost apologetic introduction to the book in order to justify its "new ideas" and aims of "social philosophy." Describing Gibran as a person who "heard and saw complaints and was affected and then complained," the publisher defended the morality of the iconoclastic characters: "Everyone has the right to search for what he sees as his happiness as long as he doesn't harm others." One must not forget that Gibran's audience was barely conscious of individualism in social and moral conduct. Already he had received criticism from members of the Maronite clergy who challenged as exaggerated and distorted the clerical posture implicit in "The Bridal Couch." "It is hard for the youth of our days," Goryeb reminded his readers, "to understand the oppression of priests in the older nations and that this still flourishes in the twentieth century." He closed by summarizing the aims of his twenty-five-year-old author: "This book is the second wall of the house which Gibran is building. The writer combines knowledge of Lebanon with work in the United States and the thought of a philosopher. He tries to depict and contrast the feelings of different classes of people—from the poor to the princely—from atheist to the priest." The introduction pleased Gibran "because it was free from personal comment." [7]

In March Kahlil sent word of himself to a cousin living in Brazil. His intense craving for personal recognition, and his awareness of and receptivity to any controversy that would make him better known, obviously dominated his thoughts.

> I feel that the fires that feed the affection within me would like to dress themselves with ink and paper, but I am not sure whether the Arabic-speaking world would remain as friendly to me as it has been in the past three years. I say this because the apparition of enmity has already appeared. The people in Syria are calling me heretic, and the intelligentsia in Egypt villifies me, saying, "he is the enemy of just laws, of family ties, and of old traditions." Those writers are telling the truth, because I do not love man-made laws and I abhor the traditions that our ancestors left us. This hatred is the fruit of my love for the sacred and spiritual kindness which should be the source of every law upon the earth, for kindness is the shadow of God in man. I know that the principals upon which I base my writings are echoes of the spirit of the great majority of the people of the world, because the tendency toward a spiritual independence is to our life as the heart is to the body. . . . Will my teaching ever be received by the Arab world or will it die away and disappear like a shadow?[8]

Later he charged Goryeb, who was traveling in the Middle East, with publicizing his name there. "But tell me, Ameen, did you mention my name when you met with the intelligentsia of Lebanon and Egypt?" He went on to interpret an unfavorable review of "Wardé Al-Hani" as an encouraging sign: "I was well pleased with the criticism because I feel that such persecution is a diet for new principles, especially when it comes from a learned man like [Lufti] al-Manfaluti." [9]

Spirits Rebellious was dedicated "To the spirit that did embrace my spirit. To the heart that did pour out its secrets into my heart. To the hand that did kindle the flame of my love." From the specific past tense, which eliminates Mary and Micheline, one can only wonder whether Gibran was secretly acknowledging Josephine's earlier influence. Also appearing in the book was the first illustration he made for any of his Arabic books, a pen-and-ink self-portrait. The mustachioed full-face view of the artist as he conceived of himself was robust and appealing. Resembling the expression and posture that Fred Holland Day had caught in an early photograph, it was not only a tribute to his old mentor but also a clear indication of his need to discover new sources and influences.

﴿ جبران خليل جبران ﴾

Self-portrait in
Spirits Rebellious.

He admitted to Mary his own lack of training. "You know that when I came to Paris I practicly knew nothing of the technical side of painting. I did things instinctively without knowing how or why. I was in darkness, and now I feel that I am walking in twilight towards light." [10] His choice of the Academy Julian was natural. Its late director, Rudolph Julian, had long lured Bostonians and others to the popular atelier on the Rue du Cherche-Midi. Lilla Cabot Perry, Edmund Tarbell, and Maurice Prendergast had studied there, and several symbolist-influenced painters including Maurice Denis, Paul Sérusier, and the Nabis Pierre Bonnard and Edouard Vuillard had been associated with it. But by the fall he was becoming reluctant to discuss his progress there except in general terms. "I am painting, or I am learning how to paint. It will take me a long time to paint as I want to, but it is so beautiful to feel the growth of one's own vision of things. There are times when I leave work with the feelings of a child who is put to bed rather early. Do you not remember . . . my telling you that I understand people and things through my sense of

Day's photograph of Kahlil.
(Madeleine Vanderpool)

hearing and that *sound* comes first to my soul? Now . . . I am beginning to understand things and people through my eyes."[11]

By November the luster of Paris was wearing off and he was feeling both homesick and uncertain about his art. "When I am unhappy, dear Mary, I read your letters. When the mist overwhelms the "I" in me, I take two or three letters out of the little box and reread them. . . . And now I am wrestling with colour: the strife is terrible and beautiful—surely one of us must triumph! I can almost hear you saying 'and what about drawing Kahlil'? . . . The professors in the academy are always saying to me 'do not make the model more beautiful than she is.' And my soul is always whispering 'O if you could only paint the model as beautiful as she *realy* is.' "[12]

He had also been ill and had recuperated with some Syrian friends, the Rahaims, in the suburb Le Raincy, which was "like a great garden divided into little gardens by narrow paths"; the red tiled roofs were "like a handfull of corals scattered on a piece of green velvet." He gratefully promised that he

179

would make a portrait of Hasiba Rahaim, "the noble Syrian lady" who had nursed him.[13]

Something else was bothering him, and he wanted Mary to feel he was worthy of her largesse:

> And now while I am in perfect helth, both physically and mentally, I wish to say that the few pictures and drawings which you have now, are all yours if I should die sudenly here in Paris. . . . I also wish to say that all the pictures and studies found after my death in my studio here in Paris are yours, and that you are free to do whatever you wish with them.
>
> The above statement, dear Mary, is not well worded but it expresses my wishes and my feelings. I hope I will be able to live long and be able to do somethings that are realy worthy of giving to you who is giving so much to me. I hope that the day will come when I shall be able to say "I became an artist through Mary Haskell." [14]

This bequest was made at a time when no other of his admirers sustained him. Micheline had returned to the States. That September, before she left Boston to assault the New York stage, she had seen Mary every day. On her last day in Boston the two looked through Kahlil's portfolio, but the closeness between him and the French teacher was beginning to fade. The strongest bond between them remained Mary, who continued to support him in Paris and began to send checks to Micheline in New York.

Kahlil also depended on Mary as a link between himself and Marianna, who was not adjusting to his absence. Mary recorded, "*November 20. Marianna Gibran found me in at 7:10 when she came to supper. She is almost ill for sheer loneliness since Kahlil left. Has had pleurisy, but is better now. Working with Miss Teahan again. Shall she visit her father? November 27. Long letter to Kahlil about what to do for Marianna. Keep her here or send to Syria on a visit.*" [15]

Lonely and depressed by the Paris damp and chill, he panicked when he received this word of his sister. "I am so very anxious about my sister. I think of nothing ells but her. She must be very ill. I dream such dreadful dreams of her. She appears to me so thin and so pale. . . . Is she very ill dear Mary? Is she dead? Will you not tell me something about her? . . . I am working as before. I work with the same feeling of one who talks in his sleep."

The crisis that he imagined did not exist. In charging Mary with watching over Marianna, he had neglected to confide that his sister was illiterate and that it was difficult for her to transmit through others the pain of being left alone. But by mid-December she had found a suitable Arabic scribe to send her brother direct word of herself, and his relief was immediate. "Few days ago I had a letter from my sister. She said nothing about her health but I gathered that she is not ill; and I feel less anxious about her than I did before.

You have no idea, beloved friend, how unhappy I feel whenever I think of her as a sick child. She, beside being a good sister, is a very near friend. We suffered so much together." [16]

The new year brought new involvements for Kahlil. He had discovered a new teacher, Pierre Marcel-Béronneau, whose methods he found more sympathetic than those at the Academy Julian. Béronneau was a visionary painter and disciple of Gustave Moreau. "He is a great artist and a wonderful painter—and a mystic. The State has bought many of his pictures: and he is known in the artistic world as 'The Painter of Salomé'. . . . I took one or two little things to show him the other day. He looked at them for a long time; and after saying few encouraging words about them, he gave me a long personal talk. He said "You must forget yourself for the time being—Do not try to give an expression to your thoughts and ideas *Now*. Wait until you have gone through the *Dictionary* of painting." In February he announced, "I am working now with Berinau [sic] only, and I have stopped working at the Julian. It is useless to divide myself between two defrent schools. M. Berinau has a smal class of 10 or 12 people. We have sometimes the nude and sometimes the draped figure. M. Berineu works with us. He wants me to see everything in values and not in lines. He said he likes my work because I am not trying to be a *small Berinau* like the others." [17]

Always practical, Mary was concerned over his peremptory dropping of the Academy Julian and over the possible loss of his tuition fees. "Make no long engagement ahead with Berinau as you did with Julian. We never know . . . when the moment may arrive when we shall . . . have learned our lesson that it lies in him to teach." "I did not leave Julian," Kahlil explained, "untill the three months term was finished, so the school owes me nothing. And as to Berinau, I pay him about fifty francs a month and so much for colours and canvases and other things. But I am paying this out of the 375 francs without any difficulties at all. So I really do not need more." [18]

Throughout this period his contact with the Arabic literary world was flourishing. On February 13 *al-Mohajer* printed a prose poem, beginning "On this day my mother bore me. . . . On this day the silence put me in the hands of this existence," which he had written the year before on the occasion of his twenty-fifth birthday. Obviously the opening lines were in his mind as he sent Mary a birthday greeting on January 6, 1909. This message, with its languid death wish from Keats, reveals in English the substance of the longer Arabic poem.

On this same day twenty-six years ago I was born.

I have already made twenty-six journeys around the Sun—and I do not know how many times the Moon has journeyed around me—and yet I do not understand the mystery of Light.

181

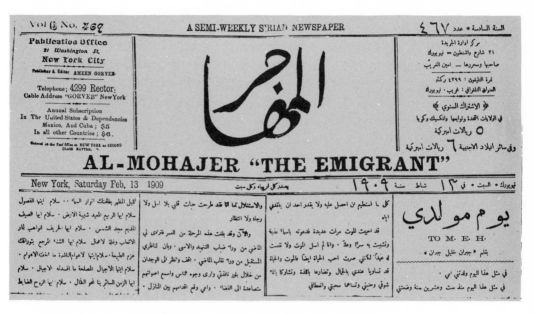

The beginning of the birthday poem to Mary, lower right.
(University of North Carolina Library, Chapel Hill)

During the twenty-six years—

"Many a time
I have been half in love with easeful Death,
Call'd him soft names in [many] a mused rhyme."

And now, dear Mary, I have not outgrown my love for Death, but I am half in love with Life. Life and Death has become equally beautiful to me. And I am beginning to look upon each day as a birthday.[19]

Pleased with this letter, Mary was even more thrilled when she saw the poem printed in *al-Mohajer*. Below the indecipherable Arabic words she was able to read the dedicatory letters *MEH*, which Kahlil had saved for her to discover: "I am sending you a prose-poem "On my birthday" which I wrote thinking of you. The soul of this poem is yours. The body belongs to other peoples of other land and of deferent language. It was published in New York and then copied by many other Arabic papers and magazines. Alas, beloved friend, I can only send you silent poetry, dumb music, veiled thoughts." And she relayed the happiness and faith given to her by the words she could not read: "I loved the poem you sent me—loved it eyeless and earless so to speak. I am like a German having faith in Keats!"[20]

The tempo of Kahlil's life was accelerating, and he was no longer so alone in a cold and alien city. He even met Auguste Rodin, once in the sculptor's studio and later briefly at an exhibition.

> I had the great pleasure of meeting Auguste Rodin the greatest sculptor of modern time, in his own studio. . . . He was indeed very kind to me and to the friend who took me to him. He showed us many wonderful things both in marble and in plaster. . . . I am sure, that you remember my telling you once of an Arab who went to Italy from the desert and saw the work of Michel-Angelo and was so moved by its power that he wrote a beautiful poem called "The Smiling Marble". When I came home from Rodin's studio I had the same feeling of that Arab, and I too wrote a sonnet on "Man the Creator". . . .
>
> April is a month of Salons and Exhibitions in Paris. One of the great Salons was open few days ago and of course I went to see it. (All the Artists of Paris were there looking with hungry eyes on the shadows of Souls of Men). . . . Great Rodin was there. He recognized me and spoke to me about the work of a Russian sculptor, saying, "This man understands the beauty of form." I would have given anything to have that Russian hear what the great master said of his work. A word from Rodin [is] worth great deal to an artist.[21]

Encouraged by his assimilation into the Paris milieu and aware of her promised role as a business agent, Mary was working on a plan to promote his work by means of a second showing at the Tau Zeta Epsilon society at Wellesley College. For help she naturally turned to Margarethe Müller who had shown his drawings there six years before. "I hope you will only let her take the few best ones," Kahlil cautioned Mary. "I mean those that are less imperfect!"[22]

Unfortunately, by the time of the show Mary was too preoccupied to worry about its details except for arranging the delivery of the works. Within one week in April both the two-year-old son of Reginald and Louise Daly and Reginald's mother died. Suddenly her outside activities were curtailed, and a few weeks later she decided to accompany the Dalys to Hawaii where Reginald would carry out geological field studies and Louise would hopefully recover from the loss of her only child.

A review in the college newspaper is the chief record of how Kahlil's second show at Wellesley was received:

> The exhibition of Mr. Kahhl Gilran's [sic] studies . . . was one of peculiar interest. The color studies were nearly all uniform . . . purple of evening shadows shading into green and lit with tiny yellows of isolated flowers. There is one picture which differed somewhat in spirit—a slight woman's figure in an orchard of blossoming apple trees. . . . The other studies were

"Souls of Men Flying before the Face
of the Inevitable," shown at Wellesley
College in 1909. (Photo Juley)

pessimistic and almost Gothic in their weird expression of pessimism. . . . .
The "Souls of Men Flying before the Face of the Inevitable" was one of
the most curious of the compositions. . . . The "Inevitable" is a huge gray
head, before whose expressionless, sightless face a flock of tiny white birds
are borne irresistibly. The contrast of the might of eternal laws and the
puny weakness of human effort is one on which he delights to dwell.
Usually the Immortal is represented by a huge figure, and the mortal by a
pygmy. . . . The characteristic of his treatment of the human form in the
color work is truth with the greatest simplicity; it is almost pure outline
work and yet the impression is rounded softness. The imaginary portraits
are interesting . . . they are still romantic but with Pre-Raphaelite rather
than Gothic romanticism. . . . The "Lost Mind" was the one most talked
of on account of its horror: a face without a mind, more vaguely suggestive
than idiocy, more haunting than madness. This face was also remarkable
for the delicacy of treatment about the eyes rendered with the utmost
simplicity. Of course the college was particularly interested in the portrait
of Fraulein Müller, a piece of work remarkable as a piece of technique but
doubly interesting in its subject.[23]

184

In the summer Charlotte visited Paris, ostensibly to find a French producer interested in her plays. It was when she and Kahlil met during June that a faint rivalry for their lady's sponsorship first surfaced between them. Both reported back to her how hard they were working. Discussing Mary's future, he led Charlotte to believe that he was involved in a whole series of liaisons, as if to deny any selfish interest he might have in what his benefactress would do. These submerged feelings seeped out only gradually to Mary in the next few years. Indeed, Charlotte sent her, now en route to Hawaii, a most optimistic report about Kahlil's progress. "His work shows an immense improvement. He has touched reality and he has learned to draw. His color sense is his own and I feel that his whole nature has matured and strengthened in this year. He is doing a portrait of me for you. No—dear, he does not—no one—loves me as you do, nor do I love anyone as I love you. He cannot understand that which is modern and occidental in me—but we get on beautifully and he will be a fine companion to see the art of Paris." [24]

In trying to please Mary, to show her that those whom she loved could love each other, the two spent much time together. They vacationed for a week at Versailles, and he started a portrait of her but could not finish it because, he complained, "Charlotte has so many ideas and scheams and dreams and she is always running—running—running after her own shadow. Her strong, beautiful soul dose not rest anywhere." [25]

Something else halted his production that June. He received word of the death of his father, who, he wrote, "died in the old house where he was born sixty-five years ago." His father's last two letters had caused him "to weep bitterly" each time he read them. The knowledge that this authoritarian man had "blessed him before the end came" strangely affected Kahlil, who for so many years had ambivalent feelings about his father's strengths and weaknesses. "I cannot but see the dim, sad shadows of the bygone days when he and my mother and my brother and my young sister lived and smiled before the face of the sun. Where are they now? . . . Are they together? . . . I know, dear Mary, that they live. They live a life more real, more beautiful than ours." [26]

In July he again immersed himself in work, and he reassured Mary that it was the most fruitful month of his life as an artist. His work, already cited at two *concours* since he had been at Béronneau's, now received a silver medal. Moreover, he had met up with Joseph Hawaiik, his friend from college days. Although the nephew of the Patriarch had come to Paris to study art, he was far more responsive to the café life of Montparnasse. He recalled Gibran at this time as a man possessed, worried about his reputation, his limited finances, and his self-imposed role as a reformer. Still the two found comfort in each other's personality and goals. "We are both trying to do something," Kahlil wrote, but we do it in two deferent ways. My friend is seeking himself in

Left: Joseph Hawaiik in Paris. (University of North Carolina Library, Chapel Hill)

Right: *The Ages of Women*, oil, 1910. (Authors)

nature, and I am trying to find myself *through* nature." [27] Confused by the aesthetic revolution taking place around them and trying to accept the ideas of the cubists and the colors of the fauves, Kahlil told his friend that they should try to understand everything and choose whatever style they wanted.

He himself was not attracted to the emerging styles but instinctively sought the ideation of the symbolist painters. His greatest treat was to walk with Hawaiik to the Panthéon and admire Puvis de Chavannes's murals *The Life of St. Geneviève*. He remembered his own childhood, when the Puvis murals decorated the new Boston Public Library and the goals of modern art were generally considered to be the translation of emotion and poetry into a picture. He still pursued this ideal, which he told Mary was "being able to give a *good* expression to a beautiful *Idea* or a high *thought*." [28]

He also discovered Eugène Carrière, who had painted in a subtle style with which he identified. "I feel now that the work of Carier [*sic*] is the nearest to my heart. His figures, sitting or standing behind the mist say more to me than anything ells except the work of Lionardo da Vinci. Carier understood faces and hands more than any other painter. . . . And Carier's life is not less beautiful than his work. He suffered so much, but he knew the mystery of pain: he knew that tears make all things shine." But the heyday of Gibran's

186

models in painting was almost over. Puvis and Moreau had died in 1898. By 1906, three years before Gibran discovered his work, Carrière was dead. Nevertheless he committed himself to their atmospheric dream world, to Carrière's "love of the manifestations of Nature" and the "mysterious haze that hung over his painting." [29]

During the fall of 1909 he and Hawaiik were working alone and sharing the costs of models. Gibran had left both Béronneau's atelier and the studio on the Avenue du Maine, where he was never happy because of the cold, and was staying in a hotel. He was finding it difficult to settle down. "I did not go back to Berinau because I feel and my friends feel that I have taken from the man all he can give. I must find someone who works more directly . . . and who is less of a dreamer. . . . I am realy tired of all fantastical lies which people call pleasures. . . . Even the idea of living in a hotel for few days is rather hateful to me." [30]

In November a new studio which had been promised him was still not available, but he was having some luck with new models and was finishing a painting called *The Young Poet*. He had also met Marie Doro, an American actress, and had received permission from her aunt to draw her. He teasingly described her to Mary. "She has a great soul and a clear mind, and she believes she has been in the Orient for many ages. I feel that too. People take us for brother and sister; . . . But Mis Doro dose not feed my heart nor I hers!!! Now you are smiling, my dear Mary; I can see you smiling." [31]

Then the whole world was smiling. Within a month Kahlil was in a Rue du Cherche-Midi studio—high, dry, warm, and light—and he was supplementing Mary's monthly checks with a part-time job teaching drawing and composition to five pupils twice a week for one hundred francs a month. "It is hard work, but I like it because it makes me sure of the few little things I know about art." [32]

He was also about to undertake a far more ambitious project. He had recently drawn the American sculptor Paul Bartlett, whose equestrian *Lafayette* stood before the Louvre and who was working on the allegorical figures that would enhance the New York Public Library. Bartlett's reaction to the portrait was so favorable that he was inspired to begin a "wonderful scheam"—a series of "drawings of the great artists of our time—the pillars of modern art and culture: I only ask thirty minutes from each man. . . . Of course I must have few of the great women like Sarah Bernhardt and Ellen Terry." Included in his list, along with his old favorites Maeterlinck and Rodin, were the dramatist Edmond Rostand and the popular novelist Pierre Loti, "who knows me." [33]

As with Puvis de Chavannes, Loti's popularity was waning, but his delicately rendered *romans de voyage*—described by Henry James as "flowers of reminiscence and imagination"—were still considered to penetrate poignantly the soul of the Middle East.[34] Day had extravagantly praised him as far back as his *Mahogany Tree* days. Loti's immortalization of his Circassian mistress, the sloe-eyed Aziyadé, mirrored Kahlil's interest in the beleaguered Middle Eastern woman. His sorties into the secluded courtyards of Levantine life remained an influence on Kahlil's portrayals of Lebanese women.

Kahlil's growing interest in liberalism in the Middle East went deeper than the superficial romanticism of Loti's writings. After the 1908 revolution of the Young Turks against the Ottoman regime of Abd-al-Hamid II, Paris was alive with small pockets of Lebanese and Syrian dissidents. Secret societies were organized to advance the cause of nationalism and home rule in Ottoman-occupied countries, and among the leaders of the movement was a Lebanese writer who had spent his adult life in Paris. Sukrui Ghanim, chiefly known for his opera *Antar*, combined his poetic writings with political publications. Although Kahlil's association with these nascent groups was peripheral, he was very conscious of them and of Ghanim. A month before Ghanim published his demands for Arabic self-determination, Kahlil was writing Mary about the older writer: "I have a Syrian poet friend. His name is Ganim. He writes bothe Arabic and French. One of his plays hase been given here this winter and it was a great success. He is about fifty years old but the flame of youth is still burning in his soul." [35]

In the same letter he described his growing list of acquaintances, for which Hawaiik was doubtless responsible. Hawaiik's abundant memories of the winter of 1910 include a parade of international students and artists and lend life to Kahlil's colorless statement to Mary: "I have several congenial friends: Syrian and French poets, English and American painters, German and Italian musicians. We meet sometimes in public places, other times in the private houses of good people who like to entertain artists."

The people whom he neglected to describe in detail remained vividly alive for Hawaiik. Forty years later he recalled the Belgian doctor who invited the two Syrians to tour the Pasteur Institute and argued with them about the ascendancy of science over religion. He described the print store where they were befriended by Monsieur Kalmy, its Romanian entrepreneur, and his two nieces Susanne and Leah. In detailing the great January flood of 1910, he pictured the rampaging Seine inundating first-floor studios. He told about sharing his studio with Olga, a Russian student committed to Tolstoy and revolution, and how he and Gibran listened to her play Beethoven sonatas and drank endless cups of tea from her samovar. He portrayed Gibran as a likable young man who was admired by this coterie. Olga presented him with a Russian cap. Leah and Susanne were curious about his love life. But even Hawaiik, who had become close enough to Kahlil to care for him during one of his recurrent illnesses, wondered about his impenetrable qualities.[36]

Gibran's driving ambition, his single-mindedness, left little room for frivolity. The absence of small talk in his letters illustrates this self-absorption. Even after he returned to Boston his conversations about how Paris had affected his life were devoid of specific examples. Only inadvertently did some local color creep into his stories, as when he told Mary about discovering his capacity for wine. "In Paris when I had to give a café party as new students all do, I drank as much as anybody. I was gay—and having a good time. And everyone of the rest was affected; some fell asleep. Some were sick—some were foolish. . . . I didn't feel it then—and next day I was fresh and ready for work as ever in my life." [37]

One of the most vivid scenes he recalled concerned the official Maronite attitude toward his works. Although after his death commentators exaggerated clerical disapproval of *Spirits Rebellious* to include his excommunication and book burning, his version of an unpleasant exchange between himself and a bishop more accurately reflected how heretical his books were considered to be.

> *Spirits Rebellious*, published while K. was in Paris, was suppressed by the Syrian government—only 200 copies got into Syria, secretly. Long since, of

course, it has entered—and the edition has been exhausted. But the church considered excommunicating K. Practically he was excommunicated but the sentence was never actually pronounced. . . . When the two representatives of the Patriarch, however, came to Paris they invited K. with other Syrians—and when he came to take leave asked him to stay and dine alone with them. He did not want to—but urged, he stayed. One bishop had a sense of humor—the other none. Humorous, I believe, was kin to K.

Non-humorous took him aside: "You have made a grave mistake—are making a grave mistake. Your gifts you are using against your people, against your country, against your church. The holy Patriarch realizes this. But he does not condemn you. He sends you a special message and loving offer of friendship. . . . And now—seek out every copy of the book—destroy them all—and let me take word from you back to Syria and the Church and to the holy Patriarch."

Then K. let himself go—furiously and with intent. He told his Holiness he had heard all that had been said, before it was uttered. Nothing in it had surprised him. Far from "returning," he was working then on a book to be called *Broken Wings*. He hoped his Holiness would read it—he hoped the holy Patriarch would read it. . . . They would see in it how entirely he disagreed with them and how he was advancing as he had begun. And he said Goodnight—did not stay for dinner.

As he passed through the outer room where the reception was still not over . . . the humorous bishop said, "Well, Effendi, have you had a good talk with his Highness"? . . . "Yes, your grace," said K., "delightful. But I am only sorry I was not able to convince him." The bishop laughed. He understood the case was hopeless. The others all understood too—that there had been a battle. The story was told—and became a current anecdote.[38]

Whether Gibran was completely candid about all the details of his verbal duel (were his antagonists really bishops? was he the only one invited to dinner?), it was true that he was receiving attention. By the spring of 1910 he was able to give Mary more concrete evidence of his progress in Paris. First, the Société Nationale des Beaux-Arts accepted the painting *Autumn* for its spring exhibit. "I never saw such a crowd in my life, nor . . . such enthusiasm," he wrote of the Salon.[39] Hawaiik's recollection is more subdued, but it is true that the reception was so large that Kahlil felt lost in the press of artists and critics. Worst of all, his painting looked dwarfed and he was dissatisfied with its location. Possibly for that reason he wrote Mary afterward that it no longer pleased him.

The second achievement was that Mary finally would be able to read a published story by him. "I have some more news, Some publishers, here in Paris, are publishing, now, a book in several volumns, containing the famous short stories by modern writers of all the living languages—To my surprise I

Autumn, oil, exhibited by the Société Nationale des Beaux-Arts in the spring of 1910. "And in one corner..," Kahlil told Mary, "your name is written. ... I shall write these two letters within that circle on every picture I will paint." (Photo Juley)

have learned that one of my prose-poems has been translated into French and will come out in the fourth volumn of the book, late in July." [40] When "Martha La Banaise" appeared in the October issue of *Les Mille Nouvelle Nouvelles,* he was disappointed because the translators had taken the liberty of deleting the ending in which Martha is buried in unconsecrated ground. Secretly, however, it must have comforted him to know he was in the company of such "auteurs célèbres contemporains" as Anton Chekhov and Arthur Schnitzler.

The description of "le jeune écrivain arabe" that preceded the story suggested the effect of Gibran's self-advertising. The writer made no mention of his early Boston days. "He first studied at the Maronite College of Wisdom in Beirut. In 1903 he left college and embarked for America. . . . J. K. Joubrane writes less to tell a story than to plead reform. Among the social problems which he addresses . . . is the emancipation of the Oriental woman from her unjust mistreatment by man: reform of marriage in the last analysis would be left to the young girl and not her family. He would also like to break

Ameen Rihani in later years.
(*Asia Magazine*, ca. 1929)

the religious yoke in Lebanon. J. K. Joubrane is read, commented on, and discussed. His novella *Wardé Al-Hani* has inspired 237 newspaper articles or reviews." [41]

In June Kahlil met, probably for the first time, Ameen Rihani, his fellow expatriate writer who was returning to America after a five-year stay in Lebanon. The older man had much greater exposure in American and Arabic letters, and he had been regularly sending articles about his travels back to American magazines. One of his favorite forums was Michael Monahan's *Papyrus*, a combination of socialist tract and bibelot which catered to the early-twentieth-century interest in Carpenter, Ernest Renan, Whitman, Wilde, Lafcadio Hearn, and Poe. Kahlil admired Rihani for his satiric wit and scholarly style. His prose was pedantic, at times excessively self-conscious as in a 1908 article on the effect of the transcendentalists in Syria. "Hence, I bring with me from the Eldorado across the Atlantic nothing more than a pair of walking shoes, a bathrobe, and three books published respectively in Philadelphia, Boston, and New York. The good Gray Poet of America, the

Sage of Concord, and the Recluse of Walden are my only American companions in this grand congé."[42] These pretensions at erudition did not bother Kahlil. In fact he was eager to polish his own vocabulary and grammar which was still sadly lacking.

The mutual admiration between the men grew from the similarity of their Maronite backgrounds. Although they both concentrated on Lebanese problems, they saw the solutions not necessarily as Beirut residents or as Parisian emigrés; there was much of the American in their views. They had come of age, aided and influenced by social progress, in Boston and New York. This infusion of a local liberalism lent a new and as yet untried quality to their style and approach to Middle Eastern affairs.

Together they set off for England early in the summer. In London they divided their time between the usual tourist attractions and the art galleries, where Gibran fell in love with the Turners at the Tate Gallery. Their personal concern with home rule for their own country directed them toward Thomas Power O'Connor, the Irish nationalist leader through whom they were able to visit the Houses of Parliament. Gibran also told Mary about going to a costume dinner and recital at the Poetry Society where he and Rihani of course dressed in their Arab costumes.

By the end of July Rihani had left for New York and Hawaiik was traveling in Italy. Kahlil returned and found Micheline in Paris. As she had predicted two years before, their initial attraction had now dwindled to a solicitous friendship. Earlier he had carefully written Mary, "Do you know, that I do not find one word to say to her. She is very sweet and very dear, and I pray that she may find peace and rest in the shadow of a good, honest man." Her aspiration to the New York theater had been without success; she was now ill and Kahlil promised that he would take care of her. Within five weeks a thoroughly objective Gibran assured Mary that she had left the city to visit her parents. "Indeed, she suffered a great deal, but she was very brave and very calm. She is yet thinking of the stage and its glory, but she knows too well the darker side of it. I hope she will get over it."[43]

He again felt isolated. He missed hearing from Mary who was in Yosemite, his friends had left Paris, and mentally he was preparing to leave. The one honor that he and Mary were still awaiting finally arrived when the Union Internationale des Beaux-Arts et des Lettres invited him to send six paintings to its Salon which would open October 1. Although he reluctantly decided against showing there since he did not want to stay in Paris "homeless with no place to work" and he hesitated to leave his studies behind, he proudly sent Mary the invitation, which she kept as evidence of his Parisian conquest.[44]

On October 22, after being delayed a week because money from her had not arrived and because of a railroad strike, he sailed for New York. Paris had nourished him and renewed his self-confidence, but he was looking forward to

Boston. "I can allmost see myself in a quiet little place working on that mystic series 'towards God' which you liked," he confided to Mary. In a way his departure committed him to America for life. "I feel, beloved friend, that I must go back to Boston and find a quiet corner in which I can work and work and work. And perhaps in few years I shall be able to come back and see Italy. . . . Syria and Italy are the two countries I love. I feel that I will be able to see Italy many times but not Syria. The songs of Lebanon will never reach my ears again except in dreams. I . . . am exiled by the nature of my work to the 'land beyond the seven seas.' " [45]

One may wonder, as Kahlil docked in New York on October 31, 1910, how convinced he was of his knowledge that he would not return to the land of the Cedars. His prophecy was in fact only half true, for with his Parisian adventures his travels abroad ended. In a sense, mostly work remained ahead.

Kahlil's invitation to the October 1910
Salon. (University of North Carolina
Library, Chapel Hill)

194

II

Talk of Marriage

Mary, back from Hawaii, met Kahlil for supper the day after he landed. Their reunion somehow lacked the warmth and spontaneity of earlier times. He showed signs of alienation; he was lonely and missed his "close friends." The evening satisfied neither of them.

The next day, still restless, he began trying to find suitable living arrangements. He wanted a studio where his sister could live with him, and this posed problems. Marianna had subsisted in an Oliver Place rooming house for the past two and a half years, and now she was yearning to set up a home for Kahlil. The news of their father's death had reawakened the pain of earlier losses and she again mourned for an entire family. Her brother's return renewed her faith in the only Gibran left for her to love. As soon as she saw him again she told him that she was determined to devote the rest of her life to him. But no matter how tenderly he felt toward her, he realized that this dedication would be burdensome. That week he discussed her decision with Mary, whose reaction was more candid: "Marianna Gibran has refused to marry, alas."[1]

Knowing Marianna's need to be near him, Kahlil was also faced with a problem in the location of his studio. For the first time since 1896 he wanted to move away from the South End. But in choosing to leave the Lebanese quarter he directly challenged his sister's will. Moreover, she refused to live in a spacious apartment; as Mary pointed out, she wanted "to touch the walls."[2]

Five days after his return he found an apartment at 18 West Cedar Street. Near the studio where he had drawn Micheline and a minute's walk away from Fred Holland Day's town apartment on Pinckney Street, the address was right for an aspiring artist. The two rooms approximated Marianna's idea of what an apartment should be, and the rent was within his, or rather Mary's, limited budget.

They moved in during the second week of November. From the start it was a disastrous arrangement. No matter how he tried to help Marianna adjust to her new surroundings, Gibran could not reconcile the differences between sedate Beacon Hill and the South End. The orderly provisions stores and genteel tearooms did not satisfy Marianna, who missed the familiar language, the open-air stands, the pickled grape leaves and puffs of wafer-thin bread, the night-time stoop-sitting of the Syrian enclave. This new world was just a ten-minute walk across the Boston Common from Oliver Place, but her daily symbols of security and survival were missing.

Even with her brother inside the studio, she felt a kind of isolation. One of the two rooms was set aside for his work, and they waged a silent war over who should be responsible for it. She believed it should be spotless, and whenever she was home she followed him around with a cleaning rag. If his papers or books became disarrayed she rearranged them; if he spilled some paint she rushed to wipe it up. For Kahlil the room never was a studio, and before long he was chafing at the lack of privacy.

Marianna inhibited him in another way by the very silence of her growing concern over Mary's presence in their lives. Although she respected the schoolteacher, her unspoken question, "Would you leave me for her?" was always there. It was one that he could not answer then, even though he was spending an increasing amount of time at Marlborough Street.

As soon as he was settled and had started to paint, he formed the habit of bringing the results to the school. He began to live for those days when he saw Mary, as he told her five years later. "You were interested in my work—but I was bringing you my heart with it all the time. I'd work in that little room and then hurry to you with whatever I had—whether it was wet or dry—those two evenings a week—and you know I just waited the days between for those evenings to come." [3]

At last his studies arrived from Paris. "With quick, ardent movements" he opened the crate in the school's kitchen. As he showed the paintings Mary crowed. "Great fun," she wrote in her diary that night. [4] He was proudest of his Temple of Art series. Besides the sculptor Bartlett he had drawn portraits of Debussy, Rostand, Rodin, and the editor and critic Henri Rochefort. He and Mary began planning whom to add to the group.

Gradually she was including him in the weekly parties she gave for her "crowd." Every Sunday evening she encouraged the teachers and any visiting Haskell sister to entertain their men friends at the school. After dining lightly they drew the curtains and danced, in defiance of the prevailing blue laws. "But one teacher told of it as a good story," Mary remembered later, "so the dancing was given up. Boston would not have stood for it—Yet the Sunday parties kept on." She showed Kahlil's paintings and sometimes he came to sketch a visiting relative or join in the fun and games. [5]

Auguste Rodin, 1910. (Photo Juley)

She always aimed to broaden a person's experience, and he escaped none of her subtle efforts at enlightenment. She soon initiated reading sessions—lessons, really—during which he read aloud to her. She began with Swinburne, whom he had told her he considered the greatest English living poet. They read "A Leave-Taking" on November 9. Her choice of a poem that dealt with death was understandable, for Alexander Cheves Haskell had died that spring. As with Kahlil, her parents were now both gone. As the oral exercises continued, Swinburne became her favorite poet too, and Kahlil perfected his spoken English by intoning from "Laus Veneris," "Atalanta in Calydon," and "By the North Sea."

Like a teacher analyzing every step of a favored pupil, Mary observed silently and without judgment his readjustment to her world. She meticulously noted his interaction at supper with two of her teachers: "A little hard to mingle—but his courtesy was lovely." One night at the home of some friends, the conversation veered toward Parisian morality, or how men and women in bohemian circles lived together. Kahlil's views ran counter to the general opinion that such men were irresponsible. Although he was "uncomfortable" and "didn't want to talk about it" for "their points of view were so far apart," he impressed her with his liberated attitude.[6]

By December Kahlil and Mary were frequently seen together. They visited Dr. Richard and Ella Cabot, went to the Museum of Fine Arts, and often attended the theater. Then, for the first time since he had known her, he confided to her the details of his background. Often she had asked him about it but he had always refrained from answering directly. Once in Paris he had tried to evade her: "I have tried more than once to write something about my past for you. I finde it rather hard. . . . There is hardly a smile in those years that are no more. I have loved a great deal—and I have always seen the beautiful: and between love and beauty I was and always shall be, a lost, hungry child of the Unknown. This is my history. This is also the history of many who come from the Infinite and go back to the Infinite in silence. And yet I must tell you more in detail. I shall surely do so some day.[7]

But he was well aware that these vague allusions could not satisfy her insatiable curiosity indefinitely. On December 7, six years after meeting her, he began to tell her the story of his origins, his family, and his early years. The evening's conversation, which followed his discussion of Christ as "the highest in creative man," derived from Ernest Renan's *Life of Jesus*, so impressed her that she used a looseleaf notebook to record it in full.[8] He started with his mother's people, elevating his maternal grandfather, Istifan Rahme, from a poor priest to a bishop. The Rahmes' meager landholdings became "properties . . . immense—whole towns, vineyards, fields." His portraits of the Gibrans were even more extravagant. He depicted his paternal grandfather as "a man of leisure, wealthy, aristocratic, athletic, brilliant—who kept lions as pets— and of whom it is said that he sent this message [to a Turkish superior]: 'Tell him Syria is the best province of the Turkish Empire, Mt. Lebanon is the most magnificent part of Syria, Bechary is the most beautiful village in Lebanon, the Gibrans are the most distinguished family of Bechary—and I am the head of that damned family.'"

One naturally wonders if the colorful model of strength and daring whom Kahlil created for Mary's wondering ears was based on a historical figure. Did he create a super-family in order to approximate the respected Haskells of whom Mary was so proud? There was of course an autocratic leader in Lebanon's recent history, Emir Bashir II. Legends of his wondrous feats, his pet lions, his bombastic rhetoric were familiar to every peasant. As Gibran embellished the fantasies about his father and grandfather over the next ten years, the image of the terrible emir often surfaced. His perception of a male parent—aggressive, dictatorial, and sometimes cruel—suggested an overlord whom he tried to respect but could never love. Whether Mary wholly believed all of this story is doubtful. One feels that as time passed she half-understood her protégé's need to compensate for his ordinary background and gently overlooked his exaggerated claims.

Yet everything he told her that night was not fabrication. Besides describing his father as "magnetic and a man of tastes" he did admit that he was "peculiar." He told how he had been wrongly accused of embezzlement, tried, and found guilty. This revelation demanded a defense of his mother's emigration to the United States, and so he created a situation where she, before leaving her husband, "began to move heaven and earth to get him cleared." Barely alluding to the subsistence years in Boston, he gave the outlines of the sickness and deaths in the family but not the details. Mary's version of the years 1902 and 1903 is confused: she identified Sultana as the older girl and encapsulated the three deaths into a period of nine months instead of fourteen. She also miscalculated by one year when she tried to recreate her own first meeting with him ("In the spring of 1903 I met Kahlil").

As faulty and misleading as this long passage is, however, its general intent is apparent. Within a month of his return Gibran's worth, both as an object of her continued patronage and as a permanent figure in her life, had been weighed and judged sufficient. Her interest in sponsoring other talented friends like Charlotte and Micheline would continue, and she would add various students to her personal scholarship list. But her preoccupation with Gibran transcended mere charity, and as of December 7, 1910, she would devote her journal to every aspect of his life. Two years later she would discontinue the abbreviated diaries and confine all her personal memoirs to the Gibran journal. Her lifelong ambition "of writing something that might serve years hence" was being realized. The subject, a restless and ambitious poet-artist who was neither comfortable in her language nor secure in his artistic expression, was a risk, but one that she was determined to take.

On December 10 Kahlil proposed to Mary. They had spent that Saturday at the Museum of Fine Arts and had planned an evening at the symphony. But there was no concert, so they returned to Marlborough Street. It was then that he told her that he "loved" her and "would marry" her "if he could." As though completely prepared to answer him, she replied that her "age made it out of the question." Her dispassionate objectivity, he recalled, cut deeply into his pride. "I came back from Paris full of this. I went and gave you my heart so simply, so frankly, so sincerely—so wholly. I was just a boy putting all I was and all I had into your hands. And you met me so coldly, so quizzically. . . . All the while I was in Paris I felt your faith and your warmth. And when I came back to Boston you were the same sweet, kind, wonderful spirit—Then the very day after I spoke to you of marriage you began to hurt me." [9]

Coincidentally, on a similar Saturday one year before, Mary had dismissed with a far greater show of emotion another ardent suitor. This time she neither shed tears nor spent a restless night agonizing over her decision. Her response was so matter-of-fact that the events of the following day took Gibran by surprise. December 11 was her thirty-seventh birthday, and just before her party he came for a visit. Whereupon she simply and unemotionally changed her mind—"I told him yes." [10]

His immediate response went unrecorded by her, but in the next weeks her consent lulled him into a new sense of security. Although she fretted about his habits—"Coffee six times a day—smoking—late hours—little exercise—all nerves"—he enjoyed a relatively placid December. He felt comfortable enough to discuss candidly and at length his waning friendship with Micheline. His painting was going well. Beside using for models Marianna and Rosie and Amelia, two younger cousins, he went to the Denison House to look for potential sitters. Through Mary's ministrations he drew Dr. Cabot, who was about to be appointed chief of staff of the Massachusetts General Hospital. A week later Charles Eliot, president of Harvard, agreed to pose for him, and they talked about Gibran's favorite subjects, art and the Middle East. As she observed his growing ability to establish rapport with men whom she deeply respected, Mary began to believe that they could share a life together. On December 28 they walked in a snowfall to see Ruth St. Denis in her Egyptian dances. Two days later he was so excited by the play *Madame X* that he borrowed three drama books from her and "went off in high spirits" to write.[11]

In observation of his twenty-eighth birthday he presented Mary with a prose poem published January 6, 1911, in the emigrant newspaper *Mirat al-Gharb* (*Mirror of the West*). *Al-Mohajer* was no longer a vehicle for his work, since Ameen Goryeb had left New York for Lebanon in the summer of 1909, but Najeeb Diab, the editor of *Mirat al-Gharb*, had eagerly accepted his writings. Like his birthday poem of 1909, "We and You" was dedicated to "MEH," and typically it contained overtones of social protest. It was a litany in contrasts between "we"—"the sons of sorrow and oppression"—and "you"—"the sons of idleness and vanity of the world."[12]

Mary and Kahlil tried with little success to render the essence of the poem into English. She felt challenged to learn Arabic, and their January evenings became filled with his descriptions of Semitic languages and the intricacies of the Arabic alphabet. This led inevitably to the problems of the Middle East. He sketched a brief history of the Arabic peoples, told her about St. Marun, the founder of his native religion, described the motivations of the Young Turks, and speculated about reports of the latest Arab efforts to win their liberty in the 1911 revolution in Yemen. Because they both had voracious appetites for listening to one another, their teacher-student roles were constantly alternating.

That month he made another effort to legitimatize his claim as a worthy husband by offering to become a naturalized citizen. But his belief that Mary might prefer him if he were an American was ill founded. The subject was dropped, and henceforth his deep loyalty to Lebanon precluded its discussion.

Mary, who usually refrained from sentiment, was beginning to surrender to a personal flood of feeling. "*January 4.* K. in after supper refreshing me utterly. *January 7.* To lunch Tante Müller and K. who drew her. I come to care much more." On January 24 she was reading Francis Thompson's poetry to find some suitable love poems for her students. "In a strange, dreamy nap on floor by fire" she saw Charlotte, who appeared and said, "Kahlil making strides in my being." [13] It was ironic that Mary's subconscious should insist on her friend's approval of Kahlil, for actually all of Charlotte's letters were expressing the fullest enthusiasm for him. Yet Mary was aware of a potential rivalry between the two people she loved so much.

Four days after the dream she told Kahlil of her concern for Charlotte's welfare and its possible effect on their plans. She revealed that she had originally sent him to Paris as a "test" of his stability and of their relationship, and that she felt "bound" to continue that test for at least two more years. He protested that he was "absolutely sure." "For the first time in my life," she went on, "I have had an impulse of deepest desire after money in order to endow Charlotte with $1,500 annually." He volunteered to share her commitment: "I could probably get work on a paper at forty or fifty dollars a month, could perhaps at once do picture work cheap which would be commercially profitable." She hurriedly rejected his offer. "No, not for a month—a day—an hour." [14]

She explained that for the past few years she had been quietly contributing to the education of two other young men. One was a Greek boy whom Sarah Armstrong had found working at a soda fountain run by a "callous Levantine shopman" and who was now enrolled in Mount Hermon, a boys' school in western Massachusetts. Her other protégé was a twenty-three-year-old senior at Harvard. Aristides Evangelus Phoutrides, also a Greek immigrant, had graduated from Mount Hermon and had embarked on a brilliant career as a classical scholar. His promise demanded her continued involvement both financially and intellectually. As Kahlil listened, he realized that her commitments would last for an indefinite time. Obviously this meant postponing their marriage. "I knew there were other 'children' though you never said it," he admitted. "But it is not forty or fifty a month that would be felt. That makes little matter. It is a case of four or five thousand dollars." [15]

The financial question was the first obstacle Mary set up to prevent their union. Almost imperceptibly their relationship began to change, and yet Kahlil was sanguine. "In the relation of husband and wife . . ," he rationalized confidently, "as in the case of most else, . . if the big thing is right—and this big thing I call understanding—all the rest can be worked out. . . . Let us trust in [God] and feel quiet assurance that all will be . . . well. If you say to me, 'Kahlil I think it is not wise for us to marry,' I will accept absolutely what you say—and believe." [16]

But in years to come he admitted how ambivalent her equivocation had seemed to him then. He already felt pressured by her relentless demands that he prove himself, and the idea of a further test was repugnant. Undeniably she was forcing him to develop a strong self-image. One night she goaded him to concede that in the Arabic world his writing was highly appreciated and compared with Gabriele D'Annunzio's. "I am sure—that if I died tomorrow some things I have said will live. But nothing I have ever done satisfies me even a short while after it is done." Certainly he was not satisfied during the winter's probationary period. "Everytime I left your house I was all filled up. That was the most unproductive year of my life. I've almost nothing of any account even in writing to show for that winter. And it was because I was being tortured all the time. If you had gone a step farther, I'd have said, I hate you!" [17]

There was another side to Mary's test. Waging a perverse campaign of alienation, she slyly tried to repulse him. "My 'disillusionment series' of camp snapshots . . . failed. I had collected all the old snapshots of myself that I had—some are ghastly—to show K. and give him a distaste for me—and he was interested but utterly unmoved." She tried the same tactic when she told him stories of all her former suitors and showed him a picture of her "first beloved. K. surprised but not changed." [18]

Charlotte visited Boston the last two weeks in February. Her presence at the school relieved the tension that was building between Kahlil and Mary. By now she had abandoned her passion for socialism and was going through a stage of mysticism. For two weeks Mary, liberated by a school vacation, was exhilarated by the dialogues whirling about her. Mornings she spent listening to Charlotte interpret dreams and expound her latest theories on Near Eastern symbols. Charlotte urged her to loosen up, to "put on coral earrings." She told her that the barrier between her and Kahlil would be removed, if only Mary would recognize her "Oriental self." [19]

Afternoons, Charlotte began to pose for Kahlil, and this time after seven hour-long sessions he managed to finish a portrait which satisfied Mary. Her admiration was not based on critical judgment, but the fact that it was by him and of Charlotte enflamed her. "I told him anew how I love Charlotte's picture and how it excites me so that I want to run about these two rooms and so that I long intensely for him." Later she wrote, "Parting I made him kiss me before Charlotte's picture." [20]

Charlotte, ca. 1911.
(Photo Juley)

Accompanying Charlotte for a sitting at 18 West Cedar Street on February 18, Mary saw the interior of his studio for the first time and carefully noted its every aspect.[21] "The room was so immaculate that I wondered whether there'd been a Marianna's housecleaning for us. . . . The yellow tapestry— one large gleam and shine . . . the death mask of the beautiful young woman found dead in the Seine . . . the red silk piece with a beautiful Japanese print . . . the two or three old bits of deep cut gilded wood carving . . . Beethoven's death mask against an oriental linen with embroidered ends." She carefully examined the contents of his small bookcase, which included the conspicuously bound Masters in Art series and the Copeland and Day edition of Rossetti's *The House of Life*. The workroom filled her with joy—"I felt as if I had seen it all before it was so characteristic."

Between sittings Kahlil made them coffee—"delicious, but devilish stuff"—and served them a salted mixture of pistachio nuts, melon seeds, and chick-peas. Often Mary read aloud as he painted. Once she chose selections from his copy of *The Singing Leaves* and made Charlotte guess who had written it. Whatever he thought when he heard her reciting Josephine's early poems can be only surmised, for he showed no outward sign. As they strolled home after the second sitting, Mary confided to Charlotte, "Kahlil and I want to be married when we can." Charlotte wholeheartedly approved; she had "hoped since she saw him in Paris that it might be." [22]

During Charlotte's visit the evenings were spent at Marlborough Street, where she tried out her plays on Mary and Kahlil. She had decided that if they were ever produced he was to help design the color schemes and costumes. Sometimes the three of them invented games. Mary read their hands or just lay on the floor drinking in the great "natural physiognomy of each." They talked about reincarnation. Mary's astonishing theory about Kahlil was simple: "Blake died in 1827, and Rossetti was born in 1828; Rossetti died in 1882 and Gibran was born in 1883." Other times they talked about spiritual messages. Mary was sure she had seen a vision while looking at a Gibran drawing, and Charlotte was always interpreting significant dreams. Kahlil tried to surpass them both with tales about his "trance-experiences." "All my life, from time to time, just as I go to sleep I have felt as if I were rising," he said. "I have been conscious of two selves—of me and me—I have never tried to separate these two personalities until very recently. I often think out things in bed, just before I go to sleep—some of my best things come that way." He went on to describe the strange sensation of rising "out of myself," of seeing his own "very pale" image, of hearing himself—"I don't know what I said." [23]

Charlotte and Mary insisted on seeing the phenomenon of "his wonderful experience." He sat on the couch and tried to recreate the circumstances. While the trance lasted Mary questioned him, but except for seeing a "round light" and "hearing music" his dream state revealed nothing. When "he came back" Charlotte advised him not to do it again. Mary refrained from comment. But when she later discussed it with her crowd, there was general agreement that such experiences were unhealthy and that Kahlil should consult Dr. Morton Prince, a Boston psychologist who had pioneered with such phenomena. Then Charlotte left Boston, and the mystical distractions came to an end.

Something else was also coming to an end: Kahlil's happiness with Boston as a place to live and work. Aware of his growing dissatisfaction, Mary forced him to admit exactly how he felt: "I read—but one can't read all the time—I go to the Museum once a week on Saturday or Sunday usually—but one gets tired going always to the same museum where one knows everything almost by heart. . . . I go a good deal to the library. But I often wish for something else than library or museum." Old friends were not filling his need for stimulation either. Day, impressed by the Temple of Art series, suggested that it be broadened to include Andrew Carnegie and other figures outside the humanities. But his enthusiasms no longer satisfied Kahlil. He found it difficult to communicate with his old mentor, who was becoming more and more eccentric. "When I came back from Paris I found him still considering photography high art, still holding Burne-Jones as an ultimate—still just where he had been ten years before." [24]

Of course he saw nothing of Josephine now. The previous year had been a triumphant one for the Markses. Their second child was born on the same day that she learned she had won first prize in an international playwriting competition at Stratford-on-Avon. From then on her reputation soared. Her award-winning *The Piper* was produced in London in the summer of 1910 and was enjoying a successful run in New York that winter. Cut off from her success, Gibran found his Boston connections moribund.

> Everything in Boston is very beautiful—except there's no art life here. Everything seems dead. . . . Even my artist friends—Royals [Rüyls], etc. seem to belong in the eighteenth century. Nothing that has been doing within the last forty or fifty years seems to be known or to meet sympathy. . . . And there's another thing that's hell—if you'll excuse my mentioning it—The people—with their faces—such faces—it's terrible. So cold—so far away—so hard. . . .
>
> My artist friends—there are people here who used to feed my very soul—I used to love beyond everything to talk with them about books and art and life and all sorts of things. And I have blamed myself because tho' I care for them I no longer find it the same to talk with them. They seem to say the same things again and again. Sentimental people talk a great deal about inspiration—it has always seemed to me we ought not to need inspiration from outside ourselves. Yet I keep on being conscious of a lack of *life* in Boston—and of a desire for the life I do not find. I used to hear people say this of Boston—but I always thought it was one of the best and most beautiful and desirable cities in the world.[25]

Mary was sure that New York would promise more, while Charlotte insisted that he could happily survive there. "Should Kahlil come to New York," she wrote, "he must live near enough me to take his meals here—his dinners. It will be home-like for both." [26]

By this time Mary was frequently at the West Cedar Street studio, and she arranged for some of the women in her crowd to pose. It was no wonder that speculation was growing about the artist and the headmistress. When Louise Daly saw how intensely her sister felt about him, she began to question her closely. For a while Mary tried "to shake off discussion by confession," but the couple "decided finally to let conjecture die instead of tackling it." For his part Kahlil was concerned about Marianna's growing suspicions. "I've told no one," he said. "I do not tell my sister because while she would say something very kind and sweet to me, afterwards I know she would go into her room and say to herself, 'Alone.'" [27]

Mary's strategy of probing continued to upset him. Later he resentfully called it "torture." She teased him to invite Josephine to sit for the Temple of Art series; in her journal she carefully pasted the salutation which was all that he had managed to write that night: "My dear Mrs. Marks." [28]

Although her intention to chronicle his life and times was being carried out with her usual thoroughness, it is interesting to note how she ignored Josephine's influence. Indeed her omission seemed to be part of a conspiracy of silence. Kahlil's reaction to her teasing is again uncertain, but if he was inwardly hurt he apparently concealed it by his own significant silence.

On the other hand Mary's aggressiveness was more often put to his advantage. By April she was organizing two plans. She told Charlotte to find a studio in New York for him, and she began trying to contact likely Bostonians who could lead him to the most powerful art patron in the city, Isabella Stewart Gardner. The Cabots suggested the Copley Greenes, who belonged to the St. Botolph Club, an influential art association. And so Mary purposefully invited her friends Mr. and Mrs. Copley Greene to dine with her and Gibran on April 14.

The evening turned out splendidly. "They really loved the work. . . . And when he said he wrote during the morning, they asked about that and cried that Mrs. Joe Smith [wife of Joseph Smith, then an illustrator and egyptologist at the Museum of Fine Arts] knows Arabic and he must know Mrs. Joe Smith. So they took his address and phone number and next Friday at luncheon or supper tis Mrs. Joe Smith he shall meet! The three went off together a little after nine—finding each other a joyful discovery and the Greenes saying they wanted him to paint their Francesca." So confident was Mary that she added, "It was the moment of the opening of the door between K. and the world that shall love him . . . I *think* his future is not far away now." [29]

She then made the cerebral decision that would affect their lives forever. "And so I made up my mind to follow what seems to me the final finger of God—I put definitely from myself the possibility of being his wife. . . . My age is simply the barrier raised between us and the blunder of our marrying, not my age constitutes the objection—but the fact that for K. there waits a very different love from that he bears me—an apocalypse of love—and that shall be his marriage. His greatest work will come out of that—his greatest happiness, his new, full life. And it is not many years distant. Towards the woman of that love, I am but a step. And tho' my susceptible eyes weep, I think of her with joy." [30]   The next day, April 15, she prepared for the moment of truth with Kahlil. She "wanted so much to think" that all morning she sat at the piano and "practiced hard new hymns" and then walked up and down the Back Bay streets, rehearsing how she would tell him. He arrived at the school after Symphony and they "swapped news." When they were sitting on the library sofa and she "could command her voice," she began. "Everything in me protests against my saying it, except the one thing that makes me say it. But I know the one thing is right. You will acquiesce in what I say—but my heart longs to be overpersuaded. Still I know in the end, I should not be persuaded."

"What is it, Mary?" he interrupted. "Is it something bad?"

"Bad for me—Good for you—Don't mind if I cry," she told him. "I've shed many tears since I saw you last night."

"You won't cry," he reassured her, and held her hand hard.

"I've stopped thinking that I shall ever be your wife and I want to be."

Kahlil went white and still as he listened to her carefully prepared logic. She told him how, since December, whenever she visualized their marriage she felt "obscurely" it was wrong. Her "great passion for him" had grown slowly; until March she had adhered to her lifelong conviction that she needed "great physical strength in a lover or husband." This had changed, but nevertheless her age remained "insuperable." Although she knew that she still possessed "a certain youthfulness and great vigor," she would be "soon on the downward path" while he was "still long climbing upwards." While she talked he wept. "Mary, you know I cannot say things when I am this way."

When she finished, sobbing, they held one another, and when it grew late she kissed his hand—"as I have often longed to do, but as I have not before." At the door she cried again and it was Kahlil's turn to wipe her tears. "And as he went he said as well as he could, 'You've given me a new heart tonight.' " [31]

Both of them remembered their roles that night for many years. Mary interpreted Kahlil's immediate acquiescence as proof that "he never wanted marriage. . . . And through his silence I think I hear that K. knows I'm right." On the other hand he argued that her vacillation had destroyed their marriage plans. "What hurt me so was that you couldn't see *me*. You couldn't believe in me. You were interested in my work but a man's work isn't the man. There's a peculiar essence in any real person that is his reality. . . . You stood off from the real me like an indifferent spectator. I had no core to you." [32]

A day passed, and he stayed away from the Sunday night gathering. When she found an excuse to visit him on Monday, he was involved in a study that he called *Chaos*. They refrained from alluding to Saturday night. Then Marianna arrived "with the big black bag she carries everywhere." She was rarely around when Mary visited, and now the schoolteacher eagerly seized the opportunity to make her drop the formal title "Miss Haskell." She got the shy young woman to whisper "Mary" over and over until she felt relaxed enough to call her by her first name. As she studied her she decided that Marianna looked thin, "but not badly for her." She also noticed that her voice was "still melancholy itself—the seat of tears" and realized that the thought of Kahlil's going away represented "a terror to her."

"When Kahlil goes to New York I'll see much of you," she promised.

"Ah! When Kahlil goes to New York! Shall you go with him?"

"What do you think?"

Marianna hesitated. "Well, I'm sure he'd like it." And then the phone rang. Miss Teahan wanted her, and although she was weary Kahlil's sister prepared to walk back to the shop. Mary carefully searched her face. "For the first time I realized how like his her eyes are." [33]

The next day Mary contrived another reason to go to the studio. For *Broken Wings*, a painting he was doing of Marianna, Kahlil had mentioned his need to study some birds. She hurried to the market, bought two doves, and walked over to West Cedar Street. No one was home so she hung them on the door. The implications of her recent decision overwhelmed her: "Gradually realizing life without living with Kahlil in its future outlook—I in Boston or California—he abroad—It hurts!" [34]

Gibran went to the Copley Greenes that night. Mary's prediction about his future being settled as a result of meeting them was sadly exaggerated. At dinner he managed to conduct himself pleasantly; he met Mr. and Mrs. Joseph Smith and exchanged amenities, although certainly not in Arabic. It was just another evening out, an insignificant cultural dalliance.

Kahlil did learn of the Greenes' interest in Eugène Carrière and borrowed some reproductions of his work to take to Mary the next night. As he showed them to her, they discussed Charlotte's latest theatrical involvement. Disillusioned with the frustrations of trying to sell her plays, she had accepted an offer from the producer Walter Hampden to travel with a repertory group, The Lyceum Players. She had a minor part as Lady Parchester in Alfred Sutro's *The Walls of Jericho*. She also invited Kahlil to use her Greenwich Village apartment when she was on tour. He wavered—"if she were a man I shouldn't hesitate—but a woman—it seems like intrusion"—but at last Mary persuaded him to take advantage of the offer.[35] On April 26 he took the Joy Line boat from Boston to New York and arrived at 164 Waverly Place early the next morning.

April and May in New York were "alltogether too good. . . . New York is not the place where one finds rest." But, he asked Mary, "Did I come here for rest? I am so glad to be able to run." He especially reveled in the Metropolitan Museum: "America is far greater than what superficial people think." [36]

"Too many friends and too many callers and too many things to see" prevented him from doing much work on Waverly Place. He immediately re-identified himself with the New York Syrian community, and the activists there rekindled his passion for the nationalist struggle. Within a week he had met the Turkish ambassador at a dinner given by Naum Mokarzel, an editor of the emigré newspaper *al-Hoda* (*The Guidance*). "The ambassador was trying all the time to be *sweet* and *gentle*. We talked about art, and he even invited me to go and see him in Washington. That is the Turkish way of leveling and smoothing down the things that stay in the way!" [37]

Ameen Rihani's presence in New York was an important reason for Kahlil's relocation, and re-establishing their friendship became his chief pursuit. He saw the other writer every day and proudly related his achievements: "Read Rihani's poem 'The Song of Siva' in May number of *The Atlantic Monthly*. . . . I want to bring Charlotte and Rihani together. They will like each other." [38]

All through May Kahlil confidently and adroitly balanced his contacts and friendships in his two separate worlds. With Mary's letter of introduction he reached her old friend, the composer and musicologist Arthur Farwell. He drew Farwell on May 5 and in turn Farwell took him around New York galleries. As a result he met William Macbeth, the art dealer who specialized in contemporary American painters.

Charlotte in the meantime had decided that The Lyceum Players was a "dry experience," and she returned to New York on May 15. She at once made sure that Kahlil met everyone in her Greenwich Village circle. She wrote Mary that the minute she arrived at Waverly Place she had contacted him and another freelance writer—"and we three *with you so present!* spent the evening, as I felt on the threshold of a new life for all of us." She also mentioned how much Kahlil had changed and become "full of reposeful power." [39] Although she had heard of their broken engagement, she was convinced that it was only a temporary setback. She remained sure that if only Mary would relax, Kahlil would take the initiative and insist upon marriage.

He moved into the rooming house at 28 West Ninth Street where Rihani was staying. The quarters were cramped but he was able to use Rihani's larger room to paint in. Every morning he walked over to Charlotte's for breakfast. In spite of her difficulties in finding sponsors for her own work, she did possess amazing catalytic powers. He met her close friend Charles Edward Russell, the defeated Socialist candidate for governor of New York. Knowing how much Mary respected this man's reform politics, Kahlil immediately notified her about his latest conquest.

Rihani also introduced Kahlil to his friends, American as well as Syrian—the poet Edwin Markham whom Kahlil drew; Michael Monahan, the editor and publisher of *Papyrus* ("he is Irish and possesses rare charms"); and Richard Le Gallienne, the critic and chronicler of the Yellow Decade when Wilde and Beardsley had shocked English and American sensibilities. Then in New York,

Rihani, 1912. (Authors)

Le Gallienne sat for Kahlil who was able to report that his study of the oft-misunderstood "Golden Boy" was "so real that it made him sad." [40]

Back in Boston, after school commencement on May 26, Mary turned her attention toward New York. But first she had Micheline for a visit. The Frenchwoman, who was now teaching at the Ely School in Greenwich, Connecticut, had seen Kahlil in New York that month, and after assessing her emotional growth Mary concentrated on hearing about him. "We talked K. for hours. It is very fresh still and she [envisages] him just the same as always." Micheline also met Marianna that weekend. True to her word, Mary conscientiously met the lonely woman at least once a week and enlivened her days by treating her to plays, operas, and concerts. Marianna had responded by giving her "the best" of Kamila's bangle bracelets, the proudest possession of any Syrian matriarch. Thereafter the schoolmistress proudly wore this symbol of her affection. Micheline found Marianna so much like Kahlil that she made friends with her at once, and Marianna responded by coming "out full blown to her." [41]

Arriving in New York on June 1 for a twelve-day visit, Mary rushed to Waverly Place. Kahlil had started another painting of Charlotte and she could hardly wait to see it. Envisioning a female cupbearer or "Sakia," he posed Charlotte nude amidst swirling "green, apricot and orange veils" and holding "a brazen jewelled bowl of incense." In his words she was "a goddess, an image . . . so many prayers have risen to her that at last she is coming to life." When he had begun the painting two weeks earlier, Charlotte had told Mary how much they had wanted her there: "Kahlil said beautifully that he never began his work in here before he had summoned you. And yet I feel we need that wonderful eye of yours, to see critically and creatively." Now for the next three days their world revolved around the picture. "Charlotte trips about in her veils, stepping on the ends, lifting them again—wrapping them interval-wise about her." [42]

On June 3, a Saturday night, Kahlil brought Rihani for dinner. Charlotte had met him two nights before, but this was the first time Kahlil had introduced Mary to any of his Lebanese colleagues. At Charlotte's instigation the two women wore costumes, Mary an alluring black satin dress and Charlotte her Lady Parchester costume with "puffs and night gown." "The men were stunned." Rihani wore "an abba [a Middle Eastern shirt] and a turban." He good naturedly scribbled bits of Arabic and English so Mary could read his hand. They burned incense and listened to his poetry.[43]

Once during the evening Gibran gave Mary a lengthy, piercing look. She remembered it for a long time for what she felt was its painful quality of hunger. When over the next few years they analyzed the turning points in their relationship, he always recalled "the night they painted up" as a fiasco.[44] What had annoyed him most were Charlotte's mischievous efforts at matchmaking, and his penetrating look turned out to be only his expression of sulky uneasiness.

Two days later Charlotte left for Denver. For the next five days, twelve hours a day, Mary and Kahlil roamed unencumbered through New York.[45] They visited the Cathedral of St. John the Divine and Columbia University, the Metropolitan Museum and the Brooklyn Museum. In Prospect Park they watched President Taft review an assembly of children. "When the crowd pressed suddenly to the band stand to see Taft enter his auto, the vibration was so wonderful that K. said, 'Chaos that's what it means to me chaos out of which anything may come.'" They ate at workingmen's lunch counters, went to Ferard's, a meeting place for artists, ate goulash at a little Romanian place, and found their favorite restaurant on Eighth Street—Gonfarone's, where the waiters sang and the prix fixe with wine was fifty cents.

Their "feast of experiences" also included reading from Nietzsche's *Thus*

Mary and Kahlil reading Nietzsche, 1912. (University of
North Carolina Library, Chapel Hill)

Spake Zarathustra, which Kahlil had borrowed from Rihani. He drew Mary a
sketch of Renan—"the fattest thing in the world and one of the loveliest.
When he was in Syria they couldn't find a mule big enough to carry him." One
day it rained, and they stayed in the apartment from one in the afternoon to
one the next morning. He spent much of the time drawing a series of motifs of
how various poets "seemed" visually to him. "Swinburne—rising alone in
great simple curves from the sea. . . . Keats in the blue lighted groves, deep
yet clear—Shelley treading the fields as if they were air—Rodin a simple
massive harmony of line—Dante loneliness with serpent—Shakespeare colos-
sus, the heavens passing by his head, and mankind clustered about his feet and
knees—Michelangelo, a big sculptor head holding an image. . . . And a wee
rectangle 'K. G.' in the corner."

After Mary returned to Boston Kahlil visited her before she left for the West on June 18. She proposed that she stop sending him monthly checks and replace them with a lump sum of $5,000, the amount bequeathed him in her will. He would be free to invest the money as he chose (she suggested her own brokers Moors & Cabot, whose investments she figured were yielding a healthy eight percent). After they settled these details they sat down on June 17 and made out his will. Earlier that month he had said, "Speaking of wills, I want to do something that will stand in law about my pictures. If I should die, I don't want anyone else to touch my work or have anything to say about it, but you. I want it all in your hands. How can I do this? And how can I go about returning the money I have used?"[46]

Mary saved the first draft for her journal, and Kahlil copied it. On the first page appeared the names of nine persons who they agreed would receive, at her discretion, a memento of him. With the exception of William Hunt Diederich (a grandson of William Morris Hunt and a sculptor Kahlil had known in Boston), all were instrumental figures in his development. First was Fred Holland Day, followed by Charlotte Teller, Ameen Rihani, Diederich, Emilie R. Michel, Mrs. Louis Rüyl, Mr. and Mrs. Joseph Rahaim, and Joseph Hawaiik. Although simple in form, the terms regarding his artistic and literary estate were thoughtful and concerned for posterity:

> I, Kahlil Gibran being in sound mind and body, do herein make my last will and testament, and this will shall render void any previous wills, testaments or memoranda. All pictures, drawings, and studies made by me I leave to Mary E. Haskell as her sole property. If before my death I become insane they shall thereupon be at once her property.
>
> I leave my literary manuscripts to my sister Marianna Gibran, advising her to consult about their publication with Ameen Rihani, N. Diab, and Ameen Goryeb, Beirout Syria. My manuscripts on politics and sociology I leave in the hands of Ameen Goryeb. Whatever money remains to me I leave to Mary E. Haskell. To her I leave all the letters written in English to me. All letters written to me in Arabic or French I desire my sister to keep unread for five years after my death—and during that time to allow the writers of them to claim any or all of their own if they wish. At the end of the five years I desire her to put those which have not been claimed into the hands of Joseph Hawaik [sic].
>
> If Mary Haskell is living I desire the heart to be taken from my body and given to her, and my body to be sent to Bechary Syria to be buried in Mar (St.) Mema. If she is not living, my heart shall not be removed from my body and the body shall be buried in Mar Mema.
>
> I leave my books that are in Bechary to the Bechary Society's Reading Room. I leave my books in America to the Golden Links Society, Boston—with the exception of books concerning art; these I leave to Mary Haskell, with all prints.
>
> I leave all my personal effects to my sister Marianna, except my two smaller Chinese silver rings: these to Mary Haskell.

If Mary E. Haskell is not living at the time of my death, I desire my friend Fred Holland Day to take charge of all pictures, drawings and studies made by me. My wish is that in this case they shall become eventually the property of the public in a museum—and that they shall be kept together as far as is possible; but also that by means of them my sister Marianna shall be provided for. I should, Mary Haskell being dead, be willing to let them become the property of any museum or society which would undertake for their sake to provide for my sister.[47]

Then they talked about his summer. While Mary was away he was planning to stay in Boston and work. First he wanted to revise *The Broken Wings*, a book he had started in 1906. "It is how I felt five years ago—I don't feel that now. But it is well done and I don't want to discard it." He was also beginning a series of essays about a "Madman" and had promised to illustrate a book by Rihani. When Mary worried about what he would do for a vacation, he answered, "Lie on the grass." "How long?" she laughed. "About two minutes." [48]

The next morning she almost missed her train for Chicago. As she boarded she spotted an artist with an obviously older wife. The train sped west and she recorded in her journal the lengthy entries for the past month. The task was not finished until she reached Salt Lake City, where she contentedly summed up her feelings: "Wholly at peace with our situation—especially when I see fading wives on train!" [49]

12

A Concord Soul

While Mary climbed mountains in California with her Sierra Club companions, Gibran stayed in Boston with Marianna. He had planned to visit Fred Holland Day at Five Islands, but by the end of June he learned of his friend's frenzied involvement in what would be his final obsession. Day was building an imposing chalet on Five Islands, and he complained to Mary that his plans for Maine had been postponed. "Oh what a June this is! It is dark and cold and dreary. I feel as if I am in a prison." [1] And yet the lonely summer was productive.

Dodd, Mead paid him $50 for illustrating Rihani's forthcoming *The Book of the Khalid*. Having finished Charlotte's portrait, now called *Isis*, he worked on four more paintings. But his most meaningful work was the revision of *The Broken Wings*. The longest of his Arabic novellas, it was based on his usual theme of the alienating effects of corrupt power. All his devices of melodramatic plot and characterization reappeared. The platonic love between a poor young visionary and the beautiful Selma Karema was thwarted by her forced betrothal to the nephew of a villainous bishop. Her fate, although relieved by forbidden trysts with her poet-lover, was inevitably doomed. Evidence of the bishop's growing suspicions crumbled even their pretense at freedom. The story ended with her death in childbirth, and the grief-stricken narrator symbolically burying his heart in her grave.

Gibran called *The Broken Wings* a spiritual autobiography, but when he outlined the story to Mary later that year he insisted, "Not one of the experiences in the book has been mine. Not one of the characters has been studied from a model, nor one of the events taken from real life. . . . I say this because the book dealing with a young man's awakening to life and with a love affair is sure to be called autobiographical—indeed it has already been called so—but although of course I have had love affairs and waking, nothing

Illustration for *The Book of the Khalid.*

personal to me is in this book." [2] However, there are two aspects which seem to be taken from his life.

In the chapter "Between Christ and Ishtar" the lovers' meeting place, which Arabic critics considered sacrilegious, depicted the doubly symbolic walls of a secluded temple. On one side, "speaking wordlessly of past generations and the evolution of religions," was shown a Byzantine bas-relief of the agonized Christ with his sorrowing mother and Mary Magdalene. The other showed a Phoenician carving of "Ishtar, goddess of love seated on her throne, surrounded by seven nude virgins." The insertion of Ishtar or Astarte, the queen of goddesses in the Assyrian panoply, was due not so much to Gibran's firsthand observation of his native countryside but to his early exposure to the Pre-Raphaelite poets. Within this context the lines of Rossetti's poem "Astarte Syriaca (For a Picture)" become significant: "Mystery: lo! betwixt the sun and moon/ Astarte of the Syrians; Venus Queen/ Ere Aphrodite was."

Gibran was indebted to another, more personal source. "Oh, Lord God, have mercy on me and mend my broken wings," was the anguished, helpless cry of both Selma and her lover. It resembled the final words uttered by the ascetic figure in Josephine's one-act play *The Wings*. When the idealistic monk was reunited with King Aelfric he pleaded, "Not yet know I enough of God,—or men / Ah, Thou! Have pity on all broken wings." Gibran was frequently at Josephine's during the winter of 1904 when she was writing this work, and there can be little doubt that the essence of her lines echoed in his mind when he wrote the lovers' cry. In this sense *The Broken Wings* was autobiographical.

By telling this long pent-up story Gibran seemed to repay old obligations. The ghosts that had haunted him since 1906 were fading away. He deliberately became more outgoing and less other-worldly. Abandoning his trances ("nothing came of them") and his cane, he paid more attention to his health and spoke of taking a course in economics. Mary received word of his firmer grasp on "Reality" while she was in Wenatchee, Washington, working some farm land that she owned with her brother Tom. Later he described his transformation in more detail:

> This is a condensation of what he told: that all his life his deepest desire had been to give pleasure to people—bring joy—happiness—show it, create it; but himself has never laid hold on it; he shrank from evil—feared it—longed to escape it—wept at the world's woes—almost especially perhaps in the past six or seven years. One day last summer he was alone in the country with a book—and suddenly bethought him—why should he go on always pointing others to joy and himself not enjoy it? Then his fear went and he laid hold on Reality as the goal of life—and life itself as the greater art—and the man as bigger than the new work—And now in his writing and painting—and speech, and all expression he wants to make Reality clear. How he shall do it is not clear to him—it will take a few months yet probably, for him to know. But knowledge will come—and he will be come able to express what he desires to express.[3]

Back in Boston, bronzed and strengthened by her outdoor vacation, Mary rejoiced at Kahlil's vitality. On September 16, their first evening together, they met in the Italian North End and ate at the Hotel Napoli. Kahlil looked "better than ever—young, carefree, assured, happy." Wearing a new light brown suit "from Hollander's—the nicest thing they had, 25.00 reduced from $55.00" and "a tie to match—15 cents," he also approved of her "rig." She celebrated the night out by wearing "Charlotte's blue dress with my black and silver scarf and the brown velvet wild rose from my last winter's hat—and my brown hat with the two brown wings—and black feather boa." [4]

For two days and nights they carried on a constant dialogue. He brought her "Slavery," his article just published in *Mirat al-Gharb*. Then he renewed his search for a New York studio. With a smile of "calm mitglauben" when Mary forecast a big year, he left on the Joy Line. He stayed at the West Ninth Street rooming house and a few days later was able to report that he had found an apartment at 51 West Tenth Street with good light, a low rent ("only twenty dollars"), and a small balcony.[5] The building he moved into was the famous Tenth Street Studio. Designed by Richard Morris Hunt, for fifty years it had served many leading American artists as home, studio, and gallery space. In New York Gibran also settled with his publisher, Naseeb Diab, some details about *The Broken Wings*, which was to appear that winter.

Returning to Boston on the twenty-sixth to pack and take leave of the West Cedar Street apartment, he brought Mary his latest picture, saying, "This painting is the parting of the ways in my life." She immediately christened it *The Beholder*, and after sitting up with it the entire night agreed that "it was his best so far." During her vigil with the painting of a figure lost in an ethereal dream world, she wrote four pages of interpretation: "He looks not down nor up; earth and heaven are together in his eye. . . . He is Will. . . . Low behind him . . . lurks a shifty giant face with straining brow and eye compressed to the rocks as if to eavesdrop on a master—the earth spirit made servant. And from the cloud-flight ahead a vast obscure young face turns startled—the future, feeling him afar." Earlier that month she had asked him to paint Nietzsche's Zarathustra, and now she could write, "Here is Zarathustra—here is the hand hungry and wearying to give." [6]

For the next two weeks Kahlil and Mary moved together as if caught in mutual ecstasy. Nothing surfaced of the uncertainty or bickering which had clouded so much of their time together. "He is handling every human and social activity . . ," she noted. "No man talking with him now would find him sentimental or dreary or unpractical—but full of actuality—alert—and critical, wary, judgmatical." One day they saw "The Irish Players under Yeats" perform Synge's *The Well of the Saints* and Lady Gregory's *The Workhouse Ward*. Afterward they visited Kahlil's studio and evaluated his summer's work. She noted a not quite successful self-portrait with herself—"poor of me as the attendant spirit face that he always puts near." [7] Still euphoric over *The Beholder*, which renewed their hopes for a Boston show, they stopped to see the Copley Greenes. The next day they heard Yeats address the Drama League at the Plymouth Theater. Kahlil went backstage, saw George Pierce Baker, then professor of drama at Harvard, and made an appointment to draw Yeats.

The meeting with Yeats on October 1 at the Hotel Touraine reinforced his new mood. The drawing took under an hour but the two men talked for three. Yeats confided that Boston bored him. "He can't work here," Kahlil related. "Lady Gregory can. . . . But he can't and he wants to get away." According to Mary, Kahlil caught in his portrait the "homely, spirituelle, real" qualities of

The Beholder, oil, 1911. (Photo Juley)

the Irish poet along "with the complexities of Yeats practico-aeriality with the lack-shave look of his chin." Although the encounter did not lead to a sustained friendship it deeply impressed Kahlil. He told Mary of his conviction that Yeats would "do work of absolute worth" and identified with the conflict in his life: "One very bad thing is spoiling Yeats' work. He is a patriot—and he ought to be simply an artist. He knows it. I believe he will work out of it." [8]

The same opposing forces were beginning to pull at Kahlil. Ever since his return from Paris he had belonged to The Golden Links Society, a group of young Syrian men brought to his attention by Mrs. Tebbutt, a social worker from the Denison House. The Boston branch was one of many in New York, Egypt, Syria, Constantinople, London, and elsewhere. The club's purpose was the improvement of life for Syrian citizens everywhere. As he became involved with it, he gradually took a position favoring national and individual self-reliance. Not only did he believe that "the Syrian looks in vain to Turkey

Yeats, pencil, 1911.
(Photo Juley)

for help," but he applied this concern to the Syrian immigrant's position in American society: "He errs to look to any government in any country to solve his problem—for he must help himself. He must be himself as a man." [9]

One of the ongoing debates in The Golden Links was over assimilation in the host country, "whether tis better for Syrians who are living in other countries to settle into Syrian colonies or to mix with the foreigners." In Boston colonies were favored, although Kahlil called for assimilation, based upon his own closeness to the Western world. Yet in trying to realize himself essentially as a creator, his final decision was "to move away from partisan causes: I have known each [world] well enough to stand now outside of both at will." [10]

But this professed objectivity was impossible to achieve, for he was intensely patriotic. During the last week in September 1911 Italy declared war on Turkey to gain colonies in North Africa, and hope for home rule revived in

Turkish-occupied countries. And so, despite his criticism of Yeats's political involvement, he was likewise trapped. Mary clearly saw this paradox. After he spent an entire night talking about the Italian-Turkish conflict, she observed, "More and more I see him ceasing to be remote even while his remoteness grows." [11]

Perhaps because they both were anticipating their separation by his move to New York, or because he was more self-assured than ever before, the first two weeks in October continued to be remarkably free of tension. One night as they were looking through a stack of magazines two items caused him to reminisce. Stopping at a poem by Louise Imogen Guiney, he recalled the days when she had inspired him. Then they saw a picture of Josephine Peabody Marks. Once again Mary's handling of his reaction is fraught with ambivalence. In her journal, which was increasingly becoming an official voice, she impersonally glossed over the incident. "[This] led K. into saying he believes that if something different had been her environment she might have done work with a touch of the Absolute. To his mind, the promise of her first achievements is unfulfilled—tho' her craftsmanship is improved." But in her diary she wrote about their discussion of Josephine's successful career as a result of her marriage. Then in a hand even more cramped than usual she revealed the real substance of that talk: "I was aware that K. had made a stride in loving, when in discussing Jos., he spoke of *the* love in such simple tenderness—and then [said]: 'next after that came a good love that is friendship mixed with passion.' Something seems added to him—wide, restful and enduring—as if he had *attained* in loving as in painting." [12]

Despite the tantalizingly fragmented quality of these three entries, her hesitancy to discuss the friendship with Josephine had at last left her. Nevertheless these few words are the only occasion in all her writings when she portrayed Kahlil speaking tenderly about Josephine. Upright and independent as she was, Mary after all was only human. Doubtless she harbored a secret resentment toward the animated and talented Posy. As meticulous as the journals are, they still portray Kahlil from this unconsciously biased point of view.

On Friday, October 6, the Greenes, the Cabots, and two art-minded women were to join Kahlil and Mary for dinner. Because the Cabots and Mrs. Greene pleaded sick only Mr. Greene appeared with the two friends. "It was the devil of an evening." Mary reproached herself for the complete failure of Kahlil's chance to score socially or professionally. "Poor management!" she brooded. "The hostess-touch fails me! . . . I think it was my first time of *pain* in attempted social intercourse. K. and they seemed of such different worlds— and I of his, rather than of theirs—But the remoteness was so much completer than I had expected, that I was unprepared to meet it. K. is used to it: he handles it better. But I've realized only so recently the absoluteness of the gulf between him and most other minds. . . . An illuminating experience for me at his cost." [13]

Seemingly unconcerned about her failure, a few days later Kahlil brought her three more paintings, which they titled *Pain*, *Where the Dead Gods Lie*, and *The Two Crosses*. He told her that the scenery in *Dead Gods* was conceived after he had heard about her "mountain summer." When she saw the "wide billowing mountains and far mists," she cried, "How I wish I could walk over that pass!" "Don't you suppose I thought of that when I was painting it?" he explained.[14]

As their days together grew shorter they both became apprehensive about the year ahead. On October 10 Mary was "swallowing lumps all the time because conscious of K.'s near departure. He was so conscious of it all last evening." For distraction they finished organizing a "world-soul" course in literature for her to teach. Their final choices included selections from the Egyptian Book of the Dead, Job, Aeschylus, Sophocles, Euripides, the Koran, Dante, Shakespeare, *Faust*, Balzac, Nietzsche, Ibsen, and Whitman (despite Miss Dean's admonishments that inclusion of the last four writers would "damn" both Mary and the school).[15] Kahlil held out for a medieval miracle or mystery play and Swinburne, but finally agreed that neither fitted their concept of a supreme expression.

By including Kahlil in her curriculum planning, Mary was involving him more for his own sake than for her students' instruction. The simple reading aloud lessons were now sessions in which she forced him to think and express himself in English. If he disagreed with her he had to substantiate his arguments. He covered the blackboard with diagrams and illustrations, and before erasing them for the morning classes she carefully copied them into the burgeoning journal.

Lady Gregory had been impressed with the Yeats portrait, and on Kahlil's last day in Boston, October 13, she sat for him. While he drew her at the Hotel Touraine other admirers flocked to her side. "Mrs. Gardner came in and recognized me," he told Mary that night. "I saw her a few years ago, and her face was very much better. She has aged a great deal." He described how she was "like a bee . . . talking with Lady Gregory and reading her a letter—emphatically and with much animation." Also present was Ezra Pound, whom Mary had met at Charlotte's apartment earlier that year. When she and Kahlil had discussed his work then, he "had criticized the lack of music in it—especially since E. P. is young and youth is preeminently singing time." [16]

Their last evening together was again spent at the Irish Players since Lady Gregory, "pleased with her portrait," had given Kahlil two tickets. They saw her own *The Image* and Shaw's *The Shewing Up of Blanco Posnet*. Then they parted. "I'll send you sketches of everything I do in New York," he promised.

After he left Mary rededicated herself to her "world-consciousness" course. But she found it hard to concentrate: "K. in N.Y., no doubt had Sun. in part with Charlotte. Ach! Next Chapter." [17]

She intended that for her part the next chapter was to arrange a show at the St. Botolph Club. To this end Kahlil had left behind all his paintings, drawings, and sketchbooks. Unfortunately, the Greenes' interest in his latest work was wavering, and for the rest of the month she bustled to get other responses to *Where the Dead Gods Lie* and *The Two Crosses*. They were not encouraging. "Dead Gods!" one woman shuddered. "No wonder it is terrible. Dead humans are bad enough—but dead Gods!" But such complacence only strengthened her will. "I feel as tho' war has just been declared between us and the world. . . . And in the name of the Absolute we will win." [18]

She invited Frances Keyes, the art teacher who had originally suggested that she show Gibran at the school and who was now the confidante of the elusive Mrs. Gardner, to view the entire work. "She will know whether Mrs. Gardner might be interested," she wrote Kahlil. "If Mrs. G. would be, and would come on Miss K.'s suggestion, and if she approved, the exhibit could almost surely be at the St. Botolph." [19]

On October 23 Miss Keyes arrived and proceeded to deliver what Mary later described as a "solar-plexal swatting." "She ripped them all to pieces technically—no color in shadows—further outlines always meaningless—no care taken of edges of his work—unevenly studied." As painful as it was, Mary recorded every devastating word. The two friends who accompanied Miss Keyes were mortified at her embarrassment and tried to make polite amends. But she accepted no sympathetic noises. Her plan for securing Mrs. Gardner as an ally was wrecked. "I didn't mention Mrs. Gardner—felt it would be useless, especially since Mrs. G. saw K. at Lady Gregory's and could have followed up his work had she been interested." [20]

For the next three days she carried the burden of how much of the evaluation she should reveal to Kahlil, and then she wrote him a candid fifteen-page letter. The criticism wounded her more than it did him. After writing the letter she noted, "I miss him continually—and never felt lonelier than I do when I look at his pictures with someone indifferent to them—deaf to the imaginative call in them." But he delivered a scathing counterattack.

> All artists think that severe, unsympathetic critics are absolutely wrong. Now I do not think that Miss Keyes is wrong. . . . She is a *slave* of the old accepted forms of expression—and slavery is not a vice; it is only a misfortune. She and I belong to two different worlds and we see art and life from two different point of view. . . . I know to well what is wrong with my work and I am to trying to make it right—but Miss Keyes dose not know—and she thinks it is the technique. But I am almost sure that even when my style or technique becomes perfect Miss Keyes will not like my

work. She is too old in flesh and to young in spirit to accept new forms and new thoughts. . . . Now Mary, if I was a *famous* artist and Miss Keyes had read much about me and my work, she would not have dared to criticize the last three pictures and the series of drawings. Her fear of other people's opinion would have made her swallow her own thoughts! But I am unknown in this land, and people like Miss Keyes *must* try their wits on me. . . . And as to exhibiting, you know I realy have no body of work to show. I wanted to exhibit because there is always a chance of selling a picture or two. I am anxious to make my living one way or the other.[21]

Meanwhile Mary had asked Day to advise her on arranging an exhibit. But by then he was too far removed from the art world and her plea went unanswered. When she received Kahlil's letter she was pleased at his resilience. "I want to tell you how my habitual contentment in you brimmed into a great singing repose when I realized once for all that criticism will not shake you. *You* know . . . how justly I say my estimate of you is not faith, but knowledge." Lest he be overtaken with hubris, however, she inserted a lesson about objective criticism and the right of dissent. "And apropos to acclaiming, let me reveal to you the old-fashioned Concord Soul—Miss Keyes is a Concord Soul—If the world think one thing, their unanimity makes the Concord Soul suspect this thing: and when the Concord soul differs from the world, the more it may suffer from expressing the difference, the more bound it feels to express it. There is a noble side to this conceit—and Miss K. would criticize you not less loudly if you were famous, but more loudly. Believe this or not, at your will—it is true. Concords are rare—Miss Keyes is one of them." [22]

"I did not know that Miss Keyes paints," was his undaunted reply. "She never seemed like a painter to me—but if she realy insist on cutting out burnt siena, umbers, and ochers, I, too, will insist on saying that she never had a real pallete in her hand! And as to her being a Concord soul—Well—have I not known all the *Concord* souls in the Arabic world? Have I not fought them for the last seven years?" [23]

That he was arrogant and stubborn and did not appreciate the nuance of her message, Mary could not deny. But despite her partisan commitment to his future she became for him his level self, his honest appraiser, in truth his "Concord Soul."

13

A Three-Cornered Friendship

While Mary endured loneliness and frustration in Boston, Kahlil was finding a new purpose away from the influences that had smothered his maturity. He became busy making his studio comfortable. It was left to Charlotte to describe their times in New York, for she was so close to selling her plays to David Belasco that autumn that she exuberantly spilled out to Mary every detail of her life and of anyone else's whom they knew. Recognizing how removed the schoolteacher was, she tried to relieve some of her anxieties about her own and Kahlil's intimacy.

> Kahlil . . . is looking better than I have ever seen him, and is even more firmly fixed than before. We had no chance to go to depths for I was stupid from a cold and he had his studio on his mind. But . . . I am afraid if he and I were the two only on the much-abused (literally) desert-island I could not feel him as a man. This seems almost a slander—but you know that I believe that attraction is a matter of Chemistry. The Chemistry that does appeal to me is in the big strong phlegmatic blonde stupids who don't know enough to appreciate anything of my purposes or prayers. . . . The near presence of Kahlil will keep me from anything rash, and I shall not be lonely in one sense—but I do not want him to touch my hand even, and I should love to be beaten by the blonde beast.

Once after touching on Kahlil's vulnerability to love—"You are right, he has his problems before the altar of the Cyprian [but] his power to say no to his old ways is his new power in work"—she hastened to assure Mary that she had meant nothing specific by her reference to Venus:

> I was so vague that I doubt not you thought K. had said something of some love; it was not that—He said—with Oriental reserve too—that he had reached the place where the "little creatures" had to be shut out of his life.

He did not hint of any positive worship tho'; and I think he is feeling a sense of relief and release which may explain the note in his letters you speak of. He is a great help to me in thinking *absolutely* these days; but I am on no pedestal and it does me good to have him "reprove" me. Yesterday he said he wished we were brother and sister—since then he could say anything: we would quarrel—and yet we would still be brother and sister. I told him to go ahead.[1]

Because she was so generous with her time, friends, and personality, Charlotte's Waverly Place visitors both stimulated and amused Kahlil. We can glimpse how he acted at one "pancakes, bacon, coffee" breakfast with Micheline: "With M. he is like an angel," wrote Charlotte, "chained by one ankle to earth and hopping uncomfortably though trying to be airy and easy as tho' from a dance of his own choosing. What I like best in Kahlil . . . is his latest growth—is the new stoniness—philosophical—the definite acceptance of Good and Evil." When his studio was ready for visitors he first showed it off to Charlotte, who of course described it to Mary. "It is different—but it has the same atmosphere as his room in Boston. He said 'Won't Mary love this color?'—a rug for his couch. He brought me a pomegranate—his skin has become etherealized and the rug, the fruit and his face all had the same colors in them." [2]

Torn both by Kahlil's messages of devotion—"and now let me cry out with all the voices in me that I love you"—and by Charlotte's provocative inferences, Mary could hardly wait to plunge herself again into the excitement of New York. She accepted an invitation for Thanksgiving at Waverly Place, which Charlotte promised would be "a simple Syrian meal." [3]

On the night before she departed she treated Marianna to dinner and the theater. Since Kahlil had left she conscientiously saw his sister at least once a week. This kind of caring which he so blithefully ignored made Marianna trust her more and more, even to the point of letting her see where she lived. At the expiration of the West Cedar Street lease, Marianna had moved back to 15 Oliver Place. There she tried to forget her loneliness by sharing a tenement with a cousin, Maroon George, and her husband Assaf and, spurred by Kahlil and Mary, by enrolling in classes at the Denison House. But the settlement house could not satisfy her, she complained that the "talk was trivial and stale that is meant to be elevating for the Syrian Club," and even Mary was forced to realize that what mattered to this woman—"so sincere, and so mediocre but *real*"—was simple survival. "I never knew a woman so passionately and consciously longing for the age-long woman work. 'I have to take somebody to the hospital,' she says—'to go to them when they're sick—and make their bed—and wash them and fix their room and nightgown and cook for them. O, I just love to do that.'" Still, she was shocked when she finally saw Oliver Place: "It is a regular shabby slum." Marianna saw Mary off on the midnight

The West Tenth Street Studio. (Courtesy The New-York
Historical Society)

train to New York with "tears raining from her eyes at Miss Teahan's
brutality—heart wrung with longing to see Kahlil—and inexpressible messages
to him—Her last words were resolutions to leave Miss Teahan—but I was not
to tell Kahlil." [4]

In New York, Mary for the next four days forgot the school and the South
End in her joy at staying with Charlotte and seeing Kahlil secure in his studio.
Before their Thanksgiving dinner the two women rushed to see him at the
Tenth Street Studio—"such a personal old simple building with its low-arched
wide black windows and the irregular reliefs in the white air-shaft that seem to
say, 'He was a living fellow put us here and made a courtyard of us.'" To
understand him in his new setting Mary naturally had to inspect everything:
the "four candlesticks that light seems to melt upon, sold him by the pound,
his tapestries from the Paris rag-fair for a few francs, . . a hanging
lamp—marvels of old iridescent Syrian glass—one plate of it hanging up and

three small shelves of smaller pieces." Oriental rugs, "sent and lent by Mme. Kuri [Marie El-Khoury] from Atlantic City," added to his pleasure dome. He identified this woman, along with Ameen Rihani, "as the nucleus of a growing circle of friends." A gem dealer, she was a noted hostess and sometime sponsor of Arabic literary efforts. They drank coffee and savored the incense-laden air while he showed them his three latest pictures. "Charlotte lay like a fourth picture on the dark rug by the red-mouthed little stove—in her winey velveteen—vine-like, with arm, and face pale gold. Then K. sat under the high window and read from *The Broken Wings* in the Arabic . . . we were hearing a song—but the invisible was so thick about me, lights and sounds came from such far times and spaces, that from centre to circumference I trembled with the excessive life-sense." [5]

Mary hardly slept at all that weekend. They visited the Metropolitan Museum twice, she read the faces and hands of Charlotte's visitors, and they all went to the Hippodrome and watched "a wonderful Oriental world" of acrobats, elephants, and dancers. Drumming time to the music on her "contented arm," Kahlil confessed how proud he was to see the Syrian dancers—"It could be done only in America." Then they went back to Charlotte's and sat up till three listening to her read her latest play. "Your stimulating mentality knocked Kahlil out for a day or two at least," wrote Charlotte after the weekend. "At least that is *my* version of his 'weariness.' You must not take the pace that kills others you wonder of womankind." [6]

Three days later Mary suddenly became aware of a new dimension in the threesome's delicately balanced friendship when she received an eleven-page letter from Charlotte devoted to Kahlil's friend Rihani. He had recently returned from six months in Lebanon, bringing her a copy of his just-published *The Book of the Khalid*, a long autobiographical tale of a Syrian antihero's wanderings in New York City and the Middle East. From the moment Charlotte read the breezy picaresque adventures she developed a startling obsession for the author.

> I want to talk to you of Rihani's book, which is directly and indirectly the cause of my wakefulness. . . . My impression of him last spring . . . was of a light-weight fellow, given to an obvious sort of Bohemianism, and full of pluck in his pain [a chronic back ailment]. If I could now detach myself from its Syrian charm and its American-satirized-malice I might judge it with some coherence. As yet I cannot. . . . To be quite frank Kahlil has never made me *feel* Syria, the book does. The book makes me feel Kahlil and his quiet persistent search for the Absolute. And yet—how much more I feel Rihani because of his stiletto like satire and humor. . . . Rihani's personality has suddenly become large enough to conceal most of the rest of Existence. His pain . . . is powerful. . . . Rihani must be cured. He has too much work to do to go to pieces now. So I lead him *tomorrow* for diagnosis, to an osteopath of whose delicacy I am assured (and who will

wait for his money) and I lead him to oxygen to sustain him while he suffers this pain. Kahlil, I think, will hardly reassure him on his work as I do, for one reason—Kahlil has not the lash of humor . . . and he will take Rihani for flippant when he is throwing his tortured body into a pool of mockery. . . . He will probably never do the limpid work of Kahlil—although it is for clearness and simplicity I shall drive him along one trail, *Satire!!* If anyone knew how I believed in its destructiveness! . . . But the beginning of this letter to you began last week before Rihani's return—in an hour with Kahlil. He needs you. . . . His work needs you! . . . Can't you spend Christmas with me—with US—Out of such a visit great work may come—four people may come to live in Paris and later in the desert—and who knows—but one of the four, or two of the four, or four of the four may give birth to the Child who is to unite the East and the West—by its Genius. . . . [I] pray that you will accept my invitation and the Invitation of Destiny.[7]

Mary decided against playing midwife to Charlotte's scheme for literary immortality but planned to travel south and visit a relative. She also persuaded Gibran to spend the vacation with Marianna in Boston. Before she left he helped her distribute bags of candy on the last day of school. One night he described for two hours the story of *The Broken Wings*. The book was delayed in press and he had not bothered to find a substitute Christmas present for her. On the other hand he approved of her gifts for him: the works of Swinburne and Rossetti and some little things for his studio—Hawaiian salt boxes, a Chinese spoon, Japanese straw slippers. Together they wrapped up a neckpiece of furs, their gift to Marianna, who they agreed needed this symbol of luxury to buoy her spirits.

But most of their talk was about the deepening relationship between Charlotte and Rihani. Unfortunately Mary's journal was not privy to all they said: "His remarks were based on too intimate knowledge of R. and observation of C. to be put on paper." Yet because Kahlil described him "as never before having had a woman friend" their general impression was that the most bewildered figure in the growing web must have been Ameen himself.[8]

Kahlil took Mary to the midnight train on December 22, but she did not proceed directly to Georgia. She stopped in New York to assess the complexities personally. "Charlotte's face was shining, trembling, with Rihani—the biggest thing that has come to her." They talked over the situation, which Charlotte admitted was too "big to handle." Finally Mary "dared to advocate withholding" herself from anything short of marriage. Then she resumed her trip, considered the audacity of her meddling, and sent a telegram and card recanting all that she had advised. For the remainder of the train ride she read Rihani's book. Certainly fierce loyalty to Gibran colored her opinion of it: "It is absolutely honest but limited as if the mind had wearied of the effort to see—had just accepted sensation and chance thoughts and fruits of mere courage." [9]

After a hurried reunion with Southern friends and cousins she returned to Boston, again by way of New York. Kahlil heard her report at Marlborough Street on January 2: Charlotte was now "skeptical," although she was certain that Rihani was "truly in love with her." His attentions were draining her and she had not been able to work for the past week. "There may be some great glorious fights ahead of those two yet," Kahlil predicted. Then while Mary quizzed him he defended his failure to paint a promised self-portrait during the holiday. Pleading his miserable quarters on Tyler Street, he added, "Well, you see, that is really very uninteresting work to me." "I don't give a straw for the uninterestingness," Mary exclaimed. "I want the picture done." [10]

The vacation ended with a readjustment of their mutual bequests. This practice of swapping precious objects and books to be received after death always fascinated them. They decided that he should have her pieces of embroidered Chinese silk, the encyclopedias, and her big Japanese carving of Fujiyama. He added to his will her earlier gift of two Chinese rings and "all the things of the sub-balcony in the studio." [11]

That night he reluctantly left for New York, with a look that haunted Mary for a month. "There are a few looks on K.'s face that I want to record," she finally wrote. The look of January 2, 1912, was the tenth of a remarkable list of expressions. "At parting he said, 'This is terrible,' and tho' my arms were around him, I could see his face all darkened and its spaces deepened and filled with what his words expressed—and when he turned at the door again—as he does not usually do, and with a look so different from the exquisitely comradely laugh with which we commonly part. His color had changed from ivory tints to brown and olive; the face looked large and strong and full of grief and there was something great investing it like a shadow and a light—as if he were listening with me to a strange lofty music and looking with me into something unsounded. It was the terrible again—pain, joy and vision." [12]

Mary lived a double life throughout January, while Kahlil worked and sent dutiful notes and Charlotte became more involved with Ameen and sent rambling letters. Impatience with the school and its demands on her time began to show. The three in New York filled her inner life and she tried to see how she fit into their world: "For my share of the rectangle, I've my old recipe of more loving and more trusting and less consciousness of myself as other than incidental in the life of each." As if to compensate for her absence, she behaved in some ways like an infatuated schoolgirl. Her choice of dress had for many years been simple and utilitarian; her favorite clothes were her camping togs which she often wore when Kahlil visited. Now she "bought two adornments . . . that induce lover-tho'ts: huge black chiffon veil . . . and pale blue silk knit thing that clings." [13]

Her rational decisions about the impossibility of marriage with Gibran were disappearing. Each letter from Charlotte describing the intimacy between herself and Rihani made her torment all the more painful. "I love K. yet age and homeliness would make me fearful to marry him even if he had means and desired it. . . . Kahlil is to me far more than ever to be desired—but every pang of knowledge that that shall not be has become dear to me. . . . And like David who wept only when his child was dead, I who have wept not during the struggle of these months to put marriage from my thoughts, showered tears last night." [14]

On January 26 he sent her a copy of *The Broken Wings*, in which he had translated the chapter titles and the dedication to her. The homage was more than she had expected: "In reply—I could only say out of my speechlessness: "To him who turns eyes sunward; who brings fire; who gives the Absolute a voice; whose immortality my name exults to wear—Acknowledgment." [15]

But other messages from him reflected unrest in New York. He whose polite reserve prohibited "indiscretion" was becoming resentful of the teetering Charlotte-Ameen affair. He saw very little of them, he wrote. "In fact I don't see much of anybody. I feel rather funny with other people—even those whome I care for. . . . I took luncheon with Charlotte today. Rihani and Barney were there too—All three seemed so strange to me. They made me feel as if they have nothing to do save to be tired of life. Charlotte and Rihani are coming to see me this afternoon. I hope they will bring a different spirit with them. . . . You see, Mary, after seeing you, or after reading one of your great letters, I look around and find everything and everybody so *slow*—so helplessly slow. . . . Reading the above I find that I was not *discreet* in making some remarks! But I need not worry about that. I talk to you, Mary, even as I would talk with my own heart." [16]

She welcomed his complaint as a new sign of freedom and maturity. "First time I ever knew him with a criticism indiscreet of others—that he felt no fear to do it gave me great pleasure." She was well aware of how complicated matters were, for Charlotte had already been far franker than he: "Kahlil is openly disappointed tho' he is doing nobly to conceal the true human qualities of envy and criticalness. . . [Rihani] and Kahlil discuss me—that I know—and I have some funny bits to tell you when I see you. Kahlil feels that I am playing a part or that I am not being true to my 'own true self'—Rihani is perfectly honest and outspoken—but what Oriental is *frank?* Their reserves have, at times, the appearance of mendacity. And the unconsciously-mendacious do not trust anyone. I only hope they won't ball each other up, for their friendship will have great value for each—and serve the world." [17]

Soon afterward there occurred what Kahlil had predicted as "the inevitable misunderstanding" between the couple. It led to Charlotte's banishment of Ameen, despairing outbursts, and her shattering avowal to abandon playwriting and return to her family in Denver. She begged for Mary's stable presence:

> I feel very guilty as to Rihani, for in spite of all I have said, he has continued to live in the expectation that I would marry him ultimately. But I shouldn't, even if he had money or fame. We are too highstrung to be mated. . . . He does not arouse any particular emotions beyond the mental ones and I *am* dead—finished as a woman. I can't tell you the bleakness of prospect. Indeed before I migrate I shall give you copies of "Pittsburgh" and the others [scripts] if you wish—as well as a copy of my will—so that you shall not lose the money you have so generously been giving me for the sojourn. I do not know why I have failed, but I have—for the time being at least. . . . Cut your Friday classes in a good cause and we'll burn incense here in the flat and go up in smoke—as inhabitants of the one world we have dwelt in.[18]

Torn by Kahlil's sharpened, jealous loneliness and at the same time alarmed by Charlotte's depression, Mary felt trapped at the school. But duty forced her to stay. "Thank God for Fridays," she wrote, "and that to-night I don't have to look at Wordsworth, Ruskin, Chaucer, or even Sophocles or Shakespeare. . . . Today—this afternoon—I have been strapped down to a grim floor of ugliness—and when I turned my head, it was still ugliness I saw . . . everywhere the sandy ache of ugliness 'lay like a load on my weary eye'. . . . Thank God I know Kahlil. . . . Thanksgiving that you aren't a business man or professor or cowboy or planter or critic—but what you are—Life—Space—Beauty—Warmth." [19]

Winter vacation finally released her and she hurried to New York. Matters there were not so drastic as she had been led to suspect. Kahlil was suffering from the inevitable cold, and Charlotte and Rihani were still jousting. Seeing them all together caused her to yearn for something more. One night she and Charlotte talked until four about Rihani. She slept restlessly for two hours and then woke with a "long, sobbing cry." A voice in her dream had aroused her: "Kahlil says this has gone far enough. He must have all or nothing." [20] The thought of an extra-marital affair had been dogging her for a year. Now, despite her personal distaste for it, she knew that she and Kahlil must discuss it.

Fatigued by lack of sleep and her revelation, she stumbled through the next day. Ameen joined Charlotte and her for breakfast. Then Micheline arrived. In the past year she had returned to teaching, giving up all her aspirations for the stage. Her year at the Ely School had been good for her. For lunch she took Mary to meet a young attorney whom both Charlotte and Kahlil were predicting she would marry. As Mary studied Lamar Hardy, she too decided he was suitable. And then the moment for confrontation with Kahlil arrived.

> From Micheline in p.m. I came to studio, for nearly three hours time enough for much talk. I told him the dream, and asked if our non-union seemed hard and otherwise unlovely. I was tired. He got coffee and rolls—We eat. I napped—it was quiet and the light soft—K. was moved. I told him the cowardice I felt in a man's letting a woman be his mistress; It was new to him. . . . He made the great refusal and for minutes and minutes shook—but recovered.
> "Now I know you love me," he said.
> "Did you not know it before today?"
> "Yes but differently."
> I too was profoundly touched and felt even far nearer than ever before.[21]

But the problem remained unresolved. That night she refused to join him and Micheline at a soirée given by the art patrons Alexander and Marjorie Morten. The next day she stopped by the studio before leaving for Boston and challenged Kahlil to take the initiative. She began, "I have put you and me in your hands!"

"I wish I'd said that first," said he.

"You've always said it. The key's been in my hands; now I hand it over."

Kahlil was "agitated." "No, that's too hard on me. Why haven't we ever talked about all this before?"

"We wouldn't have talked about it now," said Mary, "if I hadn't begun it."

They argued about who did take the initiative in their friendship. "He seemed to think he took it habitually—said he was tired of leading a ruling woman." [22] For the first time he did not see her to the station.

Back at school the "upheaving talk" tore at her nerves. She did not attempt to record the unsettling events in the journal but made a rambling entry in her more personal diary. One day how deep was the split in her life was brought home to her. Her sister Louise "came to lunch and asked who I'd seen in New York and whether I saw Adam [their youngest brother]. I realized how of another world my list sounded and how incomprehensible to her *my* world is *out* of this one here." Soon afterward this realization was bolstered by Charlotte, who finally wrote, "Romance is throttled. . . . I am giving up even the pretense of friendship with Rihani." Gibran, who had tried to be loyal to both, also lost favor in her eyes and she urged Mary to reconsider their relationship. "When you and I say these two men are too young for us, as women, we are not making them less, nor ourselves more—we are simply growing more conscious that the steps by which we grow (and, let us hope, by which *they* grow) are not, after all—the goal itself. . . . You will be released anew into great joy by giving up the spiritual hope of union with—yes, with a Mohammedan. That is the sane and right category for both." [23]

On March 8, a few days later, Mary suggested to Kahlil a complete break. "Shall I say to you dear Old Man what has been in my thought ever since I left N.Y.?—that if it is more pain than pleasure to you to see me I don't want you to see me—but to let time and absence begin right now their sure cure. The feeling that has come in fifteen months may go in much less—if never fed—and then seeing or not seeing will be easy—This is not said lightly—but in simple earnest." Small wonder that he was upset by this letter. Not only his friendship with Mary but his very livelihood and survival as an artist were imperiled. Immediately he protected himself and his future with a carefully weighed answer.

> Mary, dearest Mary, how could you, in the name of Allah, ask me if my seeing you gives me more pain than pleasure? What is there in heaven or earth to inspire such a thought?
>
> And what is pain and what is pleasure? Could you seperate one from the other? The power which moves you and me is composed of both pleasure and pain—and that which is realy beautiful gives nothing but delicious pain or painful joy.
>
> Mary, you give me so much of pleasure that it is painful—and you give me so much of pain too—and that is why *I love you.*

For the rest of the month he avoided any mention of their mutual friends and distracted her by listing new acquaintances of his own. The artist Adele Watson, Mrs. Alexander Morten, the sculptor Ronald Hinton Perry, "Mrs. Benette, a society lady who writes poetry," and a Spanish count in the diplomatic service all came to his studio. "I have met more people during the last week than I ever did in one year of my life." [24]

From now on the only individuals whom he described to Mary were those connected with his work. Never again would he repeat what he finally realized was the fatal error of introducing her to those to whom he was personally close.

On April 3 he came to Boston, intent on repairing the damages of the past months. Their first evening together was full of the old fondness. He did not look well. "He has never been at so low an ebb physically," Mary noted. "Nor so active and productive mentally." She ministered to him. "Went with me to the bathroom and bathed eyes, douched nose, and gargled with Boric Acid—and was at once better—tho' he almost lost the new coolness by smoking a cigarette later. . . . There was so much to say about the pictures since I left N.Y. and about the new friends that we did not touch on our personal matter—but when Kahlil lowered the tell tale lights and took me in his arms he knew." [25]

234

Two days later they walked to the Public Garden and sat on a bench facing the pond. The afternoon was "sweet and balmy," wrote Mary. "While we talked a beggar came and got ten cents—and a rosy little Jew boy in kilts chased pigeons with a musical 'Whoo Whoo!' around us." In this setting Kahlil was totally unprepared for her topic of conversation. "We sat till after six—and our vital talk was on Kahlil's mind and habits in sex things." For the past two years she had stored a long list of impressions about his sexuality. There was Micheline's assessment—"Kahlil is like other men. He must always be in love with someone"—and her accusation of his lack of consideration for women in Paris, "where he used to let her and Rachel wash the dishes while he smoked or go to the car alone with a suitcase of things for him." Then came Charlotte's warning of his "inflammability," coupled with her scathing lumping together of him and Rihani as untrustworthy "Mohammedans." His own words on free love had also incriminated him: "And when he said in N.Y. intercourse was no more than picking a flower—I could only say to myself that there were mysteries beyond my apprehension in the possible attitudes towards sex of clean minds." [26]

When she confessed that she had never been able to reconcile rumors of his successive affairs with his "unifiedness and stability and fastidious reserve," he was confused. "So I gave him a list of his remarks from time to time and their inevitable significance to me. He was astounded—and didn't see at all that what he had said meant what to the English-speaking it must mean. Ignorance of certain English connotations explained some—his way of unconcreteness in matters that might give offence if in concrete words explained some—and his extreme brevity others." His defense of his conduct was masterful. He explained that "he had connection with very few women in his life" and offered "to tell how many." Mary refused to hear the details. When she sat down to record the talk in her diary she did briefly allude to his first sexual experience, "how he was initiated and carried far while not yet fifteen by a married woman twice his age—after which, with his temperament, he might have been well expected to play the devil instead of shrinking." He also described his "physical reserve—how few people he can touch without shrinking and how impossible intimacy with many women would always be." [27]

Gradually he made her see how literal he had been when he had so often said, "I'd never say this to anyone else—or I never thought I could speak to anyone about these things." "Hawaiik, it seems, is the only friend who knows his life and mind in the matter of sex. Rihani, Madame El-Khoury, Charlotte, Micheline, all consider him a man of 'affairs.' He doesn't undeceive them—simply because he shrinks more from talking about his intimate concerns than from being misconceived." Finally she was satisfied. "I believe as he does that sex-relations except as regards health and scourge of children, are properly the affairs of the persons concerned—not of society—and he knows this—Yet he has never given me a request by word or deed for intercourse—though I feel—as who could help it, with the freedom that is between us and the great love—how great is his desire." [28]

For her the dialogue "had changed the world." When he came to Marlborough Street that night "for the first time I knew the peace and sweetness of his touch and his kiss on my body. He caressed me; that was all but there was an infinite feeling of expansion and freedom of heart now that not even the fastening of my garments said, 'Thou shalt not. . . .' My old walks on Commonwealth Ave. that have made the air about the Vendome thick with ghosts of battle were spent I thought in trying to give up the idea of marriage. . . . But now I find this easy; so it wasn't marriage I had been longing for—but nearness." [29]

They came back to the school the next night after the Saturday symphony. There followed a scene which bothered Mary briefly but which continued to enrage Gibran for several years.

> After we got home the door was tried by someone from outside. Policeman, I thought and heeded not; but presently another attempt made me go there . . . and there were Adam and Nattie! My telling how I avoided Louise last year because I felt so much comment about Gibran returned to me in a rush—I was horribly embarrassed—couldn't have brought myself to let them in had they been angels—whispered a bluff to N. and got her to take Adam off. But next morning . . . I went around and found her and Adam at breakfast and made a clean breast of it—that Gibran had been here last night—that we loved each other—couldn't marry. . . .
>
> Adam said, "I'm glad you came and told me because I saw him when you opened the door."
>
> Nattie said, "I'm glad you told us because I'm glad you have that in your life—and if you didn't take it and get all you could of him—I should think you were less yourself! [30]

Thus relieved, she met Kahlil at Copley Square, where the wind drove them into the library. Sitting and whispering in the most remote corner of the special libraries room, they had good reason not to be overheard. First she told him of her confession to her brother and sister-in-law. Kahlil "greatly approved" of it but worried whether she had made them understand that his love equaled hers for him. They then probed the question of intercourse, the unreliability of contraceptive devices, and the consequences. He spoke out for marriage—"as soon as I've conquered my work and a little of the world"—and again she explained that impossibility. He "simply laughed" when she said she had studied loves like theirs "from Oedipus married to his mother, to

236

Mahomet and his old Kadjah [Khadija], through Browning to Elizabeth Barrett." [31]

But ten years later he blurted out how Adam's visit and then her hesitancy had discouraged any hope of their ever forming a physical union.

> And so I . . . waited and kept on hoping and hoping. . . . And then came the crash. One night while we were spending the evening at Marlborough Street, the bell rang—It was your brother and his wife. You hesitated about letting them in—but decided to do so. There was a peculiar feeling about their finding me there and you felt very uncomfortable. When we met two days later you were still a good deal upset—And you said something about your brother's attitude toward me—that he would consider me in the light of such foreigners as you call dagos. That finished me—And the very *next* time we met you were your very sweetest self—just as if nothing had happened. But with me something had happened. The man in me towards you had to change for self protection. But until I learned that, I couldn't work. I couldn't see friends normally—I couldn't be sane and keep going through what you continually were putting me through. And after awhile, I said to myself, "On any personal, intimate daily plane, relations with this woman are impossible. They must be restricted to the spirit and the soul." [32]

When Kahlil returned to New York his letters reflected his changed outlook. Again he wrote Mary of impersonal matters. He told her about meeting and drawing Abdul Baha, the leader of the Bahai movement for world unity, on the morning of the Titanic tragedy. Charlotte complained that he was neglecting her, but even when she and Rihani were temporarily reunited in the spring he refused to discuss them.

Charlotte's preoccupation with dreams and symbols was taking a constructive turn. In March she had met Dr. Beatrice Moses Hinkle, one of the first women doctors in public health and formerly city physician in San Francisco. As early as 1904 she was publishing articles on psychoanalysis, and when she became interested in mental health she started at Cornell Medical College the first psychotherapeutic clinic in America. Now a widow of thirty-eight, she had just returned from three years in the Orient and Europe. Her studies had led her to Carl Jung, and she had attended the historic Weimar Congress in September 1911.

"She knows *scientifically* all those things you and I discuss," Charlotte had written to Mary in March. The idea of psychotherapy was not new to Charlotte. Indeed in 1909 she had envisioned a kind of world therapy session that she and Mary would run. "Who knows, Mary, but you and I in later years (perhaps not so late, either) may have a place to which the world will come to hear and see and know themselves thru' us. Can't you see a well-proportioned room in green or yellow with only one object in it for the eye to rest on—as the Japanese have it—and in this room, one at a time the patients relaxing, emptying themselves before coming in for their lesson in—what would we call it?—self-knowledge, or unself-knowledge. Then an expert in psychology like Dr. Cabot to call in for morbid cases: baths, gymnasium, osteopathy, oxygen, music—all these things harmonized and unified for each peculiar individual." [33]

Charlotte's depression fled. She regained confidence in her talents and rededicated herself to playwriting and journalism. But even after she met Marianna on a weekend visit to Boston, Kahlil was steadfast in his disapproval of her and her latest fad. He liked Dr. Hinkle, but Charlotte's dream swapping, which dangerously included him, was to be avoided at all costs.

When school was out at the end of May he came to Boston and stayed at Tyler Street for two weeks. "I so hate his Tyler Street rooming and knocking about," Mary wrote, but he refused to stay at the school. "Said it couldn't help being known if he were here and would be inevitably misinterpreted." His apprehension was in a way borne out by a dream of Charlotte's, which she described to Mary on May 23. "You were so disappointed in Kahlil and me that you were almost out of your head—so wild and weird. Finally to shock you back to reason I tried to pretend that *I* was a maniac. Whenever I mentioned K.'s work you actually spit at me—for you knew something I didn't." She added that Micheline and others were talking about their friendship as a possible basis of marriage and warned, "You may be sure that Miss Dean and some of your associates are conjecturing all things." [34]

Mary and Kahlil spent the two weeks together walking and talking. There was a new hardness in his tone when they discussed their intimacy. "He spoke of the change that has come to him—how he has come to his own road—become a man instead of a boy and firm instead of vague. I feel that beyond expression—the definition in him and the rock quality. . . . When I offered to try a preventative of conception so that we may have sex intercourse, the other day, he refused so simply explaining what I had not known he knew—the profound change abortion might make "in your whole being," in case prevention failed and how all pleasure and joy would be destroyed by the least uncertainty. . . . 'It is so much to touch, to talk—just to be *intimate*. That intimacy is the precious thing. Life is a continued intercourse.' " [35]

On June 10 she "put him on the rack" when she revealed how she had become skeptical of his self-understanding when he had spoken of marriage in December 1910.

> Then K. told me his story—for the first time. Two months before he left Paris he determined to return and ask me to marry him: "I was a dizzy person," he confessed. "I am one-sided as you know, I could not see all

238

sides of a thing. But I knew what I wanted—and you did not put the words into my mouth that night in December. . . . I was very happy for two or three hours. But that very night when I went home a world of things came to me in a rush. How I had nothing to offer you—was only a poet in a strange land—with some fame in another country . . . no money—no anything to ask you to share. I had a big thing to do. . . . I was daring to take up another big thing—and I realized suddenly that I was not equal to more than one of them."

"Why didn't you say so?" . . .

"Because I hoped I should see the way that was the right way and I did not yet see it. I was too uncertain to move again in any direction." [36]

When they argued, sometimes over ludicrous things, Kahlil protested, "You say things that cut and hurt—and you are the only person in the world who has the power to do this to me. Is it a rubbery quality in me that tempts your strong arm—for you have a strong arm—just to see me bound back again?" They also talked much about Charlotte, her restlessness, her reluctance to face work, her endless theorizing. Mary finally got him to admit why he was avoiding her: "It is at bottom because she regards him and speaks of him as having sex relations with women, he said." [37] When he left on June 16, a détente had been achieved in their wordy war of nerves.

By July 1 Mary was in the Sierras. As a special treat she took along Aristides Phoutrides. Rihani had left for Lebanon and Charlotte had seen him off, "looking like a young lord in purple and fine silk. He left his typewriter with me and his incense cup. I made him a pillow for the voyage." [38] More important, she had moved from Greenwich Village to a new apartment on East 77th Street. It was the end of their era. Within five years all of them except Kahlil and Mary would be estranged.

Halfway through the summer Mary and Kahlil agreed to meet, but not at Marlborough Street. "I don't know how much you were seen there in June," she wrote, "but I suspect about as much as you *were* there—so it is better for me not to begin this year with your *visible* presence." When they saw each other in New York on September 7, the strains of the past months were fading. Sex, which both fascinated and frightened her, was no longer an issue. "I debated intercourse and the possibility of being called his mistress—with great distress of uncertainty—at last I left it to our larger selves—and dear me! When K. came there was no question even. He simply ignored intercourse—and made me feel a thousand times more loved than ever before. He has shamed me out of my self-protectiveness." [39]

He on the other hand was learning how to cope with her intrusions, however well meaning, into his life. She chastised him for smoking too much and eating too little, and spoke of her plan for him to go west to recover his health. His refusal was "wholesouled." Perhaps he was afraid of the

Mary and companions after a Sierra knapsack trip. Phoutrides is on the left. (University of North Carolina Library, Chapel Hill)

condescension she had shown for Phoutrides the past summer. This gifted man "lost, forgot, overlooked most things," she complained. "Phoutrides is as yet a simple head as well as a simple soul! I overtook him at the Grand Canyon—making innocent waste of his money, losing and forgetting his stuff. . . . He dropped his leggins down the Grand Canyon—and had no soap to wash clothes with in camp."[40] Instinctively Kahlil recoiled from any endurance test in the Grand Canyon or on the slopes of Mount Whitney. He was beginning to understand exactly how much closeness he could tolerate.

Charlotte's absence from Waverly Place, forcing Mary to rent a room at 25 West Eighth Street in order to be near the studio, was the greatest change. When they had dinner at her new place an outsider, Gilbert Hirsch, was there. Charlotte had already written about this young Harvard graduate and journalist and about how profoundly he was helping her. "I nearly touched bottom . . . I am being supported by a spirit (in Hirsch) which has for me as a man what you have had for me as a woman and friend. He is so close to you. If I do love him I shall marry him altho hark ye! He is only twenty-five." Kahlil wished they would marry, but Mary's assessment was more penetrating. "Hirsch and the Freudian-Jung psychoanalysis have been making Charlotte over. Hirsch loves her wholly and holily: Has guided her . . . and sustained her through a fierce nervous breakdown. . . . They have been together, practically all summer in adjoining flats. . . . has been searching out every bluff and every evasion . . . from her third year onward and is becoming healed and sound—no longer itching for a scheme for the universe or to prove Woman greater than Man." [41]

Then, after meeting Jung in New York and writing a long article about him for the *Times*, Charlotte sailed out of Gibran's and Mary's lives. She and Gilbert Hirsch were quietly married on October 16 and left for Europe the next day. At long last Kahlil had no fears about her as a competitor or matchmaker. The intrigue and jealousy which had risen to nearly incestuous heights the past year were dispelled.

"Then, you stopped . . . hurting me. You were never brutal again—but always gentle," he told Mary later. "And then Charlotte married and went away—and all our meetings were just blessed." [42]

Gibran at work in his studio. (Madeleine Vanderpool)

14

The Birth of a Legend

Kahlil's relief at Charlotte's marriage was rather naive. Misunderstandings and doubts between him and Mary continued long after the newlyweds had left New York. At issue now was his financial dependence. He could not attend to his health, he explained, because "many things are burdening my mind, weighing there."

"*What* so burdens you?" she asked.

"Being in two worlds. Were I in Syria, my poetry would ensure notice to my pictures, were I an English poet, it would ensure them English notice. But I am between the two—and the waiting is heavy. I want to be independent—to have enough to fulfill my work—to help my sister and to entertain a friend." [1]

She understood.

> How thankful I felt to hear the words and the tears as he said it. . . . . I could only say it would always hurt, till it was over—and that I hoped he'd express the hurt every time we met because expression relieves. Later, thinking it over, I realized that dependence need not hurt; but that just as it is sweet to eat and drink from God, it may be sweet to take means at each other's hand—and we can feel richer, not poorer for it. Long after, looking back, one will see sweetness in this relation of guest and host, and know its core was good. Why not see it *now* in its eternal verity? And I believe K. came too to look more thus on it; for in our other glimpses in 1912, I felt little of that former sense of unendurableness—as if, realizing that he is choosing dependence for his work's sake which is dearer than independence, he had stopped crying for independence. [2]

This mutual acceptance of their interdependence had taken eight years to realize. For the twelve remaining years of their intimacy Mary not only relieved Gibran's guilt over her patronage but equipped him intellectually and linguistically to bridge his two separate worlds. Within four years he would publish in English; within ten, he would compose most of his work in English.

Although she continued to try to act as his agent in order to introduce his work to Americans, she was never quite successful in this role. She was too didactic a personality, too unbending to be able to match artist and admirers. Charlotte with her instinct for the right introduction was in fact responsible for his initial contacts in New York. But she was fully aware of how indispensable Mary was to his development. "Kahlil . . . has a big writer's work to show in concept and visions, but [it] has not grown in *vigor* as it should. How I long for your nurturing eye upon it. As [Rihani] says of himself 'The oriental has flashes of power, but short duration of power. He conceives in grandeur—but grows weary in working it out.' That is why I believe only in Kahlil's work if it is one *with* you. You *sustain*—your whole being is sustenance and maintenance!"[3]

Another person was aware of Kahlil's dual allegiances. In the fall of 1912 the French novelist Pierre Loti was in New York for the production of his play *The Daughter of Heaven*. Kahlil described to Mary his re-encounter with Loti, whose popularity and eccentric appearance were beginning to wear. More significant was Loti's appraisal of the changes he perceived in the younger man.

> Pierre Loti is here and I had a charming hour with him on Thursday. We talked about the East, "his beloved East." He said he saw my "Broken Wings" and other things and he ended by saying "You are becoming more brutal and less oriental—and it is too bad, too bad!"
>
> I told him that I loved my country too well to be like her other children. But he dose not see that; he is too delicate, too sensitive. He has all the *beautiful* Oriental diseases in his artistic soul. And he will not be drawn. "Oh no, no! I, I sit before an artist? No, no, never, *jamais, abadun* (in Arabic)—anything but that; it will kill me."
>
> Loti is 62 years old—but he is wonderfully powdered and rouged and pencilled—yes, rouged and pencilled—and he looks pathetically much younger.
>
> I want to see him again. It makes me feel *good* to see such a dreamer of shadowy dreams. It makes me feel real to be with such an orientalized occidental.[4]

The writer's much-heralded visit to the United States foundered. Within a month Kahlil wrote, "Pierre Loti is gone back to live in the shadow of some temple in the East. . . . His last words to me were 'Now, Gibran, let me tell you in behalf of Syria that you must *save your soul* by going back to the East. America is no place for you!'"[5]

Mary would have financed a trip to France or even to Lebanon if Kahlil had wanted it. But work, not travel, was his satisfaction. After he had six teeth pulled in the fall of 1912, she made plans for him to recuperate in Vermont, but he declined. A year later, sure that he was "a candidate for consumption," she carefully plotted a winter vacation in Bermuda for both him and Marianna. But although she took care of schedules, hotel reservations, and insurance, he again refused. "Please do not be angry with me," he wrote. "When winter comes one wants to think and work—regardless of how one feels. And besides, I am naturally stupid about going to a *different place.* I always feel as though I am leaving my reality behind me. Even in the summer I love to stay where my pictures and books are. Perhaps it is a form of physical laziness." [6]

"Indeed, dearest K. G.," Mary had already assured him, "I understand with all my heart your desire to be alone, your *need* to be alone. . . . Even when two people are actually together, is it not a pulse-beat of meeting—&—parting, meeting—&—parting. . . . Sometimes the parting from a person needs to be very long—but however long it may be for you and me, meeting will come again—and with new Kahlils and new Marys." [7]

Slowly they worked out a formula for visits—Boston for the holidays, New York for the beginning and end of Mary's summer trips and for the annual November meetings of the Head Mistress Association. They no longer shared their life together with others. As this pattern became clearly defined, Mary rededicated herself to the school. The Haskell–Dean partnership had been dissolved in the spring of 1912, and she relished "the new freedom in having the reins again in my hand . . . my interest has come all to life again." At first she contemplated expanding her facility by buying a larger building and including a Montessori program for younger children, but she settled for the rented Marlborough Street quarters and a broadening of her philosophical goals. She evolved her own innovative approach to learning history, literature, and art in an integrated way. To this end she initiated weekly trips to the local museums. "I think no school has done this before—using a real live museum. Watercolors, clay, embroidery: the children can use all these—copying what they see. Think how they will love it!" [8]

With this new challenge she became convinced that her contribution to progressive education was paralleling Gibran's creative endeavors, and on November 10, 1912, she spelled out in a letter their separate but equal roles. "Aren't children—isn't the begetting of children—the Larger Being's resource with us when we are ourselves unfinished instruments of expression?—We become links then in the development of finished instruments. C'est tout. Those who create neither works nor children are neither links nor completions I suppose—probably less as yet than either. . . . Great works *must* initiate new human varieties, just as new human varieties *may* initiate great works." [9]

Thus settled, they worked apart but with special acknowledgments to the other. After she gave a speech in a public school to about a thousand children, she wrote, "A fourteen-year old boy in school yesterday reminded me of you—and we made friends straightway, with looking at each other and with my showing him once or twice that he knew what he thought he didn't know." And Gibran told her, "Mary, you have never seemed 'absent' to me. You are always near me. There are times when I talk to you by the hour. And of cours there is Telepathic communication between us. I knew that ages ago. How could two beings, such as we are, understand one another without *that* silent communication? When we are together we simply talk—but when we are apart we understand . . . the things we have talked about." [10]

Their first visit after Charlotte's marriage came on November 9 when Mary journeyed to New York for the annual meeting of headmistresses. She spent a morning at the studio, noticing "the hum of the building and the movement" but also its inconveniences—the cramped quarters, the lack of central heating, the inadequate plumbing ("no hot water and twenty-five cents a bath"). "I had not been all A.M. in the studio before. Today I caught . . . more of the atmosphere in which K. lives and works—more vivid realization of how the twenty-four hours sound and feel as they go by. His rugs are never shaken . . . and the place looks dingier as months pass—but its spirit is so noble in the spare setting and so masculine and clear and labor filled. I feel a home likeness and a bachelordom at once—bareness, quietness, intense thought, life rubbed to the bone and loneliness." [11]

Almost thirty, Gibran was losing the buoyant good looks that had so attracted attention in turn-of-the-century Boston. "K. ages very quickly. His face shows now so much strain and stress—shows privation and loneliness and burden and intensest concentrated effort." Each time they met they meticulously reviewed the events in their lives. Mary began by reciting school problems or what was happening to the several members of her family, and he followed with accounts of his latest New York acquaintances. They both understood the importance of these contacts. "New York is a strange place," he once said. "It has its own technique in bringing a man out. It is to begin him socially and end him professionally. I want to begin professionally. But I can't change New York technique, and I don't feel the strength to combat it besides doing my work. So to a certain extent I accept it and am being known in the New York way." [12]

Since the spring of 1912 when Micheline had taken him to the party at the Mortens', he had been learning to socialize. The friendship with Alexander and Marjorie Morten was an important start. Later that year Charlotte had observed, "Last night I dined at Mrs. Morten's and some of Kahlil's incense was burned, so I knew he had been there enough to be friends. Mrs. M. has money and taste and ought to be a good friend to him." [13]

The Mortens were pioneering patrons of contemporary American art. Among their favorite painters were Arthur B. Davies, Albert Pinkham Ryder, and Childe Hassam. Early in 1913, just before the Armory Show, Alexander Morten arranged for Davies to visit Gibran's studio. As founder and president of the Association of American Painters and Sculptors and prime organizer of the Armory Show, he was one of the most influential tastemakers in New York at that time. Kahlil, who in Boston had been introduced to his work by the Rüyls, immediately sent Mary a joyful report of the visit.

> Mr. Davies kept repeating the word "wonderful—wonderful" as he gazed at the paintings and drawings, then he said to Mr. Morten, "This man is going to surprise the world as he surprised me." And then he told me how sorry he is that he did not see my work a month ago—he said he would have asked me to send half a dozen pictures to the large exhibition which will open tomorrow (Monday).
>
> "But," he said, "I will see to your having an exhibition by yourself. I shall speak to Mr. MacBeth about it."
>
> Mr. Morten, who owns more of Davies' pictures than any other man in New York, said that he, too, will see MacBeth.
>
> Mr. Davies said, as he was leaving, "I want to see these things again and I hope you will come and see me—I am sure we are going to be great friends—In the meanwhile do not be anxious about exhibiting—that is quite secondary—the thing is to keep on working. And do not be like me—Here I am at the age of fifty and I have not done much—I have lost so much time fooling around!" The next day Mr. Morten said to me over the phone "I have never heard Davies' speaking of anybody's work as he did of yours—you should feel very happy." [14]

During 1913 Gibran also made friends with several others in Charlotte's circle. He met Jung several times and drew a pencil portrait of him. He remained close to Dr. Beatrice Hinkle. To Mary he described "her vitality, power and magnetism. . . . I became aware that she was making a study of me. That made me conscious. I did not tell her before leaving that I was aware. And I have been sorry that I did not. Yet perhaps it was as well, after all, for she probably perceived I was conscious and just included that in her study. She admires Jung immensely, and so do I." [15]

His circle was growing. If knowing the Mortens led to acceptance in the art world and friendship with Dr. Hinkle introduced him to others exploring Jungian psychology, a third acquaintance now involved him with literary figures. Julia Ellsworth Ford, the wife of the hotel owner Simeon Ford and a longtime admirer of the Pre-Raphaelites, began to invite him to her Friday night literary dinners. There he formed enduring friendships with several American poets and writers, among them Witter Bynner, the peripatetic poet and former editor of *McClure's Magazine* who would play a most important role in his career.

But time and again he swore to Mary that no one knew him as well as she did. In terms of his origins this was undoubtedly true. Oliver Place and his privations there were far from the image that he created for his metropolitan admirers. His mystique among his new friends was based not on the real-life story of an immigrant adolescent's progression from one interested patron to another, but on the tale of a sudden descent into New York by a Levantine cosmopolite, fluent in French and English, sprung full blown from a mysterious past.

It was inevitable that speculation should arise about his source of income, and he enjoyed telling Mary about people's conjectures. Mrs. Ford's comments were typical of the growing legend. "I'd like to help that young man," she allegedly said. "Has he any money? Where does he get it from? I'm afraid of him. I don't even dare ask him the price of a picture." [16]

To be the secret source of his support appealed enormously to Mary, and in February 1913 a letter from him caused her to contribute even more solidly. "There is a chance of my getting a fine, large studio here in this building [51 West Tenth Street]. It is three times as large as mine and it has north light, south light (sunshine) and skylight—very cheerful and very good for work. The rent is forty-five dollars! Now I have been debating with myself for the last few days and I do not know what to do! I shall have to spend some money to make the place look nice and clean—about fifty dollars. May I take it if they would let me have it?" His solicitousness pained her and she deliberated her next move: "May I take it? *May I?* That made me think with fire and sword in my heart. Stop it I must. K. would never fulfill himself until he could be free at last." [17]

Thus she proposed an "arrangement," an advance to Kahlil of $1,000 toward what they would call the Haskell–Gibran Collection. With this newest gift, she proposed that all her former "loans" to him be canceled. In turn she was to receive ten of his paintings (by June he insisted that the total be raised to fourteen). These pictures were to be chosen "according to intrinsic merit and to representativeness of development." She also decided to transfer some securities to him to "carry him through until he is independent." [18]

Relieved and grateful that he was now free to move to more spacious quarters, he responded, "My getting into a larger studio is indeed a fine thing. Putting aside the physical comfort, I know it will mean very great deal to the work. [He would continue to refer to "the work" or "the collection" in terms of an investment shared by both of them.] Humanity is afraid of the work of a starving artist who lives in a 'dark little hole.' *Respectable* people, and it does not matter how broad they are, can never really be themselves save in respectable places! To be a victim of the respectability of people is a fine thing from the *artistic* point of view—but somehow, Mary, it is not in me to be a victim of anything or anybody; and I am *not* artistic." By the end of April he wrote, "I received this morning a blank order for the payment of dividends from the American Telephone & Telegraph Co. . . . Now for the first time in my life I find myself a stockholder and it all seems so strange." [19]

248

That spring some dollars-and-cents details of their lives were sporadically revealed in her diary. He lived on $1,500 to $2,000 a year, which included a small amount forwarded monthly to Marianna. His earnings from articles in the Syrian newspapers were minimal. Royalties from the first-year sales of *The Broken Wings* amounted to $75. As for Mary's capital worth, it was forever strained to accommodate her generosity. That year she estimated her share of the income from her and her brother Tom's orchards in Washington State to be between $2,000 and $3,000. With Miss Dean's departure, profits from the current school year were lean. A modest bequest from her father's estate supplemented her income but in no way justified her largesse. A year before, at Charlotte's suggestion, she had begun to send another immigrant teenager to Mount Hermon. This time her charge was the pitifully handicapped Jacob Giller, a Russo-Jewish boy from New York City. By 1913, though her payments to Charlotte and Micheline had ceased, she was responsible for two tuitions at Mount Hermon, was continuing to aid Aristides Phoutrides, and had just endowed Gibran with a sizable stock portfolio.

How she managed can be explained only by her scrupulous devotion to her budget and to her enormous self-denial. She scrimped on clothes ("My spring hat cost me half a nineteen-cent bottle of colorite—clothes nothing") and saved on food. One economy was the habit of Katy, her devoted cook, of cadging leftovers from the well-provided kitchen of a nearby Back Bay mansion. Indeed, Mary turned this savings into high comedy when she related it to Kahlil.

> *After Supper.* I wonder what the rich old lady across the alley would think if she knew that . . . I had her asparagus for lunch today and more of it for supper, with her fried chicken, mushrooms, rice and ice cream? And on Friday her strawberry cream? On Tuesday a fry of her pineapple? . . . I sin with open eye—for I know all that's bought in this house, and recognize the Avenue Superior brands! And my only comment is Solicitude to Katy to return like courtesies. Cooks commonly feed their friends—but I know no other case of feeding their ladies![20]

Years later, when Mary's philanthropy toward Gibran was revealed, she was written off as a wealthy patron. This description belittles the self-imposed sacrifices that supported her magnanimity. During the spring of 1913 she and Kahlil carefully totalled up her "loans" to him thus far. They found that "he had had up to date $7,440, as well as we could recall." This was less than one-fourth of her total gifts to her protégés: "When I told K. that in the last seven years I had spent nearly $40,000, he looked as approving as if I had said I had improved the mind of man—and said it was splendid." [21]

Although by now she often neglected to fill in more confidential entries in the abbreviated diary (October 1913 would see her last note in it), her devotion to recording Gibran's widening activities in the journal became an obsession that year. In April the first issue of *al-Funoon* (*The Arts*) appeared in New York. It marked the beginning efforts of the Arabic-speaking community to publish a periodical devoted to literary and artistic affairs. Although it was edited by Naseeb Arida and N. Nasseem, it reflected Gibran's taste and style. His designs, illustrations, prose poems, and articles helped give it an immediate appeal. Many of his poems during the first year became the nucleus for his "Madman" writings, and he initiated a series of simple essays and imaginative drawings about pre-Islamic and Islamic poets and philosophers. Through his efforts al-Maarri, ibn-al-Farid, ibn-Khaldun, al-Ghazali, ibn-al-Muqaffa, and ibn-Sina were portrayed and introduced to the mostly Christian Arabic readership.

He was also keeping up with his Temple of Art series. In September 1912, he had drawn the playwright Alice Bradley and on May 26, 1913, he drew Sarah Bernhardt. "At last the divine Sarah is caught! The drawing which I made of her yesterday, though it does not show her *real age*, is a great success. But if I am to go through the same process with the rest of the great men and women, I might as well give up art and become a diplomate! She wanted me to sit at a distance so that I may not see the *details* of her face. But I *did* see them. She made me take off some of the wrinkles. She even asked me to change the shape of her huge mouth! . . . I think I understood her yesterday—and I behaved accordingly, and perhaps that is the reason why she liked me a little!" [22]

Another subject who appealed to his revolutionary sympathies was Giuseppe Garibaldi. He had met and drawn the soldier-adventurer at Mrs. Ford's and for a while had fantasized about Garibaldi's leading a regiment of immigrant Syrians to overthrow the Turkish yoke. "I met General Garibaldi, the grandson of the great Garibaldi. He is the man who goes from one part of the world to another to fight with the people against any form of slavery. He has taken a part in six deferent wars—the last being with the Greeks against the Turks." [23]

During that active spring he urged Mary to see the Armory Show or, as it was officially called, the International Exhibition of Modern Art. After its sensational reception in New York and Chicago it had traveled to Boston, abbreviated to include only European selections. Mary identified with the new spirit, made friends with the organizers, and immediately wrote him about it.

> What shall I say, what shall I say!—to tell how it has refreshed and delighted me. . . . I have heard no good word for [the pictures] from professional or layman. . . . I waited till I was free on a day when admission was twenty-five cents instead of fifty—and went just because I wanted after all to see for myself. I stood at the door of Copley Hall . . . thanking heaven that I had got there at the opening hour and could stay

Sarah Bernhardt, 1913.
(Photo Juley)

till it closed. And so I did—from one to six thirty and I made converts, about fifty, to Redon and Brancusi and Gauguin, anyhow, who are so easy to interpret in terms of common consciousness and interest—and made friends with Mr. Pach who is now alone with them in Boston. He came home with me, supped—and is going to show me Prendergast's work on Wed. if all goes well. . . . In return, I introduced Pach to you. Davies *may* come to Boston this week and if he does I may see him.[24]

Mary's hospitality to the painter-critic Walter Pach, an organizer of the show, was partially in defiance of the Boston art world's indifference toward contemporary European artists. At last her smoldering resentment over Frances Keyes's rejection of Gibran's work seemed vindicated.

And how indignant the Modern Exhibit makes me with the art teachers here! . . . But truly Kahlil, after my experience with people there this afternoon, I believe I could go daily into that exhibit, and single-handed start a tide that would in time rise above the heads of . . . Keyes and Co., and save Boston several years of waiting to see the human value of this work.

> The Cubists are coming, oho! oho!
> The Cubists are coming, oho! oho!
> All the art teachers are teaching all the
> Art students what to think when they see them—
> oho! oho!
> And Boston is humming, oho! oho![25]

"I am so glad you liked the International Exhibition of Modern Art," he replied. "It is a revolt, a protest, a *declaration of Independence*. . . . The pictures, individually, are not great: in fact very few of them are beautiful. But the Spirit of the Exhibition as a whole is both beautiful and great. Cubism, Impressionism, Post Impressionism and Futurism will pass away. The world will forget them because the world is always forgetting minor details. But the spirit of the movement will never pass away, for it is real—as real as the human hunger for freedom." [26]

When they met in New York the third week in June, he explained his personal preferences among the new painters:

> Matisse knew he could not do anything beyond mediocre in the great current of painting—too intelligent to hope against hope about it—so worked out for himself a self-expression in the decorative way which has much excellence. That was a big thing to do . . . the Cubists too cannot satisfy themselves in the great current of painting . . . they have had the cleverness, the acumen to work out a new expression which is independent of grades as pictures are not. Pictures are good, poor, or mediocre. The *Nude Descending the Staircase* is neither poor, mediocre nor good; it is different.

Of his favorites, he thought that Davies was "in a beautiful garden, full of strange forms, beautiful forms, exquisite and delicate and strong forms." Redon "has a mind and has greatness—he grasps widely, inclusively—but not completely—lacks earth the mineral." Gauguin he considered "the most interesting of the others . . . (other than Redon)." He liked best "his 'golden panel', . . . and the *Tahitians on the Rosy Sand*." [27]

Mary determinedly followed this talk with a call to Walter Pach, who invited her to lunch the following day. She met all the members of the Association of American Painters and Sculptors and toured Davies's studio "at cinematographic speed—so interesting. . . . All these men are wrapped up in what they are doing and the love of every detail of their work. I think they will not care for K.'s—it will seem too 'simple' and 'undeveloped,' 'thin,' *to them*(!)." [28]

Two days later she brought Pach to Gibran's studio. Neither man was particularly impressed with the other. "K.'s manner was new to me: it seemed cocksure, lofty, dogmatic, almost contemptuously blunt in answering from his point of view—e.g. when Pach asked whether K. was moving toward less color, as in 'Summit,' or more, as in 'Sitting Boy,' K. said there was more color in the 'Summit.'" When Pach left and she berated Gibran for his "air of superiority," he refused to accept her criticism. "If it was childish and contemptuous, he would still stand for it; it was his. Once or twice he answered me as he had answered Pach . . . he seemed unable to stick to the exact issue—excited and troubled." She had never heard him this way before and they argued until she became aware of his extreme tension. "Nervousness was another point that came up—K. had seemed so nervous. . . . And I had the roughness to tell that to K. in the course of our talk." [29] Finally she relented.

A week later she was in the Sierras, where she always found peace. "The East is greenhorn, though sweet and fresh—the Middle West is fertility in gestation—my mind wearies of the incubator—the West is Super earth." The letters that Kahlil received from her every summer were a course in geography, sociology, and aesthetics. In the sweltering heat of New York he soaked up impressions of a world of untampered mountain and desert.

> Dear Man. . . . From Colorado on South—the earth spreads pure like a star, fierce and delicate. Life does not puff out from it—but is lightly inscribed—in sparse sage and cactus and low tenacious grass—just color for the skin—Here the bones count—and bones of beasts as well lie in tight dried skin up on the plains—Death does not hide. The poorer and lovelier houses are adobe (A-dō-be)—just brick of the same dun clay the house stands on—square, flat-roofed, oriental—as dignified as the mesas on the horizon. Indians are the dark people you see everywhere—still shadowed with their race nimbus like worn gilding.
>
> And on man and all that from man springs, on earth and all her infant ovaries the Santa Fe Railroad has laid hand, to lift so high and say "no higher!" No church ever cared more economically for its own nor took from them so surely all surplus. . . . And the newspapers out here seem more Taft-bought-up than in the East—less trouble taken to hide the blood-money.
>
> At every step, in every social stratum, our corporations are making us pay our souls; for no less price are we allowed to keep alive our bodies. Our thought—our will—our desires—these are powers that will not serve; therefore they must not live. . . . Our hope is in the farmers, the schools, the women perhaps—and in the tyranny itself that makes revolution.[30]

She spent a month of camping alone in the mountains "with Arabic. And I'll tell you why. I want Arabic. . . . I began it on the train and studied every moment." On July 6 she found her camping spot, "near a great waterfall and rapids—at the head of a high mountain basin . . . with only a foottrail for fishermen leading near, and that little used—and a tract full of beautiful hidden places on the mountainside where I can sleep, read, cook—unseen, unguessed at. . . . I can get down for mail in four hours—back again in five!" [31]

By the time she returned to New York on August 29, Gibran had escaped the city three times. He had visited friends in Vermont and Marianna in Boston. What most impressed him was a week spent at the Japanese-style estate of the Alexander Tisons in Denning, New York. Tison was a lawyer who had taught for several years at the Imperial University in Tokyo. The exotic house and gardens were Kahlil's first taste of luxurious American country living. Although Mary thought he looked older, "his first holiday for years" had exhilarated him. "One can live a hundred years in one moment of life in certain lovely places," he told her.[32]

But within two days she began to chastise him for making contacts with wealthy people. "And I spoke out in irritation . . . said the rich had a chance at all artists through riches; the poor and the professional had no chance for lack of riches. . . . It was through money, I said, that I too had happened to be able to keep connection with him." The ensuing scene nearly obliterated the arrangement arrived at during the previous spring. Reviewing this latest blowup, she quoted his explosive reaction:

> Just tell me what really was your idea in giving me the money and I shall know where I stand. Tell me simply so that I shall not mistake. Was it a gift? If so, I will see what I shall do. Was it a loan? If so, I will adjust myself to that. Was it meant to make a bond between us? Tell me and I shall know what to do. Whatever your intention was, whatever your attitude is, I will try to meet it and am glad to. But I can't stand the uncertainty. It has been one of the hardest things of my life. You have said opposite things with equal earnestness and I really do not know which you mean. Months at a time I have suffered terribly from it.[33]

Matters were patched up temporarily when Mary offered an after-dinner apology. "If ever I trouble you again as I did about money—just cut me off. You've given me chances enough. If I'm so dense and so careless and can so hurt you, it is not worthwhile to stick to me. . . . And I shan't complain if you tell me. I know justice when I see it and I'm willing for justice. And I know mercy too—when it is shown me." Kahlil "looked, smiled and patted my arm." Sure that he would forgive and forget, she closed, "I believe he has no hanging to a past grief or injury." [34]

But just as he had secretly resented the night when Adam and Nattie

Haskell had surprised them, he brooded about that scene in Gonfarone's restaurant for a long time. Nine years later he would confess how their arguments about money had emibttered him.

> "When you were in New York another time, and we were walking home from Gonfarone's one night you said it was the fact that you had given me money that kept the bond between us. That night I made up my mind to raise the full sum of money that I'd received from you and send it to you and I set about it the next day—and the matter was going nicely—you had meanwhile gone back to Boston when I had a letter from you. It was the loveliest letter, so dear, so near . . . that I felt again, "how can you receive such kindness from a soul and then make such a return as you are planning to make her?" [35]

If Mary had recognized his frame of mind, the events of the next two days could have been averted. However, blithely unaware of his concealed exasperation, she went the next day to be drawn by Davies. At his studio he unexpectedly asked her to pose nude. She was surprised but not shocked: "It never occurred to me to suggest waiting til we were better acquainted. It seemed wholly impersonal. . . . We talked—it was over—we arranged that I should bring Kahlil at three next afternoon, and I went." [36]

At lunch when Kahlil heard about her posing he burst into a jealous fury. "The simplicity of my deed vanished," Mary ruefully recalled. "I felt him astounded . . . what Davies might be thinking or saying filled him with anxiety."

"You are too impersonal," he accused her, "and in some ways you are very ignorant about the world. In some ways I know it better than you."

After lunch they walked to Arnold Constable to look at some curtain material for the new studio. But first a distracted Kahlil insisted that Mary take his advice to write Davies a tactful letter. He agreed to help her word it:

> You ought to say that since the world is what it is and not what we wish it were, you feel on second thought about our delightful work this morning, that it may not be altogether unnecessary for you to make yourself clear. That you know him to be an artist of the future—as all real artists are—whose work is a strange and beautiful gift to the World—and this gave you a strange and beautiful freedom from the narrowness of the world and let you be for an hour the woman of the future. That question about such a matter will of course some day seem absurd—but since that day has not yet come—the deed needs explanation because it was before its season. I think that is enough to say.

Contritely she conceded, "I felt saved—as if suddenly my clothes had been restored to me."

All afternoon they looked at curtain materials and tried out samples at the studio. Finally, while he stayed to draft the letter, she ran back to another store, Faulkner's, and by herself lugged a heavy gray bolt back to the studio.

> It was a *big* bundle—fifteen yards, 50-inch velveteen on a roll. I feared he would reproach me . . . but I turned it inconspicuously, and a boy opened the door. So I thought it all unobserved. And he met me—not with protest, but with thanks. "Why, Mary, you are sweating—why? why? I did not know it would be so large—Aren't you good?" And he took the pleasure in the beautiful stuff that it deserved. Then we wrote a letter to Davies and mailed it on the way to Gonfarone's.[37]

When they worked on joint projects together the sparks did not fly so furiously. With the letter mailed, Kahlil relaxed and they spent the rest of the evening measuring and cutting the gray velveteeen.

Before they kept their appointment with Davies the next day she arranged to meet Walter Pach alone to discover if Davies had discussed her posing. She was relieved—"saw he had received no word . . . about me and that he was the same lovable, warm enthusiast as ever." Satisfied that the letter had not yet offended Davies' sensibilities, she met Gibran.

> From lunch to Davies—and I was wearing my Bulgarian waist with a little Bulgarian collar I got on Sixth Avenue five minutes before lunch. . . .
> Davies welcomed us with a royal completeness of display. His gorgeous Western–Indian worship-rug he had put away because of its hard colors and he ran through his pictures from youth to now—for two hours—neither man spoke much—K. hardly at all. D. said nothing of theory—of which he has spoken so much. . . . I enjoyed the time very much—the decorative quality in Davies' work suffices to give me great pleasure. . . . K. was quiet and did not feel to me unsympathetic at my side. At the end he said, "You won't forget, Mr. Davies, will you, your promise to let me make a drawing of you. It will only take an hour—and I shall be glad to come to your place or have you at mine—"
> Davies said, "You must excuse me now. I'm tired. I can't think of it. I simply can't think of it!" . . . He was brusque and positive.

No mention was made of Mary's letter, but it was obvious that Davies was not about to cooperate with the man responsible for her sudden modesty.

They left the studio and walked to Wanamaker's to buy tan velour for the couch cover. Davies's aloofness continued to irritate Gibran: "The man is very strange—a divided personality—something is morbid in him—something peculiar. . . . He is uneasy, restless—he doesn't belong here. I wish I could make you see what I mean about his work." In a fit of pique he swore that his years of frustration would someday be vindicated. "While we waited for velour, K. said 'Why did that man refuse me *that way?* There was no reason why he should—Well, some day I am going to do something for America. And I am going to *hit hard*. I can't now, for I have no arms; I have them but they are tied to my sides. Some day they will be free. Then I shall strike.' " [38]

Mary's five days in New York had exposed the caustic side of them both. In describing their every emotional nuance, she added seventy-one looseleaf pages to the journal. Money and a rival artist were not their only basis for arguing. Their quarrels escalated from the sublime to the ridiculous. Such was the scene when she insisted "in case of his death, I wanted to go to Mt. Lebanon with his body—go authorized by him." It recalled their argument of the year before, when he had objected to her intention to will her body to medical research and leave her heart to him. Now he chided her, "I'm not going to die for a long time—probably at least twenty years—And you make me feel as if I had to die tomorrow! And why do you care about these matters of the body after death?—Why?"

Mary began to cry. She told him how she deserved to be identified publicly with him. "How I used to wish people might know he loved me because it was the greatest honor I had and I wanted credit for it—wanted the fame of his loving me. He wants it known that I had faith in him—and made his start possible—that I backed him financially—And he has no desire to conceal our friendship. But he does not want it to be called a mistress and lover affair as it might be. Somehow he got me into at least no more tears—But it had taken it out of him—and I realized how stupid I had been to introduce such a topic." [39]

On their last night together, after they had carefully balanced accounts for the new studio accessories and admired the work accomplished, Kahlil admitted he was tired. "There have been things in my visit to tire you," she said. Even more pointed was her journal summary of the five discordant days, "Marriage! the wonder is that we are friends!" [40]

Kahlil at age thirty-five in a portrait by his studio neighbor,
George W. Harting. Mary once wrote, "The photos Harting
did of him are interesting and good—ever so many views.
The best all-round one he sent me awhile ago. Some are
beautiful—and several give a heightened impression of his
great crown." (Authors)

15

Conquering New York

Just at the time that their friendship, strained by his resentments and her suspicions, seemed most endangered, its ambivalence ended. Mary's tenuous role of unfulfilled mistress and mentor changed to that of collaborator, the cause of Kahlil's decision to write in English.

The turning point came when, three weeks after their latest skirmish, he sent her some lines in English. They read simply, "From 'The Diary of a Madman'— Last night I invented a new pleasure. And as I was giving it the first trial, an Angel and a Devil came rushing toward my house. They met at my door and fought with one another over my newly created pleasure. The one crying 'It is a sin,' the other 'It is a vertue.' Now, Mary, will you not translate this into English!" [1]

Ever since his return from Paris she had known about his work on "The Madman." In June 1911 she had noted, "K. G. is writing the 'Madman' in English." A year later she inserted into her journal some lines from Stephen Crane's *The Black Riders*: "In the desert I saw a man, naked, bestial, crouching upon the ground—who held his heart in his hand and ate of it. 'Is it good?' I said to him. 'It's bitter,' he said, 'bitter, but I like it—because it is bitter—and because it is my heart.'—Crane." [2] Since this poem was first published by Copeland and Day in 1895, it is probable that Kahlil had been haunted by it since reading it sixteen years before.

If these lines were his earliest literary source on madness, his personal fascination with the mad sprang from witnessing the medieval treatment of the insane in Lebanon. As late as the twentieth century those called *mejnun*, literally "posssessed by a jinn," were considered the responsibility of the Church. Priests were in charge of exorcising the devil in aberrant personalities. In 1912 the archaeologist Frederick Jones Bliss described a site near Besharri, the monastery of Mar Antanius Qozhay'ya in the Qadisha Valley, as a typical depository for the insane.

> Here, so runs the legend, once slept St. Anthony himself, when he came from Egypt to visit the Lebanon hermits. Hence to this convent and cave are brought the "possessed" of all creeds, including Moslems and Druzes, that St. Anthony may drive out the evil spirit. . . . Sometimes the patients are cured by simply passing under the arch and cross, . . . and still others in the church, where a priest exorcises the evil spirit. . . . If the spirit will not leave the man, he is taken into the cave, where an iron collar is fastened around his neck. If violent, his limbs are shackled. A number of mad men may be chained in the cave at the same time. The priest in charge visits the cave occasionally, giving the patients to drink of the holy water which drops from the roof, but feeding them very little. The cure is assured when the patient is found without the collar.[3]

Gibran had visited a monastery madhouse, and the memory of it had seared his consciousness and impressed him with the innate wisdom of society's outcasts. He told Mary,

> In Syria madness is frequent. There has been much contemplative life there for several hundreds of years—and it results in various things: sometimes in extreme nervousness; sometimes in madness; sometimes in just apparent idleness; sometimes in wonderful wisdom.
>
> I've told you, haven't I, about the man who called me by my first name? . . . It was at a monastery in Syria. They had a little madhouse there and mad people were brought from even far away in the country. They treated them badly—but somehow they made them well. One day I was at this monastery and the monk who was talking with me said they had a madman from the mountains. I said, "Take me at once then to see him. I'd be very much interested." As we came near we heard chains—he had chains on his legs—and then he appeared. He came straight to us—and he had one of the most remarkable human faces I ever saw.
>
> Just about that time there was a great dispute going on in that part of the world about the Song of Songs. The Church held that it was a mystic symbol of Christ and that the Church was the beloved. And others held that the Song was pure poetry. As the Madman came up to us he called out: "Kahlil Gibran! Go and tell (the name of a man prominent in a dispute on the Church side)—that Solomon loved a real woman as you and I would—I myself know the Shulamite very well."
>
> Then he went away and did not come back. You can imagine how the whole thing thrilled me. I can see that wonderful face now.

In another incident he identified with the mad.

> Once when I was riding with a companion we came upon a madman who was well known in all the country round, as mad, but harmless. It was the

time of year when all the people were busy, getting in the harvests. But he was standing on a rock—twenty or thirty feet above the road—where we were riding. . . .

I called out, "What are you doing there?"

"I'm watching Life," he said.

"Is that all?" said my companion.

"Young man, isn't that enough?" said he. "Could you do better? I am extremely busy. I have spoken."

Then he spoke no more . . . I was thrilled through and through.[4]

When Gibran sent Mary those few English lines he had ventured into a territory for which she had long waited. As much as she admired his Arabic writings, this side of his creative talents made her feel alien and helpless. Together they had occasionally tried to translate his poems, but the results were never satisfactory and certainly not publishable. For a while she had thought that the problem would be solved if she learned Arabic in order to translate his work, but by 1913 she realized this was an impossible dream. Her goals of studying alone in the mountains, of traveling someday to Constantinople or Syria were equally unrealistic.

As an educator she was aware of the problem of English as a second language for the millions of immigrants in America, and she urged the retention of the mother tongue for second-generation children. "I've just got off a batch of mail," she once wrote Gibran, "and written for Phoutrides my reasons for urging on all Greeks in U. S. to speak Greek with their children at home. Think of having a double Psyche to transmit and giving but one! My teeth gnash at the sight." Nevertheless her motivation in grooming Kahlil to write in English was mostly selfish. She wanted desperately to read him. The only solution seemed to be his adoption of her tongue.

Laboring to learn English, he had progressed through many stages. Although his speech and writing were less obviously flawed than when he had first met her in 1904, he still needed her advice on pronunciation, fluency, and colloquial vocabulary. "He read in Nietzsche of . . . Poets, of Scholars. I never liked to have anyone else read aloud to me: and K. reads to no one else in English—very naturally; for he still makes what for an English-born would be many mis-stresses. . . . 'If I gave up six months to studying English, I think I could master it idiomatically'. . . . 'But how can I give up six months!' " [5]

Mary prepared a special tutorial program that worked in two directions. First she helped him compose letters in English. His requests to artists and performers for sittings were always supervised by her. Gradually most of the serious spelling and grammatical errors disappeared, but she admitted to herself that even his brief letters to her were stilted in expression. "He is a silent person and has the masculine desire to write little—his expression in letters is so meager compared to his speech. He is a *talker* on general art subjects with me but not a *writer* on anything." [6] She methodically saved his letters to show him where he made mistakes. But her most important contribution was in exploring literature with him. Because he had always been a voracious reader it was easy to turn him toward her favorites.

By 1912 he had revised his opinion of Maeterlinck. Although he still regarded his youthful idol as "of the first rank," he admitted, "but there are grades in that rank . . . do you know my definition of Maeterlinck?—oatmeal and milk—but not meat. . . . He is great as an essayist [but] not as a creative artist—nothing in his plays—he worked for effect of unlimited form by repetition of phrases, and people called it rhythm. Two hundred years hence he'll be reckoned as one of the first rank of end of nineteenth century—not as a thinker, but as a perceiver and popularizer—a student." [7]

Two writers who had replaced Maeterlinck in his favor were Ibsen and, with reservations, Nietzsche. "Nietzsche probably [was] the loneliest man of the nineteenth century—surely the greatest because he not only created, like Ibsen, but also destroyed. The conception of Superman was not new with him, but the degree of realization of Superman was new with him, though Ibsen wrote with Superman in mind, and Christ *was* Superman." [8] Even though he was drawn to Nietzsche's will to power, his interpretation of Christ was clearly opposed to Nietzsche's portrayal of Jesus as a weak figure. From other conversations Mary noted how Kahlil's affinity to the philosopher had developed, and how he was infatuated with his style rather than every aspect of his thought.

> Nietzsche he has loved since he was twelve or thirteen. "His form always was soothing to me. But I thought his philosophy was terrible and all wrong. I was a worshipper of beauty and beauty was to me the loveliness of things—the harmony and music and lyric qualities of them. What I wrote before I was twenty-three or twenty-four was liquid and musical. I had not learned to catch the greater rhythm of life, that includes it *all* so I thought the philosophy of destruction was all wrong. . . . When I was in Paris, I appreciated his wonderful style and form and various things in his spirit—but I had not grasped the totality of the man. Gradually I came to realize, however, that when we accept a man's form, we also accept his thought, whether we know we do or not. For they are inseparable". . . . [He] agrees with Nietzsche's conception of returning cycle of identical experience—feels cyclical return but "similar" is almost an impossible word. The return will be always in different form. "Spring returns but no two springs are alike." [9]

Other forces were pulling Gibran away from his earlier obsessions with truth and beauty. Mary asked him

whether he really believes he did waste his early life— "Yes, years and years of it," he said—when he was swallowing the sentiments of his forbears. . . . I asked K. with whom he had begun "that strange hunger". . . . Wagner, Nietzsche, Ibsen, Strindberg, Dostoyevsky, Andreyev, Tolstoy ("though personally his work is not agreeable to me. . . .)—Maeterlinck, Renan, Anatole France, Rodin and Carrière of course, and the greatest, Carpenter ("though I can't read him any longer"), Walt Whitman ("though there is a great deal in Whitman that I don't care for") and William James.[10]

Supplementing his preoccupation with modern writers, Mary's discoveries soon became his. "Montessori is epochal," he stated. Mary sent him Symonds's translation of Michelangelo's sonnets, to which he gratefully responded, "There is something in these sonnets of Michael Angelo—something that moves me as no other thing does. Perhaps they would have moved me much less if they [were] writen by someone else: but this is a case where it is so hard to divide between the man and his work." If she was unable to send him an especially inspirational book she would sit up till dawn copying lines and lines of poetry. She did this in April 1913, when she wrote out six pages of poems by the metaphysical poet Thomas Traherne. This devotion to Kahlil's growing literary awareness was in a way her own form of creativity. "Personally, I've no impulse to creative expression—but to appreciative expression— Yes! I long to make known my joy to its sources—to God and you—I want your hand and His on my heart, that you may hear its extremity of speech. It is as if I had a present for you served up in my pocket and couldn't get it out." [11]

Gibran's training period was nearly over when he asked Mary to "translate" his lines on "a new pleasure." The couple would, of course, continue their literary dialogue, but their talks would not be so didactic, so purposefully directed to his enlightenment. At the same time her suggestions for his reading were evolving toward the contemporary, such as the *Song Offerings* of Rabindranath Tagore. In November 1913 she charged him with reading William English Walling. This old and brilliant friend, the brother-in-law of her sister Frederika Walling, was to her the ideal of the complete thinker. Social reformer, historian of Russia before the revolution, and a founder of the National Association for the Advancement of Colored People, he was "a spirit like the North Star and honester than day or the surgeon's knife." Kahlil enjoyed his book *Larger Aspects of Socialism*, especially the chapter on "Nietzsche and the New Morality," and wrote Mary, "I, too, have been reading a good deal about socialism. To me it is the most interesting human movement in modern times. That does not mean I agree with all its details. It is a mighty thing and I believe it will go through many changes before it becomes a form of government." [12]

Would Gibran have survived as a creator without Mary's passionate nourishment of logic and reason, her efforts to round out his education? He himself doubted it.

> We talked more frankly and fully than ever before about the suffering of our lesser selves in the money relation—mine because it is a barrier to the sort of love I want, his because he is not sure I shall have enough in my years to come and is sure I deprive myself now. He said his work in Arabic no less than his painting, was my gift— "Had I ever realized it?"
> "No."
> "You have *literally* given me life for I believe I should have ceased to exist, if I had not been able to do this work," said K.
> "But if you had died that would have been no calamity to you. Whereas if you had not been in my life, I should yet have lived—a life so much less, that it would have been a calamity."
> We both see that apropos to the collection, our course is absurd commercially for we change so constantly—but it is wise in a larger way. . . . *I think* money heartaches are probably nearly over for us . . . for it *is* simply just the working out of our inner partnership, which we discover more and more fully as we grow towards our larger selves that are so at one." [13]

If their physical and social relationships had failed, their partnership of ideas had just begun. Her journal reflected the change by becoming only a record of Gibran. In October she abruptly ended her more intimate diary. Perhaps she stopped recording the personal events of her day because she was weary of details, or perhaps during an attack of painful neuritis that fall she was tired. The closing lines were wistful and sad: "*Back* in *school*—Everybody so *Lovely*—lay down in P.M. No energy or strength." [14]

In January 1914 hopes for a New York show of Gibran's work crystallized when Alexander Morten brought William Macbeth to his studio. But although the art dealer "said the work interested him very much," Kahlil relayed to Mary the disappointing verdict. It caused in him the usual debilitating symptoms. "Mr. Mackbeth [*sic*] will not exhibit my pictures . . . he cannot see his way to showing so many nude figures to the public. . . . No, beloved Mary, I am not ill. I am simply tired out. . . . But it will not last long. I think the end of this winter will bring the beginning of calmer and freer life for your Kahlil. I shall try to live my own life and not that of 'an interesting young man from the East.' " [15]

Ironically it was this foreignness that fascinated New Yorkers and gained him proximity to more successful performers and writers. He attended the opening of Percy MacKaye's play *A Thousand Years Ago* as a guest of the Fords. Among the party in the box were the MacKayes and Ruth St. Denis, and later he added the playwright and the dancer to his growing Temple of Art series. "Ruth St. Denis danced for me yesterday afternoon—almost nude," he wrote Mary. "I liked her. She knows a very great deal about dancing. I

Ruth St. Denis, 1914.
(Photo Juley)

made a few little drawings of her while she was moving and whirling in her fine, large studio. . . . Miss St. Denis is *many persons* besides a wonderful dancer. She knows how to listen and she knows how to receive. People do not like her because she does not tolerate their stupidity. They call her queer because she lives her own life." [16]

Slowly the people he met at Julia Ellsworth Ford's on Friday nights began to recognize him as an artist. Percy MacKaye used his portrait as the frontispiece to a special edition of his masque *St. Louis*. Gibran's favorite in the entourage was Judge Thomas Lynch Raymond, a bibliophile and art-minded scholar who soon would be elected mayor of Newark, New Jersey. While drawing him in 1914 he took pleasure in listening to him describe the problems of a fast-growing city. That spring Raymond began to invite him to his home in Newark and suggested that since he was having trouble finding a New York gallery he could arrange a show at the Newark Library–Museum. It was not to be, but the news buoyed Mary: "I like it that you should exhibit in Newark—as I like it that Christ was born in Bethlehem." Even old friends and acquaintances turned up at Mrs. Ford's that spring. Gibran encountered Yeats, still with that "sad, sad look in his dim eyes." [17] He was happy that Yeats had remembered their talk in Boston three years before; this time they talked about Tagore.

At the end of February he saw a far more familiar face. Josephine Peabody Marks, now the proud mother of two and still very much present in the world of poetry, came to New York for a literary vacation. They saw each other at Percy MacKaye's production *A Bird Masque* at the Hotel Astor on February 24, 1914. Posy's diary shows that for a brief week that winter she and Kahlil, thrust together for the last time in the same literary flurry, had an opportunity to see how each had grown. After so many years his brief re-entry into her life seemed ironic, and yet for a while they must have enjoyed seeing each other.

> *February 24.* At Masque in evening—encountered ꦠ et al. *February 25.* Had tea with ꦠ and showed him pictures of children. *February 27.* Took LaFollettes to his studio [Fola LaFollette, the daughter of Senator Robert LaFollette and wife of George Middleton, president of the Dramatist's Guild, was Joesphine's close friend]. Later dined at Mrs. Ford's with Witter Bynner and ꦠ . *February 28.* Dinner party with EAR [Edwin Arlington Robinson] and ꦠ.[18]

Judging by Mary's subtly biased accounts, Kahlil was little moved by seeing Josephine. Although he did not tell Mary how often he had seen her, he did write that she had not grown and "seemed to be of Cambridge not of the world." Later that year she must have pressed him for details, and he expressed dissatisfaction with Josephine's conversation: she had talked mostly about herself and about her children. Still favoring the tight bodices and full skirts of her Edwardian youth, she had not moved into modern ways. "It was just like her *being,* that was wearing the same clothes," he complained. "No new day—no change . . . and just think! for three . . . years I used to go to see her twice a week! She was writing her best things then and though I was only eighteen, I say frankly that I believe I influenced her work."

"Did you love her?" Mary asked.

"Yes."

"And she you?"

"Yes, I think she loved me first. You see she was a woman, and I was a youth."

"No wonder you loved her. She was *so pretty* and so studied and had gifts."

Then as in a deliberately prejudiced afterthought, Mary added, "She was twelve years his senior." [19] In fact Josephine was only eight and a half years older. It was only human for Mary to blur the fact that someone prettier and more imaginative had first encouraged Kahlil. But this refusal to recognize Josephine's role continued to mar the objectivity of her journal.

By June 1914 Gibran's progress in painting and drawing was eclipsing his memories of Boston. Even his contributions to the Arabic world were not preeminent. He had continued to write for *al-Funoon* but when the magazine ceased publication in June he seemed little concerned. Nor was he particularly impressed with his latest book *Kitab Damah wa Ibtisamah*, a retrospective anthology of his youthful work published by Naseeb Arida. In August he presented Mary with the first copy, translating the title for her as *Tears and Mirth* and the dedication as "To M. E. H. I dedicate this book, which is the first zephyr of my life's tempest, to the noble spirit who loves the zephyrs and runs with tempests. Gibran." But his comments on it betrayed a disenchantment with his earlier outpourings. "Love and Death and Beauty—Love and Death and Beauty—it's all full of that. You know I don't like this book now." [20]

What did excite him was that Alexander Morten had at last brought N. E. Montross to the studio, and that perceptive dealer had promised him a show in his Fifth Avenue gallery. When he saw Mary on her way west that June, he was able to tell her that their mutual charade of his financial independence was finally paying off.

"It was a strange story," said K. "Mr. Morten brought Mr. Montross. He had given him a strange idea of me before hand—which I have since learned is what people have very generally felt about me. 'That fellow will consider himself to be doing you a favor when he shows you his pictures. He doesn't care a darn whether he sells or not. He's independent.'"

"And it was amusing to see Mr. Montross go about it when Mr. Morten left. 'Of course,' he said, 'I understand that you paint these pictures for the satisfaction of expressing your poetic imagination. But after they have passed out of your vision and you are on other things, I suppose you have no objection to selling them.'

"'Certainly not,' I said. 'I thought his twenty-five per cent pretty steep, but I find that is usual and that it is better financially in the long run to give him twenty-five per cent than to give others less because he has a clientele with whom he can get the best prices—he asked me about my prices.'

"'What would you say for this [painting] for instance?' [asked Montross].

"I said, 'fifteen hundred dollars' [twice the value Kahlil and Mary had agreed upon for each painting]—

"'Very good, good,' said he, 'but we can easily do a little better than that.' . . . He is an elderly man. He is very shrewd but very able. He called *Let Me Go* the biggest thing I had done, and then I knew he knew. His whole idea is business but then he *is* a dealer. . . . Afterwards he said to Mr. Morten—Morten told me—'Several ladies had been into my place and talked about Mr. Gibran's pictures and I said to myself, "That man must be doing rotten work."' But when Morten went to him it was different." [21]

With the exhibit set for December, Kahlil and Mary's time together was spent planning. "You do my thinking," she told him. "Think what years you've saved me, speeding me." "And think what you've saved me!" said he. "You've been my exhibitor, my agent, my editor." Laughing, she retorted, "I'd have thought I was your cook, your laundress." [22] Working on "The Madman" and going over frames, invitations, the choice of works, distracted them from much of the nagging gossip of other years.

Yet the old ties with Charlotte and Micheline were not completely broken. By 1914 the Hirsches had shared an exciting year and a half in England, Germany, and France. They had spent time with Yeats, and in Paris discovered Leo and Gertrude Stein and Marsden Hartley. Charlotte still sent Mary confidential chapters about the creative or Freudian streams in which she dipped. She candidly analyzed their "six years together" as a "sublimated love affair," an interpretation that must have hurt Mary after her years of generosity. "If such a woman writes every detail, tells every detail to her woman friend—you have the readiest evidence as to where her real interest lies," wrote Charlotte. She confessed that she was pregnant. "I'm a sight. . . . Four inches of my hair is brown mixed plentifully with gray—and the rest is still peroxide gold." [23]

Unlike Mary, Kahlil's response to Charlotte's latest theory was carefully controlled.

> I told him Charlotte had had a dream about me from which she interprets the friendship between herself and me as a sublimated love affair—during which her confidences showed her heart was fixed on me—while her body outraged by sublimation in my direction sought elsewhere. I've no objection to the terminology if she likes it. If such friendships are called love-affairs, why so they are called, that's all. But what was *my* outraged and starved body doing all those years? And what now? It gets no food that is not sublimated. Yet no ravages have followed. [24]

As for Micheline, her romance with Lamar Hardy was advancing along with his career; in 1914 he was appointed special counsel to the recently elected Mayor John Mitchell of New York, and she became friends with the Mitchells. By April Kahlil had visited her twice but what Mary learned from him about his old friend was predictably impersonal. "A recent evening with Micheline . . . and [he] felt the hours wasted," she noted. " 'She kept on talking of the Mitchells. Told me how to make money—to draw this big man—and then his friends will want to be drawn.' " [25]

But during this period Micheline still forwarded Mary her impressions of his development. "How changed he is—his face has no longer that indefinable expression made of illusions, of longings and hopes for a radiant future, etc etc that only belong to Youth! He is a man now, a man that life has touched with a little cynicism, or rather bitterness. The boy in him appealed to me

268

tremendously, Mary, the man in him brings to my heart a vague feeling of fear. How foolish, is it not? . . . I should like to see him often, and yet I hesitate to." [26] Two years before, this kind of candor would have provoked Mary to re-evaluate her own understanding of Kahlil, but now the opinion of others was secondary to their goals.

Both enjoyed their own withdrawal from society. That summer Mary retreated farther than ever into the mountainous West and lived "in the cleft of a pile of boulders. Like five fingers and a palm." She had reached a stage where all of her Yosemite experiences, stripped of civilized trappings ("and as long as it is warm enough in the day I wear no clothes either"), were shared by Gibran. "And it will seem natural to you that you are like my hands and eyes—as truly here as I, as these trees and rocks and sky and the sound of the river and the three naked mountains in the meeting of whose feet we are. And we are all that is apparent, except a few jays, a mouse, a rat, a harsh little squirrel—and many insects." [27]

In New York "because nobody else is in it and I want to be alone as much as I can," or in Boston, "trampled upon by good people with whom I have little in common. I enjoy being with my sister—but we are not left alone for one single hour at a time," he worked to prepare for the show. Always Mary was in his mind. That summer he described a "strangely beautiful dream" he had, where they were standing on a green hill overlooking the sea:

> You turned to me and said "We must throw *her* back, Kahlil, we must throw her into the sea." I knew you were speaking of a beautiful marble statue of Aphrodite that we had just unearthed—and I said: "But how can we? She is so lovely. The rosy tint is still on her lips, and there is so much blue in her eyes." Then you said: "But do you not see, Kahlil, that she would be much happier and more comfortable in the sea?" And I sadly said, "Yes."
>
> Then we carried the large goddess as if she were a light thing—and from the top of a high white rock we threw her into the sea. And we were both glad. Just then a flock of white birds flew before our eyes. And as they came near us they caught fire and were changed to flying flames. Then you said, "Do you not see I was right?" And I said, "Yes, you are always right." [28]

This symbolic rejection of a physical relationship satisfied her. Even in Wenatchee his spirit went with her as she threw herself into chores on her brother's farm. "What I do is cook food and wash a year's wash, and recover the buggy seat . . . and mend and gather fruit." In August she wrote,

> It has been so continuously a growing . . . this solitude—a growing in life together. . . . My soul folds you to herself for your beautiful dream of Aphrodite. Your spirit made it from what has been in both our hearts. We

have found a sea, Kahlil beloved, beautiful enough for her and great enough to hold her . . . we are not denying life: we are seeking it—and we are finding it. . . .

Between sunset and night I walked up on . . . the irrigation ditch that makes the valley grow halfway between the big Columbia River and the top of the desert foothills. . . . Below us are the young orchards and the alfalfa fields and little houses, the wide river and the road white like moonstone,—and above are the mounded sagebrush and dust of the ages— That is what you and I love best.[29]

When Mary returned to New York on August 31 they spent a week working on "The Madman" and the exhibit. Gibran had read some of "The Madman" in English at Judge Raymond's, where it had especially moved Rose O'Neill. Formerly married to Harry Leon Wilson, the literary editor of *Puck*, this latest admirer was at the apex of her career as a popular magazine illustrator, writer, and designer of the Kewpie doll. In imported bisque, domestic celluloid, and edible chocolate, the dolls were sweeping the country, and their glamorous creator could afford to indulge her natural bent toward the arcane and mystic. She and her sister Callista welcomed Kahlil to their free-spirited salons in Greenwich Village and Cos Cob, Connecticut.

Although Mary recorded his friendship with Rose O'Neill, the journal did not reflect the colorful personalities of his newest friends but mentioned them merely to chronicle his increasing popularity. The main thrust of the journal was devoted to their growing collaboration on "The Madman." She was moved by the latest piece even more than by the earlier ones.

> "But you know," said K., "I am always doing the same thing in my Madman, from many points of view. He is destroying veils and masks and laughing at absurdities, and exposing folly and falseness and stupidity and cowardice—and always saying I am here, I am there, I am everywhere, I am now. I am life."
>
> The Madman he read glorious new things from: his "I am like thee, O Night," his seven selves conversing about their hard lots—the one about the Scarecrow—and the seeking of soul and self for a bathing place.

Sometimes he saved special problems for them to solve together. About the parable that would become "The Greater Sea" he sought her advice: " 'I want to add another type of foolishness to the people in the Madman and Soul seeking a place to bathe,' said K. 'I have six and I want seven—the saint, the realist, the philosopher, the scholar—somebody. I think I'll take the saint.' Then he . . . chose the realist. We decided he should be listening to the conch shells and calling it the sea. We got it over very quickly." [30]

They had evolved a system of working. "When we write together, he dictates and I write, because my spelling is quicker and surer," noted Mary.

"When we are not satisfied with an expression, we make tries at it until we get it, both of us. He gets it oftener, I think, than I. But when he has completed a thing before I hear it, there is little or no change needed." She was encouraged by his improvement in English.

> K.'s English is remarkable—has a final quality that I for instance could not get if I were translating from his original— Simply a structure occasionally wrong. And this three pages of Night and The Madman he wrote off in less than an hour. . . . It will not be long before he will be so a master of English that he need look nothing over with anybody. . . . And his English prose is poetry-prose—"the voice of a voice" is in it . . . he does not mind the English seeming as if a foreigner did it.[31]

Efforts to find a publisher for "The Madman," they decided, could wait until after the show. In the next three and one half months Gibran finished three large drawings and four paintings and added to the portrait series a drawing of Marjorie Morten. Just before the show opened on December 15 he panicked and thought that grippe would incapacitate him, but Mary, on the sidelines in Boston, kept him supplied with encouraging letters, pills, and sweets. "Four years ago," she reminded him on December 8, "you were dreaming of 'conquering New York' to use the old phrase. And now!—New York—and so much more, already!" [32]

The night before the opening he was addressing invitations and wrote her how he was already planning new work. "I have finished those pictures and I am finished with them. They are no longer a part of my soul. They belong to my past. I shall only use them as a means. My whole being is directed toward a fresh start. This exhibition is the end of a chapter." [33]

Ryder, pencil, 1915. (The Metropolitan Museum of Art, Gift of Mrs. Mary H. Minis, 1932)

16

Learning to Think
in English

Kahlil's show opened at the Montross Gallery on Fifth Avenue on Monday, December 14, 1914, and Mary came to New York five days later. Sales in the first week were encouraging. Of the forty-four paintings and drawings, five paintings had been purchased for a total of $6,400: *Nebula* to the Mortens for $1,200, *Ghosts* to Cecilia Beaux (the popular portrait painter whom Kahlil had met earlier that year) for $700, *Silence* to Julia Ellsworth Ford for $1,000, *The Elements* to a Mrs. Gibson for $1,000, and *The Great Solitude* to Rose O'Neill for $2,500.

It had been a long time since Mary had seen Kahlil interact with strangers, and as he escorted her through the gallery she eagerly observed how he conducted himself. "I have seen him only with Pach and Davies and Montross since he left Boston and became his adult self. . . . I feel him sensitive at every pore, with people—as if raw edges were being touched . . . all through him, I understand why he says it takes him three hours to get back to himself and his own 'quiet life' after one hour with people."

After reviewing the familiar series of portraits (Rodin, Debussy, Rochefort, Rostand, Abdul Baha, Lady Gregory, Le Gallienne, Paul Bartlett, Percy MacKaye, Judge Raymond, Ruth St. Denis, and Sarah Bernhardt), she gasped over the latest drawings. "I was thunderstruck! The new ones clashed like a great orchestra in my ears—Fourteen in ten days! I felt weak in the knees and glad of my umbrella to lean on. I can't get over them." Later in the day she denied to Kahlil that she still found his drawings more interesting than his paintings, while admitting, "It seems to me you have gone farther in the use of that medium!" "I have," he interrupted. "I've always drawn." "And I *never* found your drawings more interesting than your paintings, after you began really to paint," she insisted. "But I do think that you've done something new, even for you, in these latest drawings."

Afterward they had lunch at Child's—"wee lamb chops for thirty cents and coffee"—and then she returned alone to the drawings. Although she tried to avoid it, she met people from Gibran's new world.

In the gallery Mr. Montross soon came and talked. From time to time he went to look after a guest. Then he would come back. About 3:30 I heard a lady say, "Has Miss Haskell from Boston come?"

I turned and caught M.'s eye and laid my finger on my lips. Soon he came up and said, "It is Mrs. Morten. Shall I introduce her?" I was glad to meet her. She is direct and real and sensitive—in her early thirties. . . . We talked about the pictures and about her portrait. I told her why I liked it so much.

"It is my potential self," she said.

"Isn't that our real self?" said I. "Our past is gone—our present goes—our potential is our only real self."

I said to her, Mr. Morten, who also came, and Mr. Montross, that I consider K. a *very great genius*, such as the world sees only once in a long time. Mrs. Morten said she thought so, too—and was pleased.

At the studio that evening, after Kahlil and Mary tried to define their "master-passion for the Great Reality," which they believed to transcend merely being "in-love," she revealed a secret dimension of herself.

At night he asked me apropos to my saying I had got a woman who was in love with me this fall to see The Total Life—telling her as clearly as I could what I meant and how I love it and find it *the* bond with people—about Lesbianism. . . . He has no dislike of it—as so many people have—but he says it is one of the things he's never been able to get into the mind of and understand. . . . So I told him I thought Lesbianism was based on the diffusion of sex in woman—through all her life—from dress to child-bearing—and that a woman was determined into Lesbianism of-tenest probably by being sex-ripe and meeting no fit eligible man, but a congenial woman. I asked if he'd like to know my own experience with ——. He said yes, and I told him.

That with —— was a very beautiful and illuminating experience for me—but I had felt all along it was not the final kind—and I had never got repose out of being sexually caressed by her—though *she* got repose—I got only excitement—whereas simply *being* with K., even without *any* caress, reposes me utterly.

There is the thing that makes K. suspect Lesbianism to be the product of the civilization which has been man's mood for six thousand years. If sex were free—conception so understood and preventable that men and women might be together with as little outcome as is left "after a bird has sung"—wouldn't Lesbianism gradually die? except in rarest sporadic cases? "For more and more I feel that sex is basic," he said, "is one of the final things." [1]

In their determined progression toward platonic love the poignancy of unfulfilled desires caused anguish for them both. Such episodes in the journal undermined her definition of their Greater Love and revealed her fears of aging and his concern with outsiders' opinions. Sometimes her desolation emerged with no forewarning, as in a scene earlier that spring. "On Monday we were at the Madman about dusk and a hurdy-gurdy began to play and suddenly I noticed a beautiful something in the sky and the real grief of the limitation on us returned to me suddenly. K. noticed my face and said, 'Why is your face so sad?' . . . I asked, to evade answering, if all faces weren't sad in repose. K. said, 'Yes,' quietly—but in a few minutes I told him the truth." [2]

During the first weekend of the exhibition they abandoned their reserve. Spurred by his telling her that she was too thin, Mary decided to prove that she was "well-covered all over—we warmed the room and I undressed for him. 'I'm astonished,' said K., 'you aren't thin . . . you don't need to add. . . . You are exactly right. . . .' K. put his arms round my neck and kissed me on the breast, as we stood, and I felt that touch all night and for three days after." And then she dressed again, "for we don't want the sex complication." That night she contemplated the incongruity of her act: "I had not realized before that K. had never seen me. I've undressed to change my clothes in his room—and I've seen him. But I was so glad that he did see me now. It was strange to have stood for Davies and remain unknown to the eyes of Kahlil." [3]

A week later they met in Boston. So that he could be away from the distractions at Oliver Place, she found him lodgings in a Newbury Street rooming house. Their project that week was to find a gallery that would show his paintings, and they spent hours going up and down Back Bay streets. She was unusually preoccupied—"chilled and barren and sad"—and tried to evade his questions. Finally she told him

> how the lack of freedom kept raising protest in me—how the other night in New York and every sex-stirring made me feel more what I missed; how I had thought of saying, "Let us be free" and had finally settled it again in my mind and was all right.
>
> "There," he said, "you've said it. You've called it settled—and it's not settled. . . . It *is crooked* . . . it is against nature. . . . We've called it settled because that feels pleasanter."
>
> "It sounds strange," he went on, "to say to you who are the honestest being alive that you aren't honest. But you haven't faced this simply enough yet. We want intercourse—"
>
> "We can't have it because the risk is too great."
>
> "Yes, and we've always been saying it in many more words."

How intimidated Kahlil was by public censure was made clear that night: "An accident would have to end so much for us. I tell you truly, I would leave this country and never come back again." But Mary was aware more than ever of her forty years, although he tried to assure her that their "difficulty" was "a little thing" compared to the "big thing, the ensemble." "As he said this, he looked at me. I was gray and lined and old looking." [4]

It is difficult to know how Bostonians may have viewed the closeness between the two. What did neighbors say when they saw the diminutive Syrian enter the halls of the Haskell School at eight in the evening and leave at three the next morning? Next to the school, at 312 Marlborough Street, there still resided Thomas Sergeant and Lilla Cabot Perry, whom Kahlil had visited after Day had first sponsored him. Certainly Lilla Perry, who had expressed so much interest in the boy, must have followed the friendship with interest. Once that week, he and Mary deliberately avoided the Perrys and embarrassment in a public place. As Mary described it,

> To the Guild [of Boston Artists] we went. It was full of visitors. . . . I saw the elder Miss Perry ahead, and told K. . . . "Mrs. Perry's here," said he, "and I don't want to speak to her." So I met the eye of neither Perry— But I saw Mlle. hurry to tell her mother K. was there—and felt the old eyes looking at him intensely. Doubtless they were both shocked—for K. was looking white and drawn—with absorption in the puzzle of his quest. He was enthusiastic about this gallery . . . liked both rooms and liked the *reclame* of its fervent following. . . . I wonder whether his having been a Boy in Boston would admit him to membership.[5]

His boyish precocity would not admit him; Mary learned upon discreet inquiry the following spring that the Guild was not interested in showing him. Then the Boston Art Club agreed to exhibit his work in May, but that promise was inexplicably canceled shortly before the show was to open. Boston had changed its mind about the interesting young Syrian. Probably many secretly wished that Miss Haskell also would curtail her insistent championing of him.

Not only were Bostonians disenchanted with Gibran but Mary was confronted with implicit criticism about him from other sources. Earlier she had asked Montross to arrange an anonymous gift of one of the paintings to the Metropolitan Museum, and now she learned from him that the museum had turned down the offer. Two days after Christmas she received a letter from Charlotte. The Hirsches, who had returned from Europe, had attended the Montross opening, and from their fleeting encounter with Kahlil Mary learned that recent motherhood agreed with her old friend. But when Mary pressed him for details about Charlotte's expression or self, he declined comment: "Well I saw them for such a moment only—there were so many people. I can't say." In her predictably frank way Charlotte now wrote that she had turned away from the East.

> Orientalism is the sleeping sickness of the Universe—it is the soft, sweet-scented night. No one can deny its beauty—nor the beauty of death.

That is what we found in Kahlil's pictures the other day. They would be very dangerous if they were a little stronger: They are like Yeats' poetry and Debussy's music, but lack a certain clear-cut something which those two have; for that reason they may be more perfect in their way, the Orient Way. . . . He came West for the spirit of the West—but he is the East as it works upon us. If I wrote an art criticism for him—I could make him famous.[6]

When Mary read the letter to Kahlil she laughed, "Still explaining the Universe." But the promise of a splendid review must have seemed somewhat cruel in view of the fact that several critics were not sympathetic. He had already warned Mary to expect this reaction. "This is how my work stands: I am an excellent draughtsman; I cannot draw at all; I am early Italian—and modern French; I am obscure and childishly imitative; and I am a pupil of Rodin, of Davies, of Miller." [7]

The opinions of three newspapers were mostly negative. "Cloudy visions of striving and unhappy humanity with literary suggestions," wrote the anonymous critic of the *Times*. The *Tribune* characterized him as influenced by Rodin, "a kind of feeble Arthur Davies," and the *Evening Post* reviewer confessed that the pictures "wrapped in foggy symbolism" produced "a feeling of irritation—something like trying to read in a room where the lights are turned down." [8]

Joseph Edgar Chamberlain of the *Evening Mail* was kinder. He had formerly been associated with the Boston *Evening Transcript*, had written two books for Copeland and Day, and had followed Gibran's career since the early days. Along with a favorable review he sent him a personal note congratulating him on his steady growth: "Your pictures interest and delight me very much, and it has been a matter of great pleasure to see you getting along so well, and 'arriving' so serenely among the great." Even more encouraging was Charles H. Caffin's article in the *American*. Calling the exhibit "very unusual and highly interesting," he treated the "dreamscapes" with special consideration. "It is a world of original creation that unfolds itself," he wrote, "a world mostly composed of mountains, vegetation, and sky. . . . It is remarkable, as showing how an artist, influenced by the modern tendency to revert to the primitive and elemental, can direct it, if he have high capacity of imagination, into channels of deep significance." [9]

The *Evening Sun* found Kahlil's personality colorful enough to feature an interview on the women's page. The reporter was mostly concerned with his comments on woman, love, and marriage. "Women's influence," he observed,

is to be found somewhere behind all the creations of man throughout the centuries. I do not state this as a theory. For me it is a psychological fact, its manifestation being perfectly palpable throughout history. . . . Romance! The world is stuffed with romance. In my opinion little can be hoped of marriage based on the sentimental idea of love. . . . A [successful] marriage has its foundation on comradeship not romance . . . it is the attraction of complement and supplement, invariably the coming together of two great natures for whom there is no other choice but marriage, from which eternal recreating is the only result.[10]

What intrigued the interviewer and so many like her was not Gibran's paintings or his role as an Arabic writer but his simple and direct conversation about the rites of life—birth, marriage, and death.

But the perceptive art critic for the *Sun*, Henry McBride, was less impressed with the message of the paintings. "The style has been greatly influenced by that of the late Eugene Carrière . . ," he noted. "The work on display is certainly sufficiently earnest to make all visitors sympathize with the artist in his pursuit. . . ." But he deplored "the pessimism" symbolized by "the crushed mortal striving for he doesn't know what; pushing on for an unknown destination, and leaning in his bitterest moments upon a female as blind and as hopeless as himself." [11]

Shortly afterward McBride again visited the Montross Gallery and unexpectedly found Albert Pinkham Ryder standing alone in front of one of Kahlil's pictures. McBride, who admired the elusive sixty-seven-year-old painter and had tried unsuccessfully to meet him, introduced himself. Ryder apologized for having broken their appointments—"Explanations," McBride later recalled, "that were like the Gibran paintings, rather vague." Desperately trying to make conversation, McBride waved to the paintings. "How do you like these? He seems to be after something mysterious. All of them are the same."

"He seems to mean it at any rate," Ryder said. "That's the main thing." [12]

Ryder's attendance at his show impressed Gibran more than any review. Eight months before, he had told Mary how eager he was to meet him. "The big person in this country is Ryder. He has painted little and nothing new for a long time. But there is so much *in* what he has done. And the *man* is the great thing. He is very hard to see. If he says you may see him next Thursday, he will be a week preparing for the visit—he is so sensitive—preparing himself, preparing his place. . . . I do hope to get him for my series—but I have to approach him carefully—so carefully." [13]

Kahlil still hesitated to approach Ryder, but during the first week of January he decided to write a prose poem to him as a sort of tribute and thanks to the older man who had taken the time to see the work of a younger man. He sent it to Mary for correction, promising, "If you like the poem I will publish it separately on Japanese paper and send it to him." [14]

Staying up most of the night to correct the two pages, she immediately returned them. As usual, she began her criticism gently: *"The English of your Ryder poem has no fault, save three letters in spelling!* Ah!!! (ecstasies; wherein; forgotten)."

But she followed her abundant praise with seven pages of suggestions. At times her ideas completely revised his original wording, as in the third stanza which read, "And yet thou are not alone, for thine is the Giant-World of super-realities, where souls of unborn worlds dance in rhythmic ecstasies; and the silence that envelops thy name is the very voice of the Great Unknown." She changed the entire section. " 'Super-realities' I feel I can't stand. . . . If it weren't for objectionable 'super-realities' we shouldn't have objectionable 'rhythmic ecstasies' or 'thy name.' This was the best I could do tonight." [15]

Although Kahlil rejected most of her changes, he agreed with several of them. He used her phrase "whose nights are big with high and lustrous days" instead of the original "whose nights are pregnant . . ," and his "unrecorded deeds of a forgotten race" became her "unrecorded deeds of unremembered races."

The two-page poem, his first publication in English, was privately printed by the Fifth Avenue firm of Cosmus & Washburn within two weeks of the time Mary had corrected it. On January 28 he was able to send her the rough sheets embellished simply with brown lettering and orange motifs. "The Poem to Ryder delights me in every way," she answered. She was also pleased with his objective assessment of her revisions. "And I am so glad you changed it little. Just from memory I disliked most of my comments the next day. But I said to myself, 'Kahlil will not be moved by suggestions that don't really improve. He will disregard them—nor feel annoyed that I made them. And when the poem satisfies him it will be right.' And sure enough the very things I regretted, you ignored." [16]

His independence was growing in other ways as well. When Mary asked if she should visit him during her upcoming winter vacation, he delicately suggested that they postpone their next meeting until the spring. Although she had waited for five years to hear him say no to her beck and call, this knowledge of his growing away from her must have been hard to bear. A still harsher blow was a defiant letter from Charlotte, who assailed her for neglecting her old friends while concentrating on Kahlil. It was true that he had emerged Mary's undeniable favorite. With the marriage of Micheline to Lamar Hardy at the home of Mayor John Mitchell in October 1914, her responsibility toward the French woman was discharged. Also dwindling was her commitment to Phoutrides, who was earning his doctorate at Harvard that spring. Her remaining charge was Jacob Giller. Although he had not proven himself as a scholar, she agreed to stake him for a while longer by helping him finance a bookstore on New York's East Side.

"To Albert Pinkham Ryder," 1915. (Authors)

Charlotte was hurt when she realized that Mary had not called on her during her stay in New York. She gave vent to her outrage by indicting her for her unwavering loyalty to Kahlil. To Mary's defensive claim, "He bears off the palm among human beings I know for sheer strength to think, to labor, to create," she retorted,

> I ought to [be] glad that you feel such satisfaction with him and his work. I do not. . . . If anywhere in this last letter you had said "I do not agree with your criticism of Kahlil's work and this is why—" then I should feel that you and I were talking together. . . . You think you can admire Kahlil's work and still have faith in me. You believe that the "understanding" for which you have always prayed and have so consciously cultivated can make you see truth in all things and overlook, if not deny, the evil in anything . . . you chose Kahlil and not me. . . . I will tell you what Kahlil seems to me—what I *know* he is: He had his chance to be a man when he asked you to marry him—when he gave that up, he died. Your vanity made

you keep on with friendship in order to show that you were bigger than the hurt he gave you . . . his work shows it. It is wonderful in the Oriental Gift of color; it is supine—There is not one iota of self-respect in his work; fluent and gracious as it is. You won't see that. Can he draw a soul looking square at life? No. Not even when he tries—He blurs the eyes—He does not want to see.[17]

Certainly the understanding that Charlotte accused Mary of abusing must have been strained by the supreme egoism of both Kahlil and Charlotte. However, Charlotte was partially right. Kahlil's expanding career did satisfy Mary more than her own unfulfilled promise, although despite Mary's disavowal of the debt she was insistent about repaying the estimated $12,000 with interest. Somehow Mary's answer allayed her resentment for a while and they cautiously resumed their longtime but fragile friendship.

By early 1915 Mary had no delusions about Kahlil, and yet despite his assertions of independence and her friend's warnings her life with him defied actuality. "Your own treasured letter," she wrote, "tells me again that it is not my fancy, but reality, that this life of ours is together. . . . I long with all my soul to see you—but I understand so well that we had better wait. . . . But tell me how you are—And what more about Ryder. That was such a wonderful hour with him. I fairly eat up all you told me of it." All her satisfactions centered vicariously on Kahlil's description of a new friend or conquest. Of Ryder he had written,

One of the most creative hours in my life was that which I have spent with Ryder the other day. I found him on a cold day in a half heated room in one of the most poor houses on 16th street. He lives the life of Diogeneus, a life so wreched and so unclean that it is hard for me to discribe. But it is the only life he wants. He has money—all the money he needs—but he does not think of that. He is no longer on this planet. He is beyond his own dreams. And he read the poem. Oh what a thrilling moment. His face changed, and there were tears in his old eyes. Then he said, "It is a great poem. It is too much for me. I am not worthy of it. No, No, I am not worthy of it."

then after a long silence, he said, "I did not know that you were a poet as well as a painter. . . ." He promised to sit for a drawing. I shall go to him tomorrow. And if I do not find him I shall go again and again untill I make a drawing. It must be done. His head is wonderful—very much like that of Rodin—only it is unkept.

Later he told her about how he managed to arrange a sitting with Ryder for the Temple of Art series.

I don't try to make appointments with him because if he has an appointment it keeps him anxious for days beforehand. I just start when I am ready to try for him—and take my chances. This day I put my portfolio under my arm, and started for Ryder's—Near 16th street I saw him on the street, walking along very slowly—you know he takes steps about two inches long. I waited to see what he would do. He went into a restaurant, and ordered lunch. He ordered corn beef and cabbage and ate it very slowly—

It took him till quarter past four to eat his lunch—his hands are so feeble. I waited till he was through and it was a cold day. Then he came out. And he said, "O Mr. Gibran. I saw you through the window. Have you been waiting all this time for me?" I said I had, and I walked along with him. In a step or two we passed by a saloon and he said, "Will you have a drink?"

I said no but I would be glad to wait for him in his studio. He went in and took one. He went into two on his way home. . . .

I have made two drawings of Ryder. To me they are finer than anything I have done. One of them is not finished yet and I must go to him again. But, oh, Mary, how tired and weary he is—and how aloof. He told me the last time I saw him that he is painting pictures in his mind. He can use his hands no more.

When Mary came to New York in April, much of their conversation concerned the older painter.

He is sixty to sixty-four and seems eighty to ninety. . . . K. says Ryder used to be a beautiful creature and rather a dandy, used to wear white a great deal, and was a conspicuous figure on Fifth Avenue. But he loved a woman whom his friends thought not worthy of him, and they planned to part him from her and her influence. They got him to go abroad and when he came back she had disappeared. Ryder was never himself again.

"Probably he hasn't bathed since," said K.

He has two rooms—one on 14th and one on 16th street—but he received K. in the room of an old English lady of eighty—because his own room was too cold. He sleeps at 16th street on three chairs with old clothes on them—of money he has quite enough, but seems lost to comforts.

"He made me ashamed of being clean," Kahlil confessed. "He is so gentle and courteous—'May I take it for you?' he said when he saw my portfolio, though he uses his hands with such difficulty . . . has no will of his own . . . no skill for contact with people."

When K. had finished drawing him, he took the picture and looked at it. "So carefully," K. recounted, "it was a great revelation to me—such looking—as if he were looking to see what life was in it."

Then he said, "Wonderful work. You've drawn what's inside me—the bones and brain."

"He hadn't been to an exhibition for eight years when he went to mine," Kahlil said. "Mrs. Morten sent him—the Mortens have several of his pictures."

"Your pictures have imagination," Ryder said, "and imagination is art. Art is nothing else. . . ."

"Ryder has been a great lesson to me," concluded Kahlil. "He is full of wonder—of that wonder that is the mark of the real and great ones." [19]

Gibran mailed copies of the poem to his friends, and it attracted the attention of those who had previously considered him only a painter and an interesting conversationalist. That spring Percy Grant, an old friend of Charlotte's and the liberal vicar of the nearby West Tenth Street Church of the Ascension, read it from his pulpit. "This is the second time Doctor Grant spoke of me and my work in his 'church,' " Kahlil said. He also reported that two of the long poems in "The Madman" were read to the Poetry Society of America. Although reaction to these pieces was mixed, it was significant that American poets were criticizing his English work despite the fact that it had never been published in a magazine. One of his first supporters in the Poetry Society was Mrs. Douglas Robinson, the sister of Theodore Roosevelt. Corinne Roosevelt Robinson first thought the work "diabolical stuff—contrary to all our forms of morality and true beauty." [20] However, this initial reaction was soon replaced by admiration, and Gibran had found another influential supporter.

In June he went to Boston, again staying at Miss DeWolfe's rooms at 9 Newbury Street. He settled into a pattern of alternating evening visits between Marianna and Mary. Most of the time with Mary was now spent in polishing his English work. On this visit she captured the essence of the subtle change in their relationship. "Pale and burned out he looked. . . . The Powers have no pity. And he works as if he were to die young and would finish before the hour. I never saw his creative life at such close hand before. I would no more touch or move him than a man would approach sexually his wife in childbirth." On the third she presented him with two bronze laurel leaves. Her annual ritual of sending him a fresh branch of pungent laurel from the Sierras was now incorporated into the school's honors program: the small cast leaves based on designs he had sent to her that spring were awarded for scholastic

Bronze laurel leaf designed by Kahlil for Mary. (Agnes Mongan)

merit and achievement. The slight charms were unsigned, and only she knew the source of the design. Like a school pin he had long ago drawn, a bronze shield bearing honor students' names, and a sketch for the class ring (an open hand holding a rose), the leaves were secret reminders of Kahlil with which Mary was filling the school. She turned to him for advice and succor whenever educational concerns pressed too deeply. At three o'clock one morning she had written to him about her divided loyalties.

> It is early early morning, and I am defying bed in the interests of M. E. H.—mine is life like a submarine's—in the day, I come to the surface and cruise actively in school waters. At night I go into the depths whose fascination *makes* me a submarine. . . . And life like an aeroplane's: all day in the hangar—after sunset in the sky. . . . These two waking lives are as far apart as awakeness and dreams are.[21]

After he read his latest poem, "The Perfect World," she identified completely with him. "And the English of it is superb . . . I felt we had been sharing an actual conception—for I had been living it in school while he had set it in a poem and made it so complete." What made it different from his earlier efforts was his process of writing it. "I *wrote* this in English," he said. "It is the first thing I have written in English instead of translating it from Arabic. . . . But I tell you, this writing in English is *very hard* for me. . . . I've been finding out that the English is a very wonderful language if I can learn how to use it." [22] He showed her a large notebook in which he had started another series of poems in English, which would eventually become *The Earth Gods.*

And so Mary was called upon to edit with him material from two unfinished works. " 'The Perfect World' we hardly touched—it was so perfect. And then we worked at the passages not yet final in the Prologue. . . . We must have spent three hours on it. . . . K. had long been tired but he kept on and on—and I was the one to stop him at last. He called it his 'lesson'—though it assuredly was mine." That week they also added several poems to "The Madman." The more they removed themselves from the personal, the more productive their evenings became.

> From drawing the face, Kahlil went straight into writing the story of the man with the valley full of needles ["On Giving and Taking," *The Madman*]. When we had done that, he wrote about the cat who said that for prayer it would rain mice and the dog who despised their superstition, knowing it would rain bones ["The Wise Dog," *The Madman*]. And then the story of the two hermits and the earthen bowl ["The Two Hermits," *The Madman*]. He gave always every idea and I simply found the phrases sometimes. But it was astounding—for him I'm sure even more than for me—to be able to do anything with another person. It would be torment for me to try that with anybody else.[23]

284

After he returned to New York Mary followed him there, first spending two days with Charlotte and her family. Without the strictures of a work schedule, these times seemed to be marred by recriminations and accusations. "But the past came up again," she wrote on June 20, "because I had found Charlotte's letter taking me to task for seeing K.'s pictures instead of her . . . thought to read it to him, then realized I'd no right to—Charlotte was thus naturally up again—and her condemnation of K. In our talking, I learned much more of how I had lacerated K. in 1910–1911; of how I kept telling him Charlotte was nearer to me than he—though I had said I'd marry him." An additional contention was Kahlil's continued refusal to travel West. "I said it had taken me a long time to get over being miserable because K. didn't want to travel with me or go into the mountains with me, or do anything but just 'visit.' It was a foolish thing to say—since I understand now how he couldn't want such constant association with me. And I felt that K. was hurt." [24]

That summer she reversed her usual schedule by spending July with her brother Tom in Washington and then traveling south to Little Yosemite. The turbulence of their five years together haunted her, and from Wenatchee she sent Kahlil a statement in which she castigated herself for inhibiting his personal life. "Never in all these years have I let you be yourself, save as by one of these hopes, whose shattering meant more pain. . . . I said I wanted you to be free with me. But if, ever you were free, I hit you. With your Self I was like one in a room in the dark, who knocks everything down. But this room *was* Your Self and the things were the most sensitive things of the soul." [25]

Acknowledging her admission, he predicted a new era for them both.

All is well now, beloved Mary, all is well. . . . Indeed, we have had five long years of great pain. But those years were extremely creative. We grew through them and though we came out of them covered with deep wounds, yet we came out with stronger and simpler souls. Yes, simpler souls, and that to me is a very great thing. . . . I feel that God is the simplest of all powers.

And you know, Mary, that each and every human relation is divided into seasons of thoughts and feelings and conduct. The passt five years were a season in our friendship. Now we are at the beginning of a new season, a season less cloudy and perhaps more creative and more eager to simplify us.

And who can say, "This season is good and that season is bad?" All seasons are natural to life. Death itself is part of life. And though I have died many times during the passt five years yet I feel now that the marks of death are not upon me and my heart is without bitterness. I know deep in my soul that my work is just beginning to free with the freedom of loneliness. The past five years taught me how to work and now I am beginning to use the power of work as an instrument to express my soul. I am not very strong physically but with the little physical strength I have I could go on and do all the things that I want to do. And I know deep in my soul that I have your blessings and that to me is the best element in my life.

"Beloved Kahlil, I asked Life to give me words for what was in my heart—and Life gave me your words," she responded gratefully. "My desire, beloved Kahlil, is to discover you and to become one with your spirit. It is for this I am alone in the mountains and alone everywhere, and this is why I sit still 'doing nothing'. . . . All division from you has been for me division from Life and all oneness with you oneness with life." [26]

Yet never again would she imagine that she sat with him "in our canyon," "under a great pine and great cedar that grow above the forest," or walked to the river with him and together waited for trout leaping up "the long rapids and falling back, water-ousels tipping and dipping all on the banks," or watched "little dark lizards" darting by. For the final time she felt his presence as she saw the jays, flickers, and hawks visit the "same three bird pans that we watched last summer." Mary's mountain summer had heightened her self-awareness, so that the following year she was able to summarize her life in an alumnae report: "My life has looked simple and uneventful from the outside. Inside year by year has developed a larger more sensitive drama. The age our class has reached begins a second life for women. I want to sound this life from forty to seventy as eagerly as I sounded life from fifteen to forty. Visibly less, I long to be invisibly more." [27] And so she remained Gibran's strength, as the divergence of their paths became more imperceptible.

17

The War Years

It was not until June 1915, eleven months after the events at Sarajevo, that Mary and Kahlil interrupted their self-absorbed dialogues to discuss their attitudes toward World War I. "Do you realize, Kahlil," she said, "that we've never talked of the War, yet we are both living it? I live it all the time."

"We did talk about it at first," he answered. "I know it is changing my subconsciousness."

Both of them agreed that the war was contributing to an evolutionary process that would change the "subconsciousness of the world." They believed that narrow nationalism would eventually breed a global awareness of "collective national personalities as members of the world personality—not like body members, but like family members—each different and separate—yet with *the* stamp and bond." [1]

Gibran, however, could not conceal his nationalistic leanings, and he had committed himself to war long before 1914. As early as 1912, when the Ottoman Empire had been successfully challenged by the Balkan States, he was convinced that Turkey's hold on Lebanon and Syria could be broken only by a general Allied attack. "Treat poetically with the Turkish government!" he once told Mary. "You might as well sing the songs of Keats to the Standard Oil!" His commitment to war as a means of gaining his country's freedom caused him to guard closely his Arabic ties at just the time when he was forming commitments within the American literary community. His conflicting loyalties caused him anguish and guilt. The distance between Arab nationalists and his pacifist American friends was to him a "gulf that had to be crossed every day," and this tore at him. [2]

Soon after he had drawn Abdul Baha and had met many Americans, including the Mortens, who were Bahaist pacifists, a large reception for Abdul Baha prompted him to question the growing peace movement in America.

Abdul Baha, pencil, 1912. (Photo Juley)

"Why should man speak of Peace when there is so much of *ill-at-easiness* in his system that *must go out* one way or another? And was it not the Peace disease that crept into the Oriental nations and caused their downfall?" In October 1912 he told Mary how violently he opposed nonalignment.

I have been made *sick* and *tired* by those passionless statesmen of Europe. Because they are free and tranquil they think that the whole world should be satisfied. Mary, there is a sort of cruelty in the optimism of happy people. Rich and happy people protest against the young Balkan States because they fear that they might "break the peace of the world"—And why should they not break the hypocritical peace of the world? They have suffered enough under that one-sided peace, and I pray to God that this war may bring about the dismemberment of the Turkish Empire, so that the poor crushed nations of the Near East may live again. . . . I am not patriotic, Mary; I am too much of an Absolutist, and Absolutism has no country—but my heart burns for Syria. Fate has been most cruel to her. . . . Her Gods are dead, her children left her to seek bread in far away lands . . . and yet she is still alive—and that is the most painful thing.[3]

For the duration of the war he lived a dream life as a revolutionary and fighter. Politically and financially impotent, he began to fantasize his importance as a romantic figure leading his people to victory. The roots of this ambivalence began in 1913. In June his friends Najeeb Diab and Ameen Rihani represented the emigrant Lebanese at the First Arab Congress in Paris. His resentment at not participating in this historic event was obvious.

> Well, beloved Mary, your Kahlil came very near going to Paris! Does it sound very strange!
> During the last week of this month a conference will take place in Paris. More than 30 Syrians will meet and discuss Home Rule in Syria . . . Diab and myself were asked by a committee of Syrians to go as two representatives. The idea is fine—but after talking the thing over with these good people, I found that they do not agree with me on any point, nor I with them. They were to pay my expenses and I was to speak theire minds—not mine! And since theire minds and my mind are so different, there is no way of representing them without being insincere and cowardly.[4]

Two weeks later he explained to her the difference between "the old school of dealing with Turkish problems" and his ideas on political change. "They would appeal to the Powers of Europe and by diplomacy seek Home Rule. . . . But their very asking for it diplomatically obliges them to accept Turkey's consent diplomatically given. And Turkey *will* consent; will promise; and will not keep the promise." That night she noted, "K. wants Revolution. He feels that even if it fails, Home Rule will result." She chided him for not asking her to send him to Paris when she saw how he brooded in New York while his friends were making history. "This battle with his own people, his sense of their waste of time, his *not* going to Paris—have made it a time of great anguish, sleepless, unspeakably solitary—He is indignant with himself for weeping; but it is like the leading Thinker left out of the Thought-Meeting!" [5]

But on July 10 his conviction of the futility of the conference was borne out.

> I think the conference of Paris is a failure. Those patriots are altogether too wise and too considerate. . . . I have made up my mind to be alone. I can't agree with anyone on anything unless I swallow nine tenth of my thoughts—and just now I am not in the mood of swallowing anything. In order to work in harmony with those men, one must be as patient as they are—and patience, Mary, has been, and *is* now the curse of all the Oriental races. Oriental people in general are fatalists—they believe in an inevitable necessity overruling their fortune and their misfortune. . . . They resist

passion and think by resisting passion they become victorious over themselves. And they *do* become victorious over themselves—not over the others! Passion, Mary, is the only thing that creates a nation.[6]

If Gibran's activist plans, conceived with his friend General Garibaldi, were only dreams, he was able to sublimate some of his passion in his writing. Five months after the Paris conference he published in *al-Funoon* "An Open Letter to Islam," which the magazine titled "To the Muslims from a Christian Poet." This prose poem called for an alliance of the disparate religious factions in Ottoman-occupied countries. In extolling a common purpose between those who read the Koran and those who read the Bible, his personal attitude became clear.

> I am Lebanese and I'm proud of that,
> And I'm not an Ottoman and I'm also proud of that.
> I have a beautiful homeland of which I'm proud,
> And I have a nation with a past—
> But there is no state which protects me. No matter how many days I stay away
> I shall remain an Easterner—Eastern in my manners,
> Syrian in my desires, Lebanese in my feelings—
> No matter how much I admire Western progress.

Implicit in the "open letter" was a warning to Arabs, both Christian and Muslim, that unless they combined forces to destroy the Ottoman Empire "the yellow-haired blue eyes" would conquer it and the Middle East would be controlled by new European masters. It was followed in March 1914 by a more violent attack on the Ottomans. This time he chose a dramatic form in which two intellectuals, a Mohammedan and a Christian, met in a Beirut coffee house to discuss peacefully the inherent disease of their occupied country and the need for cooperation between their religions. He called this piece, which was unsigned, "The Beginning of Revolution." Characteristically, he overdramatized the effect of his political influence. "My 'Open Letter to Islam' created the feeling which I wanted to create," he boasted in March. "It was that short letter which I kept in my pocket for two years before publishing it. But there are some friends in the East who think that in publishing that two page letter I have signed my death warrant with my own hand! *I do not care!*" [7]

When Mary saw him in August she recounted how he envisioned the disposition of the Middle East by the Western Powers:

> If Turkey joins Germany, a protectorate of Syria will come, by France and England—England taking the lower part, because she wants both ends of the Canal and France the upper—And twenty to twenty-five years of such government will be a governing school for Syria and she will learn to govern herself and become free. He would prefer England, but Syria has so

many close bonds with France and French protection will be very acceptable to the Syrians as a whole.

The war was filling him—"I'm always drawing lines about the fighting in my head"—and she tried to identify with his partisanship although the atrocities of battle smote her conscience. "Sometimes it drives me up and down the floor . . . till daylight comes," she wrote him in October, "and more and more the pains suffered by women and children and by soldiers mutilated on the field live in me. Something in me weeps all the time and makes me want to stop everything. I do try to *understand*—to catch the Realities of that struggle." Forced to strengthen her resolve, he answered, "Listen, Mary. Man is part of nature. Each and every year the elements in nature declare war on each other. . . . Man is elemental. He must fight and he must die for what he does not fully understand. And it is the fight and the death of any seed in the fields. . . . Man fights for a thought or a dream. Who can say that thoughts and dreams are not a part of the elements that once came together to make up this planet?" [8]

A month later, as he was preparing for the Montross exhibition, she realized how his political involvements were interfering with his artistic production. Often he was called from his studio to the phone downstairs, and she wondered how he arranged his time to allow for this double life. "The Syrians are after him all the time since the war—see him every day or almost every day. 'I've got used to it now—to adjusting my mind to one thing quickly after another,' he said. 'But it was very trying at first. The minute my model goes they are at the door. Sometimes they come ahead and wait outside my door till the model goes. For I never let anything interfere with my model.' "

Another time, when he repeated his secret desire to go to Syria and foment an uprising, she tried hard to conceal her doubt about his real influence. "Have you men in mind who would do the work if you started them?" she asked. "A few," he replied, "and more might be found." She observed that "he has no desire to be killed, because though his death for Syria just now would effect something, the something would be very small: smaller than his *living* can effect." Finally she got him to admit, "Syria is not the purpose of my life . . . perhaps I shall find myself as much an alien there as anywhere else. But I should be glad to know whether this is the case or not." [9]

At their next meeting, the weekend of the show, she again subtly broached the subject. She wondered, "Now that Turkey is in the war, do any leaders appear in Syria?" "No," he answered. "Then wouldn't it be a waste for you to go there to try to do anything? With the *possible* quickening of her freedom—which will in course of time come anyhow—be worth your trying—worth being your job?" [10] He was not to go. In the end, they both understood that. But he tried to compensate by sending small sums of money to Syria. He promised that he would contribute whatever he received from his latest book, *Tears and Laughter.*

By 1915 communications between Lebanon and the rest of the world were minimal. A successful blockade of the Syrian coast by the French on the one hand, and the Turkish military occupation with its strict censorship on the other, made wary emigrants fear for the liquidation of those left behind. Added to the political uncertainty was the specter of famine and disease. Early in 1915 rumors of widespread atrocities by the Turks had reached the Lebanese community in New York. Under a reign of terror religious leaders were being deported, while those suspected of anti-Turkish sentiments were subject to arrest and imprisonment. Six men, including Dr. Ayub Tabet, organizer of the First Arab Congress, had been charged with treason and sentenced to death in absentia. Dr. Tabet was one of Gibran's best friends from college, a physician, and the brother of Sultana "Tabit" with whom Gibran had been infatuated in Beirut. He managed to escape to New York, and now Gibran was meeting daily with him. His presence as an exile allowed him to rally the emigrants around a pro-French position, and Gibran observed much of the intrigue and local plotting.[11]

By May 1916 Gibran was actively soliciting funds for his beleaguered country. "Beloved Mary. My people, the people of Mount Lebanon, are perishing through a famine which has been planned by the Turkish government. 80,000 already died. Thousands are dying every day. The same things that happened in Armenia are happening in Syria. Mt. Lebanon being a Christian country, is suffering the most." This plea elicited a $400 check from Mary. But the amount was too extravagant, he wrote back. "I want the Syrians here to feel that they must unite and help themselves before others can help them." On June 29 he notified her that he had given in her name $150 to the Syrian–Mount Lebanon Relief Committee. "It is the largest contribution from an American so far." [12]

On the same day he sent her a formal letter and receipt. As secretary of the Relief Committee, of which Rihani was assistant chairman, he was proud to be at last an official voice of his people. Earlier that year he had received a personal tribute. Several Arab-American writers and editors (Naseeb Arida, Abdul Massih Haddad, Najeeb Diab, Elias Sabagh, Wadi Bahout) had presented him with a ruby ring, which he proudly wore on his index finger.

More significantly *al-Funoon*, which had been defunct for two and a half years, was revived that spring. He was spurred to organize a society of the contributing authors. When the magazine reappeared in June several of them showed their association by signing "Arrabitah" ("Pen Bond") next to their names. He spoke to Mary about his ideal of creating a forum where younger writers could exchange ideas about trends in modern Arabic literature. "There are a few young Syrians: Arida, Haddad, Sabagh, Bahout, that love to come about once a week in the evening—and I love to have them. . . . The other day about thirteen of them asked to come to my room—all poets, writers, artists, and they were so eager—they wanted to form a sort of little society, and they did—to meet once every two weeks in one room or another. And if any of them haven't the right room, I told them they'd be welcome to my room." [13]

Anxious to see Kahlil in his latest role, she stayed in New York for three days in July before she traveled south to visit a cousin, "Aunt Loulie" Minis. She tried to sort out his confusion and despair over the latest reports which were filtering into New York. Fourteen Christians and Moslems had been hanged in Beirut that May, and although details were confused and exaggerated, it was quite clear that being a Syrian nationalist was now dangerous. Gibran linked the Turkish atrocities with recent British retaliations against the Irish Home Rule movement. As he explained them, he showed extreme anxiety.

> You remember the conference in Paris, when I didn't go? . . . They drew up a proclamation, signed it and would have presented it to the French Government. But France then was thick with Turkey. The proclamation was not published. . . . A copy of the Proclamation was given to the French Consul at Beirut. War broke out. . . . The Turkish Government took the papers and the signers of the Proclamation were killed—about fifty of them were known to me personally. Doctor Tabet . . . feels terribly because of these deaths.[14]

The emotional strain of the war news seemed to reach a crisis in the summer and fall of 1916. Each time Mary saw him she objectively recorded his fragmented statements, many of which she obviously did not understand. They sounded as if he were being pursued by heartless diplomats, suspicious countrymen, and diabolical enemy agents.

> Turkish spies are of course watching everything that is done here. But Doctor Tabet comes in a great deal, gives his ideas, which are invaluable, and writes a few letters.

> I can't get away from Syria, I never shall, I am a Syrian—and yet this work is almost more than I can bear. Rihani—and all the others—they understand one another so well—they get along so well—but I don't understand them and they don't understand me—they say, "O, you just come down there and sit, and all will be well"—they are taking care, as it were, of the bird that lays golden eggs—I can get money when no one else can. Because the work of Turkey has been to divide those she governs— the Syrians do not trust one another. They fear that if they give money to the Committee the money won't reach those who are suffering in Syria. . . . I have to talk to all these people to explain, to convince them. . . . I

can make them weep—and they do what I ask them to. . . . Spies watched the Committee's every movement in New York and if *any* Syrian in U. S. displeases Turkey, his relatives are killed. That is why the U. S. Syrians are so infinitely cautious and watchful.[15]

The prominent theme in all of his confusion was death. In the October number of *al-Funoon* he published a prose poem, "Dead Are My People." It began as an elegy dedicated to the victims of the recent horrors, evolved into an indictment of his own helplessness and the general malaise of the Middle East, and closed with an appeal to his fellow exiles to support the Relief effort.

> The knolls of my country are submerged
> By tears and blood,
> . . . .
> What can an exiled son do for his
> Starving people, and of what value
> Unto them is the lamentation of an
> Absent poet?
> . . . .
> This is my disaster, and this is my
> Mute calamity which brings humiliation
> Before my soul and before the phantoms
> Of the night.
> . . . .
> Yes, but the death of my people is
> A silent accusation; . . .
> And if my People had attacked the despots
> And oppressors and died as rebels,
> I would have said, "Dying for
> Freedom is nobler than living in
> The shadow of weak submission . . ,"
> . . . .
> But my people did not die as rebels;
> . . . .
> Death was their only rescuer, and
> Starvation their only spoils.
> . . . .
> . . . Remember, my brother,
> That the coin which you drop into
> The withered hand stretching toward
> You is the only golden chain that
> Binds your rich heart to the
> Loving heart of God. . . .[16]

A month before the poem's publication Kahlil had left New York and the pressures of the Relief Committee to spend some time with Marianna. The year before they had found a small cottage in Cohasset, a seaside village twenty-five miles south of Boston. There they, along with visiting relatives, had enjoyed their first vacation together. And so when he escaped the city in 1916 he returned to the house on Jerusalem Road. Writing from there to Witter Bynner, he again expressed anxiety. "I am ill in bed. I came to

Cohasset about two weeks ago with a wingless body and a weary soul—and now my sister and a good doctor are taking care of me. This house is between the deep woods and the deep sea; but I have not been strong enough to sit in the green shadows or dip my pale self in the blue water. I fear, Witter, that I shall remain a songless thing for a long while."

Several days later he further described to Bynner what seemed to be a psychosomatic ailment. "Bless you for the wonderful letter. It did so much good. It is a nervous breakdown. Overwork and the tragedy of my country have brought a cold, dull pain to my left side, face, arm and leg. It will pass away, Witter, and I shall be well again. Here I sit in the sun all day turning the left side of my body to its warm, healing rays. And the left side of my face is darker, much darker, than the wright side. The effect is strangely queer—not unlike the jesters of the xvth Century!" [17]

Mary was shocked when she saw Kahlil in Boston on October 5. "More than forty years are graven now into his 33-year-old face. Even his hands look older than he is—and this time he has gained no flesh. . . . In his run-down state, his left side, always susceptible, from his childhood injury, had been almost paralyzed—and he has given it sun treatment. In New York he had taken some electrical treatments—but the rest has done more for him."

To distract him from the Relief Committee she introduced several subjects that night. They talked about his growing interest in astronomy, which led them to their mutual belief in extraterrestrial life. "Suppose fish should believe that above the water is no life," he queried, "because they don't know such life: that would be as natural, and no more reasonable, than for us to believe there is no life in elements impossible to human existence." A magazine article about Amy Lowell prompted Mary to deliver a short seminar on psychiatry and modern literature. "Then we read 'The Opal' and another little poem of hers. I showed him how the psychoanalysts find sex and masturbation in them. Kahlil was not entirely convinced. 'I think psychoanalysis is a wonderful thing but why call everything *sex?* Everything *may be* sex—but I can't feel that it is.'" Later she asked him to draw her "own vision of a far-winged soul impeded by a clinging small-winged soul." He complied by filling four of her journal pages with winged figures until he grew bored. "And now I'll draw Amy Lowell," he announced. Sketching the full figure of the poet amused him. "Of course I'm undressing her—what would she say if someone told her, 'That Syrian has been drawing you?'"

It was a long disjointed session, which ended with Mary's wistful vigil as he left the school. "He took Jung's *Psychology of the Unconscious* to read. And he ate a slice of pineapple and two wee ginger-snaps—and smoked four or five cigarettes—and between 12:00 and 1:00 started for—I don't know where he was staying. I watched him down the street, as always—through the window—his walk so unchanged—but no cigarette lighted, as it usually is, as

Marianna, Kahlil, and Maroon George
at Cohasset. (Authors)

long as he was in sight. He walks with a peculiar little rocking—a sort of swing
and dip—very springy." [18]

The chief reason for his borrowing *On the Psychology of the Unconscious*
was that the text had been translated by the psychiatrist Beatrice Hinkle, who
had retained her interest in Gibran and his work. When she first met him she
had introduced him to James Oppenheim. Early in 1916 this young writer
became a regular visitor to the Tenth Street Studio and was impressed with
portions of "The Madman." Despite their disparate backgrounds, Kahlil found
a common bond with him. Born in 1882 in St. Paul, Minnesota, Oppenheim
had suffered the death of his father when he was six years old. His early years
had not been easy. Like Kahlil, his education—high school and two years as a
special student at Columbia University—had been spotty. His entrance into
the intellectual mainstream had been nurtured in the settlement houses of
New York, where he worked as assistant headworker at the Hudson Guild
Settlement and as a teacher at the Hebrew Technical School for Girls. To
make a living he had turned to hack journalism and magazine fiction. At the
same time he had published by 1914 eight books of poetry and prose, all
infused with a fervent social idealism. When Kahlil met him he was in analysis
with Dr. Hinkle and was preparing to publish a magazine that would embrace
the visions of the new literary movement in America.

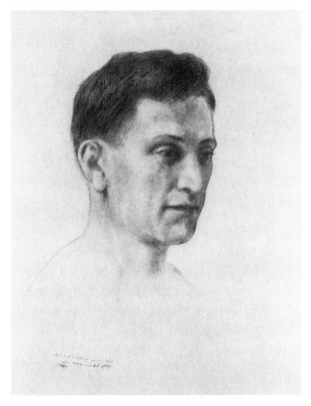

N'oula Gibran, pencil, inscribed "In memory of a week spent between the forest and the sea — in Cohasset on Jerusalem Road, August 1917. Gibran." (Authors)

To Oppenheim Gibran's unorthodox approach to literature, the very fact that passion rather than reason moved him to self-expression, was enormously appealing. What mattered was not that he misspelled simple words but that he possessed a primitive and intuitive sense of rhapsody. When Oppenheim, encouraged by Dr. Hinkle and sponsored by Mrs. A. K. Rankin, a wealthy patron, founded *The Seven Arts* he chose as the associate editors Waldo Frank and Van Wyck Brooks, and included Gibran on the advisory board along with Robert Frost, Louis Untermeyer, Robert Edmond Jones, Edna Kenton, and David Mannes. The only immigrant on the staff, Gibran was a sort of resident seer representing the antimaterialism of the Middle East.

Kahlil first mentioned *The Seven Arts* to Mary in July 1916 when he gave her a copy of the magazine's prospectus. Its message sent forth a spirited challenge to young American writers:

> It is our faith and the faith of many, that we are living in the first days of a renascent period, a time which means for America the coming of that national self-consciousness which is the beginning of greatness. . . . We have no tradition to continue; we have no school of style to build up. What we ask of the writer is simply self-expression without regard to current magazine standards. We should prefer that portion of his work which is done through a joyous necessity of the writer himself.

He did not know any of the other writers except Oppenheim. "He likes the things I do—and I like his ideas. . . . He wants to publish all I've written in English. . . . And some of the Syrians are angry because I have given him my name." [19]

Even before *The Seven Arts* was launched Kahlil knew that his association with a potentially pacifist venture would infuriate his Arab associates. Yet he continued actively to support Oppenheim and even requested copies of the prospectus to send abroad. "Everyone of my friends is quite enchanted with 'The Seven Arts.' The need has been felt for years." In August he worked with Oppenheim on a possible design for the magazine's cover. Similar in concept to his hand and flame motif for *al-Funoon*, it was never used. But he cheerfully accepted the rejection and assured Oppenheim, "You are quite right. The hand was not strong enough in the first design, and the flame did not look like a flame. . . . I am more than glad I can be of some use to 'The Seven Arts.' I am very much interested and I want to see that everything in it is right." [20]

The first issue appeared in November 1916. For Mary the inclusion of Kahlil's work in such an impressive format was so far his most significant accomplishment. "The Seven Arts has come—and for 'Night and the Madman' I prize it—Give something to each issue, do please, if you can K. G.—the one greater voice among the many honorable lesser voices." [21] Those voices whom she rated below Kahlil's would influence American letters for the next generation. Along with Lowell and Frost, Oppenheim assembled a stunning galaxy of prose writers. Eugene O'Neill, D. H. Lawrence, Sherwood Anderson, Theodore Dreiser, John Dos Passos, and H. L. Mencken all contributed to the new effort. The success Kahlil would soon enjoy when he began publishing books in English was related to his identification with this movement, as he himself realized early on.[22] "The Greater Sea" appeared in the December issue, and two shorter pieces, "The Astronomer" and "On Giving and Taking," in January 1917.

His depression had vanished. Involvement in his work seemed to have cured his obsession with revolutionary schemes and the psychosomatic side effects. When Mary saw him in November she noted, "He looked well as his handwriting had led me to expect." Indeed, because of his relaxed attitude they both seemed to enjoy this visit. She had seen the Hardys and the Hirsches, and she told him of "Micheline's fine Beatrice . . . and of Charlotte's dainty boy, and how Charlotte and Gilbert had earned $3,000 in the past year." Even Charlotte's news sounded "splendid" to him. "We talked on most comfortably and warmly at dinner and I can't remember what we said—save that K. too loves the Russian music." [23]

Mary learned that he was preoccupied not with his old fears about the Middle East but with getting together a show to be held at M. Knoedler & Co.

early the next year. She helped him choose the forty wash drawings for it. "Knoedler's is the biggest art dealer in the world," he observed. "Everybody is astonished at Knoedler's exhibiting my drawings. 'Why should they?' they wonder." [24] The impetus had come from Mrs. Albert Sterner, a gallery employee, who had visited his studio and had liked his work.

The sketches represented a departure in style and objective from the earlier pastels and paintings. Simpler and freer in form and more vibrant in color, they bore more resemblance to watercolors by Rodin than to his earlier attempts at symbolism. He had made most of them during his past two summer vacations. "At Cohasset I did 75. . . . Sometimes I'd come in from the woods at 5 o'clock and do 3 or 4 before dinner—and I didn't know beforehand what they would be . . . while I worked I hardly knew what I was doing. I'd go to sleep . . . the next morning I would sometimes not remember their look—and they would surprise me when I saw them." The entire series was built around three motifs—centaurs, mothers and children, and dancers.

Wash drawing from the centaur series. (Photo Juley)

299

"I want this [exhibit] to be just the human form in its relation to other forms—trees, rocks—other forms of life—that peculiar wiry something," he explained.[25]

This new breakthrough so involved them that for the first time in six years Kahlil did not see Mary during the Christmas holidays. During his first months of Relief work he had stopped sending her English poems, but by the new year his letters reflected a resurgence in literary as well as artistic production.

> Beloved Mary, I am having a hard time with the frames and some of the drawings. But I think I can get everything ready by the 29th. And I am in a working mood. My heart is full of moving forms. . . . I am sending you this with a poem which I wrote a few days ago ["God," *The Madman*]. Will you not look it over, Mary, and correct its English? I feel that this poem is the beginning of something I want to do.

> I am sending you another little thing—a parable—["The Three Ants," *The Madman*] to read and correct its English—when you have the time. You see, Mary, I go to your school, too, and I am sure that I could not have written a word in English if it were not for you. But I must learn a great deal more before I can give form to my thoughts in this wonderful language. The poem on God which I have sent you is the key to all my feeling and thinking. And if need be I will change its present form, because I want it to be simple and clear. This little parable . . . too, belongs to what I have been going through during the passt year. But these short glimpses are not enough. Large thoughts must be expressed in a large way before they are felt by others. My English is still very limited but I can learn.[26]

The show opened on Monday, January 29, 1917. Kahlil's note inviting Mary to it showed that his spirits had never been higher. "*The Seven Arts* and this exhibition are making my dayly life as full and as rapid as I want it to be. . . . It is all so wonderful—even when I am not working: and it is even wonderful when I am so physically tired. Life is sweetly rich—not less rich when it is painful." A final request symbolized his growing independence: "Will you not telephone me on Friday or Saturday? I have my own telephone now and I do not have to run up and down those stairs all day long! The number . . . is 9549 Chelsea." [27]

Mary saw the Fifth Avenue exhibition alone. Her unannounced presence was far different from her visits to the Montross Gallery in 1914, and she enjoyed eavesdropping on some Syrian visitors who knew Kahlil. Later that day she "told him about the group who evidently knew him . . . and he identified one of them as Mme. El-Khoury. . . . They had said he was the 'greatest thing we have here,' that he 'had the divine in him,' that he and Rihani were 'rivals,' but in different veins." The promise of sales and favorable reviews had softened him. "This exhibition has done a great deal for me, for

300

my own life. . . . *The Seven Arts* publication . . . means a great deal in my life too. It has given me something. I find myself here now being introduced somewhat as I was in my own country fifteen years ago. There, of course, it was all easy. . . . Here I have done far more work, and waited longer. But I don't know here either just why it has come. I simply find that I am known." [28]

Earlier that year, through Bynner, Gibran had met and drawn John Masefield and Laurence Housman, the brother of A. E. Housman. Now Mary learned that he had dined with Frederick MacMonnies, the sculptor of the *Bacchante* for the Boston Public Library, where he had encountered art in America twenty-one years before.

At the studio the next day she learned more about his New York life while overhearing some phone conversations. "Mrs. Ford telephoned. . . . Oppenheim called up too—and they talked of [William Marion Reedy] of the St. Louis *Mirror* whom both liked very much. Reedy wants to have K.'s drawings in St. Louis and it has been suggested that K. publish a dozen of his drawings with Mrs. E.'s article . . . we decided that this and St. Louis were not for him. . . . In due course both things will come." Obviously Gibran's spiritual mentor still influenced his decisions. She insisted that his highest priority should be a show in Boston, and he meekly agreed to speak to Knoedler about the possibility.[29]

"Mrs. E."—Alice Raphael Eckstein—had written an article about Gibran for *The Seven Arts.* Oppenheim's generosity in championing his work continued to invigorate him. As he told Mary, " 'He's growing all the time in his work and he comes to talk things over constantly with me. You see,' said K. with a smile, 'I boss someone else as you boss me.' " New York reviewers had been kind to the exhibit, but it was Mrs. Eckstein, a scholar of Goethe and also a close friend of Dr. Hinkle, who elevated Gibran's purpose and message to astral planes.

> It is at the dividing line of East and West, of symbolism and representation, of sculptor and painter, that the work of Mr. Kahlil Gibran . . . presents itself as an arresting force in our modern conception of painting. . . . We see the body of a woman who rises out of the vast forms of the *Erdgeist* carrying in her arms man and woman. . . . Erda, Amida, Ceres, Mary, it is a matter of choice and of temperament. The meaning is universal. . . . His centaurs and horses have a charm utterly apart from their natures, so that they are never wholly animal in character . . . so in these centaurs we sense the beast that is yet man and again that in man which is and must be animal, that evolution upward which is in itself a miracle but which will forever prevent us from clutching the stars.[30]

In March J. Dudley Richards, owner of the Boston gallery Doll and Richards, agreed to exhibit the wash drawings. Before the opening, however, the death of Ryder on March 28 added to Gibran's exposure. He had kept in touch with the elderly artist since meeting him in 1915. When Ryder was seriously ill in St. Vincent's Hospital he had visited him and described to Mary how he looked.

> Ryder had K. telephoned to from the hospital and K. went to see him almost every day. . . . "He looked so beautiful in the hospital, all gone away here (cheekbones) so that the bony structure showed through the thin flesh—and the hands were so beautiful—he talked slowly, but clearly. His memory is feeble so that he tells you a thing and then repeats it."
>
> Ryder loves K.'s poem to him and talks a great deal about it—"and to think," the artist said, "he had to come 'way from Mt. Lebanon and I am here—and we found each other. Nobody introduced us."
>
> "The truth was," said K., "that I went to him."

The comfort Kahlil derived from this association added much to his self-identity. Somehow Ryder's alienation from society mirrored his own feelings, and he had often tried to analyze his reverence for the solitary man. "I count my knowing him one of the great things of my life—that I was able to get through to his real life and have him in my real life," he later confided to Mary.

> I stopped going to see him in the last months because of the effort it was to him. . . . You know how about twenty years ago, or so, he was in the world. . . . But I seem to know why he left it—I understand the course of Ryder's life. It is such a struggle to meet the world—to pull the mind and the heart away from their own objects in order to answer the words that are meaningless. . . . He just gave it up . . . left the society of gentlemen and ladies, and he sought the low life of New York that made no demand on him. That was a refreshment—a rest from the effort. And since his mind had stopped the struggle, his body went too. . . . No one else had such a vision of the earth.[31]

In his memorial article Henry McBride mentioned meeting Ryder at the Montross Gallery and concluded with Kahlil's tribute to him. "The following is the first poem addressed to Albert Pinkham Ryder that I have seen. It is by Kahlil Gibran, a Syrian artist and writer. It is too bad that we have to go all the way to Syria to sing the praises of Ryder. However, I rather like the verse that begins: 'Thine is the Giant-World of primal truth,' though I hardly dare to recommend so many 'we's' and 'thee's' as Mr. Gibran uses in the last verse of all. Here is the poem." National publications picked up the poem. Mary recorded that the lines were quoted in the Toledo *Blade*, a Chicago newspaper, and three other newspapers. *Current Opinion* not only included an excerpt but also reproduced the portrait. "We are indebted to Mr. Kahlil

Gibran, the Syrian poet, mystic and artist, for this striking portrait study . . . ," the caption read.[32]

Amid this recognition Kahlil's show in Boston opened on April 16. He did not go to see it but waited for Mary to send reports. "Doll and Richards have hung the wash-drawings in their small room between the gallery at the back and the large front room. . . . The light is good—the space too small, and the hanging order fair only." Of the people whom he knew, her sister Louise had been most appreciative, saying, "To me they were most wonderful as presenting Man as a work of Earth's, an earth-product or many earth-products—Man the root, man the rock, man the vine, the flower, man the animal."

Another interested commentator was Charles Peabody, who had bought a pastel from Day's 1904 show. He and his wife Jeannette were good friends of Mary; he had photographed her a few years ago and now his daughters were attending the Haskell School. "Mr. Peabody didn't care for the form, but thought the color glorious—glorious—perfect. It made him think of 'the finest old Pompeian.' " [33]

The Boston reviews were heavily influenced by Alice Eckstein's article. But one astute writer had the historical sense to recall Kahlil in his turn-of-the-century setting, in an article entitled "Syriac Suggestions."

> This Syrian artist, who came to Boston in 1903 [*sic*] is favorably recalled as assistant at the Harcourt Street studio of F. Holland Day. Of late years he has worked in New York. More than perhaps any of the then group of symbolists he has carried forward the sort of vague, mystical expression that was the beau ideal of advanced Boston in the days when white roses were worn on the birthday of Charles the Martyr and when wealthy ladies scrubbed church steps. Into a super-refined atmosphere of revolt from the prosaic and literal came the young Arab and found himself breathing congenially.
>
> The phase passed locally. Mr. Day left and no one hereabout has carried on his cult of photo-secessionist Christs. Erstwhile wearers of the white rose now build imperishable cathedrals and interest themselves in model housing for East Boston and the South end [probably a reference to Ralph Adams Cram]. But Mr. Gibran in literary New York has run true to the quest of the inchoate. Still, as of yore, he pulls a pencil point around and round in sweeping lines and then fills in the shaggy contours with nearly flat washes of dull color. A faint gleam here of red and blue: the least bit of accenting to indicate construction; but for the rest, all is flow and flux, is rhythm and mystery. The Philistine titters. A student of race psychology, on the contrary, feels sure that here is an expression of the same kind of mentality that produced the delightful "Automatics" of Saracen art or the exquisite Persian miniatures. . . . Art conceived in a sublimated ether this of Gibran's surely is.

The review's candor irritated Mary, who called it "stupid." [34] Slowly the facts of Kahlil's artistic beginnings in Boston were being submerged. To replace the reality of settlement houses and the now unfashionable Day there was being created the official image of a Middle Eastern, francophile New Yorker who had neither struggled nor suffered to survive.

Another significant figure from his past also saw the show. Josephine Peabody Marks went on April 24. In noting her attendance in her diary, she did not record her reaction, but if it was negative it would not have been surprising. Mary reported that many of his Boston admirers preferred his earlier style; this was especially true of an unnamed former friend who regretted that he had departed from what she called the "purely and exclusively ideal."

But America's long-awaited entrance into the World War now superseded any concern Gibran might have had about opinion in Boston. "Beloved Mary," he wrote on April 20, "I am now downtown working for Syria. Since the day America made a common cause of the Allied Governments, the Syrians and the Lebanese in this country have decided to join the French Army which is almost ready to enter Syria. With the help of some Syrians in the city, I have been able to organize a 'Syrian–Mount Lebanon Volunteer Committee.' *I had to do it*, Mary. The moral side of this movement is what the French Government sees and cares for." [35]

The League of Liberation that preoccupied him until the end of the war actively encouraged young Lebanese and Syrians to bear arms against Turkey. Words by Woodrow Wilson, "No People must be forced under sovereignty under which it does not wish to live," were the slogan it adopted for its letterhead.[36] Affiliated with similar groups in Paris, London, and Egypt, the American movement openly crusaded for Middle Eastern autonomy. The editors of several leading Syrian papers—Elia D. Madey and Diab from *Mirat al-Gharb* (*Mirror of the West*), Haddad from *as-Sayeh* (*The Traveler*), Arida of *al-Funoon*—were on the executive committee. Dr. Tabet was president, Rihani was vice-president, and Mikhail Naimy, a recently arrived writer, was secretary of Arabic correspondence. Gibran was chosen secretary of English correspondence.

His renewed commitment to the cause of his people again seriously conflicted with his role on *The Seven Arts*. By the summer of 1917 the magazine had become a passionate forum where Oppenheim, John Reed, and Randolph Bourne were violently denouncing the war. Caught in a crisis of conscience, he tried to justify his ambivalent position when he saw Mary in July.

> You know I like Oppenheim—though I feel so oppositely to him about what to do in this war. . . . I'm anti-war—but for that very reason I use this war. It is my weapon. I'm for justice—and so I make use of this great

injustice. . . . And Oppenheim knows how I feel. He's come to me—you know he always comes to talk things over—and I've told him. I don't want to hurt the magazine and they want to keep my name. I can't, somehow, hurt them—so I think perhaps it is better to let things drift. My Syrian friends don't like it—and many of them haven't understood my still being on the Board since the magazine has been printing its recent editorials.

His dilemma was shared by countless other Americans that summer. The diverse positions held by Charlotte, a staunch pacifist, and Mary, becoming more and more an ardent patriot, widened the rift between these old friends. Mary's Relief efforts, at first personal, were by now directed at the whole school. On April 22 she had written, "[The] school has sent more than $1,000 so far since October—to various needs in Syria, France, Belgium—and I think we shall reach $1,500 before the year ends. In 1914–15 we sent $215; in 1915–16, $420 . . . next year I believe we can extend the work." To all of this Charlotte was unsympathetic: "And you, I fear, like Aunt Rose, glory in Red Cross, service badges, thrift—and the whole subtle armament which war begets for the enthusiastics." [37]

Another exchange between an American forced to accept the Allied course and one who still held out for a new order was articulated in several letters between Amy Lowell and James Oppenheim in the summer of 1917. To her the one distracting feature in the otherwise "splendid magazine" was his insistence "to keep snarling at the war." [38] Under fire from all sides, he eventually agreed with his backer Mrs. Rankin and Miss Lowell to subdue his pacifist ardor. But despite the poet's pledge of $200 to support the magazine in its financial plight, the effort to rally support for *The Seven Arts* and to curtail its anti-government invective was too late. In the issue of October 1917 he was forced to announce the demise of his bright venture. Most of the literary vigor engendered·by it was transmitted to another publication, *The Dial*. But in its brief life of a year *The Seven Arts* had been an appropriate springboard for Gibran.

Although his release from the magazine might have seemed fortunate, a restlessness took the place of the activity which it had offered. Again he began to fantasize about being at the front. "If I enlist," he argued, "others also will enlist. . . . But they might decide that my mind was the part of me most useful. . . . I can't do any regular work with this war going on—work of my own. . . . And if it all ends, and I'm still here, you know what my life will be then—just trying to do things." [39]

In December he visited Boston, where Marianna had finally found an apartment at 76 Tyler Street, a clean and warm building next to the Maronite church. When Mary saw him the day after Christmas she deplored his appearance—"His face in repose has no laugh beneath it. A deep restless suffering underlies it—and the cause is Syria—is, more specifically, Mt. Lebanon." For the next two nights his conversation centered on the complexities of the war. "It is this constant sense of Syria and her uncertain fate—and the checking of all those free currents in himself—of creative work, that has leached his face again of its good color and given it that look of unquiet burning." The old uncertainty that had disappeared during the past year was re-emerging.

> I know I'm of use because a new price has been set on my head—not that I mind that. . . . The other day a letter was sent me—anonymous—and a similar one to Doctor Tabet in English. "Turkey is not dead—and she has a long arm—if you do not stop what you are doing—" (I forgot the closing threat, [interpolated Mary] but the sense was you'll soon not be alive to do it—and the usual blood-dripping dagger was added). Of course . . . I know that if the agents of Turkey were really planning to kill me in New York they wouldn't say anything about it—but just the same I made use of that letter, I telephoned straight to the Department of Justice.

The Department was unable to help. Mary received his wildest stories with equanimity. Even his latest claim did not upset her. "He showed me the scar on his arm that a shot in Paris had given him—a Turkish attempt on his life. . . . He had never told me of that before—the shot was fired too close—and had been a failure. But threats and plots do not affect him. It is the non-personal things that he thinks about and worries over." [40]

"No, I haven't always faith," he answered when she asked his opinion of the outcome of the fighting. "Sometimes I think Syria may quite perish. Sometimes I see the coast of America bombarded with submarines and zeppelins." Gradually she drew him away from his preoccupation. "K. seems only one-third living in his conscious; two-thirds in his subconscious. This war dethrones all life except its own and it holds him captive. I get the sense that when we are together something of that raging restlessness is quieted even if not very deeply." [41]

Because of a bitterly cold spell he did not return to his icy New York studio until January 12, and all during his visit she coaxed him to write and draw. Toward the end they began to collaborate again, and they finished an elegy to Rodin (who had died the past November) and worked on four parables ("The Pomegranate," "Ambition," "The Eye," and "Other Seas"). By the time he left, Kahlil had regained his composure and his will to work. "K. loves everything lovable and everything and everybody—loves all life that is alive," she wrote after their final meeting. "Poverty of spirit on the left never blinds him to what rich things may be on the right. . . . He looks much better for the three weeks of removal from his working scenes, in the comfort Marianna knows how to make."

306

The evenings spent with Mary had produced many drawings, for which she told him she was "rich." "I can no more help drawing them than I can help breathing," he told her, "and I come here and draw instead of talking and I leave the drawings because I don't want to carry them away with me." [42] She had brought him back to reality with Blake and Turner and magazines, and by her own quiet assurance.

Illustrations from *The Procession.* (Authors)

Gibran in the country. (Authors)

18

The Prophet

By the end of January 1918 demand for Gibran's presence at literary gatherings in New York was increasing. That month at the request of Mayor Raymond he spoke about Syria to a group in Newark. He had read at the Poetry Society of America and was promised an entire evening there. He accepted an invitation for another evening at the home of Corinne Roosevelt Robinson. "Music and poetry," he wrote in his acceptance, "are the only two elements that can remind us of calmer yesterday and kinder tomorrow." [1]

As his craving for recognition was satisfied, the signs of his disorientation were disappearing. He attributed the change within himself to external sources. "Talking to people about poetry and reading to them give me a great deal of real pleasure," he wrote Mary on February 5. "It seems that human beings have changed remarkably during the past three years. They are hungry for beauty and for truth and for that other thing—that other thing which lies beneath and beyond beauty and truth. And people are so kind and so sweet to me. Sometimes it makes me very shy." [2]

As the deprivations and shortages of the war reached home, Mary fretted about his drafty studio. "May you get enough coal to keep warm! I think of you all through the bitter days and such part of the bitter nights as I'm awake in—and wonder how it feels in the studio—doubtless there'd be 'plenty' of coal if the government had allowed us all to be stuck $20 a ton for it!" However, profiteering and inflation did not depress him. "These are hard days indeed. . . . But we are learning so much about Life and about ourselves— and we are learning about clothes and food and fuel. And when better days come the things we have learned will be of great value to us all. Personally—I am doing well. . . . Life, Mary, is altogether too kind and too gracious to me. . . . I am often unhappy because . . . others—millions and millions—are handled so roughly. And I am quite conscious that this feeling, this form of unhappiness is not free from self-glorification." He no longer envisioned a zeppelin bombardment of the North American coast. "I believe the end will be good, though just now all looks darker than ever before. . . . In all these years, man has been thinking locally—in terms of himself, of his family, of town, of country, of continent. Now he is beginning to think in terms of the planet—not just the great man—but many men. His speech has become planetary—in telegraph and telephone and movie." [3]

When Mary visited New York in March to see a memorial exhibition of Ryder's work, she learned how Kahlil's own reputation was spreading beyond the city. "There were four big audiences," he told her, "and I've read twice at Mrs. Robinson's . . . 40 at dinner! And at the reception at [the Jasper Baynes']. . . . I couldn't go to Chicago [for a reading before the Poetry Society]. . . . I didn't want to take that trip for a two-hour thing. You know about [Haniel] Long who teaches poetry at the Carnegie Institute of Pittsburgh. He's a very real being—a poet—and he wants me to come out there to talk." He showed Mary his latest portrait drawings of Witter Bynner and Pierre de Lanux. De Lanux, a representative of the French high commission in Washington, was a writer interested in nationalistic movements. He had just published a book on Serbia and had made a critical study of the new wave of American poets. But for her the best news was his statement, "I've submitted the book to a publisher." [4] The book was "The Madman," and for the first time in his career he was looking for an English-language publisher.

One morning she waited to see him until some visitors had left the studio. One of them was a writer, Mrs. Marie Tudor Garland from Boston. She divided her time between a Greenwich Village house, a place in New Hampshire, and a rambling estate in Buzzards Bay, Massachusetts. A widow for ten years, she had turned the responsibility of bringing up six young children into a rich adventure. All her houses were open to her several children, their friends, and her many artist friends. The coterie of Rose O'Neill especially responded to her charm and entertainment. Now Kahlil had decided to accept an invitation to her Bay End Farm, where he would be able to work undisturbed in a cottage.

That morning he read Mary an embryonic English poem, which she called "Passage to Men and Women." Praising it as beautiful and true, she recorded a fragment in the journal:

> Love each other—and
> Let your love be as a sea between
> The shores of yourselves—
> Fill each other's cup—but drink not from
> One cup—Give bread to each other—
> But share not the same loaf—
> Be each alone in your togetherness—

This unresolved, untitled passage would become the core of the celebrated statement on marriage in *The Prophet*. Moved by it, she confessed a recurrent feeling of ennui toward her school. This time it was he who comforted her.

> When I told him I was troubled at times because my whole heart isn't in my work, he said like a flash, "No, and my whole heart isn't in my work—and nobody's whole heart is just in his work—Your whole heart isn't in anything—in any one thing. It's in everything. . . . There's just one thing our work needs—and that's Love. That's what pupils want, what friends want, what strangers want, what an audience wants—what we all want. . . . And that's so easy to do—and yet we don't do it—For I don't mean an emotion, when I say 'love'—I mean just freedom and welcome and want and being all there with all of one's self. Not with a philosophy and lots of ideas—that will make people say 'What an interesting hour!'—but just with ourselves—the dearest thing we have—but the thing we don't give. And it's the only thing people want. . . . We are not very loving beings, Mary—I mean we Humans." [5]

Everywhere they walked that day his elation accompanied them. He welcomed the changing New York skyline as a sign of growth—"We've seen these buildings grow up. . . . It's a great thing to see again and again as if we'd never seen them before." At dinner "he was saluted gayly" by one of his models, and he explained how he was determined to be friendly with everyone including models—"to treat them nicely and make them feel. O it's so nice to work then!" [6]

This euphoric mood was influencing his production. He continued to work on a long lyrical poem in Arabic that he had begun in Cohasset the summer before. He described "Processions" as a contrast in two voices—"one of the woods . . . the other more mental, more philosophical." He showed Mary several new drawings and spoke anew of a work to which he had often alluded before: "My island man has changed a great deal in these years. I'm not so sure as I was about some things!" he smiled. "Now when all these groups come out to him, instead of meeting them with a 'Oh! so you've come out here, have you? Well come on, and I'll give you a piece of my mind that will show you just how rotten such and such ideas are,' he greets them and meets them with his whole self, his loving self." [7]

The first reference to Gibran's "island man" had appeared in Mary's journal six years earlier.

> *June 12, 1912.* Today K. got the first line—or first motif, rather—for his Island God. For he has finally decided that his Promethean exile shall be an island one—instead of a mountain one.
>
> "I can put a mountain on the island—but I couldn't put an island on the mountain. And an island gives so many possibilities—especially if it is near

enough the mainland for a city to be visible." The first part is to be named with the name given in Arabic to the rising of the new moon [Ielool]. At the end of seven thousand years from the shore near the city he puts off in his boat alone—and we learn why he had left the Gods to be an exile among men, and why now he leaves men as an exile to solitude: because he must await a new race that shall be able to accept the fire. K. has done a good day's work on it. [In a marginal note she added, presumably at a later date, the name of the god: "Almustafa of *The Prophet*."]

This is the book he means when he says "My Book." Some of the separate songs or prose poems he writes . . . he is keeping to bring from the lips of this exile. So that there is a slowly growing body of material for the book. Similarly, the Madman grows. . . . When he has completed a thing he keeps it for months and then returns to it with critical sense, . . . then he revises and may put away again—either to revise finally, or never to publish, but just to keep for a few lines in it worth using in something he shall care to publish. Thus he has much he never will publish.

Three months later he had again mentioned the project. "Speaks of Island Man–Mustafa as my book. 'It will be with me probably five years more—but it is complete now in structure in my mind. I shall probably get out two or three other books in the interim.' "[8]

As the years passed, Mary sporadically referred to both the Island God and a new work called the "Commonwealth."

April 6, 1913. Three chapters are added to Mustafa.

September 4, 1914, New York. He had been all night in visions of his Commonwealth, sleeping not at all but making notes [about] "the big aspects of human life. Birth, education, marriage, death—and the other big details though not the biggest, like expression which is art, and labor, which is construction—these are in it."

"Have you any personalities or characters as mouthpieces in it?"

"No. It is the prophetic form. That is the really great form. You remember what I said about punishment was very simple. [They had agreed that Harry Thaw, the murderer of Stanford White, should be made to give $2 million-worth of buildings or other works as compensation for having taken White from America.] Let a man restore to the world as much life as his crime destroyed. . . . Let a man who kills a farmer add to his own work what the farmer would have produced if he had lived—or an equivalent. This is simple, and it is really a solution. I have taken other aspects of life, and reduced each to its simple reality. And just as to be simple and real as in an individual, is called madness, so simple reality in the state will be called madness."

"Your Commonwealth is the Mad State then."

"Exactly."

"Do you treat of interstate relations or is it all of internal affairs?"

"I've thought about that. It seems to me it is not complete without relations between different states. But treated briefly. Everything will be short. You know I believe the realest books *are* short. How short *Job* is!"

November 14, 1914. "I've written more than I've drawn and painted—in Arabic—some on my War—some on my Commonwealth, and some separate pieces."

April 11, 1915. "You treat of marriage in your Commonwealth, don't you?"

Yes, he does [she answered herself], as he treats of all big things in common life—The Commonwealth is to be one of his life works—like his Mustafa—one of the things he wants to leave behind as life work.[9]

After April 1915 no mention of the "Commonwealth" or Almustafa appeared in the Journal until April 21, 1916, when he proposed combining the two works.

"Perhaps I shan't ever publish the Commonwealth, but . . . put all that is in [it] into the mouth of Mustafa. And that really is my work. I am not a thinker. I am a creator of forms. The Commonwealth is not in my language. Only what I say in that language . . . is what I want to say—And only what I say in that language is going at last to matter to other people. . . . There is absolute language, just as there is absolute form—An expression may be absolute just as a triangle is absolute." [He drew a tiny triangle and beside it a wavy-lined triangle.] "People may add this and that—but the eye will perceive in it the triangle. I am always seeking the absolute in language. And I shall find it. There is nothing to do but wait. It will come. I am finding it more than I used to." [10]

If then Gibran anticipated an "absolute language" in which to execute his life's work, what led him to compose in English? Over a year later, when Mary showed him a copy of *Lights of Dawn*, the recently published poetry of Aristides Phoutrides, he was still questioning whether any poet could successfully use a second language. He "was much interested in Phoutrides' book," she wrote, ". . . but . . . he said, 'He's word ridden—But after all, foreigners can't write English poetry. . . . Yet I keep on trying.'" She defined his style as "a sort of universal English—the simplest structure, 'pure line' English, that he uses, in choosing the Bible style." He explained his attraction to that style: "The Bible is Syriac literature in English words. It is the child of a sort of marriage. There's nothing in any other tongue to correspond to the English Bible. And the Chaldo-Syriac is the most beautiful language that man has made—though it is no longer used." [11]

An important influence on his decision to write "Almustafa–Commonwealth" in English was the attention and support he was receiving from his American friends. "The Madman" had been turned down by one publisher but he submitted it to a second. He wrote Bynner, still his most faithful champion:

I am sending you some of the parables you like. But you have heard them so often that I should think you must be quite weary of them. The Poetry

Society gave me a most generous reception and everybody was really more than kind. Yet our friend Mr. Morrow [William Morrow, a partner at Frederick A. Stokes, the firm that had just published Bynner's *Greenstone Poems*] does not want to publish the little collection. He does not think the book will sell enough! I have turned the mss. to the macmillan Company.[12]

In April 1918, when he sent Mary word of his trip to Mrs. Garland's farm, he announced that his next work would be composed entirely in English: "One *large thought* is filling my mind and my heart; and I want so much to give it form before you and I meet. It is to be in English—and how can anything of mine be really English without your help?"[13] During the twenty-four days he spent at Bay End Farm he outlined and finished most of the first draft of that "large thought." He and Mary called it "The Counsels" and by June 1919 it had evolved into its final form—*The Prophet*.

The letters he wrote during this April vacation show how deeply satisfied he was amid the family and farm life of Bay End. For part of his stay Rose O'Neill, swathed in her filmy Grecian robe, came with her everpresent coterie: her sister Callista, the Hindu poet Dhan Mukerji, and his English wife. Kahlil felt free to wander by the seashore or to the freshwater pond, to inspect the herds of Welsh ponies and sheep, or to watch animals in the pine forest. Each guest was encouraged to search out a special place to create or think in solitude, outdoors or in one of the several houses scattered over the estate. Meanwhile Marie Garland's family of six and her eight adopted children offered him amusing distractions. Hope, the fourteen-year-old daughter, later recalled that he made a roseleaf cake with them and took time to talk with them and look at their artistic efforts.[14]

Although he was accomplishing much work, the weeks were like a vacation. "Regards from the trees and the flowers," he wrote Marianna. "I am a royal guest in a royal house in a royal countryside. I can work here, ride horses and can drive the auto whenever I want. . . . Please send me two pounds of halvah and two hundred cigarettes." To Mary he exclaimed, "I would like to stay here forever!! because I am free to be what I want and to do as I like. And I feel that I shall be able to do some good work." She answered him with a long-felt wish of her own: "Some of your pictures . . . and some of your English things would be dear to the soldiers in a pocket-sized book. I think, for instance, of 'God' and of the 'Hand in the Cloud' you showed me in March. They would be like God's reserves in a man's heart. And I wish the prisoners of war could have them, for love and light and space."[15]

On May 6 he returned to Boston with what would be the realization of that dream. "Kahlil . . . looking marvelously well—solid, browned, bright-eyed and unnervous, unworn. 'I've had a glorious time,' he began. 'I felt like work and was able to do it.'" He praised Mrs. Garland's ability to combine a vigorous intellectual life with the practical role of a farm owner and, most of all, her emancipated attitude in handling her children: "That's one of the things I admire most . . . the freedom she gives others. With the boys, for instance, she frankly says to them that she tries to learn from them instead of teaching them." Finally Mary got him to talk about what he had accomplished in that idyllic community. He had done no painting but "did about two thirds of the big piece of English work I wrote you about. It has been brooding in me for eighteen months or more—but I've had the feeling that I wasn't big enough yet to do it . . . but in the past few months it has been growing and growing in me and I began it. It is to have 21 parts—and I've written 16 of them. . . . This was a great deal of work." He described the prologue:

> In a city between the plains and the sea, where ships come in, and where flocks graze in the fields behind the city—there lives and wanders about the fields and somewhat among the people, a man—poet, seer, prophet— who loves them, and whom they love—but there is an aloneness, an aloofness, after all, about him. They are glad to hear him talk—they feel in him a beauty and a sweetness—but in their love of him they never come very close—even the young women who are attracted by his gentleness do not quite venture to fall in love with him. And while the people count him as a part of the city, and like it that he is there, and that he talks with their children in the fields, there is a consciousness . . . that this is all temporary. And one day out of the blue horizon comes a ship towards the city—and somehow everyone knows, though nothing is told, that the ship is for the hermit-poet. And now that they are going to lose him—the feeling of what he is in their life comes to them—and they all crowd down to the shore, and he stands and talks with them.
>
> And one says, "Tell us about Children," and another, "Speak to us of Friendship"—and he speaks of these things. . . . It is what he says about them that I've been writing. There are 21 or maybe 24 parts—And when he has ended—he enters into the ship—and the ship sails away into the mist.[16]

He read Mary the parts on children, friends, clothes, eating and drinking, talking, pain, men and women, death, time, buying and selling, teaching and self-knowledge, houses, and art. "And at the end," she noted, "one says to the poet, 'Tell us about God,' and he says, 'of Him I have been speaking in everything.' "[17]

They immediately began to make the "very slight needed changes" in seven of the parts. "I'm not trying to write poetry in these," he said. "I'm trying to express thoughts—but I want the rhythm and the words right so that they shan't be noticed, but shall just sink in, like water into cloth—and the thought be the thing that registers." "He didn't read the one on Love at first," she wrote, but when he did begin, "When love beckons to you, follow him,

Though his ways are hard and steep," she was transfixed. There was "none more beautiful." "Do you notice how full these things are of what we have said in talking together sometimes years ago?" he asked. "There's nothing in them that hasn't come from our talks. Talking about them with you has made them clear to me. And one writes these things in order to find in them his own higher self. This poem . . . has made me better."

That night they began to call the work "The Counsels." After he left, borrowing a book and a black rubber coat against the rain, she mused, "And when he described the Hermit poet of the Counsels and the relation of the people of the city to him—it was a description, to the very heart, of the way people are towards himself. And he expressed it with an accuracy, a mastery, complete—the words fitted as close as light. . . . It is a solemn thing, and incredible, to look into his eye and hear him say as a poem what is in his deepest heart and in his consciousness during solitude." [18]

The next working session occurred on May 11. She felt that six of the parts they had worked on were now complete, but she had reservations about his language in others. "I oughtn't really to be writing English, anyhow," he confessed. "But I talk English so much—and all my friends write—write all the time. It's all around me. But I still think in Arabic . . . when I've been writing in Arabic, English is oh! so far away. I have to think out how to spell even the slightest word." Partially to dispel his doubts, but more to clarify her own aims, she outlined her general method of criticizing his language:

> I am going to give you a little reading matter for Monday. . . .
>   I. When you read your things, I'm always listening with three ears—
>   1. of my own soul.
>   2. of the ordinary man—and others—of today who might read it or to whom it might be read.
>   3. of the simple man generations hereafter.
>   II. I don't report on 1.—and I can't . . . so I only say "I love it," or "It is beautiful". . . .
>   III. I report on 2 and 3.
>   1. Will it say to 2 what you mean it to say?
>   2. Will it be solid still to 3—and is there anything in it that time will discard?

While admitting her "sledge-hammer" tactics, she ended her lesson by acknowledging that there was a better way of criticism—"and truer to a larger reality." [19]

By the third week in May he was back in New York. His creative surge continued and he mailed five packets of poems and pieces of "The Counsels" to 314 Marlborough Street. "I hope that you do not mind my sending you these things, now that you are so busy," he apologized. "Please do not give them a thought untill you have nothing else to do." [20]

316

It was true that Mary's life had never been so full, for she was closing down her school. For the past few years she had expressed doubts about its direction and her own role as an educator. After one meeting of headmistresses she observed, "I spoke a different language from all but the *young* women in the association . . . we at 314 are doing a different work because we here have to meet To-Day and be worth while to girls of To-Day only—whereas the fashionable schools can live with less vital work, because of the social desirability of their clientele." She blamed herself for failing to win the support of the elite of Boston society. One night she showed Kahlil an outfit which she thought would allow her the freedom her active life demanded. When he speculated about how the parents would react to its "different" look, she retorted,

> Boston has already sized me up and turned me down, so I need not hope for advantage in Boston through any conformity. . . . I am ranked next to Miss Winsor [another headmistress]—with her by some—in spirit and in some gifts—but they don't want to send their children to me because I am different—and they don't want their girls to be different and they do want to know just what they are sending them to; . . . Girls get something here which they don't get elsewhere. . . . But I queered myself with the Back Bay in 1903 when I rode the bare-backed horse and walked the trapeze-top in the Lees' yard at Cohasset—with never a notion that these things would affect my desirability as caretaker of girls in parents' eyes. They enjoyed watching these things in me, but they didn't want their girls to do them. They don't trust me. I'm not discreet for them.[21]

In April she had accepted an opportunity to realize more fully her vision of what a school should be. She was asked to head the Cambridge School, founded in 1886 by Arthur and Stella Gilman, the pioneers in women's education who had also begun the Cambridge Society for Collegiate Instruction, which eventually became Radcliffe College. Kahlil thought it would be a good move. When she described the school's wanting her as "like a request, 'Come and love us. We want to be loved,'" he agreed, "Of course. It's the one thing we all want." [22]

And so she left her school, the place smothered by narrow brick buildings, the detested back alley, and the busy street. The Cambridge School, a sprawling Victorian mansion surrounded with flowering trees and broad lawns, was located at 36 Concord Avenue. She viewed her new responsibility to give it a higher reputation within the community as challenging, and with its light and spaciousness she felt "aerated all over." Her final letter to Gibran from Marlborough Street summed up the years from 1903: "This is our last night in this old house . . . the years fill my heart up with thankfulness . . . and for what is best and farthest and deepest in the change I . . . bless and thank God

Mary at a Cambridge School graduation, 1919.
(Mrs. Thomas J. Durham)

for our friendship more than for all the other things. . . . When I think of it as a whole—fifteen years—for after all it is just the same period as my life in this house and this school—for we met, my first winter—it has been like a single moment." [23]

"I have blessed you a thousand times for that letter, the last from 314 and the first from Cambridge," he answered. "It tells me so many wonderfully sweet things about the past fifteen years. . . . 314 was indeed the stream from which I drank the water of life, and I shall always think of that large room as the birthplace of all that is worth while in me and in my life. But, Mary, wherever you are is 314. It is the spirit of the house not the house." [24]

Just as she was beginning a new life in Cambridge, so in a way was he. Sometime between the middle of May and the end of June he was introduced to Alfred A. Knopf, a young publisher whose reputation, though less than three years old, was attracting many unusually talented writers. James Oppenheim, whose *The Book of Self* had recently come out under the Knopf imprint, arranged a luncheon in Greenwich Village. Also present were Bynner

318

and de Lanux, who was enthusiastic enough about "The Madman" (which Macmillan had rejected) to offer to translate it into French. Before the meeting Gibran had reported, "Alfred Knopf, the publisher, wishes to bring out my 'Parables.' It is a good house and more interested in placing a book before the public than the other firms." Mary approved: "Knopf seems rather new to fame, but he is getting out many interesting books by people of other countries, and I shall be much interested to know if he is solid and desirable." Within a month, on the same day that Mary moved to the Cambridge School, he was at last able to announce triumphantly,

Mr. Knopf and I have gone over almost everything concerning my little book "The Madman—His Parables and Poems." The contract was signed yesterday, and the frontispiece was given to the engraver while I was there. The book will come out sometime in mid October. The more I see of Mr. Knopf the more I like him. He is young and has an eye for the beautiful, and though he is no philanthropist! yet he is honest—he does not leave anything unsaid. Of course I want the book to be a success commercially, for both Mr. Knopf's sake and for the sake of my next book, "The Counsels." But I think we can make it a success. There will be three drawings in the book, the frontispiece and two others, and they should make the book more interesting.[25]

At around the same time there appeared another indication that he was becoming more confident about his writing ability. "Defeat, my Defeat," a poem he had recently written in English, was included in a pamphlet advocating self-determination for the fragmented countries in Eastern Europe. The publication was sponsored by Franklin Nicola, a Pittsburgh financier and friend of Marie Garland whom Gibran had met through Haniel Long. Mary saw the poem only after it was published. "I am sending you two copies which I hope you will like," he wrote. "And if you should find any faults in the English, please let me know them. It is never too late to know mistakes." But later, when he had decided to include it in "The Madman" and she volunteered to work on it, he refused her offer. "It's all printed now, and can't be changed. And it doesn't matter much after all. Perhaps I oughtn't ever to have included it in the book." [26]

Throughout July he alternately pleaded weariness and overwork whenever Mary suggested a visit together. Her response to the obvious implication that he preferred the country retreats of his friends—the Fords in Rye, the Baynes on Long Island, the Mortens in Connecticut—was typically self-effacing. No longer feeling slighted if he behaved inconsiderately, she seemed to live only for the lines he sent her. "God bless you and make Rye and Long Island lovely and refreshing and sweet and free to you—and always show you more and tell

"Defeat, my Defeat," and the
cover of the pamphlet in
which it was printed. (Authors)

you more and love you more. . . . I've been saying to myself all day, 'What else in the world is so delicious as the coming of these Counsels.' " [27]

Even though their times together were becoming fewer, he still counted on her to look after Marianna. When his sister finally moved into the three-room apartment at 76 Tyler Street, both he and Mary began to encourage her to leave Miss Teahan's establishment. Mary had once summarized its drabness by noting how "soured and bilious and disappointed with all memories Miss Teahan looked—sitting sewing with little smooth-cheeked Ethel at the other end of the same filmy stuff." But it was difficult for Marianna, now thirty-three, to tear herself away from the only life she had ever known. Finally Kahlil threatened not to visit anymore, Mary insisted that sewing seams for others was "not dignified," and she was forced to retire. Mary still guided the younger woman, supervised her important purchases, and regularly reported on her health. "Marianna Gibran has a winter coat!" she wrote that summer. "New, blue, big, beautiful. The warmest and best we've seen at all! Our dream come true—and she is going to have an Oxford grey suit made, and don't mention it—but we're taking treatment with a fine woman osteopath who is straightening the spinal rotation that keeps her from her native vigor." [28]

Kahlil was preparing to leave New York for his annual vacation in Cohasset, and Mary offered to show off her latest skill by driving him there. "I can run an automobile, now, K. G. . . . It's simple—and I like it better than being driven. I got a car for the school—perforce to bring girls out from Boston." But she cheerfully accepted his evasion of her offer. "I'm just so glad you won't stop in Boston or Cambridge, for I am myself such a desert of solitude . . . but I will see you before you go back to New York, anyhow." [29]

They did not see each other at all that summer. He finished his long Arabic poem "Processions," which was scheduled for publication in the fall by Naseeb Arida, the former editor of the again defunct *al-Funoon*. He left Cohasset hurriedly because "both the Syrian committee and Mr. Knopf seemed to think I am very much needed," notifying her that he would be free to see her in New York the following weekend. More and more his letters revealed an unprecedented quality of independence. For many years it had been she who announced the time and place of their visits; now he began to assume the dominant role, and she was content to follow. He added that his vacation had been "rather fruitful. I have added seven new processions to the original Arabic poem. But each one of the new processions calls for a new drawing. So you see, Mary, that I am not only hard pressed by things outside myself but also by things inside." [30]

After she finally saw him at the studio on August 31 her journal revealed, perhaps unconsciously, a definite shift in their roles. It became a series of monologues by him instead of the animated conversations in which she had participated equally. Fast disappearing was the quality of give and take, the intimate gossip, that had enlivened it for the past eight years. She seemed happy just to record his point of view or his activities and became more and more reluctant to insert herself. Of "Processions" she wrote:

The processions are aspects of life as seen by Man in two selves [she called them Civile and Foreste]—the self of civilization . . . and the spontaneous simple self like certain shepherd lads of the Near East—or man as he accepts and chimes in with life, not analyzing, doubting, debating, or defining. The two meet where their two worlds also meet—on a ridge of land just outside the city and at the edge of the forest . . . and each says what the given thing is in his experience. . . . There are three processions of love: one of summer lust, hated by Civile, but called by Foreste just a disease somewhere between the bones and the skin, that will pass away; one of great and overwhelming passion, which to Civile is madness, but of which Foreste says, "If it is madness to forget all in the rage of love, then in the forest there is none who is sane; and one of understanding (oh! I can't recall this one—even though it is probably the permanent and child-of-God fellowship one). That Civile expressed a noble and large thing and that Foreste made it at once unlimited, simple, and forever moving. And Foreste says there is no death in the forest. Foreste uses bubbling lyrical meters, many of them—always different. Civile uses always the same—and every other line of his throughout ends with the same rhyme—a *wra*.

Both Kahlil and Mary had anticipated the coming fall as the time when he would publish nearly simultaneously an English and an Arabic book. However, a paper shortage delayed "Processions" in press. He was anxious that this poem, his first serious attempt to write a traditionally rhymed and metered work in Arabic, should be presented to the world as an example of exquisite bookmaking, and he decided to wait for Arida to locate a good stock. As for his American publisher, he told Mary, "Knopf is such a sweet being and he wears well. He is very beautiful in his openness to suggestions, too, when you are working with him. He's twenty-five—married to a nice good wife and they have a dear little child. I dined with him two nights ago."

By now he accepted the rifts between himself and his pacifist American friends. He was finding a new kind of role for himself—an empathetic, understanding attitude which attracted even strangers. He wrote "Defeat, my Defeat," he explained, to give courage to people who thought they were failures. "And you know, I've heard more from that poem than from any of the others?" He continued,

> People are so lonely. Of the hundreds who weep on my shoulder, so to speak, and tell me their life histories, almost all say, "I'm a failure, and I'm alone," whether they are married and successful and beloved at home, or not. They've found the truth. That each one of us is eternally alone—and alone with imaginative life—and they don't know what to do with their imaginative life. They shrink from the vagueness and the labor of thinking into it and feeling into it. They just wish they could change things so that its presence wouldn't make itself felt. They haven't got in touch with the whole so that they can dwell with it. They are baffled and puzzled.

One night as they walked up Fifth Avenue after dinner, they saw a white cat lying in a doorway. "Dead!" said a man who had just touched it with his cane. "I thought it was a little too beautiful to be alive," remarked Kahlil. This led to their talking "about the look that comes so divinely when people die." He reminisced about his mother's last days: "She died . . . with the most frightful suffering. Yet her face gave never a sign that she suffered. . . . She was for a while in the Massachusetts Hospital—and the head physician there used to get as quickly through with his other cases as he could, and come and sit a while with her to talk. Her talking was always so delightful—She had the golden tongue." [31]

Mary must have recalled another version of Kamila's illness, which had been told to her four years earlier. According to Marianna, her tongue, instead of being "golden," had been swollen for lack of an Arabic-speaking person to talk to while in quarantine. Although the apparent disparities must have registered on Mary's retentive mind, she made no effort to challenge him. His extravagances were like a protective skin, which she had ceased trying to penetrate. She accepted all of him—his peccadilloes, fabrications, evasions— and continually blessed him.

On October 22, 1918, he sent her a copy of *The Madman*. The handwritten inscription was simple: "To M.E.H. This also I owe to you. K.G." Two weeks later he shot out word of an event more splendid than any personal victory:

> Thursday—the seveneth Day of November. One Thousand nine hundred and Eighteen.
>
> Mary. Out of the dark mist a new world is born. It is indeed a holy day—The most holy since the birth of Jesus.
>
> The air is crowded with the sound of rushing waters and the beating of Mighty Wings. The voice of God is in the wind. Kahlil.

His enthusiasm, sparked by news of the false Armistice, was premature by four days. On November 17, six days after the real Armistice was signed, he was still euphoric. "Long ago, Mary, I said to myself, 'God dwells within a thousand veils of light,' and now I am saying, 'The world has passed through one of the thousand veils of light and is nearer to God.' Everything is different. Everybody is different. The faces on the streets and in shops and on cars and trains are different." [32] They had waited four years for this peace, and the publication of *The Madman* the same month made their peace all the sweeter.

Cover designed by Gibran for an Arrabitah publication.
(Authors)

19

Arrabitah: The Pen-Bond

Weren't you going to send me some leaflets about *The Madman*?" asked Mary when she received her copy. "I'd like very much to have them—I could easily use one hundred." [1]

In pursuing her own publicity campaign on Gibran's behalf, she never challenged the lead statement in the flyer, which read, "Auguste Rodin said of Kahlil Gibran, 'He is the William Blake of the Twentieth Century.' " It is true that as early as 1904 reviewers in Boston were linking Gibran's work with that of Blake, but he himself had never reported Rodin's words during his stay in Paris. It is probable that the quotation was invented by him, and it certainly was used more in the spirit of promotion than of truth. Yet Mary, whose devotion to frankness was intense, heartily approved the apocryphal statement.

The Knopf circular was not the first time Kahlil deliberately confused his readers. Two years earlier he had written a biographical sketch for *al-Funoon* that began, "Gibran was born in the year 1883 in Besharri, Lebanon (and more precisely, it is said, Bombay, India)." It went on to invest him with official honors. His fragmented studies in Paris became a distinguished degree from the Ecole des Beaux-Arts; the acceptance of a painting at the 1910 Salon was exaggerated into full-fledged membership in the Union Internationale des Beaux-Arts et des Lettres.[2]

It was evident that Mary often secretly questioned his embellishments. "Why was your 'Letter to Islam' so hard for Marianna to read?" she asked him once, and she silently suspected his sister's illiteracy after his unconvincing answer about the poem's difficult style. They had often discussed his reticence and the fact that American inquisitiveness repelled him. In 1912 he had first tried to define his concept of "creative truth versus dead truth." "The Arabs distinguish between the two kinds," he told her. "They dislike impertinent questions and the trivial. Ask one what he had at a supper, and he may tell you nectar and birds of heaven—and you may find it was really potatoes, mushrooms and beans. But he's not lying; he's refusing to answer—what he doesn't like is your asking." He avoided giving answers that might reveal his background:

> I meet curiosity a great deal—and I hate it. There isn't anything about me that can't be seen—in my work—in my face, in me. But people don't want to find it out—they want me to tell them in words. They don't want to work for it. . . . There are many things in me that I don't want any human being to know. They are mine—and no one else's. . . . There is a gulf between each soul and other souls . . . it is not meant to be bridged. I feel nearer to people who are a little remote—who have in themselves that aloofness. Curiosity is one of the most hateful qualities of the human mind. And the pleasant mask it assumes is Sympathy. Curiosity is everywhere and so often it calls itself Sympathy even to itself.[3]

Thus by the time *The Madman* was reviewed, Gibran had been introduced to Americans as a mysterious hero and a ready-made genius—the Middle Eastern counterpart of Tagore. All references to his adolescent days as a "street fakir," to his precocious ties with the Boston decadents, were erased. "This book introduces to English readers the work of the greatest poet of Arabia . . . ," wrote the reviewer for the New York *Call*. "In the opinion of many critics, he is a far greater poet than Tagore."

In the *Sun* Howard Willard Cook, who was also a member of Mrs. Ford's Friday dinner group and who later included Kahlil in the dedication of an anthology of poetry, added to the growing myth. "It is proper that out of Lebanon in Syria should come a new psalmist and writer of fables, who gives to us of the Western world a note too seldom found in the writings of our own poets." The *Evening Post* reviewed *The Madman* together with a translation of Chinese poetry by another young writer, Maxwell Bodenheim:

> Kahlil Gibran's volume, exquisitely embellished by three symbolic drawings by the author, reflects beauty of an entirely different calibre. It is the power of the parable that Gibran uses, and he employs it with great skill. . . . It seems like a blend of Tagore, La Fontaine, Nietzsche, and Dr. Sigmund Freud—a blend which, in *The Madman*, is surprisingly successful. Gibran, the publisher assures us, is as much read in his native Arabia as Tagore is in India. This seems rather improbable for where Tagore furnishes his readers pleasant and palatable sweetmeats, . . . Gibran offers them strong and often acrid doses of disillusion and truth, a tonic enjoyed by but few. A poem like "The Sleep Walkers" might have been taken directly out of Jung's revealing "Wandlungen und Symbole der Libido." [4]

So enthusiastic was the *Post* that a month later it featured an interview with Gibran by Joseph Gollomb. Again he was compared with Tagore in terms of his popularity, exotic origins, and use of the parable. "But there resemblance ends," Gollomb wrote, "and differences appear."

> Tagore . . . is a figure from some canvas Sir Frederic Leighton might have painted of a religious mystic. Gibran is Broadway or Copley Square or The Strand or the Avenue de L'Opera—a correctly dressed cosmopolitan of the Western world.
>
> His dark brows and moustache and somewhat curly hair above a good forehead; the clear brown eyes, thoughtful but never abstracted in expression; the sensibly tailored clothes, smart but not conspicuous—there seemed to me a chameleon-like ease of adaptiveness about him. In his studio in West Tenth Street he looked a sensible denizen of Greenwich Village—for such there be. But had I seen him at a congress of economists, or in a Viennese cafe, or in his native Syria, I feel sure he would look equally in the picture in each instance.
>
> It is not a case of lack of individuality with him but on the contrary, an unusual common sense and sympathy which transcend differences and enable him to understand so well each environment in which he finds himself that he neither feels nor looks the stranger. . . . Notwithstanding his citizenship in the world as a whole, Mr. Gibran feels himself a Syrian. To him there is no contradiction here. He is working to bring about a world in which there is a great fellowship of mutual understanding and sympathy. "But in that great process the task of each people will be not to do away with the national character, but to contribute to it," he said to me.

He then was quoted at length about the historical contributions of the Arabic-speaking people. He was optimistic that with self-determination "our people will have much to give." Gollomb closed by speculating that his influence on the "English-reading people . . . remains to be seen. But he has come to stay, if one is to judge by the impression created by his first work. . . . He is emerging into the citizenship of the whole new world. Is it Kahlil Gibran, the individual, who is thus emerging? Or is it the voice and genius of the Arabic people?" [5]

The more critical magazines doubted the lasting appeal of his poems, but even their faint praise underscored the legend. *The Dial* observed, "It is not strange that Rodin should have hoped much of this Arabian poet. For in those parables and poems which Gibran has given us in English he curiously seems to express what Rodin did with marble and clay. The English language never seems a fit medium for work of this nature. It is too angular, too resisting to hold the meanings which Oriental literature crowds as thickly and dazzlingly [*sic*] as jewels on an encrusted sword-hilt." *The Nation* was also skeptical: "Disciples of the modern cult of things Eastern will possibly welcome the

Day in his third-floor seclusion in the 1920s. Here he
received Amy Lowell and other devotees of Keats.
(Norwood)

specimen of the work of the Arab sage, Kahil [*sic*] Gibran. . . . We think,
however, that most Westerners will find the work repellent in its exotic
perversity, and will lay it aside with an uncomprehending shake of the head,
for East is East and West is still West, and Tagore has not really succeeded in
bridging the chasm between them, nor do we think Gibran will do so." But
only Harriet Monroe, the perceptive editor of *Poetry*, doubted the image
conjured up by the promotion blurb. "If Auguste Rodin actually called this
Syrian poet 'the William Blake of the Twentieth Century' as the slip cover
reports, I can only smile in remembering from personal acquaintance with the
great Frenchman, his serene amiability toward all fellow-artists; and in this
case it was the fellow-artist—the limner, not the poet—that Rodin's alleged
remark must have referred to." [6]

The Madman elicited a far more interesting private reaction. Fred Holland
Day, who by 1918 had not only abandoned art photography but quite literally
the world, still was aware of events in publishing. A general malaise attributed
by some to the terrors of war, by others to the failing health of his mother, had
driven him farther from active life. Five months after the publication of *The
Madman* he permanently retreated to his bed and spent the remaining
fourteen years of his life in splendid exile on the third floor of his family's
Norwood estate. His only contact with the outside world came through the
experience of family retainers, occasional visits by faithful friends, and
correspondence with a chosen few. In December he sent a copy of *The*

Madman to his former partner, Herbert Copeland, whose literary activity had also deteriorated since the halcyon days of their publishing venture. After the partnership ended he edited Booker T. Washington's *The Future of the American Negro* but then spent the intervening years drifting down through minor posts in publishing houses, and by now he was working as a clerk at the Boston City Hospital. His letter thanking Day is a pertinent assessment of Gibran's development.

> I am glad to have Kahlil's book. Thank you. I disagree with you about it. I think it really clever, surprisingly so. I should hardly say "The William Blake of the Twentieth Century" for it is so utterly lacking in simplicity; but I honestly think it is very good indeed, really good in the abnormal way which seldom attains to greatness, but of its kind I think remarkably good and "smart." I would not have said he had it in him, though I have not seen him for years, of course. Where is he nowadays? In this part of the world? Do you ever hear from him? It has quite aroused my interest—and enthusiasm.

Day received another letter during the Christmas season. Signed only by the initials S. A. L., it confirms the image of the eccentric publisher now neglected by all but his oldest associates. "Kahlil Gibran seems to continue to be quite *it*. Do you see him? Does he remember all you did for him, or is he too one of those who forgets?" Day answered by sending a copy of *The Madman* to the inquirer, who in turn wrote, "I liked the poems very much, perhaps not so much the parables." [7] What Day himself thought of the book remains an enigma. Whether his sensibilities approved or not, at least he had the satisfaction of knowing that his turn-of-the-century apprentice was succeeding in the world to which he had introduced him.

That same Christmas, Mary received a critique from Charlotte, who was now living in Washington, D.C. Their correspondence had long since lost its intimate ardor—the last word from Charlotte, six months before, had conveyed her nearly hysterical fear of an impending earthquake and the news that as an "act of sacrifice" toward the war and society she had burned up 250 pounds of her manuscripts. Now, came the final chapter of the twelve-year correspondence. After describing her growing practice as a lay psychoanalyst she wrote,

> When I saw your handwriting on the announcement of "The Madman" I was so glad—and then so disappointed when I found no slightest note of you—except your implied pleasure and interest in K.'s success. . . . The War has changed my feeling about fiction and drama. . . . [Allegory is] permissible—so would Kahlil's be in form, were not the content so dangerously Oriental, perfectly done I admit—but so full of the auto-erotic—I take it with [Ralph Adams] Cram that the Gothic is the only Christian form we have had—in living and in expression—the spire, the

alert, the eager, not the bent head and nerveless hand and satire. All this at one time held me as it holds you. But now I am afraid of it.[8]

All vestiges of her or Kahlil's rapport with Charlotte disappeared with this exchange. Mary's closest friend and the indispensable social contact of Kahlil's early days in New York receded into the background. The breach had been growing for five years. Certainly Charlotte's unshakable pacifism had incurred mutual distrust. Mary's journal revealed another rift: by 1919 Gibran no longer included Ameen Rihani among his favorite Arabic friends. When he married an American artist late in 1918, Kahlil rather grudgingly passed the news on to Mary, who in turn told Charlotte. He never mentioned Rihani's new career of writing criticism for American art magazines, and within two years he would completely disassociate himself from his old friend. It is not clear whether professional jealousy or friction resulting from Ameen's affair with Charlotte caused the rupture. What is obvious is that in dissolving old ties—first with Josephine, then Day, next Charlotte, and finally Rihani—Kahlil was also discarding old identities, or "masks." In the words of his Madman, "I woke from a deep sleep and found all my masks were stolen. . . . I cried, 'Blessed, blessed are the thieves who stole my masks.' " [9] The choice for his final decade would be primarily a benign and gentle identity about which a growing band of disciples would exclaim and write.

Mary first observed this gracious public posture early in 1919, while he was visiting Marianna in Boston. On January 10 he read to the school from *The Madman* and the unpublished "Counsels."

> Before we went in, four of the tiny ones were in the hall—and I let them shake his hand. "Hello!" he said, quite delightedly, to them. . . . He read very charmingly—just exactly as he reads when in his studio. . . . The girls were amused, and delighted, and moved, by turn. He began very directly when he was before his audience—and at the close simply vanished—no chance to speak with him—and waited in the office. . . . "That was the sweetest audience I ever had," he said.[10]

The kinds of people who were responding to his first book in English were diverse. Alfred Hoernle of the philosophy department at Harvard liked it but objected to the figure in the drawing of the soul moving upward. Many supporters of the new Imagism admired the construction of the poetry. "Kahlil Gibran is writing poems and parables that have an individual music, a naive charm and distinction and a structural symmetry based on symbol, contrast, repetition and parallelism," wrote Marguerite Wilkinson in an anthology of contemporary poetry. "[It] is almost entirely a poetry of symbolism. His poems are parables, not designs in rhyme, rhythm or imagery, although his rhythms are clear and pleasing. In . . . *The Madman*, we have the best parables that can be found in contemporary poetry. And each may be interpreted according to the whimsy of the reader." [11]

Perhaps the range of possible interpretations was the secret of his success. He was also praised by social reformers. One in particular was Rose Pastor Stokes, the nonconforming activist whose devotion to material revolution was as intense as his was to spiritual evolution. Although she believed in violent change while he held out for the exercise of sincere, intelligent love, they established a rapport and he began to understand and lean toward the socialist position as a method "for more justice in the condition of life—for a better distribution of opportunity." One of his then unpublished parables, "The Capitalist," depicted "a man-headed, iron-hoofed monster who ate of the earth and drank of the sea incessantly." When he read it a year later, "there was a dead silence—except for a single person who applauded. And who do you think that was? Rose Pastor Stokes—and I said I was just waiting for the applause—well then they just shouted. . . . I've changed the name to 'The Plutocrat.' " [12]

Occasionally in 1919 Mary saw him in the milieu of his New York associates. She treasured the briefest glimpse.

> We saw Oppenheim in the little French restaurant on Sixth Avenue and Ninth Street—such a lovely face! K.'s look as they greeted was so lively and affectionate that I knew he must be speaking to a real friend. O. has not power in his face, but he has infinite gentleness and sensitiveness and receptivity and lovingness and earnestness. . . . He simply turned a hose of sunshine on Kahlil when he looked at him.
>
> As we were walking to supper a big automobile full of people suddenly whirled round and drew up to the sidewalk with the apparent intention of asking a question. But instead the uniformed naval man at the wheel called out, "Hello Darling! Hello little Darling!" to K. And they all laughed and K. laughed and stepped out to shake hands with them. "That's Birger [Lie]," he said to me afterwards; "a Norwegian and a fine composer. And the woman on the front seat is Rose O'Neill."
>
> It was a nice crowd, and the atmosphere of their greeting was delicious—like the atmosphere one feels among the groups of young friends in Shakespeare's plays. [13]

Kahlil's attraction to the Titania-like presence of Rose O'Neill probably prompted him to tell Mary, "I am more interested in people than ever before and I like them better," whereupon she added, "I see plainly the change within the last eighteen months. Life hurts him less and gives him more. He is freer with his kind and from his kind." Evenings at Rose O'Neill's Washington Square studio were a kind of theatrical utopia, called Zanzos, where the password was creativity and poets ruled. "Kahlil Gibran was of the court, telling legends of Syria," she recalled in her unpublished autobiography. "The Syrian poet-painter took me to his countrymen for rugs, lanterns, large decorated brass trays and carved taborets to set them on." Her fey letters revealed the symbolic role of each performer. "Come back to Zanzos, where you cannot tell the woman from the nightingales . . . ," she wrote Birger and Matta Lie. "Could we have made a Zanzos out of this New York! With a princely stab of intelligence, a 'sweet musicianer,' a court fool or two, a dark gleaming from the East, a fairy child, a little elephant, a smouldering flame of an architect, Syria to proclaim it, and poetry to *convince it!* More immediately! More Zanzos! Let there be no geography but Zanzos!" [14]

An escape into Zanzos was a release for Kahlil. Here he could remain aloof from personal involvements and yet still feel the warmth of comradeship. Rose's sister Callista was dubbed "the little elephant" because of a little stone Ganesha, the Hindu god of wisdom, that he gave her. The illustrious figures whom he began to describe to Mary—Padraic Colum, Lord Dunsany, Leonora and Edgar Speyer—were first encountered at the O'Neills. In Zanzos the most serious demand on him was the commissioning of a poem: "Darling Prince, here is Kahlil's poem to the Princess [Matta Lie]. I think the first three stanzas are very lovely with 'all things gentle,' 'all things sweet,' and 'all things golden.' I am enchanted that radiant Kahlil adored my darlings with me." [15]

Like many successful illustrators, Rose O'Neill compensated for the popularity of her lucrative Kewpies with an attempt at fine art. Her serious drawings she called "sweet monsters." Although Gibran never mentioned that he criticized her work, her biographers were probably correct in attributing her titanic, brooding figures to his influence. "She spoke of her incentives on more than one occasion to Kahlil Gibran while he viewed her drawings of Man Aboriginal and Creature Anthropoid. . . . Her drawings, not in theme but in certain aspects of execution, resembled his own. The kinship gave Gibran a sense of having taught her, somehow. It was a source of quiet satisfaction to him, as he listened; his darkly flushed face and kindling eyes encouraged her confidences." [16]

In November 1919 Mary observed still another facet of his broadening world when the Reverend William Norman Guthrie, former editor of *The Drama*, displayed a group of wash drawings at his church, St. Mark's-in-the-Bouwerie. "I've talked and read at his church," said Kahlil, "and I like him and his work." Liberal ministers in New York, many of whom belonged to poetry societies, heard Gibran recite, and became friends of his, were eventually to represent the most solid source of his popularity. Although his reception sometimes embarrassed him—"I am going now to a church to read to a large group of people. May God forgive me for talking and reading so often!"—there can be no doubt that he thrived on attention from these open-minded congregations. [17]

Al-Mawakib (*The Procession*) was published by Mirat al-Gharb in March 1919. In December Knopf brought out a handsome edition of *Twenty Drawings* (for which Kahlil designed a borzoi colophon), prefaced by Alice Raphael Eckstein's *Dial* article. Work on "The Counsels," however, was not progressing, although in April Gibran was still confident that the book would soon be published. "I'm going really to work at the Prophet (Counsels), brood over it and get it in shape during the summer and it will be published next winter." [18] This statement is the first appearance of the new title, a decision for which he offered Mary no explanation. Whether he had in mind Josephine's prophecy of seventeen years before is unknown, but it seems that Mary instinctively preferred "The Counsels," which she often continued to use.

When he came to Boston in July he still had hopes of meeting a deadline: "The Prophet to come out in October." But two factors were impeding his progress. First were his commitments to Arabic publications. His publisher in Egypt, Emile Zaidan of *al-Hilal*, was pressing him for an anthology of the prose poems he had written during the war, which meant revising each one. He had also agreed to contribute to a local magazine called *Fatat–Boston* (*Young Women*), for which he wrote an article exhorting the children of first-generation Arabs to preserve proudly their heritage in their quest for citizenship. "I believe that you can say to Emerson and Whitman and James, 'in my veins runs the blood of poets and wise men of old, and it is my desire to come to you and receive, but I shall not come with empty hands.'"

Second, his growing popularity was distracting him.

> From the making of my bed in the morning—to going to bed at night— . . . my life has ceased to be anything but labor. And most of it is not the labor that I am longing to do and must get out of my system if I am not actually to explode . . . and the truth is, it has come before I expected it. . . . I thought in ten more years to be where I find myself now. It's come all of a sudden—with the Madman and the Arabic world, also—where I used to get six letters—I now get thirty-six—and I answer them all. . . . I need time, say six more months or so, before I can adjust to the tempo of this new life.[19]

Throughout August he and Mary saw each other in Cambridge at least once a week. Instead of working on "The Prophet" he started a new set of parables in English, which would become *The Forerunner*. Together they finished "The Dying Man and the Vulture," "The Small Nations and the War," "God's Fool," "Values," and "Knowledge and Half Knowledge." At one meeting he traced the development of his major effort, now temporarily set aside.

> I found the other day a composition of mine when I was sixteen, that is an embryo of the Prophet. . . . It is the work of sixteen but it has a faint hint

of style . . . not at all in the classical style—you know I always rebelled against the classical. A group of people are at an inn and they talk about all sorts of things and one man in particular disagrees with the rest and gives his philosophy about the food and various things. Then they depart . . . and I linger with this man to draw him out. And we walk out into the fields and meet a company of peasants. And he delivers little sermons. You see the idea is there that I have now in the Prophet. And there is my island man Mustafa—he too is a development of the same thing.

His block continued after he returned to New York in the fall. For three months Mary had no word from him. When she saw him in November she detected "a temporary veiling of himself . . . it was as if he had packed his besieging absorptions into a bureau drawer." He had decided first to finish the other book of poems and parables and possibly another volume of drawings during the coming year. "And after those I'll publish The Prophet. You know The Prophet means a great deal in my life. All these thirty-seven years have been making it—and I have the Arabic original of it, in elementary form. It is full of what is the sweetness of my inner life. . . . I began it, and it's always been in me. But I couldn't hurry it. I couldn't do it earlier." [20]

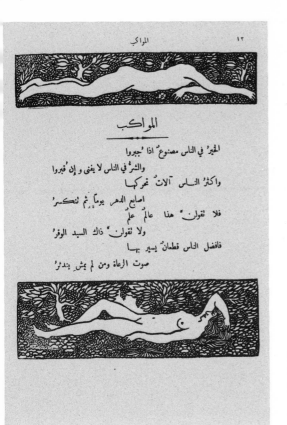

المواكب

الخيرُ في الناسِ مصنوعٌ اذا جُبِروا

والشرُّ في الناسِ لا يفنى و إن قُبِروا

واكثرُ النـاسِ آلاتٌ تحركها

اصابعُ الدهرِ يوماً ثم تنكسرُ

فلا تقولنَّ هذا عالمٌ علمٌ

ولا تقولنَّ ذاك السيدُ الوقرُ

فافضلُ الناسِ قطعانٌ يسيرُ بها

صوتُ الرعاةِ ومن لم يمشِ يندثرُ

Spread from the Arabic edition of
The Procession. The flute, or *nay*, is
featured in the refrain. (Authors)

He showed no signs of progress in Boston at Christmas, either. He had made a drawing for Mary's newly renovated children's school, and he seemed to enjoy the audiences of teachers and pupils who came in to watch him. But although he talked a lot, he avoided any discussion about his English work and read to her only one parable, that of the Lark and the Serpent ("The Poet and the Scholar," *The Forerunner*), about which he explained, "There are two great classes of people in the world—the Life Seekers and the Truth Seekers—those who would live more and those who would understand more—the poet (you know I don't mean only the man who writes poetry) and the scholar." Again silence followed his return to New York. Finally he wrote Mary that he would be able to see her in New York in mid-April. "It has been the most terrible winter that I have known—terrible in many ways," he admitted. "But somehow, when I feel like a little, helpless fish in a muddy lake I cannot help but say to myself, 'The air, which is above the water, is not muddy. I cannot lose my faith in the God-Element.' " [21]

During her visit that spring of 1920, he appeared less dependent on her judgment than before. "I've a great glorious piece of news for you!" he greeted her.

You know how the housing situation has become. . . . Twenty-five thousand families in New York are living on the streets—in tents and in the open—well, I've pretty nearly been turned out of this building. A group came along to buy the building and our rent was to be put up 300%—so we bought it ourselves—the twelve artists who live here. Now we are safe. The Jacobses who live below me and I will put in bathrooms and share the expense of plumbing—and we shall do the few things we want to make the whole place livable.

"The Forerunner," with its five accompanying drawings, was at Knopf ready for press, and he was full of news about his growing popularity. "I've accepted Pond's [the lecture bureau] offer to make a lecture tour next winter. And I've given five readings . . . three of them I was paid for—but I gave the money back for one—my reading in the Public Library—for them to buy more Arabic books with." *The Dial* had reproduced two drawings, "Mountain and Cloud" and "Study," in its April issue. *Twenty Drawings* had received a penetrating review in *The Nation*, which observed in part, "Gibran's message is not one of arcane transcendencies, but one of graceful emotional exposition of form. There his work is valuable and secure." [22]

Mary also heard about a portrait of the popular Norwegian writer, Johan Bojer, which he had just finished. The session, described later that year by Howard Willard Cook, had delighted the artist: "Bojer says it is the first thing of himself he really likes." Bojer's novels, with their themes of spiritual realization, were becoming popular in America, and Cook's comparison of Gibran and Bojer was enormously satisfying to Kahlil.

> As I sat in [Gibran's] studio one day last April, on the occasion of Bojer's first visit to America, and saw him dip into the soul of the man who had written *The Great Hunger* . . . I knew that Gibran's genius was two-fold—the poet and artist were inseparable. . . . Bojer was manifestly nervous. He folded and unfolded his hands as he talked and his talk was mostly about fairy tales, tales of his own saga that declared his kinship with Hans Andersen. . . . The sitting lasted more than an hour, and when it was over Bojer stood before the drawing with his hands behind his back, balancing himself upon his toes. Turning to Gibran, he said: "You are a sculptor. Your work should be in marble! Your drawing resembles works by Michelangelo and Rodin." [23]

This flurry of interest which strengthened Kahlil's purpose ironically continued to weaken Mary's position. After she had looked over the finished illustrations for "The Forerunner," she heard its epilogue, which he had titled "The Last Watch." The need for her corrections had diminished.

> Now he read it all—how he had loved Man . . . loved them absolutely— and none heard his love or saw it or felt it or understood it—and he had

neither one to love, nor many, but loved alone. Only this I had not known: that when he upbraided men and denounced them, then they had begun to love him. . . .

When I was dictating from K.'s ms. of the "Last Watch" . . . I cried—and when I said, "Don't mind my crying," K. answered, "Mary, don't think I mind your crying. Probably nobody in the world has cried more than I. I cry a great deal, here alone, and you see I can give free rein to tears because I *am* here alone. . . ."

It needed hardly a word changed. K.'s English is the finest I know for it is creative and marvelously simple. And now he rarely misspells a word—though he still uses the dictionary as aid—and rarely misses an idiom. "I'm getting to feel safer! . . . And now my whole being is going into The Prophet. That is to be my life until it is done. Everything that I have done is already over for me. And they have all been just my schooling. But in The Prophet I have imprisoned certain ideals—and it is my desire to live these ideals. It is not writing them that is my interest. Just writing them would seem to me false. I can only receive them by living them."

Their meetings of April 20 and 21 became a series of monologues which Mary conscientiously recorded. "I'm working, you know on the Counsel, 'Crime and Punishment,'" he said. "The subject is very near to me. I can never divorce myself from the Criminal. When I read of a forgery, I feel that I am the forger—and of the murder, that I too have committed murder. If one of us does a thing, we all do it—and what collective humanity does, is done by each of us." [24]

It is revealing that in defining his vision of "world consciousness," Kahlil did not also tell Mary specifically how he was trying to implement this theme among his Syrian associates. For during the week of her visit he was in the process of uniting the *al-mahjar* literary world. The Golden Links and *Fatat–Boston* had been futile efforts. *Al-Funoon*, even with his and Rihani's support and with some editorial participation by Mikhail Naimy, had appeared intermittently from 1913 to 1918 before it too had failed. Now once again he was trying to establish an official mouthpiece for the self-proclaimed avant-garde of the Arabic immigrants. Ironically, at the height of his success in American letters he was confronted with unexpected success in the Arabic world. This was due largely to the critical ability and organizational efforts of Naimy, who had recently returned from military service in France.

Naimy had first appeared in Mary's journal in 1914 when Gibran had described him as an unknown critic who "praises to Heavens and damns to Hell." Although she did not mention the title of his review, it must have been "The Dawn of Hope after the Night of Despair" in *al-Funoon*. In it Naimy, a recent immigrant to America and then a law student at Washington State University, had analyzed Gibran's effect on Arabic literature. His own literary background, including education at the Greek Orthodox Russian Teachers'

Institute at Nazareth and four years at theological seminaries in Russia, was far more scholarly than Kahlil's. In this twenty-page analysis he carefully refrained from either raising Gibran "to the level of Shakespeare as some have done" or "throwing him into the first circle of Dante's Hells and stripping him of his fame." In fact he was the first critic to treat the author of *The Broken Wings* as something more than a cause célèbre. Pointing out his role in the emigré newspapers, he identified him as the first authentic voice of his exiled countrymen and the first Arab novelist to employ successfully native names, customs, and backgrounds. He detected, however, a veneer in Gibran's use of national characteristics. The heroine of *The Broken Wings* was not "Syrian in mind or heart." Stripped of the superficial jasmine blossoms and lemon scents, Selma Karema could easily have been "French, English, Russian, Italian or Austrian." But Naimy welcomed Kahlil's attempts, "though incomplete and deformed," as the beginning of a dawn of Arabic literature.[25]

By 1916 "Mischa" Naimy was a salesman based in New York and had met Gibran at the offices of *al-Funoon*. For the remaining years of their friendship his initial objectivity became blurred. Partially as a result of his evaluation, the man whom he had once faintly praised became acknowledged as the leader of the Arab emigré writers. On the evening of April 20, 1920, Naimy reported on a gathering hosted by Abdul Massih Haddad, the editor of the semiweekly newspaper *as-Sayeh*, and his brothers.

> The discussion arose as to what the Syrian writers in New York could do to lift Arabic literature from the quagmire of stagnation and imitation, and to infuse a new life into its veins so as to make of it an active force in the building up of the Arab nations. It was suggested that an organization be created to band the writers together and to unify their efforts in the service of the Arabic language and its literature. The suggestion was met with warm approval by all the poets and writers present. . . . The time not permitting to work at details and by-laws, Gibran invited the company to spend the evening of April 28 at his studio.

On that night eight men came to 51 West Tenth Street and, continued Naimy,

> after a thorough discussion the following points were unanimously agreed upon:
> 1. The organization to be called in Arabic AR-RABITATUL QALAMYIAT (meaning the pen-bond), and in English ARRABITAH.
> 2. It is to have three officers: A president who shall be called "Chieftain," a secretary who shall be called "Counsellor," and a treasurer.
> 3. The members shall be of three categories: Active, who shall be known as "Workers," supporters, who shall be known as "Partisans," and correspondents.
> 4. Arrabitah to publish the works of its own members and other Arab

writers it may consider worthy, as well as to encourage the translation of world literature masterpieces.

5. Arrabitah to foster new talent by offering prizes for the best in poetry and prose.

The worker Mikhail Naimy was charged with the final drafting of the by-laws. The present then unanimously elected G. K. Gibran for Chieftain, Mikhail Naimy for Counsellor, and William Catzeflis for Treasurer.[26]

Years later Catzeflis, a frequent contributor to immigrant publications, was to recall Gibran's influence in this venture:

> Ar-Rabitah was not a society, not a literary club in the accepted sense of the word, but rather, a small round-table gathering of kindred souls and minds whose aim was to help reform the then stagnant Arabic literature and who aided and encouraged one another towards that goal. Arabic literature had fallen into the depths of stagnation. With the fall of their Empire its culture remained stationary, shackled by rigid and obsolete rules and regulations. Purism was the god of the writers and poets. Steeped in traditionalism of the narrower sort, there were hundreds of versifiers but few poets. They sacrificed substance to form and no one dared to deviate from the trodden path.
>
> Into this spiritual morass, Ar-Rabitah, with Gibran in the lead, threw a bombshell by saying, "If the meaning or beauty of a thought requires the breaking of a rule, break it. . . . If there is no known word to express your idea, borrow or invent one. . . . If syntax stands in the way of a needed or useful expression, away with syntax."
>
> Gibran was never a purist, although he took extreme care in furbishing and refurbishing his phrases. His Arabic was never orthodox and he broke the rules right and left: however, this beautiful and fecund Arabic was the right vehicle for his winged words.[27]

For the next few years, each member signed his work with the phrase "a worker in Arrabitah" next to his name. Kahlil designed the society's logotype—an open book inscribed in a circle and bearing a saying of Mohammed: "How wonderful the treasures beneath God's throne which only poets' tongues can unlock."

A month after Arrabitah was launched he visited Boston. He admitted to Mary that work on "The Prophet" was still stalemated. This procrastination, she thought, was due to the work of refinishing his studio and small "things that had accumulated." He indicated to her the responsibility he felt toward his native culture, but he said nothing about the society. "Something is going to come out of that Mountain (Lebanon) that will surprise the world—out of the shepherds and simple people and princes of Lebanon. And it's up to me to organize a body of work. I'm doing some of the folk songs of Lebanon into English for two women." Back in New York, he blamed the studio for his

Members of Arrabitah. Left to right, top row: Abdul Massih Haddad, William Catzeflis, Ameen Rihani, Wadi Bahout, Nudra Haddad. Bottom row: Naseeb Arida, Raschid Ayoub, Mikhail Naimy, Elia D. Madey, and Kahlil Gibran. (Authors)

continued silence. "Yes, indeed, I am coming to Boston this summer but not before I put this studio in order. . . . My sister and I cannot get the rooms at Cohasset this summer. The old lady had given them to her married daughter. But it does not matter. I shall come to Boston and we will make the best of it. I can always do more work in the city than the country. And I *must* do a great deal of work this summer or else be snowed under." [28]

He finally appeared at the school on August 20. In their next four visits during that month, he and Mary spent some time on "The Prophet," but mostly he described his recent activities. He told her about his latest long prose poem, one he had written for *al-Hilal* (*The Crescent*) in Egypt—"my political farewell—the meaning of it was, your Syria is not my Syria and my Syria is not your Syria. The sheep-tending shepherd in Lebanon is more to me than the deeplaid scheming of men in the government. I love the Syria that was real generations ago and will be real ages from now." He showed her another drawing, "Breath on a Windowpane," that *The Dial* had reproduced. They looked at *al-Awasif* (*The Tempests*), his anthology which had just arrived from Egypt. "Naimy has written a very beautiful thing on that book. I think no one else could have done what he has done. He is writing a book on me." [29]

He introduced an idea for yet another book. "I have about 500 short sayings—too short for The Madman—most of them in Arabic—but I can put 300 or 350 of them into English; and they would make a very nice little volume." Mary began randomly to record the sayings, which she called "The Way of The Seven Days." Sometimes she would elaborate on them. "He read me a number of the short sayings—very fine. Of the one, 'Once I saw at the gate of the temple a dog biting a dead lion. Then I lost my fear of the dead and my respect for the living,' he said, 'That's bitter. That was written about six years ago—And I was bitter then. But there's no bitterness in me now.'" She listened again to the Counsels on "Good and Evil" and "Crime and Punishment" and questioned an apparent disparity: "In 'Good and Evil' K. used the word 'your giant self' wherein in 'Crime and Punishment' he had used 'God-self.' I was talking of the English use of 'giant' as so different from the sense in which K. uses it—and the use of 'God'. . . . As to what word I shall use when I mean God—I shall use God—not 'Life' or 'Law' or 'Love,' even though those all mean the same thing. If in my consciousness the word is God I shall say 'God.'" [30]

Three days later he arrived at the school, saying excitedly:

> I've a perfectly good idea for these sayings. You know some of them are bitter and these bitter things are very distant from me now—they aren't myself at all, but if I throw away everything I outgrow, I'll throw away a very great deal. And all these things were real to me when I wrote them. Well I've thought of a form that will hold them all—in a setting that would use them for just what they are: the story of a consciousness—I am on a journey to the Holy City. In the morning I overtake a stranger, . . and we naturally fall into a conversation. He is sad and bitter and all day we talk. He says the bitterest things. The next day he is a little less bitter—and we are a little nearer to the Holy City. The third day he says things still less bitter—and so he changes—on to the fourth, the fifth and the sixth—and on the seventh he is saying the planetary things . . . and we arrive to the Holy City. As we come near to the Kaabah, I lose sight of him—in the evening, I see him dead, near the wall of the temple.

The aphorisms poured out, and Mary continued to edit them: "I closed my hand and when I opened it, in it was a soft mist. I closed it again and opened it—and lo it was a worm." "I desire eternity because there I shall meet my unpainted pictures and read my unwritten poems." This exercise broke his year-long silence about "The Prophet." On September 7 she was able to sum up its opening. "And so today, though he is still almost in fragments bodily—he had brought the beginning of The Prophet—how Almustafa had waited twelve years for the ship of purple sails and when he saw it come, how he spoke to himself of the dearness with which his pain had clothed the city in his heart—so that he sorrowed to depart." When she gently objected to the repetition of the pronoun "he" for the Prophet, Gibran replied, "I thought that I would use [Almustafa] once only in the book—at the very beginning— and through all of the rest of it say 'he.' Almustafa in Arabic means something very special—the Chosen and the Beloved too—really between them both—there is no name in English with any such significance." He then debated whether to add "the Chosen and Beloved" after the name.[31]

Although she also questioned the meaning of the phrase used by Almitra—"land of your memories"—he defended this choice. "All that is written here is written with many things in mind. Each thing is a symbol of man's life as a whole—and the "land of his memories" is all our historic past—Life bears us from our great past towards our greater future." But he agreed with her suggestion of deleting "purple sails" from his description of the ship. "I may find something other than the 'purple sails' . . . but of old, vessels with purple sails were actually used for certain sacred errands—and this fact has clung to my memory from somewhere—so I used it." After they had analyzed the introduction he returned to his collection of sayings:

"I don't know what date to set for either The Prophet or The Way of The Seven Days," he mused. "I can't publish anything later than The Prophet which shall be any way less than The Prophet. This would mean that if the Sayings come later, a good many of them would have to be left out. . . . I won't hurry about either of these books. It doesn't matter how long they take." [32]

On September 14 Mary summarized the success of the visit.

> Never before has he written so systematically on an English book while in Boston—nor has he paid Marianna so long a visit. So we are doing more than usual. It is the pressure of The Prophet to be finished this autumn. Usually, too, he keeps things to show me, until he has completed them or almost completed. But this Prophet prologue he brings in its first or second writing down. . . . Our method is: first, K. reads it through aloud to me. Then we look together at the text—from the beginning of the new part or from an earlier section; and if we come to a bit that I question, we stop then and there until the question is settled. K. uses me as the reader embodiment of his English speaking audience. When he waits, to read me only the final draft, it is rare that the English ear would dream of desiring any change. . . . If he lives many years yet—he said the other day, "You will outlive me—I know that"—he *will* know what he may not say in English! Even in the short time he has written, he has gained so much. And his hand writes English twice as fast as twelve or eighteen months ago . . . he writes like lightning now save for an occasional word which he hesitates to spell.

He had remained in Boston longer than usual because the collaboration was going smoothly. Yet he worried about being away from his Arabic colleagues, and this anxiety moved him to tell Mary for the first time about Arrabitah.

> We founded what is practically an academy of Arabic in New York—and in Boston too—and probably it will get branches in the Arabic world

also—at Beirut or Damascus or Cairo. It will publish in Arabic yearly the best that has been published in the other languages of Europe . . . they have elected me president and Naimy as secretary—we need money too—and I have to be in New York to ask money from certain of the Syrians who will give it to me more readily than to other people. They had planned the first autumn meeting this Saturday—but I wrote Naimy yesterday that I'd like to stay a little longer here and I hoped he could have the meeting put off one more week.[33]

When he left on September 17 he assured her that he would return to Boston within a month to finish "The Prophet." But he could not keep that promise. *The Forerunner* appeared in October, and when she saw him in November he had nothing to show her. She visited his studio again in December, but he was too involved with the production of the Arrabitah New Year's issue of *as-Sayeh* even to mention the material they had worked on that summer. "Of late I have been lost in my own mist," he wrote her, "and whenever I feel lost I turn to writing Arabic poetry. Going back to one's own race is a good way of finding another dawn." [34]

Title of *Fatat-Boston*. (Authors)

"The Traveler," cover of *as-Sayeh*, January 1921. (Authors)

20

No Longer Apart

M ore than ever Gibran was finding himself a poet between two worlds—his native land and his adopted country. He saw himself as a spokesman for each, and he often found the role a difficult one. When Mary visited him in New York in December 1920, he mentioned a recent meeting with Rabindranath Tagore: "I . . . gave Tagore the dickens. . . . You know [he] has talked about America as a money-grabbing land without a vision—he talks as so much of the East talks about the West. I tried to say—and I think I succeeded—that spirit may be manifest in machinery . . . and in everything."

He described his latest writings in Arabic. The most important piece was a play, "Iram, City of Lofty Pillars," which was about a seeress and a prophetess who lived in Iram, "the city of imagination." He told her also about the reception of his work in the Middle East. "The Political Farewell" in particular was receiving unprecedented attention, but his stance as an advocate of independence was also clearly recognized by his enemies.

> You know I told you about the thing I wrote for *al-Hilal*, "You have your Lebanon and I have my Lebanon." Well, the censorship in Syria cut it out of the magazine and out of the Syrian papers that printed it, and out of the papers coming into Syria from New York and Cairo and South America. . . . But they didn't cut my name and the title out of the table of contents so now everybody knows the piece was there—and they are determined to get it—and it will do more than if the government had let it alone.

In a letter to Emile Zaidan he apologized for the excitement over the relatively mild poem.

> I didn't know that censorship in Syria has become so bad. . . . It makes me laugh and cry at the same time—I feel that those who have extracted that

article out of *al-Hilal* have praised me and I don't deserve their praise. They insulted themselves and they don't deserve the insults. . . . In the twenty years I've spent until now, I've really done nothing that deserves to remain eternal. My vine has only yielded sour grapes and my net is still covered with water. Please ask my friends to give me more time.[1]

Although this denial of his accomplishments might seem merely a gesture of Oriental self-effacement, he confessed to Mary a similar feeling of inadequacy.

> I want some day not to write or paint but simply to live what I would say, and talk to people. I want to be a Teacher . . . I want to wake their consciousness to what I know it can know. Because I have been so lonely, I want to talk to those who are lonely—and so many are lonely. . . . I've moved very slowly. I ought to have been ten years ago where I am now. But there are certain streaks in me that held me back—a certain inheritance. In my father's people is much temper, and restlessness, and vainness. And I have all these and they held me back for long: The caring for fame and what people said and thought. But they will not hold me back longer. For I know them now. Therefore, I shall be free of them.[2]

In Boston for Christmas, his preoccupation with the challenges facing the new countries in the Middle East continued. For *al-Hilal* he was writing an article on "the two consciousnesses in the Near East: the creative consciousness, simple, direct, that everyone, workmen and all, can have, and the other consciousness—complex, often political or economic or social—that is a thing of the moment and not creative." Soviet Russia and America seemed to him to be the greatest exponents of the "new consciousness," which he characterized as wanting "goodness and reality." He himself desired to influence the ideals and goals of emerging nations: "A young country can produce a new form of self . . . and it seems to be coming to me to lead this new consciousness—and not to keep silence. . . . I don't want to speak about political things: they don't interest me. But this new consciousness, new desire, new vision—that is my business."

The embodiment of these beliefs was the article "The New Era," which appeared in April 1921. Although his Arabic writings were delaying "The Prophet," by now three-quarters finished, he was at last able to tell Mary that his lifelong ambivalence, his painful search for identity, was yielding to the realization of integrated goals.

> I used to think I was a fragment of something else—something different from the rest of Life—and in everything I wrote was something that expressed, directly or indirectly, aloneness. But that was really false. There is no such thing as aloneness and difference from the rest of life. I know now that I am a part of the whole—a fragment of a jar, so to speak, and

not a fragment from another jar. Now I've found where I fit, and in a way I *am* the jar—and the jar is I. Feeling myself always different and alone, I was self-centered. . . . Now I feel humiliated to remember how I always considered myself as one apart. You know, if one is in a room, one can either dig into one corner of the room—or can project himself to fill the room. Filling the room is harder, but it is realer . . . and when one really *accepts* the whole room, or accepts all of life, with its suffering and its pain, and its relations with other peoples—then one finds one's place in the whole, and one feels the whole life.[3]

This affirmation was one demonstration of Gibran's real talent for the pertinent aphorism. Publication in *The Dial* of some of the sayings that Mary and he had worked on the summer before enhanced his reputation still more. But he still hedged when it came to working on "The Prophet." This was due in part to a recurrence of his mysterious general malaise, which this time he described as heart trouble. Mary had never seen him so exhausted from overwork as she did in New York the first week in February. He kept up his practice of dictating three or four hours' worth of material for Arab newspapers and journals, but he complained that his "personal life seems absolutely still. . . . I've lost even my dreams when I sleep. . . . I don't want to do anything. I'm tired, played out—I need six months' rest." [4]

When he showed her Arrabitah's first annual issue, he described his intentions in illustrating the cover. "The Great Traveler, God. I invented the letters beneath [squared Arabic letters]. I like it but I haven't got quite enough in the movement of what I wanted . . . I wanted absolute evenness." She recorded two of his other illustrations:

One of two faces in a mountain . . . a wash drawing, blue, which Mme. El-Khoury bought a few years ago; and another . . . a youth with his back turned to crouching figures hedged with thorn-vine bonds, himself beholding a lily that grows up beside him. "This illustrates a poem of Naimy's ("If Thorns But Realized"), really I believe one of the great poems of the Twentieth Century. I'm sorry, I can't give you that original—but I felt I ought to promise it to Naimy. You know he practically devotes his life to me. He says he considers me his work."

One nagging decision she helped him with was whether to finish "The Prophet" immediately in order to begin the long-planned lecture tour. Pond had recently asked Gibran if he was ready to give his first public reading in New York, but he had waited to seek her advice. When she said that she "wouldn't for a moment consider doing it," he replied, "I'm so glad to hear you say that. . . . I *could* 'order' a Farewell to the Prophet. . . . But noth-

Naimy and Gibran at Cahoonzie. (Authors)

ing in me wants either to end the Prophet to order, or to do that kind of reading." [5]

In April Mary came to New York again, and once more she had little to report besides Kahlil's concern over his health and the pressure to complete the book. Knopf wanted to publish it in the fall. "I told him no," Kahlil said. "I want to read it next winter—and then it can be published the next fall—Knopf says, 'Mr. Gibran, you don't go about enough. People ask you here and ask you there. You ought to accept. It would increase the sale of the book.' Ye Gods! . . . They are all the same way. The young woman in the office says, 'Mr. Gibran, if you'd give an exhibit of pictures and drawings, it would make the book sell yet better.' And they say it in kindness." [6]

After leaving New York she did not hear from him for three months. These periods of silence no longer bothered her, but because of them the sequence of his activities becomes increasingly obscure in the journal. She never described, for instance, his escape with three other members of Arrabitah to upstate New York. Fortunately, Naimy recalled how Gibran found a measure of relaxation that June, at a hamlet in the Catskills called Cahoonzie. "Gibran, Arida, Haddad and myself decided to spend a short vacation in the country. . . . We put up at a large two-story farmhouse, located on the top of a most pleasant hill. In that solitude . . . we spent ten days which passed like ten minutes."

One day after they hiked to a waterfall the four shared a memorable experience. Inspired by the majesty of the forest, along with the *arak* they drank, they sang native folksongs which led to their composing on the spot verses of Arabic poetry. As they headed back, Gibran and Naimy fell behind and talked in English. "We walked a distance to the time beat of our silent thoughts," Naimy recalled. "Suddenly Gibran stopped, struck the road with his cane, and called aloud, 'Mischa!' I, too, stopped. Looking at my companion I was abashed to see the change in his face. The glowing picture of the waterfall and the hours we spent with it had entirely evaporated from his eyes. Instead there was a cloud of bitter sadness. 'Mischa!' he called again, 'I'm a false alarm.' Saying that, he bent his head and fell silent." Naimy regarded this scene as "the most touching and dramatic of all the moments I had with Gibran during the fifteen years of our comradeship." [7]

Naimy responded to his friend's display of anxiety in a letter written shortly afterward, and its lavish praise should have reassured Kahlil. "Dear Brother Gibran: O Lamb of Christ at heart, O Jupiter of mind, My heart is sad because I didn't see you before [a trip]. I felt in a vacuum that night when the brothers wished me farewell, because the main link of the chain was not there. . . . Hoping that I will see you safe and sound, creating pearls and spreading them before people as usual." [8]

Through July, August, and September, Kahlil stayed with Marianna and visited Mary in Cambridge thirteen times. "I've come to Boston to finish that book and finish The Prophet," he explained. "That book," or "that awful book," was another anthology of his Arabic writings that Zaidan and another publisher, Yusuf Bustani, were preparing. Kahlil had agreed to edit it, and the details of its publication were burdensome and complex. "Never again will I give my word to finish a thing by a certain date!" he fumed.[9] But the commitment had been made, and he spent half of July polishing his most recent articles and finishing "A Ship in the Mist," his latest Arabic story, which dealt with a man's love for an invisible companion.

Each time they met he drew something for Mary. Often he voiced dissatisfaction with his earlier oil paintings and described his preparation for a new series:

> You know I haven't been painting now for a long time . . . I can't paint again now until I am free from writing. . . . When I was younger I used to do them both together—would just draw at any time; but now I can't do that . . . I have been learning about putting form and color together. . . . I knew there was something radically wrong with my work. . . . It didn't say what I wanted it to say and that something was color. . . . When I have painted these [new] pictures, I will destroy everything else that didn't lead up to them.[10]

On August 8 she filled two notebooks with their conversations about Ouspensky's *Tertium Organum*, H. G. Wells's *Outline of History*, and the natures of Christ, Buddha, and Mohammed. From this Kahlil turned again to "The Prophet." " 'Man's needs change: but not his love, nor his desire that his love shall satisfy his needs.' That's from the Farewell. Do you like it? It's not written yet. Write it down," he told Mary, "and I'll put it in my pocket." She copied it and another aphorism that appealed to her, "Teach never what you know—but always how the child may find a path for himself." [11]

On his next visit she brought up a longtime anxiety of hers. At forty-eight she feared the specter of old age and the prospect of inactivity. But Kahlil was in his element. He insisted,

> When people dread age, they are thinking in a very local way. If elderly people seem less alive to *you*, there's something wrong with your way of consciousness. . . . I sometimes imagine myself, my bodily part, after death, lying in the earth and returning to the elements of earth: the great loosening, the change everywhere, the opening into simpler things—the widening out into those things from which anything may be built up again—the Great Return—such deep quietness and a passing into the substance of things. . . . It is the autumn of the body—that leads to the winter . . . and this winter is necessary to another spring. . . . If you remember little things that I say, Mary, remember this . . . the [planetary]

sense of old people doesn't restrict itself into intellectual forms. . . .
Rather it pervades and contemplates and reorganizes life. . . . [It] may be
rich, and yet the means of expressing that consciousness may be lost. It
may be impossible of performance of any kind, just as impossible as it is
with mad people.

He also relieved her doubts about her skill as an administrator. "It is the *being*
that teaches, not the ideas, and not the organizations we create. . . . Plato
organized nothing—yet he lives, and lives among people who actually know
none of his ideas." [12]

Mary's crucial role as a sympathetic critic again gave him impetus. For the
last three weeks in August he cloistered himself in the Tyler Street tenement,
and when he finally returned to the school she jubilantly exclaimed:

Kahlil was looking lovely in every one of his thousand aspects when I came
in a little late today and found him waiting in the office. The day was hot.
He was doubtless hot and his skin was soft and transparent—his eyes
shining—and he was full of that radiant smile of his—the freshest, gentlest,
brightest play of light in any human life.

He has written the Farewell of The Prophet and read it to me. His same
message—of the Greater Self and the Oneness of Life and the lovingness
of the Greater Self—put again in words and figures that reach where one
has thought words and figures could not reach.

"If its general structure is right, I can change any detail in it," said K.
when he had ended. "If it isn't right, I'll rewrite the whole thing. . . ."
But it was the very soul of rightness and such a mirror of the prophet's
soul. And how absolutely the Prophet is Kahlil—although Kahlil has
several times said, "This is not I but the Prophet."

Immediately after the reading we went over the whole in detail—about
sixteen pages—and only a word here and there to transpose—or a
connective to omit. . . . The perfect tense . . . is about the only common
English construction which he does not yet fully sense. It was the longest
piece of writing that we have ever taken at a sitting.

They spent two more afternoons polishing the Farewell. On September 6 she
dictated from the "exceedingly careful and accurate and clear" manuscript,
and he copied it.[13]

Three days later they went over the whole manuscript because he was
concerned about the "quantity-proportions" of the book. "I may have said this
or that very badly," he admitted, "but I feel that the *amount* in this opening
ought to be kept. . . . The beginning, middle, and the end has each its proper
weight, and if we misjudge any one of them, a certain harmony is lost." In his

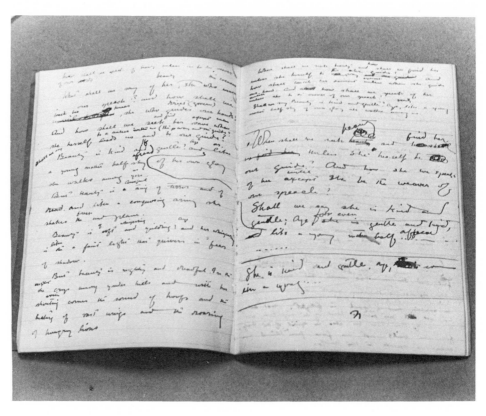

Manuscript of *The Prophet*. (Authors)

deliberate evaluation of each section, he both acknowledged his indebtedness
to Nietzsche and pointed out differences between Zarathustra and Almustafa.

> The mistake of making too short a beginning has been often made. Take
> Zarathustra, for instance—probably I sound almost sacrilegious, for
> Zarathustra has much beautiful poetry, and I *love* it and love the
> book—But Zarathustra comes down from the mountain. He talks two or
> three minutes to an old hermit on the way—that is all—Then he finds the
> townspeople waiting to see a tightrope dancer, and to this crowd in their
> present mood he begins to talk—like a god or a superman. Of course they
> couldn't hear his real meaning. And there's a certain *twist* in his doing it
> that way. There *was* a twist in Nietzsche—a lack of balance in him as an
> artist. He had an analytical mind. . . . And the analytical mind always says
> too much.

Because it was his last visit to the school that summer, Mary recorded
seventeen pages of his comments that day and still apologized to her future
and unknown audience for her brevity. "And more than ever does he express

realities wonderfully in talking—But I retain less vividly and fully than of old—even though I record as promptly as possible." She noted his version of two important names in "The Prophet": "Almitra's name has in it the ancient Mithras-root—that is in the name Mitras, or Mithraic—a very early religion, about which we know little. And the city of Orphalese has in it the Orpheus-root. Apparently there were two Orpheuses—a musician, one—and a really great prophet, the other—We have lost the actual details of him but he must have told profoundly upon man's life at one time."

Although she would continue her journal for the next three years, this entry marks the end of Mary and Kahlil's face-to-face collaboration. They were, of course, both unaware of the changes in her life that would alter their friendship. But during that final session he digressed and in a few phrases seemed to summarize the ambiguity of life: "There is no mystery; there is no lie; there is no truth; in a certain sense we may say that. Unless a tree is a truth." [14]

Although she had planned to see him in New York in November, she did not attend the meeting of headmistresses. Her older cousin Louise Gilmer Minis, whom she always had called "Aunt Loulie," died on November 16. Mary traveled to Savannah for the funeral and returned south during Christmas vacation to visit with the widower, Jacob Florance Minis.

In Cambridge on January 5, 1922, she saw Kahlil, who had spent the past ten days with Marianna. He appeared restless; he spoke of traveling but seemed unable to pull himself away from everyday commitments. "I shall have many things to do in England and France and Italy . . . ," he told her. "Perhaps after those countries, I might go to the East—certainly not earlier!" "When he spoke of the East," she wrote "there was the look of real trouble in his face, of real suffering—but I don't know what his thoughts were."

Her keen involvement in every detail of his life was diminishing, for she was facing a crucial decision of her own. Florance Minis, then sixty-nine years old and afraid of loneliness and death, had asked her to come live with him as his companion and hostess. Formerly president of the Southwestern Railroad and the Savannah Cotton Exchange, he was a large landowner and enjoyed a luxurious life. Tempted by this way out of her general weariness, Mary told Kahlil that she was debating going to live with him but that she could not decide whether to leave the school. His first reaction was "Wait. You will know presently. . . . Perhaps you won't have to sacrifice school to uncle or uncle to school. You may be able to harmonize them and keep both . . . just don't feel you have to hurry your decision—and it will come." [15]

Ten months before, even two months before, they would have discussed at length the show of his wash drawings, which was to open at the Women's City Club on Beacon Street four days later. But in her state of self-preoccupation Mary referred to it only obliquely, by way of quoting him: "I brought another picture that I think ought to go in the Exhibition. . . . I gave it to Mrs. Speyer [Leonora Speyer, violinist, poet, wife of the international financier Sir Edgar Speyer]." As for the other details that had always intrigued her—their friends' reactions to his pictures, the possibilities of sales, reviews in the local papers—she noted nothing.

The day before the opening Mary and Jeannette Peabody hung his drawings. In the afternoon he met Mary at the club to see the show. "The rooms were very disappointing," she wrote, "reading rooms, in the first place, and full of furniture and ornaments—no quality of exhibit in them. Had K. known what they were, he would not have sent the pictures, but he was very philosophical about it, very kind and unirritated—we went for a walk—the length of the Esplanade and back to Park Street for my car—our first walk for a long time." Unfortunately she did not record the responses of any critics.

On January 11 she was to discuss his work and read from *The Forerunner* at the City Club, and normally she would have spent hours telling him what she was going to say. But she did not once allude to this event. Instead they again concentrated on her "subject of inner debate." She wanted Kahlil to meet Minis. "Yes," he said, "I'd like to see your uncle too—but if you like him there is no question about my liking him too." Quietly he began to answer her arguments against living with someone who did not fully "understand" her. "You'll never find congenial people to live with—never the one in a million to whom you can always say everything. But what does that really matter after all? The relation with people can still be very sweet. And what is ordinarily called being understood does enslave something in us. And what does being understood really matter? The great thing is increase of realization."

The momentousness of her decision seemed to lower his defenses, and in an unexpected burst of candor he told her why he had broken with Charlotte when she had come to the Montross exhibition in 1914.

> C. said, "Kahlil, I could write something about you that would make you famous in 24 hours from one end of the country to the other,"—and "instead of answering her sweetly, chiming in with her, I answered her with just what was in my mind. I said, 'C.—there is only one way to fame—and that is to do work worthy of it. And when one does that, the fame matters little'. . . . You know, Mary, that work is a sacred thing to me. . . . Well C. didn't like it because she wasn't ready for the steady effort of real work, and she wasn't ready to confess her unwillingness. She put veils before her own eyes—and at the stage she was in she doubtless couldn't help doing so. But I would not treat the veil as a reality, and she felt a resentment because I wouldn't." [16]

They saw each other three more times that month, and they dwelt almost completely on Mary's irresolution. In describing Minis, she spared none of his faults and confided that she hoped to change some of the attitudes that irritated her. She had been angered at Christmas when she had felt obliged to criticize him for making unfavorable comparisons of the prices of presents. Kahlil gently tried to curb her reforming zeal, and in a way he became the champion of his unknown rival, as he summarized the older man's positive qualities:

> If I went to live with a person like that—one thing I'd never do. I'd never criticize. But I'd show by doing and perhaps by doing with a bit of overemphasis. I'd trust that to teach him, but I believe criticism won't teach him. The man who faces his age so squarely, and who writes to you as he does, and who loved his wife so genuinely, who did so good a part by his parents, and adds to servants' wages secretly because he thinks them too low, must be fundamentally kindly. Talking about prices may be a very superficial thing. The people he is talking to may think just as much about them, without mentioning them.

Well aware that he was no longer contributing to her life as he once had, Kahlil encouraged her to break away from the school. She professed still to have the energy and vision necessary to develop a perfect environment for learning. For several years, however, she had been increasingly aware of her own shortcomings. He had tried to persuade her of how unimportant it was to succeed in complex meaningless, administrative duties. In turn he defined his own attitude toward institutions: "I am an individualist of the Eastern type, as you know. I believe every living organization is . . . made by one individual whom the others follow. The fault I find with the mammoth organization is that it has only one head and too many tails, too many ins and outs, hands and feet. Many of those tails should be heads. They should develop as individuals. The work of life is to make individuals." [17]

Only eighteen months before, he had urged her to submit to pressure when some mothers and teachers had objected that the nude figures in his pictures "might feed undesirable impulses or thoughts—and that girls cannot feel the 'spiritual' quality of the drawings." Although he was hardly touched by the criticism, he begged her to take down every drawing of which she had heard the slightest unfavorable remark. Such censorship greatly increased her disenchantment with running a school. The doubts about "the effect of these drawings on girls seems to me just a part of the very complicated and fear-beset and harassed mind toward life that people are giving me glimpses of . . . ," she wrote to him at that time. "But what I do not quite know is how fully to meet it—or when to disregard it—when school is concerned." For a while she had entertained hopes of introducing her ideas to less fashionable or affluent children, "but alas one has no freedom in our public schools." [18]

Doubtless Gibran made it easier for her to abandon her lifelong work. "I can't have an opinion about your going to live with your uncle," he said to her on January 14, 1922. "I can only say, 'don't hurry.' I know the school work doesn't hold you. You've outgrown it." Again he showed her how to use praise instead of criticism when trying to influence Minis.

> I've tried the same thing with my Syrian friends. There is a group of really creative men [in New York] now. . . . But when these men first came to N.Y. they were all separated. I made up my mind to get them to meet at least once in two weeks—apart from the Society—to talk and read together. . . . At first they used to criticize one another's work—just as the Americans did—just as we all do—by pointing out the flaws. . . .
>
> Well—I deliberately do this: when a man reads a poem, I pick out the best thing in it—it may be only a line—and I talk about that line. . . . And presently the man himself *feels* that line as his best. . . . Next time he's keener for his own best. . . . After a year and a half with these men it has come to this: A man will say "I've written a poem—but there is only a line or two that matters." He's become his own critic.[19]

After his last visit that month she watched him as he walked from the school. An unconscious weariness crept into her perception of him, as though she knew that their days together would be ending. "It was seven when K. left—he missed a car—didn't run hard for it. He does not run hard for things now—because he is determined to be fit for his work and to get his heart in good shape." In February she wrote him that she was coming to New York for a committee meeting and asked if she could visit for an evening. "Precious Kahlil. When I see you this time, let's look at a good many of your pictures. Wear your rags—so that we shan't mind dust—and keep a sheet or a towel out of the laundry to cover me with too." [20] At his insistence they saw each other three times during her stay. The retrospective showing she had planned was put aside for three nights of retrospective talk. On March 12 she wrote,

> Our third evening from 5:30 to 3:45 A.M.—and K. said, "This has been the most wonderful of all our evenings—and I thank God for it. We have made many things clear to each other." . . . I won't attempt to separate what he said this evening from what he said on Friday or Wednesday. We talked so much each time and I've had so little chance to record and have so poor a memory.
>
> K. told me the whole story of our relation from his side—because something led me, I forgot what, to confess I had thought that he must have cared for me because over here he had not found many people he could be near to, despite his army of friends . . . and that near, personal love for me had been killed in him by me, and that he had such patience with me always because he felt—as he said to me once years ago—"I want to die your friend, Mary"—and that he had sometimes seen me just for my sake when he had found it a task.

"Well!" said K.—"I'm going to *tell* you things, hereafter." And he told me much then and there.

He reviewed their entire friendship and described how after 1908 he had learned to accept her support. "I never could take anything like that from anybody except from you. But you looked at money so wonderfully—and you said something about money then that I've remembered ever since. . . . You said money was impersonal, that it belongs to none of us, but simply passes through our hands; a responsibility not a possession; and that our right relation to it is to put it to rightness." He recalled the time of self-discovery in Paris and his return to Boston. "Many people thought I was in Paris for a political purpose . . . because I wrote political articles. . . . The only thing I was really caring about was the unknown in Kahlil Gibran." Then came the account of their stormy years—the indecision over marriage, Charlotte's influence, the real and imagined hurts. He concluded,

But it was only the lesser thing in me that changed toward you. The deepest thing of all never was moved. That deepest thing, that recognition, that knowledge, that sense of kinship began the first time I saw you, and it is the same now—only a thousand times deeper and tenderer. . . . I shall love you to eternity and I know I loved you long before we met in this flesh. . . . Nothing can shake us apart . . . if I'd been able to love other women, I've had plenty of chances. In Boston I knew them, as attractive, as intelligent, as well bred as Boston had. In Paris I met many of the nicest sort—some Americans, some French and Italian, and some Syrian. . . . And in New York, I meet them all the time . . . I know some women who are more brilliant than you and some who are more interesting . . . but I tire of them. . . .

And I tell you this plainly, and I want you to remember it always. You are the dearest person in the whole world to me. And that kinship, that togetherness, in our spiritual being wouldn't be changed if you should marry seven times over to seven other men.

Sex things are temporary—always. And if we had had a so-called sex relation, it would have parted us by this time. For we would certainly have outgrown it. And marriage would have parted us too. . . . If we had married, you wouldn't have put up with my wanting solitude for ten days at a time. Either would have been destructive. . . .

I can't ever visualize it when you tell me . . . that nobody loved you as a child. Because you certainly are now an unusually lovable person. I hear people call you lovable almost as often as I hear you spoken of at all and by people who don't know that I know you well. . . .

And another thing I want to say to you. You speak of yourself as if you were homely. Surely you know that you have a very remarkable face—and that there is a beauty in it all your own. . . . Don't you know I use your face again and again in my drawings?

357

This long summary led to a discussion of subjects outside their relationship, and Kahlil even mentioned Day—a figure who had been conspicuously absent from the journal for many years.

> Mr. Day is one of the sweetest men living. But my not seeing him is largely a matter of temperament. He doesn't move with the rest of life. . . . But he does beautiful photographs. He is practically the father of the so-called art photography. And he published some very fine books when he was in Copeland and Day. And he loves fine things and beauty. His Keats collection is one of the finest in America. And he has a wonderful place out in Norton [sic]. I must go to see him when I come to Boston again, soon.

The conversation was so decisive for Mary's future that her usual analysis of his health did not appear until the end of the entry. "He's tired much—and has pain often—especially about the heart. Stays in bed regularly till about noon. Interested in Berman's new book *The Glands Regulating Personality*. I got him one and he was glad." [21]

A month later his failing health drove him from New York to Cambridge. As he approached the school Mary noticed that "he walked slowly—and when we met at the door, he was dark and thin, and his face full of shadows. He is not so well—his heart a constant trouble—and his nerves feeling shattered." He had made up his mind to get away from New York and with Marianna to find a little place in the country. He agreed to see a specialist Mary recommended, but while she was making inquiries he interrupted her, "Couldn't you do that sometime when I'm not here, Mary? I'd rather talk with you."

Because he was planning to stay in Boston for several months he urged her to accompany Minis to Europe that summer. Already he had postponed his book for another year. "Knopf says The Prophet is too late for next fall; that it can't come out before spring. I think perhaps I'll say next fall—and give it to Knopf next February. It's not ready yet, and I won't hurry it—and I like the fall best for publishing." [22]

It had been years since she had interfered with his personal habits. They both had outgrown her regimens of lotions, Turkish baths, and nasal douches, but now she sent him some thyroid medicine, which he declared made him sleep better than he had for two months. For a while the dosage seemed to work. After his physical examination on April 25, she reported, "Dr. William H. Smith . . . had found nothing organically wrong—no enlargement, no valvular trouble—Had called it a nervous heart and had asked K. to go to the Mass. General for some further examination. . . . 'He gave me a little dissertation on the artistic temperament . . . and said I might be paying now for irregular eating and sleeping during all my long working life. The thing he didn't tell me was why I'm so nervous. I don't know myself why I am.' " [23]

Kahlil felt the need to stop working for a year "and learn just how to live," but the manuscript of "The Prophet" was then in typescript and the final polishing weighed heavily on him. On April 21 he reluctantly told Mary, "We've an awful thing soon to do—to go over all The Prophet and paragraph the typewritten sheets. I want the paragraphs as short as they can be made—Some even one line only. The appeal to the eye and to the spirit is so much simpler and more direct." A year and a half before, Mary had noted, "Kahlil hasn't decided whether to have any quotation marks in the book or not. Indenting may be used instead—and the whole thing may be in capitals." [24] He had admired the all-uppercase typography in the Copeland and Day edition of *The Black Riders*. Now he decided to reject both quotation marks (a natural deletion, since Arabic does not use them) and the capitalization of all words.

On May 5 he brought the typed manuscript to Cambridge. He had been at the Massachusetts General Hospital that morning for "an examination of breathing. I had to breathe into something and evidently a record was mechanically made somewhere, for a little pointer was moving." Before they began the spacing he and Mary read each Counsel over. "Let us make the divisions by ideas," he stated, "so that each division, whether it is one line or several, shall be in itself a complete thought and can be taken alone. . . . I want the division to be a natural one—not according to rule—but just the actual pauses of the thing itself—the freedom of free verse without its eccentricities. . . . Let's not copy the Bible but we can bear it in mind." [25]

They saw each other six more times that month, and along with phrasing the manuscript they carried on their endless dialogue, mainly about her dilemma and his health. After his second examination by Dr. Smith revealed nothing, he was forced to admit that his discomfort was not organic. "Neither he nor any other doctor seems to notice much the pain that I have in my heart," he complained. "The dull sort of pain. But my greatest pain is not physical. There's something big in me . . . I've always known it, and I can't get it out. It's a silent greater self, sitting and watching a smaller somebody in me do all sorts of things. But none of those things are what the greater self would say. All the things I do seem false to me." About this latest attack of anxiety, she wrote, "K. was walking up and down and talking in bits—His face was moved—It was dark between the brows—He had never spoken before so directly and avowedly of the pain of his long waiting. 'All that I can say and do say is foreign to the real thing that I would say and cannot. Only this one book, The Prophet, has as it were a shadow of that thing—a bit every now and then.' " [26]

Despite their progress on the book, throughout May his uneasiness continued. "I've worked so much on The Prophet," he said on the nineteenth, "that I can't hear it any longer." The same day he found distraction in making a small sculpture: "He was carving two small faces in wood—with the little

One of Gibran's
small woodcarvings. (Authors)

white knife he had found—a bearded man, and a face—like mine . . . he found the wood in the Arboretum." [27]

On May 30 Mary could at last write, "We worked on the line-spacing of the Counsels and finished it." He was already thinking of his next book, and before he left that day he described its theme and quoted some lines he had already conceived: " 'Yes, I've done a little on the talking to the Mist. That's different from the Counsels, you know.' It's personal, his experiences and feelings—more lyrical with less wisdom—he [the Prophet] talks to his Sister Mist: 'We too shall not part again until you are dew in a garden and I a babe on the breast of a woman'—and of the Mist, he says, 'all my smiles were on her face and all her tears were in my eyes' " [*The Garden of the Prophet*]. He could at last acknowledge the completion of "The Prophet," whose theme he summarized: "The whole Prophet is saying just one thing: 'you are far far greater than you know—and All is well.' " [28]

All spring Mary's anguish over whether to leave Cambridge strained them both. Over and over he told her not to hurry and to follow her own feelings. Sometimes it seems that if he had uttered one word of restraint, one indication that he himself needed her, she would have discarded all plans of moving. Once she showed him a letter from Minis, who was hurt by her procrastination. "When I said, 'I'm rough sometimes' K. looked me straight in the eye for just a second's pause and then said, 'Yes,' and laughed." [29]

On June 16, their last day together, he talked again about the ambivalence he felt toward traveling to the Middle East:

> The East is in sad need of everything and of men most of all . . . but I know that if I do go I can't stand it physically . . . and the East isn't really my work. Movements of all kinds—political, literary, artistic even—do not concern me. I want to make things . . . things that will be seen by people who will never hear my name. I have to be alone. The slightest presence of another mind destroys things for me. I am most worth while alone. One is near to everyone by being near to no one.

As he left "he looked badly still. When he boarded his car on leaving, his shoulders looked 40 years old, for the first time. An unutterable pain and sadness filled my heart all through our visit." [30]

Mary's trip to Europe was her first since 1908 when she had seen Kahlil in Paris. Her years of self-denial were ending. She who had so carefully saved pennies was about to savor first-class indulgence. He seemed relieved and told her how much it meant to him that she was thinking more of lavishness. She took down his measurements so she could buy him overcoats, suits, and ties. "And you may write brown over them all, for that's my color," he instructed her. "What fits you will fit me." Within two months she returned, excited by the ease of luxury and laden with gifts for him. He and Marianna had spent the summer in a spacious house in Scituate, south of Boston. In mid-September he arrived at the school with "an expression as if his mind were elate[d] with incessant creation," and with twenty-six watercolors under his arm. Concern over his health had vanished. "Yes, the people at the beach must have known I wanted solitude," he said, "for the grown ones have hardly come at all. There are ninety-seven children on that hill . . . and I must have made sixty or seventy kites for them. . . . And the other day they came to me and said, 'We've left you alone all summer. But won't you come now and be a judge at the Children's Parade?' So I was a judge—and the children paraded—and they gave me quite a little ovation!" [31]

Mary felt that his latest drawings were "as far beyond all his previous work as that most recently previous is beyond the work of his boyhood. These pictures can stand by the finest hitherto painted in the world and be honored with them!" He had made some of them expressly for "The Prophet." Others he would save for poems yet unwritten. " 'And this I made for the very end of the book all in pencil.' And he showed me the ring of wings, around the hand in whose palm is an open eye—and the celestial equator of souls engirdling. 'And this is the Tree of Heaven, that man feeds [on] as does the lamb and the fruit [*Jesus, Son of Man*]; and Joy and Sorrow [*The Wanderer*]. Here is the archer with the parents who are the Bow in his hand' " [*The Prophet*].

Then it was Mary's turn. She gave him overcoats, ties, a tooled leather bookcover from Paris, a cigarette case, a leather box, and lastly "our jewel—the opal chain and pendant. 'Why Mary—glorious . . . but you must wear it. Wear it for me. Of course I'll accept it—and call it really mine. But you must wear it for me.' " He reciprocated by offering her the original drawings of "The Prophet" "to do what you wish with."

In the midst of this exchange of presents she unemotionally revealed what they had both been waiting to hear: "I told him about my decision to go to live with my uncle. He is glad because I am glad to do it." He immediately assured her that he did not consider this a betrayal. "When I said F. was always asking whether I loved him better than anyone else in the world—best of all—K. said, 'Every love is the best in the world, and the dearest. Love isn't like a pie that we can cut pieces of, large or small. It's all one. . . . Of course, you can say he is the dearest thing in the world to you. . . .' And he laughed—so serenely." [32]

By October 7 they were making the final choice of illustrations for "The Prophet." "We fastened a string along the wall, so as to stand the pictures in a row grouped according to color—the ones with purple in the long row—and three of the blue-green colors only on the big candlestick. . . . We assigned different pictures to different Counsels . . . using about fifteen of them . . . of all of them, Kahlil liked 'Pain' the best—'the woman form with hands outstretched as [if] crucified against the breast of two men.' " He conceded that the Archer would be the most popular picture ("objective people like objective things"), thought the composition of Death most successful, and criticized his winged hand as being "too large, too definite, too limited." [33]

Because Mary had decided to leave the school during Christmas vacation, this was also his last visit to Cambridge. In November, faithfully attending the annual meeting of headmistresses, she saw him twice in New York. If she had any doubts about his ability to run his life without her, his words and appearance now convinced her of his complete self-possession. He was still benefiting from the freedom and solitude of Scituate: "Those three months were the best I've ever had in my life. . . . Everything came easy and it's still coming easily. I get up and have my coffee, and then I go right to work without effort and stick at it for four or five hours—and what I produce is what I want. The mistake I used to make was that . . . I kept myself busy every moment—until activity became a disease." [34]

He continued to make small sculptures.

> His carvings were on the table—all in settings of his making also. A
> circular portico of columns, Greek, carved from wood, held one; another

had a square curtain-like background of grained wood put together in a design of tree stems and clouds. The head lay in a soapstone tomb, with a setting cut out to show it—and a raised entablature—and he has made two most beautiful settings from stones found on his beach at Rosecliff.

They went to the Metropolitan Museum "to see the Chinese collection—especially the room with the black head and the [bronze] hand and the boddisatva that is so simple and supreme." Mary did not admit it, but she was possessed by a powerful and deep weariness, which shows implicitly in the journal. The notes from these meetings hold less description and less observation than before. Upon her return to Cambridge she was faced with packing and distributing the accumulations of twenty years. Many of her precious objects—the familiar decorations of Marlborough Street and a large selection of books—she sent to Kahlil. As he thanked her a week before Christmas, he admitted, "And now, with your last letter before me, I no longer feel like a loved guest, but rather like a child in my mother's house." [35]

He had already written of his hope that she would come once more to New York. She could not stay away, of course, and so before her new life began she spent three days with him. The day of New Year's Eve, 1922, was "a full, full time—from 1:00 P.M. to 1:00 A.M.—a wonderful twelve hours that seemed not five hours." That afternoon they enjoyed a pilgrimage to one of their favorite spots, the Museum of Natural History. From her passionate recital of the minerals and fossils they saw, she seemed to be formally taking inventory of all the wonders they had shared together. They spent the evening in the studio, silently reading "The Prophet"—"to see if anywhere it sounded preachy." (This concern probably had been prompted by a review of *The Forerunner*: "Parables and prose poems like [these] . . . will have all the unpopularity of sermons outside the pulpit.") "It did not. We only changed a spacing occasionally." [36]

Again Kahlil begged her to take anything she wanted from the studio. Two days later came their last meeting before she left, and she was more conscious than ever of the impending farewell. "I looked long at that wonderful face of his—and the mouth—the mouth of patience and of all feeling—that changes almost as the pupil of the eye changes—so different is it at one time and another. . . . I think all the tides of human life and planetary life flow through the mind that informs that face." They would miss collaborating on his next book, in which "it is of the simplest things he speaks—a drop of dew, the light from a star. In The Prophet he has talked of things in human life but in the next book his subjects will be more general."

Her final gesture that night was to reassure him when he confessed, "I have a fear about my English. For years I have wondered about this, but I have not said it to you. Is my English, modern English, Mary, or is it the English of the past? For English is still to me a foreign language. I still think in Arabic only. And I know English only from Shakespeare and the Bible and you." "I told him the simple truth," she answered, "that like his Arabic, his English too is creative. It is not of any one period. It is his own." [37]

Then she left. They had both agreed to write, and he had promised to visit her in Savannah. That winter they kept in close touch, and on March 19 he sent her the galley proofs of "The Prophet." "I have gone through them and made a few corrections, but with the feeling that they need your keener eye for punctuations and other *niceties*. . . . The frontispiece—the face of Almustafa—is also finished. I have a feeling, Mary, that you will like it more than any other face I [have] drawn." Within a month he had received and responded to her final changes: "The punctuations, the added spaces, the change of expressions in some places, the changing of 'Buts' to 'Ands' and the dropping of several 'Ands,' all these things are just right. The one thing which I thought a great deal about, and could not see, was the rearrangement of paragraphs in Love, Marriage, Children, Giving, and Clothes. I tried to read them in the new way, and somehow they seemed rather strange to my ear . . . I want very much to talk to you about it when we meet." [38]

They met in New York for three days at the end of May and then twice in June. The first night they had supper together, went for a bus ride, and returned to the studio. Mary was full of talk about her new life, but Kahlil also had news. Commissions for portraits were becoming a good source of income. One couple was interested in commissioning him to do a stained-glass window based on his watercolor "The Tree of Life." He also showed her his "partly unauthorized" latest Arabic anthology, *al-Badai wa al-Taraif,* which he translated as *Best Things and Masterpieces.* But because so much friction existed between the publishers, *al-Hilal* and Bustani, he had lost interest in the book and treated it as an unwanted stepchild. In a sense nothing that he had written in Arabic or English concerned him now except *The Prophet.* He called it "the first book in my career—my first real book, my ripened fruit." [39]

What excited him most was the opportunity to supervise closely the photography and engraving of the twelve drawings for the book. The engravers were "really interested in these pictures," he told her. "When I went there to see them, they crowded around . . . they said they'd never seen such pictures and they loved having them to work with. . . . They couldn't believe I'd done them without models—and most of them in twenty-five or thirty minutes apiece. They just *made* me talk about them. . . . I don't see how I could ask better for a book that is not to cost more than $2.25." Knopf's integrity continued to please and reassure him. "The big publishers don't publish their books," he had once said, "and Knopf does publish. So does Mosher in Maine." [40]

Mary was planning to travel to Egypt later that year with Minis, and as she listened to his plans for his next books—"the second part of *The Prophet* will be between the Prophet and his disciples—and the third part will be between the Prophet and God"—she was fully satisfied with his self-sufficiency. On May 30 she had a chance to observe him apart from her presence.

I [saw] K. at the *Cherry Orchard*—sitting with Sir [Edgar] Speyer and two ladies in the fifth row orchestra. He did not see me—but I stood in the first balcony *near* him—and saw him for the first time since youth with a group—and for the first time ever, followed his reaction to a fine play when he was full in my eye. Between acts one of the women would ask him a question and that would start him and then he'd talk right along . . . they would all hang on what he was saying . . . they were a very quiet group, yet the busiest and most animated in the house . . . and once, at a very touching moment, in the last act, K. leaned way over and put his head down in his hands—in the most spontaneous gesture of the understanding of sorrow and despair that I ever saw. He has not a bit of self-consciousness. Once or twice between acts, too, he illustrated some point by sketching or diagramming on a program in his ardent way. I was happy beyond words watching him.[41]

The Prophet was in the hands of the typesetters. As she watched Kahlil that night at the theater, Mary silently acknowledged that she was no longer needed.

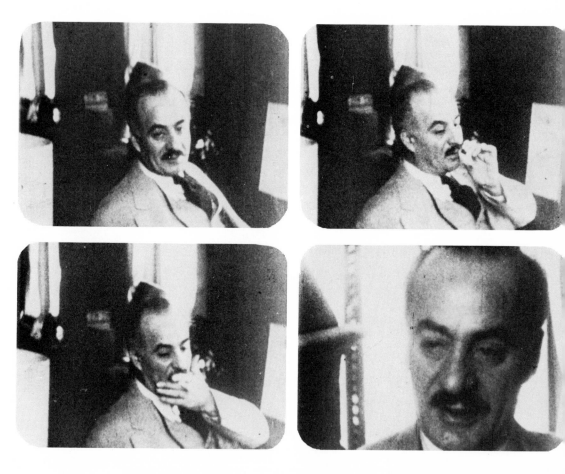

Stills of Gibran from the 16 mm. motion picture taken by
Alfred A. Knopf, *A Publisher Is Known by the Company He
Keeps*, 1929. Produced by Louis DeRochemont Associates,
distributed by McGraw-Hill. (Alfred A. Knopf, Inc.)

21

Cosmopolite

I had a strange dream a few nights ago," Kahlil told Mary in May 1923.

> I dreamt I was falling. I often dream that and have dreamt it ever since I
> had that terrible fall when I was twelve. This time I was falling over a
> precipice—and about half-way down the precipice a tree stuck out. I
> lighted on the tree, on my feet, and stood there for about two seconds.
> Then I just spread out my two arms and flew—as easily and quietly as
> anything you can imagine. And all of a sudden there was below me a sea of
> people, all looking up at me—and then I performed for them—showing
> off—soaring straight up, by a great effort—and then sliding along—again
> and again—enjoying myself hugely while I was doing it.[1]

The dream was transparently significant. During the eight remaining years
of his life, Gibran's need for personal recognition must have been satisfied. His
reputation in America and abroad was soaring. In the Arabic world his
writings were reprinted in innumerable editions. Not only would Lebanese-
Americans claim him as the voice of *al-mahjar,* but transplanted Arabs in
South America, Africa, and Australia would identify with him.

As his audience broadened, his dialogues with Arabic intellectuals grew.
Foremost among the writers with whom he corresponded was May Ziadeh,
known to avant-garde Arabs as Miss May.

She was like many of the intellectual women whom he admired, and his
attraction to her was predictable. Seven years younger than he, she was a
Middle-Eastern counterpart of the American suffragette. She had been born in
Nazareth in Palestine, had received a classical education in Roman Catholic
convent schools, and in 1908 had moved with her family to Cairo. There her
Lebanese father had started a daily newspaper. Exposed to an active literary
life at home, she became fluent in French, English, and Arabic. In 1911 she

published her youthful poems, *Fleurs de Rêve*, under the pseudonym Isis Copia. That year, too, her lifelong concern with the emancipation of the Middle-Eastern woman surfaced in her first essay in Arabic, which appeared in her father's paper.

In 1912 the appearance of *The Broken Wings* moved May to write Gibran. Although she regarded Selma Karema as too liberal a character, she admitted that she shared his objectives of freeing women from the rigid proscriptions prevalent in the Middle East. A year later, at the request of a Lebanese publisher, he composed a poem in honor of a well-known Lebanese writer, Khalil Mutran. May read this piece, "The Poet from Baalbek," at a testimonial gathering held for Mutran at the Egyptian University in Cairo in April 1913. Response to the reading was overwhelming, and thereafter she became an active champion of Gibran's writings.

With the outbreak of the war, letters between them stopped. However, by 1919 she had written a long and penetrating criticism of *The Procession* for *al-Hilal*. A year later Kahlil felt he knew her well enough to ask for her photograph, and by July 1921 he considered their relationship important enough to mention it to Mary. A discussion about telepathic experiences prompted his description:

> There is a young Syrian woman, Lebanese, in Egypt, very gifted—whom I have never seen. . . . She admires my work very much—and this time she had sent me a book of her own—a remarkable book [*Bahithat al-Badya*, or *The Desert Inquirers*]. In writing to her in reply—I told her of a dream of her I had had the night before, in which she was suffering great pain or sorrow. I told her the dream, just as we say whatever we can to make a letter. After she received that letter from me, she wrote again, saying at the time of my dream, she and her family were just undergoing the worst trouble that had ever befallen them. The hour of the accident to her father . . . was the hour of my dream.[2]

With Mary's departure, Kahlil in some ways substituted for her sympathetic ear May's sympathetic eye. Spiritually and intellectually, the Lebanese woman was close enough to understand him, while her physical remoteness allowed him the freedom he required. Perhaps theirs was the kind of bond that he described to her. This version, probably a first draft of a letter, was found among his papers:

> Since I wrote you, you have been on my mind and I spend long hours thinking of you, addressing you, trying to get answers about your hidden aspects and deducing your secrets. Strangely I felt many times the existence of your noble self in this room talking to me and arguing, expressing your opinion on my work and how it relates to my life.
> You are puzzled with what I am saying. I am puzzled with my need and

my compulsion to write you. . . . You said once, "Isn't there between minds a recorder, between ideas, an exchanger that is not realized by reason but which cannot be denied by people of the same homeland?"

In this statement there is a fundamental truth which I have known by analogy for a long time. Lately I have come to realize the existence of a strange bond which differs in motive, characteristic and influence from every other bond. It is stronger than blood and racial bond . . . it can exist between two people who have not been together in the past or the present and whom the future will not bring together.[3]

Along with personal relationships, Gibran remained involved with political events in his native country. Following the October 1918 landing of a French naval division in Beirut, a series of armistices and treaties had led to French authority throughout Syria. Now Lebanon was gradually achieving autonomy through the provisions of the League of Nations mandate. As he abandoned his illusions of actively participating in politics, his published messages to his Arab audience became less specific and more philosophical in tone. "But whatever the nations agree upon the Syrians themselves must make or unmake the future of Syria," he told Mary in February 1919 at the time of the Peace Conference. "No matter what happens in Paris I, among many Syrians, shall go on fighting for my country. Perhaps the best form of fighting is in painting pictures and writing poetry." [4]

All through the early twenties he held fast to this statement. Following the publication in 1920 of "You Have Your Lebanon and I Have My Lebanon," there appeared in *al-Hilal*, over the next four years, a series of his thoughts on the rebirth of Arabic culture through the language, writing, and creative growth of the people. His predominant theme was the need for the emerging nations to adopt only the constructive aspects of Western society. In 1923 he explained to Mary his motives for writing the articles:

The Near East has a disease—a disease of imitation, of the cheaper things of the West—especially of America—but not of your railroads, and your fine sanitation, and your educational system—but of your dress and your guns. They have taken to heart that if the greatest philosopher in the world and the smallest gun in the world are pitted against each other, the philosopher has no chance. And so Syria and Armenia and Mesopotamia and Persia want to combine in one great federation and be *strong* with army and navy like those of a Western power. They want to be safe. I want to show them that such safety is destruction for them. For it is not their real life, their creative life, their natural contribution.

The Near East has been conquered from time to time . . . and so they were turned to a more contemplative life. And they developed a consciousness of life, and of self, and of God—that the West has not yet developed. I would rather have them still conquered, still subject, and developing that consciousness, than have them free, with that consciousness becoming less.[5]

369

Not all Arabic intellectuals held Gibran's pronouncements in esteem. Ever since the appearance of *The Broken Wings*, *al-Mashriq*, the influential Lebanese literary journal, had attacked his books. In 1912 it labeled his antagonism toward the Church hierarchy as "dirty sayings that belittled the sayer." By 1923 its tone had not softened. "Who can imagine this poet?" wrote the Jesuit critic Louis Cheikho. "Is he a poet or an idiot? He seems childish, empty like his Great Sea. . . . In his heart is the irreligious microbe." This polemic gave the members of Arrabitah a splendid opportunity to counterattack, and soon immigrant writers and conservative Arabists were pitted against one another. In a defense of Cheikho's criticism *al-Mashriq* warned that Gibran's ideas were "lustful and cheap" and his influence pernicious. "Stop reading him!" traditionalists instructed their faithful flocks.[6]

Gibran, of course, thrived on this kind of controversy. However, the judgment passed on the form and language of his poetry did inhibit his Arabic production, and finally ended it. His last truly creative poem had been *The Procession*, and this work, so important to him, was attacked not only for its "corrupt images" but for its linguistic and metrical weaknesses. Faced with the choice of continuing to struggle for acceptance by the Arabic world of letters or of confining himself to expression in English, he took the latter course. With this decision he resolved the last major dichotomy in his life.

He made a similar decision in his art as well. No longer did he create paintings for exhibition; he directed his talent for draughtsmanship to pencil portraits and wash drawings for his books. At the same time he narrowed his literary horizons to the writing of self-contained passages, soulful and satisfying to countless people whom he realized needed spiritual solace to face an increasingly complex society. By combining these strengths he created a successful package, which he described to Mary. "You know I feel ideally a book should be small. I'm hipped on unity. . . . I want you to be able to read it at a sitting—before you go to sleep at night—or to put it in your pocket and take it out on an afternoon walk." [7]

This purpose then was the secret of his success—and by 1923 he had few doubts that his little English books would be successful. Years later, when asked to account for the ever-multiplying sales of the slim volumes, Alfred Knopf would recall their author's confidence in their potential. "*The Prophet* is another one of those books the appeal of which seemed to be well known to its author before it was published. . . . Whenever I saw Gibran in the few years of life that remained to him after 1923 and gleefully reported how well *The Prophet* was doing, his reply was always the same—he shrugged his shoulders and said: 'What did I tell you?' " [8]

Part of Kahlil's expectations must have been due to Mary's predictions, which she made when she received her copy at the Minis country home in Clarkesville, Georgia. On October 2, 1923, she wrote him,

370

The Prophet came today and it did more than realize my hopes. For it seemed in its compacted form, to open yet new doors of desire and imagination in me. . . .

This book will be held as one of the treasures of English Literature and in our darkness and in our weakness we will open it to find ourselves again and the heaven and earth within ourselves.

Generations will not exhaust it—but instead, generation after generation [will] find in the book what they would feign be—and it will be better and better loved as men grow riper and riper.

It is the most loving book ever written—in any language known to me, anyhow—and, I believe, in any language. And it is so, because you are the greatest lover—who ever wrote—But you know, Kahlil, that the same thing happens finally, whether a tree is burned up in flame, or falls silently to dust in the woods. . . . And you are starting a conflagration! For more and more will love you as years go by, long long after your body is dust. They will find you in your work. For you are in it as visibly as God is.[9]

During her first year away from him Mary tried to adhere to their old pattern of regular meetings. They saw each other in New York one month after *The Prophet* was published and again in 1924. But the brief reunions were greatly inhibited by her traveling companion. "And we had no meal together," she wrote on November 26, "because I am here with my uncle and am always wanted for meals." She did, however, observe the trend that would make *The Prophet* the all-time best selling book in America. Within one month the first edition of 1300 copies was sold. When Kahlil showed her a favorable review in the Chicago *Post*, he told her about the general reception.

I have been actually overwhelmed with letters about it, and many of the letters from people I never heard of. . . . Twenty days after the book appeared some Syrian publishers tried to buy a number of copies and there was not one left. . . . I read from it at the Poets' Club. . . . And it was read in a church—St. Mark's—first of all by [Butler] Davenport. To my regret he read the whole book . . . but his spirit was ever so good—and the reading gave people some idea of the book. . . . You know, I had wanted it first read in a church.[10]

A clue to its success was that although the postwar avant-garde was tiring of Gibran, popular individual response was overwhelming. *The Prophet* received much less literary attention than had *The Madman* and *The Forerunner*. It was his only book in English that the *Times* did not review. Typical of the critical lack of interest was the review in *Poetry*:

Kahlil Gibran has written a third book, *The Prophet*, following two others of the same genre, a book that will have a deep appeal for some readers and leave many others cold. It is a bit of Syrian philosophy, a mode alien to our culture and yet one in which many restless and unsatisfied spirits of our race and generation find a curious release. . . .

The discourse on beauty ends with the following lines:

> Beauty is eternity gazing at itself in the mirror.
> But you are eternity, and you are the mirror.

This seems to relapse into the sheerly mystical, and as the poem curves on to its end, one feels that it could never be a satisfying interpretation of our world. Moreover, the book lacks vigor. . . . One feels that the poem could be a sort of decoration for us, like a faded Buddhist painting, that it could hang on our walls, but it would never be part and parcel of our house. . . .

Doubtless this book will awake response in many readers, for it is not without beauty, but the essence of the book, which is its spiritual significance, cannot satisfy the robust hunger of the occidental spirit.

But the book comforted thousands of anonymous Americans. A month after its publication Gibran told Mary that Knopf planned to print a flyer with quotations from readers' letters. Although this publicity effort did not materialize and there was no advertising campaign at all, the book's sales doubled in the next year by word-of-mouth recommendation. When he saw Mary in June 1924, he portrayed for her the kind of person who made up the growing readership. As she described it,

> "I've received a beautiful letter," and he showed me one from a woman in Michigan—just saying he was blessed for having written and *in* having written The Prophet—and thanking him "in the name of thousands of children."
>
> "I have answered it of course," said K.—"and I think I can see almost the very face of that woman, from her letter. She is not intellectual, but she feels deeply—and she is genuinely religious, and a very sweet being." [11]

The meeting in November 1923, and eight days in May and June 1924 were their last fully recorded visits. Life in Georgia had altered Mary's habits and activities. She used her still abundant energies to be the effective mistress of a Savannah mansion and a country estate. Her lifelong propensity for guiding young men and women was as strong as ever, but instead of helping promising students and creators she inserted herself into the lives of her several nieces and nephews, and especially into the lives of her servants. With the exception of Kahlil, time and tragedy had removed her most promising protégés from her view. Micheline Hardy was happily married and maintained friendly but purely social contact from New York. Aristides Phoutrides had been appointed assistant professor of classical literature at Yale University, but at the very beginning of a promising career he was the victim of a drowning accident in

August 1923. And that November, when Kahlil asked if she had received any word from Charlotte, she tersely answered, "I had not." [12]

Another death marked the end of an era for both Kahlil and Mary. After two years of an agonizingly slow deterioration of body and spirit, Josephine Peabody Marks had died on December 4, 1922. Mary alluded to his reminiscing about her during one of their conversations in June. "We talked about Josephine—her youth and her later work and self—her dying when she did. And he told me a story of the old days—how at a salon . . . one day a beautiful woman, friend to Mr. Day, came and on going out, Kahlil spoke of her beauty—Josephine grew excited at once, 'And do you consider her more beautiful than you think me?' " Her premature and painful death had occurred at a time when a new generation of poets was displacing the earlier twentieth-century romantics. This fact must have been uppermost in Kahlil's mind when he recalled having seen her in 1914: "and how years and years later at a poet meeting in New York when no special notice was paid her, she said to him at parting—'I see you've made a hit.' "

These brief references to Posy, his spiritual guardian during his youthful bereavements and muse to his first songs, were devoid of sentiment and regret. Whether he spoke more wistfully than Mary was willing to hear or record can only be conjectured. But she added, "He has been looking for some of her letters to him in the old days—because Mr. Marks wants them for a biography of her. 'I can't find them. But I surely have them somewhere. I will look in Boston.' " [13] A year later, when the *Diary and Letters of Josephine Preston Peabody* was published, his name was mentioned in it three times. Sadly, her letters to him were not included—and the story of her ministrations remained all but unknown to the outside world.

Mary's last descriptions of Kahlil were not as clear or penetrating as they once had been. She mentioned that his favorite clothing to work in was a long, loose garment similar to his native abba, and she tried to note the change in the studio. In it hung a Byzantine tapestry of a crucifixion that he had bought from the recently widowed Mrs. Morten and a carved screen made by N'oula, who then was living in Boston with his growing family. She quoted him on his outside life—"I'm the most social human being in the world but the most unsociety person." She tried to identify more of his friends—the Hutchinsons (Hesper Hutchinson was the daughter of Richard Le Gallienne) and Mariita Lawson, a young model whose beautiful face he had been using in his latest drawings. Of an article Naimy had written about him, she commented, "We decided against using it. . . . Kahlil observed, 'There is something peculiar to himself in each poet—his own-*ism*, his individual element. . . . In N.'s article there is no suggestion of that—and that in any poet is the main thing.' " [14]

She did record how the promised sequel to *The Prophet* was developing:

"I'm going to tell you the plan of the Second Book of the Prophet—and the Third Book—the Second Book is in the Garden of the Prophet and the Third is the Death of the Prophet—you know that he has gone to his island—and there he goes to his mother's house—and he spends a great deal of his time in his mother's garden. And he has nine disciples, who come from time to time to talk with him in the garden. And what he talks about to them is how the small things and the great things are connected—of man's kinship with—his actual sharing in the other things of the universe. He talks of the Dewdrop and the Ocean, the Sun and Fireflies, of the Air and Ways and Space, of the Seasons, of Day and Night, of Light and Darkness. . . . And it ends with not a farewell like The Prophet but in a closing part which expresses Peace. . . . In the third book he returns from his island—and talks with various groups as they come to him. . . . The Prophet is put into prison. When he is freed again, he goes into the marketplace and they stone him." [15]

She tried to continue her sixteen-year-old habit of recording the books he was reading ("*The Golden Bough* is a delight," he said. "It has not left my bed since it came"), and mentioned, without giving its title, a book on the apocryphal sayings of Jesus he had just bought. But a choppiness and a diminution of the journal's narrative style give indications that she was distressed with the knowledge of yet another change in their relationship.

There is a sort of pervasive sadness, a sense of final farewell, in her evocative description of Kahlil as he read some aphorisms from his forthcoming book. He had decided to publish them separately, without the story "The Way of The Seven Days."

> We had a magical evening together. But there is only one more together now before I go—and the coming to an end of this sweet period is so present with me that it is hard to remember much that we said. . . . He . . . told me the little introduction to the book—very lovely—how the shores of the Great Sea are of sand, and [the sayings] are a few grains of that sand, and a handful of bubbles from the foam. . . . He sat by his table—I on his sofa facing the fireplace. At his left in the glass covering the green-bodiced lady of his seventeen years—was reflected the purple rosy light of the colored lamp—like a moon rising far away. Past his right—shone the golden tapestry and the golden things upon it—the bits of carving, the stained head of the Paris days—the wash drawing shellacked of lovers dovelike with arms spread in the mountain valley—it was all like the Great Earth glowing in the twilight sky—with K. bathed in the glow of it, reading from the vault of the inner sky.

This passage could easily have been the last one in her fourteen-and-a-half-year-old journal. But she wrote some more on June 8, and it was not until June 18 that the journal ended. The last paragraph was a bit of practical advice from Kahlil. He assured her that age would not impair her relationship if she decided to marry J. Florance Minis—the question that would weigh heavily upon her for the next year. "Sex life doesn't stop at 50 in all right thinking women—any more than in men," he said. "I have read in an Arab [book] of the twelfth century that many women after that age are happier than before in sexual intercourse—because they do not then fear conception." [16]

Now that he was on his own, Gibran felt free to run his own affairs. Neither he nor Mary, however, predicted how his financial affairs would suffer in her absence. Ever since her gift of $5,000 in 1911, he had periodically consulted her about financial matters. At first he had used her stockbroker, but gradually he started to invest any extra cash with his Lebanese friends in Boston. Most of his old colleagues in The Golden Links had become small businessmen, and as early as 1912 he began to lend the local baker, Adolph Nahass, or the community tobacconist, Dimitri al-Khoury, money which they would pay back with good interest upon demand. Mary countenanced and even collaborated in this plan. In fact it was upon her suggestion that he used the interest to endow Marianna with a regular income, for he complained that without it he could never get her to take much.

After the war, as his royalties increased, Mary had suggested that real estate was the only safe investment during inflationary times. On May 21, 1924, he told her that he and a partner, Faris Malouf, had bought a building on Marlborough Street at Massachusetts Avenue. If she had been in Boston when he agreed to invest in the twin brownstones at 409–411 Marlborough Street, she probably would have cautioned against too big a plunge. But it was a time of speculation, and with a shared capital outlay of about $24,000, he acquired seven stories of prime real estate on one of the city's busiest corners. Along with this unmanageable ark he also assumed a seemingly endless series of mortgages and personal debt.

Almost from the first the "Marlborough Chambers Co.," as the venture was known, was doomed. The houses were mostly empty and had to be renovated before they could yield a profit. The partners scraped and borrowed every available bit of cash for plumbing, electricity, and elevators, but by midsummer Gibran was sending Mary warning signals. He was being forced to spend much time in Boston, and he even begged to see her. "I have many things to tell you and many questions to ask you. You are the only one in the world who could advise me about 'me.'" Early in September he gave her all the details.

We have leased the building . . . for ten years to Miss Josephine M. Quimby and Miss Harriette M. Fowler. These two ladies conduct the Fenway Business Women's Club. The 150 rooms in our building will eventually be occupied by business women only. This *fat* piece of good luck came to us about a month ago when it was least expected.

I am sending you a copy of the lease. The alterations and repairs, detailed on the first page, will cost us from ten to twelve thousand dollars. . . . My partner, Mr. Malouf, rebels against such a high rate, and I too feel it is too much. So we are trying to raise as much money on the basis of 6% interest as we possibly can.

In October, faced with unpaid insurance bills, taxes, and mortgage payments, he again sought her help. He had lost his initial enthusiasm for the project.

We have no securities for the rent of our lessees. Miss Quimby and Miss Fowler cannot give any. And because the lease is not secured we have not been able to raise any money for repairs and alterations. . . . We have contracted for all sorts of things, and men are now working. . . .

I realize now our error. It is the error of small people trying to do big things. It is the error of the greedy or the stupid. I have been both, and I am very sorry. . . .

Do you know of any banking institution that would be willing to lend us ten or fifteen thousand dollars on the strength of the good future of the building? Or do you know someone who would trust us enough to take a fourth mortgage?

Please tell me what to do, Mary. I know I am involved in something quite foreign to whatever intelligence I have. I have made a mistake, a grave mistake, in trying to move in a world so different from my own world. But it seems to me that I should not be utterly crushed by that mistake.[17]

Her advice was to refrain from further involvement. Instead of producing a fourth mortgage she immediately sent her personal check to cover the most outstanding demands. She was scheduled to be in Boston the next month for a routine health checkup, and she asked him to draw up an accounting of unpaid bills for her to review. This rescue placed her in an awkward position. Gibran was well aware that Minis resented his friendship with her, and she was naturally unwilling to admit to her companion the full extent of her patronage of Kahlil. For the first time in their correspondence, she warned him to hide all evidence of her support and began to use the agreed-upon initials "C. J." when noting down payments to him.[18]

In a like way he was also concealing his blunders from the outside world. He pleaded illness when he canceled a long-promised appearance at the dedication of a Lebanese orphanage in Albany. He was unable to enjoy the success of *The Prophet* except for a banquet given by Lebanese and Americans in Detroit, an obligation he could not escape since it had been made before he had become, in his words, "a little boy who catches on behind a truck to run." [19] It was probably the only concession to his career that he made while he owned the building.

When he returned from Detroit in October, Mary was in Boston reviewing the entire affair. His share of the outstanding bills as of the first of December was $6,045. She juggled her assets and finally conceived a way of meeting the debts, which meant recovering some personal loans of hers. Although they saw each other in New York on November 16, she did not record what must have been one of their most difficult meetings. In his letters acknowledging the stream of checks she was sending, Kahlil appeared humiliated, anxious to draw up a will that would assure her of some repayment in case of his death, and yet still hopeful that the promised occupancy of the businesswomen would save the property. His prediction was disastrously wrong. The overambitious Misses Quimby and Fowler defaulted, the partners were overextended, and the banks began to foreclose in February 1925. When she heard the news, Mary's response was predictably serene and loving.

> Beloved Kahlil, I'm just as sorry as sorry can be, for the loss—and for all its sad and hard and humiliating disappointing circumstances. And my heart just aches for You—there is not the strange sort of nourishing quality and strength in money troubles that there is in other and deeper troubles. . . .
>
> But that is all there is to this—a mistake. . . . And money loss leaves the soul intact after all. . . . I've nothing to forgive—nothing. When you're in trouble I'm just a thousand times more standing by you.

He answered her soberly two weeks later:

> After all the debts are paid I shall get about three thousand back. This sum I shall put in a saving bank in my sister's name. Other money, lent or invested here and in Boston, is still where it was before the unfortunate affair started. My sister will receive one hundred or more from Khoury each month. A good part of that she will put also in the saving bank. . . . I am trying to return to my own world so that I may be able to do some work. I have forgiven everyone who made me pay so much for being what I am. May God help them all.

To Marianna he was even more laconic. He had always sent her brief notes which Maroon or Assaf George or N'oula Gibran would read to her. They showed his concern for her ease—"Wealth is good . . . . When I touch sand it turns to gold . . . . Take some money and go to the movies." But by January 1925 he was forced to restrain even her small indulgences. "Enclosed is money order for six hundred dollars," he wrote at Easter. "I send it as pocket money for your needs. I will not come for the holidays for many reasons. I am at present drowning in a sea of work and do not want to change the direction of my thoughts. I should do the work I was created for. Everything else is bad." [20]

Later that year he wrote Mary of how carefully he had kept the story of his losses from his American associates. "Even if I go to Boston [in August] and spend my days in Franklin Park it will be better than staying here or visiting my formal friends. Most of my friends are most loving and most considerate; but they do not know what I have gone through, and I do not want them to know. It is better that they should think of my work rather than thinking of me or my problems." [21]

His stratagems worked. During the worst of the venture Konrad Bercovici, a Romanian-born writer living in New York, portrayed Gibran as Kahlil wanted the world to know him. In an article on the Syrian quarter he wrote,

> I have passed many hours with the poet and artist, listening to his musical voice, which makes English as sonorous as if it were Italian as he read me his poems. Faultlessly attired, Kahlil Gibran looks more like a cultured Frenchman than a Syrian. But at home, in his large studio on Tenth Street, discussing with me the Orient, he instinctively bends his knees under him as he sits down on the divan to sip the thick coffee, the preparation of which is his particular pride, when he makes his guests feel at home. Everything Occidental is forgotten on entering his room and facing him. Instantly all feeling of hurry is banished. The day seems to be longer; the hours seem to be slower; even the rumbling below, in the street, the noise coming through the heavily shuttered windows, seems to be more distant than it actually is.

Even Witter Bynner, who had known Gibran for ten years and had dedicated his play *Cycle* to him, became confused when he portrayed him in honor of Knopf's ten years of publishing. In April 1925 Gibran replied to Bynner's request for information with all the enigmatic reserve that made him so elusive:

> It is very hard for me . . . to tell you what my position is in the Arabic world. The Eastern peoples like to say that I have founded a new school of literature. If I had, I certainly was not conscious of doing so. Writers and critics like to repeat two words: The first is "a Gibranite" meaning a *new* or a *different* person; the other is "Gibranism" meaning *freedom in all things*. . . . There have been many fights about me in the East—and always between the old and the young. I think I still live because the young were not conquered.

Much of Kahlil's self-description ran through Bynner's published piece. Although Bynner had known him as well as any American writer had, he was vague about his personality. He related one anecdote about "the Gibran manner"—"I have known the maids, in a house where we have dined, to gather behind a screen and forget to serve dinner. 'How can we remember to do anything,' said their spokesman, 'when Mr. Gibran is talking!' "—and then,

378

adding to the ever-growing legend, he closed, "May he continue contributing to the largeness of this America! until the young are conquered." [22]

Kahlil had nearly abandoned his Temple of Art series, but he still enjoyed drawing portraits of his friends and illustrating their books. He offered to illustrate Bynner's latest volume of poetry. In 1922 he had decorated *Companions*, an anthology of American poetry (including works by Le Gallienne and Rihani), and had illustrated a book of verse by a young writer, Madeline Mason Manheim, who three years later would translate and publish *The Prophet* in French.

The division between his Arabic and American circles seemed to widen in 1925. Perhaps his business failure made him more secretive. When Mary visited him in the spring it was obvious too that her role of confidante had been ruled out for her. At the beginning of the year she had started a shortened diary, and her brief notes revealed how her new life was forbidding any observation on his growth: "*May 20, 1925.* Dined and spent evening with Gibran. F. much distressed at homecoming." This cryptic remark heralded the final, secret stage of their long relationship. Later that summer, while enjoying the baths at Karlsbad, Germany, she began to use "C. J." in every reference in her diary. "*July 11, 1925.* Letter to C. J. while F. slept."

In early September Kahlil met her briefly upon her return and received his two gifts, figures of a Madonna and a Christ. Wherever they saw each other—in Pennsylvania Station or at a Thompson's Spa—the substance of their talk was no longer made a matter of record. Her few cramped diary entries were in abbreviated German script and mostly illegible. In Europe she had decided to marry Minis, and a sense of propriety forbade her the disloyalty implied in openly chronicling another man's life. Her own days were quietly spent shopping, reading, and caring for her future husband. And yet for the next six years she would continue surreptitiously to record Kahlil and his work.

In June of 1925 Sulayman Bustani, a leading Arabic scholar and writer who was known for his translations of the Greek classics, died while in New York. Kahlil, who had entertained him the year before in Boston, drew a series of posthumous sketches. *As-Sayeh* featured one of them in an issue devoted to Bustani, and several members of Arrabitah, including Kahlil, wrote tributes. Arrabitah had been unable to sustain its professional goals, and except for such formalities the organization, and Kahlil's role within it, had become almost entirely social. His concerns were mostly writing in English and being with his American friends.

What he especially enjoyed was his annual trip to Henderson House, Corinne Roosevelt Robinson's summer home in Herkimer, New York. "I think that the genius of the Roosevelt family is in its simple and wholesome *family* life," he wrote Mary. "They are very clannish and strangely devoted to one another. And they know so much, and they are interested in so many things." Another couple whose hospitality he enjoyed was Frederick and Margaret Lee Crofts. A publisher of textbooks, Crofts had purchased that division from Alfred Knopf. Gibran drew several portraits of the ebullient Mrs. Crofts; it was at places like their summer home in Stamford, Connecticut, and the Robinsons' that he felt most wanted and could relive his childhood days.

"I was recently in the country visiting friends," he told Mary in one of their last meetings of 1924. "And in the morning about six o'clock I got up and looked out of my window. The trees were budding, the birds were singing, the grass was wet—the whole earth was shining. And suddenly I was the trees and the flowers and the birds and the grass. I was all of it and there was no I at all." [23]

22

The Last Years

Gibran's real estate venture took a year out of his creative life. In its aftermath he was forced to simplify his affairs and to concentrate on writing and painting. Previously he had translated many of his works for Arabic periodicals, but now he turned over the task of translating his books to Antony Bashir. This brilliant young Syrian Orthodox priest, scholar, and translator was archimandrite of North America.

Because the second volume of the promised trilogy was only an idea, Gibran gathered his short sayings—many of which had already been published in Arabic or English—into a ready-made book for his American following. It was at the time of this compilation of *Sand and Foam* that he met the woman who would lighten the burden of organizing, transcribing, and typing during his remaining years of productivity. After his death she would assume an even more dominant role.

Henrietta Boughton née Breckenridge was forty-five years old in the fall of 1923 when she first heard Butler Davenport read *The Prophet* at St. Mark's-in-the-Bouwerie. Like so many of Gibran's most ardent disciples, she was an idealist and an avowed pacifist. A graduate of the normal school in her home town of Albany, she had taught English in private schools before moving to Manhattan. Here she pursued her true avocation as a writer.

"Netta" Boughton had survived an unhappy marriage which had ended in desertion, raised her only child, and was able to catch a foothold in the precarious world of poetry by writing steadily for the New York *Times* poetry page. Her special talent was chameleon-like adaptability: upon demand she could compose a Shakespearean sonnet, a bit of doggerel, or some modern verse. She wrote under several pseudonyms, among them Ben Brigham and Barbara Young. Except on her passport and legal transactions she adopted the latter name as her own.

Like Gibran's anonymous reader from Michigan, she was deeply moved when she first heard *The Prophet*, and she began to include her favorite Counsels in her own poetry readings, which she gave to supplement the meager stipend forthcoming from newspaper poetry pages. In March 1925 she learned that Kahlil was not a mystic secluded in the Middle East but a writer living and working in Greenwich Village. She wrote him a letter of praise and requested an audience, which he granted.

Of all the women with whom Gibran allied himself, Barbara Young was the least attractive. Tall and angular, she was endowed with little of Josephine's beauty, Charlotte's charisma, or Mary's intelligence. She was not affluent like many of his social acquaintances nor beautiful like his models. She was reliable, fiercely loyal, and very impressionable. One of the immediate bonds between the two was their belief in reincarnation. She was convinced that she had lived in Africa and had written a poem on these origins—"I Was A Brown Girl Once." She also shared his complete disdain for scholarship or historical perspective—a quality that was to prove disastrous when she later determined to write his biography. He recognized a kindred spirit and, more important, a devotee who was qualified and eager to help him.

Twenty years later she mistakenly recalled that her first session as his amanuensis occurred in the autumn of 1925 when he dictated "The Blind Poet" to her.[1] Although the poem had in fact already been published in *The New Orient*, it can safely be assumed that sometime that fall he started to organize the aphorisms, and her role as secretary began. Over the next three years she not only published a book of verse, *The Keys of Heaven*, and opened the Poetry House bookshop on 12 East Tenth Street, but she promoted Gibran by sponsoring a public reading of his poetry at the Brevoort Hotel and arranging for him to read before a meeting of the Fifth Avenue Bookstores Association.

When the Indian editor Syud Hossain asked Gibran to be an officer of The New Orient Society in New York and to contribute to its quarterly journal, he was undoubtedly honored. His commitment to *The New Orient* symbolized his growing identity as a citizen of the world. The magazine was international in outlook and cosmopolitan in its choice of supporters. Within the context of "a new synthesis: for the East and West each to bring its quota of inspiration and aspiration to the common service of an indivisible humanity," he had found his place. In turn Hossain commented on his appointment, "There is no more sincere and authentic or more highly gifted representative of the East functioning today in the West than Kahlil Gibran."

Gibran served on the society's board of directors alongside such Americans as the distinguished Orientalist Arthur Upham Pope and his old friends Julia Ellsworth Ford and Witter Bynner. Most of the writers were international in origin as well as spirit. First among them was Mahatma Gandhi, whom Kahlil

Gibran, Julia Ellsworth Ford,
and Syud Hossain. (Authors)

believed to be "one of the greatest men living. He teaches nonresistance. He says 'accept nothing from the English—neither office nor title, and do no commerce with them; neither resist if they kill or abuse you.' " [2] Others were Annie Besant, Ananda Coomaraswamy, John Dewey, Yone Noguchi, Bertrand Russell, and H. G. Wells. Several of them, including A. E. (George Russell), Claude Bragdon, Charles Fleischer, John Haynes Holmes, Alma Reed, and Sarojini Naidu, knew Gibran through the society and became associated with him or wrote about him during his cosmopolitan years.

By 1926 he had reached a professional plateau; there he remained for the rest of his life. Writing and publishing were facilitated by Barbara's secretarial tasks; his public image was steadily becoming that of an international figure; and he was beginning to produce some new work, much of which he began in 1926 in Boston, where he remained long after his usual Christmas vacation.

Along with finishing a few pieces for "The Garden of The Prophet" there, he was writing two plays in English. As with most of his English works, the seeds for "Lazarus and His Beloved" had been sown long before. He had originally worked it out in Arabic, and Mary had mentioned it briefly eleven years earlier:

> *April 26, 1914.* His next book of four long poems all yet unpublished is going to be satisfactory: The Devil; Sit Balkis; The Poet; Lazarus and The

Only Love. . . . Lazarus is new to me—I don't know when K. wrote it. I think both that and Sit Balkis were probably fairly recently worked out. It is the Lazarus of the Bible and the 3 days during which he was dead. He went then into his own soul world. There he met the woman he loved and lived with her. But the power of the world-god compelled him back to earth and earth-life.

"In the near East," he told her, "was formerly the belief that every poet has his djinia or tabia . . . even though he have also a woman love—this djinia is his real mate; for humanly his real self is alone." [3] By 1926 he had chosen, instead of prose poetry, a straightforward dramatic form for Lazarus' quest. In the second one-act play, "The Blind," he made his first attempt to create a piece completely devoid of Oriental imagery.

Mary and Florance were wed on May 7. The couple came to New York, and Kahlil read "Lazarus" to her on the thirteenth. Three days before, they had also met at his studio, but her marriage must have preoccupied both of them, and whatever transpired during that visit was carefully veiled in her notes: "F. went downtown to see about passports . . . he stayed for lunch in Wall Street—I returned to lunch with Micheline and then saw J. Grinch. Much moved—almost tears—showed 'Sand and Foam,' a few of 300 aphorisms—'I have more than a 1000: chiefly Arabic'—and picture of the blind poet and the bit on Dew for The Garden of The Prophet." By May 13 Florance must have sanctioned his bride's openly visiting the studio: "F. had —— to lunch while I saw Gibran. F. alright about it now. G. read me his 'Lazarus' . . . and told me about 'Blind Man' . . . and 'Snow' for 'The Garden of The Prophet.' Greatly moved in reading Lazarus whose three days of release mirror his own dreams." [4]

The Minises left for Europe, and Kahlil went to Boston to finish the remaining details on "Sand and Foam." Drawing on his experiences at Copeland and Day, he enjoyed overseeing virtually every detail of the design and reminded his editor, "I would like the book . . . to be printed in the same manner as the manuscript, that is in regard to the number of aphorisms on *one* page and the number of pages it should contain." [5] At the same time he was redesigning for Knopf a special edition of *The Prophet*. The book's sales, especially for gift giving, continued to climb. He then turned to what would become his most ambitious work in English. Without his usual inner debate, and with an advance of $2,000, he abandoned "The Garden of The Prophet" and settled down for a year to work on a life of Jesus.

To write this life had been an ambition of his for nearly twenty years. Mary's journal since 1908 had devoted pages to his dreams and musings about Jesus and the role of the Son of Man. From Paris he had written her, "My greatest hope now is to be able to paint the life of Jesus as no one did before.

My life can finde no better resting place than the personality of Jesus." He read "everything about him I could ever lay hands on. And I have been all through his country from Syria to Lower Palestine. And all my life the wonder of him has grown on me." In particular, Ernest Renan's philosophy and *Life of Jesus* influenced his conception of Jesus as "the greatest of all artists in as much as he was the greatest of poets. . . . To call him God makes so light of him. Because as God's his wonderful sayings would be small but as man's they are most perfect poetry."

The appearance of Jesus—Gibran never called him Christ—as a human being in ordinary surroundings characterized his dreams. Far from visions, they are concrete, if submerged, longings to return to his homeland. They abound in details that are specifically Lebanese. In 1911, when he was having between two and four of the dreams each year, he told Mary that they usually occurred in one of three settings—"a slope near Besharri where there are many big stones and pieces of columns," "near a big spring, where a river rises up quietly out of the rock," or "in a little garden near Beirut, full of flowers—with a wall and a gate where I used to study while at college."

In one dream he met Jesus at a Phoenician tomb outside Besharri. "The walnuts and weeping willows arched over the road, and I could see the patches of sunlight falling through on his face." Sitting and talking on a large carved stone in front of the tomb, they could hear an old Franciscan monk, a friend of Kahlil's grandfather, chopping trees with a "tremendous sound that filled all the valley . . . like a great bell—as if the tree were of metal." Sometimes he could recall the words of Jesus, always simple and ordinary. "I was sitting on a log near the pool. He came along and sat down too. . . . His skin had the look of the petals of those very dark roses—so clear and soft and living—with that strange olive green color. And dust lay on it as you've seen—a sort of gold on a butterfly's wing. Then he half lay down on the ground, with his staff. . . . I said to him: 'Is your staff of fig?' 'No,' he said. 'It's shahbi.' Shahbi is a hard wood common in Mt. Lebanon." [6]

Over the years he told Mary stories about Jesus that had been told in Lebanon ever since Jesus' day. "There are enough of such stories," he said, "to make a large book and it will be a very wonderful book. They ought to be collected." The last dream that she reported appears late in the journal, on May 27, 1923.

> It was in Lebanon, as it always is that I see him—in Mar Mema [a monastery near Besharri], that beautiful place where if I care to be buried anywhere, I would choose to be. A stream runs down, and weeping willows border the stream at one spot where we boys often used to play. . . . I was by the stream, gathering watercress . . . and he came from the west and the light was behind him and made his outline glow. . . . And I took some cress in my two hands and held them out to him and said,

"Master, will you not have some of this watercress?" And he took a bunch of it, and put it into his mouth. . . . His whole face smiled. . . . And he ate it with relish, as if the crispness was delicious to him. And he said, "Nothing is more beautiful than green—and this is the most *greeny* watercress"—and then he went down to the stream and knelt and put his head down and drank . . . and when he rose, the water was sparkling on his moustache and his beard at the lips.[7]

According to Barbara, Gibran began the first of seventy monologues about Jesus on November 12, 1926. She created a theatrical picture of him. "He stood, very still and erect. His face had the look of a tormented angel. There was anguish and exultation upon him. Then with an almost blinding illumination of his changeful face he cried out, 'I can begin writing That Book tonight!' " Ignoring or perhaps unaware of all the notes that he and Mary had made over the years, she turned the writing of *Jesus, The Son of Man* into a long mystical vision in which he agonized, lights appeared, and she took notes. After eighteen months, "when it was finished, . . . it was as though both the poet and the one whose hand had transcribed the record had come through a mighty and terrible struggle."[8]

What she failed to report was that Kahlil was spending more and more time in Boston, where he wrote much of the first draft. By 1927 he had become a respected and popular figure in the Syrian community there. This was not due to the message of his Arabic writings but was simply a result of his success in America, an acceptance to which all immigrants aspired. When he came to town Marianna's apartment was always smoke filled as countless visitors paid their respects. Next to 76 Tyler Street was Our Lady of the Cedars, and although Kahlil never attended its incense services, he and its pastor, Stephen El-Douaihy, were close friends. The pastor could easily enter the adjoining house—not by coming in the street entrance but by climbing onto the adjacent roof and walking down the stairwell to the second-floor studio.

Another institution that kept a close watch for Gibran's return was the Denison House. By the twenties it had become Boston's most important social agency for Syrian children as well as for the growing Chinese community. In 1919, because of Kahlil's stature, Marianna was selected as one of four neighborhood representatives to serve on the board of directors. He rarely came to Boston without paying respects to that building diagonally across from her apartment, and in the spring of 1926 Louisa McCrady, then the headworker and ironically an old labor union friend of Mary Haskell's, gave a dinner in honor of him.

Still, he remained ambivalent about the role of social workers and their intrusion in the lives of others. In 1922 he complained to Mary,

> You know I don't love the sort of thing—settlements. I don't love missions—and I think the approach made to the Syrians is stupid. The

Americanization of the Syrians will result in just a cheap imitation by the Syrians of the surface things American. . . . They say that . . . the whole House has changed—and is very much better—really friendly and alive. Formerly these people used just to try to get into the Syrian houses, and then they'd sit down and ask questions. And the Syrians are a shy people. They don't understand that.

After one afternoon there, when he met Joseph Hitti, brother of the Arabist Philip K. Hitti, he asked, "What did it all amount to? Each one of those women came with a question and I had gone without an answer. . . . Once there I throw my whole heart into it for the hour or two hours or three hours and I enjoy it. Then I go home and it is all over and I say to myself, 'Why did I go to that place? What was it worth to anybody?' " [9] But in spite of his protestations he continued to visit the settlement workers, answer questions, and probably he secretly welcomed their attention.

In 1927 while he was working on his life of Jesus, he and Mary Haskell became almost estranged. On her return from Europe in August 1926, she had tried to see him in New York, only to learn that he was in Boston. No word about "C. J." appeared in her diary for eight months thereafter, but then, on April 16, 1927, she noted a lessening of her husband's possessive attitude. Two days later she broke her long silence with a letter: "Kahlil—? Ever so many questions. How is your book of Jesus? How has the winter been? What has happened with you? Please write me a letter. Are you in Boston or New York for the next two weeks?" In the next pages she described her placid life of formal entertaining, and then she recounted a touching scene. "And the other day an Alabama woman, a stranger, dining here and looking at my portrait, suddenly said, 'It reminds me of another painter—I wonder if you know any of his work—named Gibran.' I took her upstairs to my room and showed her the twenty-seven pictures on the walls. . . . Wherever your work meets its own, here as elsewhere, its own recognize it and love it." [10]

If Kahlil answered this message, she did not save his letter. The few notes from him which she kept during this period became more and more impersonal. Unless they were in contact by telephone, it comes as something of a surprise to find that with no apparent forewarning or accompanying letter, he sent her the manuscript of "Jesus, The Son of Man" in the second week of December 1927. In a way she must have considered it a special greeting, for she received it the day after her fifty-third birthday. Surreptitiously departing from the genteel duties of a Southern hostess, she began at once to edit the work. All during the winter and early spring of 1928 he continued to send her revisions and additions, which she worked on when she could. To judge from her diary, this was sometimes not easy, and often she worked while her household slept. "*March 8, 1928. Remainder of 'Son of Man' arrived. March*

30. 'Son of Man' 3:00 A.M. to 7:00 A.M. April 4. At night I finished 'Son of Man'—so as to return it before leaving."

On April 25 she mailed back the remaining pages. Four days later the Minises were in New York preparing to embark on another continental tour, and in the midst of shopping, theater-going and family reunions, she slipped away to 51 West Tenth Street. "Work with C. J. on S. of Man and saw the beautiful drawings for the book—to be 250 pp." On May 2 they met for the last recorded time—"Return to Gibran [his name was spelled out and then deliberately blurred] his 'Beautiful Necessity.'" [11]

Though she said nothing, Mary must have been shocked by Kahlil's appearance. His ambitious work had taken its toll. In the past December premonitions of death and an overwhelming compulsion to retreat from the world had invaded a series of his poems.

> Pity it is
>   We drowse too soon;
> Pity it is
>   We fall asleep
> Ere our song
>   Encompass the height,
> And ere our hand
>   Inherit the deep.
>
> Thanks unto the Lord,
> We have no possessions,
> Nor have we a possessor.
> And we have no mate nor descendant nor kin.
> We walk the earth a shadow
> Seen only by those in whose eyes the shadow is hidden.
> We laugh for the tragedy and the day;
> And we weep for the laughter thereof.
> And we are a spirit,
> And you say "How strange."
> But we say, "How strange is your body." Farewell.

One way to escape physical pain was through alcohol. Pain was besetting him, for by 1928 he was drinking to excess. In almost every letter to Marianna he requested *arak*, which at the height of Prohibition Assaf George had to seek out in the clandestine home stills of the South End. Many of his pleas were couched in jest. "New York is a wasteland," he wrote his sister. "There is not a drop of arak to drink before dinner and no song by Maroon after dinner. . . . If you have a little, send my share." [12]

He was entrusting Assaf George with more responsibilities than the supplying of his means of escape. First, he jointly purchased two buildings with George and put them in Marianna's name. This real estate was more modest than his mistake of four years earlier, and he made sure that he would in no way be involved in its management. The houses at 180–182 Broadway were not far from Tyler Street, and agreement for mutual ownership ensured that Marianna would always have somewhere to go if she was forced to leave their tenement. He also commissioned George to investigate a monastery near Besharri that was for sale. It was not Mar Mema but a similar site owned by the Carmelites. "I was very happy because you called about Mar Sarkis," he wrote George. "We must obtain that holy piece of land. And I beg you to do all you can about that matter." [13]

When Mary saw him in New York, he had gained weight and there were signs of bloat in his formerly trim physique. That summer in Boston painful symptoms began to debilitate him. His legs and feet swelled. His appetite, always small, dwindled to nothing. Marianna was replacing empty *arak* bottles at an alarming rate. He remained inside 76 Tyler Street all through July and August, and regretfully refused Corinne Roosevelt Robinson's annual invitation to Henderson House. When she sent her consolations, he thanked her and added, "I did not mind a bit my not going to Russia to attend the Tolstoy Fete. I only wanted to be once again under your roof. Life has its own rhymes; I did not rhyme this year in any of the words that Life has written. I think I shall *rhyme* next year! They tell me that 'Jesus,' my little book, will be out on the 12th of October. Of course I shall send the very first copy that reaches my hand to you." [14]

Mary did not know until November how sick Kahlil had been. While he was suffering from what he called summer rheumatism, Florance too was ailing and occupying her time. She made no attempt to communicate with Kahlil until after the book's publication, and by then he was back in New York and somewhat cheered by its reception. On November 7 he wrote to tell her that she had been sent a copy.

> I hope you will like it, when you see it, in spite of the many little mistakes. My publishers seem to be extremely happy over it, and my friends here, as well as others throughout the country, say such kindly things about it. . . . My summer was not a happy summer. I was in pain most of the time. But what of it? I wrote much in Arabic, songs and prose poems. . . . I did more than that, while in pain. I told the people of Mt. Lebanon that I have no desire to go back and govern them. They wanted me to do that and, you know, Mary, that I am homesick and that my heart longs for those hills and valleys. But it is better that I should stay here and work. I can do better in this strange, old room than anywhere else. [15]

Out of context, with no supporting documentary evidence, one would tend to regard this vague reference to a mandate from the Lebanese as mere fantasy. However, it is entirely possible that Dr. Ayub Tabet, his close friend during the war years, had asked him to join him in some capacity in the newly formed Republic of Lebanon. By 1928 Tabet was active in a reform movement there and for a while he served as minister of the interior and health.

Certainly, however, Gibran did not exaggerate the "kindly" remarks about his latest work. In contrast to the mainly negative reception of *Sand and Foam* ("arid and thin," the *Herald Tribune* called it), it was receiving general acclaim. The *Times*, which had ignored *The Prophet*, devoted the front page of its Christmas book review section to two books on the life of Christ: *The Master* by Walter Russell Bowie and *Jesus, The Son of Man*. "It is as a fellow-countryman that [Gibran] approaches the Man of Nazareth," wrote P. W. Wilson. "What we have in his case is not history but drama, a series of soliloquies, poetic in structure and beauty, which are attributed to the contemporaries of Jesus. . . . Here is a treatment, certainly unusual, possibly unique." John Haynes Holmes, the former minister of the Community Church in New York, wrote probably the most sincere appreciation.

> Readers of Mr. Gibran's earlier work *The Prophet*, published in many editions in this country and translated into more than twenty languages, will know what to expect in this book. Here is the same poet, with the same austere purity of thought, the same amplitude and beauty of phrase, the same wisdom, serenity and lofty vision. . . . [He] has attempted a unique and daring experiment. He has told the story of Jesus . . . episode by episode . . . somewhat after the fashion of Browning in *The Ring and The Book*. . . . It is as though a contemporary sat down, at a belated hour, to write another and different gospel.
>
> Nor is this as imprudent as it sounds, for Gibran is, secondly, a poet. It is difficult to describe the mystery of his verse. It has a simplicity which is disarming and yet a majesty which at times is overwhelming. . . .
>
> Now and again the poet dares a direct comparison with the New Testament, as in the parable of the shepherd in South Lebanon. I heard Mr. Gibran read this parable once and I thought then as I think now that it matches the Scripture standard.[16]

That December a feature article in the *Herald Tribune* by Claude Bragdon, architect and critic, further broadcast the myth of Gibran. The two had met at a fashionable tea party given by Henriette Sava-Goiu, later the wife of William Saxe, Gibran's lawyer. At the instigation of the poet, Bragdon inadvertently added to the romance of his background. "He was what is called in the East of 'fortunate birth,' for he was brought up in an atmosphere of love, beauty and abundance. Not only were his people affluent and cultured, but his mother's family, from far back, was the most musical in all the countryside." He went on to give currency to the quality of "Gibranism" that critics had been trying to define:

> Just what this word means Gibran's English readers will have no difficulty in divining: mystical vision, metrical beauty, a simple and fresh approach to the so-called "problems" of life. . . . His major interest is in *life*. He aims to discover some workable way of feeling, thinking, living, which shall lead toward *mastery*—how to serve the forces which enslave us until they are by us enslaved. . . . To him "nothing is higher than the human."

Apologizing for his favoritism, he closed,

> He is compact, strong, swarthy . . . he loves society as well as solitude, is
> an enjoyer of small things as well as great, of things physical as well as
> metaphysical; although he is austere in one sense, there is none of the
> ascetic about him. . . . I shall have to leave the description stand as it is
> with the assurance that he isn't, after all, quite like it—he evades me and
> escapes me, if you-know-what I mean.[17]

It is interesting to note that following the article, which was elaborately
illustrated with six Gibran drawings, came Gibran's celebration of Christmas,
a piece called "The Great Recurrence."

On January 5, 1929, Gibran was the recipient of tributes from the
Arabic–American colony. In honor of his twenty-five years as a contributor to
Arab letters, Arrabitah sponsored a testimonial dinner at the Hotel McAlpin in
New York. Among the eighteen speakers was Philip K. Hitti, who summarized
in English the pride that his countrymen took in the man and his works.

> The influence which Gibran exercises in modern Arabic literature can be
> measured, in a way, not only by the multitude of people who have been
> benefited by reading him but also by the big crop of would-be Gibrans,

Arribitah banquet, Jan. 5, 1929. Gibran is under the
portrait, to the right of the flag. (Authors)

quasi-Gibrans and Gibran-imitators who have in recent years, mushroom-like, sprung up and flourished all over the Arabic speaking world. So much so that you can hardly nowadays pick up an Arabic paper printed in Beirut, Cairo, Baghdad, São Paulo or Buenos Aires without finding somebody consciously trying to write Gibran-like. Of course, the esoteric, figurative, imaginative style . . . is not a new thing in Arabic literature. . . . But our hero of tonight, through his unmatched mastery of this art, through his pure and rich imagery, through his lofty and noble idealism, through his unexcelled diction and composition—be it in Arabic or in English—has become the father of a new school of thought all of his own. While others use empty words, are affected and artificial, Gibran unfailingly produces gems of thought and is always natural and sublime.

The toastmaster, William Catzeflis, presented Kahlil with gifts and tributes from organizations all over the country. Issued for the occasion was a specially bound edition of *al-Sanabil* (*The Spikes of Grain*), a commemorative anthology of his earlier works. "With visible emotion," as one observer described it, "Gibran then spoke of his pride in his race." [18]

The next day, his forty-sixth birthday, he was honored again, this time at the studio of the Mexican painter José Clemente Orozco. Worn from the formal dinner, he showed signs of an emotional breakdown. Alma Reed, the journalist and archaeologist who was Orozco's sponsor in New York, was a prime mover in the so-called Delphic group, a group of artists and writers involved with Oriental mystery religions and modern poetry of the "cosmology." Years later when she remembered the evening at the studio, she gave a rare glimpse of Gibran within that international coterie. Her account of his guarded friendship with Orozco highlighted the ties that the two artists shared. Champions of the peasant in their native lands, both were living in Manhattan. Their studios, Orozco's Ashram and Gibran's so-called Hermitage, were meeting places for thinkers, revolutionaries, and socialites. Uncomfortable labels had been stamped on their respective talents—the "Mexican Goya" and the "Blake of the twentieth century." Each artist cherished the friendship of a devoted American woman—Orozco, that of Alma Reed; Gibran, that of Mary Haskell.

"From the very beginning of their acquaintance," wrote Mrs. Reed,

> there had existed a well-controlled but active antagonism between the two artists. While Orozco maintained a discreet and somewhat ominous silence on the subject of Gibran's pictures, Kahlil would indulge in an occasional defensive fling at what he called "the violent art of Mexico." He asked me how I could endure living in the Ashram when Orozco's scenes of horror and tragic death covered the walls. Widely divergent views of art, however, did not seem to prevent their enjoyment of each other's company at their frequent meetings.

Their mutual regard was never more in evidence than at Gibran's birthday party, which launched the Ashram's international social activities for the New Year.

Among the members of the Delphic group who gathered that night were Sarojini Naidu, Syud Hossain, Mrs. Alice Sprague, the poet Estelle Duclo, the critic José Juan Tablada, and members of the New York Craftsman's Poetry Group, headed by Elizabeth Crittenden Percy. "Also present . . . was Judge Richard Campbell, genial New York host to visiting Irish intellectuals and patron of the Abbey Theatre Players. In high spirits, Orozco occupied his customary seat in a quartet composed of the poet Van Noppen, Claude Bragdon, and Dr. Demetrios Callimachos."

Mrs. Belle Baker, who was known for her public recitals of Gibran's poetry, read from *The Prophet*, the unpublished "Lazarus," and *Jesus, The Son of Man*. Gibran himself read from his early English works, *The Madman* and *The Forerunner*. He also read parables, which Orozco had always admired. Then, Alma Reed recalled,

in their appreciation of Kahlil's delightful fantasy, the guests kept pressing him for more parables and aphorisms. He continued to read in a voice that betrayed deep emotion, until at last he appeared no longer able to control his feelings. Abruptly he asked the company to excuse him. He rushed into the dining room where he sat down and wept. Shaken by sorrow, he explained to me between heavy sobs that as he read the parables he suddenly realized there was nothing in the much publicized books of his maturity to equal these spontaneous little works of his youth.

"What a tragedy," he said. "I have lost my original creative power. I know the truth and I face it. I can no longer write as I once did." I tried to console him by pointing out that creative periods are never duplicated in any true artist's life. I assured him that we all thought *The Prophet* and . . . Lazarus . . . as great as the parables, if in a different way. But he continued to weep and, as he sat there, Orozco joined us to see "what was wrong with the poor man." In a few moments, he succeeded in giving Kahlil a more hopeful outlook.

"Hombre," he said, as he held the poet in one of those cordial, familiar *abrazos* that pass between men friends in Spain and Latin America, "don't regret that your latest work is different from your early work. I find it good—in fact, wonderful—that you change. It would indeed be a calamity if you did not. Who knows—your new work may be even better than your old. Give it time. You are not the sole judge of its worth. Meanwhile, be happy that you are still young enough to grow—that you are not an ossified academician. To stagnate even at a good point is living death for the artist!" They talked for a little while and Kahlil regained his poise. Then together they walked back into the living room, their faces wreathed in smiles.[19]

The birthday program went on.

Unknown to the party, Gibran had shortly before learned from his doctor how seriously ill he was. He soon left for his Tyler Street refuge, but the disease he was trying to evade followed him relentlessly. By the end of January X rays revealed an ominous enlargement of the liver. But on the day he was scheduled for a thorough examination, all of the Gibrans gathered at the Tyler Street studio. Marianna was hysterical. Her impressions of the hospital were mingled with death and bereavement. Maroon and Assaf George were both loath to let him leave for what could end in a fearful operation or worse. And so he decided to avoid further diagnosis and turned away from medical help. The cirrhosis continued to ravage him, but meanwhile he tried to work. In March he wrote Naimy from Boston and continued the masquerade of a sick man who expected to recover—"My ailment is seated in something much deeper than muscle and bone. I have often wondered if it was not a state of health instead of illness." [20]

Publicly he would not admit to his weakened state, and in April he announced in *The Syrian World* the fall publication of "The Garden of The Prophet." But its organization continued to elude him. From Boston a month later he wrote Mary about his fatigue, distractions, and lack of resolve. Soon afterward he again abandoned the book. He turned instead to a work which, like so many of his last efforts, was conceived when he was young and ideas were flowing. In February 1911, back from Paris, he had asked Charlotte's opinion about an idea for a poem: "The earth-God has gone mad, and destroyed all life save one man and one woman. The earth is in the form and likeness of a skull—its hollows dry, riverbeds, gray—its surface cinders—gray. The man and woman are to water it with their tears, make it fruitful again and repeople the earth." Wrote Mary, "C. thought it too ghastly." [21]

Over the years the one earth god had become three gods; in 1915 the prologue depicted them as the "three moods one has in his different selves and at different times." Years later he wrote his editor at Knopf, Elizabeth Selig, that "the three Earth Gods in my poem symbolize the three primal elements in man, the desire for power, the desire to rule a greater world, and Love, a greater desire for Now and this Here." In 1923, after finishing *The Prophet*, he had reminded Mary of this old theme and read her the version as it then stood—three gods watching the drama of two human beings falling in love and one god's belief in man as the "fourth divinity." "It's perhaps the best *English* that I have written," he said. "I'm going to change every *thou* in it to *you*—as in *The Prophet* and my other English books—and I'll cut out some of the phraseology—shorten the way of saying things—and someday finish it and it will be a good thing." [22]

In the fall of 1929, after seeking solitude in Boston for almost ten months, Gibran felt able to return to New York and attend to the world he had neglected. The studio was becoming cluttered with magazines, books, drawings, and paintings, which he had always promised Mary would someday go to a little library he was planning for Besharri. It was time literally to put his house in order, and he wrote Mary of his situation and also of his intention to remain uninvolved with Middle Eastern political affairs.

> My responsibilities in the East are over. . . . It was in my heart to help a little because I was helped much, and I am glad of it all. The next time I shall measure, and measure well, the distance between my desire and my ability. . . . I have had the studio repainted. It is now so clean and shiney, and there is in it some kind of order. My Arabic work, my English work, my drawings and my paintings are so separated and arranged so I can put my hand on anything without going through the torture of finding it. And I am going on with the work; rather slowly to be sure, but with a certainty in my heart.[23]

He continued to force himself to work. In December "Snow," a poem he had been saving for "The Garden of The Prophet," appeared in the *Herald Tribune* magazine section, which was edited by his friend Madeline Mason Manheim. It was one of his last published pieces.

He tried hard to convince his closest friends that his condition was improving, and they in turn screened from the outside world his growing and secret dependency on alcohol—the only thing that killed the pain and hastened the disease. His drinking was not publicly acknowledged until 1934 when Naimy referred to it in his biography. Later Idella Purnell, a friend who had featured him in her Mexican poetry magazine *Palms*, drew a pathetic scene of the poet trying to entertain admirers early in 1930. The Chilean poet Gabriela Mistral had told her

> that there was one person she wished above all others to see in New York, Kahlil Gibran. I arranged the interview and acted as interpreter. . . . Gabriela was very humble with Kahlil; she addressed him throughout the evening as "maestro" and questioned him closely about eternal verities which she felt he understood better than she. . . . Because of her eager, child-like faith, I did not mention until 1948 . . . that during the course of the evening when her prophet excused himself for a moment and stepped behind an oriental screen, it was to take a swig out of a bottle which, in the unfortunately arranged mirror, didn't look like a medicine bottle! [24]

In March 1930 Gibran made the final copy of his will, which provided for Marianna, Mary, and Besharri. This along with his few securities he entrusted to Edgar Speyer. By July he was in Boston with Marianna, and his "Earth Gods" was in Mary's hands.

After her jottings about *Jesus, The Son of Man*, no apparent reference to

Kahlil had occurred in Mary's diary. She had carefully avoided mention of the few letters between them. All throughout 1929 the Minises had remained close to home, but by 1930 they started to travel again and by June were in New York. Always before in the city she had made some cryptic mention of him, but this time an entry for June 18 read only, "Jaunt to see Micheline." The next day was "quiet." In the afternoon her husband rested and she "went atop a V Ave. bus to 135th Street and back." Three weeks later, ensconced at their country home in Rockwood, Georgia, she began a series of coded entries at the top of each page. "L.1" was written beside July 12, "L–1–2" beside July 13. They became more complicated as the summer progressed—"*August 2. 8L–62–P3, PH.4*"—and could have easily been disregarded except for a note in her hand, added years later, under her August memoranda: "The pencilled cap. Letters & numerals atop of pp. Are a code to record work with K. Gibran's mss." [25]

With this realization, one is tempted to assume that if she did take that long Fifth Avenue bus ride she took it with Kahlil. They had often ridden together on the open-air bus in the past, and since her husband so objected to her visiting the studio it is probable that Kahlil gave her his manuscript on a double-decker bus ten months before his death.

While she was faithfully editing it, he tried to maintain a normal schedule in Boston. As he had the summer before, he refused all invitations and a note from his most beloved hostess, despite his constant assurances, showed real anxiety over his health. "I have thought of you so often," wrote Mrs. Robinson, "and asked my son to telephone and find out how you were. . . . All my F. D. R. family are hoping you are coming sometime. . . . I was greatly worried about you, dear Kahlil, and felt so helpless to be of assistance. Yours with real affection and concern." [26]

In Boston that summer of 1930 he was longing to recreate the days he and Marianna had spent by the sea. With the help of his cousin Zakia Gibran Diab, who located a house on the water near Boston, he and his sister stayed for two months at 122 Ocean Street in Squantum. He lingered there far into the fall, and although he wrote Knopf that he was working hard, he rejected his publisher's suggestion that he return and attend to some business. "It is not possible for me to go back to New York just now in order to have new negatives made of the original drawings of *The Prophet* for the Czechoslovakian publishers." [27]

Leaving Squantum was hard, but leaving his sister was harder. He commissioned Zakia to look for an apartment for her, some place within the city and near public transportation, where she could live a good and healthy life. By 1930 many of the South End's ethnic groups were dispersing into the greenbelts around Boston, and he insisted to a reluctant Marianna that it was time for her to leave the crowded streets. When a comfortable apartment was found across the street from Franklin Park, he stayed until mid-October to be sure that she was settled in, and he promised to return for Christmas.

On November 2 Mary wrote in her diary the final coded reference to her summer's work. With the editing accomplished, "The Earth Gods" went to press. Before the month ended Gibran signed another contract with Knopf. He knew there was no time now for "The Garden of The Prophet," for already the bloat of the past two years was giving way to a sudden wasting away of his body. He worked on some parables left over from *The Madman*. His last book was to be *The Wanderer*—"a man with but a cloak and a staff, and a veil of pain upon his face." When Christmas came he did not want Marianna to see him, and he stayed in New York, pleading work. By January he was confined to the studio, but to old friends he still insisted he was having a temporary setback. Only to May Ziadeh, just before leaving Squantum, had he admitted his agony while he waited for death.

> My health at present is worse than it was at the beginning of the summer. . . . This strange heart that used to quiver more than one hundred times a minute is now slowing down and is beginning to go back to normal after having ruined my health and affected my well-being. . . . I am, May, a small volcano whose opening has been closed. If I were able today to write something great and beautiful, I would be completely cured. If I could cry out, I would gain back my health. . . .
>
> Please, for God's sake, don't tell me, "You have sung a lot, and what you have already sung was beautiful." Don't mention to me my past deeds, for the remembrance of them makes me suffer, and their triviality turns my blood into a burning fire, and their dryness generates thirst in my heart, and their weakness keeps me up and down one thousand and one times a day. Why did I write all those articles and stories? I was born to live and to write a book—only one small book—I was born to live and suffer and to say one living and winged word, and I cannot remain silent until Life utters that word through my lips. I was unable to do this because I was a prattler. . . . However, my word is still in my heart, and it is a living and a winged word which I must utter in order to remove with its harmony the sins which my jabbering has created.
>
> The torch must come forth. Gibran.[28]

In mid-March *The Earth Gods* was published. He sent Mary a copy and added, "No, I have not been so very well but getting on nicely now. I am preparing another book, The Wanderer. . . . My publishers wish to bring it out next October. I thought it is going to be too soon after the publication of *The Earth Gods*; but . . . I must turn over the manuscript and the drawings within a month. I wonder if you should care to see the manuscript with your seeing eyes and lay your knowing hands upon it before it is submitted?" By March 31 she had received it. "*Saturday, April 4.* Reading The Wanderer since last Tuesday. It goes slowly." Two days later she sent her final message to Kahlil. "Ever so happy with The Wanderer—and will return it as soon as I possibly can." [29]

Easter Sunday came on April 5 that year, and he must have received her note the day before his last serious attack. Disregarding published reports of his final days, the following letter from Barbara Young to Margaret Lee Crofts seems to be the most spontaneous account of the events following Easter.

> For some weeks . . . he had been keeping [to] his bed most of the time, getting up and down, but seldom dressing as for the street. Easter evening I spent with him, and he was feeling much better, his voice was strong and he got up and walked about but was pitifully thin and with a drawn look in the darling face. I had a habit of calling him every day on the phone. Monday I called and his voice was fine, he said he had Syrian friends coming in the evening. Tuesday he sounded tired, but said he had letters to dictate. Then he would go to sleep early. I told him I would be out of town for the day Wednesday if he was *sure* he would be all right. He laughed and said "I *will* be all right."
>
> Thursday I called and his voice frightened me, so I went at once and found that the janitor's wife [Anna Johansen, who daily brought Kahlil his breakfast] had sent for Mrs. Jacobs that morning—Leonebel Jacobs, who used to live in the building. [Mrs. Jacobs, a painter, and her husband had long been his neighbors; she had exhibited her portrait of him.] They had brought a doctor and would take him to St. Vincent's Hospital Friday morning. I sat beside the precious being doing all that there was to do. He talked and was playful, perfectly himself, sleeping a little—and just a short time before the ambulance came in the morning there was a sudden change. Before he went downstairs he said—seeing my terrible anxiety— "Don't be troubled. *All is well*," and these were his last conscious words. He breathed away at eleven that night. I had wired Marianna but she did not get there until eight in the evening. [30]

Marianna, whose last long trip had been her journey to Boston in 1895, was helpless. It was up to Assaf George and Zakia Gibran to organize the details and accompany her to New York. When she arrived, a sea of foreign faces greeted her. The only one she knew was Kahlil, and by then he could not speak.

The news had spread. Two other American friends, Mrs. William Brown Meloney and Adele Watson, and Mikhail Naimy joined the vigil. Barbara became the intermediary for them. She told Naimy that when a nun had asked Gibran if he were a Catholic, he had gruffly answered, "No." By the time a pastor of St. Joseph's Maronite Church had arrived, Gibran was unconscious. At 10:55 P.M. on April 10, 1931, the poet was dead.

The myth became more alive than ever, but when he died few people remembered the man. Fewer still remembered the boy. But for the alertness of an elderly spinster eking out the Depression years in a Beacon Hill room, the boy would have been completely lost. Jessie Fremont Beale was then feeble and genteelly poor. But she remembered, and she wrote the one who was responsible for recognizing the boy's genius. Of all the letters, memorials, and tributes written over the next year, hers was the most knowing.[31]

January 11, 1932

Dear Mr. Day:

Miss Brown [the poet Alice Brown] passed on to me the Kalil clipping [*sic*]. That dear little Syrian boy did a lot of thinking! His interest in his fellowman was great. Did you see him when he was in Boston the year before his death, I think? He was visiting his sister on Tyler Street or somewhere in that neighborhood. The Congregational book store on Beacon Street was interested in keeping his books on sale. I hope sometime to read his Life of Christ.

Jessie Fremont Beale

"Nude Figure Kneeling among Clouds," watercolor.
(Courtesy Museum of Fine Arts, Boston, Gift of Mrs. Mary
Haskell Minis)

Epilogue

I often think of his death—and of myself after that. This Sunday night before I left for my train I lay by his side . . . looked at his profile . . . and thought again of the day when it will not turn to me." Mary Haskell had written this seventeen years earlier, and when she finally learned of Gibran's death she reacted as serenely as though she had been emotionally ready for years. Unaware of his last days, she had been hostess to a convention of the Southern States Arts League, but on Sunday, April 12, at 11:30 A.M. Marianna's telegram finally reached her. Two hours later Mary was on the northbound train.

Meanwhile Marianna had agreed to a two-day vigil in New York. On Saturday and Sunday the body lay at the Universal Funeral Parlor on Lexington Avenue, "where hundreds filed by . . . in a continual stream." [1] The next day Marianna brought it to Boston. Members of Arrabitah, Barbara Young, and a few other American friends accompanied the cortege.

Several metropolitan newspapers published romanticized obituaries. In an editorial the *Sun* identified Gibran as the "chief poet and artist of the Arabic-speaking peoples of the world." Within a week educational, religious, and other socially involved journals across the country were remembering him. "Kahlil Gibran is dead," was a lead article in the Ohio *Penitentiary News.*[2] Thousands consoled by his message of love began publicly and privately to pay tribute.

Within the small family circle there was fear that the Catholic Church would not allow a consecrated burial, for rumors of Gibran's refusal to receive the last rites had reached Boston. A few hours after he had met the train at South Station, Monsignor Stephen El-Douaihy assured a frantic Marianna that her brother would receive the proper ritual.

Mary arrived on Monday evening and went immediately to Marianna.

Friends and relatives gathered at South Station. Front row, left to right: Marianna Gibran, Zakia Gibran Diab, Maroon George, Rose Gibran, Amelia Parent. Back row: Barbara Young, Assaf George, Mike Eblan, N'oula Gibran, Stephen El-Douaihy. (Authors)

"Found her waiting for me. She had on her mother's . . . black lace scarf. We went by cab to 44 West Newton Street—Syrian Ladies Club, where Kahlil was laid out." To her he looked "stern, determined, kind, remote, concentrated." Among the "numberless Syrians" that night were the relatives about whom she had heard for years—N'oula and Rose Gibran, Maroon and Assaf George. She also saw for the first time his Arab and New York associates—Naseeb Arida, Najeeb Diab, Mikhail Naimy, Barbara Young, Adele Watson, and a writer, Gertrude Stern. Then they "persuaded [Marianna] to go down for a little supper—we called it a Last Supper for K.—and broke bread for him and sipped coffee." [3]

The next day hundreds of South Enders followed the cortege through the streets to the church of Our Lady of the Cedars. "And as the cortege passed by many dropped upon their knees . . . and the scores of traffic officers of Boston stood at salute as the flag-draped casket went by. It was impossible for the many hundreds of friends to find places inside the little church, and they waited in silence on the sidewalk during the service." [4]

Mary remarked on the ancient Syriac chanting and the scene at the hillside vault in Mount Benedict cemetery where Marianna cried "Habibi" ("Beloved") and several of Gibran's friends stepped forth and spoke. Calm and dry-eyed, she noted with impatience the words spoken by Gertrude Stern, who seemed to her "hysterical." At the end of the ceremonies she accompanied Marianna to her house and convinced her that legal complexities required her immediate presence in New York.

Two days later, shepherding Gibran's sister and his cousin Zakia to New York, Mary began the long process of establishing that the document which Kahlil had written in March 1930 and had given Marianna in July was his last will and testament. The provisions that he had made for Marianna and Mary differed little from his earlier wills:

> In the event of my death I wish that whatever money or securities Mr. Edgar Speyer has been gracious enough to hold for me should go to my sister Mary K. Gibran who now lives at 76 Tyler St., Boston, Mass.
> There are also 40 (forty) shares of the Fifty-one West Tenth St. Studio Association stock lying in my safe deposit box with the Bank of Manhattan Trust Company, 31 Union Square, New York. These shares are also to go to my sister. . . . Everything found in my studio after my death, pictures, books, objects of art, etcetera go to Mrs. Mary Haskell Minis, now living at 24 Gaston Street West, Savannah, Ga. But I would like to have Mrs. Minis send all or any part of these things to my home town should she see fit to do so.

Two more paragraphs turned this straightforward bequest into a legal nightmare.

> There are in addition to the foregoing two (2) bankbooks of the West Side Savings Bank, 422 Sixth Avenue, New York, which I have with me in my studio. I wish that my sister would take this money to my home town of Becharri, Republic of Lebanon, and spend it upon charities.
> The royalties on my copyrights, which copyrights I understand can be extended upon request by my heirs for an additional period of twenty-eight years after my death, are to go to my home town.[5]

Friends and relatives refused to believe that this largesse to Besharri was Gibran's true intention. News traveled fast, and in New York the three women were soon besieged by several interested parties who swore that he had personally assured them that they were mentioned in his will. Only Mary, who had heard his secret dream of helping his village, understood what he had wanted. On May 29, 1923, he had told her,

> If I had 50,000 dollars to spend, I could get three or four hundred acres in Lebanon . . . and make a model agricultural station of it. And Syria needs

that. For in Syria, as all over the world the people are leaving the country
. . . and many of the farms are abandoned. . . . Syria needs one man with
five or ten millions who will deliberately work for her growth and
development and consciousness of her self. I could get any amount of
money from the Syrians here—but I don't want to do that and go over
there. They would say, "Gibran the poet has turned farmer"—But I could
be back of the project if the money were my own—and really help it by
my interest.

There is a valley in the Lebanon—at the northern end of the
range—like a platter in shape—the mountains rise around the sides of
it—and from the far end a bold stream comes that waters it all. . . . The
Gibrans owned that valley—and it was let out in farms where people had
lived for ages. . . . But now all that is changed. All the Gibrans but one
have moved away. . . . The lands are sold . . . wild again and feeding no
one.[6]

On April 17 Mary, Marianna, and Zakia visited Edgar Speyer's office, where
his assistant Henry Lorch produced a copy of the 1930 will and confirmed that
he and an associate had witnessed it. The women, joined by Barbara, spent the
rest of the day in the studio, where no later document was found. A similarly
futile search was conducted on Saturday at the bank. Accompanied by Walter
Shea, assistant to Gibran's lawyer William Saxe, they found in his safe deposit
box only the West Tenth Street Studio shares.

For Mary, however, the search in the studio had been successful. She
turned up among the hundreds of papers the notebooks and manuscripts that
she had worked on, as well as several packets of her letters. By now Marianna
was distraught from the pressures of retrieving documents, manuscripts, and
correspondence. Faced with a studio crammed with printed material, she was
assaulted with the secret knowledge that she was helpless, and she was afraid
to admit the grim implications of illiteracy. So Mary agreed to accompany her
and Zakia to Boston, after she had received a tentative promise from the
confused Marianna that she would take her brother's body to Lebanon.

Back in New York early Monday morning, Mary asked Naimy to meet her
at a Thompson's Spa near Grand Central Station. She knew that he was
planning to write a biography in Arabic, and her paramount concern was that
he should understand Gibran's growth from her viewpoint. Naimy, who had
been close to Kahlil ever since the early days of Arrabitah, was completely
ignorant about his Boston years. For four hours she explained to him the entire
story of her sponsorship. From Thompson's Spa they moved on to the studio,
where their conversation continued. "Mischa asked many wonderful questions
about Kahlil," she wrote Marianna that night as she traveled to Savannah,
"and I was glad it is he who will write Kahlil's life for the Arabic speaking
world. I understood as we talked why Kahlil trusted him to write above even
other men friends." [7]

After Naimy left her she tried unsuccessfully to reach Barbara to ask her to help secure the studio. "My fears were for the safety of his writings, his drawings and paintings," she continued to Marianna. "First I went out and bought two rather large locked suitcases. Then I had [the caretaker] put latches on the windows and a padlock on the closet door. . . . Until 6 p.m. I worked alone. Then Naimy came back and we worked together till 9:55 . . . and now in the closet, locked up, are all the portfolios, . . . all the small treasures . . . all the manuscripts that we found; and in my 2 suitcases I put my notebooks that had been found on Saturday and *all* the letters, mine, his, and other peoples, locked them up and marked them with my name."

With the knowledge that immediate problems had been met and local tradespeople had been paid, Mary left feeling secure. But in Savannah she encountered difficulties in trying to oversee the estate from seven hundred miles away. Not only was she still editing "The Wanderer," but she was in constant communication with Saxe and had to act as intermediary between him and Marianna. Turning to Barbara for help, she soon sent her the keys and detailed instructions about organizing the studio and making it ready for dispersal. She also charged her to act as her representative in dealing with Knopf about "The Wanderer." Another responsibility that Barbara had agreed to assume was the answering of all expressions of sympathy.

Barbara also became the unofficial consultant for the several memorial services. On April 29 Charles Fleischer, whom Kahlil had met in November 1902 when he first visited Josephine, organized the American tribute, held at the Roerich Museum in New York. Since leaving Temple Israel in Boston ten years before, he had been an editor on the New York *American* and was well known as a lecturer and writer about the brotherhood of man. Gibran's passing "from our sight and ken," he said in tribute, "is really only a reclamation by the Eternal Spirit of the Cosmos. Therefore, we mourn not, because we can easily take as the keynote . . . his own words from *Sand and Foam*: "Mayhap a funeral among men is a wedding-feast among angels." Claude Bragdon and Syud Hossain delivered eulogies, Naimy read his elegy "The Mystic Pact," and Barbara read her "Valedictory." [8]

Death had raised Gibran's popularity among his countrymen to adulation. "The Arabic press of Egypt, Syria, Lebanon, Iraq and other Arabic-speaking countries eulogized him as they have no other Syrian emigrant before, and as they have few of the outstanding literary personalities of the homeland in recent times," boasted *The Syrian World*.[9] On May 24 two major memorial meetings were held within the Syrian community. The tribute in Brooklyn included official representation from several Arab countries; at the Municipal Building in Boston's South End one thousand Syrian and Lebanese gathered to remember their native son. Both services were marked by hyperbole.

Over the next six months Barbara became the leader of a cult that exalted

Gibran as a near-immortal presence and destroyed the man. From the beginning Mary had advised her to act objectively, especially with the surviving documents that described his life. Barbara had been at the studio when Mary's letters had been discovered, and when she first saw them and realized that they revealed his all too mortal side, she had recommended burning all the correspondence. This had so worried Mary that she had taken some letters to Savannah with her.

Within a few weeks, however, Mary had entrusted her with enough duties to ask her to replace the letters in the studio. "They should not be published," she wrote, "but certainly they should not be destroyed at this time." A week later Barbara reluctantly agreed to leave them untouched: "I am only fearing anything that may happen to you or to me. . . . You know what desecrations have been committed in the name of 'Literature' upon the most sacred remembrances and tokens of the loves of poets in the past. I have the feeling that we must put our wings about the rapture and tragedy in *this* past and keep it from all eyes, even our own." [10]

By the end of May Mary was becoming more dependent upon Barbara's physical presence in New York, and a decision was reached that she would live in the studio and catalogue all the material for appraisal. Both women were by this time anxious about Marianna's lack of resolution to go to Lebanon. In gratitude she had made Mary a hat after the funeral. She had also again asked for her judgment: "Mary Please advice me on this problem I recieved a Telegram from Bacherri Mt. Lebanon Syria asking for Khalil body to be buried in the cedars of Mt Lebanon I do not know what to do I hope that Khalil spirit will help you to tell me what to do." [11]

For over twenty years Mary had known how ardently Gibran had wanted to be buried in Lebanon. In June 1911 he had described the grotto chapel of Mar Mema "because it is there I came to myself, I learned, was shown. There I went oftenest and I loved it most. . . . Is it selfish, extravagant, for me to want to be buried in Syria? Is it a waste of a great deal of money?" "A gift to Syria," she called it. He also had told her and Charlotte about "the temple I'm going to have in my house." Then he had envisioned it as a square room of gray stone, "simple, with one narrow door like the Egyptians', and light from above only." Opposite the door would be an old Buddha from India, with a crucifix hanging above. On the right wall he planned to paint his own Prometheus and on the left Zarathustra. A Moslem prayer rug would cover the floor and on the rug would stand a silver incense bowl. He concluded, "When I die, of course my friends will bury me under the stones of the floor." Although Charlotte had teased him out of this conceit by calling it "his little egoist temple," Mary must have had these conversations in mind when she answered Marianna: "Yes, I think that the town of Becharri . . . has the right . . . idea. . . . It seems to me, as I know it seems to you, that it will be the most beautiful thing, for his body to rest in Lebanon. Let them have it for a shrine. And there should be also a collection there . . . some pictures, some treasures from the studio, some mementoes of the poet—in some fit (and fireproof) housing." [12]

By June 1 Marianna again was forced to go to New York, where she and Saxe were appointed administrators of the estate. The lawyer advanced her $2,000, half for charity in Besharri and half for expenses, and with this assurance she relented. "I am preparing for my trip with the Body it is a hard task for me," she wrote Mary on June 4. Two weeks later she confessed how she resented Barbara's encroachments: "Barbara mentioned about going with me but I talked her out of the idea and now she is not going." [13]

In some ways Marianna was more successful in avoiding Barbara's intrusions than was Mary. Early in May Mary had forwarded the finished manuscript of "The Wanderer" to Barbara: "You will be appalled I fear at the changes," she explained, "but they are just what I was doing while Kahlil was alive. . . . Always it has been a matter of making his English so idiomatic that it should not sound like the English of a foreigner. . . . It is ready for Knopf." Barbara rejected most of the work, returning the manuscript so that Mary might see how she had "gone back to the words of the blessed one." Mary finally accepted "her changes back to original . . . and wrote her to that effect." With this concession Mary seemed to surrender symbolically her control of the estate. But she still trusted Barbara and tried to convince a suspicious Marianna of her valuable service. "I feel sometimes as if I would have smothered or almost died, these days since Kahlil went, if Barbara were not there, loving everything of his, and so *able* to do what he would want done." [14]

Gibran's last journey began on the morning of July 23. A long line of cars accompanied the casket and the embarking party—Marianna, the Georges— to Providence, where speeches were read before several hundred Bostonians and New Yorkers, and Gibran's poems were read by Barbara. Music was played while the casket was lowered into the ship S.S. *Sinaia* of the Fabre Line, and at two the ship sailed.

In Lebanon preparations for the homecoming were just beginning. When the *Sinaia* arrived at Beirut on August 21 an official delegation boarded, and before a guard of honor the casket was transferred to a government launch. On shore the coffin was opened and the minister of education pinned on the poet's breast the decoration of Fine Arts conferred posthumously by governmental decree. From the port began the long march to the Maronite cathedral. "Walking in the procession were the Minister of the Interior and representatives of the High Commissariat, the French Admiralty and the army of occupation. Following them were representatives of the consular corps, the benevolent societies of all creeds, Christians, Moslems and Jews, and thousands of school children." [15] Archbishop Ignatius Mobarak blessed the body at the Cathedral of St. George, and that evening Charles Dabbas, president of the Republic, officiated at the government reception. Probably the most moved of all the speakers was Ameen Rihani, who sincerely recalled his friendship with Gibran.

The greatest public outpouring occurred the next day. The fifty-mile route from Beirut, along the coast, and up the steep mountain to Besharri was lined with townspeople. Twenty times the swelling cortege stopped for local ceremonies. Following the body streamed men chanting martial songs and improvising poetry, while wailing women beat their breasts. At a town near Gebail ancient Byblus ceremonies evoking ancient rites to the local goddess Astarte were enacted as young men in native dress brandished swords and dancing women scattered perfume and flowers before the hearse. Impressed by the evergreen arches erected at each town and by the companies of Bedouin horsemen, one vacationing American wrote back that the entire event appeared "more like a triumphal entry than a funeral." [16] After two more days of ecclesiastical and lay ceremony, the body remained at St. John's in Besharri, while Marianna and the Georges negotiated with the Carmelite Mission to purchase Mar Sarkis.

Accounts of the welcome were published in the New York *Times* on September 20. That his old friends must have appreciated the exaggerated

A ceremony honoring Gibran in Besharri. (Authors)

drama surrounding Gibran's return was evident in a Christmas letter Rose O'Neill sent Birger and Matta Lie in Norway: "Kahlil died this year. . . . I said, if *he* could lay down his heavy tools, any of us can lay down ours. For no one was so faithful to his tools. . . . I send you a clipping of his return to Lebanon. Isn't this charming about the young men in native dress engaging in sword-play before the hearse? How Kahlil would have loved that." [17]

Back in New York, Barbara's management of his affairs was becoming a Byzantine tangle. Her correspondence with Mary throughout the spring and summer of 1931 documents her methodical alienation of his Arab friends. Whenever Mary recommended consultation with one of the members of Arrabitah, Barbara would at once malign the suggested helper. She finally revealed her intentions: "I'd like to put *all the Arabic* away for five years—until I can do it myself." [18] But she was in no way prepared, linguistically or otherwise, to compile a life. When asked to prepare a short biographical sketch for the *National Cyclopedia of Biography*, she was forced to call upon Mary for simple biographical data. Mary sent information on his birthdate, his arrival in America, Day, the show at the Haskell School, and the fire at the Harcourt Studios. In July she generously sent extracts from the journal, clippings, and programs. By September Barbara, who was already receiving a monthly stipend from her, announced that she was ready to write a biography if Mary would advance her the cash.

This was not her only project. That month she retained enough ties in the Syrian community as a result of her friendship with Salloum Mokarzel to be hired as poetry editor of his *The Syrian World*. She also agreed to collaborate with Andrew Ghareeb, a young Syrian newspaperman, in his translation of some of Gibran's early poems, was writing a movie scenario based on *The Prophet*, and was planning a studio exhibit of Gibran's art. *A Study of Kahlil Gibran: This Man from Lebanon* was the first labor completed. This forty-five page brochure, published in November by Mokarzel's press, outwardly appeared to be the author's recollections of conversations with Gibran. It was in fact a carefully designed paraphrase of Mary's journal extracts and portions of early newspaper interviews.

By this time Barbara's uncritical approach was beginning to estrange American friends as well. To loyal friends like Witter Bynner and Marie Tudor Garland, both of whom inquired about pencil sketches Gibran had made of them, she quoted exorbitant prices. When a representative from the Newark Museum expressed interest in the drawing of Mayor Thomas Raymond (who had died in 1928), she asked $1,000. Those close to the poet—Alice Raphael Eckstein, Margaret Lee Crofts, Marjorie Morten, Adele Watson—were discouraged from participating in the forthcoming show. "Alice Raphael has offered to be of any possible service in regard to the paintings," she wrote Mary. "I will ascertain her fitness to advise. . . . Adele Watson knows *nothing*.

. . . There ought to be someone in the building. If not—*we will be led to the one.*" Marie El-Khoury, who had arranged for a death mask and hand to be made shortly after Kahlil had died, was also dismissed. "I don't feel like consulting El-Khoury. Something is constantly warning me against her and I think it is Kahlil's voice."[19] Not surprisingly, Barbara soon appointed herself manager and dealer.

In September Micheline Hardy died. Moved by this further loss, Mary told Barbara how close Micheline and Gibran had been. This was the kind of fact that Barbara easily dismissed. "I knew she had been a dear friend long ago. But I only knew her first name. Kahlil only mentioned her once or twice." Even Gibran's American publisher of thirteen years did not escape her scorn, and when Knopf did not respond to her idea of publishing a book of fifty drawings, Barbara announced she would find someone else. "I know good people in Scribner's and Macmillan's and Brentano's." She encountered little pressure from the Boston Gibrans while Marianna was in Lebanon. One

The death mask.
(Authors)

interested relative she called "another persistent and not always intelligent voice." [20]

By early January 1932 word finally reached the States that Marianna had negotiated the purchase of Mar Sarkis. Amid more eulogy and chanting, Gibran's body was moved from the Maronite church to its final resting place on January 10. Details of the exhibition at the studio were also completed that month. Mary was obliged to assure the estate's administrators that she would bear all expenses, and the show opened on January 21. Many of Gibran's closest associates were missing from the list of thirty-two patrons in the program. Salloum Mokarzel was the only Arabic name to appear, and William Saxe, his wife Henriette Sava-Goiu, and Ruth St. Denis were the only members of Gibran's coterie whom Barbara had deemed worthy of inclusion. On the front cover she quoted his own words: "If I should die tonight remember that one of the dearest dreams of my heart is this dream—that sometime, somewhere a body of work, perhaps fifty or seventy-five of the paintings shall be hung together in a gallery in a large city, where people may see them, and perhaps love them. Kahlil Gibran in 1930."

The author was indeed Gibran; however, he wrote the statement not in 1930 but in 1913, when Mary and he were making their financial arrangement. His version had begun, "One of the dearest dreams of my heart is this—somewhere, somewhen a body of work, say fifty or seventy-five pictures will be hung together in a museum." [21] Again, by carefully arranging his words to Mary, Barbara was becoming known as his confidante.

Barbara had promised that the show would be a financial success, but by February Mary was worried. She was committed to paying two rents at 51 West Tenth Street, monthly salaries to both Barbara and her daughter Margery Haney, and she had agreed to assume the large expense of having all the paintings and drawings photographed by the well-known firm of Peter A. Juley & Son. Ever pragmatic, she was depending upon sales to offset her expenditures, but Barbara unabashedly preferred to admire the appearance of the candlelit studio and the comments of interested visitors: "Isn't that better than selling pictures?" she asked Mary.

Mary was growing more uneasy, and on February 9 she noted, "Wrote Young we must open door for Naimy to do biographical work and work with mss. in studio." Two days later Barbara replied with a scathing attack. Just as she had pointedly informed Mary that Naimy had ignored the ceremonies when the *Sinaia* sailed, she now mentioned that he had not bothered to attend the exhibit. She accused him of a malicious intent. "If you could have seen his face and heard his voice as he said, 'Gibran was a very earthy person.' There was blackness in both face and voice. Every attitude such as, 'I too am famous in Syria,' and 'Now that I know what he never wanted me to know,' was

411

Barbara and her daughter in the studio at the time of the exhibit. (Photo Juley)

arrogant, and depreciative of one who was an archangel in comparison to him. . . . Dear Mary, the reason Naimy resents me, is that I read him too well . . . he began almost immediately after Marianna's and your departure to say very sweet and flattering things to me, and to practice his suave Eastern technique as though a covert love-making might accomplish my confidence. . . . He is not a good nor a trustworthy man, and I will never trust him with anything that was precious to Kahlil." [22]

Within a week and against her husband's wishes, Mary arrived in New York to straighten out the confusion. She immediately lowered the unrealistic prices of the work and with her sister Louise Haskell Daly arranged to offer some of it as gifts to New York and Boston museums. She soon realized that the Depression and a lack of response from many of Kahlil's old admirers prevented her ever recovering her considerable investment, so she decided to supervise the dismantling of the studio and to ready its contents for shipment to Lebanon. She met with Bryson Burroughs, curator of paintings at the Metropolitan Museum, who chose five representative drawings, and she arranged that the Boston Museum of Fine Arts and the Fogg Art Museum should receive some work. She saw Naimy at the studio, and with Salloum Mokarzel sorted and packed Kahlil's Arabic notebooks and library. When she left on February 28, she took with her the suitcases containing the notebooks and the Gibran–Haskell correspondence to look through before returning them to Barbara.

Chafing under Mary's reassertion of authority, Barbara complained petulantly and bitterly over her insistence that some of Gibran's work remain in the States, and inferred that her intentions were mercenary. "I have honestly tried to understand how you can let them go for money, but I can't. . . . You said in your letter that you would decide which pictures shall go to Becharre, but I feel certain that you will wish us to decide together . . . I believe I have a peculiar sense of what will be appropriate for the Monastery." However, Mary gave Mayor Raymond's portrait to the Newark Museum, and Barbara was forced to sell Witter Bynner his drawing for $50 and Marie Garland hers for $150.

Barbara still needed Mary, though, and at the end of March while the show was being dismantled she asked her to send her to Lebanon. "You are there in the midst of great plenty, your husband a rich man . . . who and what takes care of me? Nothing and nobody. It is a bitter situation to have to face, and you will have to forgive me if I cannot feel that is just." Mary's reply was sweet but firm: "And for the transportation of the collection to Becharre, I will get Mr. Minis to advance me from my allowance for the year to come. I had hoped to finance you, too, dear, in your work if the Fellowship [a Guggenheim Barbara had unsuccessfully sought] were not yours, but that too was through the pictures, and without them I cannot. I will see you back to your strength, and to your peace of mind until you reach England." [23]

The same letter revealed that Mary's attitude toward Barbara's chosen role as a martyr to Gibran's cause also had hardened. "Kahlil is in the care of Life," she advised her. "All of time still lies before him; he stands in his own power, and does not depend on the service or the upholding of another. Those who are ready will hear him, whether you serve him or not. . . . And one of the things one can learn from Kahlil is a certain firmness in self preservation. He was his own first responsibility . . . and I know of no instance where he sacrificed that responsibility to anyone else. . . . The whole tenor of his writing is to value one's self and to expect others to value themselves."

She also rejected Barbara's request that everything in the studio be shipped to Besharri. "I do not, however, give Becharre any unpublished English mss. nor the washes intended for publication but not yet published. Those, as I have previously written to you, I wish sent to me here, without reservation; also the mss. of the Wanderer, in all stages, and including the one that I first returned to you and which was not used for publication. . . . I wish for the present to assume complete responsibility in the matter of all unpublished English that he has left; . . . And for the present, I will not turn over anything more to you to do, nor to anyone else to do." [24]

By the end of June Mary had fulfilled almost all of her responsibilities. Thirty crates holding most of the studio effects along with 73 paintings, 366 drawings, and the hundreds of books from the library had arrived at Beirut on the *Sinaia*. Marianna was back from Lebanon, where she had been asked incessantly for money. Although Saxe reported that her income from the studio and stock shares was "meager," she was able to support herself. The one obstacle to Mary's serenity was Barbara, who since she had left for London in May had not heeded her advice.

In reply to Mary's request to send the English manuscripts to Savannah, Barbara had sent a trunk, but upon its receipt Mary noted that "The Wanderer" and the unfinished "Garden of The Prophet" were missing. In response to Mary's challenge that she would retrieve them by legal means, Barbara sent a complex story. Its main thrust was that the manuscripts had never been in the studio but had been in her possession at the time of Gibran's death. "He had so often said, 'Take this and keep it for me. Then I shall know it is safe.'" She continued,

> As to the letters which you took back to S. and sent back you yourself wrote me, and I believe I still have the letter, to destroy if I saw fit. I did so. The bulk of English letters I went through, returned literally several hundred to Marjorie Morten—hers were by far the great majority, a large packet to Hesper Le Gallienne; Leonora Speyer's she asked me to destroy, which I did, and the letters of several other people who wrote asking me to do the same. The Wanderer Ms. which you had worked on you also asked me to destroy. At first I did not do it. But when the book came out, it seemed the only thing to do. . . . I shall withhold nothing that was left in the Studio of Kahlil's work. But I shall keep everything that he had given with his own blessed hands into my keeping. I know this is as it must be. . . .
>
> Marianna has written me. I learn that she had a long conversation with Naimy, who is now in Syria, the day before she sailed. He is there for no good. But I am not afraid . . . Kahlil's work shall not suffer so long as I can listen to what comes to me in the deep stillness of the night.[25]

With these astonishing admissions, Barbara lost both Mary and Marianna's trust. "You have the power to be impersonal," Mary wrote her in August, "and therefore can see that all that was present to me was: my entrusting all to you; my request for a small but vital portion; my reception of but a futile fragment of that portion. Now I know, that that vital portion was not left to me. That knowledge removes all desire from me, to have it."

414

In July Marianna was trying to cope with Barbara's meddling and begged Mary to prevent her from going to Besharri. "It is worrying me to death of her idea of going to live in Becharri because she thinks she is going to make money there. It was a great mistake for me to go there myself." Three weeks later Marianna again repeated her suspicions: "Please write Barbara not to open the things. . . . Barbara thinks that I have a home or a place in Becharri but I haven't . . . and Mar Sarkis is not ready. . . . If Barbara wants to go to Becharri let her try for herself. I have tried the journey I wish to God, I did not go there at all."

Thereupon Mary sent a letter to the mayor and township of Besharri. In formally presenting the mementoes to the town, her words characterized her lifelong generosity: "This complete gift comes to Becharre in the name of Gibran himself, and of his sister Marianna—and I am but a loving instrument." In gentle terms she forbade Barbara's opening the crates. "It is not intended, however, that Mrs. Barbara Young, nor the authorities of Becharre, shall at present open these cases. Miss Marianna Gibran begs me to request that they be placed unopened at Mar Sarkis, and kept there unopened until she herself arrives there again or until she sends you authorization." [26] Upon learning of the prohibition Barbara abandoned her plans and returned to the States. Almost immediately correspondence between her and the two other women ceased.

Mary still was intensely interested in the Gibran estate, but she wrote Marianna of how her independence was now curtailed. "I can very, very rarely write because Mr. Minis is now far from well. . . . Nor have I ever become able to speak to him about Kahlil's affairs or my part in them—except that I told him in the winter that I had to go to New York to look after things. He consented unwillingly. . . . Only when I got back again he said he would never never let me leave him again; and except for a matter of life and death I think I never shall be able to." [27]

As for Marianna, the complex events of the past year had left her numb. Besieged by letters in Arabic and English that asked for information, for charitable donations, for personal reminiscences, she could handle none of them. Gradually she retreated from the public eye and answered nothing that came her way. In October 1933 word reached her that the townspeople of Besharri had waited over a year for her authorization to open the crates, and that on a pretext of "preventing them from mice" four men "made themselves the committee," opened the crates, and began charging the other residents admission to see the contents. [28] When visitors returned with disturbing reports of the neglected tomb and the deteriorating works of art, Marianna cried and did nothing.

Meanwhile Barbara relentlessly pursued her mission. In 1933 she published *I Go A-Walking*, a book of poetry illustrated by Gibran drawings which she owned. That year she also completed editing *The Garden of The Prophet* and wrote the foreword to Ghareeb's translation of *Prose Poems*, which appeared in 1934.

Isolated from what was happening, Mary wrote Marianna in March 1933, "It does not seem nearly two years ago when I had the telegram from you and went on to Boston. . . . Sometimes I feel like a river that has slipped out of sight and is running far down underground—quite shut away from that part that is flowing still above ground." Still she bore Barbara no malice and was more than charitable toward her editing of the sequel to *The Prophet*. "I have 'The Garden of The Prophet,' " she wrote Marianna in June 1934, "and am so glad Barbara could get it out, and I think she did a beautiful loving work in it. If you know about her, please tell me what you can."

She also asked Marianna's advice about the writings that she had rescued from the studio. "I have never had a word from Becharre in reply to all the things sent, nor to a letter I wrote the officials of the town. . . . Therefore I feel in the dark about Becharre, and dare not name Becharre to take charge of these remaining things." Revealing that she had originally named Barbara to care for the journals but that she now feared they might "go astray" with her, Mary suggested that Naimy or "one or more of his intimate friends"—Arida or Mokarzel—should be entrusted with them. "If you have any advice you can give me, dear Heart, please write it to me," she implored.[29] Suspicious of all literary endeavors, Marianna remained mute.

Still Mary secretly kept in touch with developments. In March 1935 Barbara opened a Gibran Gallery in the mezzanine of the Grand Hotel at Thirty-first Street and Broadway, advertising "50 examples of Gibran art . . . including wood carvings and manuscript examples," and Mary read of the event in the New York *Times*. She relieved her curiosity by charging one of her oldest friends to report on details of the exhibit. The woman sent back several brochures that described the "Barbara Young collection" and mentioned that "from time to time other examples from the collection of 150 items will be placed on view." A letter from Barbara which was forwarded to Mary revealed that she called herself "literary executor to this great poet and painter" and the collection "a private one, my own." Offering to tour the southern states, she had put together a package of lectures, poetry reading, art exhibition, and available photographic reproductions. "Do you know this Miss Barbara Young at all?" innocently inquired Mary's friend.[30]

By July 1936 Mary was intent on dispersing her personal belongings among her several nieces and nephews. While giving away jewelry and family books, she again begged Marianna for a word about the journal. "I think it would be better to keep Kahlil's letters for the Syrian men writers—especially since Barbara knows I have them, and has never written me to ask for or about any of them. I have not heard from her since her salary, which was necessary when she was taking care of things for him, stopped by degrees. . . . Maybe you would rather have me send Kahlil's letters to you, yourself, . . . I will do according to your wish, whatever it is. Only be sure that whoever is to write a real Life of Kahlil will get these. . . . Write me when you have made up your mind." [31]

On September 3, 1936, Jacob Florance Minis died at his summer estate in Clarkesville, Georgia. Within two weeks Mary was back in Savannah, had settled the preliminary details of the Minis home there, and had moved to a modest apartment of her own. For the next eight months she meticulously attended to the dispersal of two great houses while relishing her liberty. The following June she traveled to New York, where she went directly to the Grand Hotel. Finding no gallery there, she began to visit her old haunts. On the twenty-third she had lunch with George Kheirallah, an Arabic scholar who earlier that year had sent her his translation of *The Procession*. In a biographical sketch he had outlined Gibran's life, including his simple origins. It was he who gave Mary the present address of the Gibran Gallery. Later she walked to 572 Madison Avenue and peered inside. "I saw her and her Gibran exhibit through her window at night," she wistfully noted. "Chiefly photos but some fine originals." [32]

Her reunion with Marianna was more gratifying. In Boston she recorded two bits of information—"M. has no more faith in Barbara—nor do other Syrians seem to have—and Naimy is anathema." Naimy's fall from favor among the Boston Syrians was due to his treatment of Gibran in his Arabic biography, which had been published in 1934. When copies reached the United States, Arabic reaction was fierce. Naimy stated that when he returned to the East a year after Gibran's death, he found that his "friend had already become a mythical personality." Suggesting that his "long and close association with Gibran" enabled him "to learn of some intimate sides of his life which he jealously kept secret from others," he argued that his inclusion of "certain outspoken passages" was to prove that "the best and noblest in [Gibran's] life was his stubborn, incessant struggle with himself to cleanse his soul from all impurities." [33]

With an understanding of his obsession for privacy, however, it is clear that it was not Gibran who had shared his secrets with Naimy but Mary, when she had tried to encapsulate the life in a few hours in 1931. Equipped mostly with Mary's synopsis, Naimy created a portrait of a man who was torn between the "God pole" of spiritual aims and the "man pole" of physical weaknesses. But his conclusions and chronology were often flawed: Day's early influence was diminished; the first Boston show was labeled a failure; and Josephine's role was ignored, probably reflecting Mary's conversation. Mary's patronage and the introduction to Micheline were misdated by four years. The involvement of Charlotte and Rihani, the roles of Witter Bynner, Marie Tudor Garland,

and Rose O'Neill were all missing. What had most angered friends and relatives were Naimy's lurid revelations of Gibran's weakness for alcohol and women. (Although friendships between Gibran and many women can be established, the extent of the intimacy cannot be determined because of his personal reserve. After his death Mary wrote, "About personal letters and love letters, we all feel . . . as he felt himself. His private life must never be desecrated by an unreserve which he abhorred." [34]) Naimy embroidered accounts of imagined studio trysts and excessive drinking with made-up conversations. Rihani was the first of several Arabic writers to rally to Gibran's defense, and in a blistering letter published in a Beirut newspaper he accused Naimy of inventing entire scenes to support his man–god thesis and of sacrificing historical perspective. Joining in the fracas were loyal members of Arrabitah who implied that the biographer was motivated only by personal gain and jealousy.

Throughout the thirties this controversy remained unknown to the Western world. Gibran's popularity steadily increased despite the fact that most of his early friends were dead or forgotten. Day had died in 1933, Oppenheim in 1932, and Marie Garland, Rose O'Neill, and Witter Bynner were out of fashion by the end of the thirties. A few literati remembered his personality. "Kahlil Gibran as well as Tagore has expressed the mystical faith of Asia much better than Krishnamurti . . . ," recalled George Russell in 1938. "I do not think the East has spoken with so beautiful a voice since the Gitanjali of Rabindranath Tagore as in *The Prophet*." In the same year Claude Bragdon described Gibran in his autobiography *More Lives Than One*, but no major literary movement, no critic, and few anthologies recognized Gibran as worthy of discussion.

Yet in the publishing world the books' persistent sales were beginning to be noticed. *Publishers Weekly* was the first magazine to acknowledge the strange history of the public's fascination with all of Gibran's writings, and in 1938 debated why, in the middle of the Depression, *The Prophet* was enjoying its largest sale to date. With more than 12,000 copies sold in 1936 and over 13,000 sold in 1937, book merchandisers began to tote up numbers. The total on December 31, 1937, was 129,233 copies.

Although the Arab world knew about Mary's association with Gibran, few Americans even by the late thirties knew of her role. One of course was Jeannette Peabody, who in 1937 gave her one of Gibran's early drawings, "The Vision of Adam and Eve." "I thought you ought to have this because you loved him." [35] Cherishing these rare instances of recognition, Mary continued to live an active and full life. When she returned to Savannah that fall she sent Marianna a carton of documents, which included all the English manuscripts and unpublished material that remained in her possession. She kept the art, the journal, and letters, and on her infrequent visits to Boston she continued to press Marianna for advice about their disposition.

In May 1939 a graduate student at Columbia University learned of Mary's existence through Louise Haskell Daly. For the next three years Neva Marie Wright, who had completed a master's thesis on Gibran at the University of New Hampshire, conducted with her a correspondence mostly devoted to the intricacies of getting Naimy's biography privately translated. She spelled out the several versions of Gibran's life that were in circulation, even interviewing Marianna who by then skillfully withheld every fact of her family's origins from outsiders, and she implored Mary to verify or discredit the conflicting reports. Because she had met Gibran at a Denison House dinner given by Louisa McCrady, this young woman displayed a sincerity to which Mary responded. Before long she was helping her by secretly financing a literal translation of the biography, and in this way she at long last learned the reason for the furor about it. In Neva Wright she had an informant who regularly sent accounts of the individuals associated with Gibran, including Barbara Young. In 1937 *No Beauty in Battle*, another collection of Barbara's poems illustrated with Kahlil's drawings, had been published. Far from abandoning her projected "life," Barbara had finally traveled to Lebanon in 1939. Mary learned indirectly how disturbed she had been to see the condition of the collection. All the effects, paintings, drawings, and Arabic manuscripts were uncatalogued, untended, and unloved. The ever-growing royalties were abused and misused. Events of World War II had interfered with Barbara's plans to create some order to the material, and by the fall of 1939 she reluctantly returned to the States. Mary also heard about her management of a section devoted to Gibran at the Lebanese pavilion in the 1939 New York World's Fair.

In 1945 Barbara's "life" appeared. Entitled *This Man from Lebanon*, it differed little in style and content from the brochure. Again she used letters and extracts from the journal which Mary had sent her in 1931, and again it was implied that she herself had listened to the conversations. "He once said," she wrote, " 'I would like to see a modern city without street lights. The lower part of Manhattan would be as beautiful and terrible as the Pyramids of Egypt.' " She neglected to add that he had written this on December 8, 1921—to Mary Haskell.

Glossing over all the fin-de-siècle writers who had helped to mold Gibran, Barbara stated, "Various opinions of art and poetry were expressed by Gibran in writing at one time or another," and without citing that the year was 1913 and the statement a defense of Egyptian and Greek art, she proceeded to quote long passages of a letter to Mary. Quoting again, "The greatest literatures are probably the Arabic, or rather the Semitic—for I include the

Hebrew—the Greek and the English," she omitted the fact that he had said this to Mary in May 1923.

Barbara's omission of names and dates was more blatant than Naimy's. Except for a passing reference in the chronology Mary's name was unmentioned, and Naimy was obliquely referred to in relation to Arrabitah as "one, who shall be nameless, [who] has departed from the faith." [36] She wrote that Gibran drew Josephine during the period 1922–29 and seriously erred also in dating the Arabic works.

Altogether, Barbara stripped Gibran of all his human qualities. She touched upon no scandal within either his personal life or his family's history, and for this Marianna was grateful. In the intervening years she had come to regard strangers intent on learning about the family's origins as traitors to her brother's memory. Moreover, Barbara had dedicated the book to her, and so she was the first to forgive and forget. "Dearest Marianna," Barbara replied to Marianna's thanks, "it is such a long, long time since we have met or written, and so many things have happened to ourselves and to our world. I am happy too that you like the book about the beloved Kahlil." [37]

World War II and age were slowing down Mary, and although she served on the local ration board and volunteered at a kindergarten, her pursuit of the Gibran affair was diminishing. Still her resentment lingered for eight more years. She may have known about the exhibit of drawings that Barbara arranged at the Knoedler gallery in 1946, and if so she remained unmoved by it. A spate of translations of the early Arabic work began to appear soon after World War II. First published were Knopf's "authorized versions" of *Nymphs of the Valley* and *Spirits Rebellious* in 1948, and in 1950 came *A Tear and A Smile* with a tastefully written introduction by Robert Hillyer, whom Mary must have recalled as a young Harvard poet whom Kahlil had mentioned in the days of *The Seven Arts*. In 1949 she visited Boston and saw Marianna for the last time.

When the English edition of Naimy's biography appeared in the United States in 1950, she wrote an appreciative review of it for a local newspaper. Her satisfaction in being publicly identified with Gibran was manifest: "The talks between the two friends [Naimy and Gibran] are human documents rare to our Western experience. . . . These men honestly seek the All-Life, the Universal. They believe it can be found. And in this quest East and West do meet: a soldier of World War II told me that he had given the pocket-sized 'Prophet' to 22 of his buddies." The editor's note acknowledged that "Mrs. Minis, reviewer of this book, is the former Mary Haskell, mentioned in the book. She is the donor of the collection of Gibran's works at Telfair Academy of Arts and Sciences." [38]

With the manuscripts in Marianna's possession, and Mary's paintings and drawings at Telfair Academy, which she had once described to Kahlil as the place where as a child she had first discovered "Form," only one decision remained for her to make. At Christmas 1953 she described to Marianna her final disposition of "the greatest thing" she "had to give to life."

All those records and letters and papers I had and in Savannah my life was so occupied . . . I had not the time or the privacy to go over it all again. But since . . . I am alone because most friends are dead—I had some time; and 2 years ago I began to unpack all those papers, and the books—mostly Arabic—that Kahlil had given me. I decided to give them all to the Library of the University of North Carolina—one of the finest in the world. . . . Charlotte Teller's letters were included too—I had many from her— though now I do not even know whether she is alive. . . .

As you know, Marianna, Kahlil was reserved about his personal life, though he loved to talk about ideas and everything else. I wrote many things he said, in his own words—for I listened so attentively that for awhile I remembered perfectly—and as soon as he was gone, I would make my record—in a notebook dated. I filled about 15 large notebooks and 22 smaller ones. . . . The diaries were different, I knew, from anything else that was being written about Gibran and I knew that people who wanted to write about him would find in them much that had not been known or understood and that his conversation would add a great deal to what he wrote and would give a new and fuller understanding of much in his writings. Since, so many years later, I have read the diaries I realize that it is all true—so true, that I wish they could be published soon. . . . There are terrible things in the world today. But there are also fine and kind and brotherly things—more than we have known before. And Kahlil, in whatever form he wears now, may be influencing that increase of human goodness and that larger consciousness of the world.

She admitted that she too had made peace with Barbara. "I wrote to the N.Y. Times last spring and asked if she were alive. They sent me an address. I wrote and she answered—a dear little letter—I owe her one now." [39]

Unfortunately, Mary was unaware that Charlotte was alive in 1953. Since 1922 she and her family had lived in Europe until Gilbert Hirsch's death in 1926, when she had settled in Paris. There she brought up her son and wrote several books and articles, usually under the pseudonym John Brangwyn. Surviving the Depression and the occupation of Paris, she resolutely maintained her lifelong disdain for hypocrisy and philistinism. She died in Paris in 1954.

Barbara, Mary, and Marianna all died in nursing homes at advanced ages. In 1961 Barbara passed on at eighty-two. On October 9, 1964, Mary, whose last five years were blurred by senility and debilitating arthritis, died at the age of eighty-nine. Marianna lived a simple existence until 1968 when illness forced her to a nursing home. There she died in her eighty-eighth year on March 28, 1972.

As Mary had predicted, Gibran continued to fill a need whether or not he was served by those close to him. In 1957 the sale of the millionth copy of *The Prophet* (still identical in appearance to the first edition) placed it "among the most widely distributed books of the century." [40] Eight years later sales had reached two million copies. At each milestone journalists tried to explain the poet's popularity, but the perennial articles, misled by the misinformation in Naimy's book and repelled by Barbara's reverence, only dressed up the myth with new titles. For many, his lines became a sort of underground bible; thousands invoked him at the nuptial altar and at the death bier; in times of crisis his sayings were remembered by the young and old, by the clergyman and politician; sometimes they were plagiarized by rock groups. Critical scorn followed, but Gibran would have laughed at the inevitable puns—"Profits from the Prophet"—and at the Harvard *Lampoon* parodies—"Kahlil Gibrish."

But by the early seventies, when the four millionth book was sold, Westerners began to visit Besharri, and they gasped when they learned that "Kahlil Gibran is buried in a gift shop." [41] Ignoring the monastery where he actually lay, the volatile men of the Mountain had squandered, squabbled, and even shot one another for the golden fleece.

Yet despite the facts that the monument the Besharrians had promised was never built, that the museum they had planned was pushed into a small apartment skimmed from the royalties, that critics both Arabic and American could never fit him into a literary mainstream, Gibran's words still comforted, still lived. Gibran, a man whose life was almost forgotten, could indeed have taken comfort in words written by another poet over 2,000 years before:

> If Syrian, what the marvel then?
> stranger, we all have yet
> one fatherland, the world; all men
> one Chaos did beget. [42]

Notes

Abbreviations: JB, Jessie Beale; FD, Fred Holland Day; MH, Mary Haskell; KG, Kahlil Gibran; MG, Marianna Gibran; NG, N'oula Gibran; LG, Louise Guiney; JP, Josephine Peabody Marks; FP, Florence Peirce; CT, Charlotte Teller; BY, Barbara Young. References to MH are followed by the volume number of her papers at Chapel Hill: nos. 32–40 and 69–71 refer to the "line-a-day" diary, nos. 41–68 to the journal about Gibran. JP followed by a date refers to her journals at Harvard; JP followed by diary refers to her "line-a-day" diaries in the possession of Alison P. Marks. Unless otherwise stated, all JB, FD, and FP papers are at Norwood. Short titles indicate works listed in the bibliography. Bracketed dates are those supplied by the authors or by MH at a later time from envelopes.

1 POOR IN BESHARRI

1 Marianna Gibran quoted Gibran's statement repeatedly to the authors. However, at a time when he was redesigning the circumstances of his birth, his friend Mary Haskell questioned him closely as to how a French magazine had been able to publish 1883 as his definite birth year. He defensively retorted, "My birth year is known." MH 45, June 9, 1915.

In 1883 Lebanon, officially Mount Lebanon, was an autonomous province of Turkey. It was commonly known to Westerners as Syria, and Gibran himself sometimes referred to the Lebanese people as Syrians.

2 Jessup, in Riley, *Syrian Home-Life*, p. 97.
3 Karam, *Muhadarat fi Jubran Khalil Jubran*, p. 10.
4 Reminiscences, NG.
5 MH 41, Mar. 22, 1911.
6 John Carne, *Syria, the Holy Land* (London: Fisher, 1836), p. 47.
7 MH 59, Jan. 14, 1922.
8 MH 46, Nov. 1915.
9 Ms., 1913, MH folder 68.
10 MH 46, Aug. 27, 1915; 44, Aug. 29, 1913; 68, June 1, 1924; 46, July 26, 1916.
11 MH 45, June 30, 1915.
12 Abdul Latif Tibawi, *American Interests in Syria 1800–1901* (Oxford: Clarendon Press, 1961), p. 16.
13 Jessup, p. 158.
14 MH 41, Dec. 7, 1910.
15 Ibid.
16 Reminiscences, Zakia Gibran Rahme and NG.
17 The date of MG's first entrance to the U.S. was stamped on her passport when she returned to Lebanon in 1931 (Certificate of Registry, no. 27256, file R-33017).

2 A CITY WILDERNESS

1 Review of Robert Woods, *The Poor in Great Cities*, in *Wellesley Prelude* 7 (May 14, 1892): 391.
2 Woods, ed., *The City Wilderness*, pp. 7, 36, 37.
3 Quoted in ibid., p. 46.

4 *Twentieth Annual Report of the Associated Charities of Boston* (1899), pp. 56, 57.
5 Ibid., p. 58.
6 Ibid., p. 57.
7 Ibid., p. 58.
8 MH 46, Sept. 19, 1915.
9 Quincy School records now at Abraham Lincoln School, Boston, show that "Kahlil Gibran Jr. alias Assad" entered Sept. 30, 1895, and was discharged Sept. 22, 1898. The source of the name Assad is uncertain.
10 Woods, p. 40.
11 MH 46, July 23, 1916.
12 MH 41, Mar. 22, 1911; 45, Apr. 11, 1915.
13 MH 40, Apr. 29, 1911.
14 MH 46, Sept. 19, 1915.
15 MH 52, Sept. 3, 1920.
16 Woods, pp. 234–35.
17 Ibid., p. 235.
18 Ibid., pp. 184, 197.
19 Ibid., p. 111.
20 Emerson, "Self Reliance."
21 Woods, p. 245.
22 Paine, in *Twentieth Annual Report*, p. 2.
23 Ibid.
24 *Time and the Hour* 3 (Nov. 7, 1896): 15.
25 *Time and the Hour* 3 (Nov. 28, 1896): 7.
26 *Time and the Hour* 5 (June 12, 1897): 1.
27 *Twenty-Sixth Annual Report of the Boston Children's Aid Society* (1890), pp. 13–15.
28 Descriptive statement, p. 2, Denison House Papers, Schlesinger Library, Radcliffe College.
29 JB to FD, Nov. 25, 1896.

3 THE SICK LITTLE END OF THE CENTURY

1 *Statement of the Boston Children's Aid Society for the Year 1897*, p. 4.
2 The phrase was first used by LG in a letter to Louise Chandler Moulton, Sept. 10, 1894. See Parrish, "Currents of the Nineties," p. 95.

3 Louis Holman and Ferris Greenslet, "The Life of Fred Holland Day," 5 pp. typescript, Norwood.

4 *Lamb's Biographical Dictionary of the United States* (Boston, 1900), 2:390.

5 LG to FD, Mar. 6 and Jan. 30, 1890 (Parrish, pp. 108–09).

6 LG to FD, Jan. 25, 1892. (ibid., p. 120).

7 FD to Norton, Jan. 25, 1892 (ibid., p. 121).

8 Gosse to FD, June 27, 1894 (ibid., p. 167).

9 Cram, *My Life in Architecture*, p. 90.

10 *The Mahogany Tree*, May 28, 1892, p. 345.

11 Ibid., Jan. 2, 1892.

12 Ibid., Feb. 27, 1892, pp. 13–15.

13 Ibid., July 9, 1892, p. 411.

14 Cram, pp. 85–86.

15 *Letters of Louise Imogen Guiney*, 1:32.

16 Boston *Daily Advertiser*, Apr. 27, 1892.

17 Boston *Transcript*, Apr. 2, 1892.

18 *Publishers Weekly* 65 (Feb. 17, 1894): 213 (Parrish, p. 213).

19 Boston *Evening Transcript*, May 13, 1899, p. 9.

20 William Dana Orcutt, "Frederick Holland Day," *Publishers Weekly* 125 (Jan. 6, 1934): 54.

21 *Time and the Hour* 3 (Dec. 5, 1896): 16.

4 THE YOUNG SHEIK

1 FP to FD, "Tuesday evening," 1896.

2 FP to FD, "Tuesday evening" (the following week), 1896.

3 FP to FD, Jan. 9 [1897].

4 Day, "Photography Applied to the Undraped Figure," *American Annual of Photography and Photographic Times Almanac*, 1898, p. 192.

5 *Photograms of 1900* (London), p. 114.

6 Edward Steichen, *A Life in Photography* (New York: Doubleday, 1963), chap. 2.

7 Boston *Evening Transcript*, Mar. 9, 1898, p. 6.

8 Herbert White Taylor, "F. Holland Day," *Photo Era* 4 (March 1900): 77.

9 Sadakichi Hartmann, "A Decorative Photographer," *The Photographic Times* 32 (March 1900): 105.

10 MH 46, Aug. 27, 1915 and Apr. 21, 1916.

11 Sadakichi Hartmann, "A Purist," *The Photographic Times* 31 (Oct. 1899): 451.

12 [Minna A. Smith] to FD, Dec. 24, 1917.

13 [Minna A. Smith] to FD, Dec. 11, 1917.

14 Day, "Photography Applied to the Undraped Figure," p. 194.

15 FP to FD, May 21 [1897].

16 JB to FD, June 10 [1897].

17 JB to FD, July 9 [1897].

18 JB to FD, Sept. 22 [1897].

19 *Time and the Hour* 5 (July 17, 1897): 9.

20 JP Dec. 8, 1898.

21 Ibid.

22 Claude Bragdon, "Maeterlinck," *The Critic* 45 (Aug. 1904): 156.

23 MH 43, Sept. 7, 1912.

24 Maeterlinck, *The Treasure of the Humble*, trans. Alfred Sutro (New York: Dodd, Mead, 1899), pp. 52, 25, 79, 164.

25 *Time and the Hour* 6 (Dec. 4, 1897): 14–15.

26 Examples are in the authors' collection.

27 MH 46, Apr. 21, 1916.

28 *Annual Report of Trustees of the Public Library* (1896), p. 22.

29 Perry to FD, undated.

30 *Time and the Hour* 7 (Mar. 19, 1898): 11–12.

31 Boston *Evening Transcript*, Mar. 9, 1898, p. 6.

32 MH 46, Aug. 27, 1915.

33 Ibid.

34 MH 59, Apr. 18, 1922.

35 JP Dec. 8, 1898.

36 Perry to FD, Mar. 12, 1899.

37 *The Critic*, no. 841 (Apr. 2, 1898), p. 232.

38 Day, "Photography Applied to the Undraped Figure," p. 188.

39 Reminiscences of MG and interview with Zakia Gibran Rahme.

40 LG to FD, Aug. 4, 1898, Library of Congress.

41 FP to FD, "Monday evening," 1898.

42 LG to FD, Sept. 4, 1898, Library of Congress.

43 FP to FD, Sept. 10, 1898.

44 JP Sept. 15, 1898.

45 JP to FD, Sept. 15, 1898.

5 MISS BEABODY

1 JP to Frederick Sherman, 1898 (*Diary and Letters of Josephine Preston Peabody*, p. 5).

2 JP May 1891 (ibid., p. 10).

3 JP May 1893 (ibid., p. 18).

4 JP to Abbie Farwell Brown, Mar. 5, 1894 (ibid., pp. 29–30).

5 JP May 1894 (ibid., p. 35).

6 JP Mar. 1892, Jan. and Feb. 1893 (ibid., pp. 11–13).

7 JP diary, Aug. 1893, Nov. 1893 (ibid., pp. 14, 20).

8 JP diary, Feb. 1895; JP to Scudder, Sept. 7, 1894; JP diary, Oct. 1895, July 1895 (ibid., pp. 56, 48, 73, 59).

9 JP to Scudder, Jan. 6, 1895; JP diary, Apr. 1896 (ibid., pp. 55, 77).

10 JP to Scudder, idem.

11 JP Oct. 1895.

12 JP diary, May 1897 (*Diary*, p. 83).

13 JP Oct. 28, 1898, June 17, 1896.

14 JP June 17, 1896.

15 JP Feb. 1, 1897.

16 JP diary, Nov. 1903 (*Diary*, p. 187); JP May 30, 1897.

17 JP Dec. 19, 1898. Inscription translated by a Prof. Toy.

18 Karam, *Muhadarat fi Jubran Khalil Jubran*, p. 26.

19 Marun Abbud, *Judud wa Qudama*, pp. 118–21.

20 JP Oct. 5, 1898.

21 JP Nov. 22, 1898, Dec. 1, 1898.

22 JP Dec. 8, 1898.

23 JP Aug. 18, 1898.

24 JP Dec. 12, 1898.

25 JP Dec. 8, 1898.

26 JP to KG, first draft, Dec. 12, 1898.

27 JP Mar. 24, 1899.

28 JP to FD, Mar. 25, 1899.

29 JP Mar. 30, 1899.

30 MH 46, July 23, 1916.

31 Khalil S. Hawi, *Kahlil Gibran*, p. 87n.

32 MH 43, June 5, 1912.

33 Hawi, p. 87n.

34 MH 41, Apr. 19, 1911.

35 MH 41, Mar. 24, 1911.

36 Reminiscences, NG.

37 William M. Murray, "F. H. Day's Exhibition of Prints," *Camera Notes* 2 (July 1898): 22.
38 Ibid., p. 21.
39 LG to FD, Oct. 3, 1898, Library of Congress.
40 Day, "Portraiture and the Camera," *American Annual of Photography and Photographic Times Almanac*, 1899.
41 Hartmann, "Decorative Photographer," p. 105.
42 Murray, p. 21.
43 Alvin Langdon Coburn, "American Photographs in London," *Photo Era* 6 (Jan. 1901): 209–15.
44 Program, Royal Photographic Society, Nov. 8, 1900. A "Portrait of M. G. K. G." was reproduced in *American Annual of Photography and Photographic Times Almanac*, 1901, p. 36.
45 Hartmann, "Decorative Photographer," p. 103; Thomas Bedding, "The English Exhibitions and the American Invasion," *Camera Notes* 4 (Jan. 1901): 163; Hartmann, "Decorative Photographer," p. 106.
46 Robert Demachy, "The American New School of Photography in Paris," *Camera Notes* 5 (July 1901): 41.
47 FD to LG [Apr. 23] 1901, private coll.
48 *Kahlil Gibran: A Self-Portrait*, trans. Anthony Ferris, pp. 17–18.
49 MH 44, Mar. 10, 1914.
50 Ibid.
51 Ibid.

6   PEGASUS HARNESSED TO AN ASH-WAGON

1 JP Nov. 6, 1902.
2 JP Dec. 1901; JP to Scudder, 2 Sept. 1901 (*Diary*, pp. 161, 158).
3 JP May 1899; JP Oct. 1899 (ibid., p. 123).
4 JP Mar. 30, 1899; JP to Mary Mason, July 8, 1899.
5 JP Sept. 13, 1900.
6 Mason, *Music in My Time*, pp. 118–19.
7 JP Jan. 1, 1901; JP Sept. 1901 (*Diary*, p. 159), JP to Dreyfus, June 1902 (*Diary*, pp. 169–70).
8 JP to Mason, Sept. 30, 1899 (*Diary*, p. 122); JP Mar. 3, 1900.
9 JP Nov. 17, 1902. Dr. Charles Fleischer, in 1902 rabbi at Temple Israel, Boston, would serve as chairman of a memorial service for Gibran twenty-nine years later.
10 JP Nov. 21, 1902.
11 Ibid.
12 JP Nov. 25–27, 1902. JP later wrote a different poem titled "Return."
13 JP diary, Dec. 6, 1902.
14 JP diary, Dec. 1902; JP Dec. 13, 1902.
15 JP Dec. 13 and 22, 1902.
16 JP Dec. 13 and 23, 1902.
17 JP Dec. 23, 1902.
18 JP Jan. 1 and 12, 1903.
19 The month of KG's birth may have been December (*Kanoon I*) or January (*Kanoon II*). In transliteration the two are easily confused. He chose to observe his birthday on Twelfth Night, or Epiphany.
20 KG to Müller (JP Jan. 6, 1903).
21 FD to KG, Jan. 6, 1903, authors' coll.
22 *Twenty-third Annual Report of the Associated Charities of Boston* (1902), p. 23.
23 MH 44, Mar. 10, 1914.
24 JP diary, Jan. 15 and 19, 1903.
25 Ibid.
26 JP Jan. 26, 1903.
27 JP to Mason, Jan. 25, 1903.
28 Written in Arabic in a dummy copy of *Lyrics of Earth*, authors' coll.
29 JP Feb. 21, 1903.
30 JP Feb. 24, 1903.
31 JP Mar. 7, 1903.
32 JP to Mason, Mar. 9, 1903.
33 MH 44, Mar. 10, 1914.
34 KG to FD, Mar. 12, 1903.
35 JP Mar. 13, 1903.
36 JP diary, Mar. 16, 1903.
37 JP Mar. 24, 1903.
38 KG to FD, Apr. 13 and 10, 1903, authors' coll.
39 JP Apr. 19, 1903.
40 JP Apr. 21, 1903.
41 JP May 9, 1903.
42 Written in *Lyrics of Earth*.
43 *The Iris* (Wellesley College, Tau Zeta Epsilon Society, 1903), pp. 4–5.
44 JP May 30, 1903.
45 JP June 15, 1903 (*Diary*, p. 177).
46 JP June 9, 21, and 24, 1903.
47 KG to FD, authors' coll.
48 MH 44, Mar. 10, 1914.

7   A GALLERY OF GRACIOUS AND NOVEL HEADS

1 JP to LG, July 5, 1903, Dinand Library, College of the Holy Cross.
2 LG to FD, May 8, 1903, Library of Congress; LG to JP, summer 1903, Harvard College Library.
3 JP Aug. 9, 1903.
4 KG to FD, Aug. 20, 1903, authors' coll.
5 JP to Mary Mason, Sept. 6, 1903.
6 JP Sept. 13 and Mar. 23, 1903.
7 JP Aug. 21 and Sept. 13, 1903.
8 JP Sept. 13, 1903.
9 JP Sept. 24, 1903.
10 JP diary, Oct. 2, 1903; JP Oct. 21, 1903.
11 JP diary, Oct. 10, 12, 13, 1903.
12 JP diary, Oct. 23, 1903.
13 JP diary, Oct. 25 and 29, 1903.
14 Written in *Lyrics of Earth*.
15 Lilian Whiting, *Boston Days* (Boston, Little, Brown, 1902), pp. 352–53, 358.
16 Smith to FD, Nov. 3, 1903.
17 Draft of letter to JP, in *Lyrics of Earth*.
18 JP Dec. 25, 1903.
19 MH 35, Jan. 1, 1904.
20 JP Jan. 8, 1904.
21 JP Jan. 27, 1904.
22 JP diary, Mar. 11, 1904.
23 KG to FD, Feb.–Mar. 1904 (authors); JP diary, Mar. 9, 1904.
24 JP to Dreyfus, Apr. 29, 1904.
25 Boston *Evening Transcript*, May 3, 1904, p. 10.
26 MH 71, Aug. 16, 1937.
27 MH 41, Dec. 7, 1910; JP diary, May 10, 1904.
28 MH 35, May 10, 1904; 41, Dec. 7, 1910.
29 MH 60, Mar. 12, 1922.

8   STRANGE MUSIC

1 MH 41, Dec. 7, 1910.
2 Daly, *Alexander Cheves Haskell*, p. 173.

3 MH folder 67, undated.
4 JP diary, July 1903 (*Diary*, p. 179).
5 MH 32, Feb. 9, 1894.
6 *The Wellesley Magazine* 2 (Apr. 14, 1894):372–73; *Wellesley College News*, Nov. 1896, p. 110.
7 MH 32 Feb. 12, 1894.
8 MH 32, Jan. 27, 1894.
9 MH 35, May 14, 1904.
10 MH 35, May 17–20, 1904.
11 JP diary, May 23, 1904.
12 MH 35, June 17, 1904.
13 JP diary, June 27, 1904; MH 35, June 29, 1904, and "Addresses."
14 JP July 1, 1904; JP diary, July 5, 1904; JP July 8, 1904.
15 JP diary, July 4, 1904; JP July 1, 1904.
16 Ms. attributed to T.R. Barabee, "My Expaients [*sic*] with Mrs. J.M. Sears," July 1904, Norwood.
17 N.D. [probably Najeeb Diab], "The Story of a Young Syrian," *The Independent*, Apr. 30, 1903, pp. 1007–13.
18 Goryeb, "Jubran Khalil Jubran."
19 *A Tear and A Smile*, pp. 30–31.
20 JP Diary, Oct. 15, 1904.
21 KG to FD, Oct. 29, 1904, authors' coll.
22 Boston *Herald*, Nov. 12, 1904, pp. 1, 5; Boston *Sunday Herald*, Nov. 13, 1904, p. 6.
23 Boston *Sunday Globe*, Nov. 13, 1904, p. 5.
24 JP to Müller, Nov. 19, 1904, Wellesley College; JP Nov. 26, 1904; JP to FD, Nov. 27, 1904; MH to FD, Nov. 28, 1904, Norwood; KG to MH, undated.
25 JP diary, Feb. 23 and Mar. 1, 1905.
26 Draft of letter written in a dummy copy of *The Arabella and Araminta Stories*, authors' coll.
27 *A Tear and A Smile*, pp. 32–34.
28 Ibid., pp. 5–8.
29 JP diary, Apr. 7, 1905.
30 *A Tear and A Smile*, pp. 58 ff.
31 Illuminated birthday greeting, coll. Lionel P. Marks.
32 Copy at Harvard College Library.
33 JP diary, July 1, 1905.
34 Ibid.
35 JP Nov. 29, 1905.
36 MH 36, Aug. 20, Sept. 17, Oct. 31, 1905.
37 MH 36, Nov. 10, 1905; 37, Apr. 23, 1906.
38 KG to JP, Dec. 25, 1905; JP Dec. 28, 1905.
39 JP Jan. 11, 1906.
40 MH 37, Feb. 11, 1906; JP Feb. 13, 1906.
41 KG to JP, Feb. 25, 1906.
42 JP diary, Feb. 27, 1906.
43 JP May 2, 1906; JP diary, May 30, 1906.
44 JP *Diary*, p. 202; "Wedding Book," coll. Alison P. Marks.

9   THE PRESENCE OF A SHE-ANGEL

1 KG to NG, Dec. 28, 1905, authors' coll.
2 See Khalil al-Ghurayyib, "Dhikrayat Jubran, al-Rihani, Rustum, Mukarzil, al-Ghurayyib," pp. 6–10, and "Marakat al-Tan al-Samit bayn Jubran wa Asad Rustum," pp. 56–63.
3 *A Tear and A Smile*, pp. 38–41.
4 Ibid., pp. 18–20.
5 Ibid., pp. 82–84.
6 Ibid., pp. 14, 24.
7 Ibid., p. 60.
8 Ibid., pp. 27, 37, 44.
9 al-Ghurayyib, pp. 57–58.
10 *A Tear and A Smile*, pp. 89–91.
11 JP to FD, May 3, 1907.
12 MH 32, Sept. 3, 1894.
13 MH to Armstrong, Aug. 23, 1906.
14 MH 38, Jan. 11, 1907.
15 On Dewey, Richard Teller Hirsch to authors. Review of *The Cage, The Independent*, Mar. 7, 1907, pp. 559–60.
16 MH 38, Dec. 7, 1907.
17 CT to MH, Nov. 25, 1907.
18 MH 39, Jan. 27, 1908, and partly in space for Dec. 7, 1910.
19 KG to MH, Jan. 26, 1908.
20 MH 39, Jan. 30, 1908; JP Jan. 30, 1908.
21 CT to MH, [Jan. 29] 1908.
22 MH 43, Dec. 25, 1912.
23 MH 39, Feb. 4, 1908.
24 MH 39, Feb. 6 and 11, 1908.
25 KG to Goryeb, Feb. 12, 1908 (*Kahlil Gibran: A Self-Portrait*, pp. 22–24).
26 KG to MH, between Feb. 17 and 20, 1908.
27 KG to MH, Jan. 28, 1908; CT to MH, Jan. 22, 1908.
28 CT to MH, Mar. 7 and Jan. 22, 1908.
29 MH 39, Mar. 26, 1908.
30 Copies at Chapel Hill.
31 KG to MH, Mar. 25, 1908.
32 MH 39, Mar. 27, 1908.
33 MH 39, Mar. 28, 1908.
34 KG to MH, Apr. 2, 1908.
35 MH 39, Apr. 17, 1908.
36 MH 39, Apr. 26, 1908.
37 KG to MH, Jan. 28, 1908.
38 MH 39, Apr. 1908.
39 MH misc. folder, visit on May 5, 1908, recorded on May 10.
40 Ibid.
41 Ibid.
42 MH 39, May 19, 1908.
43 *A Tear and A Smile*.
44 KG to FD, June 1908, authors' coll.

10   LE JEUNE ECRIVAIN ARABE

1 MH misc. folder, May 5, 1908.
2 KG to MH, July 9, 1908.
3 KG to MH, July 13, 1908.
4 KG to MH, July 29, 1908.
5 *Al-Arwah al-Mutamarridah*.
6 MH 52, Aug. 20, 1920.
7 Goryeb, in *Al-Arwah al-Mutamarridah*, p. 7.
8 KG to NG, March 15, 1908 (*Kahlil Gibran: A Self-Portrait*, pp. 27–28).
9 KG to Goryeb (ibid., p. 32).
10 KG to MH, July 4, 1909.
11 KG to MH, Oct. 2, 1908.
12 KG to MH, Nov. 8, 1908.
13 KG to MH, Oct. 2 and Nov. 8, 1908.
14 KG to MH, Oct. 2, 1908.
15 MH 39, Nov. 20 and 27, 1908.
16 KG to MH, Dec. 20, 1908; Jan. 2, 1909.
17 KG to MH, Jan. 2 and Feb. 7, 1909 (the latter formerly at Chapel Hill, now missing).
18 MH to KG, April 3, 1909; KG to MH, April 17, 1909.
19 *A Tear and A Smile*, p. 137; KG to MH, Jan. 6, 1909.
20 KG to MH, Mar. 14, 1909; MH to KG, Apr. 3, 1909.

21 KG to MH, Feb. 7 and Apr. 17, 1909 (the former now missing).
22 KG to MH, Mar. 14, 1909.
23 *Wellesley College News*, May 26, 1909, p. 4.
24 CT to MH, June 2, 1909.
25 KG to MH, June 23, 1909.
26 Ibid.
27 KG to MH, July 31, 1909.
28 KG to MH, Mar. 14 and June 23, 1909.
29 Frances Keyzer, "Eugène Carrière," *The Studio* 8 (Aug. 1896): 135–42.
30 KG to MH, Oct. 20, 1909.
31 KG to MH, Nov. 10, 1909.
32 KG to MH, Dec. 19, 1909.
33 Ibid.
34 James, introd. to Loti, *Impressions* (Westminster, 1898), p. 4.
35 KG to MH, May 10, 1910.
36 Hawaiik, *Dhikrayati ma Jubran, Baris 1909–1910.*
37 MH 44, Sept. 2, 1914.
38 MH 44, Sept. 3, 1914.
39 KG to MH, May 10, 1910.
40 Ibid.
41 *Les Mille Nouvelle Nouvelles*, p. 142.
42 Rihani, "A Syrian Symbolist," *Papyrus* 8 (Feb. 1908): 18–22.
43 KG to MH, Dec. 19, 1909, and Aug. 30, 1910.
44 KG to MH, Aug. 30, 1910.
45 KG to MH, June 5, 1910, and Dec. 19, 1909.

11 TALK OF MARRIAGE

1 MH 40, Nov. 1 and 6, 1910.
2 MH 41, Apr. 17, 1911.
3 MH 45, Apr. 10, 1915.
4 MH 40, Nov. 7, 1910.
5 MH 41, Mar. 1, 1911.
6 MH 40, Nov. 16, 1910; 41, Nov. 28, 1910.
7 KG to MH, Jan. 2, 1909.
8 MH 41, Dec. 7, 1910.
9 MH 40, Dec. 10, 1910; 45, Apr. 10, 1915; 60, Mar. 12, 1922.
10 MH 41, event of Dec. 11 entered under Dec. 10, 1910.
11 MH 40, Dec. 26 and 30, 1910.
12 "We and You," in *Treasury of Kahlil Gibran.*
13 MH 40, Jan. 4, 7, and 24, 1911.
14 MH 40, Jan. 28, 1911.
15 MH's annotation on letter from John Polos to her; ibid.
16 MH 41, Jan. 28, 1911.
17 MH 41, Jan. 26, 1911; 45, June 20, 1915.
18 MH 41, Dec. 21, 1910; 40, Feb. 3, 1911.
19 MH 40, Feb. 17, 1911.
20 MH 41, Mar. 17 and 22, 1911.
21 MH 41, Feb. 18, 1911.
22 MH 41, Feb. 19, 1911.
23 MH 41, Feb. 21 and 22, 1911.
24 MH 41, Mar. 22, 1911; 60, Mar. 12, 1922.
25 MH 41, Mar. 17 and 22, 1911.
26 CT to MH, Nov. 1, 1910.
27 MH 41, Mar. 1 and 9, 1911.
28 MH 41, Apr. 6, 1911.
29 MH 41, Apr. 14, 1911.
30 Ibid.
31 MH 41, Apr. 15, 1911.
32 Ibid.; MH 45, Apr. 11, 1915.

33 MH 41, Apr. 17, 1911.
34 MH 40, Apr. 18, 1911.
35 CT to MH, Apr. 18, 1911; MH 41, Apr. 20, 1911.
36 KG to MH, Apr. 27 and May 1, 1911.
37 KG to MH, May 1 and 2, 1911.
38 KG to MH, May 2 and 16, 1911.
39 CT to MH, May 15, 1911.
40 KG to MH, May 16 and 22, 1911.
41 MH 40, May 28 and 24, 1911.
42 MH 41, June 1, 1911; CT to MH, May 20, 1911; MH 41, June 3, 1911.
43 MH 40, June 3, 1911.
44 MH 45, Apr. 11, 1915.
45 MH 41, June 7–24, 1911.
46 MH 41, June 6, 1911.
47 "K.G.'s memo of bequest and direction in case of his death," MH 41, June 7, 1911. The final version is missing.
48 MH 41, June 10 and Mar. 29, 1911.
49 MH 40, June 24, 1911.

12 A CONCORD SOUL

1 KG to MH, June 28, 1911.
2 MH 42, Dec. 20, 1911.
3 MH 42, Dec. 2, 1911.
4 MH 42, Sept. 16, 1911.
5 Ibid.; KG to MH, Sept. 22, 1911.
6 MH 42, Sept. 26, 1911.
7 MH 42, Sept. 29 and 28, 1911.
8 MH 42, Oct. 1, 1911.
9 MH 41, Feb. 26, 1911.
10 Ibid.
11 MH 42, Sept. 29, 1911.
12 MH 42, Oct. 2, 1911; events of that day partly entered under Sept. 30.
13 MH 40, Oct. 6 and 7, 1911.
14 MH 40, Oct. 9, 1911.
15 MH 40, Oct. 10 and 19, 1911.
16 MH 42, Oct. [13] 1911; 41, Feb. 14, 1911.
17 MH 42 [Oct. 1911] and Oct. 17, 1911.
18 MH 40, Oct. 19 and 21, 1911.
19 MH to KG, Oct. 18, 1911.
20 MH to KG, Oct. 28, 1911; MH 40, Oct. 23 and 24, 1911.
21 MH 40, Oct. 25–26 and 29, 1911.
22 MH to KG, Nov. 3, 1911.
23 KG to MH, Nov. 10, 1911.

13 A THREE-CORNERED FRIENDSHIP

1 CT to MH, Oct. 18, Nov. 3 and 10, 1911.
2 CT to MH, Oct. 23 and Nov. 3, 1911.
3 KG to MH, Oct. 31, 1911; CT to MH, Nov. 27, 1911.
4 MH 40, Nov. 6 and 17, 1911; 42, Nov. 31, 1911.
5 MH 42, Nov. 31, 1911.
6 MH 42, Dec. 1, 1911; 40, Dec. 2, 1911; CT to MH, Dec. 10, 1911.
7 CT to MH, Dec. 13, 1911.
8 MH 42, Dec. 21–22, 1911, and Jan. 2, 1912.
9 MH 40, Dec. 23 and 24, 1911.
10 MH 40, Jan. 1, 1912; 42, Jan. 2, 1912.
11 MH 42, Jan. 2, 1912.
12 MH 40, Jan. 21, 24–25, 1912.
13 MH 40, Jan. 5 and 13, 1912.
14 MH 40, Jan. 17 and 31, Feb. 1, 1912.

15 MH 42, Jan. 28, 1912.
16 KG to MH, Jan. 26 and 31, 1912.
17 CT to MH, Jan. 21, 1912.
18 CT to MH, Feb. 2, 1912.
19 MH to KG, Feb. 8, 1912.
20 MH 40, events of Feb. 23 entered under Feb. 19, 1912.
21 MH 40, events of Feb. 23 entered under Feb. 20, 1912.
22 MH 40, events of Feb. 23 entered under Feb. 25, 1912.
23 MH 40, Feb. 26, 1912; CT to MH, Mar. 1 and 2, 1912.
24 MH to KG, Mar. 8, 1912; KG to MH, Mar. 10 and 24, 1912.
25 MH 42, Apr. 3, 1912; 40, events of Apr. 4 entered under Mar. 19, 1912.
26 MH 40, events of Apr. 5 entered under Mar. 30–31, 1912; 42, Apr. 5, 1912; 40, Mar. 23, May 20 and 17, 1912; 42, Apr. 5, 1912.
27 MH 42, Apr. 5, 1912; 40, Apr. 14–15 and Mar. 27, 1912.
28 MH 40, Mar. 27, 28, 24–25, 1912.
29 MH 40, Mar. 31-Apr. 2, 1912.
30 MH 40, events of Apr. 6 entered under Apr. 3–5, 1912.
31 MH 40, events of Apr. 7 entered under Apr. 8, 1912; 42, Apr. 7, 1912.
32 MH 60, Mar. 12, 1922.
33 CT to MH, Mar. 17, 1912, and Jan. 12, 1909.
34 MH 40, events of May 31 entered under May 29, 1912; CT to MH, May 23 and 30, 1912.
35 MH 40, events of first and second weeks in June entered under June 27–28, 1912.
36 MH 40, events of June 10 entered under June 22–24, 1912.
37 MH 40, undated events of June entered under June 13–14 and May 31, 1912.
38 CT to MH, June 25, 1912.
39 MH to KG, Aug. 16, 1912; MH 40, events of Sept. 7 entered under Aug. 26–27, 1912.
40 MH 43, Sept. 7, 1912; 40, retrospective account of the summer and fall written on Nov. 9 and entered under June 30, 1912; MH to KG, June 25, 1912.
41 CT to MH, July 1912, undated; MH 40, retrospective account written on Nov. 9 and entered under July 9–11, 1912.
42 MH 60, Mar. 12, 1922.

14 THE BIRTH OF A LEGEND

1 MH 40, events of Sept. 7 entered under Aug. 6, 1912.
2 MH 40, events of Sept. 7 entered under Aug. 6–9, 1912.
3 CT to MH, May 21, 1912.
4 KG to MH, Sept. 29, 1912.
5 KG to MH, Oct. 22, 1912.
6 MH 43, Dec. 1, 1912; KG to MH, Dec. 7, 1913.
7 MH to KG, Nov. 27, 1913.
8 MH 40, May 2–3, 1912; MH to KG, Sept. 22, 1912.
9 MH to KG, Nov. 10, 1912.
10 MH to KG, Mar. 15, 1912; KG to MH, Dec. 19, 1913.
11 MH 40, events of Nov. 9 entered under Oct. 3, 1912; 43, Nov. 9, 1912.
12 Ibid.; MH 44, Jan. 10, 1914.
13 CT to MH, Apr. 13, 1912.
14 KG to MH [Feb. 16] 1913.
15 MH 44, Dec. 21, 1913.
16 MH 44, June 20, 1914.
17 KG to MH [Feb. 14, 1913]; MH 40, events written at "the end of April" entered under Feb. 6, 1913.

18 MH 43, Apr. 6, 1913; 40, events written at "the end of April" entered under Feb. 12, 1913.
19 KG to MH, Feb. 18, 1913; ibid.; KG to MH [April 30, 1913].
20 MH to KG, Easter 1913 and May 5, 1912.
21 MH 43, June 26, 1913; 40, events of Apr. 6 written at "the end of April" and entered under Mar. 20–21, 1913.
22 KG to MH, May 27, 1913.
23 Ibid.
24 MH to KG, May 11, 1913.
25 Ibid.
26 KG to MH, May 16, 1913.
27 MH 43, June 25, 1913.
28 MH 43, June 23, 1913.
29 MH 43, June 25, 1913.
30 MH to KG, July 13, 1913, and June 20, 1912.
31 MH to KG, June 18 and July 6, 1913.
32 MH 44, Aug. 29, 1913.
33 MH 44, Aug. 31, 1913.
34 Ibid.
35 MH 60, Mar. 12, 1922.
36 MH 44, Sept. 2, 1913.
37 Ibid.
38 MH 44, Sept. 3, 1913.
39 MH 44, Aug. 30, 1913.
40 MH 44, Sept. 3, 1913.

15 CONQUERING NEW YORK

1 MH folder 69, "from letter of Sept. 21, 1913."
2 MH 43, undated, ca. June 1912.
3 Bliss, The Religions of Modern Syria and Palestine, pp. 121–22.
4 MH 45, June 11, 1915.
5 MH to KG, Feb. 6, 1912; MH 43, June 12 and 15, 1912.
6 MH 40, Feb. 8, 1912.
7 MH 43, Sept. 7, 1912.
8 Ibid.
9 MH 43, June 10 and Dec. 27, 1912.
10 MH 43, Apr. 6, 1913.
11 Ibid.; KG to MH, Feb. 8, 1912; MH to KG, Apr. 19, 1913.
12 MH to KG, Dec. 7, 1913; KG to MH [Nov. 4, 1913].
13 MH 44, Dec. 21, 1913.
14 MH 40, Oct. 27, 1913.
15 KG to MH [Jan. 19] and Jan. 21, 1914.
16 KG to MH, Jan. 21 and Feb. 8, 1914.
17 MH to KG, May 1914; KG to MH [Mar. 8, 1914].
18 JP diary, Feb. 24–28, 1914.
19 KG to MH [Mar. 8, 1914]; MH 44, Sept. 6, 1914.
20 Inscribed copy at Chapel Hill.
21 MH 44, June 20, 1914.
22 Ibid.
23 CT to MH, Apr. 7, 1914.
24 MH 44, Apr. 26, 1914.
25 MH 44, June 20, 1914.
26 MH 44, original letter inserted into journal before Mar. 10, 1914.
27 MH to KG, July 13, 1914.
28 KG to MH, July 22, Aug. 7, and July 23, 1914.
29 MH to KG, Aug. 12, 1, and 16, 1914.
30 MH 44, Aug. 30, 1914.
31 MH 44, Sept. 2, Aug. 31, 1914.
32 MH to KG, Dec. 8, 1914.
33 KG to MH, Dec. 13, 1914.

1 MH 45, Dec. 19, 1914.
2 MH 44, June 20, 1914.
3 MH 45, Dec. 20, 1914.
4 MH 45, Dec. 28 and 29, 1914.
5 MH 45, Dec. 28, 1914.
6 MH 45, Dec. 19, 1914; CT to MH, Dec. 25, 1914.
7 MH 45, Dec. 27 and 20, 1914. KG may have been referring to the painter Kenneth Miller.
8 See bibliography.
9 Chamberlain to KG, Dec. 24, 1914, Chapel Hill; see bibliography.
10 Hamilton, "Woman's Influence," p. 8.
11 McBride, N.Y. *Sun*, Dec. 20, 1914, p. 2.
12 McBride, N.Y. *Sun*, Apr. 1, 1917, sec. 5, p. 12.
13 MH 44, Apr. 26, 1914.
14 KG to MH [Jan. 11, 1915].
15 MH to KG, Jan. 12, 1915.
16 MH to KG [Feb. 2, 1915].
17 CT to MH, Feb. 28, 1915.
18 MH to KG, Feb. 23, 1915; KG to MH [Feb. 9, 1915].
19 MH 45, Apr. 11, 1915; KG to MH [Mar. 14, 1915]; MH 45, Apr. 11, 1915.
20 KG to MH [Mar. 14, 1915].
21 MH 45, June 3, 1915; MH to KG, Apr. 22, 1915.
22 MH 45, June 3, 1915.
23 MH 45, June 11, 1915.
24 MH 45, June 20, 1915.
25 MH to KG, mid-July 1915.
26 KG to MH, Aug. 2, 1915; MH to KG, Aug. 9, 1915.
27 MH to KG, Aug. 9, 1915; MH misc. folder.

17 THE WAR YEARS

1 MH 45, June 20, 1915.
2 MH 43, June 22, 1913; KG to MH [June 21, 1918].
3 KG to MH [May 16, 1912].
4 KG to MH [Oct. 22, 1912, and June 10, 1913].
5 MH 43, June 22, 1913.
6 KG to MH, July 10, 1913.
7 "Min Sharit Masihi Il al Muslimin," *al-Funoon* 1 (Nov. 1913): 37–39; "Bad Thawrah" [The Beginning of Revolution], *as-Sayeh*, Mar. 9, 1914 (clipping, MH folder 71); KG to MH [Mar. 8, 1914].
8 MH 44, Aug. 30, 1914; MH to KG, Oct. 2, 1914; KG to MH [Oct. 14, 1914].
9 MH 45, Nov. 14, 1914.
10 MH 45, Dec. 20, 1914.
11 *Syria during March, 1916* (London: Causton, 1916), p. 22. A collection of articles reprinted from the Cairo journal *Mokattam.*
12 KG to MH [May 26 and 29, June 29, 1912].
13 MH 46, Apr. 23, 1916.
14 MH 46, July 21, 1916.
15 Ibid.; MH 46, Oct. 5, 1916.
16 "Dead Are My People," *Treasury of Kahlil Gibran*, pp. 339–45. Originally appeared as "Mata Ahli," *al-Funoon* 2 (Oct. 1916): 385–90.
17 KG to Bynner, Sept. 22, 1916, and undated, 1916, Harvard College Library.
18 MH 46, Oct. 5, 1916.
19 Hoffman et al., *The Little Magazine*, p. 87; MH 46, July 23, 1916.

20 KG to Oppenheim, July 12, 1916, and undated, 1916, N.Y. Public Library.
21 MH to KG [Nov. 2, 1916].
22 KG to MH [Nov. 5, 1916].
23 MH 47, Nov. 11, 1916.
24 MH 47, Feb. 3, 1917.
25 MH 46, Sept. 19, 1915; 47, Nov. 12, 1916.
26 KG to MH [Jan. 3 and 12, 1917].
27 KG to MH [Jan. 31, 1917].
28 MH 47, Feb. 3, 1917.
29 MH 47, events of Feb. 4 entered under Feb. 3, 1917.
30 Ibid.; Raphael, "The Art of Kahlil Gibran," pp. 531–34.
31 MH 46, Aug. 27, 1915; 47, May 9, 1917.
32 McBride, N.Y. *Sun*, Apr. 1, 1917, sec. 5, p. 12.
33 MH to KG, Apr. 18 and [22–23] 1917.
34 F.W. Coburn, "Syriac Suggestions," Boston *Sunday Herald*, Apr. 22, 1917, p. 5; MH to KG, Apr. [22–23, 1917].
35 MH 47, May 9, 1917; KG to MH [Apr. 20, 1917].
36 Letter sent Apr. 5, 1918, to Theodore Roosevelt, reel 271, Roosevelt Collection, Harvard. The letterhead reads, "Syria–Mount Lebanon League of Liberation."
37 MH 47, July 27, 1917; MH to KG, Apr. 22, 1917; CT to MH, June 2, 1918.
38 Lowell to Oppenheim, July 30, 1917, Harvard College Library.
39 MH 47, Nov. 10, 1917.
40 MH 47, Dec. 26, 1917.
41 MH 47, Dec. 28, 1917.
42 MH 42, Jan. 12, 1918.

18 THE PROPHET

1 KG to Robinson, Jan. 26, 1918, Harvard College Library.
2 KG to MH [Feb. 5, 1918].
3 MH to KG, Feb. 10, 1918; KG to MH [Feb. 26, 1918].
4 MH 47, Mar. 22, 1918.
5 MH 47, Mar. 24, 1918.
6 Ibid.
7 MH 47, Sept. 10, 1917, and Mar. 24, 1918
8 MH 43, June 12 and Sept. 7, 1912.
9 MH 43, Apr. 6, 1913; 44, Sept. 4, 1914; 45, Nov. 14, 1914.
10 MH 46, Apr. 21, 1916.
11 MH 47, July 30, 1917.
12 KG to Bynner, Mar. 15, 1918, Harvard College Library.
13 KG to MH, Apr. 10, 1918.
14 Interview, Mrs. Hope Garland Ingersoll, July 24, 1973.
15 KG to MG, undated, authors' coll.; KG to MH [Apr. 14, 1918]; MH to KG [Apr. 17, 1918].
16 MH 47, May 6, 1918.
17 Ibid.
18 Ibid. The line from *The Prophet* is from the Knopf edition, p. 18.
19 MH 47, May 11, 1918; MH to KG, May 12, 1918.
20 KG to MH [June 5, 1918].
21 MH 46, Nov. 13 and Dec. 30, 1915.
22 MH 47, May 11, 1918.
23 MH to KG, June 20, 1918.
24 KG to MH [July 11, 1918].
25 KG to MH [May 29, 1918]; MH to KG [June 4, 1918]; KG to MH [June 21, 1918].
26 KG to MH [May 21, 1918]; MH 48, Aug. 31, 1918.
27 MH to KG, June 20 and [June 4] 1918.

28 MH 45, June 20, 1915; 42, Apr. 3, 1912; MH to KG, June 20, 1918.
29 MH to KG, July 24 and [Aug. 9] 1918.
30 KG to MH [Aug. 26, 1918].
31 MH 48, Aug. 31, 1918.
32 Copy at Chapel Hill; KG to MH, Nov. 7 and 17, 1918.

19 ARRABITAH: THE PEN-BOND

1   MH to KG [Oct. 27, 1918].
2   *al-Funoon* 2 (Sept. 1916).
3   MH 44, June 20, 1914; 43, Sept. 7, 1912; 44, Sept. 4, 1914; 46, Sept. 19, 1915.
4   See bibliography.
5   Gollomb, "An Arabian Poet in New York," N.Y. *Evening Post*, Mar. 29, 1919, book sec., pp. 1, 10.
6   See bibliography.
7   Copeland to FD, Dec. 29, 1918; S.A.L. to FD, Dec. 16 and 27, 1918.
8   CT to MH, Dec. 23, 1918.
9   *The Madman*, pp. 7–8.
10 MH 48, Jan. 11, 1919.
11 Marguerite Wilkinson, *New Voices* (New York: Macmillan, 1929, rev. ed.), pp. 27, 95.
12 MH 49, Apr. 14, 1919; 51, Apr. 20, 1920.
13 MH 49, June 9, 1919; 50, Nov. 9, 1919.
14 "Story of Rose O'Neill: An Autobiography," pp. 204, 198 (unpublished ms., coll. The International Rose O'Neill Club, Branson, Mo); O'Neill to Lie, undated, coll. Jean Cantwell, Branson, Mo.
15 O'Neill to Lie, undated, coll. Jean Cantwell.
16 McCanse, *Titans and Kewpies*, p. 137.
17 MH 50, Nov. 8, 1919; KG to MH, May 4, 1919.
18 MH 49, Apr. 14, 1919.
19 MH 49, July 30, 1919; "To Young Americans of Syrian Origin," *The Syrian World* 1 (July 1926): 4–5 (orig. pub. in *Fatat-Boston*); MH 49, July 30, 1919.
20 MH 49, Aug. 4, 1919; 50, Nov. 8, 1919.
21 MH 50, Dec. 30, 1919; KG to MH [Apr. 10, 1920].
22 MH 50, Apr. 17, 1920; *The Nation* 110 (Apr. 10, 1920): 485–86.
23 Cook, introd., Gad, *Johan Boher*.
24 MH 50, Apr. 17, 1920; 51, Apr. 18 and 20, 1920.
25 MH 45, Nov. 15, 1914; "Fajr al-Amal ba'ad Layl al-Ya's," *al-Funoon* 1 (July 1913): 50–70.
26 Naimy, *Kahlil Gibran*, pp. 154–55.
27 Catzeflis, introd., Kheirallah, *The Life of Gibran Khalil Gibran and His Procession*.
28 MH 51, May 20 and 22, 1920; KG to MH [July 19, 1920].
29 "Lakum Lubnanukum wa Li Lubnani," *al-Hilal* 29 (Aug. 31, 1920): 19–23; MH 52, Aug. 31, 1920.
30 MH 52, Aug. 20 and 25, 1920.
31 MH 52, Sept. 3, 1920; 53, Sept. 7, 1920.
32 MH 52, Sept. 7 and 14, 1920.
33 MH 53, Sept. 14 and 7, 1920.
34 KG to MH [Dec. 12, 1920].

20 NO LONGER APART

1   MH 54, Dec. 18, 1920; KG to Zaidan, published in *al-Hilal* 42 (Mar. 1934): 517.
2   MH 54, Dec. 18, 1920.

3   MH 54, Dec. 30, 1920.
4   MH 55, Feb. 5, 1921.
5   Ibid.
6   MH 56, Apr. 1924.
7   Naimy, *Kahlil Gibran*, pp. 168–69, 171.
8   Naimy to KG, July 21, 1921, authors' coll.
9   MH 57, July 12, 1921.
10 MH 57, July 22, 1921.
11 MH 56, Aug. 8, 1921.
12 MH 58, Aug. 12, 1921.
13 MH 58, Aug. 30 and Sept. 6, 1921.
14 MH 58, Sept. 9, 1921.
15 MH 58, Jan. 5, 1922.
16 MH 58, Jan. 9, 1922.
17 MH 59, Jan. 12, 1922.
18 MH to KG, Oct. 10, 1920.
19 MH 59, Jan. 14, 1922.
20 MH to KG, Feb. 22, 1922.
21 MH 60, Mar. 12, 1922.
22 MH 59, Apr. 14, 1922.
23 MH 60, Apr. 25, 1922.
24 Ibid.; MH 59, Apr. 21, 1922; 53, Sept. 17, 1920.
25 MH 61, May 5, 1922.
26 MH 61, May 9, 1922.
27 MH 61, May 19, 1922.
28 MH 62, May 30, 1922.
29 MH 60, Apr. 25, 1922.
30 MH 62, June 16, 1922.
31 MH 61, May 12, 1922; 62, Sept. 11, 1922.
32 MH 62, Sept. 11, 1922.
33 MH 63, Oct. 7, 1922.
34 MH 64, Nov. 12, 1922.
35 MH 64, Nov. 9 and 12, 1922.
36 MH 65, Dec. 31, 1922; review is from *Poetry* 18 (Apr. 1921): 40–41.
37 MH 65, Jan. 2, 1923.
38 KG to MH, Mar. 19 and Apr. 17, 1923.
39 MH 66, June 16, 1923.
40 MH 66, June 23 and 16, 1923.
41 MH 66, May 30, 1923.

21 COSMOPOLITE

1   MH 66, May 27, 1923.
2   MH 57, July 12, 1921.
3   Draft of letter, KG to Ziadeh, July 25, 1919, authors' coll.
4   KG to MH, Feb. 27, 1919.
5   MH 65, Dec. 31, 1922.
6   *al-Mashriq* 15 (1912): 315–16; Cheikho, "Badai Jubran Khalil Jubran wa Taraifuh," pp. 487–93; Fuad al-Bustani and Edward Sab, "Bayn al-Mashriq wa al-Saih," pp. 910–19.
7   MH 53, Sept. 7, 1920.
8   Knopf, *Portrait of a Publisher*, 1:48.
9   MH to KG, Oct. 2, 1923.
10 MH 67, Nov. 26, 1923.
11 Marjorie Allen Seiffert, *Poetry* 23 (Jan. 1924): 216–18; MH 68, June 5, 1924.
12 MH 67, Nov. 26, 1923.
13 MH 68, June 1, 1924.
14 MH 67, May 21, 1924; 68, June 18, 1924.
15 MH 67, Nov. 26, 1923; 68, June 18, 1924.
16 MH 68, June 5 and 18, 1924.
17 KG to MH, Aug. 28, Sept. 4, and Oct. 3, 1924.

18 The first mention of "C.J." occurs in a letter from MH to KG. Oct. 19, 1924.

19 KG to MH, Oct. 16, 1924.

20 MH to KG, Mar. 19, 1925; KG to MH [Mar. 30, 1925]; KG to MG, undated, authors' coll.

21 KG to MH, July 8, 1925.

22 Bercovici, *Around the World in New York*, p. 40; KG to Bynner, Apr. 14, 1925, Harvard College Library; Bynner, "Kahlil the Gibranite," pp. 43–46.

23 KG to MH, Sept. 4, 1924; MH 67, May 23, 1924.

22 THE LAST YEARS

1 Young, *This Man from Lebanon*, p. 85.

2 Hossain, editorial, *The [New] Orient* 2 (May–June 1924): 96; Hossain, "Between Ourselves," *The New Orient* 2 (July–Sept. 1924): vii; MH 57, July 22, 1921.

3 MH 44, Apr. 26, 1914; 46, Nov. 14, 1915.

4 MH 69, May 10 and 13, 1926.

5 KG to Mr. Smith, May 22, 1926.

6 KG to MH, Apr. 29, 1909; MH 41, Dec. 7, 1910, and Apr. 19, 1911; 44, Jan. 10, 1914; 41, Apr. 19, 1911. *Shahbi* means "my people"; KG may have said, "wood of my people," meaning "cedar," and MH may have misheard or left out the phrase.

7 MH 54, Dec. 30, 1920; 66, May 27, 1923.

8 Young, *This Man from Lebanon*, pp. 100, 103.

9 MH 61, May 19, 1922; 62, May 26, 1922.

10 MH to KG, Apr. 14, 1927.

11 MH 69, Mar. 8–Apr. 4 and Apr. 30–May 2, 1928.

12 Unpublished poems, MH folders 68 and 69 (the first poem is dated Dec. 15, 1927; the second is undated and is titled "The Sufist"); KG to MG, undated, authors' coll.

13 KG to Assaf George, undated, authors' coll.

14 KG to Robinson, Sept. 11, 1928, Harvard College Library.

15 KG to MH, Nov. 7, 1928.

16 See bibliography.

17 Bragdon, "A Modern Prophet from Lebanon," pp. 16–18.

18 Philip K. Hitti, "Gibran's Place and Influence in Modern Arabic Literature," *The Syrian World* 3 (Feb. 1929): 31–33; unsigned article probably by Mokarzel in idem., p. 52.

19 Reed, *Orozco*, pp. 67, 102–05.

20 Dr. Samuel A. Robins to Dr. William J. Brown, Jan. 24, 1929, reporting results of roentgen examination; reminiscences, Mary Kawaji, Zakia Gibran, NG; KG to Naimy, Mar. 26, 1929 (*Kahlil Gibran*, p. 260).

21 MH 41, Feb. 24, 1911.

22 MH 45, June 3, 1915; KG to Selig [Nov. 25, 1930]; *The Earth Gods*, p. 14; MH 66, June 16, 1923.

23 KG to MH, Nov. 8, 1929.

24 Purnell, "Gift for Mimicry Harms Poet," review of English edition of Naimy's biography, Los Angeles *Daily News*, Nov. 4, 1950, p. 9.

25 MH 70, June 18 and July 12–Aug. 2, 1930.

26 Robinson to KG, July 28, 1930, authors' coll.

27 KG to Mr. Stimson, Sept. 18, 1930.

28 *The Wanderer*, p. 3; KG to Ziadeh, 1930 (*Kahlil Gibran: A Self-Portrait*, pp. 91–92).

29 KG to MH, Mar. 16, 1931; MH 70, Apr. 4, 1931; MH to KG [Apr. 6, 1931].

30 BY to Crofts, Apr. 23, 1931, authors' coll; JB to FD [Jan. 11, 1932].

EPILOGUE

1 MH 44, Jan. 11, 1914; "The Last Days of Gibran," *The Syrian World* 5 (Apr. 1931): 21.

2 "A Seer Departed," N.Y. *Sun*, Apr. 15, 1931, p. 37; Ohio *Penitentiary News*, Apr. 18, 1931, p. 1.

3 MH 70, Apr. 13, 1931.

4 Young, "Gibran's Funeral in Boston," *The Syrian World* 5 (Apr. 1931): 23–25.

5 Authors' coll.

6 MH 66, May 29, 1923.

7 MH to MG, Apr. 21, 1931, authors' coll.

8 "Americans Pay Tribute to the Spirit of Gibran," *The Syrian World* 5 (Apr. 1931): 28–29.

9 "The Arabic Speaking World Mourns Gibran," *The Syrian World* 5 (May 1931): 50.

10 MH to BY, May 2, 1931; BY to MH, May 9, 1931.

11 MG to MH, Apr. 29, 1931. All MG's letters were written for her by Assaf George or Zakia Gibran.

12 MH 41, June 17 and 4, 1911; MH to MG, May 2, 1931, authors' coll.

13 MG to MH, June 4 and 18, 1931.

14 MH to BY, May 8, 1931; BY to MH, May 19, 1931; MH 70, May 29, 1931; MH to MG, July 1, 1931, authors' coll.

15 Young, "A Poet Returns Home," *The Syrian World* 6 (Sept. 1931), pp. 14–17.

16 Harte, letter to the editor, *The Christian Century*, Sept. 30, 1931, p. 1212.

17 O'Neill to Lies, Christmas 1931, coll. Jean Cantwell.

18 BY to MH, July 3, 1931.

19 BY to MH, Nov. 15, 1931.

20 BY to MH, Sept. 28, Dec. 20 and 30, 1931.

21 KG to MH, Feb. 18, 1913.

22 BY to MH, early Feb. 1932; MH 70, Feb. 9, 1932; BY to MH, Feb. 11, 1932.

23 BY to MH [Mar. 3] and 28, 1932; MH to BY, Mar. 30, 1932.

24 MH to BY, Mar. 30, 1932.

25 BY to MH, July 20, 1932.

26 MH to BY, Aug. 7, 1932; MG to MH, July 2 and 21, 1932; MH to township of Besharri, July 28, 1932.

27 MH to MG, July 17, 1932.

28 Joseph G. Rahme of Besharri to MG, Oct. 17, 1933, authors' coll.

29 MH to MG, Mar. 30, 1933, and June 21, 1934, authors' coll.

30 "His Wish Fulfilled," *Art Digest* 9 (June 1, 1935): 19; Ethel Hutson to MH, July 18, 1935; BY to Hutson, Aug. 1, 1935; Hutson to MH, Aug. 6, 1935.

31 MH to MG, July 16, 1936, authors' coll.

32 MH 71, June 23, 1937.

33 MH 71, June 29, 1937; Naimy, *Kahlil Gibran*, pp. vii–ix.

34 MH to BY, May 2, 1931.

35 MH 71, Aug. 16, 1937.

36 Young, *This Man from Lebanon*, pp. 135, 168–69, 34. Cf. KG to MH [Dec. 8, 1921], KG to MH, Jan. 26, 1913, and MH 66, May 1923.

37 BY to MG, May 14, 1945, authors' coll.

38 Savannah *Morning News*, Nov. 19, 1950, p. 50.

39 MH to MG, Christmas 1953, authors' coll.

40 J. Donald Adams, "Speaking of Books," N.Y. *Times Book Review*, Sept. 29, 1957, p. 2.

41 Sheila Turner, "Tales of a Levantine Guru," *Saturday Review*, Mar. 13, 1971, p. 54.

42 *Fifty Poems of Meleager*, trans. Walter Headlam (London: Macmillan, 1890), poem XLIX, p. 99.

Selected Bibliography

A careful search of the major depositories of Arabic periodicals in the United States and Lebanon failed to reveal the early twentieth-century publications *al-Mohajer, Mir'āt al-Gharb,* and *as-Sayeh.* For the primary sources of Gibran's first articles we have therefore depended upon clippings found in the Haskell collection at Chapel Hill and in the authors' collection. We have cited only articles that we have seen. From 1910 on Gibran's prose poems and essays were often reprinted in Middle Eastern magazines. Because most of this material was later included in the anthologies *Tears and Laughter, The Tempests,* and *Best Things and Masterpieces,* we have not always indicated the titles of the articles. In citing books by Gibran we have given the date of the first authorized publication, followed by the authorized translation. Not included are the countless foreign translations and unauthorized versions. We have included only the most important reviews of Gibran's books and exhibitions. Anthologies and books with illustrations by Gibran have generally not been listed. Manuscript collections are noted in the introduction.

Books by Kahlil Gibran

1905 *Nubdhah fī Fan al-Mūsīqá* [Music]. New York: al-Mohajer.
1906 *'Arā'is al-Murūj.* New York: Al-Mohajer. *Nymphs of the Valley,* Trans. H. M. Nahmad. New York: Knopf, 1948.
1908 *Al-Arwāh al-Mutamarridah.* New York: al-Mohajer. *Spirits Rebellious,* trans. H. M. Nahmad. New York: Knopf, 1948.
1912 *Al-Ajnihah al-Mutakassirah.* New York: Mir'āt al-Gharb. *The Broken Wings.* In *A Second Treasury of Kahlil Gibran.*
1914 *Kitāb Dam'ah wa Ibtisāmah.* New York: Atlantic. *A Tear and A Smile.* Trans. H. M. Nahmad. New York: Knopf, 1950. Also known as *Tears and Laughter.* Review: Robert Hillyer, N.Y. *Times Book Review,* Apr. 3, 1949, p. 7.
1918 *The Madman: His Parables and Poems.* New York: Knopf. *Al-Majnūn,* trans. Antonius Bashīr. Cairo: al-Hilal, 1924. Reviews: D.K., N.Y. *Call Magazine,* Nov. 24, p. 6; *The Dial* 65 (Nov. 30): 510; Howard Willard Cook, N. Y. *Sun,* Dec. 15, p. 4; *The Nation* 107 (Dec. 28): 812; Boston *Evening Transcript,* Jan. 25, 1919, p. 9; N.Y. *Evening Post,* Feb. 1, 1919, p. 6; Joseph Gollomb, N.Y. *Evening Post,* Mar. 29, 1919, book sec., pp. 1, 10; [Harriet Monroe], *Poetry* 14 (Aug. 1919): 278–79.
1919 *Al-Mawākib.* New York: Mir'āt al-Gharb al'Yawmīyah. *The Procession.* In George Kheirallah. *The Life of Gibran Kahlil Gibran and His Procession.* New York: Arab-American Press, 1947. Introduction by William Catzeflis.
       Twenty Drawings. New York: Knopf; reprinted 1974. Review: Glen Mullin, *The Nation* 110 (Apr. 10, 1920): 485–86.
1920 *Al-'Awāṣif* [The Tempests]. Cairo: al-Hilal. English translations are in *A Treasury of Kahlil Gibran* and *A Second Treasury of Kahlil Gibran.*
       The Forerunner: His Parables and Poems. New York: Knopf. *As-Sābi,* trans. Antonius Bashīr. Cairo: Yūsuf Bustānī, 1925. Reviews: Boston *Evening Transcript,* Nov. 3, p. 6; *Poetry* 18 (Apr. 1921): 40–41; *The Dial* 70 (May 1921): 594.
1923 *Al-Badā'i' wa al-Ṭarā'if* [Best Things and Masterpieces]. Cairo: Yūsuf Bustānī. English translations are in *A Treasury of Kahlil Gibran* and *A Second Treasury of Kahlil Gibran.*
       The Prophet. New York: Knopf. *Al-Nabī,* trans. Antonius Bashīr. Cairo: Yūsuf Bustānī, 1926. Review: Marjorie Allen Seiffert, *Poetry* 23 (Jan. 1924): 216–18.
1926 *Sand and Foam.* New York: Knopf. *Ramal wa Zabāt,* trans. Antonius Bashīr. Cairo: [probably Yūsuf Bustānī], 1927. Reviews: N.Y. *Herald Tribune Books,* May 22, 1927, p. 12; *The Dial* 83 (Sept. 1927): 265.
1927 *Kalimāt Jubrān,* ed. Antonius Bashīr. Cairo: Yūsuf Bustānī. *Spiritual Sayings of Kahlil Gibran,* trans. Anthony R. Ferris. New York: Citadel, 1962.
1928 *Jesus, The Son of Man.* New York: Knopf. *Yasū' Ibn al-Insān,* trans. Antonius Bashīr. Cairo: Elias's Modern Press, 1932. Reviews: Paul Eldridge, N.Y. *Evening Post,* Nov. 24, p. 8; N.Y. *Herald Tribune Books,* Dec. 2, p. 6; M.S.M., Boston *Evening Transcript,* Dec. 22, 1928, sec. 6, p. 1; P. W. Wilson, N.Y. *Times Book Review,* Dec. 23, pp. 1, 18.
1929 *Al-Sanābil* [The Spikes of Grain]. New York: as-Sā'iḥ.

1931   *The Earth Gods.* New York: Knopf. *Alihāt al-Arrd*, trans. Antonius Bashīr. Cairo: Elias's Modern Press, 1932. Review: N.Y. *Herald Tribune Books*, May 3, p. 23.

1932   *The Wanderer: His Parables and His Sayings.* New York: Knopf.

1933   *The Garden of The Prophet.* New York: Knopf.

1934   *Prose Poems.* New York: Knopf. Selections from *al-Funoon* and *as-Sayeh*, trans. Andrew Ghareeb.

1951   *A Treasury of Kahlil Gibran*, ed. Martin L. Wolf, trans. Anthony R. Ferris. New York: Citadel.

1959   *Kahlil Gibran: A Self-Portrait.* New York: Citadel. Letters, trans. Anthony R. Ferris.
        Al-Majmūʻah al-Kāmilah li Muʻallafat Jubrān Khalīl Jubrān [Complete Works], ed. Mikhail Naimy. Beirut: Dār Beirut.

1962   *A Second Treasury of Kahlil Gibran*, trans. Anthony R. Ferris. New York: Citadel.

1965   *Mirrors of the Soul*, trans. Joseph Sheban. New York: Wisdom Library. Essays from various Arabic sources.

1973   *Lazarus and His Beloved*, ed. Kahlil and Jean Gibran. Greenwich, Conn: New York Graphic Society.

ARTICLES AND POEMS BY KAHLIL GIBRAN

1905–09   *al-Mohajer*, New York. "Hayāt al-Hubb," Apr. 1, 1905; "Yawm Mawlidī," Feb. 13, 1909.

1910   "Martha La Banaise." *Les Mille Nouvelle Nouvelles* (Paris) 10 (Nov. 1910): 141–50.

1911–12   *Mir'āt al-Gharb*, New York. "Nahnu wa Antum," Jan. 6, 1911; "Yasū' al-Maṣlūb," Apr. 14, 1911; "al-ʻUbūdīyah," Sept. 13, 1911; "Abnā' al-Alihah wa Ahfād al-Qurūd," Apr. 5, 1912.

1911–34   *al-Hilal*, Cairo. Widener Library, Harvard. Gibran's early articles were reprints from *Mir'āt al-Gharb*. From 1920 to 1924 he wrote an annual article. Vols. 19 (Feb. 1, 1911): 302–04; 20 (Nov. 1, 1911): 118–20; 24 (Apr. 1, 1916): 554–56 (from *as-Sayeh*); 28 (May 1, 1920): 745–52; 29 (Oct. 1, 1920, Mar. 1 and Apr. 1, 1921): 19–23, 599–600, 936–40; 30 (Mar. 1, 1922): 520 (from *as-Sayeh*); 31 (Feb. 1, 1923): 463–69; 32 (Nov. 1, 1923, and Apr. 1, 1924): 20–23, 690–91; 33 (Oct. 1, 1924): 21–24; 34 (Oct. 1, 1925): 35–37; 40 (Dec. 1, 1931): 238; 41 (May 1, 1933); 42 (Mar. 1934): 513–17.

1913–18   *al-Funoon*, New York. New York Public Library. Vol. 1 (Apr.–Dec. 1913): Apr. pp. 1–4; June, pp. 17–21; Aug., pp. 1–3; Sept. pp. 57–58; Nov., pp. 1–3 and 37–39; Dec., p. 70. Vol. 2 (June 1916–May 1917): June 1916, pp. 61–63 and 70–71; July, pp. 97–99 and 152–54; Aug., pp. 211–12 and 258–59; Sept., pp. 289–91; Oct., pp. 385–90; Nov., pp. 481–86; Dec., pp. 589–90; Jan. 1917, p. 673; Feb., pp. 781–82; Mar., pp. 885–87 and 931–32; May, pp. 1201–03. Vol. 3 (Aug. 1917–Feb. 1918): Aug. 1917, pp. 1–6; Sept. pp. 81–95 and 143–44; Oct., pp. 163–64, 171–72, and 191–93; Nov., pp. 275–76; Jan. 1918, p. 465.

1914   "Bad' Thawrah." *as-Sayeh*, Mar. 9, 1914.

1915   "To Albert Pinkham Ryder." New York, privately printed by Cosmos & Washburn. Review: McBride, N.Y. *Sun*, Apr. 1, 1917, sec. 5, p. 12.

1916–17   *The Seven Arts*, New York. "Night and the Madman," 1 (Nov. 1916): 32–33; "The Greater Sea," 1 (Dec. 1916): 133–34; "The Astronomer" and "On Giving and Taking," 1 (Jan. 1917): 236–37; "The Seven Selves," 1 (Feb. 1917): 345; "Poems from the Arabic," 1 (May 1917): 64–67.

1918   "Defeat, my Defeat." In "Serbia. 'O Grave Where Is Thy Victory?' " Privately printed.

1919   Article in *Fatat-Boston*, Oct.–Nov. Printed by Wadi Shakir, 40 Tyler Street.

1920   "War and the Small Nations." *The Borzoi*. New York: Knopf.

1921   "Seven Sayings." *The Dial* 69 (Jan. 1921).

1925–26   *The New Orient*, New York. New York Public Library. "The Blind Poet," 2 (July–Sept. 1925); "Lullaby," 3 (July 1926): 68.

1926–31   *The Syrian World*, New York. New York Public Library. In these years Gibran submitted monthly articles. They are all reprints of his published English work except for "To Young Americans of Syrian Origin," 1 (July 1926): 4–5 (from *Fatat-Boston*), and his translation of Syrian folksongs, "O Mother Mine," 1 (Mar. 1927): 13, "I Wandered among the Mountains," 1 (May 1927): 11–12, and "Three Maiden Lovers," 2 (Aug. 1927): 13.

1928   "The Great Recurrence." N.Y. *Herald Tribune Magazine*, Dec. 23, 1928, p. 19.

1929   "Snow." N.Y. *Herald Tribune Magazine*, Dec. 22, 1929, p. 3.

EXHIBITION CATALOGUES AND REVIEWS OF KAHLIL GIBRAN'S ART

1903   Wellesley College. Tau Zeta Epsilon Society. May. Review: *The Iris*, 1903 pp. 4–5.

1904   Boston. Harcourt Building. *Drawings, Studies and Designs by Gibran Kahlil Gibran with a Small Collection . . . by the Late Langrel Harris.* Apr. 30–May 10. 4 pp. Review: Boston *Evening Transcript*, May 3, 1904, p. 10.

1909   Wellesley College. Tau Zeta Epsilon Society. May. Review: *Wellesley College News*, May 26, p. 4.

1910   Paris. Société Nationale des Beaux-Arts. *Catalogue illustré.* No. 548, *L'automne*.
        Paris. Grand Palais. *Catalogue des ouvrages de peinture. . . .* Apr. 15–June 30. No. 125.

1914 New York. Montross Gallery. *Exhibition of Pictures by Kahlil Gibran*. . . . Dec. 14–30. 4 pp. Reviews: N.Y. *Herald Tribune*, Dec. 20, p. 3; [Henry McBride], N.Y. *Sun*, Dec. 20, p. 2; Charles H. Caffin, N.Y. *American*, Dec. 21, p. 9; N.Y. *Evening Post*, Dec. 26, p. 12; N.Y. *Times*, Dec. 27, sec. 5, p. 11; Jean Hamilton, "Woman's Influence Is To Be Found . . . behind All the Creations of Man . . ," N.Y. *Evening Sun*, Dec. 28, p. 8.

1917 New York. M. Knoedler & Co. *Exhibition of Forty Wash-Drawings by Kahlil Gibran*. . . . Jan. 29–Feb. 10. 4 pp. Reviews: N.Y. *Tribune*, Feb. 4, sec. 3, p. 3; Charles H. Caffin, N.Y. *American*, Feb. 5, p. 8; N.Y. *Times*, Feb. 25, sec. 5, p. 12; Alice Raphael [Eckstein], "The Art of Kahlil Gibran," *The Seven Arts* 1 (March 1917): 531–34 (reprinted in *Twenty Drawings*). Boston. Doll and Richards. *Exhibition of Thirty Wash Drawings by Kahlil Gibran*. . . . Apr. 16–28. 4 pp. Reviews: Boston *Evening Transcript*, Apr. 17, p. 13; *Christian Science Monitor*, Apr. 20, p. 11; F. W. Coburn, Boston *Sunday Herald*, Apr. 22, p. 5.

1922 Boston. Women's City Club. *Exhibition of Wash Drawings by Kahlil Gibran*. Jan. 10–31. 4 pp. Review: Boston *Sunday Herald*, Jan. 15, p. 7.

1930 New York. 51 West Tenth Street Studio. *The Gibran Gallery. Exhibition of Pencil- and Wash-Drawings by Kahlil Gibran*. Jan. 21–March. 4 pp.

1946 New York. M. Knoedler & Co. Review: Wolf, Ben. "Knoedler Presents." *Arts Digest* 21 (Dec. 1, 1946): 15.

NON-ARABIC BIOGRAPHY AND CRITICISM

Adams, J. Donald. "Speaking of Books." New York *Times Book Review*, Sept. 29, 1957, p. 2.

Bercovici, Konrad. *Around the World in New York*. New York: Century, 1924. Reprints "The Syrian Quarter," *The Century Magazine* 86 (July 1924): 354.

"Bisharri Youth Violent over Gibran Committee." *Lebanese American Journal* 20 (Apr. 29, 1971): 1–2.

Bragdon, Claude. *Merely Players*. New York: Knopf, 1929.

———. "A Modern Prophet from Lebanon." New York *Herald Tribune*, Dec. 23, 1928, pp. 16–18.

———. *More Lives Than One*. New York: Knopf, 1937.

Bushri, Suheil B. *An Introduction to Kahlil Gibran*. Beirut: Gibran International Festival, 1970. Good bibliography, especially for posthumous criticism in Arabic.

Bynner, Witter. "Kahlil the Gibranite." *The Borzoi*. New York: Knopf, 1925.

Chapin, Louis. "Another Side of Gibran." *Christian Science Monitor*, Feb. 7, 1973, p. 17. Drawings at Telfair Academy of Arts and Sciences.

Cooley, John K. "A Man with a Flair in His Soul." *Christian Science Monitor*, June 4, 1970, p. 19.

"Fifteen Years of Mounting Sales." *Publishers Weekly* 133 (Apr. 2, 1938):1451–52.

Gad, Carl. *Johan Bojer, The Man and His Works*. New York: Moffat, Yard, 1920. Introduction titled "Johan Bojer and Kahlil Gibran" by Howard Willard Cook.

Ghougassian, Joseph P. *Wings of Thought. Kahlil Gibran, the People's Philosopher*. New York: Philosophical Library, 1973.

"Gibran's Legacy of Love is Twisted by His People into Hatred and War." Boston *Globe*, Dec. 14, 1972, p. 48.

Hanna, Suhail. "Gibran and Whitman: Their Literary Dialogue." *Literature East and West* 7 (Dec. 1968): 174–98.

Hawi, Khalil S. *Kahlil Gibran: His Background, Character and Works*. Beirut: American University of Beirut, 1963.

Hilu, Virginia, ed. *Beloved Prophet: The Love Letters of Kahlil Gibran and Mary Haskell and Her Private Journal*. New York: Knopf, 1972.

Kanfer, Stefan. "But Is It Not Strange That Even Elephants Will Yield—and That The Prophet is Still Popular?" New York *Times Magazine*, June 25, 1972, pp. 8–9ff.

Knopf, Alfred A. *Portrait of a Publisher, 1915–1965: Reminiscences and Reflections*. 2 vols. New York: The Typophiles, 1965.

———. *Some Random Recollections: An Informal Talk Made at The Grolier Club*. New York: The Typophiles, 1949.

Kratschkovsky, Ign. "Die Literatur der arabischen Emigranten in Amerika (1895–1915)." In *Le Monde Oriental*, vol. 21, pp. 193–213. Uppsala: Lundequistska, 1927.

Lecerf, Jean. "Djabran Khalil Djabran et les origines de la prose poétique moderne." *Orient* 3 (July 1957): 7–14.

"The Lounger." *The Critic*, no. 841 (Apr. 2, 1898), p. 232.

Metz, Homer. "In Perspective: Memories of Gibran." Providence *Journal*, March 14, 1973.

Naimy, Mikhail. *Kahlil Gibran: A Biography*. New York: Philosophical Library, 1950.

Naimy, Nadeem N. *Mikhail Naimy: An Introduction*. Beirut: American University of Beirut, 1967.

Obituaries, Tributes, and Accounts of Burial in Besharri. Boston *Evening Transcript*, Apr. 14, 1931; Boston *Post*, Apr. 15, 1931; *Publishers Weekly* 119 (Apr. 25, 1931):2111; *The Syrian World* 5 (Apr., May 1931): 7–48, 50–51; New York *Times*, Sept. 30, 1931; A. C. Harte, letter to the editor, *Christian Century* 48 (Sept. 30, 1931):1212.

Otto, Annie Salem. *The Parables of Kahlil Gibran*. New York: Citadel. 1963.

434

Pilpel, Harriet, and Zavin, Theodora. *Rights and Writers.* New York: Dutton, 1960. "The curious will of Mr. Gibran" is treated on pp. 153–55.

"Poor Gibran." *Lebanese American Journal* 20 (Apr. 29, 1971): 4.

"Profits from The Prophet." *Time*, May 15, 1972, p. 50.

Sherfan, Andrew Dib. *Kahlil Gibran: The Nature of Love.* Secaucus, N.J.: Citadel, 1972.

Reed, Alma. *Orozco.* New York: Oxford University Press, 1956.

Ross, Martha Jean. "The Writings of Kahlil Gibran." Unpublished M.A. thesis, University of Texas, 1948.

Russell, George W. [A.E.]. *The Living Torch.* New York: Macmillan, 1938.

Saal, Rollene W. "Speaking of Books: The Prophet." New York *Times Book Review*, May 16, 1965, p. 2.

"Tributes to Gibran . . . at the Hotel McAlpin in New York . . . on the Occasion of the Twenty-fifth Anniversary of the Publication of His First Literary Work." *The Syrian World* 3 (Feb. 19, 1929):29–33.

Turner, Sheila. "Tales of a Levantine Guru." *Saturday Review*, Mar. 13, 1971, pp. 54–56f.

Wright, Neva Marie. "Gibran Kahlil Gibran. Poet, Painter and Philosopher." Unpublished thesis, University of New Hampshire, 1938.

[Young, Barbara]. "The Son of Man." *Pictorial Review* 36 (Dec. 1934): 15.

Young, Barbara. "The Great Survival." *The Poetry Review* 23 (London, 1932): 343–47.

———. *A Study of Kahlil Gibran: This Man from Lebanon.* New York: Privately printed by the Syrian American Press, 1931.

———. *This Man from Lebanon: A Study of Kahlil Gibran.* New York: Knopf, 1945.

ARABIC BIOGRAPHY AND CRITICISM

'Abbūd, Mārūn. *Judud wa Qudamā'; Dirāsāt, Naqd wa Munāqashāt.* Beirut: Dār al-Thaqāfah, 1954.

———. *Mujaddidūn wa Mujtarrūn.* Beirut: Dār al-Thaqāfah, 1961.

———. *Ruwwād al-Nahdah al-Hadīthah.* Beirut: Dār al-Thaqāfah, 1966.

al-'Aqqād, 'Abbās Mahmūd. *al-Fusūl.* Beirut: Dār al-Kitāb al-'Arabī, 1967.

al-Bustānī, Fu'ād. "'Alá Dhikr Jubrān." *al-Mashriq* 37 (1939): 241–68.

———, and Sa'b, Edward. "Bayn al-Mashriq wa al-Sā'ih." *al-Mashriq* 21 (1923): 910–19.

Cheikho, Louis. "Badā'i' Jubrān Kahlīl Jubrān wa Tarā'ifuh." *al-Mashriq* 21 (1923): 487–93.

———. "Difā' al-Sā'ih 'an Jubrān Khalīl Jubrān." *al-Mashriq* 21 (1923): 876–77.

Dāghir, Yūsuf. *Masādir al-Dirāsah al-Adabīyah.* Beirut: Manshūrāt Ahl al-Qalam, 1956.

al-Ghurayyib, Khalīl. "Dhikrayāt Jubrān, al-Rīhānī, Rustum, Mukarzil, al-Ghurayyib." *Awrāq Lubnānīyah*, Jan. 1958, pp. 6–10.

———. "Ma'rakat al-Ta'n al-Sāmit bayn Jubrān wa As'ad Rustum." *Awrāq Lubnānīyah*, Feb. 1958, pp. 56–63.

———. "Min Mudhakkarāt al-Rassām Khalīl al-Ghurayyib 'an Zamīlih Jubrān Khalīl Jubrān." *Al-Baidar*, Jan. 31, 1960, pp. 14–15.

Ghurayyib, Rose. *Jubrān fī Athārih al-Kitābīyah.* Beirut: Dār al-Makshūf, 1969.

Goryeb, Ameen [Ghurayyib, Amīn]. "Jubrān Khalīl Jubrān." *al-Hāris* 8 (1931): 689–704.

———. "Mahrajān Jubrān fī Lubnān." *al-Hāris* 9 (1931): 139–147.

Hawaiik, Joseph [al-Huwayyik, Yousef]. *Dhikrayātī ma' Jubrān, Bārīs 1909–1910.* Ed. Edvic Shaybūb. Beirut: Dār al-Ahad, n.d.

'Intābī, Fu'ād. "Jubrān wa Atharuh fī al-Adab al-'Arabī." *al-'Irfān* 17 (1929): 337–41.

Jabr, Jamīl. *Jubrān, Siratuh, Adabuh, Falsafatuh wa Rasmuh.* Beirut: Dār al-Rīhānī, 1958.

———. *Mayy wa Jubrān.* Beirut: Dār al-Jamāl, 1950.

Ja'ja', Aghnātiyūs. "Bisharrī Madīnat al-Muqaddamīn." *al-Mashriq* 30 (1932): 464–69, 538–44, 685–91, 779–87.

"Kalimah 'an Udabā' al-Funūn." *al-Funoon*, Sept. 1916.

Karam, Antūn Ghattās. *Muhādarāt fī Jubrān Khalīl Jubrān.* Cairo: Ma'had al-Dirāsāt al-'Arabīyah, 1964.

Karāmah, Nabīl. *Jubrān Khalīl Jubrān wa Athāruh fī al-Adab al-'Arabī.* Beirut: Dār al-Rābitah al-Thaqāfīyah, 1964.

Khūrī, Alfred. *al-Kalimah al-'Arabīyah fī al-Mahjar.* Beirut: Dār al-Rīhānī, n.d.

Khūrī, Ra'īf. "Jubrān Khalīl Jubrān." *al-Tariq* 3 (1944): 4–5.

Madey, Elia D. "Jubrān Tahta Mabādi' al-Nu'ayma'." *as-Sameer* 18 (Jan. 15, 1935): 17–23. Review of Naimy's biography.

Majmū'at al-Rābitah al-Qalamīyah li Sanat 1921. Beirut: Dār Sādir, 1964.

Mas'ūd, Habīb, ed. *Jubrān Hayyan wa Mayyitan.* São Paulo, 1932.

Naimy, Mikhail [Nu'aymah, Mikhā'īl]. "Fajr al-Amal ba'd Lail al-Ya's." *al-Funoon* 1 (1913): 50–70.

———. *al-Ghirbāl.* Cairo: al-Matba'ah al-'Asrīyah, 1923.

———. *Jubrān Khalīl Jubrān, Hayātuh, Mawtuh, Adabuh, Fannuh.* Beirut: Dār Sādir, 1960.

———. *al-Majmū'ah al-Kāmilah.* Beirut: Dār al-'Ilm, 1970.

———. *Sab'ūn.* Beirut: Dār al-'Ilm, 1970.

al-Nā'ūrī, 'Isá. "Bayn Jubrān wa Nu'aymah." *al-Adīb* 15 (1956): 12–15.

Rabbāṭ, Anṭūn. "al-Muhājir al-Sūrī." *al-Mashriq* 13 (1910): 926–29.

Reviews of *The Broken Wings. al-Hilāl* 20 (1912): 383; *al-Mashriq* 15 (1912): 315–36.

Reviews of *The Madman. Majallat al-Majma' al-'Ilmī al-'Arabī* 4 (1924): 468–69; *al-Mashriq* 22 (1924): 555.

Review of *The Procession. al-Mashriq* 22 (1924): 75.

Review of *The Prophet. al-Mashriq* 24 (1926): 633.

Sabagh, Elias [Sabbāgh, Ilyās]. *Wahi al-Ku'ūs.* Boston: al-Matba'ah al-Suriyyah, 1932. Lists members of The Golden Links Society.

Ṣā'igh, Tūfīq. *Adwā' Jadīdah 'alá Jubrān.* Beirut: al-Dār al-Sharqīyah, 1966.

Sarrāj, Nādirah Jamīl. *Dirāsāt fī Shi'r al-Mahjar, Shu'arā' al-Rābiṭah al-Qalamīyah.* Cairo: Dār al-Ma'ārif, 1964.

Sukīk, 'Adnān Yūsuf. *al-Naz'ah al-Insānīyah 'inda Jubrān.* Cairo: al-Hay'ah al-Miṣrīyah al-'Ammah, 1970.

al-Talīsī, Khalīfah Muhammad. *Al-Shābbī wa Jubrān.* Tripoli: Maktabat al-Farjānī, 1957.

Yakun, Walīy al-Dīn. "al-Ajniḥah al-Mutakassirah." *al-Muqtataf* 40 (1912): 297–298.

Zakkā, Ṭansī. *Bayn Nu'aymah wa Jubrān.* Beirut: Maktabat al-Ma'ārif, 1971.

al-Zayn, Aḥmad al-'Arif. "Lailah fī al-Arz, hawla Ḥflat Jubrān." *al-'Irfān* 22 (1931): 410–16.

Ziadeh, May [Ziyādeh, Mayy]. "Jubrān Khalīl Jubrān li Munāsabat Ṣudūr Kitābih Yasū' Ibn al-Insān." *al-Muqtataf* 74 (1929): 9–13.

————. "Jubrān Khalīl Jubrān Yaṣif Nafsah Biyadih fī Rasā'ilih." *al-Hadīth* 5 (1931): 363–66.

————. "al-Mawākib." *al-Hilāl* 27 (1919): 874–81.

GENERAL BACKGROUND

Annals of an Era. Percy MacKaye and the MacKaye Family 1826–1932. Washington, D.C.: Pioneer Press under the Auspices of Dartmouth College, 1932. Valuable index.

Ansara, James Michael. "The Immigration and Settlement of the Syrians." Unpublished thesis, Harvard University, 1931.

Arnett, Mary Flounders. "Marie Ziyada." *Council for Middle Eastern Affairs* 7 (Aug.–Sept. 1957): 288–94.

Bliss, Frederick Jones. *The Religions of Modern Syria and Palestine.* New York: Scribner's, 1912.

Brockelmann, C. *Geschichte der arabischen Litteratur.* 3rd supp. vol., pp. 457–71. Leiden: E. J. Brill. 1942.

Brown, Milton W. *The Story of the Armory Show.* New York: Joseph H. Hirshorn Foundation, 1963.

Cole, William I. *Immigrant Races in Massachusetts: The Syrians.* Boston: Massachusetts Department of Education, n.d. (ca. 1919).

Cook, Howard Willard. *Our Poets Today.* New York: Moffat, Yard, 1923.

Cram, Ralph Adams. *My Life in Architecture.* Boston: Little, Brown, 1936.

Daly, Louise Haskell. *Alexander Cheves Haskell: The Portrait of a Man.* Norwood, Mass.: Privately printed at the Plimpton Press, 1934.

Doty, Robert M. *Photo-Secession: Photography as a Fine Art.* New York: George Eastman House, 1960.

Fairbanks, Henry G. *Laureate of the Lost.* Albany: Magi Books, 1972. Treats Guiney and Day.

Gibb, H.A.R. "Studies in Contemporary Arabic Literature I-IV." *Bulletin of The School of Oriental Studies* 4 (1926–28): 745–60; 5 (1929): 311–21, 445–67; 7 (1933–35): 1–22. Vols. 4 and 5 published by the London Institution, vol. 7 by the University of London.

Guiney, Louise Imogen. *Letters.* Ed. Grace Guiney. 2 vols. New York: Harper, 1926.

Hinkle, Beatrice M. *The Recreating of the Individual.* New York: Dodd, Mead, 1923.

Hitti, Philip K. *Lebanon in History: From the Earliest Times to the Present.* London: Macmillan, 1957.

Al-Hoda 1898–1968. The Story of Lebanon and Its Emigrants Taken from the Newspaper al-Hoda. New York: al-Hoda Press, 1968.

Hoffman, Frederick J.; Allen, Charles; and Ulrich, Carolyn F. *The Little Magazine: A History and a Bibliography.* Princeton: Princeton University Press, 1946.

Jacobs, Samuel A. *Companions: An Anthology.* New York: Samuel A. Jacobs, 1922.

Kraus, Joe Walker. "A History of Copeland & Day (1893–1899); with a Bibliographical Checklist of Their Publications." Unpublished M.A. thesis, University of Illinois, 1941.

Longrigg, Stephen Hemsley. *Syria and Lebanon under French Mandate.* New York: Oxford University Press, 1958.

McCanse, Ralph Alan. *Titans and Kewpies: The Life and Art of Rose O'Neill.* New York: Vantage, 1968.

The Mahogany Tree. 26 issues: Jan. 2, 1892–July 9, 1892.

Manheim, Madeline Mason. *Hill Fragments.* New York: Brentano's, 1925.

Mason, Daniel Gregory. *Music in My Time and Other Reminiscences.* New York: Macmillan, 1938.

Miller, Lucius Hopkins. *Our Syrian Population: A Study of the Syrian Communities,* n.d. Reprint, San Francisco: R & E Research Associates, 1968.

Naef, Weston. *The Painterly Photograph, 1890–1914.* New York: Metropolitan Museum of Art, 1973.

Papyrus. Ed. Michael Monahan. Issues of Jan., July 1904; Aug. 1905; May, June, July 1906; Feb. 1908; March 1911.

Parrish, Stephen Maxfield. "Currents of the Nineties in Boston and London: Fred Holland Day, Louise Imogen Guiney, and Their Circle." Unpublished Ph.D. dissertation, Harvard University, 1954.

Peabody, Josephine Preston. *The Collected Plays.* Boston: Houghton Mifflin, 1927.

———. *Collected Poems.* Ed. Katharine Lee Bates. Boston: Houghton Mifflin, 1927.

———. *Diary and Letters.* Ed. Christina Hopkinson Baker. Boston: Houghton Mifflin, 1924.

Residents and Associates of the South End House. *The City Wilderness: A Settlement Study.* Ed. Robert A. Woods. Boston: Houghton Mifflin, 1898.

Riley, Isaac. *Syrian Home-Life.* New York: Dodd, Mead, 1874. Taken from materials furnished by Henry Harris Jessup.

Rollins, Hyder Edward, and Parrish, Stephen Maxfield. *Keats and the Bostonians.* Cambridge: Harvard University Press, 1951.

Stevens, E. S. *Cedars, Saints and Sinners in Syria.* London: Hurst & Blackett, 1927. Description of Mar Sarkis as it was in the 1920s.

"Syrians in the United States." *Literary Digest* 61 (May 3, 1919): 43.

Index

Page numbers in italics refer to illustrations.

438

439